HISTORY OF THE CONQUEST OF PERU

Francisco Pizarro, Conqueror of Peru

• THE BARNES & NOBLE LIBRARY OF ESSENTIAL READING •

HISTORY OF THE CONQUEST OF PERU

With a Preliminary View of the Civilization of the Incas.

William H. Prescott

Introduction by Mary Powlesland Commager

BARNES & NOBLE

NEW YORK

THE BARNES & NOBLE
LIBRARY OF ESSENTIAL READING

Introduction and Suggested Reading Copyright © 2004
by Barnes & Noble Publishing, Inc.

Originally published in 1847

Cover Design by Pronto Design, Inc.

2004 Barnes & Noble Publishing, Inc.

ISBN 13: 978-0-7607-6137-3
ISBN 0-7607-6137-X

Printed in China

3 5 7 9 10 8 6 4 2

CONTENTS

VOLUME II
BOOK III
CONQUEST OF PERU. — CONTINUED

BOOK IV

CIVIL WARS OF THE CONQUERORS

BOOK V

SETTLEMENT OF THE COUNTRY

INTRODUCTION

EVEN before his *History of the Conquest of Mexico* was published in December of 1843, William Hickling Prescott had begun to plot the research and writing of *History of the Conquest of Peru*, which was destined to join its companion volume as a classic in American literature and history. Berating himself repeatedly in his private journal for being lazy and too easily distracted by good company, Prescott often chafed at the slowness of his progress. Finally he sent the manuscript to its English and American publishers in the spring of 1847. That done, he worried about its fate: The work had been written in such haste that its style and historical accuracy had been sacrificed. However, to his relief, the "good natured public received the work as kindly as either of its predecessors;" moreover, the critics demonstrated "friendly character." The author, just celebrating his fifty-first year, already a member of the French Institute, the Royal Academy of Berlin, and the Spanish Academy of History, could relax and pride himself on his recent election to membership in the American Antiquarian Society and the Royal Society of Literature in London, the last an honor bestowed "on no other Yankee."

Both the public and the critics were justified. Prescott's *History of the Conquest of Peru* deserved its kind reception in 1847 as it does our attention and admiration today. Whatever our opinions about the rightness or evil of conquest, or the character of the invading Spaniards, we suffer with Francisco Pizarro and his followers as they wait, forlorn and famished, for reinforcements during their ill-fated first and second expeditions in the 1520s which failed to discover the fabled land of the Inca. We marvel, too, and feel their fear, as they first set eyes on the encampment of the emperor Atahuallpa outside the city of Cajamarca in November of 1532. What chance of success had this small band against the Inca's army numbering in the tens of thousands? How had they let themselves be lured by dreams of great wealth and glory into such a dangerous situation?

The power of Prescott's descriptive talent is impressive, even more so considering his physical limitations. As a young man, studying at Harvard, he suffered an injury to his left eye as the result of a food fight. From that time on, he would be subject to repeated infections, often of both eyes, and spend weeks at a time in a darkened room. Self-effacing as was proper of any Bostonian of his day, Prescott in his preface to the *History of the Conquest of Peru* seeks to dispel the idea that he was completely without sight. He wanted no false credit of "having surmounted the obstacles which lie in the path of the blind man." Nevertheless, we need not be so modest in our appreciation of his work and what he overcame to complete it.

True, Prescott enjoyed certain advantages in life. He came from a distinguished family. His grandfather, William Prescott, earned a place in history for his heroism at Bunker Hill. His father, a respected lawyer and judge, was a success financially as well. His mother's father after establishing himself as a merchant served for many years as American consul in the Azores. Young William lived comfortably. Once he had centered on a career as an historian, family funds indulged his desire to amass a grand collection of original manuscripts and engravings from European and South American archives and personal collections. They provided, too, the wherewithal to hire translators and transcribers in England and Spain and secretaries and readers in the United States. All the same, it remains remarkable that a man who often had to "work chiefly with the ear, a snail-like process" left us such a rich literary legacy.

Even under the best of circumstances, working with early Spanish sources is not easy. Sixteenth-century Spaniards were by no means uniform in their writing or their spelling. While Prescott's friends and acquaintances searched out the materials he required, the more difficult task often was finding someone who could render the document into intelligible Spanish. Once that happened, he then had to find someone who could read to him in a foreign language. Indeed, difficulties meeting that need almost caused him to abandon his proposed histories of the conquests of Mexico and Peru in favor of an historical overview of English literature.

How fortunate for us that he continued to explore the "most brilliant passages of Spanish adventure in the New World." But how did this New Englander, come to be acknowledged worldwide as one of the foremost authorities on Spanish history, especially the Spanish conquests in America? Prescott's own passage from fledgling lawyer to leading historian boasts some of the characteristics of adventure. When he embarked on his career, the field of Spanish history was largely uncharted. No historian since, even if disagreeing with Prescott's conclusions, has failed to follow in his wake.

The young Prescott did not leap suddenly into this new field. Nor was he trained formally in its pursuit. Before penning the first word of his first book, *The Reign of Ferdinand and Isabella, the Catholic,* which appeared in 1837, he spent almost a decade reading and studying history, rhetoric, English, French, Italian, and Spanish language and literature.

Spain was just then re-emerging into the consciousness of the English-speaking world as a result of the Napoleonic Wars and the Independence struggles in the Americas. The long-standing animosity engendered by Spain's failed invasion of England in 1688 had faded. England had found common cause with Spain. British soldiers fought successfully to oust Bonaparte from the Iberian Peninsula. Her merchants crossed the Atlantic to explore opportunities in the newly independent countries of South America. Many veterans of the Peninsula wars had proceeded them, fighting to bring about that independence. One of those, William Miller, proved indispensable to Prescott.

In order to accomplish his goals William Prescott, by necessity, had to depend on others. His family and secretaries often read to him; the latter also had the charge of transcribing his notes whether dictated or written in the near dark on his noctograph, a curious writing instrument created to aid those with failing sight, consisting of a tablet laced with wires which kept an ivory stylus between the lines. Beyond this immediate circle stood a wide group of friends who encouraged Prescott in his labors. There were those of his Boston boyhood such as George Ticknor who began the Modern Languages program at Harvard and Arthur Middleton, who in the 1840s was United States Minister to Spain. There were those who first approached Prescott to laud his work but stayed in his life as firm friends such as Pascual de Gayangos, an expert on Arabic Spanish history, and don Angel Calderón de la Barca who served briefly as Spanish consul in Boston. All became engaged in aiding him in his research. It was don Angel's wife, the Scottish born Frances Inglis, who supplied her Boston-bound friend with much of the colorful detail of the Mexican countryside. It was William Miller who did the same for Peru.

Miller fought with both José de San Martín and Simón Bolívar, the great liberators of Spanish South America. Honored in Peru as Gran Mariscal in 1834, the one-time hero of Ayacucho later fell victim to changing political fortunes. Exiled in 1839, he traveled to Hawaii and Mexico. By the summer of 1840 he was in Boston, where he encountered Prescott, who found him a godsend and "a very gallant & intelligent Englishman." Miller provided the author with the intimate knowledge of Peru's terrain and peoples that he lacked. Their friendship — or, we might say collaboration — continued through letters as Miller went on to become her Majesty's Commission and Consul General in the Pacific, based in Honolulu. It appears that he faithfully continued to honor Prescott's plea "to think of other people's hobbies" when he had the leisure, offering suggestions and praise as the Peruvian manuscript took form.

The work moved swiftly in comparison to his earlier books. The secondary reading had been done during the writing of Mexico; the outline was much the same. Yet, the author found his new theme less sympathetic. A lover of the ancient epics and romantic tales, Prescott in his preface to the *History of the Conquest of Mexico*, confessed that the story of Hernán Cortés' triumph over the Aztec emperor Moctezuma had more the "air of romance than sober history." In Cortés, Prescott discovered a hero. The siege and fall of the ancient Mexican capital of Tenochitlán provided a dramatic conclusion to the tale of conquest. All happened within a few years: Spurred on by earlier expeditions,

Cortés landed at Veracruz in 1519; he and his men triumphed over Tenochitlán in 1521. While Prescott found much to admire about the Aztecs and was not blind to the faults of the Spaniards, the bloody religious rites of the former excused many of the excesses of the latter. The story of the Spanish conquest of Peru did not lend itself so easily to that stirring narrative which is one of Prescott's greatest talents.

Working long before the professional disciplines of anthropology and archeology added so much to our knowledge of the ancient peoples of the Andean region, Prescott struggled as he had with the Aztecs to understand and explain the rise of their empire in the new world. Whatever errors — born of ignorance and lack of information — he committed to the printed page, he continues to receive credit as the first historian to attempt a comparison between the two. While judging the Aztecs far more accomplished in the arts and sciences, Prescott found more to admire about the Incas. Their religious rituals depended far less on human sacrifice and cannibalism, their political organization was superior, their control of conquered territories more complete. Subject peoples lived under the royal scepter, not as in the Aztec case, under the yoke. Thus at the outset, Prescott appears less comfortable with the triumph of the Spanish in Peru as he was with their success in Mexico. Too much a product of protestant New England, too securely rooted in the intellectual inheritance of the Enlightenment which saw natural laws governing the conduct of man, he never completely abandons his conviction that Christianity must triumph over paganism if mankind is to progress. Nevertheless we hear his regret that the development of the Incan civilization was not allowed to progress further on its own. Coupled with a greater measure of admiration for the vanquished, is a larger measure of disapproval, if not disdain, for the victors than evidenced in the *History of the Conquest of Mexico.*

Although Francisco Pizarro stands alone in the minds of most as the conqueror of Peru, his position during his own life was never so firmly established. He fails to achieve the status of hero. Granted, he was the one who captured the Incan emperor at Cajamarca in 1532. Clearly, here he emulated the actions of Cortés, whom he had met in Spain. He, alas, was also the one who alone had the blame for executing the hapless Atahuallpa rather than honoring his pledge to release him once a ransom was paid. Cajamarca, however, was but one city on the northern frontier of the Incan empire. The real seat of power lay to the south in the capital city of Cuzco. Taking that city proved relatively easy. Holding onto it was another matter. Eventually the indigenous peoples rallied around a new Inca, Manco Capac, and fought furiously to oust the invaders. Spaniards would retake the city, but opposition to Pizarro came not only from the Peruvians.

Spanish unity quickly dissolved into factions. The task of conquest incomplete, Pizarro and his one-time partner Diego Almagro became locked into a conflict of their own. As the Spanish conquerors spread out from Cuzco —

Benalcazar northward to Ecuador, Valdivia south to Chile—the political squabbles deteriorated into Civil War. In 1538, Pizarro's brother, Hernando, defeated Almagro at Cuzco. The hero of many battles would meet death alone, strangled in his prison cell. Three years later followers of Almagro's son, another Diego, broke into the aging Pizarro's home, swords drawn, and took their revenge. Whatever his successes on the battlefield, whatever his talent for seizing the advantage of the moment, it seems as if Prescott was correct. "The power of Pizarro was not seated in the hearts of his people." As the assassins made their way through the streets, their purpose clear, no one rallied to the defense of the hero of Cajamarca. This stands in stark contrast to the hundreds of unharmed followers of Atahuallpa who gave their own lives willingly in their vain effort to protect their ruler from capture.

Rivalry amongst the Spaniards left their would-be historian with what he referred to as an embarrassment of riches of historical materials. As they fought physically against each other, the combatants and their followers engaged in a war of words seeking to justify their actions and win approval from the distant monarch, Charles V, king of Spain and Holy Roman Emperor. Sorting through these often-contradictory materials was no mean feat. Prescott wisely suffered "the scaffolding to remain after the building has been completed." Thus we are allowed to either concur or disagree with his own conclusions as he reviews for us what he sometimes despairingly referred to as the "motley story" of the *History of the Conquest of Peru.*

In telling the story of Mexico, Prescott chose to end the *Conquest* with the fall of the Aztec capital. That he truncated the tale for the sake of drama is one of the more persuasive criticisms of that book. The political consolidation of that conquest was less dramatic and far less heroic as royal authority in the person of a viceroy took hold and Spanish adventurers, removed from political power, pushed the limits of that authority to the old boundaries of Aztec rule and beyond. Faced with the slow pace of Spanish success in Peru and the rapid disintegration of the Spanish unity, Prescott had no alternative but to seek a less bold, if still "brilliant," conclusion worthy of the historian. Thus he ends his tale with the arrival of Viceroy Gasca—"a fine theme—the triumph of moral power over the physical."

While modern writers try to avoid such judgments, considering morality as being the concern of the philosopher rather than the historian, nineteenth-century practitioners of the craft, assumed a responsibility to seek out the moral of the tale. Prescott's moralizing and his anti-catholic bias, more pronounced in the Peruvian volumes than those devoted to Mexico, are sure to strike some of today's readers as heavy handed and "unscientific." However, rather than dismissing the rest of his scholarship as outdated and unsound, we do well to remember his own approach to the *History of the Conquest of Mexico:* ". . .while on the one hand, I have not hesitated to expose in their strongest colors the excesses of the Conquerors; on the other, I have given them the benefit of such mitigating reflections as might be suggested by the circumstances and the period in which they lived." Prescott lived in nineteenth-century New England. He took for granted much of what today is held in dispute. Not an overly religious man nor a historian who plied his pen aggressively in defense of American nationalism, he was, nevertheless, comfortable with who he was and might well have believed as it has been humorously said of the Unitarians in the "Fatherhood of God, the Brotherhood of Man and the Neighborhood of Boston." While he labored hard to sort out the "truth" of the tale, reading and ruminating over as many contradictory accounts of the conquest as he could amass, and adhered faithfully to the rigorous standards of scholarship of his day, his historical impartiality did not mean that he had to be without opinion as to the relative goodness or evil of an event or a person.

Whatever the flaws of the *History of the Conquest of Peru,* it remains the classic account and a good read. Prescott introduces us to the realm of the Inca and those who would destroy it. He engages our emotions as well as our attention and whets our appetite to learn more. His book remains the starting point for all historians—professional and amateur alike—of the period. As literature, it will not disappoint. This new edition doubtless will prove an exciting companion for many as they struggle to get through long winter evenings or pass lazy summer days at the beach.

Mary Powlesland Commager returned to her native Massachusetts in 1976 after crisscrossing the country studying and teaching Latin American history. Now retired, she divides her time between Amherst, Massachusetts, and Cancun, Mexico, where she is working on a popular history of the Yucatan Peninsula.

PREFACE

THE most brilliant passages in the history of Spanish adventure in the New World are undoubtedly afforded by the conquests of Mexico and Peru, — the two states which combined with the largest extent of empire a refined social polity, and considerable progress in the arts of civilization. Indeed, so prominently do they stand out on the great canvas of history, that the name of the one, notwithstanding the contrast they exhibit in their respective institutions, most naturally suggests that of the other; and, when I sent to Spain to collect materials for an account of the Conquest of Mexico, I included in my researches those relating to the Conquest of Peru.

The larger part of the documents, in both cases, was obtained from the same great repository, — the archives of the Royal Academy of History at Madrid; a body specially intrusted with the preservation of whatever may serve to illustrate the Spanish colonial annals. The richest portion of its collection is probably that furnished by the papers of Muñoz. This eminent scholar, the historiographer of the Indies, employed nearly fifty years of his life in amassing materials for a history of Spanish discovery and conquest in America. For this, as he acted under the authority of the government, every facility was afforded him; and public offices and private depositories, in all the principal cities of the empire, both at home and throughout the wide extent of its colonial possessions, were freely opened to his inspection. The result was a magnificent collection of manuscripts, many of which he patiently transcribed with his own hand. But he did not live to reap the fruits of his persevering industry. The first volume, relative to the voyages of Columbus, was scarcely finished when he died; and his manuscripts, at least that portion of them which have reference to Mexico and Peru, were destined to serve the uses of another, an inhabitant of that New World to which they related.

Another scholar, to whose literary stores I am largely indebted, is Don Martin Fernandez de Navarrete, late Director of the Royal Academy of History. Through the greater part of his long life he was employed in assembling original documents to illustrate the colonial annals. Many of these have been incorporated in his great work, "Coleccion de los Viages y Descubrimientos," which, although far from being completed after the original plan of its author, is of inestimable service to the historian. In following down the track of discovery, Navarrete turned aside from the conquests of Mexico and Peru, to exhibit the voyages of his countrymen in the Indian seas. His manuscripts, relating to the two former countries, he courteously allowed to be copied for me. Some of them have since appeared in print, under the auspices of his learned coadjutors, Salvà and Baranda, associated with him in the Academy; but the documents placed in my hands form a most important contribution to my materials for the present history.

The death of this illustrious man, which occurred some time after the present work was begun, has left a void in his country not easy to be filled; for he was zealously devoted to letters, and few have done more to extend the knowledge of her colonial history. Far from an exclusive solicitude for his own literary projects, he was ever ready to extend his sympathy and assistance to those of others. His reputation as a scholar was enhanced by the higher qualities which he possessed as a man, — by his benevolence, his simplicity of manners, and unsullied moral worth. My own obligations to him are large; for from the publication of my first historical work, down to the last week of his life, I have constantly received proofs from him of his hearty and most efficient interest in the prosecution of my historical labors; and I now the more willingly pay this well-merited tribute to his deserts, that it must be exempt from all suspicion of flattery.

In the list of those to whom I have been indebted for materials, I must, also, include the name of M. Ternaux-Compans, so well known by his faithful and elegant French versions of the Muñoz manuscripts; and that of my friend Don Pascual de Gayangos, who, under the modest dress of translation, has furnished a most acute and learned commentary on Spanish-Arabian history, — securing for himself the foremost rank in that difficult department of letters, which has been illumined by the labors of a Masdeu, a Casiri, and a Conde.

To the materials derived from these sources, I have added some manuscripts of an important character from the library of the Escurial. These, which chiefly relate to the ancient institutions of Peru, formed part of the splendid collection of Lord Kingsborough, which has unfortunately shared the lot of most literary collections, and been dispersed, since the death of its noble author. For these I am indebted to that industrious bibliographer, Mr. O. Rich, now resident in London. Lastly, I must not omit to mention my obligations, in another way, to my friend Charles Folsom, Esq., the learned librarian of the Boston Athenæum; whose minute acquaintance with the grammatical structure and the true idiom of our English tongue has enabled me to correct many inaccuracies into which I had fallen in the composition both of this and of my former works.

From these different sources I have accumulated a large amount of manuscripts, of the most various character, and from the most authentic sources; royal grants and ordinances, instructions of the Court, letters of the Emperor to the great colonial officers, municipal records, personal diaries and memoranda, and a mass of private correspondence of the principal actors in this turbulent drama. Perhaps it was the turbulent state of the country which led to a more frequent correspondence between the government at home and the colonial officers. But, whatever be the cause, the collection of manuscript materials in reference to Peru is fuller and more complete than that which relates to Mexico; so that there is scarcely a nook or corner so obscure, in the path of the adventurer, that some light has not been thrown on it by the written correspondence of the period. The historian has rather had occasion to complain of the *embarras des richesses;* for, in the multiplicity of contradictory testimony, it is not always easy to detect the truth, as the multiplicity of cross-lights is apt to dazzle and bewilder the eye of the spectator.

The present History has been conducted on the same general plan with that of the Conquest of Mexico. In an Introductory Book, I have endeavoured to portray the institutions of the Incas, that the reader may be acquainted with the character and condition of that extraordinary race, before he enters on the story of their subjugation. The remaining books are occupied with the narrative of the Conquest. And here, the subject, it must be allowed, notwithstanding the opportunities it presents for the display of character, strange, romantic incident, and picturesque scenery, does not afford so obvious advantages to the historian, as the Conquest of Mexico. Indeed, few subjects can present a parallel with that, for the purposes either of the historian or the poet. The natural development of the story, there, is precisely what would be prescribed by the severest rules of art. The conquest of the country is the great end always in the view of the reader. From the first landing of the Spaniards on the soil, their subsequent adventures, their battles and negotiations, their ruinous retreat, their rally and final siege, all tend to this grand result, till the long series is closed by the downfall of the capital. In the march of events, all moves steadily forward to this consummation. It is a magnificent epic, in which the unity of interest is complete.

In the "Conquest of Peru," the action, so far as it is founded on the subversion of the Incas, terminates long before the close of the narrative. The remaining portion is taken up with the fierce feuds of the Conquerors, which would seem, from their very nature, to be incapable of being gathered round a central point of interest. To secure this, we must look beyond the immediate overthrow of the Indian empire. The conquest of the natives is but the first step, to be followed by the conquest of the Spaniards,—the rebel Spaniards, themselves,—till the supremacy of the Crown is permanently established over the country. It is not till this period, that the acquisition of this Transatlantic empire can be said to be completed; and, by fixing the eye on this remoter point, the successive steps of the narrative will be found leading to one great result, and that unity of interest preserved which is scarcely less essential to historic than dramatic composition. How far this has been effected, in the present work, must be left to the judgment of the reader.

No history of the conquest of Peru, founded on original documents, and aspiring to the credit of a classic composition, like the "Conquest of Mexico" by Solís, has been attempted, as far as I am aware, by the Spaniards. The English possess one of high value, from the pen of Robertson, whose masterly sketch occupies its due space in his great work on America. It has been my object to exhibit this same story, in all its romantic details; not merely to portray the characteristic features of the Conquest, but to fill up the outline with the coloring of life, so as to present a minute and faithful picture of the times. For this purpose, I have, in the composition of the work, availed myself freely of my manuscript materials, allowed the actors to speak as much as possible for themselves, and especially made frequent use of their letters; for nowhere is the heart more likely to disclose itself, than in the freedom of private correspondence. I have made liberal extracts from these authorities in the notes, both to sustain the text, and to put in a printed form those productions of the eminent captains and statesmen of the time, which are not very accessible to Spaniards themselves.

M. Amédée Pichot, in the Preface to the French translation of the "Conquest of Mexico," infers from the plan of the composition, that I must have carefully studied the writings of his countryman, M. de Barante. The acute critic does me but justice in supposing me familiar with the principles of that writer's historical theory, so ably developed in the Preface to his "Ducs de Bourgogne." And I have had occasion to admire the skilful manner in which he illustrates this theory himself, by constructing out of the rude materials of a distant time a monument of genius that transports us at once into the midst of the Feudal Ages, — and this without the incongruity which usually attaches to a modern-antique. In like manner, I have attempted to seize the characteristic expression of a distant age, and to exhibit it in the freshness of life. But in an essential particular, I have deviated from the plan of the French historian. I have suffered the scaffolding to remain after the building has been completed. In other words, I have shown to the reader the steps of the process by which I have come to my conclusions. Instead of requiring him to take my version of the story on trust, I have endeavoured to give him a reason for my faith. By copious citations from the original authorities, and by such critical notices of them as would explain to him the influences to which they were subjected, I have endeavoured to put him in a position for judging for himself, and thus for revising, and, if need be, reversing, the judgments of the historian. He will, at any rate, by this means, be enabled to estimate the difficulty of arriving at truth amidst the conflict of testimony; and he will learn to place little reliance on those writers who pronounce on the mysterious past with what Fontenelle calls "a frightful degree of certainty," — a spirit the most opposite to that of the true philosophy of history.

Yet it must be admitted, that the chronicler who records the events of an earlier age has some obvious advantages in the store of manuscript materials at his command, — the statements of friends, rivals, and enemies, furnishing a wholesome counterpoise to each other; and also, in the general course of events, as they actually occurred, affording the best commentary on the true motives of the parties. The actor, engaged in the heat of the strife, finds his view bounded by the circle around him, and his vision blinded by the smoke and dust of the conflict; while the spectator, whose eye ranges over the ground from a more distant and elevated point, though the individual objects may lose somewhat of their vividness, takes in at a glance all the operations of the field. Paradoxical as it may appear, truth founded on contemporary testimony would seem, after all, as likely to be attained by the writer of a later day, as by contemporaries themselves.

Before closing these remarks, I may be permitted to add a few of a personal nature. In several foreign notices of my writings, the author has been said to be blind; and more than once I have had the credit of having lost my sight in the composition of my first history. When I have met with such erroneous accounts, I have hastened to correct them. But the present occasion affords me the best means of doing so; and I am the more desirous of this, as I fear some of my own remarks, in the Prefaces to my former histories, have led to the mistake.

While at the University, I received an injury in one of my eyes, which deprived me of the sight of it. The other, soon after, was attacked by inflammation so severely, that, for some time, I lost the sight of that also; and though it was subsequently restored, the organ was so much disordered as to remain permanently debilitated, while twice in my life, since, I have been deprived of the use of it for all purposes of reading and writing, for several years together. It was during one of these periods that I received from Madrid the materials for the "History of Ferdinand and Isabella," and in my disabled condition, with my Transatlantic treasures lying around me, I was like one pining from hunger in the midst of abundance. In this state, I resolved to make the ear, if possible, do the work of the eye. I procured the services of a secretary, who read to me the various authorities; and in time I became so far familiar with the sounds of the different foreign languages (to some of which, indeed, I had been previously accustomed by a residence abroad), that I could comprehend his reading without much difficulty. As the reader proceeded, I dictated copious notes; and, when these had swelled to a considerable amount, they were read to me repeatedly, till I had mastered their contents sufficiently for the purposes of composition. The same notes furnished an easy means of reference to sustain the text.

Still another difficulty occurred, in the mechanical labor of writing, which I found a severe trial to the eye. This was remedied by means of a writing-case, such as is used by the blind, which enabled me to commit my thoughts to paper without the aid of sight, serving me equally well in the dark as in the light. The characters thus formed made a near approach to hieroglyphics; but my secretary became expert in the art of deciphering, and a fair copy—with a liberal allowance for unavoidable blunders—was transcribed for the use of the printer. I have described the process with more minuteness, as some curiosity has been repeatedly expressed in reference to my *modus operandi* under my privations, and the knowledge of it may be of some assistance to others in similar circumstances.

Though I was encouraged by the sensible progress of my work, it was necessarily slow. But in time the tendency to inflammation diminished, and the strength of the eye was confirmed more and more. It was at length so far restored, that I could read for several hours of the day, though my labors in this way necessarily terminated with the daylight. Nor could I ever dispense with the services of a secretary, or with the writing-case; for, contrary to the usual experience, I have found writing a severer trial to the eye than reading,—a remark, however, which does not apply to the reading of manuscript; and to enable myself, therefore, to revise my composition more carefully, I caused a copy of the "History of Ferdinand and Isabella" to be printed for my own inspection, before it was sent to the press for publication. Such as I have described was the improved state of my health during the preparation of the "Conquest of Mexico"; and, satisfied with being raised so nearly to a level with the rest of my species, I scarcely envied the superior good fortune of those who could prolong their studies into the evening, and the later hours of the night.

But a change has again taken place during the last two years. The sight of my eye has become gradually dimmed, while the sensibility of the nerve has been so far increased, that for several weeks of the last year I have not opened a volume, and through the whole time I have not had the use of it, on an average, for more than an hour a day. Nor can I cheer myself with the delusive expectation, that, impaired as the organ has become, from having been tasked, probably, beyond its strength, it can ever renew its youth, or be of much service to me hereafter in my literary researches. Whether I shall have the heart to enter, as I had proposed, on a new and more extensive field of historical labor, with these impediments, I cannot say. Perhaps long habit, and a natural desire to follow up the career which I have so long pursued, may make this, in a manner, necessary, as my past experience has already proved that it is practicable.

From this statement—too long, I fear, for his patience—the reader, who feels any curiosity about the matter, will understand the real extent of my embarrassments in my historical pursuits. That they have not been very light will be readily admitted, when it is considered that I have had but a limited use of my eye, in its best state, and that much of the time I have been debarred from the use of it altogether. Yet the difficulties I have had to contend with are very far inferior to those which fall to the lot of a blind man. I know of no historian, now alive, who can claim the glory of having overcome such obstacles, but the author of "La Conquête de l'Angleterre par les Normands"; who, to use his own touching and beautiful language, "has made himself the friend of darkness"; and who, to a profound philosophy that requires no light but that from within, unites a capacity for extensive and various research, that might well demand the severest application of the student.

The remarks into which I have been led at such length will, I trust, not be set down by the reader to an unworthy egotism, but to their true source, a desire to correct a misapprehension to which I may have unintentionally given rise myself, and which has gained me the credit with some—far from grateful to my feelings, since undeserved—of having surmounted the incalculable obstacles which lie in the path of the blind man.

BOSTON, April 2, 1847.

VOLUME I

BOOK I

INTRODUCTION

VIEW OF THE CIVILIZATION OF THE INCAS

CHAPTER I

PHYSICAL ASPECT OF THE COUNTRY. — SOURCES OF PERUVIAN CIVILIZATION. — EMPIRE OF THE INCAS. — ROYAL FAMILY. — NOBILITY

OF the numerous nations which occupied the great American continent at the time of its discovery by the Europeans, the two most advanced in power and refinement were undoubtedly those of Mexico and Peru. But, though resembling one another in extent of civilization, they differed widely as to the nature of it; and the philosophical student of his species may feel a natural curiosity to trace the different steps by which these two nations strove to emerge from the state of barbarism, and place themselves on a higher point in the scale of humanity. — In a former work I have endeavoured to exhibit the institutions and character of the ancient Mexicans, and the story of their conquest by the Spaniards. The present will be devoted to the Peruvians; and, if their history shall be found to present less strange anomalies and striking contrasts than that of the Aztecs, it may interest us quite as much by the pleasing picture it offers of a well-regulated government and sober habits of industry under the patriarchal sway of the Incas.

The empire of Peru, at the period of the Spanish invasion, stretched along the Pacific from about the second degree north to the thirty-seventh degree of south latitude; a line, also, which describes the western boundaries of the modern republics of Ecuador, Peru, Bolivia, and Chili. Its breadth cannot so easily be determined; for, though bounded everywhere by the great ocean on the west, towards the east it spread out, in many parts, considerably beyond the mountains, to the confines of barbarous states, whose exact position is undetermined, or whose names are effaced from the map of history. It is certain, however, that its breadth was altogether disproportioned to its length.[1]

The topographical aspect of the country is very remarkable. A strip of land, rarely exceeding twenty leagues in width, runs along the coast, and is hemmed in through its whole extent by a colossal range of mountains, which, advancing from the Straits of Magellan, reaches its highest elevation — indeed, the highest on the American continent—about the seventeenth degree south,[2] and, after crossing the line, gradually subsides into hills of inconsiderable magnitude, as it enters the Isthmus of Panamá. This is the famous Cordillera of the Andes, or "copper mountains,"[3] as termed by the natives, though they might with more reason have been called "mountains of gold." Arranged sometimes in a single line, though more frequently in two or three lines running parallel or obliquely to each other, they seem to the voyager on the ocean but one continuous chain; while the huge volcanoes, which to the inhabitants of the table-land look like solitary and independent masses, appear to him only like so many peaks of the same vast and magnificent range. So immense is the scale on which Nature works in these regions, that it is only when viewed from a great distance, that the spectator can, in any degree, comprehend the relation of the several parts to the stupendous whole. Few of the works of Nature, indeed, are calculated to produce impressions of higher sublimity than the aspect of this coast, as it is gradually unfolded to the eye of the mariner sailing on the distant waters of the Pacific; where mountain is seen to rise above mountain, and Chimborazo, with its glorious canopy of snow, glittering far above the clouds, crowns the whole as with a celestial diadem.[4]

The face of the country would appear to be peculiarly unfavorable to the purposes both of agriculture and of internal communication. The sandy strip along the coast, where rain never falls, is fed only by a few scanty streams, that furnish a remarkable contrast to the vast volumes of water which roll down the eastern sides of the Cordilleras into the Atlantic. The precipitous steeps of the sierra, with its splintered sides of porphyry and granite, and its higher regions wrapped in snows that never melt under the fierce sun of the equator, unless it be from the desolating action of its own volcanic fires, might seem equally unpropitious to the labors of the husbandman. And all communication between the parts of the long-extended territory might be thought to be precluded by the savage character of the region, broken up by precipices, furious torrents, and impassable *quebradas,*—those hideous rents in the mountain chain, whose depths the eye of the terrified traveller, as he winds along his aërial pathway, vainly endeavours to fathom.[5] Yet the industry, we might almost say, the genius, of the Indian was sufficient to overcome all these impediments of Nature.

By a judicious system of canals and subterraneous aqueducts, the waste places on the coast were refreshed by copious streams, that clothed them in fertility and beauty. Terraces were raised upon the steep sides of the Cordillera; and, as the different elevations had the effect of difference of latitude, they exhibited in regular gradation every variety of vegetable form, from the stimulated growth of the tropics, to the temperate products of a northern clime; while flocks of *llamas*—the Peruvian sheep—wandered with their shepherds over the broad, snow-covered wastes on the crests of the sierra, which rose beyond the limits of cultivation. An industrious population settled along the lofty regions of the plateaus, and towns and hamlets, clustering amidst orchards and wide-spreading gardens, seemed suspended in the air far above the ordinary elevation of the clouds.[6] Intercourse was maintained between these numerous settlements by means of the great roads which traversed the mountain passes, and opened an easy communication between the capital and the remotest extremities of the empire.

The source of this civilization is traced to the valley of Cuzco, the central region of Peru, as its name implies.[7] The origin of the Peruvian empire, like the origin of all nations, except the very few which, like our own, have had the good fortune to date from a civilized period and people, is lost in the mists of fable, which, in fact, have settled as darkly round its history as round that of any nation, ancient or modern, in the Old World. According to the tradition most familiar to the European scholar, the time was, when the ancient races of the continent were all plunged in deplorable barbarism; when they worshipped nearly every object in nature indiscriminately; made war their pastime, and feasted on the flesh of their slaughtered captives. The Sun, the great luminary and parent of mankind, taking compassion on their degraded condition, sent two of his children, Manco Capac and Mama Oello Huaco, to gather the natives into communities, and teach them the arts of civilized life. The celestial pair, brother and sister, husband and wife, advanced along the high plains in the neighbourhood of Lake Titicaca, to about the sixteenth degree south. They bore with them a golden wedge, and were directed to take up their residence on the spot where the sacred emblem should without effort sink into the ground. They proceeded accordingly but a short distance, as far as the valley of Cuzco, the spot indicated by the performance of the miracle, since there the wedge speedily sank into the earth and disappeared for ever. Here the children of the Sun established their residence, and soon entered upon their beneficent mission among the rude inhabitants of the country; Manco Capac teaching the men the arts of agriculture, and Mama Oello[8] initiating her own sex in the mysteries of weaving and spinning. The simple people lent a willing ear to the messengers of Heaven, and, gathering together in considerable numbers, laid the foundations of the city of Cuzco. The same wise and benevolent maxims, which regulated the conduct of the first Incas,[9] descended to their successors, and under their mild sceptre a community gradually extended itself along the broad surface of the table-land, which asserted its superiority over the surrounding tribes. Such is the pleasing picture of the origin of the Peruvian monarchy, as portrayed by Garcilasso de la Vega, the descendant of the Incas, and through him made familiar to the European reader.[10]

But this tradition is only one of several current among the Peruvian Indians, and probably not the one most generally received. Another legend speaks of certain white and bearded men, who, advancing from the shores of Lake Titicaca, established an ascendency over the natives, and imparted to them the blessings of civilization. It may remind us of the tradition existing

5

among the Aztecs in respect to Quetzalcoatl, the good deity, who with a similar garb and aspect came up the great plateau from the east on a like benevolent mission to the natives. The analogy is the more remarkable, as there is no
trace of any communication with, or even knowledge of, each other to be
found in the two nations.[11]

The date usually assigned for these extraordinary events was about four
hundred years before the coming of the Spaniards, or early in the twelfth
century.[12] But, however pleasing to the imagination, and however popular,
the legend of Manco Capac, it requires but little reflection to show its
improbability, even when divested of supernatural accompaniments. On the
shores of Lake Titicaca extensive ruins exist at the present day, which the
Peruvians themselves acknowledge to be of older date than the pretended
advent of the Incas, and to have furnished them with the models of their
architecture.[13] The date of their appearance, indeed, is manifestly irreconcilable with their subsequent history. No account assigns to the Inca dynasty
more than thirteen princes before the Conquest. But this number is altogether too small to have spread over four hundred years, and would not carry
back the foundations of the monarchy, on any probable computation,
beyond two centuries and a half, — an antiquity not incredible in itself, and
which, it may be remarked, does not precede by more than half a century the
alleged foundation of the capital of Mexico. The fiction of Manco Capac and
his sister-wife was devised, no doubt, at a later period, to gratify the vanity of
the Peruvian monarchs, and to give additional sanction to their authority by
deriving it from a celestial origin.

We may reasonably conclude that there existed in the country a race
advanced in civilization before the time of the Incas; and, in conformity with
nearly every tradition, we may derive this race from the neighbourhood of
Lake Titicaca;[14] a conclusion strongly confirmed by the imposing architectural remains which still endure, after the lapse of so many years, on its borders. Who this race were, and whence they came, may afford a tempting
theme for inquiry to the speculative antiquarian. But it is a land of darkness
that lies far beyond the domain of history.[15]

The same mists that hang round the origin of the Incas continue to settle
on their subsequent annals; and, so imperfect were the records employed by
the Peruvians, and so confused and contradictory their traditions, that the
historian finds no firm footing on which to stand till within a century of the
Spanish conquest.[16] At first, the progress of the Peruvians seems to have
been slow, and almost imperceptible. By their wise and temperate policy,
they gradually won over the neighbouring tribes to their dominion, as these
latter became more and more convinced of the benefits of a just and well-
regulated government. As they grew stronger, they were enabled to rely
more directly on force; but, still advancing under cover of the same beneficent pretexts employed by their predecessors, they proclaimed peace and
civilization at the point of the sword. The rude nations of the country, with-

out any principle of cohesion among themselves, fell one after another before the victorious arm of the Incas. Yet it was not till the middle of the fifteenth century that the famous Topa Inca Yupanqui, grandfather of the monarch who occupied the throne at the coming of the Spaniards, led his armies across the terrible desert of Atacama, and, penetrating to the southern region of Chili, fixed the permanent boundary of his dominions at the river Maule. His son, Huayna Capac, possessed of ambition and military talent fully equal to his father's, marched along the Cordillera towards the north, and, pushing his conquests across the equator, added the powerful kingdom of Quito to the empire of Peru.[17]

The ancient city of Cuzco, meanwhile, had been gradually advancing in wealth and population, till it had become the worthy metropolis of a great and flourishing monarchy. It stood in a beautiful valley on an elevated region of the plateau, which, among the Alps, would have been buried in eternal snows, but which within the tropics enjoyed a genial and salubrious temperature. Towards the north it was defended by a lofty eminence, a spur of the great Cordillera; and the city was traversed by a river, or rather a small stream, over which bridges of timber, covered with heavy slabs of stone, furnished an easy means of communication with the opposite banks. The streets were long and narrow; the houses low, and those of the poorer sort built of clay and reeds. But Cuzco was the royal residence, and was adorned with the ample dwellings of the great nobility; and the massy fragments still incorporated in many of the modern edifices bear testimony to the size and solidity of the ancient.[18]

The health of the city was promoted by spacious openings and squares, in which a numerous population from the capital and the distant country assembled to celebrate the high festivals of their religion. For Cuzco was the "Holy City";[19] and the great temple of the Sun, to which pilgrims resorted from the furthest borders of the empire, was the most magnificent structure in the New World, and unsurpassed, probably, in the costliness of its decorations by any building in the Old.

Towards the north, on the sierra or rugged eminence already noticed, rose a strong fortress, the remains of which at the present day, by their vast size, excite the admiration of the traveller.[20] It was defended by a single wall of great thickness, and twelve hundred feet long on the side facing the city, where the precipitous character of the ground was of itself almost sufficient for its defence. On the other quarter, where the approaches were less difficult, it was protected by two other semicircular walls of the same length as the preceding. They were separated, a considerable distance from one another and from the fortress; and the intervening ground was raised so that the walls afforded a breastwork for the troops stationed there in times of assault. The fortress consisted of three towers, detached from one another. One was appropriated to the Inca, and was garnished with the sumptuous decorations befitting a royal residence, rather than a military post. The other two were held by the garrison, drawn from the Peruvian nobles, and commanded by an officer of the blood royal; for the position was of too great importance to be intrusted to inferior hands. The hill was excavated below the towers, and several subterraneous galleries communicated with the city and the palaces of the Inca.[21]

The fortress, the walls, and the galleries were all built of stone, the heavy blocks of which were not laid in regular courses, but so disposed that the small ones might fill up the interstices between the great. They formed a sort of rustic work, being rough-hewn except towards the edges, which were finely wrought; and, though no cement was used, the several blocks were adjusted with so much exactness and united so closely, that it was impossible to introduce even the blade of a knife between them.[22] Many of these stones were of vast size; some of them being full thirty-eight feet long, by eighteen broad, and six feet thick.[23]

We are filled with astonishment, when we consider, that these enormous masses were hewn from their native bed and fashioned into shape, by a people ignorant of the use of iron; that they were brought from quarries, from four to fifteen leagues distant,[24] without the aid of beasts of burden; were transported across rivers and ravines, raised to their elevated position on the sierra, and finally adjusted there with the nicest accuracy, without the knowledge of tools and machinery familiar to the European. Twenty thousand men are said to have been employed on this great structure, and fifty years consumed in the building.[25] However this may be, we see in it the workings of a despotism which had the lives and fortunes of its vassals at its absolute disposal, and which, however mild in its general character, esteemed these vassals, when employed in its service, as lightly as the brute animals for which they served as a substitute.

The fortress of Cuzco was but part of a system of fortifications established throughout their dominions by the Incas. This system formed a prominent feature in their military policy; but before entering on this latter, it will be proper to give the reader some view of their civil institutions and scheme of government.

The sceptre of the Incas, if we may credit their historian, descended in unbroken succession from father to son, through their whole dynasty. Whatever we may think of this, it appears probable that the right of inheritance might be claimed by the eldest son of the *Coya*, or lawful queen, as she was styled, to distinguish her from the host of concubines who shared the affections of the sovereign.[26] The queen was further distinguished, at least in later reigns, by the circumstance of being selected from the sisters of the Inca, an arrangement which, however revolting to the ideas of civilized nations, was recommended to the Peruvians by its securing an heir to the crown of the pure heaven-born race, uncontaminated by any mixture of earthly mould.[27]

In his early years, the royal offspring was intrusted to the care of the *amautas*, or "wise men," as the teachers of Peruvian science were called, who instructed him in such elements of knowledge as they possessed, and especially in the cumbrous ceremonial of their religion, in which he was to take a prominent part. Great care was also bestowed on his military education, of the last importance in a state which, with its professions of peace and good-will, was ever at war for the acquisition of empire.

In this military school he was educated with such of the Inca nobles as were nearly of his own age; for the sacred name of Inca—a fruitful source of obscurity in their annals—was applied indifferently to all who descended by the male line from the founder of the monarchy.[28] At the age of sixteen the pupils underwent a public examination, previous to their admission to what may be called the order of chivalry. This examination was conducted by some of the oldest and most illustrious Incas. The candidates were required to show their prowess in the athletic exercises of the warrior; in wrestling and boxing, in running such long courses as fully tried their agility and strength, in severe fasts of several days' duration, and in mimic combats, which, although the weapons were blunted, were always attended with wounds, and sometimes with death. During this trial, which lasted thirty days, the royal neophyte fared no better than his comrades, sleeping on the bare ground, going unshod, and wearing a mean attire,—a mode of life, it was supposed, which might tend to inspire him with more sympathy with the destitute. With all this show of impartiality, however, it will probably be doing no injustice to the judges to suppose that a politic discretion may have somewhat quickened their perceptions of the real merits of the heir-apparent.

At the end of the appointed time, the candidates selected as worthy of the honors of their barbaric chivalry were presented to the sovereign, who condescended to take a principal part in the ceremony of inauguration. He began with a brief discourse, in which, after congratulating the young aspirants on the proficiency they had shown in martial exercises, he reminded them of the responsibilities attached to their birth and station; and, addressing them affectionately as "children of the Sun," he exhorted them to imitate their great progenitor in his glorious career of beneficence to mankind. The novices then drew near, and, kneeling one by one before the Inca, he pierced their ears with a golden bodkin; and this was suffered to remain there till an opening had been made large enough for the enormous pendants which were peculiar to their order, and which gave them, with the Spaniards, the name of *orejones*.[29] This ornament was so massy in the ears of the sovereign, that the cartilage was distended by it nearly to the shoulder, producing what seemed a monstrous deformity in the eyes of the Europeans, though, under the magical influence of fashion, it was regarded as a beauty by the natives.

When this operation was performed, one of the most venerable of the nobles dressed the feet of the candidates in the sandals worn by the order, which may remind us of the ceremony of buckling on the spurs of the Christian knight. They were then allowed to assume the girdle or sash around the loins, corresponding with the *toga virilis* of the Romans, and intimating that they had reached the season of manhood. Their heads were adorned with garlands of flowers, which, by their various colors, were emblematic of the clemency and goodness that should grace the character of every true warrior; and the leaves of an evergreen plant were mingled with the flowers, to show that these virtues should endure without end.[30] The prince's head was further ornamented by a fillet, or tasselled fringe, of a yellow color, made of the fine threads of the vicuña wool, which encircled the forehead as the peculiar insignia of the heir-apparent. The great body of the Inca nobility next made their appearance, and, beginning with those nearest of kin, knelt down before the prince, and did him homage as successor to the crown. The whole assembly then moved to the great square of the capital, where songs, and dances, and other public festivities closed the important ceremonial of the *huaracu.*[31]

The reader will be less surprised by the resemblance which this ceremonial bears to the inauguration of a Christian knight in the feudal ages, if he reflects that a similar analogy may be traced in the institutions of other people more or less civilized; and that it is natural that nations, occupied with the one great business of war, should mark the period, when the preparatory education for it was ended, by similar characteristic ceremonies.

Having thus honorably passed through his ordeal, the heir-apparent was deemed worthy to sit in the councils of his father, and was employed in offices of trust at home, or, more usually, sent on distant expeditions to practise in the field the lessons which he had hitherto studied only on the mimic theatre of war. His first campaigns were conducted under the renowned commanders who had grown grey in the service of his father; until, advancing in years and experience, he was placed in command himself, and, like Huayna Capac, the last and most illustrious of his line, carried the banner of the rainbow, the armorial ensign of his house, far over the borders, among the remotest tribes of the plateau.

The government of Peru was a despotism, mild in its character, but in its form a pure and unmitigated despotism. The sovereign was placed at an immeasurable distance above his subjects. Even the proudest of the Inca nobility, claiming a descent from the same divine original as himself, could not venture into the royal presence, unless barefoot, and bearing a light burden on his shoulders in token of homage.[32] As the representative of the Sun, he stood at the head of the priesthood, and presided at the most important of the religious festivals.[33] He raised armies, and usually commanded them in person. He imposed taxes, made laws, and provided for their execution by the appointment of judges, whom he removed at pleasure. He was the source from which every thing flowed, — all dignity, all power, all emolument. He was, in short, in the well-known phrase of the European despot, "himself the state."[34]

The Inca asserted his claims as a superior being by assuming a pomp in his manner of living well calculated to impose on his people. His dress was of the finest wool of the vicuña, richly dyed, and ornamented with a profusion of gold and precious stones. Round his head was wreathed a turban of many-colored folds, called the *llautu;* and a tasselled fringe, like that worn by the prince, but of a scarlet color, with two feathers of a rare and curious bird, called the *coraquenque*, placed uptight in it, were the distinguishing insignia of royalty. The birds from which these feathers were obtained were found in a desert country among the mountains; and it was death to destroy or to take them, as they were reserved for the exclusive purpose of supplying the royal head-gear. Every succeeding monarch was provided with a new pair of these plumes, and his credulous subjects fondly believed that only two individuals of the species had ever existed to furnish the simple ornament for the diadem of the Incas.[35]

Although the Peruvian monarch was raised so far above the highest of his subjects, he condescended to mingle occasionally with them, and took great pains personally to inspect the condition of the humbler classes. He presided at some of the religious celebrations, and on these occasions entertained the great nobles at his table, when he complimented them, after the fashion of more civilized nations, by drinking the health of those whom he most delighted to honor.[36]

But the most effectual means taken by the Incas for communicating with their people were their progresses through the empire. These were conducted, at intervals of several years, with great state and magnificence. The sedan, or litter, in which they travelled, richly emblazoned with gold and emeralds, was guarded by a numerous escort. The men who bore it on their shoulders were provided by two cities, specially appointed for the purpose. It was a post to be coveted by no one, if, as is asserted, a fall was punished with death.[37] They travelled with ease and expedition, halting at the *tambos,* or inns, erected by government along the route, and occasionally at the royal palaces, which in the great towns afforded ample accommodations to the whole of the monarch's retinue. The noble roads which traversed the table-land were lined with people, who swept away the stones and stubble from their surface, strewing them with sweet-scented flowers, and vying with each other in carrying forward the baggage from one village to another. The monarch halted from time to time to listen to the grievances of his subjects, or to settle some points which had been referred to his decision by the regular tribunals. As the princely train wound its way along the mountain passes, every place was thronged with spectators eager to catch a glimpse of their sovereign; and, when he raised the curtains of his litter, and showed himself to their eyes, the air was rent with acclamations as they invoked blessings on his head.[38] Tradition long commemorated the spots at which he halted, and the simple people of the country held them in reverence as places consecrated by the presence of an Inca.[39]

The royal palaces were on a magnificent scale, and, far from being confined to the capital or a few principal towns, were scattered over all the provinces of their vast empire.[40] The buildings were low, but covered a wide extent of ground. Some of the apartments were spacious, but they were generally small, and had no communication with one another, except that they opened into a common square or court. The walls were made of blocks of stone of various sizes, like those described in the fortress of Cuzco, rough-hewn, but carefully wrought near the line of junction, which was scarcely visible to the eye. The roofs were of wood or rushes, which have perished under the rude touch of time, that has shown more respect for the walls of the edifices. The whole seems to have been characterized by solidity and strength, rather than by any attempt at architectural elegance.[41]

But whatever want of elegance there may have been in the exterior of the imperial dwellings, it was amply compensated by the interior, in which all the opulence of the Peruvian princes was ostentatiously displayed. The sides of the apartments were thickly studded with gold and silver ornaments. Niches, prepared in the walls, were filled with images of animals and plants curiously wrought of the same costly materials; and even much of the domestic furniture, including the utensils devoted to the most ordinary menial services, displayed the like wanton magnificence![42] With these gorgeous decorations were mingled richly colored stuffs of the delicate manufacture of the Peruvian wool, which were of so beautiful a texture, that the Spanish sovereigns, with all the luxuries of Europe and Asia at their command, did not disdain to use them.[43] The royal household consisted of a throng of menials, supplied by the neighbouring towns and villages, which, as in Mexico, were bound to furnish the monarch with fuel and other necessaries for the consumption of the palace.

But the favorite residence of the Incas was at Yucay, about four leagues distant from the capital. In this delicious valley, locked up within the friendly arms of the sierra, which sheltered it from the rude breezes of the east, and refreshed by gushing fountains and streams of running water, they built the most beautiful of their palaces. Here, when wearied with the dust and toil of the city, they loved to retreat, and solace themselves with the society of their favorite concubines, wandering amidst groves and airy gardens, that shed around their soft, intoxicating odors, and lulled the senses to voluptuous repose. Here, too, they loved to indulge in the luxury of their baths, replenished by streams of crystal water which were conducted through subterraneous silver channels into basins of gold. The spacious gardens were stocked with numerous varieties of plants and flowers that grew without effort in this *temperate* region of the tropics, while parterres of a more extraordinary kind were planted by their side, glowing with the various forms of vegetable life skilfully imitated in gold and silver! Among them the Indian corn, the most beautiful of American grains, is particularly commemorated, and the curious workmanship is noticed with which the golden ear was half disclosed amidst the broad leaves of silver, and the light tassel of the same material that floated gracefully from its top.[44]

If this dazzling picture staggers the faith of the reader, he may reflect that the Peruvian mountains teemed with gold; that the natives understood the art of working the mines, to a considerable extent; that none of the ore, as we shall see hereafter, was converted into coin, and that the whole of it passed into the hands of the sovereign for his own exclusive benefit, whether for purposes of utility or ornament. Certain it is that no fact is better attested by the Conquerors themselves, who had ample means of information, and no motive for misstatement. — The Italian poets, in their gorgeous pictures of the gardens of Alcina and Morgana, came nearer the truth than they imagined.

Our surprise, however, may reasonably be excited, when we consider that the wealth displayed by the Peruvian princes was only that which each had amassed individually for himself. He owed nothing to inheritance from his predecessors. On the decease of an Inca, his palaces were abandoned, all his treasures, except what were employed in his obsequies, his furniture and apparel, were suffered to remain as he left them, and his mansions, save one, were closed up for ever. The new sovereign was to provide himself with every thing new for his royal state. The reason of this was the popular belief, that the soul of the departed monarch would return after a time to reänimate his body on earth; and they wished that he should find every thing to which he had been used in life prepared for his reception.[45]

When an Inca died, or, to use his own language, "was called home to the mansions of his father, the Sun,"[46] his obsequies were celebrated with great pomp and solemnity. The bowels were taken from the body, and deposited in the temple of Tampu, about five leagues from the capital. A quantity of his plate and jewels was buried with them, and a number of his attendants and favorite concubines, amounting sometimes, it is said, to a thousand, were immolated on his tomb.[47] Some of them showed the natural repugnance to the sacrifice occasionally manifested by the victims of a similar superstition in India. But these were probably the menials and more humble attendants; since the women have been known, in more than one instance, to lay violent hands on themselves, when restrained from testifying their fidelity by this act of conjugal martyrdom. This melancholy ceremony was followed by a general mourning throughout the empire. At stated intervals, for a year, the people assembled to renew the expressions of their sorrow; processions were made, displaying the banner of the departed monarch; bards and minstrels were appointed to chronicle his achievements, and their songs continued to be rehearsed at high festivals in the presence of the reigning monarch, — thus stimulating the living by the glorious example of the dead.[48]

The body of the deceased Inca was skilfully embalmed, and removed to the great temple of the Sun at Cuzco. There the Peruvian sovereign, on entering the awful sanctuary, might behold the effigies of his royal ancestors, ranged in opposite files, — the men on the right, and their queens on the left, of the great luminary which blazed in refulgent gold on the walls of the temple. The bodies, clothed in the princely attire which they had been accustomed to wear, were placed on chairs of gold, and sat with their heads inclined downward, their hands placidly crossed over their bosoms, their countenances exhibiting their natural dusky hue,—less liable to change than the fresher coloring of a European complexion,—and their hair of raven black, or silvered over with age, according to the period at which they died! It seemed like a company of solemn worshippers fixed in devotion,—so true were the forms and lineaments to life. The Peruvians were as successful as the Egyptians in the miserable attempt to perpetuate the existence of the body beyond the limits assigned to it by nature.[49]

They cherished a still stranger illusion in the attentions which they continued to pay to these insensible remains, as if they were instinct with life. One of the houses belonging to a deceased Inca was kept open and occupied by his guard and attendants, with all the state appropriate to royalty. On certain festivals, the revered bodies of the sovereigns were brought out with great ceremony into the public square of the capital. Invitations were sent by the captains of the guard of the respective Incas to the different nobles and officers of the court; and entertainments were provided in the names of their masters, which displayed all the profuse magnificence of their treasures,—and "such a display," says an ancient chronicler, "was there in the great square of Cuzco, on this occasion, of gold and silver plate and jewels, as no other city in the world ever witnessed."[50] The banquet was served by the menials of the respective households, and the guests partook of the melancholy cheer in the presence of the royal phantom with the same attention to the forms of courtly etiquette as if the living monarch had presided![51]

The nobility of Peru consisted of two orders, the first and by far the most important of which was that of the Incas, who, boasting a common descent with their sovereign, lived, as it were, in the reflected light of his glory. As the Peruvian monarchs availed themselves of the right of polygamy to a very liberal extent, leaving behind them families of one or even two hundred children,[52] the nobles of the blood royal, though comprehending only their descendants in the male line, came in the course of years to be very numerous.[53] They were divided into different lineages, each of which traced its pedigree to a different member of the royal dynasty, though all terminated in the divine founder of the empire.

They were distinguished by many exclusive and very important privileges; they wore a peculiar dress; spoke a dialect, if we may believe the chronicler, peculiar to themselves;[54] and had the choicest portion of the public domain assigned for their support. They lived, most of them, at court, near the person of the prince, sharing in his counsels, dining at his board, or supplied from his table. They alone were admissible to the great offices in the priesthood. They were invested with the command of armies, and of distant garrisons, were placed over the provinces, and, in short, filled every station of high trust and emolument.[55] Even the laws, severe in their general tenor, seem not to have been framed with reference to them; and the people, investing the whole order with a portion of the sacred character which belonged to the sovereign, held that an Inca noble was incapable of crime.[56]

The other order of nobility was the *Curacas,* the caciques of the conquered nations, or their descendants. They were usually continued by the government in their places, though they were required to visit the capital occasionally, and to allow their sons to be educated there as the pledges of their loyalty. It is not easy to define the nature or extent of their privileges. They were possessed of more or less power, according to the extent of their patrimony, and the number of their vassals. Their authority was usually transmitted from father to son, though sometimes the successor was chosen by the people.[57] They did not occupy the highest posts of state, or those nearest the person of the sovereign, like the nobles of the blood. Their authority seems to have been usually local, and always in subordination to the territorial jurisdiction of the great provincial governors, who were taken from the Incas.[58]

It was the Inca nobility, indeed, who constituted the real strength of the Peruvian monarchy. Attached to their prince by ties of consanguinity, they had common sympathies and, to a considerable extent, common interests with him. Distinguished by a peculiar dress and insignia, as well as by language and blood, from the rest of the community, they were never confounded with the other tribes and nations who were incorporated into the great Peruvian monarchy. After the lapse of centuries, they still retained their individuality as a peculiar people. They were to the conquered races of the country what the Romans were to the barbarous hordes of the Empire, or the Normans to the ancient inhabitants of the British Isles. Clustering around the throne, they formed an invincible phalanx, to shield it alike from secret conspiracy and open insurrection. Though living chiefly in the capital, they were also distributed throughout the country in all its high stations and strong military posts, thus establishing lines of communication with the court, which enabled the sovereign to act simultaneously and with effect on the most distant quarters of his empire. They possessed, moreover, an intellectual preëminence, which, no less than their station, gave them authority with the people. Indeed, it may be said to have been the principal foundation of their authority. The crania of the Inca race show a decided superiority over the other races of the land in intellectual power;[59] and it cannot be denied that it was the fountain of that peculiar civilization and social polity, which raised the Peruvian monarchy above every other state in South America. Whence this remarkable race came, and what was its early history, are among those mysteries that meet us so frequently in the annals of the New World, and which time and the antiquary have as yet done little to explain.

CHAPTER II

ORDERS OF THE STATE. — PROVISIONS FOR JUSTICE. — DIVISION OF LANDS. — REVENUES AND REGISTERS. — GREAT ROADS AND POSTS. — MILITARY TACTICS AND POLICY

IF we are surprised at the peculiar and original features of what may be called the Peruvian aristocracy, we shall be still more so as we descend to the lower orders of the community, and see the very artificial character of their institutions, — as artificial as those of ancient Sparta, and, though in a different way, quite as repugnant to the essential principles of our nature. The institutions of Lycurgus, however, were designed for a petty state, while those of Peru, although originally intended for such, seemed, like the magic tent in the Arabian tale, to have an indefinite power of expansion, and were as well suited to the most flourishing condition of the empire as to its infant fortunes. In this remarkable accommodation to change of circumstances we see the proofs of a contrivance that argues no slight advance in civilization.

The name of Peru was not known to the natives. It was given by the Spaniards, and originated, it is said, in a misapprehension of the Indian name of "river."[1] However this may be, it is certain that the natives had no other epithet by which to designate the large collection of tribes and nations who were assembled under the sceptre of the Incas, than that of *Tavantinsuyu*, or "four quarters of the world."[2] This will not surprise a citizen of the United States, who has no other name by which to class himself among nations than what is borrowed from a quarter of the globe.[3] The kingdom, conformably to its name, was divided into four parts, distinguished each by a separate title, and to each of which ran one of the four great roads that diverged from Cuzco, the capital or *navel* of the Peruvian monarchy. The city was in like manner divided into four quarters; and the various races, which gathered there from the distant parts of the empire, lived each in the quarter nearest to its respective province. They all continued to wear their peculiar national costume, so that it was easy to determine their origin; and the same order and system of arrangement prevailed in the motley population of the capital, as in the great provinces of the empire. The capital, in fact, was a miniature image of the empire.[4]

The four great provinces were each placed under a viceroy or governor, who ruled over them with the assistance of one or more councils for the different departments. These viceroys resided, some portion of their time, at least, in the capital, where they constituted a sort of council of state to the Inca.[5] The nation at large was distributed into decades, or small bodies of ten; and every tenth man, or head of a decade, had supervision of the rest,—being required to see that they enjoyed the rights and immunities to which they were entitled, to solicit aid in their behalf from government, when necessary, and to bring offenders to justice. To this last they were stimulated by a law that imposed on them, in case of neglect, the same penalty that would have been incurred by the guilty party. With this law hanging over his head, the magistrate of Peru, we may well believe, did not often go to sleep on his post.[6]

The people were still further divided into bodies of fifty, one hundred, five hundred, and a thousand, with each an officer having general supervision over those beneath, and the higher ones possessing, to a certain extent, authority in matters of police. Lastly, the whole empire was distributed into sections or departments of ten thousand inhabitants, with a governor over each, from the Inca nobility, who had control over the *curacas* and other territorial officers in the district. There were, also, regular tribunals of justice, consisting of magistrates in each of the towns or small communities, with jurisdiction over petty offences, while those of a graver character were carried before superior judges, usually the governors or rulers of the districts. These judges all held their authority and received their support from the Crown, by which they were appointed and removed at pleasure. They were obliged to determine every suit in five days from the time it was brought before them; and there was no appeal from one tribunal to another. Yet there were important provisions for the security of justice. A committee of visitors patrolled the kingdom at certain times to investigate the character and conduct of the magistrates; and any neglect or violation of duty was punished in the most exemplary manner. The inferior courts were also required to make monthly returns of their proceedings to the higher ones, and these made reports in like manner to the viceroys; so that the monarch, seated in the centre of his dominions, could look abroad, as it were, to their most distant extremities, and review and rectify any abuses in the administration of the law.[7]

The laws were few and exceedingly severe. They related almost wholly to criminal matters. Few other laws were needed by a people who had no money, little trade, and hardly any thing that could be called fixed property. The crimes of theft, adultery, and murder were all capital; though it was wisely provided that some extenuating circumstances might be allowed to mitigate the punishment.[8] Blasphemy against the Sun, and malediction of the Inca,—

offences, indeed, of the same complexion,—were also punished with death. Removing landmarks, turning the water away from a neighbour's land into one's own, burning a house, were all severely punished. To burn a bridge was death. The Inca allowed no obstacle to those facilities of communication so essential to the maintenance of public order. A rebellious city or province was laid waste, and its inhabitants exterminated. Rebellion against the "Child of the Sun" was the greatest of all crimes.[9]

The simplicity and severity of the Peruvian code may be thought to infer a state of society but little advanced; which had few of those complex interests and relations that grow up in a civilized community, and which had not proceeded far enough in the science of legislation to economize human suffering by proportioning penalties to crimes. But the Peruvian institutions must be regarded from a different point of view from that in which we study those of other nations. The laws emanated from the sovereign, and that sovereign held a divine commission, and was possessed of a divine nature. To violate the law was not only to insult the majesty of the throne, but it was sacrilege. The slightest offence, viewed in this light, merited death; and the gravest could incur no heavier penalty.[10] Yet, in the infliction of their punishments, they showed no unnecessary cruelty; and the sufferings of the victim were not prolonged by the ingenious torments so frequent among barbarous nations.[11]

These legislative provisions may strike us as very defective, even as compared with those of the semi-civilized races of Anahuac, where a gradation of courts, moreover, with the right of appeal, afforded a tolerable security for justice. But in a country like Peru, where few but criminal causes were known, the right of appeal was of less consequence. The law was simple, its application easy; and, where the judge was honest, the case was as likely to be determined correctly on the first hearing as on the second. The inspection of the board of visitors, and the monthly returns of the tribunals, afforded no slight guaranty for their integrity. The law which required a decision within five days would seem little suited to the complex and embarrassing litigation of a modern tribunal. But, in the simple questions submitted to the Peruvian judge, delay would have been useless; and the Spaniards, familiar with the evils growing out of long-protracted suits, where the successful litigant is too often a ruined man, are loud in their encomiums of this swift-handed and economical justice.[12]

The fiscal regulations of the Incas, and the laws respecting property, are the most remarkable features in the Peruvian polity. The whole territory of the empire was divided into three parts, one for the Sun, another for the Inca, and the last for the people. Which of the three was the largest is doubtful. The proportions differed materially in different provinces. The distribution, indeed, was made on the same general principle, as each new conquest was added to the monarchy; but the proportion varied according to the amount of population, and the greater or less amount of land consequently required for the support of the inhabitants.[13]

The lands assigned to the Sun furnished a revenue to support the temples, and maintain the costly ceremonial of the Peruvian worship and the multitudinous priesthood. Those reserved for the Inca went to support the royal state, as well as the numerous members of his household and his kindred, and supplied the various exigencies of government. The remainder of the lands was divided, *per capita,* in equal shares among the people. It was provided by law, as we shall see hereafter, that every Peruvian should marry at a certain age. When this event took place, the community or district in which he lived furnished him with a dwelling, which, as it was constructed of humble materials, was done at little cost. A lot of land was then assigned to him sufficient for his own maintenance and that of his wife. An additional portion was granted for every child, the amount allowed for a son being the double of that for a daughter. The division of the soil was renewed every year, and the possessions of the tenant were increased or diminished according to the numbers in his family.[14] The same arrangement was observed with reference to the curacas, except only that a domain was assigned to them corresponding with the superior dignity of their stations.[15]

A more thorough and effectual agrarian law than this cannot be imagined. In other countries where such a law has been introduced, its operation, after a time, has given way to the natural order of events, and, under the superior intelligence and thrift of some and the prodigality of others, the usual vicissitudes of fortune have been allowed to take their course, and restore things to their natural inequality. Even the iron law of Lycurgus ceased to operate after a time, and melted away before the spirit of luxury and avarice. The nearest approach to the Peruvian constitution was probably in Judea, where, on the recurrence of the great national jubilee, at the close of every half-century, estates reverted to their original proprietors. There was this important difference in Peru; that not only did the lease, if we may so call it, terminate with the year, but during that period the tenant had no power to alienate or to add to his possessions. The end of the brief term found him in precisely the same condition that he was in at the beginning. Such a state of things might be supposed to be fatal to any thing like attachment to the soil, or to that desire of improving it, which is natural to the permanent proprietor, and hardly less so to the holder of a long lease. But the practical operation of the law seems to have been otherwise; and it is probable, that, under the influence of that love of order and aversion to change which marked the Peruvian institutions, each new partition of the soil usually confirmed the occupant in his possession, and the tenant for a year was converted into a proprietor for life.

The territory was cultivated wholly by the people. The lands belonging to the Sun were first attended to. They next tilled the lands of the old, of the sick, of the widow and the orphan, and of soldiers engaged in actual service; in short, of all that part of the community who, from bodily infirmity or any other cause, were unable to attend to their own concerns. The people were then allowed to work on their own ground, each man for himself, but with the general obligation to assist his neighbour, when any circumstance—the burden of a young and numerous family, for example—might demand it.[16] Lastly, they cultivated the lands of the Inca. This was done, with great ceremony, by the whole population in a body. At break of day, they were summoned together by proclamation from some neighbouring tower or eminence, and all the inhabitants of the district, men, women, and children, appeared dressed in their gayest apparel, bedecked with their little store of finery and ornaments, as if for some great jubilee. They went through the labors of the day with the same joyous spirit, chanting their popular ballads which commemorated the heroic deeds of the Incas, regulating their movements by the measure of the chant, and all mingling in the chorus, of which the word *hailli,* or "triumph," was usually the burden. These national airs had something soft and pleasing in their character, that recommended them to the Spaniards; and many a Peruvian song was set to music by them after the Conquest, and was listened to by the unfortunate natives with melancholy satisfaction, as it called up recollections of the past, when their days glided peacefully away under the sceptre of the Incas.[17]

A similar arrangement prevailed with respect to the different manufactures as to the agricultural products of the country. The flocks of llamas, or Peruvian sheep, were appropriated exclusively to the Sun and to the Inca.[18] Their number was immense. They were scattered over the different provinces, chiefly in the colder regions of the country, where they were intrusted to the care of experienced shepherds, who conducted them to different pastures according to the change of season. A large number was every year sent to the capital for the consumption of the Court, and for the religious festivals and sacrifices. But these were only the males, as no female was allowed to be killed. The regulations for the care and breeding of these flocks were prescribed with the greatest minuteness, and with a sagacity which excited the admiration of the Spaniards, who were familiar with the management of the great migratory flocks of merinos in their own country.[19]

At the appointed season, they were all sheared, and the wool was deposited in the public magazines. It was then dealt out to each family in such quantities as sufficed for its wants, and was consigned to the female part of the household, who were well instructed in the business of spinning and weaving. When this labor was accomplished, and the family was provided with a coarse but warm covering, suited to the cold climate of the mountains,—for, in the lower country, cotton, furnished in like manner by the Crown, took the place, to a certain extent, of wool,—the people were required to labor for the Inca. The quantity of the cloth needed, as well as the peculiar kind and quality of the fabric, was first determined at Cuzco. The work was then apportioned among the different provinces. Officers, appointed for the purpose, superintended the distribution of the wool, so that the manufacture of the different articles should be intrusted to the most competent hands.[20] They did not leave the matter here, but entered the dwellings, from time to time, and saw that the work was faithfully executed.

This domestic inquisition was not confined to the labors for the Inca. It included, also, those for the several families; and care was taken that each household should employ the materials furnished for its own use in the manner that was intended, so that no one should be unprovided with necessary apparel.[21] In this domestic labor all the female part of the establishment was expected to join. Occupation was found for all, from the child five years old to the aged matron not too infirm to hold a distaff. No one, at least none but the decrepit and the sick, was allowed to eat the bread of idleness in Peru. Idleness was a crime in the eye of the law, and, as such, severely punished; while industry was publicly commended and stimulated by rewards.[22]

The like course was pursued with reference to the other requisitions of the government. All the mines in the kingdom belonged to the Inca. They were wrought exclusively for his benefit, by persons familiar with this service, and selected from the districts where the mines were situated.[23] Every Peruvian of the lower class was a husbandman, and, with the exception of those already specified, was expected to provide for his own support by the cultivation of his land. A small portion of the community, however, was instructed in mechanical arts; some of them of the more elegant kind, subservient to the purposes of luxury and ornament. The demand for these was chiefly limited to the sovereign and his Court; but the labor of a larger number of hands was exacted for the execution of the great public works which covered the land. The nature and amount of the services required were all determined at Cuzco by commissioners well instructed in the resources of the country, and in the character of the inhabitants of different provinces.[24]

This information was obtained by an admirable regulation, which has scarcely a counterpart in the annals of a semi-civilized people. A register was kept of all the births and deaths throughout the country, and exact returns of the actual population were made to government every year, by means of the *quipus,* a curious invention, which will be explained hereafter.[25] At certain intervals, also, a general survey of the country was made, exhibiting a complete view of the character of the soil, its fertility, the nature of its products, both agricultural and mineral, — in short, of all that constituted the physical resources of the empire.[26] Furnished with these statistical details, it was easy for the government, after determining the amount of requisitions, to distribute the work among the respective provinces best qualified to execute it. The task of apportioning the labor was assigned to the local authorities, and great care was taken that it should be done in such a manner, that, while the most competent hands were selected, it should not fall disproportionately heavy on any.[27]

The different provinces of the country furnished persons peculiarly suited to different employments, which, as we shall see hereafter, usually descended from father to son. Thus, one district supplied those most skilled in working the mines, another the most curious workers in metals, or in wood, and so on.[28] The artisan was provided by government with the materials; and no one

21

was required to give more than a stipulated portion of his time to the public service. He was then succeeded by another for the like term; and it should be observed, that all who were engaged in the employment of the government— and the remark applies equally to agricultural labor—were maintained, for the time, at the public expense.[29] By this constant rotation of labor, it was intended that no one should be overburdened, and that each man should have time to provide for the demands of his own household. It was impossible —in the judgment of a high Spanish authority—to improve on the system of distribution, so carefully was it accommodated to the condition and comfort of the artisan.[30] The security of the working classes seems to have been ever kept in view in the regulations of the government; and these were so discreetly arranged, that the most wearing and unwholesome labors, as those of the mines, occasioned no detriment to the health of the laborer; a striking contrast to his subsequent condition under the Spanish rule.[31]

A part of the agricultural produce and manufactures was transported to Cuzco, to minister to the immediate demands of the Inca and his Court. But far the greater part was stored in magazines scattered over the different provinces. These spacious buildings, constructed of stone, were divided between the Sun and the Inca, though the greater share seems to have been appropriated by the monarch. By a wise regulation, any deficiency in the contributions of the Inca might be supplied from the granaries of the Sun.[32] But such a necessity could rarely have happened; and the providence of the government usually left a large surplus in the royal depositories, which was removed to a third class of magazines, whose design was to supply the people in seasons of scarcity, and, occasionally, to furnish relief to individuals, whom sickness or misfortune had reduced to poverty; thus, in a manner, justifying the assertion of a Castilian document, that a large portion of the revenues of the Inca found its way back again, through one channel or another, into the hands of the people.[33] These magazines were found by the Spaniards, on their arrival, stored with all the various products and manufactures of the country, —with maize, *coca, quinua,* woollen and cotton stuffs of the finest quality, with vases and utensils of gold, silver, and copper, in short, with every article of luxury or use within the compass of Peruvian skill.[34] The magazines of grain, in particular, would frequently have sufficed for the consumption of the adjoining district for several years.[35] An inventory of the various products of the country, and the quarters whence they were obtained, was every year taken by the royal officers, and recorded by the *quipucamayus* on their registers, with surprising regularity and precision. These registers were transmitted to the capital, and submitted to the Inca, who could thus at a glance, as it were, embrace the whole results of the national industry, and see how far they corresponded with the requisitions of government.[36]

Such are some of the most remarkable features of the Peruvian institutions relating to property, as delineated by writers who, however contradictory in the details, have a general conformity of outline. These institutions are certainly so remarkable, that it is hardly credible they should ever have been enforced throughout a great empire, and for a long period of years. Yet we have the most unequivocal testimony to the fact from the Spaniards, who landed in Peru in time to witness their operation; some of whom, men of high judicial station and character, were commissioned by the government to make investigations into the state of the country under its ancient rulers.

The impositions on the Peruvian people seem to have been sufficiently heavy. On them rested the whole burden of maintaining, not only their own order, but every other order in the state. The members of the royal house, the great nobles, even the public functionaries, and the numerous body of the priesthood, were all exempt from taxation.[37] The whole duty of defraying the expenses of the government belonged to the people. Yet this was not materially different from the condition of things formerly existing in most parts of Europe, where the various privileged classes claimed exemption—not always with success, indeed—from bearing part of the public burdens. The great hardship in the case of the Peruvian was, that he could not better his condition. His labors were for others, rather than for himself. However industrious, he could not add a rood to his own possessions, nor advance himself one hair's breadth in the social scale. The great and universal motive to honest industry, that of bettering one's lot, was lost upon him. The great law of human progress was not for him. As he was born, so he was to die. Even his time he could not properly call his own. Without money, with little property of any kind, he paid his taxes in labor.[38] No wonder that the government should have dealt with sloth as a crime. It was a crime against the state, and to be wasteful of time was, in a manner, to rob the exchequer. The Peruvian, laboring all his life for others, might be compared to the convict in a treadmill, going the same dull round of incessant toil, with the consciousness, that, however profitable the results to the state, they were nothing to him.

But this is the dark side of the picture. If no man could become rich in Peru, no man could become poor. No spendthrift could waste his substance in riotous luxury. No adventurous schemer could impoverish his family by the spirit of speculation. The law was constantly directed to enforce a steady industry and a sober management of his affairs. No mendicant was tolerated in Peru. When a man was reduced by poverty or misfortune, (it could hardly be by fault,) the arm of the law was stretched out to minister relief; not the stinted relief of private charity, nor that which is doled out, drop by drop, as it were, from the frozen reservoirs of "the parish," but in generous measure, bringing no humiliation to the object of it, and placing him on a level with the rest of his countrymen.[39]

No man could be rich, no man could be poor, in Peru; but all might enjoy, and did enjoy, a competence. Ambition, avarice, the love of change, the morbid spirit of discontent, those passions which most agitate the minds of men, found no place in the bosom of the Peruvian. The very condition of his being seemed to be at war with change. He moved on in the same unbroken circle in which his fathers had moved before him, and in which his children were to follow. It was the object of the Incas to infuse into their subjects a spirit of passive obedience and tranquillity,—a perfect acquiescence in the established order of things. In this they fully succeeded. The Spaniards who first visited the country are emphatic in their testimony, that no government could have been better suited to the genius of the people; and no people could have appeared more contented with their lot, or more devoted to their government.[40]

Those who may distrust the accounts of Peruvian industry will find their doubts removed on a visit to the country. The traveller still meets, especially in the central regions of the table-land, with memorials of the past, remains of temples, palaces, fortresses, terraced mountains, great military roads, aqueducts, and other public works, which, whatever degree of science they may display in their execution, astonish him by their number, the massive character of the materials, and the grandeur of the design. Among them, perhaps the most remarkable are the great roads, the broken remains of which are still in sufficient preservation to attest their former magnificence. There were many of these roads, traversing different parts of the kingdom; but the most considerable were the two which extended from Quito to Cuzco, and, again diverging from the capital, continued in a southern direction towards Chili.

One of these roads passed over the grand plateau, and the other along the lowlands on the borders of the ocean. The former was much the more difficult achievement, from the character of the country. It was conducted over pathless sierras buried in snow; galleries were cut for leagues through the living rock; rivers were crossed by means of bridges that swung suspended in the air; precipices were scaled by stairways hewn out of the native bed; ravines of hideous depth were filled up with solid masonry; in short, all the difficulties that beset a wild and mountainous region, and which might appall the most courageous engineer of modern times, were encountered and successfully overcome. The length of the road, of which scattered fragments only remain, is variously estimated, from fifteen hundred to two thousand miles; and stone pillars, in the manner of European milestones, were erected at stated intervals of somewhat more than a league, all along the route. Its breadth scarcely exceeded twenty feet.[41] It was built of heavy flags of freestone, and in some parts, at least, covered with a bituminous cement, which time has made harder than the stone itself. In some places, where the ravines had been filled up with masonry, the mountain torrents, wearing on it for ages, have gradually eaten a way through the base, and left the superincumbent mass—such is the cohesion of the materials—still spanning the valley like an arch![42]

Over some of the boldest streams it was necessary to construct suspension bridges, as they are termed, made of the tough fibres of the maguey, or of the osier of the country, which has an extraordinary degree of tenacity and strength. These osiers were woven into cables of the thickness of a man's body. The huge ropes, then stretched across the water, were conducted through rings or holes cut in immense buttresses of stone raised on the opposite banks of the river, and there secured to heavy pieces of timber. Several of these enormous cables, bound together, formed a bridge, which, covered with planks, well secured and defended by a railing of the same osier materials on the sides, afforded a safe passage for the traveller. The length of this aërial bridge, sometimes exceeding two hundred feet, caused it, confined, as it was, only at the extremities, to dip with an alarming inclination towards the centre, while the motion given to it by the passenger occasioned an oscillation still more frightful, as his eye wandered over the dark abyss of waters that foamed and tumbled many a fathom beneath. Yet these light and fragile fabrics were crossed without fear by the Peruvians, and are still retained by the Spaniards over those streams which, from the depth or impetuosity of the current, would seem impracticable for the usual modes of conveyance. The wider and more tranquil waters were crossed on *balsas*—a kind of raft still much used by the natives—to which sails were attached, furnishing the only instance of this higher kind of navigation among the American Indians.[43]

The other great road of the Incas lay through the level country between the Andes and the ocean. It was constructed in a different manner, as demanded by the nature of the ground, which was for the most part low, and much of it sandy. The causeway was raised on a high embankment of earth, and defended on either side by a parapet or wall of clay; and trees and odoriferous shrubs were planted along the margin, regaling the sense of the traveller with their perfumes, and refreshing him by their shades, so grateful under the burning sky of the tropics. In the strips of sandy waste, which occasionally intervened, where the light and volatile soil was incapable of sustaining a road, huge piles, many of them to be seen at this day, were driven into the ground to indicate the route to the traveller.[44]

All along these highways, caravansaries, or *tambos*, as they were called, were erected, at the distance of ten or twelve miles from each other, for the accommodation, more particularly, of the Inca and his suite, and those who journeyed on the public business. There were few other travellers in Peru. Some of these buildings were on an extensive scale, consisting of a fortress, barracks, and other military works, surrounded by a parapet of stone, and covering a large tract of ground. These were evidently destined for the accommodation of the imperial armies, when on their march across the country.—The care of the great roads was committed to the districts through which they passed, and a large number of hands was constantly employed under the Incas to keep them in repair. This was the more easily done in a country where the mode of travelling was altogether on foot; though the roads are said to have been so nicely constructed, that a carriage might have rolled over them as securely as on any of the great roads of Europe.[45] Still, in a region where the elements of fire and water are both actively at work in the business of destruction, they must, without constant supervision, have gradually gone to decay. Such has been their fate under the Spanish conquerors, who took no care to enforce the admirable system for their preservation adopted by the Incas. Yet the broken portions that still survive, here and there, like the fragments of the great Roman roads scattered over Europe, bear evidence to their primitive grandeur, and have drawn forth the eulogium from a discriminating traveller, usually not too profuse in his panegyric, that "the roads of the Incas were among the most useful and stupendous works ever executed by man."[46]

The system of communication through their dominions was still further improved by the Peruvian sovereigns, by the introduction of posts, in the same manner as was done by the Aztecs. The Peruvian posts, however, established on all the great routes that conducted to the capital, were on a much more extended plan than those in Mexico. All along these routes, small buildings were erected, at the distance of less than five miles asunder,[47] in each of which a number of runners, or *chasquis,* as they were called, were stationed to carry forward the despatches of government.[48] These despatches were either verbal, or conveyed by means of *quipus,* and sometimes accompanied by a thread of the crimson fringe worn round the temples of the Inca, which was regarded with the same implicit deference as the signet ring of an Oriental despot.[49]

The *chasquis* were dressed in a peculiar livery, intimating their profession. They were all trained to the employment, and selected for their speed and fidelity. As the distance each courier had to perform was small, and as he had ample time to refresh himself at the stations, they ran over the ground with great swiftness, and messages were carried through the whole extent of the long routes, at the rate of a hundred and fifty miles a day. The office of the *chasquis* was not limited to carrying despatches. They frequently brought various articles for the use of the Court; and in this way, fish from the distant ocean, fruits, game, and different commodities from the hot regions on the coast, were taken to the capital in good condition, and served fresh at the royal table.[50] It is remarkable that this important institution should have been known to both the Mexicans and the Peruvians without any correspondence with one another; and that it should have been found among two barbarian nations of the New World, long before it was introduced among the civilized nations of Europe.[51]

By these wise contrivances of the Incas, the most distant parts of the long-extended empire of Peru were brought into intimate relations with each other. And while the capitals of Christendom, but a few hundred miles apart, remained as far asunder as if seas had rolled between them, the great capitals Cuzco and Quito were placed by the high roads of the Incas in immediate correspondence. Intelligence from the numerous provinces was transmitted on the wings of the wind to the Peruvian metropolis, the great focus to which all the lines of communication converged. Not an insurrectionary movement could occur, not an invasion on the remotest frontier, before the tidings were conveyed to the capital, and the imperial armies were on their march across the magnificent roads of the country to suppress it. So admirable was the machinery contrived by the American despots for maintaining tranquillity throughout their dominions! It may remind us of the similar institutions of ancient Rome, when, under the Cæsars, she was mistress of half the world.

A principal design of the great roads was to serve the purposes of military communication. It formed an important item of their military policy, which is quite as well worth studying as their municipal.

Notwithstanding the pacific professions of the Incas, and the pacific tendency, indeed, of their domestic institutions, they were constantly at war. It was by war that their paltry territory had been gradually enlarged to a powerful empire. When this was achieved, the capital, safe in its central position, was no longer shaken by these military movements, and the country enjoyed, in a great degree, the blessings of tranquillity and order. But, however tranquil at heart, there is not a reign upon record in which the nation was not engaged in war against the barbarous nations on the frontier. Religion furnished a plausible pretext for incessant aggression, and disguised the lust of conquest in the Incas, probably, from their own eyes, as well as from those of their subjects. Like the followers of Mahomet, bearing the sword in one hand and the Koran in the other, the Incas of Peru offered no alternative but the worship of the Sun or war.

It is true, their fanaticism—or their policy—showed itself in a milder form than was found in the descendants of the Prophet. Like the great luminary which they adored, they operated by gentleness more potent than violence.[52] They sought to soften the hearts of the rude tribes around them, and melt them by acts of condescension and kindness. Far from provoking hostilities, they allowed time for the salutary example of their own institutions to work its effect, trusting that their less civilized neighbours would submit to their sceptre, from a conviction of the blessings it would secure to them. When this course failed, they employed other measures, but still of a pacific character; and endeavoured by negotiation, by conciliatory treatment, and by presents to the leading men, to win them over to their dominion. In short, they practised all the arts familiar to the most subtle politician of a civilized land to secure the acquisition of empire. When all these expedients failed, they prepared for war.

Their levies were drawn from all the different provinces; though from some, where the character of the people was particularly hardy, more than from others.[53] It seems probable that every Peruvian, who had reached a certain age, might be called to bear arms. But the rotation of military service, and the regular drills, which took place twice or thrice in a month, of the inhabitants of every village, raised the soldiers generally above the rank of a raw militia. The Peruvian army, at first inconsiderable, came, with the increase of population, in the latter days of the empire, to be very large, so that their monarchs could bring into the field, as contemporaries assure us, a force amounting to two hundred thousand men. They showed the same skill and respect for order in their military organization, as in other things. The troops were divided into bodies corresponding with our battalions and companies, led by officers, that rose, in regular gradation, from the lowest subaltern to the Inca noble, who was intrusted with the general command.[54]

Their arms consisted of the usual weapons employed by nations, whether civilized or uncivilized, before the invention of powder, — bows and arrows, lances, darts, a short kind of sword, a battle-axe or partisan, and slings, with which they were very expert. Their spears and arrows were tipped with copper, or, more commonly, with bone, and the weapons of the Inca lords were frequently mounted with gold or silver. Their heads were protected by casques made either of wood or of the skins of wild animals, and sometimes richly decorated with metal and with precious stones, surmounted by the brilliant plumage of the tropical birds. These, of course, were the ornaments only of the higher orders. The great mass of the soldiery were dressed in the peculiar costume of their provinces, and their heads were wreathed with a sort of turban or roll of different-colored cloths, that produced a gay and animating effect. Their defensive armor consisted of a shield or buckler, and a close tunic of quilted cotton, in the same manner as with the Mexicans. Each company had its particular banner, and the imperial standard, high above all, displayed the glittering device of the rainbow, — the armorial ensign of the Incas, intimating their claims as children of the skies.[55]

By means of the thorough system of communication established in the country, a short time sufficed to draw the levies together from the most distant quarters. The army was put under the direction of some experienced chief, of the blood royal, or, more frequently, headed by the Inca in person. The march was rapidly performed, and with little fatigue to the soldier; for, all along the great routes, quarters were provided for him, at regular distances, where he could find ample accommodations. The country is still covered with the remains of military works, constructed of porphyry or granite, which tradition assures us were designed to lodge the Inca and his army.[56]

At regular intervals, also, magazines were established, filled with grain, weapons, and the different munitions of war, with which the army was supplied on its march. It was the especial care of the government to see that these magazines, which were furnished from the stores of the Incas, were always well filled. When the Spaniards invaded the country, they supported their own armies for a long time on the provisions found in them.[57] The Peruvian soldier was forbidden to commit any trespass on the property of the inhabitants whose territory lay in the line of march. Any violation of this order was punished with death.[58] The soldier was clothed and fed by the industry of the people, and the Incas rightly resolved that he should not repay this by violence. Far from being a tax on the labors of the husbandman, or even a burden on his hospitality, the imperial armies traversed the country, from one extremity to the other, with as little inconvenience to the inhabitants, as would be created by a procession of peaceful burghers, or a muster of holiday soldiers for a review.

28

From the moment war was proclaimed, the Peruvian monarch used all possible expedition in assembling his forces, that he might anticipate the movements of his enemies, and prevent a combination with their allies. It was, however, from the neglect of such a principle of combination, that the several nations of the country, who might have prevailed by confederated strength, fell one after another under the imperial yoke. Yet, once in the field, the Inca did not usually show any disposition to push his advantages to the utmost, and urge his foe to extremity. In every stage of the war, he was open to propositions for peace; and although he sought to reduce his enemies by carrying off their harvests and distressing them by famine, he allowed his troops to commit no unnecessary outrage on person or property. "We must spare our enemies," one of the Peruvian princes is quoted as saying, "or it will be our loss, since they and all that belongs to them must soon be ours."[59] It was a wise maxim, and, like most other wise maxims, founded equally on benevolence and prudence. The Incas adopted the policy claimed for the Romans by their countryman, who tells us that they gained more by clemency to the vanquished than by their victories.[60]

In the same considerate spirit, they were most careful to provide for the security and comfort of their own troops; and, when a war was long protracted, or the climate proved unhealthy, they took care to relieve their men by frequent reinforcements, allowing the earlier recruits to return to their homes.[61] But while thus economical of life, both in their own followers and in the enemy, they did not shrink from sterner measures when provoked by the ferocious or obstinate character of the resistance; and the Peruvian annals contain more than one of those sanguinary pages which cannot be pondered at the present day without a shudder. It should be added, that the beneficent policy, which I have been delineating as characteristic of the Incas, did not belong to all; and that there was more than one of the royal line who displayed a full measure of the bold and unscrupulous spirit of the vulgar conqueror.

The first step of the government, after the reduction of a country, was to introduce there the worship of the Sun. Temples were erected, and placed under the care of a numerous priesthood, who expounded to the conquered people the mysteries of their new faith, and dazzled them by the display of its rich and stately ceremonial.[62] Yet the religion of the conquered was not treated with dishonor. The Sun was to be worshipped above all; but the images of their gods were removed to Cuzco and established in one of the temples, to hold their rank among the inferior deities of the Peruvian Pantheon. Here they remained as hostages, in some sort, for the conquered nation, which would be the less inclined to forsake its allegiance, when by doing so it must leave its own gods in the hands of its enemies.[63]

The Incas provided for the settlement of their new conquests, by ordering a census to be taken of the population, and a careful survey to be made of the country, ascertaining its products, and the character and capacity of its soil.[64] A division of the territory was then made on the same principle with that adopted throughout their own kingdom; and their respective portions were assigned to the Sun, the sovereign, and the people. The amount of the last was regulated by the amount of the population, but the share of each individual was uniformly the same. It may seem strange, that any people should patiently have acquiesced in an arrangement which involved such a total surrender of property. But it was a conquered nation that did so, held in awe, on the least suspicion of meditating resistance, by armed garrisons, who were established at various commanding points throughout the country.[65] It is probable, too, that the Incas made no greater changes than was essential to the new arrangement, and that they assigned estates, as far as possible, to their former proprietors. The curacas, in particular, were confirmed in their ancient authority; or, when it was found expedient to depose the existing curaca, his rightful heir was allowed to succeed him.[66] Every respect was shown to the ancient usages and laws of the land, as far as was compatible with the fundamental institutions of the Incas. It must also be remembered, that the conquered tribes were, many of them, too little advanced in civilization to possess that attachment to the soil which belongs to a cultivated nation.[67] But, to whatever it be referred, it seems probable that the extraordinary institutions of the Incas were established with little opposition in the conquered territories.[68]

Yet the Peruvian sovereigns did not trust altogether to this show of obedience in their new vassals; and, to secure it more effectually, they adopted some expedients too remarkable to be passed by in silence.—Immediately after a recent conquest, the curacas and their families were removed for a time to Cuzco. Here they learned the language of the capital, became familiar with the manners and usages of the court, as well as with the general policy of government, and experienced such marks of favor from the sovereign as would be most grateful to their feelings, and might attach them most warmly to his person. Under the influence of these sentiments, they were again sent to rule over their vassals, but still leaving their eldest sons in the capital, to remain there as a guaranty for their own fidelity, as well as to grace the court of the Inca.[69]

Another expedient was of a bolder and more original character. This was nothing less than to revolutionize the language of the country. South America, like North, was broken up into a great variety of dialects, or rather languages, having little affinity with one another. This circumstance occasioned great embarrassment to the government in the administration of the different provinces, with whose idioms they were unacquainted. It was determined, therefore, to substitute one universal language, the *Quichua*,—the language of the court, the capital, and the surrounding country,—the richest and most comprehensive of the South American dialects. Teachers were provided in the towns and villages throughout the land, who were to give instruction to all, even the humblest classes; and it was intimated at the same time, that no one should be raised to any office of dignity or profit, who was unacquainted with this tongue. The curacas and other chiefs, who attended at the capital, became familiar with this dialect in their intercourse with the Court, and, on their return home, set the example of conversing in it among themselves. This example was imitated by their followers, and the Quichua gradually became the language of elegance and fashion, in the same manner as the Norman French was affected by all those who aspired to any consideration in England, after the Conquest. By this means, while each province retained its peculiar tongue, a beautiful medium of communication was introduced, which enabled the inhabitants of one part of the country to hold intercourse with every other, and the Inca and his deputies to communicate with all. This was the state of things on the arrival of the Spaniards. It must be admitted, that history furnishes few examples of more absolute authority than such a revolution in the language of an empire, at the bidding of a master.[70]

Yet little less remarkable was another device of the Incas for securing the loyalty of their subjects. When any portion of the recent conquests showed a pertinacious spirit of disaffection, it was not uncommon to cause a part of the population, amounting, it might be, to ten thousand inhabitants or more, to remove to a distant quarter of the kingdom, occupied by ancient vassals of undoubted fidelity to the crown. A like number of these last was transplanted to the territory left vacant by the emigrants. By this exchange, the population was composed of two distinct races, who regarded each other with an eye of jealousy, that served as an effectual check on any mutinous proceeding. In time, the influence of the well-affected prevailed, supported, as they were, by royal authority, and by the silent working of the national institutions, to which the strange races became gradually accustomed. A spirit of loyalty sprang up by degrees in their bosoms, and, before a generation had passed away, the different tribes mingled in harmony together as members of the same community.[71] Yet the different races continued to be distinguished by difference of dress; since, by the law of the land, every citizen was required to wear the costume of his native province.[72] Neither could the colonist, who had been thus unceremoniously transplanted, return to his native district. For, by another law, it was forbidden to any one to change his residence without license.[73] He was settled for life. The Peruvian government prescribed to every man his local habitation, his sphere of action, nay, the very nature and quality of that action. He ceased to be a free agent; it might be almost said, that it relieved him of personal responsibility.

In following out this singular arrangement, the Incas showed as much regard for the comfort and convenience of the colonist as was compatible with the execution of their design. They were careful that the *mitimaes*, as these emigrants were styled, should be removed to climates most congenial with their own. The inhabitants of the cold countries were not transplanted to the warm, nor the inhabitants of the warm countries to the cold.[74] Even their habitual occupations were consulted, and the fisherman was settled in the neighbourhood of the ocean, or the great lakes; while such lands were assigned to the husbandman as were best adapted to the culture with which he was most familiar.[75] And, as migration by many, perhaps by most, would, be regarded as a calamity, the government was careful to show particular marks of favor to the *mitimaes,* and, by various privileges and immunities, to ameliorate their condition, and thus to reconcile them, if possible, to their lot.[76]

The Peruvian institutions, though they may have been modified and matured under successive sovereigns, all bear the stamp of the same original, —were all cast in the same mould. The empire, strengthening and enlarging at every successive epoch of its history, was, in its latter days, but the development, on a great scale, of what it was in miniature at its commencement, as the infant germ is said to contain within itself all the ramifications of the future monarch of the forest. Each succeeding Inca seemed desirous only to tread in the path, and carry out the plans, of his predecessor. Great enterprises, commenced under one, were continued by another, and completed by a third. Thus, while all acted on a regular plan, without any of the eccentric or retrograde movements which betray the agency of different individuals, the state seemed to be under the direction of a single hand, and steadily pursued, as if through one long reign, its great career of civilization and of conquest.

The ultimate aim of its institutions was domestic quiet. But it seemed as if this were to be obtained only by foreign war. Tranquillity in the heart of the monarchy, and war on its borders, was the condition of Peru. By this war it gave occupation to a part of its people, and, by the reduction and civilization of its barbarous neighbours, gave security to all. Every Inca sovereign, however mild and benevolent in his domestic rule, was a warrior, and led his armies in person. Each successive reign extended still wider the boundaries of the empire. Year after year saw the victorious monarch return laden with spoils, and followed by a throng of tributary chieftains to his capital. His reception there was a Roman triumph. The whole of its numerous population poured out to welcome him, dressed in the gay and picturesque costumes of the different provinces, with banners waving above their heads, and strewing branches and flowers along the path of the conqueror. The Inca, borne aloft in his golden chair on the shoulders of his nobles, moved in solemn procession, under the triumphal arches that were thrown across the way, to the great temple of the Sun. There, without attendants,—for all but the monarch were excluded from the hallowed precincts,—the victorious prince, stripped of his royal insignia, barefooted, and with all humility, approached the awful shrine, and offered up sacrifice and thanksgiving to the glorious Deity who presided over the fortunes of the Incas. This ceremony concluded, the whole population gave itself up to festivity; music, revelry, and dancing were heard in every quarter of the capital, and illuminations and bonfires commemorated the victorious campaign of the Inca, and the accession of a new territory to his empire.[77]

In this celebration we see much of the character of a religious festival. Indeed, the character of religion was impressed on all the Peruvian wars. The life of an Inca was one long crusade against the infidel, to spread wide the worship of the Sun, to reclaim the benighted nations from their brutish super-stitions, and impart to them the blessings of a well-regulated government. This, in the favorite phrase of our day, was the "mission" of the Inca. It was also the mission of the Christian conqueror who invaded the empire of this same Indian potentate. Which of the two executed his mission most faithfully, history must decide.

Yet the Peruvian monarchs did not show a childish impatience in the acquisition of empire. They paused after a campaign, and allowed time for the settlement of one conquest before they undertook another; and, in this interval, occupied themselves with the quiet administration of their kingdom, and with the long progresses, which brought them into nearer intercourse with their people. During this interval, also, their new vassals had begun to accommodate themselves to the strange institutions of their masters. They learned to appreciate the value of a government which raised them above the physical evils of a state of barbarism, secured them protection of person, and a full participation in all the privileges enjoyed by their conquerors; and, as they became more familiar with the peculiar institutions of the country, habit, that second nature, attached them the more strongly to these institutions, from their very peculiarity. Thus, by degrees, and without violence, arose the great fabric of the Peruvian empire, composed of numerous independent and even hostile tribes, yet, under the influence of a common religion, common language, and common government, knit together as one nation, animated by a spirit of love for its institutions and devoted loyalty to its sovereign. What a contrast to the condition of the Aztec monarchy, on the neighbouring continent, which, composed of the like heterogeneous materials, without any internal principle of cohesion, was only held together by the stern pressure, from without, of physical force!—Why the Peruvian monarchy should have fared no better than its rival, in its conflict with European civilization, will appear in the following pages.

CHAPTER III

PERUVIAN RELIGION. — DEITIES. — GORGEOUS TEMPLES. — FESTIVALS. — VIRGINS OF THE SUN. — MARRIAGE

IT is a remarkable fact, that many, if not most, of the rude tribes inhabiting the vast American continent, however disfigured their creeds may have been in other respects by a childish superstition, had attained to the sublime conception of one Great Spirit, the Creator of the Universe, who, immaterial in his own nature, was not to be dishonored by an attempt at visible representation, and who, pervading all space, was not to be circumscribed within the walls of a temple. Yet these elevated ideas, so far beyond the ordinary range of the untutored intellect, do not seem to have led to the practical consequences that might have been expected; and few of the American nations have shown much solicitude for the maintenance of a religious worship, or found in their faith a powerful spring of action.

But, with progress in civilization, ideas more akin to those of civilized communities were gradually unfolded; a liberal provision was made, and a separate order instituted, for the services of religion, which were conducted with a minute and magnificent ceremonial, that challenged comparison, in some respects, with that of the most polished nations of Christendom. This was the case with the nations inhabiting the table-land of North America, and with the natives of Bogotá, Quito, Peru, and the other elevated regions on the great Southern continent. It was, above all, the case with the Peruvians, who claimed a divine original for the founders of their empire, whose laws all rested on a divine sanction, and whose domestic institutions and foreign wars were alike directed to preserve and propagate their faith. Religion was the basis of their polity, the very condition, as it were, of their social existence. The government of the Incas, in its essential principles, was a theocracy.

Yet, though religion entered so largely into the fabric and conduct of the political institutions of the people, their mythology, that is, the traditionary legends by which they affected to unfold the mysteries of the universe, was exceedingly mean and puerile. Scarce one of their traditions—except the beautiful one respecting the founders of their royal dynasty—is worthy of note, or throws much light on their own antiquities, or the primitive history of man. Among the traditions of importance is one of the deluge, which they held in common with so many of the nations in all parts of the globe, and which they related with some particulars that bear resemblance to a Mexican legend.[1]

Their ideas in respect to a future state of being deserve more attention. They admitted the existence of the soul hereafter, and connected with this a belief in the resurrection of the body. They assigned two distinct places for the residence of the good and of the wicked, the latter of which they fixed in the centre of the earth. The good they supposed were to pass a luxurious life of tranquillity and ease, which comprehended their highest notions of happiness. The wicked were to expiate their crimes by ages of wearisome labor. They associated with these ideas a belief in an evil principle or spirit, bearing the name of Cupay, whom they did not attempt to propitiate by sacrifices, and who seems to have been only a shadowy personification of sin, that exercised little influence over their conduct.[2]

It was this belief in the resurrection of the body, which led them to preserve the body with so much solicitude,—by a simple process, however, that, unlike the elaborate embalming of the Egyptians, consisted in exposing it to the action of the cold, exceedingly dry, and highly rarefied atmosphere of the mountains.[3] As they believed that the occupations in the future world would have great resemblance to those of the present, they buried with the deceased noble some of his apparel, his utensils, and, frequently, his treasures; and completed the gloomy ceremony by sacrificing his wives and favorite domestics, to bear him company and do him service in the happy regions beyond the clouds.[4] Vast mounds of an irregular, or, more frequently, oblong shape, penetrated by galleries running at right angles to each other, were raised over the dead, whose dried bodies or mummies have been found in considerable numbers, sometimes erect, but more often in the sitting posture, common to the Indian tribes of both continents. Treasures of great value have also been occasionally drawn from these monumental deposits, and have stimulated speculators to repeated excavations with the hope of similar good fortune. It was a lottery like that of searching after mines, but where the chances have proved still more against the adventurers.[5]

The Peruvians, like so many other of the Indian races, acknowledged a Supreme Being, the Creator and Ruler of the Universe, whom they adored under the different names of Pachacamac and Viracocha.[6] No temple was raised to this invisible Being, save one only in the valley which took its name from the deity himself, not far from the Spanish city of Lima. Even this temple had existed there before the country came under the sway of the Incas, and was the great resort of Indian pilgrims from remote parts of the land; a circumstance which suggests the idea, that the worship of this Great Spirit, though countenanced, perhaps, by their accommodating policy, did not originate with the Peruvian princes.[7]

The deity whose worship they especially inculcated, and which they never failed to establish wherever their banners were known to penetrate, was the Sun. It was he, who, in a particular manner, presided over the destinies of man; gave light and warmth to the nations, and life to the vegetable world; whom they reverenced as the father of their royal dynasty, the founder of their empire; and whose temples rose in every city and almost every village throughout the land, while his altars smoked with burnt offerings, — a form of sacrifice peculiar to the Peruvians among the semi-civilized nations of the New World.[8]

Besides the Sun, the Incas acknowledged various objects of worship in some way or other connected with this principal deity. Such was the Moon, his sister-wife; the Stars, revered as part of her heavenly train, — though the fairest of them, Venus, known to the Peruvians by the name of Chasca, or the "youth with the long and curling locks," was adored as the page of the Sun, whom he attends so closely in his rising and in his setting. They dedicated temples also to the Thunder and Lightning,[9] in whom they recognized the Sun's dread ministers, and to the Rainbow, whom they worshipped as a beautiful emanation of their glorious deity.[10]

In addition to these, the subjects of the Incas enrolled among their inferior deities many objects in nature, as the elements, the winds, the earth, the air, great mountains and rivers, which impressed them with ideas of sublimity and power, or were supposed in some way or other to exercise a mysterious influence over the destinies of man.[11] They adopted also a notion, not unlike that professed by some of the schools of ancient philosophy, that every thing on earth had its archetype or idea, its *mother*, as they emphatically styled it, which they held sacred, as, in some sort, its spiritual essence.[12] But their system, far from being limited even to these multiplied objects of devotion, embraced within its ample folds the numerous deities of the conquered nations, whose images were transported to the capital, where the burdensome charges of their worship were defrayed by their respective provinces. It was a rare stroke of policy in the Incas, who could thus accommodate their religion to their interests.[13]

But the worship of the Sun constituted the peculiar care of the Incas, and was the object of their lavish expenditure. The most ancient of the many temples dedicated to this divinity was in the Island of Titicaca, whence the royal founders of the Peruvian line were said to have proceeded. From this circumstance, this sanctuary was held in peculiar veneration. Every thing which belonged to it, even the broad fields of maize, which surrounded the temple, and formed part of its domain, imbibed a portion of its sanctity. The yearly produce was distributed among the different public magazines, in small quantities to each, as something that would sanctify the remainder of the store. Happy was the man who could secure even an ear of the blessed harvest for his own granary![14]

But the most renowned of the Peruvian temples, the pride of the capital, and the wonder of the empire, was at Cuzco, where, under the munificence of successive sovereigns, it had become so enriched, that it received the name of *Coricancha*, or "the Place of Gold." It consisted of a principal building and several chapels and inferior edifices, covering a large extent of ground in the heart of the city, and completely encompassed by a wall, which, with the edifices, was all constructed of stone. The work was of the kind already described in the other public buildings of the country, and was so finely executed, that a Spaniard, who saw it in its glory, assures us, he could call to mind only two edifices in Spain, which, for their workmanship, were at all to be compared with it.[15] Yet this substantial, and, in some respects, magnificent structure, was thatched with straw!

The interior of the temple was the most worthy of admiration. It was literally a mine of gold. On the western wall was emblazoned a representation of the deity, consisting of a human countenance, looking forth from amidst innumerable rays of light, which emanated from it in every direction, in the same manner as the sun is often personified with us. The figure was engraved on a massive plate of gold of enormous dimensions, thickly powdered with emeralds and precious stones.[16] It was so situated in front of the great eastern portal, that the rays of the morning sun fell directly upon it at its rising, lighting up the whole apartment with an effulgence that seemed more than natural, and which was reflected back from the golden ornaments with which the walls and ceiling were everywhere incrusted. Gold, in the figurative language of the people, was "the tears wept by the sun,"[17] and every part of the interior of the temple glowed with burnished plates and studs of the precious metal. The cornices, which surrounded the walls of the sanctuary, were of the same costly material; and a broad belt or frieze of gold, let into the stonework, encompassed the whole exterior of the edifice.[18]

Adjoining the principal structure were several chapels of smaller dimensions. One of them was consecrated to the Moon, the deity held next in reverence, as the mother of the Incas. Her effigy was delineated in the same manner as that of the Sun, on a vast plate that nearly covered one side of the apartment. But this plate, as well as all the decorations of the building, was of silver, as suited to the pale, silvery light of the beautiful planet. There were three other chapels, one of which was dedicated to the host of Stars, who formed the bright court of the Sister of the Sun; another was consecrated to his dread ministers of vengeance, the Thunder and the Lightning; and a third, to the Rainbow, whose many-colored arch spanned the walls of the edifice with hues almost as radiant as its own. There were besides several other buildings, or insulated apartments, for the accommodation of the numerous priests who officiated in the services of the temple.[19]

All the plate, the ornaments, the utensils of every description, appropriated to the uses of religion, were of gold or silver. Twelve immense vases of the latter metal stood on the floor of the great saloon, filled with grain of the Indian corn;[20] the censers for the perfumes, the ewers which held the water for sacrifice, the pipes which conducted it through subterraneous channels into the buildings, the reservoirs that received it, even the agricultural implements used in the gardens of the temple, were all of the same rich materials. The gardens, like those described, belonging to the royal palaces, sparkled with flowers of gold and silver, and various imitations of the vegetable kingdom. Animals, also, were to be found there,—among which the llama, with its golden fleece, was most conspicuous,—executed in the same style, and with a degree of skill, which, in this instance, probably, did not surpass the excellence of the material.[21]

If the reader sees in this fairy picture only the romantic coloring of some fabulous *El Dorado*, he must recall what has been said before in reference to the palaces of the Incas, and consider that these "Houses of the Sun," as they were styled, were the common reservoir into which flowed all the streams of public and private benefaction throughout the empire. Some of the statements, through credulity, and others, in the desire of exciting admiration, may be greatly exaggerated; but, in the coincidence of contemporary testimony, it is not easy to determine the exact line which should mark the measure of our skepticism. Certain it is, that the glowing picture I have given is warranted by those who saw these buildings in their pride, or shortly after they had been despoiled by the cupidity of their countrymen. Many of the costly articles were buried by the natives, or thrown into the waters of the rivers and the lakes; but enough remained to attest the unprecedented opulence of these religious establishments. Such things as were in their nature portable were speedily removed, to gratify the craving of the Conquerors, who even tore away the solid cornices and frieze of gold from the great temple, filling the vacant places with the cheaper, but—since it affords no temptation to avarice—more durable, material of plaster. Yet even thus shorn of their splendor, the venerable edifices still presented an attraction to the spoiler, who found in their dilapidated walls an inexhaustible quarry for the erection of other buildings. On the very ground once crowned by the gorgeous Coricancha rose the stately church of St. Dominic, one of the most magnificent structures of the New World. Fields of maize and lucerne now bloom on the spot which glowed with the golden gardens of the temple; and the friar chants his orisons within the consecrated precincts once occupied by the Children of the Sun.[22]

Besides the great temple of the Sun, there was a large number of inferior temples and religious houses in the Peruvian capital and its environs, amounting, as is stated, to three or four hundred.[23] For Cuzco was a sanctified spot, venerated not only as the abode of the Incas, but of all those deities who presided over the motley nations of the empire. It was the city beloved of the Sun; where his worship was maintained in its splendor; "where every fountain, pathway, and wall," says an ancient chronicler, "was regarded as a holy mystery."[24] And unfortunate was the Indian noble who, at some period or other of his life, had not made his pilgrimage to the Peruvian Mecca.

Other temples and religious dwellings were scattered over the provinces; and some of them constructed on a scale of magnificence, that almost rivalled that of the metropolis. The attendants on these composed an army of themselves. The whole number of functionaries, including those of the sacerdotal order, who officiated at the Coricancha alone, was no less than four thousand.[25]

At the head of all, both here and throughout the land, stood the great High-Priest, or Villac Vmu, as he was called. He was second only to the Inca in dignity, and was usually chosen from his brothers or nearest kindred. He was appointed by the monarch, and held his office for life; and he, in turn, appointed to all the subordinate stations of his own order. This order was very numerous. Those members of it who officiated in the House of the Sun, in Cuzco, were taken exclusively from the sacred race of the Incas. The ministers in the provincial temples were drawn from the families of the curacas; but the office of high-priest in each district was reserved for one of the blood royal. It was designed by this regulation to preserve the faith in its purity, and to guard against any departure from the stately ceremonial which it punctiliously prescribed.[26]

The sacerdotal order, though numerous, was not distinguished by any peculiar badge or costume from the rest of the nation. Neither was it the sole depository of the scanty science of the country, nor was it charged with the business of instruction, nor with those parochial duties, if they may so be called, which bring the priest in contact with the great body of the people,—as was the case in Mexico. The cause of this peculiarity may probably be traced to the existence of a superior order, like that of the Inca nobles, whose sanctity of birth so far transcended all human appointments, that they in a manner engrossed whatever there was of religious veneration in the people. They were, in fact, the holy order of the state. Doubtless, any of them might, as very many of them did, take on themselves the sacerdotal functions; and their own insignia and peculiar privileges were too well understood to require any further badge to separate them from the people.

The duties of the priest were confined to ministration in the temple. Even here his attendance was not constant, as he was relieved after a stated interval by other brethren of his order, who succeeded one another in regular rotation. His science was limited to an acquaintance with the fasts and festivals of his religion, and the appropriate ceremonies which distinguished them. This, however frivolous might be its character, was no easy acquisition; for the ritual of the Incas involved a routine of observances, as complex and elaborate as ever distinguished that of any nation, whether pagan or Christian. Each month had its appropriate festival, or rather festivals. The four principal had reference to the Sun, and commemorated the great periods of his annual progress, the solstices and equinoxes. Perhaps the most magnificent of all the national solemnities was the feast of Raymi, held at the period of the summer solstice, when the Sun, having touched the southern extremity of his course, retraced his path, as if to gladden the hearts of his chosen people by his presence. On this occasion, the Indian nobles from the different quarters of the country thronged to the capital to take part in the great religious celebration.

For three days previous, there was a general fast, and no fire was allowed to be lighted in the dwellings. When the appointed day arrived, the Inca and his court, followed by the whole population of the city, assembled at early dawn in the great square to greet the rising of the Sun. They were dressed in their gayest apparel, and the Indian lords vied with each other in the display of costly ornaments and jewels on their persons, while canopies of gaudy feather-work and richly tinted stuffs, borne by the attendants over their heads, gave to the great square, and the streets that emptied into it, the appearance of being spread over with one vast and magnificent awning. Eagerly they watched the coming of their deity, and, no sooner did his first yellow rays strike the turrets and loftiest buildings of the capital, than a shout of gratulation broke forth from the assembled multitude, accompanied by songs of triumph, and the wild melody of barbaric instruments, that swelled louder and louder as his bright orb, rising above the mountain range towards the east, shone in full splendor on his votaries. After the usual ceremonies of adoration, a libation was offered to the great deity by the Inca, from a huge golden vase, filled with the fermented liquor of maize or of maguey, which, after the monarch had tasted it himself, he dispensed among his royal kindred. These ceremonies completed, the vast assembly was arranged in order of procession, and took its way towards the Coricancha.[27]

As they entered the street of the sacred edifice, all divested themselves of their sandals, except the Inca and his family, who did the same on passing through the portals of the temple, where none but these august personages were admitted.[28] After a decent time spent in devotion, the sovereign, attended by his courtly train, again appeared, and preparations were made to commence the sacrifice. This, with the Peruvians, consisted of animals, grain, flowers, and sweet-scented gums; sometimes of human beings, on which occasions a child or beautiful maiden was usually selected as the victim. But such sacrifices were rare, being reserved to celebrate some great public event, as a coronation, the birth of a royal heir, or a great victory. They were never followed by those canni-bal repasts familiar to the Mexicans, and to many of the fierce tribes conquered by the Incas. Indeed, the conquests of these princes might well be deemed a blessing to the Indian nations, if it were only from their suppression of canni-balism, and the diminution, under their rule, of human sacrifices.[29]

At the feast of Raymi, the sacrifice usually offered was that of the llama; and the priest, after opening the body of his victim, sought in the appearances which it exhibited to read the lesson of the mysterious future. If the auguries were unpropitious, a second victim was slaughtered, in the hope of receiving some more comfortable assurance. The Peruvian augur might have learned a good lesson of the Roman, — to consider every omen as favorable, which served the interests of his country.[30]

A fire was then kindled by means of a concave mirror of polished metal, which, collecting the rays of the sun into a focus upon a quantity of dried cot-ton, speedily set it on fire. It was the expedient used on the like occasions in ancient Rome, at least under the reign of the pious Numa. When the sky was overcast, and the face of the good deity was hidden from his worshippers, which was esteemed a bad omen, fire was obtained by means of friction. The sacred flame was intrusted to the care of the Virgins of the Sun, and if, by any neglect, it was suffered to go out in the course of the year, the event was regarded as a calamity that boded some strange disaster to the monarchy.[31] A burnt offering of the victims was then made on the altars of the deity. This sacrifice was but the prelude to the slaughter of a great number of llamas, part of the flocks of the Sun, which furnished a banquet not only for the Inca and his Court, but for the people, who made amends at these festivals for the frugal fare to which they were usually condemned. A fine bread or cake, kneaded of maize flour by the fair hands of the Virgins of the Sun, was also placed on the royal board, where the Inca, presiding over the feast, pledged his great nobles in generous goblets of the fermented liquor of the country, and the long revelry of the day was closed at night by music and dancing. Dancing and drinking were the favorite pastimes of the Peruvians. These amusements continued for several days, though the sacrifices terminated on the first. — Such was the great festival of Raymi; and the recurrence of this and similar festivities gave relief to the monotonous routine of toil prescribed to the lower orders of the community.[32]

In the distribution of bread and wine at this high festival, the orthodox Spaniards, who first came into the country, saw a striking resemblance to the Christian communion;[33] as in the practice of confession and penance, which, in a most irregular form, indeed, seems to have been used by the Peruvians, they discerned a coincidence with another of the sacraments of the Church.[34] The good fathers were fond of tracing such coincidences, which they considered as the contrivance of Satan, who thus endeavoured to delude his victims by counterfeiting the blessed rites of Christianity.[35] Others, in a different vein, imagined that they saw in such analogies the evidence, that some of the primitive teachers of the Gospel, perhaps an apostle himself, had paid a visit to these distant regions, and scattered over them the seeds of religious truth.[36] But it seems hardly necessary to invoke the Prince of Darkness, or the intervention of the blessed saints, to account for coincidences which have existed in countries far removed from the light of Christianity, and in ages, indeed, when its light had not yet risen on the world. It is much more reasonable to refer such casual points of resemblance to the general constitution of man, and the necessities of his moral nature.[37]

Another singular analogy with Roman Catholic institutions is presented by the Virgins of the Sun, the "elect," as they were called,[38] to whom I have already had occasion to refer. These were young maidens, dedicated to the service of the deity, who, at a tender age, were taken from their homes, and introduced into convents, where they were placed under the care of certain elderly matrons, *mamaconas,* who had grown grey within their walls.[39] Under these venerable guides, the holy virgins were instructed in the nature of their religious duties. They were employed in spinning and embroidery, and, with the fine hair of the vicuña, wove the hangings for the temples, and the apparel for the Inca and his household.[40] It was their duty, above all, to watch over the sacred fire obtained at the festival of Raymi. From the moment they entered the establishment, they were cut off from all connection with the world, even with their own family and friends. No one but the Inca, and the Coya or queen, might enter the consecrated precincts. The greatest attention was paid to their morals, and visitors were sent every year to inspect the institutions, and to report on the state of their discipline.[41] Woe to the unhappy maiden who was detected in an intrigue! By the stern law of the Incas, she was to be buried alive, her lover was to be strangled, and the town or village to which he belonged was to be razed to the ground, and "sowed with stones," as if to efface every memorial of his existence.[42] One is astonished to find so close a resemblance between the institutions of the American Indian, the ancient Roman, and the modern Catholic! Chastity and purity of life are virtues in woman, that would seem to be of equal estimation with the barbarian and with the civilized.—Yet the ultimate destination of the inmates of these religious houses was materially different.

The great establishment at Cuzco consisted wholly of maidens of the royal blood, who amounted, it is said, to no less than fifteen hundred. The provincial convents were supplied from the daughters of the curacas and inferior nobles, and, occasionally, where a girl was recommended by great personal attractions, from the lower classes of the people.[43] The "Houses of the Virgins of the Sun" consisted of low ranges of stone buildings, covering a large extent of ground, surrounded by high walls, which excluded those within entirely from observation. They were provided with every accommodation for the fair inmates, and were embellished in the same sumptuous and costly manner as the palaces of the Incas, and the temples; for they received the particular care of government, as an important part of the religious establishment.[44]

Yet the career of all the inhabitants of these cloisters was not confined within their narrow walls. Though Virgins of the Sun, they were brides of the Inca, and, at a marriageable age, the most beautiful among them were selected for the honors of his bed, and transferred to the royal seraglio. The full complement of this amounted in time not only to hundreds, but thousands, who all found accommodations in his different palaces throughout the country. When the monarch was disposed to lessen the number of his establishment, the concubine with whose society he was willing to dispense returned, not to her former monastic residence, but to her own home; where, however humble might be her original condition, she was maintained in great state, and, far from being dishonored by the situation she had filled, was held in universal reverence as the Inca's bride.[45]

The great nobles of Peru were allowed, like their sovereign, a plurality of wives. The people, generally, whether by law, or by necessity stronger than law, were more happily limited to one. Marriage was conducted in a manner that gave it quite as original a character as belonged to the other institutions of the country. On an appointed day of the year, all those of a marriageable age—which, having reference to their ability to take charge of a family, in the males was fixed at not less than twenty-four years, and in the women at eighteen or twenty—were called together in the great squares of their respective towns and villages, throughout the empire. The Inca presided in person over the assembly of his own kindred, and taking the hands of the different couples who were to be united, he placed them within each other, declaring the parties man and wife. The same was done by the curacas towards all persons of their own or inferior degree in their several districts. This was the simple form of marriage in Peru. No one was allowed to select a wife beyond the community to which he belonged, which generally comprehended all his own kindred;[46] nor was any but the sovereign authorized to dispense with the law of nature—or at least, the usual law of nations—so far as to marry his own sister.[47] No marriage was esteemed valid without the consent of the parents; and the preference of the parties, it is said, was also to be consulted; though, considering the barriers imposed by the prescribed age of the candidates, this must have been within rather narrow and whimsical limits. A dwelling was got ready for the new-married pair at the charge of the district, and the prescribed portion of land assigned for their maintenance. The law of Peru provided for the future, as well as for the present. It left nothing to chance.—The simple ceremony of marriage was followed by general festivities among the friends of the parties, which lasted several days; and as every wedding took place on the same day, and as there were few families who had not some one of their members or their kindred personally interested, there was one universal bridal jubilee throughout the empire.[48]

The extraordinary regulations respecting marriage under the Incas are eminently characteristic of the genius of the government; which, far from limiting itself to matters of public concern, penetrated into the most private recesses of domestic life, allowing no man, however humble, to act for himself, even in those personal matters in which none but himself, or his family at most, might be supposed to be interested. No Peruvian was too low for the fostering vigilance of government. None was so high that he was not made to feel his dependence upon it in every act of his life. His very existence as an individual was absorbed in that of the community. His hopes and his fears, his joys and his sorrows, the tenderest sympathies of his nature, which would most naturally shrink from observation, were all to be regulated by law. He was not allowed even to be happy in his own way. The government of the Incas was the mildest,—but the most searching of despotisms.

CHAPTER IV

EDUCATION. — QUIPUS. — ASTRONOMY. — AGRICULTURE. — AQUEDUCTS. — GUANO. — IMPORTANT ESCULENTS

"SCIENCE was not intended for the people; but for those of generous blood. Persons of low degree are only puffed up by it, and rendered vain and arrogant. Neither should such meddle with the affairs of government; for this would bring high offices into disrepute, and cause detriment to the state."[1] Such was the favorite maxim, often repeated, of Tupac Inca Yupanqui, one of the most renowned of the Peruvian sovereigns. It may seem strange that such a maxim should ever have been proclaimed in the New World, where popular institutions have been established on a more extensive scale than was ever before witnessed; where government rests wholly on the people; and education — at least, in the great northern division of the continent — is mainly directed to qualify the people for the duties of government. Yet this maxim was strictly conformable to the genius of the Peruvian monarchy, and may serve as a key to its habitual policy; since, while it watched with unwearied solicitude over its subjects, provided for their physical necessities, was mindful of their morals, and showed, throughout, the affectionate concern of a parent for his children, it yet regarded them only as children, who were never to emerge from the state of pupilage, to act or to think for themselves, but whose whole duty was comprehended in the obligation of implicit obedience.

Such was the humiliating condition of the people under the Incas, while the numerous families of the blood royal enjoyed the benefit of all the light of education, which the civilization of the country could afford; and, long after the Conquest, the spots continued to be pointed out where the seminaries had existed for their instruction. These were placed under the care of the *amautas,* or "wise men," who engrossed the scanty stock of science — if science it could be called — possessed by the Peruvians, and who were the sole teachers of youth. It was natural that the monarch should take a lively interest in the instruction of the young nobility, his own kindred. Several of the Peruvian princes are said to have built their palaces in the neighbourhood of the schools, in order that they might the more easily visit them and listen to the lectures of the amautas, which they occasionally reinforced by a homily of their own.[2] In these schools, the royal pupils were instructed in all the different kinds of knowledge in which their teachers were versed, with especial reference to the stations they were to occupy in after-life. They studied the laws, and the principles of administering the government, in which many of them were to take part. They were initiated in the peculiar rites of their religion, most necessary to those who were to assume the sacerdotal functions. They learned also to emulate the achievements of their royal ancestors by listening to the chronicles compiled by the amautas. They were taught to speak their own dialect with purity and elegance; and they became acquainted with the mysterious science of the quipus, which supplied the Peruvians with the means of communicating their ideas to one another, and of transmitting them to future generations.[3]

The quipu was a cord about two feet long, composed of different colored threads tightly twisted together, from which a quantity of smaller threads were suspended in the manner of a fringe. The threads were of different colors and were tied into knots. The word *quipu*, indeed, signifies *a knot*. The colors denoted sensible objects; as, for instance, *white* represented *silver,* and *yellow, gold*. They sometimes also stood for abstract ideas. Thus, *white* signified *peace,* and *red, war*. But the quipus were chiefly used for arithmetical purposes. The knots served instead of ciphers, and could be combined in such a manner as to represent numbers to any amount they required. By means of these they went through their calculations with great rapidity, and the Spaniards who first visited the country bear testimony to their accuracy.[4]

Officers were established in each of the districts, who, under the title of *quipucamayus,* or "keepers of the quipus," were required to furnish the government with information on various important matters. One had charge of the revenues, reported the quantity of raw material distributed among the laborers, the quality and quantity of the fabrics made from it, and the amount of stores, of various kinds, paid into the royal magazines. Another exhibited the register of births and deaths, the marriages, the number of those qualified to bear arms, and the like details in reference to the population of the kingdom. These returns were annually forwarded to the capital, where they were submitted to the inspection of officers acquainted with the art of deciphering these mystic records. The government was thus provided with a valuable mass of statistical information, and the skeins of many-colored threads, collected and carefully preserved, constituted what might be called the national archives.[5]

But, although the quipus sufficed for all the purposes of arithmetical computation demanded by the Peruvians, they were incompetent to represent the manifold ideas and images which are expressed by writing. Even here, however, the invention was not without its use. For, independently of the direct representation of simple objects, and even of abstract ideas, to a very limited extent, as above noticed, it afforded great help to the memory by way of association. The peculiar knot or color, in this way, suggested what it could not venture to represent; in the same manner—to borrow the homely illustration of an old writer—as the number of the Commandment calls to mind the Commandment itself. The quipus, thus used, might be regarded as the Peruvian system of mnemonics.

Annalists were appointed in each of the principal communities, whose business it was to record the most important events which occurred in them. Other functionaries of a higher character, usually the amautas, were intrusted with the history of the empire, and were selected to chronicle the great deeds of the reigning Inca, or of his ancestors.[6] The narrative, thus concocted, could be communicated only by oral tradition; but the quipus served the chronicler to arrange the incidents with method, and to refresh his memory. The story, once treasured up in the mind, was indelibly impressed there by frequent repetition. It was repeated by the amauta to his pupils, and in this way history, conveyed partly by oral tradition, and partly by arbitrary signs, was handed down from generation to generation, with sufficient discrepancy of details, but with a general conformity of outline to the truth.

The Peruvian quipus were, doubtless, a wretched substitute for that beautiful contrivance, the alphabet, which, employing a few simple characters as the representatives of sounds, instead of ideas, is able to convey the most delicate shades of thought that ever passed through the mind of man. The Peruvian invention, indeed, was far below that of the hieroglyphics, even below the rude picture-writing of the Aztecs; for the latter art, however incompetent to convey abstract ideas, could depict sensible objects with tolerable accuracy. It is evidence of the total ignorance in which the two nations remained of each other, that the Peruvians should have borrowed nothing of the hieroglyphical system of the Mexicans, and this, notwithstanding that the existence of the maguey plant, *agave*, in South America might have furnished them with the very material used by the Aztecs for the construction of their maps.[7]

It is impossible to contemplate without interest the struggles made by different nations, as they emerge from barbarism, to supply themselves with some visible symbols of thought,—that mysterious agency by which the mind of the individual may be put in communication with the minds of a whole community. The want of such a symbol is itself the greatest impediment to the progress of civilization. For what is it but to imprison the thought, which has the elements of immortality, within the bosom of its author, or of the small circle who come in contact with him, instead of sending it abroad to give light to thousands, and to generations yet unborn! Not only is such a symbol an essential element of civilization, but it may be assumed as the very criterion of civilization; for the intellectual advancement of a people will keep pace pretty nearly with its facilities for intellectual communication.

Yet we must be careful not to underrate the real value of the Peruvian system; nor to suppose that the quipus were as awkward an instrument, in the hand of a practised native, as they would be in ours. We know the effect of habit in all mechanical operations, and the Spaniards bear constant testimony to the adroitness and accuracy of the Peruvians in this. Their skill is not more surprising than the facility with which habit enables us to master the contents of a printed page, comprehending thousands of separate characters, by a single glance, as it were, though each character must require a distinct recognition by the eye, and that, too, without breaking the chain of thought in the reader's mind. We must not hold the invention of the quipus too lightly, when we reflect that they supplied the means of calculation demanded for the affairs of a great nation, and that, however insufficient, they afforded no little help to what aspired to the credit of literary composition.

The office of recording the national annals was not wholly confined to the amautas. It was assumed in part by the *haravecs*, or poets, who selected the most brilliant incidents for their songs or ballads, which were chanted at the royal festivals and at the table of the Inca.[8] In this manner, a body of traditional minstrelsy grew up, like the British and Spanish ballad poetry, by means of which the name of many a rude chieftain, that might have perished for want of a chronicler, has been borne down the tide of rustic melody to later generations.

Yet history may be thought not to gain much by this alliance with poetry; for the domain of the poet extends over an ideal realm peopled with the shadowy forms of fancy, that bear little resemblance to the rude realities of life. The Peruvian annals may be deemed to show somewhat of the effects of this union, since there is a tinge of the marvellous spread over them down to the very latest period, which, like a mist before the reader's eye, makes it difficult to distinguish between fact and fiction.

The poet found a convenient instrument for his purposes in the beautiful Quichua dialect. We have already seen the extraordinary measures taken by the Incas for propagating their language throughout their empire. Thus naturalized in the remotest provinces, it became enriched by a variety of exotic words and idioms, which, under the influence of the Court and of poetic culture, if I may so express myself, was gradually blended, like some finished mosaic made up of coarse and disjointed materials, into one harmonious whole. The Quichua became the most comprehensive and various, as well as the most elegant, of the South American dialects.[9]

Besides the compositions already noticed, the Peruvians, it is said, showed some talent for theatrical exhibitions; not those barren pantomimes which, addressed simply to the eye, have formed the amusement of more than one rude nation. The Peruvian pieces aspired to the rank of dramatic compositions, sustained by character and dialogue, founded sometimes on themes of tragic interest, and at others on such as, from their light and social character, belong to comedy.[10] Of the execution of these pieces we have now no means of judging. It was probably rude enough, as befitted an unformed people. But, whatever may have been the execution, the mere conception of such an amusement is a proof of refinement that honorably distinguishes the Peruvian from the other American races, whose pastime was war, or the ferocious sports that reflect the image of it.

The intellectual character of the Peruvians, indeed, seems to have been marked rather by a tendency to refinement than by those hardier qualities which insure success in the severer walks of science. In these they were behind several of the semi-civilized nations of the New World. They had some acquaintance with geography, so far as related to their own empire, which was indeed extensive; and they constructed maps with lines raised on them to denote the boundaries and localities, on a similar principle with those formerly used by the blind. In astronomy, they appear to have made but moderate proficiency. They divided the year into twelve lunar months, each of which, having its own name, was distinguished by its appropriate festival.[11] They had, also, weeks; but of what length, whether of seven, nine, or ten days, is uncertain. As their lunar year would necessarily fall short of the true time, they rectified their calendar by solar observations made by means of a number of cylindrical columns raised on the high lands round Cuzco, which served them for taking azimuths; and, by measuring their shadows, they ascertained the exact times of the solstices. The period of the equinoxes they determined by the help of a solitary pillar, or gnomon, placed in the centre of a circle, which was described in the area of the great temple, and traversed by a diameter that was drawn from east to west. When the shadows were scarcely visible under the noontide rays of the sun, they said that "the god sat with all his light upon the column."[12] Quito, which lay immediately under the equator, where the vertical rays of the sun threw no shadow at noon, was held in especial veneration as the favored abode of the great deity. The period of the equinoxes was celebrated by public rejoicings. The pillar was crowned by the golden chair of the Sun, and, both then and at the solstices, the columns were hung with garlands, and offerings of flowers and fruits were made, while high festival was kept throughout the empire. By these periods the Peruvians regulated their religious rites and ceremonial, and prescribed the nature of their agricultural labors. The year itself took its departure from the date of the winter solstice.[13]

This meagre account embraces nearly all that has come down to us of Peruvian astronomy. It may seem strange that a nation, which had proceeded thus far in its observations, should have gone no farther; and that, notwithstanding its general advance in civilization, it should in this science have fallen so far short, not only of the Mexicans, but of the Muyscas, inhabiting the same elevated regions of the great southern plateau with themselves. These latter regulated their calendar on the same general plan of cycles and periodical series as the Aztecs, approaching yet nearer to the system pursued by the people of Asia.[14]

It might have been expected that the Incas, the boasted children of the Sun, would have made a particular study of the phenomena of the heavens, and have constructed a calendar on principles as scientific as that of their semi-civilized neighbours. One historian, indeed, assures us that they threw their years into cycles of ten, a hundred, and a thousand years, and that by these cycles they regulated their chronology.[15] But this assertion — not improbable in itself — rests on a writer but little gifted with the spirit of criticism, and is counter-balanced by the silence of every higher and earlier authority, as well as by the absence of any monument, like those found among other American nations, to attest the existence of such a calendar. The inferiority of the Peruvians may be, perhaps, in part explained by the fact of their priesthood being drawn exclusively from the body of the Incas, a privileged order of nobility, who had no need, by the assumption of superior learning, to fence themselves round from the approaches of the vulgar. The little true science possessed by the Aztec priest supplied him with a key to unlock the mysteries of the heavens, and the false system of astrology which he built upon it gave him credit as a being who had something of divinity in his own nature. But the Inca noble was divine by birth. The illusory study of astrology, so captivating to the unenlightened mind, engaged no share of his attention. The only persons in Peru, who claimed the power of reading the mysterious future, were the diviners, men who, combining with their pretensions some skill in the healing art, resembled the conjurors found among many of the Indian tribes. But the office was held in little repute, except among the lower classes, and was abandoned to those whose age and infirmity disqualified them for the real business of life.[16]

The Peruvians had knowledge of one or two constellations, and watched the motions of the planet Venus, to which, as we have seen, they dedicated altars. But their ignorance of the first principles of astronomical science is shown by their ideas of eclipses, which, they supposed, denoted some great derangement of the planet; and when the moon labored under one of these mysterious infirmities, they sounded their instruments, and filled the air with shouts and lamentations, to rouse her from her lethargy. Such puerile conceits as these form a striking contrast with the real knowledge of the Mexicans, as displayed in their hieroglyphical maps, in which the true cause of this phenomenon is plainly depicted.[17]

But, if less successful in exploring the heavens, the Incas must be admitted to have surpassed every other American race in their dominion over the earth. Husbandry was pursued by them on principles that may be truly called scientific. It was the basis of their political institutions. Having no foreign commerce, it was agriculture that furnished them with the means of their internal exchanges, their subsistence, and their revenues. We have seen their remarkable provisions for distributing the land in equal shares among the people, while they required every man, except the privileged orders, to assist in its cultivation. The Inca himself did not disdain to set the example. On one of the great annual festivals, he proceeded to the environs of Cuzco, attended by his Court, and, in the presence of all the people, turned up the earth with a golden plough, — or an instrument that served as such, — thus consecrating the occupation of the husbandman as one worthy to be followed by the Children of the Sun.[18]

The patronage of the government did not stop with this cheap display of royal condescension, but was shown in the most efficient measures for facilitating the labors of the husbandman. Much of the country along the sea-coast suffered from want of water, as little or no rain fell there, and the few streams, in their short and hurried course from the mountains, exerted only a very limited influence on the wide extent of territory. The soil, it is true, was, for the most part, sandy and sterile; but many places were capable of being reclaimed, and, indeed, needed only to be properly irrigated to be susceptible of extraordinary production. To these spots water was conveyed by means of canals and subterraneous aqueducts, executed on a noble scale. They consisted of large slabs of freestone nicely fitted together without cement, and discharged a volume of water sufficient, by means of latent ducts or sluices, to moisten the lands in the lower level, through which they passed. Some of these aqueducts were of great length. One that traversed the district of Condesuyu measured between four and five hundred miles. They were brought from some elevated lake or natural reservoir in the heart of the mountains, and were fed at intervals by other basins which lay in their route along the slopes of the sierra. In this descent, a passage was sometimes to be opened through rocks,—and this without the aid of iron tools; impracticable mountains were to be turned; rivers and marshes to be crossed; in short, the same obstacles were to be encountered as in the construction of their mighty roads. But the Peruvians seemed to take pleasure in wrestling with the difficulties of nature. Near Caxamarca, a tunnel is still visible, which they excavated in the mountains, to give an outlet to the waters of a lake, when these rose to a height in the rainy seasons that threatened the country with inundation.[19]

Most of these beneficent works of the Incas were suffered to go to decay by their Spanish conquerors. In some spots, the waters are still left to flow in their silent, subterraneous channels, whose windings and whose sources have been alike unexplored. Others, though partially dilapidated, and closed up with rubbish and the rank vegetation of the soil, still betray their course by occasional patches of fertility. Such are the remains in the valley of Nasca, a fruitful spot that lies between long tracts of desert; where the ancient water-courses of the Incas, measuring four or five feet in depth by three in width, and formed of large blocks of uncemented masonry, are conducted from an unknown distance.

The greatest care was taken that every occupant of the land through which these streams passed should enjoy the benefit of them. The quantity of water allotted to each was prescribed by law; and royal overseers superintended the distribution, and saw that it was faithfully applied to the irrigation of the ground.[20]

The Peruvians showed a similar spirit of enterprise in their schemes for introducing cultivation into the mountainous parts of their domain. Many of the hills, though covered with a strong soil, were too precipitous to be tilled. These they cut into terraces, faced with rough stone, diminishing in regular gradation towards the summit; so that, while the lower strip, or *anden,* as it was called by the Spaniards, that belted round the base of the mountain, might comprehend hundreds of acres, the uppermost was only large enough to accommodate a few rows of Indian corn.[21] Some of the eminences presented such a mass of solid rock, that, after being hewn into terraces, they were obliged to be covered deep with earth, before they could serve the purpose of the husbandman. With such patient toil did the Peruvians combat the formidable obstacles presented by the face of their country! Without the use of the tools or the machinery familiar to the European, each individual could have done little; but acting in large masses, and under a common direction, they were enabled by indefatigable perseverance to achieve results, to have attempted which might have filled even the European with dismay.[22]

In the same spirit of economical husbandry which redeemed the rocky sierra from the curse of sterility, they dug below the arid soil of the valleys, and sought for a stratum where some natural moisture might be found. These excavations, called by the Spaniards *hoyas,* or "pits," were made on a great scale, comprehending frequently more than an acre, sunk to the depth of fifteen or twenty feet, and fenced round within by a wall of *adobes,* or bricks baked in the sun. The bottom of the excavation, well prepared by a rich manure of the sardines,—a small fish obtained in vast quantities along the coast,—was planted with some kind of grain or vegetable.[23]

The Peruvian farmers were well acquainted with the different kinds of manures, and made large use of them; a circumstance rare in the rich lands of the tropics, and probably not elsewhere practised by the rude tribes of America. They made great use of *guano,* the valuable deposit of sea-fowl, that has attracted so much attention, of late, from the agriculturists both of Europe and of our own country, and the stimulating and nutritious properties of which the Indians perfectly appreciated. This was found in such immense quantities on many of the little islands along the coast, as to have the appearance of lofty hills, which, covered with a white saline incrustation, led the Conquerors to give them the name of the *sierra nevada, or* "snowy mountains."

The Incas took their usual precautions for securing the benefits of this important article to the husbandman. They assigned the small islands on the coast to the use of the respective districts which lay adjacent to them. When the island was large, it was distributed among several districts, and the boundaries for each were clearly defined. All encroachment on the rights of another was severely punished. And they secured the preservation of the fowl by penalties as stern as those by which the Norman tyrants of England protected their own game. No one was allowed to set foot on the island during the season for breeding, under pain of death; and to kill the birds at any time was punished in the like manner.[24]

With this advancement in agricultural science, the Peruvians might be supposed to have had some knowledge of the plough, in such general use among the primitive nations of the eastern continent. But they had neither the iron ploughshare of the Old World, nor had they animals for draught, which, indeed, were nowhere found in the New. The instrument which they used was a strong, sharp-pointed stake, traversed by a horizontal piece, ten or twelve inches from the point, on which the ploughman might set his foot and force it into the ground. Six or eight strong men were attached by ropes to the stake, and dragged it forcibly along,—pulling together, and keeping time as they moved by chanting their national songs, in which they were accompanied by the women who followed in their train, to break up the sods with their rakes. The mellow soil offered slight resistance; and the laborer, by long prac- tice, acquired a dexterity which enabled him to turn up the ground to the req- uisite depth with astonishing facility. This substitute for the plough was but a clumsy contrivance; yet it is curious as the only specimen of the kind among the American aborigines, and was perhaps not much inferior to the wooden instrument introduced in its stead by the European conquerors.[25]

It was frequently the policy of the Incas, after providing a deserted tract with the means for irrigation, and thus fitting it for the labors of the husband- man, to transplant there a colony of *mitimaes,* who brought it under cultiva- tion by raising the crops best suited to the soil. While the peculiar character and capacity of the lands were thus consulted, a means of exchange of the dif- ferent products was afforded to the neighbouring provinces, which, from the formation of the country, varied much more than usual within the same lim- its. To facilitate these agricultural exchanges, fairs were instituted, which took place three times a month in some of the most populous places, where, as money was unknown, a rude kind of commerce was kept up by the barter of their respective products. These fairs afforded so many holidays for the relax- ation of the industrious laborer.[26]

Such were the expedients adopted by the Incas for the improvement of their territory; and, although imperfect, they must be allowed to show an acquaintance with the principles of agricultural science, that gives them some claim to the rank of a civilized people. Under their patient and discriminating culture, every inch of good soil was tasked to its greatest power of production; while the most unpromising spots were compelled to contribute something to the subsistence of the people. Everywhere the land teemed with evidence of agricultural wealth, from the smiling valleys along the coast to the terraced steeps of the sierra, which, rising into pyramids of verdure, glowed with all the splendors of tropical vegetation.

The formation of the country was particularly favorable, as already remarked, to an infinite variety of products, not so much from its extent as from its various elevations, which, more remarkable, even, than those in Mexico, comprehend every degree of latitude from the equator to the polar regions. Yet, though the temperature changes in this region with the degree of elevation, it remains nearly the same in the same spots throughout the year; and the inhabitant feels none of those grateful vicissitudes of season which belong to the temperate latitudes of the globe. Thus, while the summer lies in full power on the burning regions of the palm and the cocoa-tree that fringe the borders of the ocean, the broad surface of the table-land blooms with the freshness of perpetual spring, and the higher summits of the Cordilleras are white with everlasting winter.

The Peruvians turned this fixed variety of climate, if I may so say, to the best account by cultivating the productions appropriate to each; and they particularly directed their attention to those which afforded the most nutriment to man. Thus, in the lower level were to be found the cassava-tree and the banana, that bountiful plant, which seems to have relieved man from the primeval curse—if it were not rather a blessing—of toiling for his sustenance.[27] As the banana faded from the landscape, a good substitute was found in the maize, the great agricultural staple of both the northern and southern divisions of the American continent; and which, after its exportation to the Old World, spread so rapidly there, as to suggest the idea of its being indigenous to it.[28] The Peruvians were well acquainted with the different modes of preparing this useful vegetable, though it seems they did not use it for bread, except at festivals; and they extracted a sort of honey from the stalk, and made an intoxicating liquor from the fermented grain, to which, like the Aztecs, they were immoderately addicted.[29]

The temperate climate of the table-land furnished them with the maguey, *agave Americana,* many of the extraordinary qualities of which they comprehended, though not its most important one of affording a material for paper. Tobacco, too, was among the products of this elevated region. Yet the Peruvians differed from every other Indian nation to whom it was known, by using it only for medicinal purposes, in the form of snuff.[30] They may have found a substitute for its narcotic qualities in the coca *(Erythroxylum Peruvianum),* or *cuca,* as called by the natives. This is a shrub which grows to the height of a man. The leaves when gathered are dried in the sun, and, being mixed with a little lime, form a preparation for chewing, much like the betel-leaf of the East.[31] With a small supply of this cuca in his pouch, and a handful of roasted maize, the Peruvian Indian of our time performs his wearisome journeys, day after day, without fatigue, or, at least, without complaint. Even food the most invigorating is less grateful to him than his loved narcotic. Under the Incas, it is said to have been exclusively reserved for the noble orders. If so, the people gained one luxury by the Conquest; and, after that period, it was so extensively used by them, that this article constituted a most important item of the colonial revenue of Spain.[32] Yet, with the soothing charms of an opiate, this weed so much vaunted by the natives, when used to excess, is said to be attended with all the mischievous effects of habitual intoxication.[33]

Higher up on the slopes of the Cordilleras, beyond the limits of the maize and of the *quinoa,*—a grain bearing some resemblance to rice, and largely cultivated by the Indians,—was to be found the potato, the introduction of which into Europe has made an era in the history of agriculture. Whether indigenous to Peru, or imported from the neighbouring country of Chili, it formed the great staple of the more elevated plains, under the Incas, and its culture was continued to a height in the equatorial regions which reached many thousand feet above the limits of perpetual snow in the temperate latitudes of Europe.[34] Wild specimens of the vegetable might be seen still higher, springing up spontaneously amidst the stunted shrubs that clothed the lofty sides of the Cordilleras, till these gradually subsided into the mosses and the short yellow grass, *pajonal,* which, like a golden carpet, was unrolled around the base of the mighty cones, that rose far into the regions of eternal silence, covered with the snows of centuries.[35]

CHAPTER V

PERUVIAN SHEEP. — GREAT HUNTS. — MANUFACTURES. — MECHANICAL SKILL. — ARCHITECTURE. — CONCLUDING REFLECTIONS

A nation which had made such progress in agriculture might be reasonably expected to have made, also, some proficiency in the mechanical arts, — especially when, as in the case of the Peruvians, their agricultural economy demanded in itself no inconsiderable degree of mechanical skill. Among most nations, progress in manufactures has been found to have an intimate connection with the progress of husbandry. Both arts are directed to the same great object of supplying the necessaries, the comforts, or, in a more refined condition of society, the luxuries of life; and when the one is brought to a perfection that infers a certain advance in civilization, the other must naturally find a corresponding development under the increasing demands and capacities of such a state. The subjects of the Incas, in their patient and tranquil devotion to the more humble occupations of industry which bound them to their native soil, bore greater resemblance to the Oriental nations, as the Hindoos and Chinese, than they bore to the members of the great Anglo-Saxon family, whose hardy temper has driven them to seek their fortunes on the stormy ocean, and to open a commerce with the most disrant regions of the globe. The Peruvians, though lining a long extent of sea-coast, had no foreign commerce.

They had peculiar advantages for domestic manufacture in a material incomparably superior to any thing possessed by the other races of the Western continent. They found a good substitute for linen in a fabric which, like the Aztecs, they knew how to weave from the tough thread of the maguey. Cotton grew luxuriantly on the low, sultry level of the coast, and furnished them with a clothing suitable to the milder latitudes of the country. But from the llama and the kindred species of Peruvian sheep they obtained a fleece adapted to the colder climate of the table-land, "more estimable," to quote the language of a well-informed writer, "than the down of the Canadian beaver, the fleece of the *brebis des Calmoucks*, or of the Syrian goat."[1]

Of the four varieties of the Peruvian sheep, the llama, the one most familiarly known, is the least valuable on account of its wool. It is chiefly employed as a beast of burden, for which, although it is somewhat larger than any of the other varieties, its diminutive size and strength would seem to disqualify it. It carries a load of little more than a hundred pounds, and cannot travel above three or four leagues in a day. But all this is compensated by the little care and cost required for its management and its maintenance. It picks up an easy subsistence from the moss and stunted herbage that grow scantily along the withered sides and the steeps of the Cordilleras. The structure of its stomach, like that of the camel, is such as to enable it to dispense with any supply of water for weeks, nay, months together. Its spongy hoof, armed with a claw or pointed talon to enable it to take secure hold on the ice, never requires to be shod; and the load laid upon its back rests securely in its bed of wool, without the aid of girth or saddle. The llamas move in troops of five hundred or even a thousand, and thus, though each individual carries but little, the aggregate is considerable. The whole caravan travels on at its regular pace, passing the night in the open air without suffering from the coldest temperature, and marching in perfect order, and in obedience to the voice of the driver. It is only when overloaded that the spirited little animal refuses to stir, and neither blows nor caresses can induce him to rise from the ground. He is as sturdy in asserting his rights on this occasion, as he is usually docile and unresisting.[2]

The employment of domestic animals distinguished the Peruvians from the other races of the New World. This economy of human labor by the substitution of the brute is an important element of civilization, inferior only to what is gained by the substitution of machinery for both. Yet the ancient Peruvians seem to have made much less account of it than their Spanish conquerors, and to have valued the llama, in common with the other animals of that genus, chiefly for its fleece. Immense herds of these "large cattle," as they were called, and of the "smaller cattle,"[3] or *alpacas*, were held by the government, as already noticed, and placed under the direction of shepherds, who conducted them from one quarter of the country to another, according to the changes of the season. These migrations were regulated with all the precision with which the code of the *mesta* determined the migrations of the vast merino flocks in Spain; and the Conquerors, when they landed in Peru, were amazed at finding a race of animals so similar to their own in properties and habits, and under the control of a system of legislation which might seem to have been imported from their native land.[4]

But the richest store of wool was obtained, not from these domesticated animals, but from the two other species, the *huanacos* and the *vicuñas*, which roamed in native freedom over the frozen ranges of the Cordilleras; where not unfrequently they might be seen scaling the snow-covered peaks which no living thing inhabits save the condor, the huge bird of the Andes, whose broad pinions bear him up in the atmosphere to the height of more than twenty thousand feet above the level of the sea.[5] In these rugged pastures, "the flock without a fold" finds sufficient sustenance in the *ychu*, a species of grass which is found scattered all along the great ridge of the Cordilleras, from the equator to the southern limits of Patagonia. And as these limits define the territory traversed by the Peruvian sheep, which rarely, if ever, venture north of the line, it seems not improbable that this mysterious little plant is so important to their existence, that the absence of it is the principal reason why they have not penetrated to the northern latitudes of Quito and New Granada.[6]

But, although thus roaming without a master over the boundless wastes of the Cordilleras, the Peruvian peasant was never allowed to hunt these wild animals, which were protected by laws as severe as were the sleek herds that grazed on the more cultivated slopes of the plateau. The wild game of the forest and the mountain was as much the property of the government, as if it had been inclosed within a park, or penned within a fold.[7] It was only on stated occasions, at the great hunts, which took place once a year, under the personal superintendence of the Inca or his principal officers, that the game was allowed to be taken. These hunts were not repeated in the same quarter of the country oftener than once in four years, that time might be allowed for the waste occasioned by them to be replenished. At the appointed time, all those living in the district and its neighbourhood, to the number, it might be, of fifty or sixty thousand men,[8] were distributed round, so as to form a cordon of immense extent, that should embrace the whole country which was to be hunted over. The men were armed with long poles and spears, with which they beat up game of every description lurking in the woods, the valleys, and the mountains, killing the beasts of prey without mercy, and driving the others, consisting chiefly of the deer of the country, and the huanacos and vicuñas, towards the centre of the wide-extended circle; until, as this gradually contracted, the timid inhabitants of the forest were concentrated on some spacious plain, where the eye of the hunter might range freely over his victims, who found no place for shelter or escape.

The male deer and some of the coarser kind of the Peruvian sheep were slaughtered; their skins were reserved for the various useful manufactures to which they are ordinarily applied, and their flesh, cut into thin slices, was distributed among the people, who converted it into *charqui,* the dried meat of the country, which constituted then the sole, as it has since the principal, animal food of the lower classes of Peru.[9]

But nearly the whole of the sheep, amounting usually to thirty or forty thousand, or even a larger number, after being carefully sheared, were suffered to escape and regain their solitary haunts among the mountains. The wool thus collected was deposited in the royal magazines, whence, in due time, it was dealt out to the people. The coarser quality was worked up into garments for their own use, and the finer for the Inca; for none but an Inca noble could wear the fine fabric of the vicuña.[10]

The Peruvians showed great skill in the manufacture of different articles for the royal household from this delicate material, which, under the name of *vigonia* wool, is now familiar to the looms of Europe. It was wrought into shawls, robes, and other articles of dress for the monarch, and into carpets, coverlets, and hangings for the imperial palaces and the temples. The cloth was finished on both sides alike;[11] the delicacy of the texture was such as to give it the lustre of silk; and the brilliancy of the dyes excited the admiration and the envy of the European artisan.[12] The Peruvians produced also an article of great strength and durability by mixing the hair of animals with wool; and they were expert in the beautiful feather-work, which they held of less account than the Mexicans from the superior quality of the materials for other fabrics, which they had at their command.[13]

The natives showed a skill in other mechanical arts similar to that displayed by their manufactures of cloth. Every man in Peru was expected to be acquainted with the various handicrafts essential to domestic comfort. No long apprenticeship was required for this, where the wants were so few as among the simple peasantry of the Incas. But, if this were all, it would imply but a very moderate advancement in the arts. There were certain individuals, however, carefully trained to those occupations which minister to the demands of the more opulent classes of society. These occupations, like every other calling and office in Peru, always descended from father to son.[14] The division of castes, in this particular, was as precise as that which existed in Egypt or Hindostan. If this arrangement be unfavorable to originality, or to the development of the peculiar talent of the individual, it at least conduces to an easy and finished execution by familiarizing the artist with the practice of his art from childhood.[15]

The royal magazines and the *huacas* or tombs of the Incas have been found to contain many specimens of curious and elaborate workmanship. Among these are vases of gold and silver, bracelets, collars, and other ornaments for the person; utensils of every description, some of fine clay, and many more of copper; mirrors of a hard, polished stone, or burnished silver, with a great variety of other articles made frequently on a whimsical pattern, evincing quite as much ingenuity as taste or inventive talent.[16] The character of the Peruvian mind led to imitation, in fact, rather than invention, to delicacy and minuteness of finish, rather than to boldness or beauty of design.

That they should have accomplished these difficult works with such tools as they possessed, is truly wonderful. It was comparatively easy to cast and even to sculpture metallic substances, both of which they did with consummate skill. But that they should have shown the like facility in cutting the hardest substances, as emeralds and other precious stones, is not so easy to explain. Emeralds they obtained in considerable quantity from the barren district of Atacames, and this inflexible material seems to have been almost as ductile in the hands of the Peruvian artist as if it had been made of clay.[17] Yet the natives were unacquainted with the use of iron, though the soil was largely impregnated with it.[18] The tools used were of stone, or more frequently of copper. But the material on which they relied for the execution of their most difficult tasks was formed by combining a very small portion of tin with copper.[19] This composition gave a hardness to the metal which seems to have been little inferior to that of steel. With the aid of it, not only did the Peruvian artisan hew into shape porphyry and granite, but by his patient industry accomplished works which the European would not have ventured to undertake. Among the remains of the monuments of Cannar may be seen movable rings in the muzzles of animals, all nicely sculptured of one entire block of granite.[20] It is worthy of remark, that the Egyptians, the Mexicans, and the Peruvians, in their progress towards civilization, should never have detected the use of iron, which lay around them in abundance; and that they should each, without any knowledge of the other, have found a substitute for it in such a curious composition of metals as gave to their tools almost the temper of steel;[21] a secret that has been lost — or, to speak more correctly, has never been dis-covered — by the civilized European.

I have already spoken of the large quantity of gold and silver wrought into various articles of elegance and utility for the Incas; though the amount was inconsiderable, in comparison with what could have been afforded by the mineral riches of the land, and with what has since been obtained by the more sagacious and unscrupulous cupidity of the white man. Gold was gathered by the Incas from the deposits of the streams. They extracted the ore also in considerable quantities from the valley of Curimayo, northeast of Caxamarca, as well as from other places; and the sil-ver mines of Porco, in particular, yielded them considerable returns. Yet they did not attempt to penetrate into the bowels of the earth by sinking a shaft, but simply excavated a cavern in the steep sides of the mountain, or, at most, opened a horizontal vein of moderate depth. They were equally deficient in the knowledge of the best means of detaching the precious metal from the dross with which it was united, and had no idea of the virtues of quicksilver, — a mineral not rare in Peru, — as an amalgam to effect this decomposition.[22] Their method of smelting the ore was by means of furnaces built in elevated and exposed situations, where they might be fanned by the strong breezes of the mountains. The subjects of the Incas, in short, with all their patient perseverance, did little more than penetrate below the crust, the outer rind, as it were, formed over those golden cav-erns which lie hidden in the dark depths of the Andes. Yet what they gleaned from the surface was more than adequate for all their demands. For they were not a commercial people, and had no knowledge of money.[23]

In this they differed from the ancient Mexicans, who had an established currency of a determinate value. In one respect, however, they were superior to their American rivals, since they made use of weights to determine the quantity of their commodities, a thing wholly unknown to the Aztecs. This fact is ascertained by the discovery of silver balances, adjusted with perfect accuracy, in some of the tombs of the Incas.[24]

But the surest test of the civilization of a people—at least, as sure as any—afforded by mechanical art is to be found in their architecture, which presents so noble a field for the display of the grand and the beautiful, and which, at the same time, is so intimately connected with the essential comforts of life. There is no object on which the resources of the wealthy are more freely lavished, or which calls out more effectually the inventive talent of the artist. The painter and the sculptor may display their individual genius in creations of surpassing excellence, but it is the great monuments of architectural taste and magnificence that are stamped in a peculiar manner by the genius of the nation. The Greek, the Egyptian, the Saracen, the Gothic,—what a key do their respective styles afford to the character and condition of the people! The monuments of China, of Hindostan, and of Central America are all indicative of an immature period, in which the imagination has not been disciplined by study, and which, therefore, in its best results, betrays only the ill-regulated aspirations after the beautiful, that belong to a semi-civilized people.

The Peruvian architecture, bearing also the general characteristics of an imperfect state of refinement, had still its peculiar character; and so uniform was that character, that the edifices throughout the country seem to have been all cast in the same mould.[25] They were usually built of porphyry or granite; not unfrequently of brick. This, which was formed into blocks or squares of much larger dimensions than our brick, was made of a tenacious earth mixed up with reeds or tough grass, and acquired a degree of hardness with age that made it insensible alike to the storms and the more trying sun of the tropics.[26] The walls were of great thickness, but low, seldom reaching to more than twelve or fourteen feet in height. It is rare to meet with accounts of a building that rose to a second story.[27]

The apartments had no communication with one another, but usually opened into a court; and, as they were unprovided with windows, or apertures that served for them, the only light from without must have been admitted by the doorways. These were made with the sides approaching each other towards the top, so that the lintel was considerably narrower than the threshold, a peculiarity, also, in Egyptian architecture. The roofs have for the most part disappeared with time. Some few survive in the less ambitious edifices, of a singular bell-shape, and made of a composition of earth and pebbles. They are supposed, however, to have been generally formed of more perishable materials, of wood or straw. It is certain that some of the most considerable stone-buildings were thatched with straw.

Many seem to have been constructed without the aid of cement; and writers have contended that the Peruvians were unacquainted with the use of mortar, or cement of any kind.[28] But a close, tenacious mould, mixed with lime, may be discovered filling up the interstices of the granite in some buildings; and in others, where the well-fitted blocks leave no room for this coarser material, the eye of the antiquary has detected a fine bituminous glue, as hard as the rock itself.[29]

The greatest simplicity is observed in the construction of the buildings, which are usually free from outward ornament; though in some the huge stones are shaped into a convex form with great regularity, and adjusted with such nice precision to one another, that it would be impossible, but for the flutings, to determine the line of junction. In others, the stone is rough, as it was taken from the quarry, in the most irregular forms, with the edges nicely wrought and fitted to each other. There is no appearance of columns or of arches; though there is some contradiction as to the latter point. But it is not to be doubted, that, although they may have made some approach to this mode of construction by the greater or less inclination of the walls, the Peruvian architects were wholly unacquainted with the true principle of the circular arch reposing on its key-stone.[30]

The architecture of the Incas is characterized, says an eminent traveller, "by simplicity, symmetry, and solidity."[31] It may seem unphilosophical to condemn the peculiar fashion of a nation as indicating want of taste, because its standard of taste differs from our own. Yet there is an incongruity in the composition of the Peruvian buildings which argues a very imperfect acquaintance with the first principles of architecture. While they put together their bulky masses of porphyry and granite with the nicest art, they were incapable of mortising their timbers, and, in their ignorance of iron, knew no better way of holding the beams together than tying them with thongs of maguey. In the same incongruous spirit, the building that was thatched with straw, and unilluminated by a window, was glowing with tapestries of gold and silver! These are the inconsistencies of a rude people, among whom the arts are but partially developed. It might not be difficult to find examples of like inconsistency in the architecture and domestic arrangements of our Anglo-Saxon, and, at a still later period, of our Norman ancestors.

Yet the buildings of the Incas were accommodated to the character of the climate, and were well fitted to resist those terrible convulsions which belong to the land of volcanoes. The wisdom of their plan is attested by the number which still survive, while the more modern constructions of the Conquerors have been buried in ruins. The hand of the Conquerors, indeed, has fallen heavily on these venerable monuments, and, in their blind and superstitious search for hidden treasure, has caused infinitely more ruin than time or the earthquake.[32] Yet enough of these monuments still remain to invite the researches of the antiquary. Those only in the most conspicuous situations have been hitherto examined. But, by the testimony of travellers, many more are to be found in the less frequented parts of the country; and we may hope they will one day call forth a kindred spirit of enterprise to that which has so successfully explored the mysterious recesses of Central America and Yucatan.

I cannot close this analysis of the Peruvian institutions without a few reflections on their general character and tendency, which, if they involve some repetition of previous remarks, may, I trust, be excused, from my desire to leave a correct and consistent impression on the reader. In this survey, we cannot but be struck with the total dissimilarity between these institutions and those of the Aztecs, — the other great nation who led in the march of civilization on this western continent, and whose empire in the northern portion of it was as conspicuous as that of the Incas in the south. Both nations came on the plateau, and commenced their career of conquest, at dates, it may be, not far removed from each other.[33] And it is worthy of notice, that, in America, the elevated region along the crests of the great mountain ranges should have been the chosen seat of civilization in both hemispheres.

Very different was the policy pursued by the two races in their military career. The Aztecs, animated by the most ferocious spirit, carried on a war of extermination, signalizing their triumphs by the sacrifice of hecatombs of captives; while the Incas, although they pursued the game of conquest with equal pertinacity, preferred a milder policy, substituting negotiation and intrigue for violence, and dealt with their antagonists so that their future resources should not be crippled, and that they should come as friends, not as foes, into the bosom of the empire.

Their policy toward the conquered forms a contrast no less striking to that pursued by the Aztecs. The Mexican vassals were ground by excessive imposts and military conscriptions. No regard was had to their welfare, and the only limit to oppression was the power of endurance. They were overawed by fortresses and armed garrisons, and were made to feel every hour that they were not part and parcel of the nation, but held only in subjugation as a conquered people. The Incas, on the other hand, admitted their new subjects at once to all the rights enjoyed by the rest of the community; and, though they made them conform to the established laws and usages of the empire, they watched over their personal security and comfort with a sort of parental solicitude. The motley population, thus bound together by common interest, was animated by a common feeling of loyalty, which gave greater strength and stability to the empire, as it became more and more widely extended; while the various tribes who successively came under the Mexican sceptre, being held together only by the pressure of external force, were ready to fall asunder the moment that that force was withdrawn. The policy of the two nations displayed the principle of fear as contrasted with the principle of love.

The characteristic features of their religious systems had as little resemblance to each other. The whole Aztec pantheon partook more or less of the sanguinary spirit of the terrible war-god who presided over it, and their frivolous ceremonial almost always terminated with human sacrifice and cannibal orgies. But the rites of the Peruvians were of a more innocent cast, as they tended to a more spiritual worship. For the worship of the Creator is most nearly approached by that of the heavenly bodies, which, as they revolve in their bright orbits, seem to be the most glorious symbols of his beneficence and power.

In the minuter mechanical arts, both showed considerable skill; but in the construction of important public works, of roads, aqueducts, canals, and in agriculture in all its details, the Peruvians were much superior. Strange that they should have fallen so far below their rivals in their efforts after a higher intellectual culture, in astronomical science, more especially, and in the art of communicating thought by visible symbols. When we consider the greater refinement of the Incas, their inferiority to the Aztecs in these particulars can be explained only by the fact, that the latter in all probability were indebted for their science to the race who preceded them in the land, — that shadowy race whose origin and whose end are alike veiled from the eye of the inquirer, but who possibly may have sought a refuge from their ferocious invaders in those regions of Central America the architectural remains of which now supply us with the most pleasing monuments of Indian civilization. It is with this more polished race, to whom the Peruvians seem to have borne some resemblance in their mental and moral organization, that they should be compared. Had the empire of the Incas been permitted to extend itself with the rapid strides with which it was advancing at the period of the Spanish conquest, the two races might have come into conflict, or, perhaps, into alliance with one another.

The Mexicans and Peruvians, so different in the character of their peculiar civilization, were, it seems probable, ignorant of each other's existence; and it may appear singular, that, during the simultaneous continuance of their empires, some of the seeds of science and of art, which pass so imperceptibly from one people to another, should not have found their way across the interval which separated the two nations. They furnish an interesting example of the opposite directions which the human mind may take in its struggle to emerge from darkness into the light of civilization.

A closer resemblance — as I have more than once taken occasion to notice — may be found between the Peruvian institutions and some of the despotic governments of Eastern Asia; those governments where despotism appears in its more mitigated form, and the whole people, under the patriarchal sway of its sovereign, seem to be gathered together like the members of one vast family. Such were the Chinese, for example, whom the Peruvians resembled in their implicit obedience to authority, their mild yet somewhat stubborn temper, their solicitude for forms, their reverence for ancient usage, their skill in the minuter manufactures, their imitative rather than inventive cast of mind, and their invincible patience, which serves instead of a more adventurous spirit for the execution of difficult undertakings.[34]

A still closer analogy may be found with the natives of Hindostan in their division into castes, their worship of the heavenly bodies and the elements of nature, and their acquaintance with the scientific principles of husbandry. To the ancient Egyptians, also, they bore considerable resemblance in the same particulars, as well as in those ideas of a future existence which led them to attach so much importance to the permanent preservation of the body.

But we shall look in vain in the history of the East for a parallel to the absolute control exercised by the Incas over their subjects. In the East, this was founded on physical power,—on the external resources of the government. The authority of the Inca might be compared with that of the Pope in the day of his might, when Christendom trembled at the thunders of the Vatican, and the successor of St. Peter set his foot on the necks of princes. But the authority of the Pope was founded on opinion. His temporal power was nothing. The empire of the Incas rested on both. It was a theocracy more potent in its operation than that of the Jews; for, though the sanction of the law might be as great among the latter, the law was expounded by a human lawgiver, the servant and representative of Divinity. But the Inca was both the lawgiver and the law. He was not merely the representative of Divinity, or, like the Pope, its vicegerent, but he was Divinity itself. The violation of his ordinance was sacrilege. Never was there a scheme of government enforced by such terrible sanctions, or which bore so oppressively on the subjects of it. For it reached not only to the visible acts, but to the private conduct, the words, the very thoughts, of its vassals.

It added not a little to the efficacy of the government, that, below the sovereign, there was an order of hereditary nobles of the same divine original with himself, who, placed far below himself, were still immeasurably above the rest of the community, not merely by descent, but, as it would seem, by their intellectual nature. These were the exclusive depositaries of power, and, as their long hereditary training made them familiar with their vocation, and secured them implicit deference from the multitude, they became the prompt and well-practised agents for carrying out the executive measures of the administration. All that occurred throughout the wide extent of his empire—such was the perfect system of communication—passed in review, as it were, before the eyes of the monarch, and a thousand hands, armed with irresistible authority, stood ready in every quarter to do his bidding. Was it not, as we have said, the most oppressive, though the mildest, of despotisms?

It was the mildest, from the very circumstance, that the transcendent rank of the sovereign, and the humble, nay, superstitious, devotion to his will made it superfluous to assert this will by acts of violence or rigor. The great mass of the people may have appeared to his eyes as but little removed above the condition of the brute, formed to minister to his pleasures. But, from their very helplessness, he regarded them with feelings of commiseration, like those which a kind master might feel for the poor animals committed to his charge, or—to do justice to the beneficent character attributed to many of the Incas—that a parent might feel for his young and impotent offspring. The laws were carefully directed to their preservation and personal comfort. The people were not allowed to be employed on works pernicious to their health, nor to pine—a sad contrast to their subsequent destiny—under the imposition of tasks too heavy for their powers. They were never made the victims of public or private extortion; and a benevolent forecast watched carefully over their necessities, and provided for their relief in seasons of infirmity, and for their sustenance in health. The government of the Incas, however arbitrary in form, was in its spirit truly patriarchal.

Yet in this there was nothing cheering to the dignity of human nature. What the people had was conceded as a boon, not as a right. When a nation was brought under the sceptre of the Incas, it resigned every personal right, even the rights dearest to humanity. Under this extraordinary polity, a people advanced in many of the social refinements, well skilled in manufactures and agriculture, were unacquainted, as we have seen, with money. They had nothing that deserved to be called property. They could follow no craft, could engage in no labor, no amusement, but such as was specially provided by law. They could not change their residence or their dress without a license from the government. They could not even exercise the freedom which is conceded to the most abject in other countries, that of selecting their own wives. The imperative spirit of despotism would not allow them to be happy or miserable in any way but that established by law. The power of free agency—the inestimable and inborn right of every human being—was annihilated in Peru.

The astonishing mechanism of the Peruvian polity could have resulted only from the combined authority of opinion and positive power in the ruler to an extent unprecedented in the history of man. Yet that it should have so successfully gone into operation, and so long endured, in opposition to the taste, the prejudices, and the very principles of our nature, is a strong proof of a generally wise and temperate administration of the government.

The policy habitually pursued by the Incas for the *prevention* of evils that might have disturbed the order of things is well exemplified in their provisions against poverty and idleness. In these they rightly discerned the two great causes of disaffection in a populous community. The industry of the people was secured not only by their compulsory occupations at home, but by their employment on those great public works which covered every part of the country, and which still bear testimony in their decay to their primitive grandeur. Yet it may well astonish us to find, that the natural difficulty of these undertakings, sufficiently great in itself, considering the imperfection of their tools and machinery, was inconceivably enhanced by the politic contrivance of government. The royal edifices of Quito, we are assured by the Spanish conquerors, were constructed of huge masses of stone, many of which were carried all the way along the mountain roads from Cuzco, a distance of several hundred leagues.[35] The great square of the capital was filled to a considerable depth with mould brought with incredible labor up the steep slopes of the Cordilleras from the distant shores of the Pacific Ocean.[36] Labor was regarded not only as a means, but as an end, by the Peruvian law.

With their manifold provisions against poverty the reader has already been made acquainted. They were so perfect, that, in their wide extent of territory, — much of it smitten with the curse of barrenness, — no man, however humble, suffered from the want of food and clothing. Famine, so common a scourge in every other American nation, so common at that period in every country of civilized Europe, was an evil unknown in the dominions of the Incas.

The most enlightened of the Spaniards who first visited Peru, struck with the general appearance of plenty and prosperity, and with the astonishing order with which every thing throughout the country was regulated, are loud in their expressions of admiration. No better government, in their opinion, could have been devised for the people. Contented with their condition, and free from vice, to borrow the language of an eminent authority of that early day, the mild and docile character of the Peruvians would have well fitted them to receive the teachings of Christianity, had the love of conversion, instead of gold, animated the breasts of the Conquerors.[37] And a philosopher of a later time, warmed by the contemplation of the picture — which his own fancy had colored — of public prosperity and private happiness under the rule of the Incas, pronounces "the *moral* man in Peru far superior to the European."[38]

Yet such results are scarcely reconcilable with the theory of the government I have attempted to analyze. Where there is no free agency, there can be no morality. Where there is no temptation, there can be little claim to virtue. Where the routine is rigorously prescribed by law, the law, and not the man, must have the credit of the conduct. If that government is the best, which is felt the least, which encroaches on the natural liberty of the subject only so far as is essential to civil subordination, then of all governments devised by man the Peruvian has the least real claim to our admiration.

It is not easy to comprehend the genius and the full import of institutions so opposite to those of our own free republic, where every man, however humble his condition, may aspire to the highest honors of the state, — may select his own career, and carve out his fortune in his own way; where the light of knowledge, instead of being concentrated on a chosen few, is shed abroad like the light of day, and suffered to fall equally on the poor and the rich; where the collision of man with man wakens a generous emulation that calls out latent talent and tasks the energies to the utmost; where consciousness of independence gives a feeling of self-reliance unknown to the timid subjects of a despotism; where, in short, the government is made for man, — not as in Peru, where man seemed to be made only for the government. The New World is the theatre on which these two political systems, so opposite in their character, have been carried into operation. The empire of the Incas has passed away and left no trace. The other great experiment is still going on, — the experiment which is to solve the problem, so long contested in the Old World, of the capacity of man for self-government. Alas for humanity, if it should fail!

The testimony of the Spanish conquerors is not uniform in respect to the favorable influence exerted by the Peruvian institutions on the character of the people. Drinking and dancing are said to have been the pleasures to which they were immoderately addicted. Like the slaves and serfs in other lands, whose position excluded them from more serious and ennobling occupations, they found a substitute in frivolous or sensual indulgence. Lazy, luxurious, and licentious, are the epithets bestowed on them by one of those who saw them at the Conquest, but whose pen was not too friendly to the Indian.[39] Yet the spirit of independence could hardly be strong in a people who had no interest in the soil, no personal rights to defend; and the facility with which they yielded to the Spanish invader— after every allowance for their comparative inferiority — argues a deplorable destitution of that patriotic feeling which holds life as little in comparison with freedom.

But we must not judge too hardly of the unfortunate native, because he quailed before the civilization of the European. We must not be insensible to the really great results that were achieved by the government of the Incas. We must not forget, that, under their rule, the meanest of the people enjoyed a far greater degree of personal comfort, at least, a greater exemption from physical suffering, than was possessed by similar classes in other nations on the American continent, — greater, probably, than was possessed by these classes in most of the countries of feudal Europe. Under their sceptre, the higher orders of the state had made advances in many of the arts that belong to a cultivated community. The foundations of a regular government were laid, which, in an age of rapine, secured to its subjects the inestimable blessings of tranquillity and safety. By the well-sustained policy of the Incas, the rude tribes of the forest were gradually drawn from their fastnesses, and gathered within the folds of civilization; and of these materials was constructed a flourishing and populous empire, such as was to be found in no other quarter of the American continent. The defects of this government were those of over-refinement in legislation,—the last defects to have been looked for, certainly, in the American aborigines.

BOOK II

DISCOVERY OF PERU

CHAPTER I

ANCIENT AND MODERN SCIENCE. — ART OF NAVIGATION. — MARITIME DISCOVERY. — SPIRIT OF THE SPANIARDS. — POSSESSIONS IN THE NEW WORLD. — RUMORS CONCERNING PERU

WHATEVER difference of opinion may exist as to the comparative merit of the ancients and the moderns in the arts, in poetry, eloquence, and all that depends on imagination, there can be no doubt that in science the moderns have eminently the advantage. It could not be otherwise. In the early ages of the world, as in the early period of life, there was the freshness of a morning existence, when the gloss of novelty was on every thing that met the eye; when the senses, not blunted by familiarity, were more keenly alive to the beautiful, and the mind, under the influence of a healthy and natural taste, was not perverted by philosophical theory; when the simple was necessarily connected with the beautiful, and the epicurean intellect, sated by repetition, had not begun to seek for stimulants in the fantastic and capricious. The realms of fancy were all untravelled, and its fairest flowers had not been gathered, nor its beauties despoiled, by the rude touch of those who affected to cultivate them. The wing of genius was not bound to the earth by the cold and conventional rules of criticism, but was permitted to take its flight far and wide over the broad expanse of creation.

But with science it was otherwise. No genius could suffice for the creation of facts, — hardly for their detection. They were to be gathered in by painful industry; to be collected from careful observation and experiment. Genius, indeed, might arrange and combine these facts into new forms, and elicit from their combinations new and important inferences; and in this process might almost rival in originality the creations of the poet and the artist. But if the processes of science are necessarily slow, they are sure. There is no retrograde movement in her domain. Arts may fade, the Muse become dumb, a moral lethargy may lock up the faculties of a nation, the nation itself may pass away and leave only the memory of its existence, but the stores of science it has garnered up will endure for ever. As other nations come upon the stage, and new forms of civilization arise, the monuments of art and of imagination, productions of an older time, will lie as an obstacle in the path of improvement. They cannot be built upon; they occupy the ground which the new aspirant for immortality would cover. The whole work is to be gone over again, and other forms of beauty—whether higher or lower in the scale of merit, but unlike the past—must arise to take a place by their side. But, in science, every stone that has been laid remains as the foundation for another. The coming generation takes up the work where the preceding left it. There is no retrograde movement. The individual nation may recede, but science still advances. Every step that has been gained makes the ascent easier for those who come after. Every step carries the patient inquirer after truth higher and higher towards heaven, and unfolds to him, as he rises, a wider horizon, and new and more magnificent views of the universe.

Geography partook of the embarrassments which belonged to every other department of science in the primitive ages of the world. The knowledge of the earth could come only from an extended commerce; and commerce is founded on artificial wants or an enlightened curiosity, hardly compatible with the earlier condition of society. In the infancy of nations, the different tribes, occupied with their domestic feuds, found few occasions to wander beyond the mountain chain or broad stream that formed the natural boundary of their domains. The Phœnicians, it is true, are said to have sailed beyond the Pillars of Hercules, and to have launched out on the great western ocean. But the adventures of these ancient voyagers belong to the mythic legends of antiquity, and ascend far beyond the domain of authentic record.

The Greeks, quick and adventurous, skilled in mechanical art, had many of the qualities of successful navigators, and within the limits of their little inland sea ranged fearlessly and freely. But the conquests of Alexander did more to extend the limits of geographical science, and opened an acquaintance with the remote countries of the East. Yet the march of the conqueror is slow in comparison with the movements of the unencumbered traveller. The Romans were still less enterprising than the Greeks, were less commercial in their character. The contributions to geographical knowledge grew with the slow acquisitions of empire. But their system was centralizing in its tendency; and instead of taking an outward direction and looking abroad for discovery, every part of the vast imperial domain turned towards the capital as its head and central point of attraction. The Roman conqueror pursued his path by land, not by sea. But the water is the great highway between nations, the true element for the discoverer. The Romans were not a maritime people. At the close of their empire, geographical science could hardly be said to extend farther than to an acquaintance with Europe,—and this not its more northern division,—together with a portion of Asia and Africa; while they had no other conception of a world beyond the western waters than was to be gathered from the fortunate prediction of the poet.[1]

Then followed the Middle Ages; the dark ages, as they are called, though in their darkness were matured those seeds of knowledge, which, in fulness of time, were to spring up into new and more glorious forms of civilization. The organization of society became more favorable to geographical science. Instead of one overgrown, lethargic empire, oppressing every thing by its colossal weight, Europe was broken up into various independent communities, many of which, adopting liberal forms of government, felt all the impulses natural to freemen; and the petty republics on the Mediterranean and the Baltic sent forth their swarms of seamen in a profitable commerce, that knit together the different countries scattered along the great European waters.

But the improvements which took place in the art of navigation, the more accurate measurement of time, and, above all, the discovery of the polarity of the magnet, greatly advanced the cause of geographical knowledge. Instead of creeping timidly along the coast, or limiting his expeditions to the narrow basins of inland waters, the voyager might now spread his sails boldly on the deep, secure of a guide to direct his bark unerringly across the illimitable waste. The consciousness of this power led thought to travel in a new direction; and the mariner began to look with earnestness for another path to the Indian Spice-islands than that by which the Eastern caravans had traversed the continent of Asia. The nations on whom the spirit of enterprise, at this crisis, naturally descended, were Spain and Portugal, placed, as they were, on the outposts of the European continent, commanding the great theatre of future discovery.

Both countries felt the responsibility of their new position. The crown of Portugal was constant in its efforts, through the fifteenth century, to find a passage round the southern point of Africa into the Indian Ocean; though so timid was the navigation, that every fresh headland became a formidable barrier; and it was not till the latter part of the century that the adventurous Diaz passed quite round the Stormy Cape, as he termed it, but which John the Second, with happier augury, called the Cape of Good Hope. But, before Vasco de Gama had availed himself of this discovery to spread his sails in the Indian seas, Spain entered on her glorious career, and sent Columbus across the western waters.

The object of the great navigator was still the discovery of a route to India, but by the west instead of the east. He had no expectation of meeting with a continent in his way, and, after repeated voyages, he remained in his original error, dying, as is well known, in the conviction that it was the eastern shore of Asia which he had reached. It was the same object which directed the nautical enterprises of those who followed in the Admiral's track; and the discovery of a strait into the Indian Ocean was the burden of every order from the government, and the design of many an expedition to different points of the new continent, which seemed to stretch its leviathan length along from one pole to the other. The discovery of an Indian passage is the true key to the maritime movements of the fifteenth and the first half of the sixteenth centuries. It was the great leading idea that gave the character to the enterprise of the age.

It is not easy at this time to comprehend the impulse given to Europe by the discovery of America. It was not the gradual acquisition of some border territory, a province or a kingdom that had been gained, but a New World that was now thrown open to the European. The races of animals, the mineral treasures, the vegetable forms, and the varied aspects of nature, man in the different phases of civilization, filled the mind with entirely new sets of ideas, that changed the habitual current of thought and stimulated it to indefinite conjecture. The eagerness to explore the wonderful secrets of the new hemisphere became so active, that the principal cities of Spain were, in a manner, depopulated, as emigrants thronged one after another to take their chance upon the deep.[2] It was a world of romance that was thrown open; for, whatever might be the luck of the adventurer, his reports on his return were tinged with a coloring of romance that stimulated still higher the sensitive fancies of his countrymen, and nourished the chimerical sentiments of an age of chivalry. They listened with attentive ears to tales of Amazons which seemed to realize the classic legends of antiquity, to stories of Patagonian giants, to flaming pictures of an *El Dorado,* where the sands sparkled with gems, and golden pebbles as large as birds' eggs were dragged in nets out of the rivers.

Yet that the adventurers were no impostors, but dupes, too easy dupes of their own credulous fancies, is shown by the extravagant character of their enterprises; by expeditions in search of the magical Fountain of Health, of the golden Temple of Doboyba, of the golden sepulchres of Zenu; for gold was ever floating before their distempered vision, and the name of *Castilla del Oro,* Golden Castile, the most unhealthy and unprofitable region of the Isthmus, held out a bright promise to the unfortunate settler, who too frequently, instead of gold, found there only his grave.

In this realm of enchantment, all the accessories served to maintain the illusion. The simple natives, with their defenceless bodies and rude weapons, were no match for the European warrior armed to the teeth in mail. The odds were as great as those found in any legend of chivalry, where the lance of the good knight overturned hundreds at a touch. The perils that lay in the discoverer's path, and the sufferings he had to sustain, were scarcely inferior to those that beset the knight-errant. Hunger and thirst and fatigue, the deadly effluvia of the morass with its swarms of venomous insects, the cold of mountain snows, and the scorching sun of the tropics, these were the lot of every cavalier who came to seek his fortunes in the New World. It was the reality of romance. The life of the Spanish adventurer was one chapter more—and not the least remarkable—in the chronicles of knight-errantry.

The character of the warrior took somewhat of the exaggerated coloring shed over his exploits. Proud and vainglorious, swelled with lofty anticipations of his destiny, and an invincible confidence in his own resources, no danger could appall and no toil could tire him. The greater the danger, indeed, the higher the charm; for his soul revelled in excitement, and the enterprise without peril wanted that spur of romance which was necessary to rouse his energies into action. Yet in the motives of action meaner influences were strangely mingled with the loftier, the temporal with the spiritual. Gold was the incentive and the recompense, and in the pursuit of it his inflexible nature rarely hesitated as to the means. His courage was sullied with cruelty, the cruelty that flowed equally—strange as it may seem—from his avarice and his religion; religion as it was understood in that age,—the religion of the Crusader. It was the convenient cloak for a multitude of sins, which covered them even from himself. The Castilian, too proud for hypocrisy, committed more cruelties in the name of religion than were ever practised by the pagan idolater or the fanatical Moslem. The burning of the infidel was a sacrifice acceptable to Heaven, and the conversion of those who survived amply atoned for the foulest offences. It is a melancholy and mortifying consideration, that the most uncompromising spirit of intolerance—the spirit of the Inquisitor at home, and of the Crusader abroad—should have emanated from a religion which preached peace upon earth and good-will towards man!

What a contrast did these children of Southern Europe present to the Anglo-Saxon races who scattered themselves along the great northern division of the western hemisphere! For the principle of action with these latter was not avarice nor the more specious pretext of proselytism; but independence, —independence religious and political. To secure this, they were content to earn a bare subsistence by a life of frugality and toil. They asked nothing from the soil, but the reasonable returns of their own labor. No golden visions threw a deceitful halo around their path, and beckoned them onwards through seas of blood to the subversion of an unoffending dynasty. They were content with the slow but steady progress of their social polity. They patiently endured the privations of the wilderness, watering the tree of liberty with their tears and with the sweat of their brow, till it took deep root in the land and sent up its branches high towards the heavens; while the communities of the neighbouring continent, shooting up into the sudden splendors of a tropical vegetation, exhibited, even in their prime, the sure symptoms of decay.

It would seem to have been especially, ordered by Providence that the discovery of the two great divisions of the American hemisphere should fall to the two races best fitted to conquer and colonize them. Thus the northern section was consigned to the Anglo-Saxon race, whose orderly, industrious habits found an ample field for development under its colder skies and on its more rugged soil; while the southern portion, with its rich tropical products and treasures of mineral wealth, held out the most attractive bait to invite the enterprise of the Spaniard. How different might have been the result, if the bark of Columbus had taken a more northerly direction, as he at one time meditated, and landed its band of adventurers on the shores of what is now Protestant America!

Under the pressure of that spirit of nautical enterprise which filled the maritime communities of Europe in the sixteenth century, the whole extent of the mighty continent, from Labrador to Terra del Fuego, was explored in less than thirty years after its discovery; and in 1521, the Portuguese Maghellan, sailing under the Spanish flag, solved the problem of the strait, and found a westerly way to the long sought Spice-islands of India, — greatly to the astonishment of the Portuguese, who, sailing from the opposite direction, there met their rivals, face to face, at the antipodes. But while the whole eastern coast of the American continent had been explored, and the central portion of it colonized, — even after the brilliant achievement of the Mexican conquest, — the veil was not yet raised that hung over the golden shores of the Pacific.

Floating rumors had reached the Spaniards, from time to time, of countries in the far west, teeming with the metal they so much coveted; but the first distinct notice of Peru was about the year 1511, when Vasco Nuñez de Balboa, the discoverer of the Southern Sea, was weighing some gold which he had collected from the natives. A young barbarian chieftain, who was present, struck the scales with his fist, and, scattering the glittering metal around the apartment, exclaimed, — "If this is what you prize so much that you are willing to leave your distant homes, and risk even life itself for it, I can tell you of a land where they eat and drink out of golden vessels, and gold is as cheap as iron is with you." It was not long after this startling intelligence that Balboa achieved the formidable adventure of scaling the mountain rampart of the isthmus which divides the two mighty oceans from each other; when, armed with sword and buckler, he rushed into the waters of the Pacific, and cried out, in the true chivalrous vein, that "he claimed this unknown sea with all that it contained for the king of Castile, and that he would make good the claim against all, Christian or infidel, who dared to gainsay it"![3] All the broad continent and sunny isles washed by the waters of the Southern Ocean! Little did the bold cavalier comprehend the full import of his magnificent vaunt.

On this spot he received more explicit tidings of the Peruvian empire, heard proofs recounted of its civilization, and was shown drawings of the llama, which, to the European eye, seemed a species of the Arabian camel. But, although he steered his caravel for these golden realms, and even pushed his discoveries some twenty leagues south of the Gulf of St. Michael, the adventure was not reserved for him. The illustrious discoverer was doomed to fall a victim to that miserable jealousy with which a little spirit regards the achievements of a great one.

The Spanish colonial domain was broken up into a number of petty governments, which were dispensed sometimes to court favorites, though, as the duties of the post, at this early period, were of an arduous nature, they were more frequently reserved for men of some practical talent and enterprise. Columbus, by virtue of his original contract with the Crown, had jurisdiction over the territories discovered by himself, embracing some of the principal islands, and a few places on the continent. This jurisdiction differed from that of other functionaries, inasmuch as it was hereditary; a privilege found in the end too considerable for a subject, and commuted, therefore, for a title and a pension. These colonial governments were multiplied with the increase of empire, and by the year 1524, the period at which our narrative properly commences, were scattered over the islands, along the Isthmus of Darien, the broad tract of Terra Firma, and the recent conquests of Mexico. Some of these governments were of no great extent. Others, like that of Mexico, were of the dimensions of a kingdom; and most had an indefinite range for discovery assigned to them in their immediate neighbourhood, by which each of the petty potentates might enlarge his territorial sway, and enrich his followers and himself. This politic arrangement best served the ends of the Crown, by affording a perpetual incentive to the spirit of enterprise. Thus living on their own little domains at a long distance from the mother country, these military rulers held a sort of vice-regal sway, and too frequently exercised it in the most oppressive and tyrannical manner; oppressive to the native, and tyrannical towards their own followers. It was the natural consequence, when men, originally low in station, and unprepared by education for office, were suddenly called to the possession of a brief, but in its nature irresponsible, authority. It was not till after some sad experience of these results, that measures were taken to hold these petty tyrants in cheek by means of regular tribunals, or Royal Audiences, as they were termed, which, composed of men of character and learning, might interpose the arm of the law, or, at least, the voice of remonstrance, for the protection of both colonist and native.

Among the colonial governors, who were indebted for their situation to their rank at home, was Don Pedro Arias de Avila, or Pedrarias, as usually called. He was married to a daughter of Doña Beatriz de Bobadilla, the celebrated Marchioness of Moya, best known as the friend of Isabella the Catholic. He was a man of some military experience and considerable energy of character. But, as it proved, he was of a malignant temper; and the base qualities, which might have passed unnoticed in the obscurity of private life, were made conspicuous, and perhaps created in some measure, by sudden elevation to power; as the sunshine, which operates kindly on a generous soil, and stimulates it to production, calls forth from the unwholesome marsh only foul and pestilent vapors. This man was placed over the territory of *Castilla del Oro,* the ground selected by Nuñez de Balboa for the theatre of his discoveries. Success drew on this latter the jealousy of his superior, for it was crime enough in the eyes of Pedrarias to deserve too well. The tragical history of this cavalier belongs to a period somewhat earlier than that with which we are to be occupied. It has been traced by abler hands than mine, and, though brief, forms one of the most brilliant passages in the annals of the American conquerors.[4]

But though Pedrarias was willing to cut short the glorious career of his rival, he was not insensible to the important consequences of his discoveries. He saw at once the unsuitableness of Darien for prosecuting expeditions on the Pacific, and, conformably to the original suggestion of Balboa, in 1519, he caused his rising capital to be transferred from the shores of the Atlantic to the ancient site of Panamá, some distance east of the present city of that name.[5] This most unhealthy spot, the cemetery of many an unfortunate colonist, was favorably situated for the great object of maritime enterprise; and the port, from its central position, afforded the best point of departure for expeditions, whether to the north or south, along the wide range of undiscovered coast that lined the Southern Ocean. Yet in this new and more favorable position, several years were suffered to elapse before the course of discovery took the direction of Peru. This was turned exclusively towards the north, or rather west, in obedience to the orders of government, which had ever at heart the detection of a strait that, as was supposed, must intersect some part or other of the long-extended Isthmus. Armament after armament was fitted out with this chimerical object; and Pedrarias saw his domain extending every year farther and farther without deriring any considerable advantage from his acquisitions. Veragua, Costa Rica, Nicaragua, were successively occupied; and his brave cavaliers forced a way across forest and mountain and warlike tribes of savages, till, at Honduras, they came in collision with the companions of Cortés, the Conquerors of Mexico, who had descended from the great northern plateau on the regions of Central America, and thus completed the survey of this wild and mysterious land.

It was not till 1522 that a regular expedition was despatched in the direction south of Panamá, under the conduct of Pascual de Andagoya, a cavalier of much distinction in the colony. But that officer penetrated only to the Puerto de Piñas, the limit of Balboa's discoveries, when the bad state of his health compelled him to reëmbark and abandon his enterprise at its commencement.[6]

Yet the floating rumors of the wealth and civilization of a mighty nation at the South were continually reaching the ears and kindling the dreamy imaginations of the colonists; and it may seem astonishing that an expedition in that direction should have been so long deferred. But the exact position and distance of this fairy realm were matter of conjecture. The long tract of intervening country was occupied by rude and warlike races; and the little experience which the Spanish navigators had already had of the neighbouring coast and its inhabitants, and still more, the tempestuous character of the seas—for their expeditions had taken place at the most unpropitious seasons of the year—enhanced the apparent difficulties of the undertaking, and made even their stout hearts shrink from it.

Such was the state of feeling in the little community of Panamá for several years after its foundation. Meanwhile, the dazzling conquest of Mexico gave a new impulse to the ardor of discovery, and, in 1524, three men were found in the colony, in whom the spirit of adventure triumphed over every considera-tion of difficulty and danger that obstructed the prosecution of the enter-prise. One among them was selected as fitted by his character to conduct it to a successful issue. That man was Francisco Pizarro; and as he held the same conspicuous post in the Conquest of Peru that was occupied by Cortés in that of Mexico, it will be necessary to take a brief review of his early history.

CHAPTER II

FRANCISCO PIZARRO. — HIS EARLY HISTORY. —
FIRST EXPEDITION TO THE SOUTH. —
DISTRESSES OF THE VOYAGERS. — SHARP
ENCOUNTERS. — RETURN TO PANAMÁ. —
ALMAGRO'S EXPEDITION

1524-1525.

Francisco Pizarro was born at Truxillo, a city of Estremadura, in Spain. The period of his birth is uncertain; but probably it was not far from 1471.[1] He was an illegitimate child, and that his parents should not have taken pains to perpetuate the date of his birth is not surprising. Few care to make a particular record of their transgressions. His father, Gonzalo Pizarro, was a colonel of infantry, and served with some distinction in the Italian campaigns under the Great Captain, and afterwards in the wars of Navarre. His mother, named Francisca Gonzales, was a person of humble condition in the town of Truxillo.[2]

But little is told of Francisco's early years, and that little not always deserving of credit. According to some, he was deserted by both his parents, and left as a foundling at the door of one of the principal churches of the city. It is even said that he would have perished, had he not been nursed by a sow.[3] This is a more discreditable fountain of supply than that assigned to the infant Romulus. The early history of men who have made their names famous by deeds in after-life, like the early history of nations, affords a fruitful field for invention.

It seems certain that the young Pizarro received little care from either of his parents, and was suffered to grow up as nature dictated. He was neither taught to read nor write, and his principal occupation was that of a swineherd. But this torpid way of life did not suit the stirring spirit of Pizarro, as he grew older, and listened to the tales, widely circulated and so captivating to a youthful fancy, of the New World. He shared in the popular enthusiasm, and availed himself of a favorable moment to abandon his ignoble charge, and escape to

Seville, the port where the Spanish adventurers embarked to seek their fortunes in the West. Few of them could have turned their backs on their native land with less cause for regret than Pizarro.[4]

In what year this important change in his destiny took place we are not informed. The first we hear of him in the New World is at the island of Hispaniola, in 1510, where he took part in the expedition to Uraba in Terra Firma, under Alonzo de Ojeda, a cavalier whose character and achievements find no parallel but in the pages of Cervantes. Hernando Cortés, whose mother was a Pizarro, and related, it is said, to the father of Francis, was then in St. Domingo, and prepared to accompany Ojeda's expedition, but was prevented by a temporary lameness. Had he gone, the fall of the Aztec empire might have been postponed for some time longer, and the sceptre of Montezuma have descended in peace to his posterity. Pizarro shared in the disastrous fortunes of Ojeda's colony, and, by his discretion, obtained so far the confidence of his commander, as to be left in charge of the settlement, when the latter returned for supplies to the islands. The lieutenant continued at his perilous post for nearly two months, waiting deliberately until death should have thinned off the colony sufficiently to allow the miserable remnant to be embarked in the single small vessel that remained to it.[5]

After this, we find him associated with Balboa, the discoverer of the Pacific, and coöperating with him in establishing the settlement at Darien. He had the glory of accompanying this gallant cavalier in his terrible march across the mountains, and of being among the first Europeans, therefore, whose eyes were greeted with the long-promised vision of the Southern Ocean.

After the untimely death of his commander, Pizarro attached himself to the fortunes of Pedrarias, and was employed by that governor in several military expeditions, which, if they afforded nothing else, gave him the requisite training for the perils and privations that lay in the path of the future Conqueror of Peru.

In 1515, he was selected, with another cavalier named Morales, to cross the Isthmus and traffic with the natives on the shores of the Pacific. And there, while engaged in collecting his booty of gold and pearls from the neighbouring islands, as his eye ranged along the shadowy line of coast till it faded in the distance, his imagination may have been first fired with the idea of, one day, attempting the conquest of the mysterious regions beyond the mountains. On the removal of the seat of government across the Isthmus to Panamá, Pizarro accompanied Pedrarias, and his name became conspicuous among the cavaliers who extended the line of conquest to the north over the martial tribes of Veragua. But all these expeditions, whatever glory they may have brought him, were productive of very little gold; and, at the age of fifty, the captain Pizarro found himself in possession only of a tract of unhealthy land in the neigbourhood of the capital, and of such *repartimientos* of the natives as were deemed suited to his military services.[6] The New World was a lottery, where the great prizes were so few that the odds were much against the player; yet in the game he was content to stake health, fortune, and, too often, his fair fame.

Such was Pizarro's situation when, in 1522, Andagoya returned from his unfinished enterprise to the south of Panamá, bringing back with him more copious accounts than any hitherto received of the opulence and grandeur of the countries that lay beyond.[7] It was at this time, too, that the splendid achievements of Cortés made their impression on the public mind, and gave a new impulse to the spirit of adventure. The southern expeditions became a common topic of speculation among the colonists of Panamá. But the region of gold, as it lay behind the mighty curtain of the Cordilleras, was still veiled in obscurity. No idea could be formed of its actual distance; and the hardships and difficulties encountered by the few navigators who had sailed in that direction gave a gloomy character to the undertaking, which had hitherto deterred the most daring from embarking in it. There is no evidence that Pizarro showed any particular alacrity in the cause. Nor were his own funds such as to warrant any expectation of success without great assistance from others. He found this in two individuals of the colony, who took too important a part in the subsequent transactions not to be particularly noticed.

One of them, Diego de Almagro, was a soldier of fortune, somewhat older, it seems probable, than Pizarro; though little is known of his birth, and even the place of it is disputed. It is supposed to have been the town of Almagro in New Castile, whence his own name, for want of a better source, was derived; for, like Pizarro, he was a foundling.[8] Few particulars are known of him till the present period of our history; for he was one of those whom the working of turbulent times first throws upon the surface, — less fortunate, perhaps, than if left in their original obscurity. In his military career, Almagro had earned the reputation of a gallant soldier. He was frank and liberal in his disposition, somewhat hasty and ungovernable in his passions, but, like men of a sanguine temperament, after the first sallies had passed away, not difficult robe appeased. He had, in short, the good qualifes and the defects incident to an honest nature, not improved by the discipline of early education or self-control.

The other member of the confederacy was Hernando de Luque, a Spanish ecclesiastic, who exercised the functions of vicar at Panamá, and had formerly filled the office of schoolmaster in the Cathedral of Darien. He seems to have been a man of singular prudence and knowledge of the world; and by his respectable qualities had acquired considerable influence in the little community to which he belonged, as well as the control of funds, which made his coöperation essential to the success of the present enterprise.

It was arranged among the three associates, that the two cavaliers should contribute their little stock towards defraying the expenses of the armament, but by far the greater part of the funds was to be furnished by Luque. Pizarro was to take command of the expedition, and the business of victualling and

equipping the vessels was assigned to Almagro. The associates found no difficulty in obtaining the consent of the governor to their undertaking. After the
return of Andagoya, he had projected another expedition, but the officer to
whom it was to be intrusted died. Why he did not prosecute his original purpose, and commit the affair to an experienced captain like Pizarro, does not
appear. He was probably not displeased that the burden of the enterprise
should be borne by others, so long as a good share of the profits went into his
own coffers. This he did not overlook in his stipulations.[9]

Thus fortified with the funds of Luque, and the consent of the governor,
Almagro was not slow to make preparations for the voyage. Two small vessels
were purchased, the larger of which had been originally built by Balboa, for
himself, with a view to this same expedition. Since his death, it had lain dis-
mantled in the harbour of Panamá. It was now refitted as well as circumstances would permit, and put in order for sea, while the stores and provisions
were got on board with an alacrity which did more credit, as the event proved,
to Almagro's zeal than to his forecast.

There was more difficulty in obtaining the necessary complement of
hands; for a general feeling of distrust had gathered round expeditions in this
direction, which could not readily be overcome. But there were many idle
hangers-on in the colony, who had come out to mend their fortunes, and were
willing to take their chance of doing so, however desperate. From such materials as these, Almagro assembled a body of somewhat more than a hundred
men;[10] and every thing being ready, Pizarro assumed the command, and,
weighing anchor, took his departure from the little port of Panamá, about the
middle of November, 1524. Almagro was to follow in a second vessel of inferior size, as soon as it could be fitted out.[11]

The time of year was the most unsuitable that could have been selected for
the voyage; for it was the rainy season, when the navigation to the south,
impeded by contrary winds, is made doubly dangerous by the tempests that
sweep over the coast. But this was not understood by the adventurers. After
touching at the Isle of Pearls, the frequent resort of navigators, at a few
leagues' distance from Panamá, Pizarro held his way across the Gulf of St.
Michael, and steered almost due south for the Puerto de Piñas, a headland in
the province of Biruquete, which marked the limit of Andagoya's voyage.
Before his departure, Pizarro had obtained all the information which he
could derive from that officer in respect to the country, and the route he was
to follow. But the cavalier's own experience had been too limited to enable
him to be of much assistance.

Doubling the Puerto de Piñas, the little vessel entered the river Birú, the
misapplication of which name is supposed by some to have given rise to that
of the empire of the Incas.[12] After sailing up this stream for a couple of
leagues, Pizarro came to anchor, and disembarking his whole force except the
sailors, proceeded at the head of it to explore the country. The land spread
out into a vast swamp, where the heavy rains had settled in pools of stagnant

water, and the muddy soil afforded no footing to the traveller. This dismal morass was fringed with woods, through whose thick and tangled undergrowth they found it difficult to penetrate; and emerging from them, they came out on a hilly country, so rough and rocky in its character, that their feet were cut to the bone, and the weary soldier, encumbered with his heavy mail or thick-padded doublet of cotton, found it difficult to drag one foot after the other. The heat at times was oppressive; and, fainting with toil and famished for want of food, they sank down on the earth from mere exhaustion. Such was the ominous commencement of the expedition to Peru.

Pizarro, however, did not lose heart. He endeavoured to revive the spirits of his men, and besought them not to be discouraged by difficulties which a brave heart would be sure to overcome, reminding them of the golden prize which awaited those who persevered. Yet it was obvious that nothing was to be gained by remaining longer in this desolate region. Returning to their vessel, therefore, it was suffered to drop down the river and proceed along its southern course on the great ocean.

After coasting a few leagues, Pizarro anchored off a place not very inviting in its appearance, where he took in a supply of wood and water. Then, stretching more towards the open sea, he held on in the same direction towards the south. But in this he was baffled by a succession of heavy tempests, accompanied with such tremendous peals of thunder and floods of rain as are found only in the terrible storms of the tropics. The sea was lashed into fury, and, swelling into mountain billows, threatened every moment to overwhelm the crazy little bark, which opened at every seam. For ten days the unfortunate voyagers were tossed about by the pitiless elements, and it was only by incessant exertions—the exertions of despair—that they preserved the ship from foundering. To add to their calamities, their provisions began to fail, and they were short of water, of which they had been furnished only with a small number of casks; for Almagro had counted on their recruiting their scanty supplies, from time to time, from the shore. Their meat was wholly consumed, and they were reduced to the wretched allowance of two ears of Indian corn a day for each man.

Thus harassed by hunger and the elements, the battered voyagers were too happy to retrace their course and regain the port where they had last taken in supplies of wood and water. Yet nothing could be more unpromising than the aspect of the country. It had the same character of low, swampy soil, that distinguished the former landing-place; while thick-matted forests, of a depth which the eye could not penetrate, stretched along the coast to an interminable length. It was in vain that the wearied Spaniards endeavoured to thread the mazes of this tangled thicket, where the creepers and flowering vines, that shoot up luxuriant in a hot and humid atmosphere, had twined themselves round the huge trunks of the forest-trees, and made a network that could be opened only with the axe. The rain, in the mean time, rarely slackened, and the ground, strewed with leaves and saturated with moisture, seemed to slip away beneath their feet.

Nothing could be more dreary and disheartening than the aspect of these funereal forests; where the exhalations from the overcharged surface of the ground poisoned the air, and seemed to allow no life, except that, indeed, of myriads of insects, whose enamelled wings glanced to and fro, like sparks of fire, in every opening of the woods. Even the brute creation appeared instinctively to have shunned the fatal spot, and neither beast nor bird of any description was seen by the wanderers. Silence reigned unbroken in the heart of these dismal solitudes; at least, the only sounds that could be heard were the plashing of the rain-drops on the leaves, and the tread of the forlorn adventurers.[13]

Entirely discouraged by the aspect of the country, the Spaniards began to comprehend that they had gained nothing by changing their quarters from sea to shore, and they felt the most serious apprehensions of perishing from famine in a region which afforded nothing but such unwholesome berries as they could pick up here and there in the woods. They loudly complained of their hard lot, accusing their commander as the author of all their troubles, and as deluding them with promises of a fairy land, which seemed to recede in proportion as they advanced. It was of no use, they said, to contend against fate, and it was better to take their chance of regaining the port of Panamá in time to save their lives, than to wait where they were to die of hunger.

But Pizarro was prepared to encounter much greater evils than these, before returning to Panamá, bankrupt in credit, an object of derision as a vainglorious dreamer, who had persuaded others to embark in an adventure which he had not the courage to carry through himself. The present was his only chance. To return would be ruin. He used every argument, therefore, that mortified pride or avarice could suggest to turn his followers from their purpose; represented to them that these were the troubles that necessarily lay in the path of the discoverer; and called to mind the brilliant successes of their countrymen in other quarters, and the repeated reports, which they had themselves received, of the rich regions along this coast, of which it required only courage and constancy on their part to become the masters. Yet, as their present exigencies were pressing, he resolved to send back the vessel to the Isle of Pearls, to lay in a fresh stock of provisions for his company, which might enable them to go forward with renewed confidence. The distance was not great, and in a few days they would all be relieved from their perilous position. The officer detached on this service was named Montenegro; and taking with him nearly half the company, after receiving Pizarro's directions, he instantly weighed anchor, and steered for the Isle of Pearls.

On the departure of his vessel, the Spanish commander made an attempt to explore the country, and see if some Indian settlement might not be found, where he could procure refreshments for his followers. But his efforts were vain, and no trace was visible of a human dwelling; though, in the dense and impenetrable foliage of the equatorial regions, the distance of a few rods might suffice to screen a city from observation. The only means of nourishment left to the unfortunate adventurers were such shell-fish as they occasionally picked up on the shore, or the bitter buds of the palmtree, and such berries and unsavoury herbs as grew wild in the woods. Some of these were so poisonous, that the bodies of those who ate them swelled up and were tormented with racking pains. Others, preferring famine to this miserable diet, pined away from weakness and actually died of starvation. Yet their resolute leader strove to maintain his own cheerfulness and to keep up the drooping spirits of his men. He freely shared with them his scanty stock of provisions, was unwearied in his endeavours to procure them sustenance, tended the sick, and ordered barracks to be constructed for their accommodation, which might, at least, shelter them from the drenching storms of the season. By this ready sympathy with his followers in their sufferings, he obtained an ascendency over their rough natures, which the assertion of authority, at least in the present extremity, could never have secured to him.

Day after day, week after week, had now passed away, and no tidings were heard of the vessel that was to bring relief to the wanderers. In vain did they strain their eyes over the distant waters to catch a glimpse of their coming friends. Not a speck was to be seen in the blue distance, where the canoe of the savage dared not venture, and the sail of the white man was not yet spread. Those who had borne up bravely at first now gave way to despondency, as they felt themselves abandoned by their countrymen on this desolate shore. They pined under that sad feeling which "maketh the heart sick." More than twenty of the little band had already died, and the survivors seemed to be rapidly following.[14]

At this crisis reports were brought to Pizarro of a light having been seen through a distant opening in the woods. He hailed the tidings with eagerness, as intimating the existence of some settlement in the neighbourhood; and, putting himself at the head of a small party, went in the direction pointed out, to reconnoitre. He was not disappointed, and, after extricating himself from a dense wilderness of underbrush and foliage, he emerged into an open space, where a small Indian village was planted. The timid inhabitants, on the sudden apparition of the strangers, quitted their huts in dismay; and the famished Spaniards, rushing in, eagerly made themselves masters of their contents. These consisted of different articles of food, chiefly maize and cocoa-nuts. The supply, though small, was too seasonable not to fill them with rapture.

The astonished natives made no attempt at resistance. But, gathering more confidence as no violence was offered to their persons, they drew nearer the white men, and inquired, "Why they did not stay at home and till their own lands, instead of roaming about to rob others who had never harmed them?"[15] Whatever may have been their opinion as to the question of right, the Spaniards, no doubt, felt then that it would have been wiser to do so. But the savages wore about their persons gold ornaments of some size, though of clumsy workmanship. This furnished the best reply to their demand. It was the golden bait which lured the Spanish adventurer to forsake his pleasant home for the trials of the wilderness. From the Indians Pizarro gathered a confirmation of the reports he had so often received of a rich country lying farther south; and at the distance of ten days' journey across the mountains, they told him, there dwelt a mighty monarch whose dominions had been invaded by another still more powerful, the Child of the Sun.[16] It may have been the invasion of Quito that was meant, by the valiant Inca Huayna Capac, which took place some years previous to Pizarro's expedition.

At length, after the expiration of more than six weeks, the Spaniards beheld with delight the return of the wandering bark that had borne away their comrades, and Montenegro sailed into port with an ample supply of provisions for his famishing countrymen. Great was his horror at the aspect presented by the latter, their wild and haggard countenances and wasted frames, — so wasted by hunger and disease, that their old companions found it difficult to recognize them. Montenegro accounted for his delay by incessant head winds and bad weather; and he himself had also a doleful tale to tell of the distress to which he and his crew had been reduced by hunger, on their passage to the Isle of Pearls. — It is minute incidents like these with which we have been occupied, that enable one to comprehend the extremity of suffering to which the Spanish adventurer was subjected in the prosecution of his great work of discovery.

Revived by the substantial nourishment to which they had so long been strangers, the Spanish cavaliers, with the buoyancy that belongs to men of a hazardous and roving life, forgot their past distresses in their eagerness to prosecute their enterprise. Re-embarking therefore on board his vessel, Pizarro bade adieu to the scene of so much suffering, which he branded with the appropriate name of *Puerto de la Hambre*, the Port of Famine, and again opened his sails to a favorable breeze that bore him onwards towards the south.

Had he struck boldly out into the deep, instead of hugging the inhospitable shore, where he had hitherto found so little to recompense him, he might have spared himself the repetition of wearisome and unprofitable adventures, and reached by a shorter route the point of his destination. But the Spanish mariner groped his way along these unknown coasts, landing at every convenient headland, as if fearful lest some fruitful region or precious mine might be overlooked, should a single break occur in the line of survey. Yet it should be remembered, that, though the true point of Pizarro's destination is obvious to us, familiar with the topography of these countries, he was wandering in the dark, feeling his way along, inch by inch, as it were, without chart to guide him, without knowledge of the seas or of the bearings of the coast, and even with no better defined idea of the object at which he aimed than that of a land, teeming with gold, that lay somewhere at the south! It was a hunt after an *El Dorado;* on information scarcely more circumstantial or authentic than that which furnished the basis of so many chimerical enterprises in this land of wonders. Success only, the best argument with the multitude, redeemed the expeditions of Pizarro from a similar imputation of extravagance.

Holding on his southerly course under the lee of the shore, Pizarro, after a short run, found himself abreast of an open reach of country, or at least one less encumbered with wood, which rose by a gradual swell, as it receded from the coast. He landed with a small body of men, and, advancing a short distance into the interior, fell in with an Indian hamlet. It was abandoned by the inhabitants, who, on the approach of the invaders, had betaken themselves to the mountains; and the Spaniards, entering their deserted dwellings, found there a good store of maize and other articles of food, and rude ornaments of gold of considerable value. Food was not more necessary for their bodies than was the sight of gold, from time to time, to stimulate their appetite for adventure. One spectacle, however, chilled their blood with horror. This was the sight of human flesh, which they found roasting before the fire, as the barbarians had left it, preparatory to their obscene repast. The Spaniards, conceiving that they had fallen in with a tribe of Caribs, the only race in that part of the New World known to be cannibals, retreated precipitately to their vessel.[17] They were not steeled by sad familiarity with the spectacle, like the Conquerors of Mexico.

The weather, which had been favorable, now set in tempestuous, with heavy squalls, accompanied by incessant thunder and lightning, and the rain, as usual in these tropical tempests, descended not so much in drops as in unbroken sheets of water. The Spaniards, however, preferred to take their chance on the raging element rather than remain in the scene of such brutal abominations. But the fury of the storm gradually subsided, and the little vessel held on her way along the coast, till, coming abreast of a bold point of land named by Pizarro Punta Quemada, he gave orders to anchor. The margin of the shore was fringed with a deep belt of mangrove-trees, the long roots of which, interlacing one another, formed a kind of submarine latticework that made the place difficult of approach. Several avenues, opening through this tangled thicket, led Pizarro to conclude that the country must be inhabited, and he disembarked, with the greater part of his force, to explore the interior.

He had not penetrated more than a league, when he found his conjecture verified by the sight of an Indian town of larger size than those he had hitherto seen, occupying the brow of an eminence, and well defended by palisades. The inhabitants, as usual, had fled; but left in their dwellings a good supply of provisions and some gold trinkets, which the Spaniards made no difficulty of appropriating to themselves. Pizarro's flimsy bark had been strained by the heavy gales it had of late encountered, so that it was unsafe to prosecute the voyage further without more thorough repairs than could be given to her on this desolate coast. He accordingly determined to send her back with a few hands to be careened at Panamá, and meanwhile to establish his quarters in his present position, which was so favorable for defence. But first he despatched a small party under Montenegro to reconnoitre the country, and, if possible, to open a communication with the natives.

The latter were a warlike race. They had left their habitations in order to place their wives and children in safety. But they had kept an eye on the movements of the invaders, and, when they saw their forces divided, they resolved to fall upon each body singly before it could communicate with the other. So soon, therefore, as Montenegro had penetrated through the defiles of the lofty hills, which shoot out like spurs of the Cordilleras along this part of the coast, the Indian warriors, springing from their ambush, sent off a cloud of arrows and other missiles that darkened the air, while they made the forest ring with their shrill war-whoop. The Spaniards, astonished at the appearance of the savages, with their naked bodies gaudily painted, and brandishing their weapons as they glanced among the trees and straggling underbrush that choked up the defile, were taken by surprise and thrown for a moment into disarray. Three of their number were killed and several wounded. Yet, speedily rallying, they returned the discharge of the assailants with their cross-bows, — for Pizarro's troops do not seem to have been provided with muskets on this expedition, — and then gallantly charging the enemy, sword in hand, succeeded in driving them back into the fastnesses of the mountains. But it only led them to shift their operations to another quarter, and make an assault on Pizarro before he could be relieved by his lieutenant.

Availing themselves of their superior knowledge of the passes, they reached that commander's quarters long before Montenegro, who had commenced a countermarch in the same direction. And issuing from the woods, the bold savages saluted the Spanish garrison with a tempest of darts and arrows, some of which found their way through the joints of the harness and the quilted mail of the cavaliers. But Pizarro was too well practised a soldier to be off his guard. Calling his men about him, he resolved not to abide the assault tamely in the works, but to sally out, and meet the enemy on their own ground. The barbarians, who had advanced near the defences, fell back as the Spaniards burst forth with their valiant leader at their head. But, soon returning with admirable ferocity to the charge, they singled out Pizarro, whom, by his bold bearing and air of authority, they easily recognized as the chief; and, hurling at him a storm of missiles, wounded him, in spite of his armour, in no less than seven places.[18]

Driven back by the fury of the assault directed against his own person, the Spanish commander retreated down the slope of the hill, still defending himself as he could with sword and buckler, when his foot slipped and he fell. The enemy set up a fierce yell of triumph, and some of the boldest sprang forward to despatch him. But Pizarro was on his feet in an instant, and, striking down two of the foremost with his strong arm, held the rest at bay till his soldiers could come to the rescue. The barbarians, struck with admiration at his valor, began to falter, when Montenegro luckily coming on the ground at the moment, and falling on their rear, completed their confusion; and, abandoning the field, they made the best of their way into the recesses of the mountains. The ground was covered with their slain; but the victory was dearly purchased by the death of two more Spaniards and a long list of wounded.

A council of war was then called. The position had lost its charm in the eyes of the Spaniards, who had met here with the first resistance they had yet experienced on their expedition. It was necessary to place the wounded in some secure spot, where their injuries could be attended to. Yet it was not safe to proceed farther, in the crippled state of their vessel. On the whole, it was decided to return and report their proceedings to the governor; and, though the magnificent hopes of the adventurers had not been realized, Pizarro trusted that enough had been done to vindicate the importance of the enterprise, and to secure the countenance of Pedrarias for the further prosecution of it.[19]

Yet Pizarro could not make up his mind to present himself, in the present state of the undertaking, before the governor. He determined, therefore, to be set on shore with the principal part of his company at Chicamá, a place on the main land, at a short distance west of Panamá. From this place, which he reached without any further accident, he despatched the vessel, and in it his treasurer, Nicolas de Ribera, with the gold he had collected, and with instructions to lay before the governor a full account of his discoveries, and the result of the expedition.

While these events were passing, Pizarro's associate, Almagro, had been busily employed in fitting out another vessel for the expedition at the port of Panamá. It was not till long after his friend's departure that he was prepared to follow him. With the assistance of Luque, he at length succeeded in equipping a small caravel and embarking a body of between sixty and seventy adventurers, mostly of the lowest order of the colonists. He steered in the track of his comrade, with the intention of overtaking him as soon as possible. By a signal previously concerted of notching the trees, he was able to identify the spots visited by Pizarro, — Puerto de Piñas, Puerto de la Hambre, Pueblo Quemado, — touching successively at every point of the coast explored by his countrymen, though in a much shorter time. At the last-mentioned place he was received by the fierce natives with the same hostile demonstrations as Pizarro, though in the present encounter the Indians did not venture beyond their defences. But the hot blood of Almagro was so exasperated by this check, that he assaulted the place and carried it sword in hand, setting fire to the outworks and dwellings, and driving the wretched inhabitants into the forests.

His victory cost him dear. A wound from a javelin on the head caused an inflammation in one of his eyes, which, after great anguish, ended in the loss of it. Yet the intrepid adventurer did not hesitate to pursue his voyage, and, after touching at several places on the coast, some of which rewarded him with a considerable booty in gold, he reached the mouth of the *Rio de San*

Juan, about the fourth degree of north latitude. He was struck with the beauty of the stream, and with the cultivation on its borders, which were sprinkled with Indian cottages showing some skill in their construction, and altogether intimating a higher civilization than any thing he had yet seen.

Still his mind was filled with anxiety for the fate of Pizarro and his followers. No trace of them had been found on the coast for a long time, and it was evident they must have foundered at sea, or made their way back to Panamá. This last he deemed most probable; as the vessel might have passed him unnoticed under the cover of the night, or of the dense fogs that sometimes hang over the coast.

Impressed with this belief, he felt no heart to continue his voyage of discovery, for which, indeed, his single bark, with its small complement of men, was altogether inadequate. He proposed, therefore, to return without delay. On his way, he touched at the Isle of Pearls, and there learned the result of his friend's expedition, and the place of his present residence. Directing his course, at once, to Chicamá, the two cavaliers soon had the satisfaction of embracing each other, and recounting their several exploits and escapes. Almagro returned even better freighted with gold than his confederate, and at every step of his progress he had collected fresh confirmation of the existence of some great and opulent empire in the South. The confidence of the two friends was much strengthened by their discoveries; and they unhesitatingly pledged themselves to one another to die rather than abandon the enterprise.[20]

The best means of obtaining the levies requisite for so formidable an undertaking—more formidable, as it now appeared to them, than before— were made the subject of long and serious discussion. It was at length decided that Pizarro should remain in his present quarters, inconvenient and even unwholesome as they were rendered by the humidity of the climate, and the pestilent swarms of insects that filled the atmosphere. Almagro would pass over to Panamá, lay the case before the governor, and secure, if possible, his good-will towards the prosecution of the enterprise. If no obstacle were thrown in their way from this quarter, they might hope, with the assistance of Luque, to raise the necessary supplies; while the results of the recent expedition were sufficiently encouraging to draw adventurers to their standard in a community which had a craving for excitement that gave even danger a charm, and which held life cheap in comparison with gold.

CHAPTER III

THE FAMOUS CONTRACT. — SECOND EXPEDITION. — RUIZ EXPLORES THE COAST. — PIZARRO'S SUFFERINGS IN THE FORESTS. — ARRIVAL OF NEW RECRUITS. — FRESH DISCOVERIES AND DISASTERS. — PIZARRO ON THE ISLE OF GALLO

1526-1527.

ON his arrival at Panamá, Almagro found that events had taken a turn less favorable to his views than he had anticipated. Pedrarias, the governor, was preparing to lead an expedition in person against a rebellious officer in Nicaragua; and his temper, naturally not the most amiable, was still further soured by this defection of his lieutenant, and the necessity it imposed on him of a long and perilous march. When, therefore, Almagro appeared before him with the request that he might be permitted to raise further levies to prosecute his enterprise, the governor received him with obvious dissatisfaction, listened coldly to the narrative of his losses, turned an incredulous ear to his magnificent promises for the future, and bluntly demanded an account of the lives, which had been sacrificed by Pizarro's obstinacy, but which, had they been spared, might have stood him in good stead in his present expedition to Nicaragua. He positively declined to countenance the rash schemes of the two adventurers any longer, and the conquest of Peru would have been crushed in the bud, but for the efficient interposition of the remaining associate, Fernando de Luque.

This sagacious ecclesiastic had received a very different impression from Almagro's narrative, from that which had been made on the mind of the irritable governor. The actual results of the enterprise in gold and silver, thus far, indeed, had been small, — forming a mortifying contrast to the magnitude of their expectations. But, in another point of view, they were of the last importance; since the intelligence which the adventurers had gained in every successive stage of their progress confirmed, in the strongest manner, the previous accounts, received from Andagoya and others, of a rich Indian empire at the south, which might repay the trouble of conquering it as well as Mexico had repaid the enterprise of Cortés. Fully entering, therefore, into the feelings of his military associates, he used all his influence with the governor to incline him to a more favorable view of Almagro's petition; and no one in the little community of Panamá exercised greater influence over the councils of the executive than Father Luque, for which he was indebted no less to his discretion and acknowledged sagacity than to his professional station.

But while Pedrarias, overcome by the arguments or importunity of the churchman, yielded a reluctant assent to the application, he took care to testify his displeasure with Pizarro, on whom he particularly charged the loss of his followers, by naming Almagro as his equal in command in the proposed expedition. This mortification sunk deep into Pizarro's mind. He suspected his comrade, with what reason does not appear, of soliciting this boon from the governor. A temporary coldness arose between them, which subsided, in outward show, at least, on Pizarro's reflecting that it was better to have this authority conferred on a friend than on a stranger, perhaps an enemy. But the seeds of permanent distrust were left in his bosom, and lay waiting for the due season to ripen into a fruitful harvest of discord.[1]

Pedrarias had been originally interested in the enterprise, at least, so far as to stipulate for a share of the gains, though he had not contributed, as it appears, a single ducat towards the expenses. He was at length, however, induced to relinquish all right to a share of the contingent profits. But, in his manner of doing so, he showed a mercenary spirit, better becoming a petty trader than a high officer of the Crown. He stipulated that the associates should secure to him the sum of one thousand *pesos de oro* in requital of his goodwill, and they eagerly closed with his proposal, rather than be encumbered with his pretensions. For so paltry a consideration did he resign his portion of the rich spoil of the Incas![2] But the governor was not gifted with the eye of a prophet. His avarice was of that short-sighted kind which defeats itself. He had sacrificed the chivalrous Balboa just as that officer was opening to him the conquest of Peru, and he would now have quenched the spirit of enterprise, that was taking the same direction, in Pizarro and his associates.

Not long after this, in the following year, he was succeeded in his government by Don Pedro de los Rios, a cavalier of Cordova. It was the policy of the Castilian Crown to allow no one of the great colonial officers to occupy the same station so long as to render himself formidable by his authority.[3] It had, moreover, many particular causes of disgust with Pedrarias. The functionary they sent out to succeed him was fortified with ample instructions for the good of the colony, and especially of the natives, whose religious conversion was urged as a capital object, and whose personal freedom was unequivocally asserted, as loyal vassals of the Crown. It is but justice to the Spanish government to admit that its provisions were generally guided by a humane and considerate policy, which was as regularly frustrated by the cupidity of the colonist, and the capricious cruelty of the conqueror. The few remaining years of Pedrarias were spent in petty squabbles, both of a personal and official nature; for he was still continued in office, though in one of less consideration than that which he had hitherto filled. He survived but a few years, leaving behind him a reputation not to be envied, of one who united a pusillanimous spirit with uncontrollable passions; who displayed, notwithstanding, a certain energy of character, or, to speak more correctly, an impetuosity of purpose, which might have led to good results had it taken a right direction. Unfortunately, his lack of discretion was such, that the direction he took was rarely of service to his country or to himself.

Having settled their difficulties with the governor, and obtained his sanction to their enterprise, the confederates lost no time in making the requisite preparations for it. Their first step was to execute the memorable contract which served as the basis of their future arrangements; and, as Pizarro's name appears in this, it seems probable that that chief had crossed over to Panamá so soon as the favorable disposition of Pedrarias had been secured.[4] The instrument, after invoking in the most solemn manner the names of the Holy Trinity and Our Lady the Blessed Virgin, sets forth, that, whereas the parties have full authority to discover and subdue the countries and provinces lying south of the Gulf, belonging to the empire of Peru, and as Fernando de Luque had advanced the funds for the enterprise in bars of gold of the value of twenty thousand *pesos,* they mutually bind themselves to divide equally among them the whole of the conquered territory. This stipulation is reiterated over and over again, particularly with reference to Luque, who, it is declared, is to be entitled to one third of all lands, *repartimientos,* treasures of every kind, gold, silver, and precious stones, — to one third even of all vassals, rents, and emoluments arising from such grants as may be conferred by the Crown on either of his military associates, to be held for his own use, or for that of his heirs, assigns, or legal representative.

The two captains solemnly engage to devote themselves exclusively to the present undertaking until it is accomplished; and, in case of failure in their part of the covenant, they pledge themselves to reimburse Luque for his advances, for which all the property they possess shall be held responsible, and this declaration is to be a sufficient warrant for the execution of judgment against them, in the same manner as if it had proceeded from the decree of a court of justice.

The commanders, Pizarro and Almagro, made oath, in the name of God and the Holy Evangelists, sacredly to keep this covenant, swearing it on the missal, on which they traced with their own hands the sacred emblem of the cross. To give still greater efficacy to the compact, Father Luque administered the sacrament to the parties, dividing the consecrated wafer into three portions, of which each one of them partook; while the by-standers, says an historian, were affected to tears by this spectacle of the solemn ceremonial with which these men voluntarily devoted themselves to a sacrifice that seemed little short of insanity.[5]

The instrument, which was dated March 10, 1526, was subscribed by Luque, and attested by three respectable citizens of Panamá, one of whom signed on behalf of Pizarro, and the other for Almagro; since neither of these parties, according to the avowal of the instrument, was able to subscribe his own name.[6]

Such was the singular compact by which three obscure individuals coolly carved out and partitioned among themselves, an empire of whose extent, power, and resources, of whose situation, of whose existence, even they had no sure or precise knowledge. The positive and unhesitating manner in which they speak of the grandeur of this empire, of its stores of wealth, so conformable to the event, but of which they could have really known so little, forms a striking contrast with the general skepticism and indifference manifested by nearly every other person, high and low, in the community of Panamá.[7]

The religious tone of the instrument is not the least remarkable feature in it, especially when we contrast this with the relentless policy, pursued by the very men who were parties to it, in their conquest of the country. "In the name of the Prince of Peace," says the illustrious historian of America, "they ratified a contract of which plunder and bloodshed were the objects."[8] The reflection seems reasonable. Yet, in criticizing what is done, as well as what is written, we must take into account the spirit of the times.[9] The invocation of Heaven was natural, where the object of the undertaking was, in part, a religious one. Religion entered, more or less, into the theory, at least, of the Spanish conquests in the New World. That motives of a baser sort mingled largely with these higher ones, and in different proportions according to the character of the individual, no one will deny. And few are they that have proposed to themselves a long career of action without the intermixture of some vulgar personal motive, — fame, honors, or emolument. Yet that religion furnishes a key to the American crusades, however rudely they may have been conducted, is evident from the history of their origin; from the sanction openly given to them by the Head of the Church; from the throng of self-devoted missionaries, who followed in the track of the conquerors to garner up the rich harvest of souls; from the reiterated instructions of the Crown, the great object of which was the conversion of the natives; from those superstitious acts of the iron-hearted soldiery themselves, which, however they may be set down to fanaticism, were clearly too much in earnest to leave any ground for the charge of hypocrisy. It was indeed a fiery cross that was borne over the devoted land, scathing and consuming it in its terrible progress; but it was still the cross, the sign of man's salvation, the only sign by which generations and generations yet unborn were to be rescued from eternal perdition.

It is a remarkable fact, which has hitherto escaped the notice of the historian, that Luque was not the real party to this contract. He represented another, who placed in his hands the funds required for the undertaking. This appears from an instrument signed by Luque himself and certified before the same notary that prepared the original contract. The instrument declares that the whole sum of twenty thousand *pesos* advanced for the expedition was furnished by the Licentiate Gaspar de Espinosa, then at Panamá; that the vicar acted only as his agent and by his authority; and that, in consequence, the said Espinosa and no other was entitled to a third of all the profits and acquisitions resulting from the conquest of Peru. This instrument, attested by three persons, one of them the same who had witnessed the original contract, was dated on the 6th of August, 1531.[10] The Licentiate Espinosa was a respectable functionary, who had filled the office of principal alcalde in Darien, and since taken a conspicuous part in the conquest and settlement of Tierra Firme. He enjoyed much consideration for his personal character and station; and it is remarkable that so little should be known of the manner in which the covenant, so solemnly made, was executed in reference to him. As in the case of Columbus, it is probable that the unexpected magnitude of the results was such as to prevent a faithful adherence to the original stipulation; and yet, from the same consideration, one can hardly doubt that the twenty thousand *pesos* of the bold speculator must have brought him a magnificent return. Nor did the worthy vicar of Panamá, as the history will show hereafter, go without his reward.

Having completed these preliminary arrangements, the three associates lost no time in making preparations for the voyage. Two vessels were purchased, larger and every way better than those employed on the former occasion. Stores were laid in, as experience dictated, on a larger scale than before, and proclamation was made of "an expedition to Peru." But the call was not readily answered by the skeptical citizens of Panamá. Of nearly two hundred men who had embarked on the former cruise, not more than three fourths now remained.[11] This dismal mortality, and the emaciated, poverty-stricken aspect of the survivors, spoke more eloquently than the braggart promises and magnificent prospects held out by the adventurers. Still there were men in the community of such desperate circumstances, that any change seemed like a chance of bettering their condition. Most of the former company also, strange to say, felt more pleased to follow up the adventure to the end than to abandon it, as they saw the light of a better day dawning upon them. From these sources the two captains succeeded in mustering about one hundred and sixty men, making altogether a very inadequate force for the conquest of an empire. A few horses were also purchased, and a better supply of ammunition and military stores than before, though still on a very limited scale. Considering their funds, the only way of accounting for this must be by the difficulty of obtaining supplies at Panamá, which, recently founded, and on the remote coast of the Pacific, could be approached only by crossing the rugged barrier of mountains, which made the transportation of bulky articles extremely difficult. Even such scanty stock of materials as it possessed was probably laid under heavy contribution, at the present juncture, by the governor's preparations for his own expedition to the north.

Thus indifferently provided, the two captains, each in his own vessel, again took their departure from Panamá, under the direction of Bartholomew Ruiz, a sagacious and resolute pilot, well experienced in the navigation of the Southern Ocean. He was a native of Moguer, in Andalusia, that little nursery of nautical enterprise, which furnished so many seamen for the first voyages of Columbus. Without touching at the intervening points of the coast, which offered no attraction to the voyagers, they stood farther out to sea, steering direct for the Rio de San Juan, the utmost limit reached by Almagro. The season was better selected than on the former occasion, and they were borne along by favorable breezes to the place of their destination, which they reached without accident in a few days. Entering the mouth of the river, they saw the banks well lined with Indian habitations; and Pizarro, disembarking, at the head of a party of soldiers, succeeded in surprising a small village and carrying off a considerable booty of gold ornaments found in the dwellings, together with a few of the natives.[12]

Flushed with their success, the two chiefs were confident that the sight of the rich spoil so speedily obtained could not fail to draw adventurers to their standard in Panamá; and, as they felt more than ever the necessity of a stronger force to cope with the thickening population of the country which they were now to penetrate, it was decided that Almagro should return with the treasure and beat up for reinforcements, while the pilot Ruiz, in the other vessel, should reconnoitre the country towards the south, and obtain such information as might determine their future movements. Pizarro, with the rest of the force, would remain in the neighbourhood of the river, as he was assured by the Indian prisoners, that not far in the interior was an open reach of country, where he and his men could find comfortable quarters. This arrangement was instantly put in execution. We will first accompany the intrepid pilot in his cruise towards the south.

Coasting along the great continent, with his canvas still spread to favorable winds, the first place at which Ruiz cast anchor was off the little island of Gallo, about two degrees north. The inhabitants, who were not numerous, were prepared to give him a hostile reception, — for tidings of the invaders had preceded them along the country, and even reached this insulated spot. As the object of Ruiz was to explore, not to conquer, he did not care to entangle himself in hostilities with the natives; so, changing his purpose of landing, he weighed anchor, and ran down the coast as far as what is now called the Bay of St. Matthew. The country, which, as he advanced, continued to exhibit evidence of a better culture as well as of a more dense population than the parts hitherto seen, was crowded, along the shores, with spectators, who gave no signs of fear or hostility. They stood gazing on the vessel of the white men as it glided smoothly into the crystal waters of the bay, fancying it, says an old writer, some mysterious being descended from the skies.

Without staying long enough on this friendly coast to undeceive the simple people, Ruiz, standing off shore, struck out into the deep sea; but he had not sailed far in that direction, when he was surprised by the sight of a vessel, seeming in the distance like a caravel of considerable size, traversed by a large sail that carried it sluggishly over the waters. The old navigator was not a little perplexed by this phenomenon, as he was confident no European bark could have been before him in these latitudes, and no Indian nation, yet discovered, not even the civilized Mexican, was acquainted with the use of sails in navigation. As he drew near, he found it was a large vessel, or rather raft, called *balsa* by the natives, consisting of a number of huge timbers of a light, porous wood, tightly lashed together, with a frail flooring of reeds raised on them by way of deck. Two masts or sturdy poles, erected in the middle of the vessel, sustained a large square-sail of cotton, while a rude kind of rudder and a movable keel, made of plank inserted between the logs, enabled the mariner to give a direction to the floating fabric, which held on its course without the aid of oar or paddle.[13] The simple architecture of this craft was sufficient for the purposes of the natives, and indeed has continued to answer them to the present day; for the *balsa*, surmounted by small thatched huts or cabins, still supplies the most commodious means for the transportation of passengers and luggage on the streams and along the shores of this part of the South American continent.

On coming alongside, Ruiz found several Indians, both men and women, on board, some with rich ornaments on their persons, besides several articles wrought with considerable skill in gold and silver, which they were carrying for purposes of traffic to the different places along the coast. But what most attracted his attention was the woollen cloth of which some of their dresses were made. It was of a fine texture, delicately embroidered with figures of birds and flowers, and dyed in brilliant colors. He also observed in the boat a pair of balances made to weigh the precious metals.[14] His astonishment at these proofs of ingenuity and civilization, so much higher than any thing he had ever seen in the country, was heightened by the intelligence which he collected from some of these Indians. Two of them had come from Tumbez, a Peruvian port, some degrees to the south; and they gave him to understand, that in their neighbourhood the fields were covered with large flocks of the animals from which the wool was obtained, and that gold and silver were almost as common as wood in the palaces of their monarch. The Spaniards listened greedily to reports which harmonized so well with their fond desires. Though half distrusting the exaggeration, Ruiz resolved to detain some of the Indians, including the natives of Tumbez, that they might repeat the wondrous tale to his commander, and at the same time, by learning the Castilian, might hereafter serve as interpreters with their countrymen. The rest of the party he suffered to proceed without further interruption on their voyage. Then holding on his course, the prudent pilot, without touching at any other point of the coast, advanced as far as the Punta de Pasado, about half a degree south, having the glory of being the first European who, sailing in this direction on the Pacific, had crossed the equinoctial line. This was the limit of his discoveries; on reaching which he tacked about, and standing away to the north, succeeded, after an absence of several weeks, in regaining the spot where he had left Pizarro and his comrades.[15]

It was high time; for the spirits of that little band had been sorely tried by the perils they had encountered. On the departure of his vessels, Pizarro marched into the interior, in the hope of finding the pleasant champaign country which had been promised him by the natives. But at every step the forests seemed to grow denser and darker, and the trees towered to a height such as he had never seen, even in these fruitful regions, where Nature works on so gigantic a scale.[16] Hill continued to rise above hill, as he advanced, rolling onward, as it were, by successive waves to join that colossal barrier of the Andes, whose frosty sides, far away above the clouds, spread out like a curtain of burnished silver, that seemed to connect the heavens with the earth.

On crossing these woody eminences, the forlorn adventurers would plunge into ravines of frightful depth, where the exhalations of a humid soil steamed up amidst the incense of sweet-scented flowers, which shone through the deep glooms in every conceivable variety of color. Birds, especially of the parrot tribe, mocked this fantastic variety of nature with tints as brilliant as those of the vegetable world. Monkeys chattered in crowds above their heads, and made grimaces like the fiendish spirits of these solitudes; while hideous reptiles, engendered in the slimy depths of the pools, gathered round the footsteps of the wanderers. Here was seen the gigantic boa, coiling his unwieldy folds about the trees, so as hardly to be distinguished from their trunks, till he was ready to dart upon his prey; and alligators lay basking on the borders of the streams, or, gliding under the waters, seized their incautious victim before he was aware of their approach.[17] Many of the Spaniards perished miserably in this way, and others were waylaid by the natives, who kept a jealous eye on their movements, and availed themselves of every opportunity to take them at advantage. Fourteen of Pizarro's men were cut off at once in a canoe which had stranded on the bank of a stream.[18]

Famine came in addition to other troubles, and it was with difficulty that they found the means of sustaining life on the scanty fare of the forest,—occasionally the potato, as it grew without cultivation, or the wild cocoa-nut, or, on the shore, the salt and bitter fruit of the mangrove; though the shore was less tolerable than the forest, from the swarms of mosquitos which compelled the wretched adventurers to bury their bodies up to their very faces in the sand. In this extremity of suffering, they thought only of return; and all schemes of avarice and ambition—except with Pizarro and a few dauntless spirits—were exchanged for the one craving desire to return to Panamá.

It was at this crisis that the pilot Ruiz returned with the report of his brilliant discoveries; and, not long after, Almagro sailed into port with his vessel laden with refreshments, and a considerable reinforcement of volunteers. The voyage of that commander had been prosperous. When he arrived at Panamá, he found the government in the hands of Don Pedro de los Rios; and he came to anchor in the harbour, unwilling to trust himself on shore, till he had obtained from Father Luque some account of the dispositions of the executive. These were sufficiently favorable; for the new governor had particular instructions fully to carry out the arrangements made by his predecessor with the associates. On learning Almagro's arrival, he came down to the port to welcome him, professing his willingness to afford every facility for the execution of his designs. Fortunately, just before this period, a small body of military adventurers had come to Panamá from the mother country, burning with desire to make their fortunes in the New World. They caught much more eagerly than the old and wary colonists at the golden bait held out to them; and with their addition, and that of a few supernumerary stragglers who hung about the town, Almagro found himself at the head of a reinforcement of at least eighty men, with which, having laid in a fresh supply of stores, he again set sail for the Rio de San Juan.

The arrival of the new recruits all eager to follow up the expedition, the comfortable change in their circumstances produced by an ample supply of refreshments, and the glowing pictures of the wealth that awaited them in the south, all had their effect on the dejected spirits of Pizarro's followers. Their late toils and privations were speedily forgotten, and, with the buoyant and variable feelings incident to a freebooter's life, they now called as eagerly on their commander to go forward in the voyage, as they had before called on him to abandon it. Availing themselves of the renewed spirit of enterprise, the captains embarked on board their vessels, and, under the guidance of the veteran pilot, steered in the same track he had lately pursued.

But the favorable season for a southern course, which in these latitudes lasts but a few months in the year, had been suffered to escape. The breezes blew steadily towards the north, and a strong current, not far from shore, set in the same direction. The winds frequently rose into tempests, and the unfortunate voyagers were tossed about, for many days, in the boiling surges, amidst the most awful storms of thunder and lightning, until, at length, they found a secure haven in the island of Gallo, already visited by Ruiz. As they were now too strong in numbers to apprehend an assault, the crews landed, and, experiencing no molestation from the natives, they continued on the island for a fortnight, refitting their damaged vessels, and recruiting themselves after the fatigues of the ocean. Then, resuming their voyage, the captains stood towards the south until they reached the Bay of St. Matthew. As they advanced along the coast, they were struck, as Ruiz had been before, with the evidences of a higher civilization constantly exhibited in the general aspect of the country and its inhabitants. The hand of cultivation was visible in every quarter. The natural appearance of the coast, too, had something in it more inviting; for, instead of the eternal labyrinth of mangrove-trees, with their complicated roots snarled into formidable coils under the water, as if to waylay and entangle the voyager, the low margin of the sea was covered with a stately growth of ebony, and with a species of mahogany, and other hard woods that take the most brilliant and variegated polish. The sandal-wood, and many balsamic trees of unknown names, scattered their sweet odors far and wide, not in an atmosphere tainted with vegetable corruption, but on the pure breezes of the ocean, bearing health as well as fragrance on their wings. Broad patches of cultivated land intervened, disclosing hill-sides covered with the yellow maize and the potato, or checkered, in the lower levels, with blooming plantations of cacao.[19]

The villages became more numerous; and, as the vessels rode at anchor off the port of Tacamez, the Spaniards saw before them a town of two thousand houses or more, laid out into streets, with a numerous population clustering around it in the suburbs.[20] The men and women displayed many ornaments of gold and precious stones about their persons, which may seem strange, considering that the Peruvian Incas claimed a monopoly of jewels for themselves and the nobles on whom they condescended to bestow them. But, although the Spaniards had now reached the outer limits of the Peruvian empire, it was not Peru, but Quito, and that portion of it but recently brought under the sceptre of the Incas, where the ancient usages of the people could hardly have been effaced under the oppressive system of the American despots. The adjacent country was, moreover, particularly rich in gold, which, collected from the washings of the streams, still forms one of the staple products of Barbacoas. Here, too, was the fair River of Emeralds, so called from the quarries of the beautiful gem on its borders, from which the Indian monarchs enriched their treasury.[21]

The Spaniards gazed with delight on these undeniable evidences of wealth, and saw in the careful cultivation of the soil a comfortable assurance that they had at length reached the land which had so long been seen in brilliant, though distant, perspective before them. But here again they were doomed to be disappointed by the warlike spirit of the people, who, conscious of their own strength, showed no disposition to quail before the invaders. On the contrary, several of their canoes shot out, loaded with warriors, who, displaying a gold mask as their ensign, hovered round the vessels with looks of defiance, and, when pursued, easily took shelter under the lee of the land.[22]

A more formidable body mustered along the shore, to the number, according to the Spanish accounts, of at least ten thousand warriors, eager, apparently, to come to close action with the invaders. Nor could Pizarro, who had landed with a party of his men in the hope of a conference with the natives, wholly prevent hostilities; and it might have gone hard with the Spaniards, hotly pressed by their resolute enemy so superior in numbers, but for a ludicrous accident reported by the historians as happening to one of the cavaliers.

This was a fall from his horse, which so astonished the barbarians, who were not prepared for this division of what seemed one and the same being into two, that, filled with consternation, they fell back, and left a way open for the Christians to regain their vessels![23]

A council of war was now called. It was evident that the forces of the Spaniards were unequal to a contest with so numerous and well-appointed a body of natives; and, even if they should prevail here, they could have no hope of stemming the torrent which must rise against them in their progress—for the country was becoming more and more thickly settled, and towns and hamlets started into view at every new headland which they doubled. It was better, in the opinion of some,—the faint-hearted,—to abandon the enterprise at once, as beyond their strength. But Almagro took a different view of the affair. "To go home," he said, "with nothing done, would be ruin, as well as disgrace. There was scarcely one but had left creditors at Panamá, who looked for payment to the fruits of this expedition. To go home now would be to deliver themselves at once into their hands. It would be to go to prison. Better to roam a freeman, though in the wilderness, than to lie bound with fetters in the dungeons of Panamá.[24] The only course for them," he concluded, "was the one lately pursued. Pizarro might find some more commodious place where he could remain with part of the force, while he himself went back for recruits to Panamá. The story they had now to tell of the riches of the land, as they had seen them with their own eyes, would put their expedition in a very different light, and could not fail to draw to their banner as many volunteers as they needed."

But this recommendation, however judicious, was not altogether to the taste of the latter commander, who did not relish the part, which constantly fell to him, of remaining behind in the swamps and forests of this wild country. "It is all very well," he said to Almagro, "for you, who pass your time pleasantly enough, careering to and fro in your vessel, or snugly sheltered in a land of plenty at Panamá; but it is quite another matter for those who stay behind to droop and die of hunger in the wilderness."[25] To this Almagro retorted with some heat, professing his own willingness to take charge of the brave men who would remain with him, if Pizarro declined it. The controversy assuming a more angry and menacing tone, from words they would have soon come to blows, as both, laying their hands on their swords, were preparing to rush on each other, when the treasurer Ribera, aided by the pilot Ruiz, succeeded in pacifying them. It required but little effort on the part of these cooler counsellors to convince the cavaliers of the folly of a conduct which must at once terminate the expedition in a manner little creditable to its projectors. A reconciliation consequently took place, sufficient, at least in outward show, to allow the two commanders to act together in concert. Almagro's plan was then adopted; and it only remained to find out the most secure and convenient spot for Pizarro's quarters.

Several days were passed in touching at different parts of the coast, as they retraced their course; but everywhere the natives appeared to have caught the alarm, and assumed a menacing, and from their numbers a formidable, aspect.

The more northerly region, with its unwholesome fens and forests, where nature wages a war even more relentless than man, was not to be thought of. In this perplexity, they decided on the little island of Gallo, as being, on the whole, from its distance from the shore, and from the scantiness of its population, the most eligible spot for them in their forlorn and destitute condition.[26]

But no sooner was the resolution of the two captains made known, than a feeling of discontent broke forth among their followers, especially those who were to remain with Pizarro on the island. "What!" they exclaimed, "were they to be dragged to that obscure spot to die by hunger? The whole expedition had been a cheat and a failure, from beginning to end. The golden countries, so much vaunted, had seemed to fly before them as they advanced; and the little gold they had been fortunate enough to glean had all been sent back to Panamá to entice other fools to follow their example. What had they got in return for all their sufferings? The only treasures they could boast were their bows and arrows, and they were now to be left to die on this dreary island, without so much as a rood of consecrated ground to lay their bones in!"[27]

In this exasperated state of feeling, several of the soldiers wrote back to their friends, informing them of their deplorable condition, and complaining of the cold-blooded manner in which they were to be sacrificed to the obstinate cupidity of their leaders. But the latter were wary enough to anticipate this movement, and Almagro defeated it by seizing all the letters in the vessels, and thus cutting off at once the means of communication with their friends at home. Yet this act of unscrupulous violence, like most other similar acts, fell short of its purpose; for a soldier named Sarabia had the ingenuity to evade it by introducing a letter into a ball of cotton, which was to be taken to Panamá as a specimen of the products of the country, and presented to the governor's lady.[28]

The letter, which was signed by several of the disaffected soldiery besides the writer, painted in gloomy colors the miseries of their condition, accused the two commanders of being the authors of this, and called on the authorities of Panamá to interfere by sending a vessel to take them from the desolate spot, while some of them might still be found surviving the horrors of their confinement. The epistle concluded with a stanza, in which the two leaders were stigmatized as partners in a slaughter-house; one being employed to drive in the cattle for the other to butcher. The verses, which had a currency in their day among the colonists to which they were certainly not entitled by their poetical merits, may be thus rendered into corresponding doggerel:

> "Look out, Señor Governor,
> For the drover while he's near;
> Since he goes home to get the sheep
> For the butcher, who stays here."[29]

CHAPTER IV

INDIGNATION OF THE GOVERNOR. — STERN
RESOLUTION OF PIZARRO. — PROSECUTION
OF THE VOYAGE. — BRILLIANT ASPECT OF
TUMBEZ. — DISCOVERIES ALONG THE
COAST. — RETURN TO PANAMÁ. — PIZARRO
EMBARKS FOR SPAIN

1527-1528.

NOT long after Almagro's departure, Pizarro sent off the remaining vessel, under the pretext of its being put in repair at Panamá. It probably relieved him of a part of his followers, whose mutinous spirit made them an obstacle rather than a help in his forlorn condition, and with whom he was the more willing to part from the difficulty of finding subsistence on the barren spot which he now occupied.

Great was the dismay occasioned by the return of Almagro and his followers, in the little community of Panamá; for the letter, surreptitiously conveyed in the ball of cotton, fell into the hands for which it was intended, and the contents soon got abroad with the usual quantity of exaggeration. The haggard and dejected mien of the adventurers, of itself, told a tale sufficiently disheartening, and it was soon generally believed that the few ill-fated survivors of the expedition were detained against their will by Pizarro, to end their days with their disappointed leader on his desolate island.

Pedro de los Rios, the governor, was so much incensed at the result of the expedition, and the waste of life it had occasioned to the colony, that he turned a deaf ear to all the applications of Luque and Almagro for further countenance in the affair; he derided their sanguine anticipations of the future, and finally resolved to send an officer to the isle of Gallo, with orders to bring back every Spaniard whom he should find still living in that dreary abode. Two vessels were immediately despatched for the purpose, and placed under charge of a cavalier named Tafur, a native of Cordova.

104

Meanwhile Pizarro and his followers were experiencing all the miseries which might have been expected from the character of the barren spot on which they were imprisoned. They were, indeed, relieved from all apprehensions of the natives, since these had quitted the island on its occupation by the white men; but they had to endure the pains of hunger even in a greater degree than they had formerly experienced in the wild woods of the neighbouring continent. Their principal food was crabs and such shell-fish as they could scantily pick up along the shores. Incessant storms of thunder and lightning, for it was the rainy season, swept over the devoted island, and drenched them with a perpetual flood. Thus, half-naked, and pining with famine, there were few in that little company who did not feel the spirit of enterprise quenched within them, or who looked for any happier termination of their difficulties than that afforded by a return to Panamá. The appearance of Tafur, therefore, with his two vessels, well stored with provisions, was greeted with all the rapture that the crew of a sinking wreck might feel on the arrival of some unexpected succour; and the only thought, after satisfying the immediate cravings of hunger, was to embark and leave the detested isle for ever.

But by the same vessel letters came to Pizarro from his two confederates, Luque and Almagro, beseeching him not to despair in his present extremity, but to hold fast to his original purpose. To return under the present circumstances would be to seal the fate of the expedition; and they solemnly engaged, if he would remain firm at his post, to furnish him in a short time with the necessary means for going forward.[1]

A ray of hope was enough for the courageous spirit of Pizarro. It does not appear that he himself had entertained, at any time, thoughts of returning. If he had, these words of encouragement entirely banished them from his bosom, and he prepared to stand the fortune of the cast on which he had so desperately ventured. He knew, however, that solicitations or remonstrances would avail little with the companions of his enterprise; and he probably did not care to win over the more timid spirits who, by perpetually looking back, would only be a clog on his future movements. He announced his own purpose, however, in a laconic but decided manner, characteristic of a man more accustomed to act than to talk, and well calculated to make an impression on his rough followers.

Drawing his sword, he traced a line with it on the sand from east to west. Then turning towards the south, "Friends and comrades!" he said, "on that side are toil, hunger, nakedness, the drenching storm, desertion, and death; on this side, ease and pleasure. There lies Peru with its riches; here, Panamá and its poverty. Choose, each man, what best becomes a brave Castilian. For my part, I go to the south." So saying, he stepped across the line.[2] He was followed by the brave pilot Ruiz; next by Pedro de Candia, a cavalier, born, as his name imports, in one of the isles of Greece. Eleven others successively crossed the line, thus intimating their willingness to abide the fortunes of their leader, for good or for evil.[3] Fame, to quote the enthusiastic language of an ancient chronicler, has commemorated the names of this little band, "who thus, in the face of difficulties unexampled in history, with death rather than riches for their reward, preferred it all to abandoning their honor, and stood firm by their leader as an example of loyalty to future ages."[4]

But the act excited no such admiration in the mind of Tafur, who looked on it as one of gross disobedience to the commands of the governor, and as little better than madness, involving the certain destruction of the parties engaged in it. He refused to give any sanction to it himself by leaving one of his vessels with the adventurers to prosecute their voyage, and it was with great difficulty that he could be persuaded even to allow them a part of the stores which he had brought for their support. This had no influence on their determination, and the little party, bidding adieu to their returning comrades, remained unshaken in their purpose of abiding the fortunes of their commander.[5]

There is something striking to the imagination in the spectacle of these few brave spirits, thus consecrating themselves to a daring enterprise, which seemed as far above their strength as any recorded in the fabulous annals of knight-errantry. A handful of men, without food, without clothing, almost without arms, without knowledge of the land to which they were bound, without vessel to transport them, were here left on a lonely rock in the ocean with the avowed purpose of carrying on a crusade against a powerful empire, staking their lives on its success. What is there in the legends of chivalry that surpasses it? This was the crisis of Pizarro's fate. There are moments in the lives of men, which, as they are seized or neglected, decide their future destiny.[6] Had Pizarro faltered from his strong purpose, and yielded to the occasion, now so temptingly presented, for extricating himself and his broken band from their desperate position, his name would have been buried with his fortunes, and the conquest of Peru would have been left for other and more successful adventurers. But his constancy was equal to the occasion, and his conduct here proved him competent to the perilous post he had assumed, and inspired others with a confidence in him which was the best assurance of success.

In the vessel that bore back Tafur and those who seceded from the expedition the pilot Ruiz was also permitted to return, in order to coöperate with Luque and Almagro in their application for further succour.

Not long after the departure of the ships, it was decided by Pizarro to abandon his present quarters, which had little to recommend them, and which, he reflected, might now be exposed to annoyance from the original inhabitants, should they take courage and return, on learning the diminished number of the white men. The Spaniards, therefore, by his orders, constructed a rude boat or raft, on which they succeeded in transporting themselves to the little island of Gorgona, twenty-five leagues to the north of their present residence. It lay about five leagues from the continent, and was uninhabited. It had some advantages over the isle of Gallo; for it stood higher above the sea, and was partially covered with wood, which afforded shelter to a species of pheasant, and the hare or rabbit of the country, so that the Spaniards, with their crossbows, were enabled to procure a tolerable supply of game. Cool streams that issued from the living rock furnished abundance of water, though the drenching rains that fell, without intermission, left them in no danger of perishing by thirst. From this annoyance they found some protection in the rude huts which they constructed; though here, as in their former residence, they suffered from the no less intolerable annoyance of venomous insects, which multiplied and swarmed in the exhalations of the rank and stimulated soil. In this dreary abode Pizarro omitted no means by which to sustain the drooping spirits of his men. Morning prayers were duly said, and the evening hymn to the Virgin was regularly chanted; the festivals of the church were carefully commemorated, and every means taken by their commander to give a kind of religious character to his enterprise, and to inspire his rough followers with a confidence in the protection of Heaven, that might support them in their perilous circumstances.[7]

In these uncomfortable quarters, their chief employment was to keep watch on the melancholy ocean, that they might hail the first signal of the anticipated succour. But many a tedious month passed away, and no sign of it appeared. All around was the same wide waste of waters, except to the eastward, where the frozen crest of the Andes, touched with the ardent sun of the equator, glowed like a ridge of fire along the whole extent of the great continent. Every speck in the distant horizon was carefully noticed, and the drifting timber or masses of sea-weed, heaving to and fro on the bosom of the waters, was converted by their imaginations into the promised vessel; till, sinking under successive disappointments, hope gradually gave way to doubt, and doubt settled into despair.[8]

Meanwhile the vessel of Tafur had reached the port of Panamá. The tidings which she brought of the inflexible obstinacy of Pizarro and his followers filled the governor with indignation. He could look on it in no other light than as an act of suicide, and steadily refused to send further assistance to men who were obstinately bent on their own destruction. Yet Luque and Almagro were true to their engagements. They represented to the governor, that, if the conduct of their comrade was rash, it was at least in the service of the Crown, and in prosecuting the great work of discovery. Rios had been instructed, on his taking the government, to aid Pizarro in the enterprise; and to desert him now would be to throw away the remaining chance of success, and to incur the responsibility of his death and that of the brave men who adhered to him. These remonstrances, at length, so far operated on the mind of that functionary, that he reluctantly consented that a vessel should be sent to the island of Gorgona, but with no more hands than were necessary to work her, and with positive, instructions to Pizarro to return in six months and report himself at Panamá, whatever might be the future results of his expedition.

Having thus secured the sanction of the executive, the two associates lost no time in fitting out a small vessel with stores and a supply of arms and ammunition, and despatched it to the island. The unfortunate tenants of this little wilderness, who had now occupied it for seven months,[9] hardly dared to trust their senses when they descried the white sails of the friendly bark coming over the waters. And although, when the vessel anchored off the shore, Pizarro was disappointed to find that it brought no additional recruits for the enterprise, yet he greeted it with joy, as affording the means of solving the great problem of the existence of the rich southern empire, and of thus opening the way for its future conquest. Two of his men were so ill, that it was determined to leave them in the care of some of the friendly Indians who had continued with him through the whole of his sojourn, and to call for them on his return. Taking with him the rest of his hardy followers and the natives of Tumbez, he embarked, and, speedily weighing anchor, bade adieu to the "Hell," as it was called by the Spaniards, which had been the scene of so much suffering and such undaunted resolution.[10]

Every heart was now elated with hope, as they found themselves once more on the waters, under the guidance of the good pilot Ruiz, who, obeying the directions of the Indians, proposed to steer for the land of Tumbez, which would bring them at once into the golden empire of the Incas, — the El Dorado, of which they had been so long in pursuit. Passing by the dreary isle of Gallo, which they had such good cause to remember, they stood farther out to sea until they made Point Tacumez, near which they had landed on their previous voyage. They did not touch at any part of the coast, but steadily held on their way, though considerably impeded by the currents, as well as by the wind, which blew with little variation from the south. Fortunately, the wind was light, and, as the weather was favorable, their voyage, though slow, was not uncomfortable. In a few days, they came in sight of Point Pasado, the limit of the pilot's former navigation; and, crossing the line, the little bark entered upon those unknown seas which had never been ploughed by European keel before. The coast, they observed, gradually declined from its former bold and rugged character, gently sloping towards the shore, and spreading out into sandy plains, relieved here and there by patches of uncommon richness and beauty; while the white cottages of the natives glistening along the margin of the sea, and the smoke that rose among the distant hills, intimated the increasing population of the country.

At length, after the lapse of twenty days from their departure from the island, the adventurous vessel rounded the point of St. Helena, and glided smoothly into the waters of the beautiful gulf of Guayaquil. The country was here studded along the shore with towns and villages, though the mighty chain of the Cordilleras, sweeping up abruptly from the coast, left but a narrow strip of emerald verdure, through which numerous rivulets, spreading fertility around them, wound their way into the sea.

The voyagers were now abreast of some of the most stupendous heights of this magnificent range; Chimborazo, with its broad round summit, towering like the dome of the Andes, and Cotopaxi, with its dazzling cone of silvery white, that knows no change except from the action of its own volcanic fires; for this mountain is the most terrible of the American volcanoes, and was in formidable activity at no great distance from the period of our narrative. Well pleased with the signs of civilization that opened on them at every league of their progress, the Spaniards, at length, came to anchor, off the island of Santa Clara, lying at the entrance of the bay of Tumbez.[11]

The place was uninhabited, but was recognized by the Indians on board, as occasionally resorted to by the warlike people of the neighbouring isle of Puná, for purposes of sacrifice and worship. The Spaniards found on the spot a few bits of gold rudely wrought into various shapes, and probably designed as offerings to the Indian deity. Their hearts were cheered, as the natives assured them they would see abundance of the same precious metal in their own city of Tumbez.

The following morning they stood across the bay for this place. As they drew near, they beheld a town of considerable size, with many of the buildings apparently of stone and plaster, situated in the bosom of a fruitful meadow, which seemed to have been redeemed from the sterility of the surrounding country by careful and minute irrigation. When at some distance from shore, Pizarro saw standing towards him several large balsas, which were found to be filled with warriors going on an expedition against the island of Puná. Running alongside of the Indian flotilla, he invited some of the chiefs to come on board of his vessel. The Peruvians gazed with wonder on every object which met their eyes, and especially on their own countrymen, whom they had little expected to meet there. The latter informed them in what manner they had fallen into the hands of the strangers, whom they described as a wonderful race of beings, that had come thither for no harm, but solely to be made acquainted with the country and its inhabitants. This account was confirmed by the Spanish commander, who persuaded the Indians to return in their balsas and report what they had learned to their townsmen, requesting them at the same time to provide his vessel with refreshments, as it was his desire to enter into a friendly intercourse with the natives.

The people of Tumbez were gathered along the shore, and were gazing with unutterable amazement on the floating castle, which, now having dropped anchor, rode lazily at its moorings in their bay. They eagerly listened to the accounts of their countrymen, and instantly reported the affair to the *curaca* or ruler of the district, who, conceiving that the strangers must be beings of a superior order, prepared at once to comply with their request. It was not long before several balsas were seen steering for the vessel laden with bananas, plantains, yuca, Indian corn, sweet potatoes, pine-apples, cocoa-nuts, and other rich products of the bountiful vale of Tumbez. Game and fish, also, were added, with a number of llamas, of which Pizarro had seen the rude drawings belonging to Balboa, but of which till now he had met with no living specimen. He examined this curious animal, the Peruvian sheep,—or, as the Spaniards called it, the "little camel" of the Indians,—with much interest, greatly admiring the mixture of wool and hair which supplied the natives with the materials for their fabrics.

At that time there happened to be at Tumbez an Inca noble, or *orejon*,— for so, as I have already noticed, men of his rank were called by the Spaniards, from the huge ornaments of gold attached to their ears. He expressed great curiosity to see the wonderful strangers, and had, accordingly, come out with the balsas for the purpose. It was easy to perceive from the superior quality of his dress, as well as from the deference paid to him by the others, that he was a person of consideration, and Pizarro received him with marked distinction. He showed him the different parts of the ship, explaining to him the uses of whatever engaged his attention, and answering his numerous queries, as well as he could, by means of the Indian interpreters. The Peruvian chief was especially desirous of knowing whence and why Pizarro and his followers had come to these shores. The Spanish captain replied, that he was the vassal of a great prince, the greatest and most powerful in the world, and that he had come to this country to assert his master's *lawful supremacy* over it. He had further come to rescue the inhabitants from the darkness of unbelief in which they were now wandering. They worshipped an evil spirit, who would sink their souls into everlasting perdition; and he would give them the knowledge of the true and only God, Jesus Christ, since to believe on him was eternal salvation.[12]

The Indian prince listened with deep attention and apparent wonder; but answered nothing. It may be, that neither he nor his interpreters had any very distinct ideas of the doctrines thus abruptly revealed to them. It may be that he did not believe there was any other potentate on earth greater than the Inca; none, at least, who had a better right to rule over his dominions. And it is very possible he was not disposed to admit that the great luminary whom he worshipped was inferior to the God of the Spaniards. But whatever may have passed in the untutored mind of the barbarian, he did not give vent to it, but maintained a discreet silence, without any attempt to controvert or to convince his Christian antagonist.

He remained on board the vessel till the hour of dinner, of which he partook with the Spaniards, expressing his satisfaction at the strange dishes, and especially pleased with the wine, which he pronounced far superior to the fermented liquors of his own country. On taking leave, he courteously pressed the Spaniards to visit Tumbez, and Pizarro dismissed him with the present, among other things, of an iron hatchet, which had greatly excited his admiration; for the use of iron, as we have seen, was as little known to the Peruvians as to the Mexicans.

On the day following, the Spanish captain sent one of his own men, named Alonso de Molina, on shore, accompanied by a negro who had come in the vessel from Panamá, together with a present for the curaca of some swine and poultry, neither of which were indigenous to the New World. Towards evening his emissary returned with a fresh supply of fruits and vegetables, that the friendly people sent to the vessel. Molina had a wondrous tale to tell. On landing, he was surrounded by the natives, who expressed the greatest astonishment at his dress, his fair complexion, and his long beard. The women, especially, manifested great curiosity in respect to him, and Molina seemed to be entirely won by their charms and captivating manners. He probably intimated his satisfaction by his demeanour, since they urged him to stay among them, promising in that case to provide him with a beautiful wife.

Their surprise was equally great at the complexion of his sable companion. They could not believe it was natural, and tried to rub off the imaginary dye with their hands. As the African bore all this with characteristic good-humor, displaying at the same time his rows of ivory teeth, they were prodigiously delighted.[13] The animals were no less above their comprehension; and, when the cock crew, the simple people clapped their hands, and inquired what he was saying.[14] Their intellects were so bewildered by sights so novel, that they seemed incapable of distinguishing between man and brute.

Molina was then escorted to the residence of the curaca, whom he found living in much state, with porters stationed at his doors, and with a quantity of gold and silver vessels, from which he was served. He was then taken to different parts of the Indian city, saw a fortress built of rough stone, and, though low, spreading over a large extent of ground.[15] Near this was a temple; and the Spaniard's description of its decorations, blazing with gold and silver, seemed so extravagant, that Pizarro, distrusting his whole account, resolved to send a more discreet and trustworthy emissary on the following day.[16]

The person selected was Pedro de Candia, the Greek cavalier mentioned as one of the first who intimated his intention to share the fortunes of his commander. He was sent on shore, dressed in complete mail as became a good knight, with his sword by his side, and his arquebuse on his shoulder. The Indians were even more dazzled by his appearance than by Molina's, as the sun fell brightly on his polished armour, and glanced from his military weapons. They had heard much of the formidable arquebuse from their townsmen who had come in the vessel, and they besought Candia "to let it speak to them." He accordingly set up a wooden board as a target, and, taking deliberate aim, fired off the musket. The flash of the powder and the startling report of the piece, as the board, struck by the ball, was shivered into splinters, filled the natives with dismay. Some fell on the ground, covering their faces with their hands, and others approached the cavalier with feelings of awe, which were gradually dispelled by the assurance they received from the smiling expression of his countenance.[17]

111

They then showed him the same hospitable attentions which they had paid to Molina; and his description of the marvels of the place, on his return, fell nothing short of his predecessor's. The fortress, which was surrounded by a triple row of wall, was strongly garrisoned. The temple he described as literally tapestried with plates of gold and silver. Adjoining this structure was a sort of convent appropriated to the Inca's destined brides, who manifested great curiosity to see him. Whether this was gratified is not clear; but Candia described the gardens of the convent, which he entered, as glowing with imitations of fruits and vegetables all in pure gold and silver![18] He had seen a number of artisans at work, whose sole business seemed to be to furnish these gorgeous decorations for the religious houses.

The reports of the cavalier may have been somewhat over-colored.[19] It was natural that men coming from the dreary wilderness, in which they had been buried the last six months, should have been vividly impressed by the tokens of civilization which met them on the Peruvian coast. But Tumbez was a favorite city of the Peruvian princes. It was the most important place on the northern borders of the empire, contiguous to the recent acquisition of Quito. The great Tupac Yupanqui had established a strong fortress there, and peopled it with a colony of *mitimaes*. The temple, and the house occupied by the Virgins of the Sun, had been erected by Huayna Cayac, and were liberally endowed by that Inca, after the sumptuous fashion of the religious establishments of Peru. The town was well supplied with water by numerous aqueducts, and the fruitful valley in which it was embosomed, and the ocean which bathed its shores, supplied ample means of subsistence to a considerable population. But the cupidity of the Spaniards, after the Conquest, was not slow in despoiling the place of its glories; and the site of its proud towers and temples, in less than half a century after that fatal period, was to be traced only by the huge mass of ruins that encumbered the ground.[20]

The Spaniards were nearly mad with joy, says an old writer, at receiving these brilliant tidings of the Peruvian city. All their fond dreams were now to be realized, and they had at length reached the realm which had so long flitted in visionary splendor before them. Pizarro expressed his gratitude to Heaven for having crowned his labors with so glorious a result; but he bitterly lamented the hard fate which, by depriving him of his followers, denied him, at such a moment, the means of availing himself of his success. Yet he had no cause for lamentation; and the devout Catholic saw in this very circumstance a providential interposition which prevented the attempt at conquest, while such attempts would have been premature. Peru was not yet torn asunder by the dissensions of rival candidates for the throne; and, united and strong under the sceptre of a warlike monarch, she might well have bid defiance to all the forces that Pizarro could muster. "It was manifestly the work of Heaven," exclaims a devout son of the Church, "that the natives of the country should have received him in so kind and loving a spirit, as best fitted to facilitate the conquest; for it was the Lord's hand which led him and his followers to this remote region for the extension of the holy faith, and for the salvation of souls."[21]

Having now collected all the information essential to his object, Pizarro, after taking leave of the natives of Tumbez, and promising a speedy return, weighed anchor, and again turned his prow towards the south. Still keeping as near as possible to the coast, that no place of importance might escape his observation, he passed Cape Blanco, and, after sailing about a degree and a half, made the port of Payta. The inhabitants, who had notice of his approach, came out in their balsas to get sight of the wonderful strangers, bringing with them stores of fruits, fish, and vegetables, with the same hospitable spirit shown by their countrymen at Tumbez.

After staying here a short time, and interchanging presents of trifling value with the natives, Pizarro continued his cruise; and, sailing by the sandy plains of Sechura for an extent of near a hundred miles, he doubled the Punta de Aguja, and swept down the coast as it fell off towards the east, still carried forward by light and somewhat variable breezes. The weather now became unfavorable, and the voyagers encountered a succession of heavy gales, which drove them some distance out to sea, and tossed them about for many days. But they did not lose sight of the mighty ranges of the Andes, which, as they proceeded towards the south, were still seen, at nearly the same distance from the shore, rolling onwards, peak after peak, with their stupendous surges of ice, like some vast ocean, that had been suddenly arrested and frozen up in the midst of its wild and tumultuous career. With this landmark always in view, the navigator had little need of star or compass to guide his bark on her course.

As soon as the tempest had subsided, Pizarro stood in again for the continent, touching at the principal points as he coasted along. Everywhere he was received with the same spirit of generous hospitality; the natives coming out in their balsas to welcome him, laden with their little cargoes of fruits and vegetables, of all the luscious varieties that grow in the *tierra caliente*. All were eager to have a glimpse of the strangers, the "Children of the Sun," as the Spaniards began already to be called, from their fair complexions, brilliant armour, and the thunderbolts which they bore in their hands.[22] The most favorable reports, too, had preceded them, of the urbanity and gentleness of their manners, thus unlocking the hearts of the simple natives, and disposing them to confidence and kindness. The iron-hearted soldier had not yet disclosed the darker side of his character. He was too weak to do so. The hour of Conquest had not yet come.

In every place Pizarro received the same accounts of a powerful monarch who ruled over the land, and held his court on the mountain plains of the interior, where his capital was depicted as blazing with gold and silver, and displaying all the profusion of an Oriental satrap. The Spaniards, except at

Tumbez, seem to have met with little of the precious metals among the natives on the coast. More than one writer asserts that they did not covet them, or, at least, by Pizarro's orders, affected not to do so. He would not have them betray their appetite for gold, and actually refused gifts when they were proffered![23] It is more probable that they saw little display of wealth, except in the embellishments of the temples and other sacred buildings, which they did not dare to violate. The precious metals, reserved for the uses of religion and for persons of high degree, were not likely to abound in the remote towns and hamlets on the coast.

Yet the Spaniards met with sufficient evidence of general civilization and power to convince them that there was much foundation for the reports of the natives. Repeatedly they saw structures of stone and plaster, and occasionally showing architectural skill in the execution, if not elegance of design. Wherever they cast anchor, they beheld green patches of cultivated country redeemed from the sterility of nature, and blooming with the variegated vegetation of the tropics; while a refined system of irrigation, by means of aqueducts and canals, seemed to be spread like a net-work over the surface of the country, making even the desert to blossom as the rose. At many places where they landed they saw the great road of the Incas which traversed the sea-coast, often, indeed, lost in the volatile sands, where no road could be maintained, but rising into a broad and substantial causeway, as it emerged on a firmer soil. Such a provision for internal communication was in itself no slight monument of power and civilization.

Still beating to the south, Pizarro passed the site of the future flourishing city of Truxillo, founded by himself some years later, and pressed on till he rode off the port of Santa. It stood on the banks of a broad and beautiful stream; but the surrounding country was so exceedingly arid that it was frequently selected as a burial-place by the Peruvians, who found the soil most favorable for the preservation of their mummies. So numerous, indeed, were the Indian *guacas*, that the place might rather be called the abode of the dead than of the living.[24]

Having reached this point, about the ninth degree of southern latitude, Pizarro's followers besought him not to prosecute the voyage farther. Enough and more than enough had been done, they said, to prove the existence and actual position of the great Indian empire of which they had so long been in search. Yet, with their slender force, they had no power to profit by the discovery. All that remained, therefore, was to return and report the success of their enterprise to the governor at Panamá. Pizarro acquiesced in the reasonableness of this demand. He had now penetrated nine degrees farther than any former navigator in these southern seas, and, instead of the blight which, up to this hour, had seemed to hang over his fortunes, he could now return in triumph to his countrymen. Without hesitation, therefore, he prepared to retrace his course, and stood again towards the north.

On his way, he touched at several places where he had before landed. At one of these, called by the Spaniards Santa Cruz, he had been invited on shore by an Indian woman of rank, and had promised to visit her on his return. No sooner did his vessel cast anchor off the village where she lived, than she came on board, followed by a numerous train of attendants. Pizarro received her with every mark of respect, and on her departure presented her with some trinkets which had a real value in the eyes of an Indian princess. She urged the Spanish commander and his companions to return the visit, engaging to send a number of hostages on board, as security for their good treatment. Pizarro assured her that the frank confidence she had shown towards them proved that this was unnecessary. Yet, no sooner did he put off in his boat, the following day, to go on shore, than several of the principal persons in the place came alongside of the ship to be received as hostages during the absence of the Spaniards,—a singular proof of consideration for the sensitive apprehensions of her guests.

Pizarro found that preparations had been made for his reception in a style of simple hospitality that evinced some degree of taste. Arbours were formed of luxuriant and wide-spreading branches, interwoven with fragrant flowers and shrubs that diffused a delicious perfume through the air. A banquet was provided, teeming with viands prepared in the style of the Peruvian cookery, and with fruits and vegetables of tempting hue and luscious to the taste, though their names and nature were unknown to the Spaniards. After the collation was ended, the guests were entertained with music and dancing by a troop of young men and maidens simply attired, who exhibited in their favorite national amusement all the agility and grace which the supple limbs of the Peruvian Indians so well qualified them to display. Before his departure, Pizarro stated to his kind host the motives of his visit to the country, in the same manner as he had done on other occasions, and he concluded by unfurling the royal banner of Castile, which he had brought on shore, requesting her and her attendants to raise it in token of their allegiance to his sovereign. This they did with great good-humor, laughing all the while, says the chronicler, and making it clear that they had a very imperfect conception of the serious nature of the ceremony. Pizarro was contented with this outward display of loyalty, and returned to his vessel well satisfied with the entertainment he had received, and meditating, it may be, on the best mode of repaying it, hereafter, by the subjugation and conversion of the country.

The Spanish commander did not omit to touch also at Tumbez, on his homeward voyage. Here some of his followers, won by the comfortable aspect of the place and the manners of the people, intimated a wish to remain, conceiving, no doubt, that it would be better to live where they would be persons of consequence than to return to an obscure condition in the community of Panamá. One of these men was Alonso de Molina, the same who had first gone on shore at this place, and been captivated by the charms of the Indian beauties. Pizarro complied with their wishes, thinking it would not be amiss to find, on his return, some of his own followers who would be instructed in the language and usages of the natives. He was also allowed to carry back in his vessel two or three Peruvians, for the similar purpose of instructing them in the Castilian. One of them, a youth named by the Spaniards Felipillo, plays a part of some importance in the history of subsequent events.

On leaving Tumbez, the adventurers steered directly for Panamá, touching only, on their way, at the ill-fated island of Gorgona to take on board their two companions who were left there too ill to proceed with them. One had died, and, receiving the other, Pizarro and his gallant little band continued their voyage; and, after an absence of at least eighteen months, found themselves once more safely riding at anchor in the harbour of Panamá.[25]

The sensation caused by their arrival was great, as might have been expected. For there were few, even among the most sanguine of their friends, who did not imagine that they had long since paid for their temerity, and fallen victims to the climate or the natives, or miserably perished in a watery grave. Their joy was proportionably great, therefore, as they saw the wanderers now returned, not only in health and safety, but with certain tidings of the fair countries which had so long eluded their grasp. It was a moment of proud satisfaction to the three associates, who, in spite of obloquy, derision, and every impediment which the distrust of friends or the coldness of government could throw in their way, had persevered in their great enterprise until they had established the truth of what had been so generally denounced as a chimera. It is the misfortune of those daring spirits who conceive an idea too vast for their own generation to comprehend, or, at least, to attempt to carry out, that they pass for visionary dreamers. Such had been the fate of Luque and his associates. The existence of a rich Indian empire at the south, which, in their minds, dwelling long on the same idea and alive to all the arguments in its favor, had risen to the certainty of conviction, had been derided by the rest of their countrymen as a mere *mirage* of the fancy, which, on nearer approach, would melt into air; while the projectors, who staked their fortunes on the adventure, were denounced as madmen. But their hour of triumph, their slow and hard-earned triumph, had now arrived.

Yet the governor, Pedro de los Rios, did not seem, even at this moment, to be possessed with a conviction of the magnitude of the discovery,—or, perhaps, he was discouraged by its very magnitude. When the associates, now with more confidence, applied to him for patronage in an undertaking too vast for their individual resources, he coldly replied, "He had no desire to build up other states at the expense of his own; nor would he be led to throw away more lives than had already been sacrificed by the cheap display of gold and silver toys and a few Indian sheep!"[26]

Sorely disheartened by this repulse from the only quarter whence effectual aid could be expected, the confederates, without funds, and with credit nearly exhausted by their past efforts, were perplexed in the extreme. Yet to stop now,—what was it but to abandon the rich mine which their Own industry and perseverance had laid open, for others to work at pleasure? In this extremity the fruitful mind of Luque suggested the only expedient by which they could hope for success. This was to apply to the Crown itself. No one was so much interested in the result of the expedition. It was for the government, indeed, that discoveries were to be made, that the country was to be conquered. The government alone was competent to provide the requisite means, and was likely to take a much broader and more liberal view of the matter than a petty colonial officer.

But who was there qualified to take charge of this delicate mission? Luque was chained by his professional duties to Panamá; and his associates, unlettered soldiers, were much better fitted for the business of the camp than of the court. Almagro, blunt, though somewhat swelling and ostentatious in his address, with a diminutive stature and a countenance naturally plain, now much disfigured by the loss of an eye, was not so well qualified for the mission as his companion in arms, who, possessing a good person and altogether a commanding presence, was plausible, and, with all his defects of education, could, where deeply interested, be even eloquent in discourse. The ecclesiastic, however, suggested that the negotiation should be committed to the Licentiate Corral, a respectable functionary, then about to return on some public business to the mother country. But to this Almagro strongly objected. No one, he said, could conduct the affair so well as the party interested in it. He had a high opinion of Pizarro's prudence, his discernment of character, and his cool, deliberate policy.[27] He knew enough of his comrade to have confidence that his presence of mind would not desert him, even in the new, and therefore embarrassing, circumstances in which he would be placed at court. No one, he said, could tell the story of their adventures with such effect, as the man who had been the chief actor in them. No one could so well paint the unparalleled sufferings and sacrifices which they had encountered; no other could tell so forcibly what had been done, what yet remained to do, and what assistance would be necessary to carry it into execution. He concluded, with characteristic frankness, by strongly urging his confederate to undertake the mission.

Pizarro felt the force of Almagro's reasoning, and, though with undisguised reluctance, acquiesced in a measure which was less to his taste than an expedition to the wilderness. But Luque came into the arrangement with more difficulty. "God grant, my children," exclaimed the ecclesiastic, "that one of you may not defraud the other of his blessing!"[28] Pizarro engaged to consult the interests of his associates equally with his own. But Luque, it is clear, did not trust Pizarro.

BOOK III

CONQUEST OF PERU

CHAPTER I

PIZARRO'S RECEPTION AT COURT. — HIS
CAPITULATION WITH THE CROWN. — HE
VISITS HIS BIRTHPLACE. — RETURNS TO THE
NEW WORLD. — DIFFICULTIES WITH ALMAGRO.
— HIS THIRD EXPEDITION. — ADVENTURES ON
THE COAST. — BATTLES IN THE ISLE OF PUNÁ

1528-1531.

PIZARRO and his officer, having crossed the Isthmus, embarked at Nombre de Dios for the old country, and, after a good passage, reached Seville early in the summer of 1528. There happened to be at that time in port a person well known in the history of Spanish adventure as the Bachelor Enciso. He had taken an active part in the colonization of Tierra Firme, and had a pecuniary claim against the early colonists of Darien, of whom Pizarro was one. Immediately on the landing of the latter, he was seized by Enciso's orders, and held in custody for the debt. Pizarro, who had fled from his native land as a forlorn and houseless adventurer, after an absence of more than twenty years, passed, most of them, in unprecedented toil and suffering, now found himself on his return the inmate of a prison. Such was the commencement of those brilliant fortunes which, as he had trusted, awaited him at home. The circumstance excited general indignation; and no sooner was the Court advised of his arrival in the country, and the great purpose of his mission, than orders were sent for his release, with permission to proceed at once on his journey.

Pizarro found the emperor at Toledo, which he was soon to quit, in order to embark for Italy. Spain was not the favorite residence of Charles the Fifth, in the earlier part of his reign. He was now at that period of it when he was enjoying the full flush of his triumphs over his gallant rival of France, whom he had defeated and taken prisoner at the great battle of Pavia; and the victor was at this moment preparing to pass into Italy to receive the imperial crown from the hands of the Roman Pontiff. Elated by his successes and his elevation to the German throne, Charles made little account of his hereditary kingdom, as his ambition found so splendid a career thrown open to it on the wide field of European politics. He had hitherto received too inconsiderable returns from his transatlantic possessions to give them the attention they deserved. But, as the recent acquisition of Mexico and the brilliant anticipations in respect to the southern continent were pressed upon his notice, he felt their importance as likely to afford him the means of prosecuting his ambitious and most expensive enterprises.

Pizarro, therefore, who had now come to satisfy the royal eyes, by visible proofs, of the truth of the golden rumors which, from time to time, had reached Castile, was graciously received by the emperor. Charles examined the various objects which his officer exhibited to him with great attention. He was particularly interested by the appearance of the llama, so remarkable as the only beast of burden yet known on the new continent; and the fine fabrics of woollen cloth, which were made from its shaggy sides, gave it a much higher value, in the eyes of the sagacious monarch, than what it possessed as an animal for domestic labor. But the specimens of gold and silver manufacture, and the wonderful tale which Pizarro had to tell of the abundance of the precious metals, must have satisfied even the cravings of royal cupidity.

Pizarro, far from being embarrassed by the novelty of his situation, maintained his usual self-possession, and showed that decorum and even dignity in his address which belong to the Castilian. He spoke in a simple and respectful style, but with the earnestness and natural eloquence of one who had been an actor in the scenes he described, and who was conscious that the impression he made on his audience was to decide his future destiny. All listened with eagerness to the account of his strange adventures by sea and land, his wanderings in the forests, or in the dismal and pestilent swamps on the sea-coast, without food, almost without raiment, with feet torn and bleeding at every step, with his few companions becoming still fewer by disease and death, and yet pressing on with unconquerable spirit to extend the empire of Castile, and the name and power of her sovereign; but when he painted his lonely condition on the desolate island, abandoned by the government at home, deserted by all but a handful of devoted followers, his royal auditor, though not easily moved, was affected to tears. On his departure from Toledo, Charles commended the affairs of his vassal in the most favorable terms to the consideration of the Council of the Indies.[1]

There was at this time another man at court, who had come there on a similar errand from the New World, but whose splendid achievements had already won for him a name that threw the rising reputation of Pizarro comparatively into the shade. This man was Hernando Cortés, the Conqueror of Mexico. He had come home to lay an empire at the feet of his sovereign, and to demand in return the redress of his wrongs, and the recompense of his great services. He was at the close of his career, as Pizarro was at the commencement of his; the Conqueror of the North and of the South; the two men appointed by Providence to overturn the most potent of the Indian dynasties, and to open the golden gates by which the treasures of the New World were to pass into the coffers of Spain.

Notwithstanding the emperor's recommendation, the business of Pizarro went forward at the tardy pace with which affairs are usually conducted in the court of Castile. He found his limited means gradually sinking under the expenses incurred by his present situation, and he represented, that, unless some measures were speedily taken in reference to his suit, however favorable they might be in the end, he should be in no condition to profit by them. The queen, accordingly, who had charge of the business, on her husband's departure, expedited the affair, and on the twenty-sixth of July, 1529, she executed the memorable *Capitulation*, which defined the powers and privileges of Pizarro.

The instrument secured to that chief the right of discovery and conquest in the province of Peru, or New Castile,—as the country was then called, in the same manner as Mexico had received the name of New Spain,—for the distance of two hundred leagues south of Santiago. He was to receive the titles and rank of Governor and Captain-General of the province, together with those of Adelantado, and Alguacil Mayor, for life; and he was to have a salary of seven hundred and twenty-five thousand maravedis, with the obligation of maintaining certain officers and military retainers, corresponding with the dignity of his station. He was to have the right to erect certain fortresses, with the absolute government of them; to assign *encomiendas* of Indians, under the limitations prescribed by law; and, in fine, to exercise nearly all the prerogatives incident to the authority of a viceroy.

His associate, Almagro, was declared commander of the fortress of Tumbez, with an annual rent of three hundred thousand maravedis, and with the further rank and privileges of an hidalgo. The reverend Father Luque received the reward of his services in the Bishopric of Tumbez, and he was also declared Protector of the Indians of Peru. He was to enjoy the yearly stipend of a thousand ducats,—to be derived, like the other salaries and gratuities in this instrument, from the revenues of the conquered territory.

Nor were the subordinate actors in the expedition forgotten. Ruiz received the title of Grand Pilot of the Southern Ocean, with a liberal provision; Candia was placed at the head of the artillery; and the remaining eleven companions on the desolate island were created hidalgos and cavalleros, and raised to certain municipal dignities,—in prospect.

Several provisions of a liberal tenor were also made, to encourage emigration to the country. The new settlers were to be exempted from some of the most onerous, but customary taxes, as the *alcabala,* or to be subject to them only in a mitigated form. The tax on the precious metals drawn from mines was to be reduced, at first, to one tenth, instead of the fifth imposed on the same metals when obtained by barter or by rapine.

It was expressly enjoined on Pizarro to observe the existing regulations for the good government and protection of the natives; and he was required to carry out with him a specified number of ecclesiastics, with whom he was to take counsel in the conquest of the country, and whose efforts were to be dedicated to the service and conversion of the Indians; while lawyers and attorneys, on the other hand, whose presence was considered as boding ill to the harmony of the new settlements, were strictly prohibited from setting foot in them.

Pizarro, on his part, was bound, in six months from the date of the instrument, to raise a force, well equipped for the service, of two hundred and fifty men, of whom one hundred might be drawn from the colonies; and the government engaged to furnish some trifling assistance in the purchase of artillery and military stores. Finally, he was to be prepared, in six months after his return to Panamá, to leave that port and embark on his expedition.[2]

Such are some of the principal provisions of this Capitulation, by which the Castilian government, with the sagacious policy which it usually pursued on the like occasions, stimulated the ambitious hopes of the adventurer by high-sounding titles, and liberal promises of reward contingent on his success, but took care to stake nothing itself on the issue of the enterprise. It was careful to reap the fruits of his toil, but not to pay the cost of them.

A circumstance, that could not fail to be remarked in these provisions, was the manner in which the high and lucrative posts were accumulated on Pizarro, to the exclusion of Almagro, who, if he had not taken as conspicuous a part in personal toil and exposure, had, at least, divided with him the original burden of the enterprise, and, by his labors in another direction, had contributed quite as essentially to its success. Almagro had willingly conceded the post of honor to his confederate; but it had been stipulated, on Pizarro's departure for Spain, that, while he solicited the office of Governor and Captain-General for himself, he should secure that of Adelantado for his companion. In like manner, he had engaged to apply for the see of Tumbez for the vicar of Panamá, and the office of Alguacil Mayor for the pilot Ruiz. The bishopric took the direction that was concerted, for the soldier could scarcely claim the mitre of the prelate; but the other offices, instead of their appropriate distribution, were all concentred in himself. Yet it was in reference to his application for his friends, that Pizarro had promised on his departure to deal fairly and honorably by them all.[3]

It is stated by the military chronicler, Pedro Pizarro, that his kinsman did, in fact, urge the suit strongly in behalf of Almagro; but that he was refused by the government, on the ground that offices of such paramount importance could not be committed to different individuals. The ill effects of such an arrangement had been long since felt in more than one of the Indian colonies, where it had led to rivalry and fatal collision.[4] Pizarro, therefore, finding his remonstrances unheeded, had no alternative but to combine the offices in his own person, or to see the expedition fall to the ground. This explanation of the affair has not received the sanction of other contemporary historians. The apprehensions expressed by Luque, at the time of Pizarro's assuming the mission, of some such result as actually occurred, founded, doubtless, on a knowledge of his associate's character, may warrant us in distrusting the alleged vindication of his conduct, and our distrust will not be diminished by familiarity with his subsequent career. Pizarro's virtue was not of a kind to withstand temptation,—though of a much weaker sort than that now thrown in his path.

The fortunate cavalier was also honored with the habit of St. Jago;[5] and he was authorized to make an important innovation in his family escutcheon,—for by the father's side he might claim his armorial bearings. The black eagle and the two pillars emblazoned on the royal arms were incorporated with those of the Pizarros; and an Indian city, with a vessel in the distance on the waters, and the llama of Peru, revealed the theatre and the character of his exploits; while the legend announced, that "under the auspices of Charles, and by the industry, the genius, and the resources of Pizarro, the country had been discovered and reduced to tranquillity,"—thus modestly intimating both the past and prospective services of the Conqueror.[6]

These arrangements having been thus completed to Pizarro's satisfaction, he left Toledo for Truxillo, his native place, in Estremadura, where he thought he should be most likely to meet with adherents for his new enterprise, and where it doubtless gratified his vanity to display himself in the palmy, or at least promising, state of his present circumstances. If vanity be ever pardonable, it is certainly in a man who, born in an obscure station in life, without family, interest, or friends to back him, has carved out his own fortunes in the world, and, by his own resources, triumphed over all the obstacles which nature and accident had thrown in his way. Such was the condition of Pizarro, as he now revisited the place of his nativity, where he had hitherto been known only as a poor outcast, without a home to shelter, a father to own him, or a friend to lean upon. But he now found both friends and followers, and some who were eager to claim kindred with him, and take part in his future fortunes. Among these were four brothers. Three of them, like himself, were illegitimate; one of whom, named Francisco Martin de Alcántara, was related to him by the mother's side; the other two, named Gonzalo and Juan Pizarro, were descended from the father. "They were all poor, and proud as they were poor," says Oviedo, who had seen them; "and their eagerness for gain was in proportion to their poverty."[7]

The remaining and eldest brother, named Hernando, was a legitimate son, —"legitimate," continues the same caustic authority, "by his pride, as well as by his birth." His features were plain, even disagreeably so; but his figure was good. He was large of stature, and, like his brother Francis, had on the whole an imposing presence.[8] In his character, he combined some of the worst defects incident to the Castilian. He was jealous in the extreme; impatient not merely of affront, but of the least slight, and implacable in his resentment. He was decisive in his measures, and unscrupulous in their execution. No touch of pity had power to arrest his arm. His arrogance was such, that he was constantly wounding the self-love of those with whom he acted; thus begetting an ill-will which unnecessarily multiplied obstacles in his path. In this he differed from his brother Francis, whose plausible manners smoothed away difficulties, and conciliated confidence and cooperation in his enterprises. Unfortunately, the evil counsels of Hernando exercised an influence over his brother which more than compensated the advantages derived from his singular capacity for business.

Notwithstanding the general interest which Pizarro's adventures excited in his country, that chief did not find it easy to comply with the provisions of the Capitulation in respect to the amount of his levies. Those who were most astonished by his narrative were not always most inclined to take part in his fortunes. They shrunk from the unparalleled hardships which lay in the path of the adventurer in that direction; and they listened with visible distrust to the gorgeous pictures of the golden temples and gardens of Tumbez, which they looked upon as indebted in some degree, at least, to the coloring of his fancy, with the obvious purpose of attracting followers to his banner. It is even said that Pizarro would have found it difficult to raise the necessary funds, but for the seasonable aid of Cortés, a native of Estremadura like himself, his companion in arms in early days, and, according to report, his kinsman.[9] No one was in a better condition to hold out a helping hand to a brother adventurer, and, probably, no one felt greater sympathy in Pizarro's fortunes, or greater confidence in his eventual success, than the man who had so lately trod the same career with renown.

The six months allowed by the Capitulation had elapsed, and Pizarro had assembled somewhat less than his stipulated complement of men, with which he was preparing to embark in a little squadron of three vessels at Seville; but, before they were wholly ready, he received intelligence that the officers of the Council of the Indies proposed to inquire into the condition of the vessels, and ascertain how far the requisitions had been complied with.

Without loss of time, therefore, Pizarro, afraid, if the facts were known, that his enterprise might be nipped in the bud, slipped his cables, and crossing the bar of San Lucar, in January, 1530, stood for the isle of Gomera,—one of the Canaries,—where he ordered his brother Hernando, who had charge of the remaining vessels, to meet him.

Scarcely had he gone, before the officers arrived to institute the search. But when they objected the deficiency of men, they were easily—perhaps willingly—deceived by the pretext that the remainder had gone forward in the vessel with Pizarro. At all events, no further obstacles were thrown in Hernando's way, and he was permitted, with the rest of the squadron, to join his brother, according to agreement, at Gomera.

After a prosperous voyage, the adventurers reached the northern coast of the great southern continent, and anchored off the port of Santa Marta. Here they received such discouraging reports of the countries to which they were bound, of forests teeming with insects and venomous serpents, of huge alligators that swarmed on the banks of the streams, and of hardships and perils such as their own fears had never painted, that several of Pizarro's men deserted; and their leader, thinking it no longer safe to abide in such treacherous quarters, set sail at once for Nombre de Dios.

Soon after his arrival there, he was met by his two associates, Luque and Almagro, who had crossed the mountains for the purpose of hearing from his own lips the precise import of the capitulation with the Crown. Great, as might have been expected, was Almagro's discontent at learning the result of what he regarded as the perfidious machinations of his associate. "Is it thus," he exclaimed, "that you have dealt with the friend who shared equally with you in the trials, the dangers, and the cost of the enterprise; and this, notwithstanding your solemn engagements on your departure to provide for his interests as faithfully as your own? How could you allow me to be thus dishonored in the eyes of the world by so paltry a compensation, which seems to estimate my services as nothing in comparison with your own?"[10]

Pizarro, in reply, assured his companion that he had faithfully urged his suit, but that the government refused to confide powers which intrenched so closely on one another to different hands. He had no alternative, but to accept all himself or to decline all; and he endeavoured to mitigate Almagro's displeasure by representing that the country was large enough for the ambition of both, and that the powers conferred on himself were, in fact, conferred on Almagro, since all that he had would ever be at his friend's disposal, as if it were his own. But these honeyed words did not satisfy the injured party; and the two captains soon after returned to Panamá with feelings of estrangement, if not hostility, towards one another, which did not augur well for their enterprise.

Still, Almagro was of a generous temper, and might have been appeased by the politic concessions of his rival, but for the interference of Hernando Pizarro, who, from the first hour of their meeting, showed little respect for the veteran, which, indeed, the diminutive person of the latter was not calculated to inspire, and who now regarded him with particular aversion as an impediment to the career of his brother.

Almagro's friends—and his frank and liberal manners had secured him many—were no less disgusted than himself with the overbearing conduct of this new ally. They loudly complained that it was quite enough to suffer from the perfidy of Pizarro, without being exposed to the insults of his family, who had now come over with him to fatten on the spoils of conquest which belonged to their leader. The rupture soon proceeded to such a length, that Almagro avowed his intention to prosecute the expedition without further coöperation with his partner, and actually entered into negotiations for the purchase of vessels for that object. But Luque, and the Licentiate Espinosa, who had fortunately come over at that time from St. Domingo, now interposed to repair a breach which must end in the ruin of the enterprise, and the probable destruction of those most interested in its success. By their mediation, a show of reconciliation was at length effected between the parties, on Pizarro's assurance that he would relinquish the dignity of Adelantado in favor of his rival, and petition the emperor to confirm him in the possession of it; — an assurance, it may be remarked, not easy to reconcile with his former assertion in respect to the avowed policy of the Crown in bestowing this office. He was, moreover, to apply for a distinct government for his associate, so soon as he had become master of the country assigned to himself; and was to solicit no office for either of his own brothers, until Almagro had been first provided for. Lastly, the former contract in regard to the division of the spoil into three equal shares between the three original associates was confirmed in the most explicit manner. The reconciliation thus effected among the parties answered the temporary purpose of enabling them to go forward in concert in the expedition. But it was only a thin scar that had healed over the wound, which, deep and rankling within, waited only fresh cause of irritation to break out with a virulence more fatal than ever.[11]

No time was now lost in preparing for the voyage. It found little encouragement, however, among the colonists of Panamá, who were too familiar with the sufferings on the former expeditions to care to undertake another, even with the rich bribe that was held out to allure them. A few of the old company were content to follow out the adventure to its close; and some additional stragglers were collected from the province of Nicaragua, — a shoot, it may be remarked, from the colony of Panamá. But Pizarro made slender additions to the force brought over with him from Spain, though this body was in better condition, and, in respect to arms, ammunition, and equipment generally, was on a much better footing than his former levies. The whole number did not exceed one hundred and eighty men, with twenty-seven horses for the cavalry. He had provided himself with three vessels, two of them of a good size, to take the place of those which he had been compelled to leave on the opposite side of the Isthmus at Nombre de Dios; an armament small for the conquest of an empire, and far short of that prescribed by the capitulation with the Crown. With this the intrepid chief proposed to commence operations, trusting to his own successes, and the exertions of Almagro, who was to remain behind, for the present, to muster reinforcements.[12]

On St. John the Evangelist's day, the banners of the company and the royal standard were consecrated in the cathedral church of Panamá; a sermon was preached before the little army by Fray Juan de Vargas, one of the Dominicans selected by the government for the Peruvian mission; and mass was performed, and the sacrament administered to every soldier previous to his engaging in the crusade against the infidel.[13] Having thus solemnly invoked the blessing of Heaven on the enterprise, Pizarro and his followers went on board their vessels, which rode at anchor in the Bay of Panamá, and early in January, 1531, sallied forth on his third and last expedition for the conquest of Peru.

It was his intention to steer direct for Tumbez, which held out so magnificent a show of treasure on his former voyage. But head winds and currents, as usual, baffled his purpose, and after a run of thirteen days, much shorter than the period formerly required for the same distance, his little squadron came to anchor in the Bay of St. Matthew, about one degree north; and Pizarro, after consulting with his officers, resolved to disembark his forces and advance along the coast, while the vessels held their course at a convenient distance from the shore.

The march of the troops was severe and painful in the extreme; for the road was constantly intersected by streams, which, swollen by the winter rains, widened at their mouths into spacious estuaries. Pizarro, who had some previous knowledge of the country, acted as guide as well as commander of the expedition. He was ever ready to give aid where it was needed, encouraging his followers to ford or swim the torrents as they best could, and cheering the desponding by his own buoyant and courageous spirit.

At length they reached a thick-settled hamlet, or rather town, in the province of Coaque. The Spaniards rushed on the place, and the inhabitants, without offering resistance, fled in terror to the neighbouring forests, leaving their effects — of much greater value than had been anticipated — in the hands of the invaders. "We fell on them, sword in hand," says one of the Conquerors, with some *naïveté*; "for, if we had advised the Indians of our approach, we should never have found there such store of gold and precious stones."[14] The natives, however, according to another authority, stayed voluntarily; "for, as they had done no harm to the white men, they flattered themselves none would be offered to them, but that there would be only an interchange of good offices with the strangers,"[15] — an expectation founded, it may be, on the good character which the Spaniards had established for themselves on their preceding visit, but in which the simple people now found themselves most unpleasantly deceived.

Rushing into the deserted dwellings, the invaders found there, besides stuffs of various kinds, and food most welcome in their famished condition, a large quantity of gold and silver wrought into clumsy ornaments, together with many precious stones; for this was the region of the *esmeraldas,* or emeralds, where that valuable gem was most abundant. One of these jewels that fell into the hands of Pizarro, in this neighbourhood, was as large as a pigeon's egg. Unluckily, his rude followers did not know the value of their prize; and they broke many of them in pieces by pounding them with hammers.[16] They were led to this extraordinary proceeding, it is said, by one of the Dominican missionaries, Fray Reginaldo de Pedraza, who assured them that this was the way to prove the true emerald, which could not be broken. It was observed that the good father did not subject his own jewels to this wise experiment; but, as the stones, in consequence of it, fell in value, being regarded merely as colored glass; he carried back a considerable store of them to Panamá.[17]

The gold and silver ornaments rifled from the dwellings were brought together and deposited in a common heap; when a fifth was deducted for the Crown, and Pizarro distributed the remainder in due proportions among the officers and privates of his company. This was the usage invariably observed on the like occasions throughout the Conquest. The invaders had embarked in a common adventure. Their interest was common, and to have allowed every one to plunder on his own account would only have led to insubordination and perpetual broils. All were required, therefore, on pain of death, to contribute whatever they obtained, whether by bargain or by rapine, to the general stock; and all were too much interested in the execution of the penalty to allow the unhappy culprit, who violated the law, any chance of escape.[18]

Pizarro, with his usual policy, sent back to Panamá a large quantity of the gold, no less than twenty thousand *castellanos* in value, in the belief that the sight of so much treasure, thus speedily acquired, would settle the doubts of the wavering, and decide them on joining his banner.[19] He judged right. As one of the Conquerors piously expresses it, "It pleased the Lord that we should fall in with the town of Coaque, that the riches of the land might find credit with the people, and that they should flock to it."[20]

Pizarro, having refreshed his men, continued his march along the coast, but no longer accompanied by the vessels, which had returned for recruits to Panamá. The road, as he advanced, was checkered with strips of sandy waste, which, drifted about by the winds, blinded the soldiers, and afforded only treacherous footing for man and beast. The glare was intense; and the rays of a vertical sun beat fiercely on the iron mail and the thick quilted doublets of cotton, till the fainting troops were almost suffocated with the heat. To add to their distresses, a strange epidemic broke out in the little army. It took the form of ulcers, or rather hideous warts of great size, which covered the body, and when lanced, as was the case with some, discharged such a quantity of blood as proved fatal to the sufferer. Several died of this frightful disorder, which was so sudden in its attack, and attended with such prostration of strength, that those who lay down well at night were unable to lift their hands to their heads in the morning.[21] The epidemic, which made its first appearance during this invasion, and which did not long survive it, spread over the country, sparing neither native nor white man.[22] It was one of those plagues from the vial of wrath, which the destroying angel, who follows in the path of the conqueror, pours out on the devoted nations.

The Spaniards rarely experienced on their march either resistance or annoyance from the inhabitants, who, instructed by the example of Coaque, fled with their effects into the woods and neighbouring mountains. No one came out to welcome the strangers and offer the rites of hospitality, as on their last visit to the land. For the white men were no longer regarded as good beings that had come from heaven, but as ruthless destroyers, who, invulnerable to the assaults of the Indians, were borne along on the backs of fierce animals, swifter than the wind, with weapons in their hands, that scattered fire and desolation as they went. Such were the stories now circulated of the invaders, which, preceding them everywhere on their march, closed the hearts, if not the doors, of the natives against them. Exhausted by the fatigue of travel and by disease, and grievously disappointed at the poverty of the land, which now offered no compensation for their toils, the soldiers of Pizarro cursed the hour in which they had enlisted under his standard, and the men of Nicaragua, in particular, says the old chronicler, calling to mind their pleasant quarters in their luxurious land, sighed only to return to their Mahometan paradise.[23]

At this juncture the army was gladdened by the sight of a vessel from Panamá, which brought some supplies, together with the royal treasurer, the *veedor* or inspector, the comptroller, and other high officers appointed by the Crown to attend the expedition. They had been left in Spain by Pizarro, in consequence of his abrupt departure from the country; and the Council of the Indies, on learning the circumstance, had sent instructions to Panama to prevent the sailing of his squadron from that port. But the Spanish government, with more wisdom, countermanded the order, only requiring the functionaries to quicken their own departure, and take their place without loss of time in the expedition.

The Spaniards in their march along the coast had now advanced as far as Puerto Viejo. Here they were soon after joined by another small reinforcement of about thirty men, under an officer named Belalcazar, who subsequently rose to high distinction in this service. Many of the followers of Pizarro would now have halted at this spot and established a colony there. But that chief thought more of conquering than of colonizing, at least for the present; and he proposed, as his first step, to get possession of Tumbez, which he regarded as the gate of the Peruvian empire. Continuing his march, therefore, to the shores of what is now called the Gulf of Guayaquil, he arrived off the little island of Puná, lying at no great distance from the Bay of Tumbez. This island, he thought, would afford him a convenient place to encamp until he was prepared to make his descent on the Indian city.

The dispositions of the islanders seemed to favor his purpose. He had not been long in their neighbourhood, before a deputation of the natives, with their cacique at their head, crossed over in their balsas to the main land to welcome the Spaniards to their residence. But the Indian interpreters of Tumbez, who had returned with Pizarro from Spain, and continued with the camp, put their master on his guard against the meditated treachery of the islanders, whom they accused of designing to destroy the Spaniards by cutting the ropes that held together the floats, and leaving those upon them to perish in the waters. Yet the cacique, when charged by Pizarro with this perfidious scheme, denied it with such an air of conscious innocence, that the Spanish commander trusted himself and his followers, without further hesitation, to his conveyance, and was transported in safety to the shores of Puná.

Here he was received in a hospitable manner, and his troops were provided with comfortable quarters. Well satisfied with his present position, Pizarro resolved to occupy it until the violence of the rainy season was passed, when the arrival of the reinforcements he expected would put him in better condition for marching into the country of the Inca.

The island, which lies in the mouth of the river of Guayaquil, and is about eight leagues in length by four in breadth, at the widest part, was at that time partially covered with a noble growth of timber. But a large portion of it was subjected to cultivation, and bloomed with plantations of cacao, of the sweet potato, and the different products of a tropical clime, evincing agricultural knowledge as well as industry in the population. They were a warlike race; but had received from their Peruvian foes the appellation of "perfidious." It was the brand fastened by the Roman historians on their Carthaginian enemies,— with perhaps no better reason. The bold and independent islanders opposed a stubborn resistance to the arms of the Incas; and, though they had finally yielded, they had been ever since at feud, and often in deadly hostility, with their neighbours of Tumbez.

The latter no sooner heard of Pizarro's arrival on the island, than, trusting, probably, to their former friendly relations with him, they came over in some number to the Spanish quarters. The presence of their detested rivals was by no means grateful to the jealous inhabitants of Puná, and the prolonged residence of the white men on their island could not be otherwise than burdensome. In their outward demeanour they still maintained the same show of amity; but Pizarro's interpreters again put him on his guard against the proverbial perfidy of their hosts. With his suspicions thus roused, the Spanish commander was informed that a number of the chiefs had met together to deliberate on a plan of insurrection. Not caring to wait for the springing of the mine, he surrounded the place of meeting with his soldiers and made prisoners of the suspected chieftains. According to one authority, they confessed their guilt.[24] This is by no means certain. Nor is it certain that they meditated an insurrection. Yet the fact is not improbable in itself; though it derives little additional probability from the assertion of the hostile interpreters. It is certain, however, that Pizarro was satisfied of the existence of a conspiracy; and, without further hesitation, he abandoned his wretched prisoners, ten or twelve in number, to the tender mercies of their rivals of Tumbez, who instantly massacred them before his eyes.[25]

Maddened by this outrage, the people of Puná sprang to arms, and threw themselves at once, with fearful yells and the wildest menaces of despair, on the Spanish camp. The odds of numbers were greatly in their favor, for they mustered several thousand warriors. But the more decisive odds of arms and discipline were on the side of their antagonists; and, as the Indians rushed forward in a confused mass to the assault, the Castilians coolly received them on their long pikes, or swept them down by the volleys of their musketry. Their ill-protected bodies were easily cut to pieces by the sharp sword of the Spaniard;

and Hernando Pizarro, putting himself at the head of the cavalry, charged boldly into the midst, and scattered them far and wide over the field, until, panic-struck by the terrible array of steel-clad horsemen, and the stunning reports and the flash of fire-arms, the fugitives sought shelter in the depths of their forests. Yet the victory was owing, in some degree, at least, if we may credit the Conquerors,—to the interposition of Heaven; for St. Michael and his legions were seen high in the air above the combatants, contending with the arch-enemy of man, and cheering on the Christians by their example![26]

Not more than three or four Spaniards fell in the fight; but many were wounded, and among them Hernando Pizarro, who received a severe injury in the leg from a javelin. Nor did the war end here; for the implacable islanders, taking advantage of the cover of night, or of any remissness on the part of the invaders, were ever ready to steal out of their fastnesses and spring on their enemy's camp, while, by cutting off his straggling parties, and destroying his provisions, they kept him in perpetual alarm.

In this uncomfortable situation, the Spanish commander was gladdened by the appearance of two vessels off the island. They brought a reinforcement consisting of a hundred volunteers besides horses for the cavalry. It was commanded by Hernando de Soro, a captain afterwards famous as the discoverer of the Mississippi, which still rolls its majestic current over the place of his burial,—a fitting monument for his remains, as it is of his renown.[27]

This reinforcement was most welcome to Pizarro, who had been long discontented with his position on an island, where he found nothing to compensate the life of unintermitting hostility which he was compelled to lead. With these recruits, he felt himself in sufficient strength to cross over to the continent, and resume military operations on the proper theatre for discovery and conquest. From the Indians of Tumbez he learned that the country had been for some time distracted by a civil war between two sons of the late monarch, competitors for the throne. This intelligence he regarded as of the utmost importance, for he remembered the use which Cortés had made of similar dissensions among the tribes of Anahuac. Indeed, Pizarro seems to have had the example of his great predecessor before his eyes on more occasions than this. But he fell far short of his model; for, notwithstanding the restraint he sometimes put upon himself, his coarser nature and more ferocious temper often betrayed him into acts most repugnant to sound policy, which would never have been countenanced by the Conqueror of Mexico.

CHAPTER II

PERU AT THE TIME OF THE CONQUEST. — REIGN OF HUAYNA CAPAC. — THE INCA BROTHERS. — CONTEST FOR THE EMPIRE. — TRIUMPH AND CRUELTIES OF ATAHUALLPA

Before accompanying the march of Pizarro and his followers into the country of the Incas, it is necessary to make the reader acquainted with the critical situation of the kingdom at that time. For the Spaniards arrived just at the consummation of an important revolution, — at a crisis most favorable to their views of conquest, and but for which, indeed, the conquest, with such a handful of soldiers, could never have been achieved.

In the latter part of the fifteenth century died Tupac Inca Yupanqui, one of the most renowned of the "Children of the Sun," who, carrying the Peruvian arms across the burning sands of Atacama, penetrated to the remote borders of Chili, while in the opposite direction he enlarged the limits of the empire by the acquisition of the southern provinces of Quito. The war in this quarter was conducted by his son Huayna Capac, who succeeded his father on the throne, and fully equalled him in military daring and in capacity for government.

Under this prince, the whole of the powerful state of Quito, which rivalled that of Peru itself in wealth and refinement, was brought under the sceptre of the Incas; whose empire received, by this conquest, the most important accession yet made to it since the foundation of the dynasty of Manco Capac. The remaining days of the victorious monarch were passed in reducing the independent tribes on the remote limits of his territory, and, still more, in cementing his conquests by the introduction of the Peruvian polity. He was actively engaged in completing the great works of his father, especially the high-roads which led from Quito to the capital. He perfected the establishment of posts, took great pains to introduce the Quichua dialect throughout the empire, promoted a better system of agriculture, and, in fine, encouraged the different branches of domestic industry and the various enlightened plans of his predecessors for the improvement of his people. Under his sway, the Peruvian monarchy reached its most palmy state; and under both him and his illustrious father it was advancing with such rapid strides in the march of civilization as would soon have carried it to a level with the more refined despotisms of Asia, furnishing the world, perhaps, with higher evidence of the capabilities of the American Indian than is elsewhere to be found on the great western continent. —But other and gloomier destinies were in reserve for the Indian races.

The first arrival of the white men on the South American shores of the Pacific was about ten years before the death of Huayna Capac, when Balboa crossed the Gulf of St. Michael, and obtained the first clear report of the empire of the Incas. Whether tidings of these adventurers reached the Indian monarch's ears is doubtful, There is no doubt, however, that he obtained the news of the first expedition under Pizarro and Almagro, when the latter commander penetrated as far as the Rio de San Juan, about the fourth degree north. The accounts which he received made a strong impression on the mind of Huayna Capac. He discerned in the formidable prowess and weapons of the invaders proofs of a civilization far superior to that of his own people. He intimated his apprehension that they would return, and that at some day, not far distant, perhaps, the throne of the Incas might be shaken by these strangers, endowed with such incomprehensible powers.[1] To the vulgar eye, it was a little speck on the verge of the horizon; but that of the sagacious monarch seemed to descry in it the dark thunder-cloud, that was to spread wider and wider till it burst in fury on his nation!

There is some ground for believing thus much. But other accounts, which have obtained a popular currency, not content with this, connect the first tidings of the white men with predictions long extant in the country, and with supernatural appearances, which filled the hearts of the whole nation with dismay. Comets were seen flaming athwart the heavens. Earthquakes shook the land; the moon was girdled with rings of fire of many colors; a thunderbolt fell on one of the royal palaces and consumed it to ashes; and an eagle, chased by several hawks, was seen, screaming in the air, to hover above the great square of Cuzco, when, pierced by the talons of his tormentors, the king of birds fell lifeless in the presence of many of the Inca nobles, who read in this an augury of their own destruction! Huayna Capac himself, calling his great officers around him, as he found he was drawing near his end, announced the subversion of his empire by the race of white and bearded strangers, as the consummation predicted by the oracles after the reign of the twelfth Inca, and he enjoined it on his vassals not to resist the decrees of Heaven, but to yield obedience to its messengers.[2]

Such is the report of the impressions made by the appearance of the Spaniards in the country, reminding one of the similar feelings of superstitious terror occasioned by their appearance in Mexico. But the traditions of the latter land rest on much higher authority than those of the Peruvians, which, unsupported by contemporary testimony, rest almost wholly on the naked assertion of one of their own nation, who thought to find, doubtless, in the inevitable decrees of Heaven, the best apology for the supineness of his countrymen.

It is not improbable that rumors of the advent of a strange and mysterious race should have spread gradually among the Indian tribes along the great table-land of the Cordilleras, and should have shaken the hearts of the stoutest warriors with feelings of undefined dread, as of some impending calamity. In this state of mind, it was natural that physical convulsions, to which that volcanic country is peculiarly subject, should have made an unwonted impression on their minds; and that the phenomena, which might have been regarded only as extraordinary, in the usual seasons of political security, should now be interpreted by the superstitious soothsayer as the handwriting on the heavens, by which the God of the Incas proclaimed the approaching downfall of their empire.

Huayna Capac had, as usual with the Peruvian princes, a multitude of concubines, by whom he left a numerous posterity. The heir to the crown, the son of his lawful wife and sister, was named Huascar.[3] At the period of the history at which we are now arrived, he was about thirty years of age. Next to the heir-apparent, by another wife, a cousin of the monarch's, came Manco Capac, a young prince who will occupy an important place in our subsequent story. But the best-beloved of the Inca's children was Atahuallpa. His mother was the daughter of the last *Scyri* of Quito, who had died of grief, it was said, not long after the subversion of his kingdom by Huayna Capac. The princess was beautiful, and the Inca, whether to gratify his passion, or, as the Peruvians say, willing to make amends for the ruin of her parents, received her among his concubines. The historians of Quito assert that she was his lawful wife; but this dignity, according to the usages of the empire, was reserved for maidens of the Inca blood.

The latter years of Huayna Capac were passed in his new kingdom of Quito. Atahuallpa was accordingly brought up under his own eye, accompanied him, while in his tender years, in his campaigns, slept in the same tent with his royal father, and ate from the same plate.[4] The vivacity of the boy, his courage and generous nature, won the affections of the old monarch to such a degree, that he resolved to depart from the established usages of the realm, and divide his empire between him and his elder brother Huascar. On his death-bed, he called the great officers of the crown around him, and declared it to be his will that the ancient kingdom of Quito should pass to Atahuallpa, who might he considered as having a natural claim on it, as the dominion of his ancestors. The rest of the empire he settled on Huascar; and he enjoined it on the two brothers to acquiesce in this arrangement, and to live in amity with each other. This was the last act of the heroic monarch; doubtless, the most impolitic of his whole life. With his dying breath he subverted the fundamental laws of the empire; and, while he recommended harmony between the successors to his authority, he left in this very division of it the seeds of inevitable discord.[5]

His death took place, as seems probable, at the close of 1525, not quite seven years before Pizarro's arrival at Puná.[6] The tidings of his decease spread sorrow and consternation throughout the land; for, though stern and even inexorable to the rebel and the long-resisting foe, he was a brave and magnanimous monarch, and legislated with the enlarged views of a prince who regarded every part of his dominions as equally his concern. The people of Quito, flattered by the proofs which he had given of preference for them by his permanent residence in that country, and his embellishment of their capital, manifested unfeigned sorrow at his loss; and his subjects at Cuzco, proud of the glory which his arms and his abilities had secured for his native land, held him in no less admiration;[7] while the more thoughtful and the more timid, in both countries, looked with apprehension to the future, when the sceptre of the vast empire, instead of being swayed by an old and experienced hand, was to be consigned to rival princes, naturally jealous of one another, and, from their age, necessarily exposed to the unwholesome influence of crafty and ambitious counsellors. The people testified their regret by the unwonted honors paid to the memory of the deceased Inca. His heart was retained in Quito, and his body, embalmed after the fashion of the country, was transported to Cuzco, to take its place in the great temple of the Sun, by the side of the remains of his royal ancestors. His obsequies were celebrated with sanguinary splendor in both the capitals of his far-extended empire; and several thousand of the imperial concubines, with numerous pages and officers of the palace, are said to have proved their sorrow, or their superstition, by offering up their own lives, that they might accompany their departed lord to the bright mansions of the Sun.[8]

For nearly five years after the death of Huayna Capac, the royal brothers reigned, each over his allotted portion of the empire, without distrust of one another, or, at least, without collision. It seemed as if the wish of their father was to be completely realized, and that the two states were to maintain their respective integrity and independence as much as if they had never been united into one. But, with the manifold causes for jealousy and discontent, and the swarms of courtly sycophants, who would find their account in fomenting these feelings, it was easy to see that this tranquil state of things could not long endure. Nor would it have endured so long, but for the more gentle temper of Huascar, the only party who had ground for complaint. He was four or fire years older than his brother, and was possessed of courage not to be doubted; but he was a prince of a generous and easy nature, and perhaps, if left to himself, might have acquiesced in an arrangement which, however unpalatable, was the will of his deified father. But Atahuallpa was of a different temper. Warlike, ambitious, and daring, he was constantly engaged in enterprises for the enlargement of his own territory, though his crafty policy was scrupulous not to aim at extending his acquisitions in the direction of his royal brother. His restless spirit, however, excited some alarm at the court of Cuzco, and Huascar, at length, sent an envoy to Atahuallpa, to remonstrate with him on his ambitious enterprises, and to require him to render him homage for his kingdom of Quito.

This is one statement. Other accounts pretend that the immediate cause of rupture was a claim instituted by Huascar for the territory of Tumebamba, held by his brother as part of his patrimonial inheritance. It matters little what was the ostensible ground of collision between persons placed by circumstances in so false a position in regard to one another, that collision must, at some time or other, inevitably occur.

The commencement, and, indeed, the whole course, of hostilities which soon broke out between the rival brothers are stated with irreconcilable, and, considering the period was so near to that of the Spanish invasion, with unaccountable discrepancy. By some it is said, that, in Atahuallpa's first encounter with the troops of Cuzco, he was defeated and made prisoner near Tumebamba, a favorite residence of his father in the ancient territory of Quito, and in the district of Cañaris. From this disaster he recovered by a fortunate escape from confinement, when, regaining his capital, he soon found himself at the head of a numerous army, led by the most able and experienced captains in the empire. The liberal manners of the young Atahuallpa had endeared him to the soldiers, with whom, as we have seen, he served more than one campaign in his father's lifetime. These troops were the flower of the great army of the Inca, and some of them had grown gray in his long military career, which had left them at the north, where they readily transferred their allegiance to the young sovereign of Quito. They were commanded by two officers of great consideration, both possessed of large experience in military affairs, and high in the confidence of the late Inca. One of them was named Quizquiz; the other, who was the maternal uncle of Atahuallpa, was called Chalicuchima.

With these practised warriors to guide him, the young monarch put himself at the head of his martial array, and directed his march towards the south. He had not advanced farther than Ambato, about sixty miles distant from his capital, when he fell in with a numerous host, which had been sent against him by his brother, under the command of a distinguished chieftain, of the Inca family. A bloody battle followed, which lasted the greater part of the day; and the theatre of combat was the skirts of the mighty Chimborazo.[9]

The battle ended favorably for Atahuallpa, and the Peruvians were routed with great slaughter, and the loss of their commander. The prince of Quito availed himself of his advantage to push forward his march until he arrived before the gates of Tumebamba, which city, as well as the whole district of Cañaris, though an ancient dependency of Quito, had sided with his rival in the contest. Entering the captive city like a conqueror, he put the inhabitants to the sword, and razed it with all its stately edifices, some of which had been reared by his own father, to the ground. He carried on the same war of extermination, as he marched through the offending district of Cañaris. In some places, it is said, the women and children came out, with green branches in their hands, in melancholy procession, to deprecate his wrath; but the vindictive conqueror, deaf to their entreaties, laid the country waste with fire and sword, sparing no man capable of bearing arms who fell into his hands.[10]

The fate of Cañaris struck terror into the hearts of his enemies, and one place after another opened its gates to the victor, who held on his triumphant march towards the Peruvian capital. His arms experienced a temporary check before the island of Puná, whose bold warriors maintained the cause of his brother. After some days lost before this place, Atahuallpa left the contest to their old enemies, the people of Tumbez, who, had early given in their adhesion to him, while he resumed his march and advanced as far as Caxamalca, about seven degrees south. Here he halted with a detachment of the army, sending forward the main body under the command of his two generals, with orders to move straight upon Cuzco. He preferred not to trust himself farther in the enemy's country, where a defeat might be fatal. By establishing his quarters at Caxamalca, he would be able to support his generals, in case of a reverse, or, at worst, to secure his retreat on Quito, until he was again in condition to renew hostilities.

The two commanders, advancing by rapid marches, at length crossed the Apurimac river, and arrived within a short distance of the Peruvian capital. Meanwhile, Huascar had not been idle. On receiving tidings of the discomfiture of his army at Ambato, he made every exertion to raise levies throughout the country. By the advice, it is said, of his priests — the most incompetent advisers in times of danger — he chose to await the approach of the enemy in his own capital; and it was not till the latter had arrived within a few leagues of Cuzco, that the Inca, taking counsel of the same ghostly monitors, sallied forth to give him battle.

The two armies met on the plains of Quipaypan, in the neighbourhood of the Indian metropolis. Their numbers are stated with the usual discrepancy; but Atahuallpa's troops had considerably the advantage in discipline and experience, for many of Huascar's levies had been drawn hastily together from the surrounding country. Both fought, however, with the desperation of men who felt that every thing was at stake. It was no longer a contest for a province, but for the possession of an empire. Atahuallpa's troops, flushed with recent success, fought with the confidence of those who relied on their superior prowess; while the loyal vassals of the Inca displayed all the self-devotion of men who held their own lives cheap in the service of their master.

The fight raged with the greatest obstinacy from sunrise to sunset; and the ground was covered with heaps of the dying and the dead, whose bones lay bleaching on the battle-field long after the conquest by the Spaniards. At length, fortune declared in favor of Atahuallpa; or rather, the usual result of superior discipline and military practice followed. The ranks of the Inca were thrown into irretrievable disorder, and gave way in all directions. The conquerors followed close on the heels of the flying. Huascar himself, among the latter, endeavoured to make his escape with about a thousand men who remained round his person. But the royal fugitive was discovered before he had left the field; his little party was enveloped by clouds of the enemy, and nearly every one of the devoted band perished in defence of their Inca. Huascar was made prisoner, and the victorious chiefs marched at once on his capital, which they occupied in the name of their sovereign.[11]

These events occurred in the spring of 1532, a few months before the landing of the Spaniards. The tidings of the success of his arms and the capture of his unfortunate brother reached Atahuallpa at Caxamalca. He instantly gave orders that Huascar should be treated with the respect due to his rank, but that he should be removed to the strong fortress of Xauxa, and held there in strict confinement. His orders did not stop here,—if we are to receive the accounts of Garcilasso de la Vega, himself of the Inca race, and by his mother's side nephew of the great Huayna Capac.

According to this authority, Atahuallpa invited the Inca nobles throughout the country to assemble at Cuzco, in order to deliberate on the best means of partitioning the empire between him and his brother. When they had met in the capital, they were surrounded by the soldiery of Quito, and butchered without mercy. The motive for this perfidious act was to exterminate the whole of the royal family, who might each one of them show a better title to the crown than the illegitimate Atahuallpa. But the massacre did not end here. The illegitimate offspring, like himself, half-brothers of the monster, all, in short, who had any of the Inca blood in their veins, were involved in it; and with an appetite for carnage unparalleled in the annals of the Roman Empire or of the French Republic, Atahuallpa ordered all the females of the blood royal, his aunts, nieces, and cousins, to be put to death, and that, too, with the most refined and lingering tortures. To give greater zest to his revenge, many of the executions took place in the presence of Huascar himself, who was thus compelled to witness the butchery of his own wives and sisters, while, in the extremity of anguish, they in vain called on him to protect them![12]

Such is the tale told by the historian of the Incas, and received by him, as he assures us, from his mother and uncle, who, being children at the time, were so fortunate as to be among the few that escaped the massacre of their house.[13] And such is the account repeated by many a Castilian writer since, without any symptom of distrust. But a tissue of unprovoked atrocities like these is too repugnant to the principles of human nature,—and, indeed, to common sense, to warrant our belief in them on ordinary testimony.

The annals of semi-civilized nations unhappily show that there have been instances of similar attempts to extinguish the whole of a noxious race, which had become the object of a tyrant's jealousy; though such an attempt is about as chimerical as it would be to extirpate any particular species of plant, the seeds of which had been borne on every wind over the country. But, if the attempt to exterminate the Inca race was actually made by Atahuallpa, how comes it that so many of the pure descendants of the blood royal—nearly six hundred in number—are admitted by the historian to have been in existence seventy years after the imputed massacre?[14] Why was the massacre, instead of being limited to the legitimate members of the royal stock, who could show a better title to the crown than the usurper, extended to all, however remotely, or in whatever way, connected with the race? Why were aged women and young maidens involved in the proscription, and why were they subjected to such refined and superfluous tortures, when it is obvious that beings so impotent could have done nothing to provoke the jealousy of the tyrant? Why, when so many were sacrificed from some vague apprehension of distant danger, was his rival Huascar, together with his younger brother Manco Capac, the two men from whom the conqueror had most to fear, suffered to live? Why, in short, is the wonderful tale not recorded by others before the time of Garcilasso, and nearer by half a century to the events themselves?[15]

That Atahuallpa may have been guilty of excesses, and abused the rights of conquest by some gratuitous acts of cruelty, may be readily believed; for no one, who calls to mind his treatment of the Cañaris,—which his own apologists do not affect to deny,[16]—will doubt that he had a full measure of the vindictive temper which belongs to

"Those souls of fire, and Children of the Sun, With whom revenge
was virtue."

But there is a wide difference between this and the monstrous and most unprovoked atrocities imputed to him; implying a diabolical nature not to be admitted on the evidence of an Indian partisan, the sworn foe of his house, and repeated by Castilian chroniclers, who may naturally seek, by blazoning the enormities of Atahuallpa, to find some apology for the cruelty of their countrymen towards him.

The news of the great victory was borne on the wings of the wind to Caxamalca; and loud and long was the rejoicing, not only in the camp of Atahuallpa, but in the town and surrounding country; for all now came in, eager to offer their congratulations to the victor, and do him homage. The prince of Quito no longer hesitated to assume the scarlet *borla*, the diadem of the Incas. His triumph was complete. He had beaten his enemies on their own ground; had taken their capital; had set his foot on the neck of his rival, and won for himself the ancient sceptre of the Children of the Sun. But the hour of triumph was destined to be that of his deepest humiliation. Atahuallpa was not one of those to whom, in the language of the Grecian bard, "the Gods are willing to reveal themselves."[17] He had not read the handwriting on the heavens. The small speck, which the clear-sighted eye of his father had discerned on the distant verge of the horizon, though little noticed by Atahuallpa, intent on the deadly strife with his brother, had now risen high towards the zenith, spreading wider and wider, till it wrapped the skies in darkness, and was ready to burst in thunders on the devoted nation.

CHAPTER III

THE SPANIARDS LAND AT TUMBEZ. —
PIZARRO RECONNOITRES THE COUNTRY. —
FOUNDATION OF SAN MIGUEL. — MARCH
INTO THE INTERIOR. — EMBASSY FROM THE
INCA. — ADVENTURES ON THE MARCH. —
REACH THE FOOT OF THE ANDES

1532.

WE left the Spaniards at the island of Puná, preparing to make their descent on the neighbouring continent at Tumbez. This port was but a few leagues distant, and Pizarro, with the greater part of his followers, passed over in the ships, while a few others were to transport the commander's baggage and the military stores on some of the Indian balsas. One of the latter vessels which first touched the shore was surrounded, and three persons who were on the raft were carried off by the natives to the adjacent woods and there massacred. The Indians then got possession of another of the balsas, containing Pizarro's wardrobe; but, as the men who defended it raised loud cries for help, they reached the ears of Hernando Pizarro, who, with a small body of horse, had effected a landing some way farther down the shore. A broad tract of miry ground, overflowed at high water, lay between him and the party thus rudely assailed by the natives. The tide was out, and the bottom was soft and dangerous. With little regard to the danger, however, the bold cavalier spurred his horse into the slimy depths, and followed by his men, with the mud up to their saddle-girths, they plunged forward until they came into the midst of the marauders, who, terrified by the strange apparition of the horsemen, fled precipitately, without show of fight, to the neighbouring forests.

This conduct of the natives of Tumbez is not easy to be explained; considering the friendly relations maintained with the Spaniards on their preceding visit, and lately renewed in the island of Puná. But Pizarro was still more astonished, on entering their town, to find it not only deserted, but, with the exception of a few buildings, entirely demolished. Four or five of the most substantial private dwellings, the great temple, and the fortress—and these greatly damaged, and wholly despoiled of their interior decorations—alone survived to mark the site of the city, and attest its former splendor.[1] The scene of desolation filled the conquerors with dismay; for even the raw recruits, who had never visited the coast before, had heard the marvellous stories of the golden treasures of Tumbez, and they had confidently looked forward to them as an easy spoil after all their fatigues. But the gold of Peru seemed only like a deceitful phantom, which, after beckoning them on through toil and danger, vanished the moment they attempted to grasp it.

Pizarro despatched a small body of troops in pursuit of the fugitives; and, after some slight skirmishing, they got possession of several of the natives, and among them, as it chanced, the curaca of the place. When brought before the Spanish commander, he exonerated himself from any share in the violence offered to the white men, saying that it was done by a lawless party of his people, without his knowledge at the time; and he expressed his willingness to deliver them up to punishment, if they could be detected. He explained the dilapidated condition of the town by the long wars carried on with the fierce tribes of Puná, who had at length succeeded in getting possession of the place, and driving the inhabitants into the neighbouring woods and mountains. The Inca, to whose cause they were attached, was too much occupied with his own feuds to protect them against their enemies.

Whether Pizarro gave any credit to the cacique's exculpation of himself may be doubted. He dissembled his suspicions, however, and, as the Indian lord promised obedience in his own name, and that of his vassals, the Spanish general consented to take no further notice of the affair. He seems now to have felt for the first time, in its full force, that it was his policy to gain the good-will of the people among whom he had thrown himself in the face of such tremendous odds. It was, perhaps, the excesses of which his men had been guilty in the earlier stages of the expedition that had shaken the confidence of the people of Tumbez, and incited them to this treacherous retaliation.

Pizarro inquired of the natives who now, under promise of impunity, came into the camp, what had become of his two followers that remained with them in the former expedition. The answers they gave were obscure and contradictory. Some said, they had died of an epidemic; others, that they had perished in the war with Puná; and others intimated, that they had lost their lives in consequence of some outrage attempted on the Indian women. It was impossible to arrive at the truth. The last account was not the least probable. But, whatever might be the cause, there was no doubt they had both perished.

This intelligence spread an additional gloom over the Spaniards; which was not dispelled by the flaming pictures now given by the natives of the riches of the land, and of the state and magnificence of the monarch in his distant capital among the mountains. Nor did they credit the authenticity of a scroll of paper, which Pizarro had obtained from an Indian, to whom it had been delivered by one of the white men left in the country. "Know, whoever you may be," said the writing, "that may chance to set foot in this country, that it contains more gold and silver than there is iron in Biscay." This paper, when shown to the soldiers, excited only their ridicule, as a device of their captain to keep alive their chimerical hopes.[2]

Pizarro now saw that it was not politic to protract his stay in his present quarters, where a spirit of disaffection would soon creep into the ranks of his followers, unless their spirits were stimulated by novelty or a life of incessant action. Yet he felt deeply anxious to obtain more particulars than he had hitherto gathered of the actual condition of the Peruvian empire, of its strength and resources, of the monarch who ruled over it, and of his present situation. He was also desirous, before taking any decisive step for penetrating the country, to seek out some commodious place for a settlement, which might afford him the means of a regular communication with the colonies, and a place of strength, on which he himself might retreat in case of disaster.

He decided, therefore, to leave part of his company at Tumbez, including those who, from the state of their health, were least able to take the field, and with the remainder to make an excursion into the interior, and reconnoitre the land, before deciding on any plan of operations. He set out early in May, 1532; and, keeping along the more level regions himself, sent a small detachment under the command of Hernando de Soto to explore the skirts of the vast sierra.

He maintained a rigid discipline on the march, commanding his soldiers to abstain from all acts of violence, and punishing disobedience in the most prompt and resolute manner.[3] The natives rarely offered resistance. When they did so, they were soon reduced, and Pizarro, far from vindictive measures, was open to the first demonstrations of submission. By this lenient and liberal policy, he soon acquired a name among the inhabitants which effaced the unfavorable impressions made of him in the earlier part of the campaign. The natives, as he marched through the thick-settled hamlets which sprinkled the level region between the Cordilleras and the ocean, welcomed him with rustic hospitality, providing good quarters for his troops, and abundant supplies, which cost but little in the prolific soil of the *tierra caliente*. Everywhere Pizarro made proclamation that he came in the name of the Holy Vicar of God and of the sovereign of Spain, requiring the obedience of the inhabitants as true children of the Church, and vassals of his lord and master. And as the simple people made no opposition to a formula, of which they could not comprehend a syllable, they were admitted as good subjects of the Crown of Castile, and their act of homage—or what was readily interpreted as such was duly recorded and attested by the notary.[4]

At the expiration of some three or four weeks spent in reconnoitring the country, Pizarro came to the conclusion that the most eligible site for his new settlement was in the rich valley of Tangarala, thirty leagues south of Tumbez, traversed by more than one stream that opens a communication with the ocean. To this spot, accordingly, he ordered the men left at Tumbez to repair at once in their vessels; and no sooner had they arrived, than busy preparations were made for building up the town in a manner suited to the wants of the colony. Timber was procured from the neighbouring woods. Stones were dragged from their quarries, and edifices gradually rose, some of which made pretensions to strength, if not to elegance. Among them were a church, a magazine for public stores, a hall of justice, and a fortress. A municipal government was organized, consisting of regidores, alcaldes, and the usual civic functionaries. The adjacent territory was parcelled out among the residents, and each colonist had a certain number of the natives allotted to assist him in his labors; for, as Pizarro's secretary remarks, "it being evident that the colonists could not support themselves without the services of the Indians, the ecclesiastics and the leaders of the expedition all agreed that a *repartimiento* of the natives would serve the cause of religion, and tend greatly to their spiritual welfare, since they would thus have the opportunity of being initiated in the true faith."[5]

Having made these arrangements with such conscientious regard to the welfare of the benighted heathen, Pizarro gave his infant city the name of San Miguel, in acknowledgment of the service rendered him by that saint in his battles with the Indians of Puná. The site originally occupied by the settlement was afterward found to be so unhealthy, that it was abandoned for another on the banks of the beautiful Piura. The town is still of some note for its manufactures, though dwindled from its ancient importance; but the name of San Miguel de Piura, which it bears, still commemorates the foundation of the first European colony in the empire of the Incas.

Before quitting the new settlement, Pizarro caused the gold and silver ornaments which he had obtained in different parts of the country to be melted down into one mass, and a fifth to be deducted for the Crown. The remainder, which belonged to the troops, he persuaded them to relinquish for the present; under the assurance of being repaid from the first spoils that fell into their hands.[6] With these funds, and other articles collected in the course of the campaign, he sent back the vessels to Panamá. The gold was applied to paying off the ship-owners, and those who had furnished the stores for the expedition. That he should so easily have persuaded his men to resign present possession for a future contingency is proof that the spirit of enterprise was renewed in their bosoms in all its former vigor, and that they looked forward with the same buoyant confidence to the results.

In his late tour of observation, the Spanish commander had gathered much important intelligence in regard to the state of the kingdom. He had ascertained the result of the struggle between the Inca brothers, and that the victor now lay with his army encamped at the distance of only ten or twelve days' journey from San Miguel. The accounts he heard of the opulence and power of that monarch, and of his great southern capital, perfectly corresponded with the general rumors before received; and contained, therefore, something to stagger the confidence, as well as to stimulate the cupidity, of the invaders.

Pizarro would gladly have seen his little army strengthened by reinforcements, however small the amount; and on that account postponed his departure for several weeks. But no reinforcement arrived; and, as he received no further tidings from his associates, he judged that longer delay would, probably, be attended with evils greater than those to be encountered on the march; that discontents would inevitably spring up in a life of inaction, and the strength and spirits of the soldier sink under the enervating influence of a tropical climate. Yet the force at his command, amounting to less than two hundred soldiers in all, after reserving fifty for the protection of the new settlement, seemed but a small one for the conquest of an empire. He might, indeed, instead of marching against the Inca, take a southerly direction towards the rich capital of Cuzco. But this would only be to postpone the hour of reckoning. For in what quarter of the empire could he hope to set his foot, where the arm of its master would not reach him? By such a course, moreover, he would show his own distrust of himself. He would shake that opinion of his invincible prowess, which he had hitherto endeavoured to impress on the natives, and which constituted a great secret of his strength; which, in short, held sterner sway over the mind than the display of numbers and mere physical force. Worse than all, such a course would impair the confidence of his troops in themselves and their reliance on himself. This would be to palsy the arm of enterprise at once. It was not to be thought of.

But while Pizarro decided to march into the interior, it is doubtful whether he had formed any more definite plan of action. We have no means of knowing his intentions, at this distance of time, otherwise than as they are shown by his actions. Unfortunately, he could not write, and he has left no record, like the inestimable Commentaries of Cortés, to enlighten us as to his motives. His secretary, and some of his companions in arms, have recited his actions in detail; but the motives which led to them they were not always so competent to disclose.

It is possible that the Spanish general, even so early as the period of his residence at San Miguel, may have meditated some daring stroke, some effective *coup-de-main*, which, like that of Cortés, when he carried off the Aztec monarch to his quarters, might strike terror into the hearts of the people, and at once decide the fortunes of the day. It is more probable, however, that he now only proposed to present himself before the Inca, as the peaceful representative of a brother monarch, and, by these friendly demonstrations, disarm any feeling of hostility, or even of suspicion. When once in communication with the Indian prince, he could regulate his future course by circumstances.

On the 24th of September, 1532, five months after landing at Tumbez, Pizarro marched out at the head of his little body of adventurers from the gates of San Miguel, having enjoined it on the colonists to treat their Indian vassals with humanity, and to conduct themselves in such a manner as would secure the good-will of the surrounding tribes. Their own existence, and with it the safety of the army and the success of the undertaking, depended on this course. In the place were to remain the royal treasurer, the *veedor,* or inspector of metals, and other officers of the crown; and the command of the garrison was intrusted to the *contador,* Antonio Navarro.[7] Then putting himself at the head of his troops, the chief struck boldly into the heart of the country in the direction where, as he was informed, lay the camp of the Inca. It was a daring enterprise, thus to venture with a handful of followers into the heart of a powerful empire, to present himself, face to face, before the Indian monarch in his own camp, encompassed by the flower of his victorious army! Pizarro had already experienced more than once the difficulty of maintaining his ground against the rude tribes of the north, so much inferior in strength and numbers to the warlike legions of Peru. But the hazard of the game, as I have already more than once had occasion to remark, constituted its great charm with the Spaniard. The brilliant achievements of his countrymen, on the like occasions, with means so inadequate, inspired him with confidence in his own good star; and this confidence was one source of his success. Had he faltered for a moment, had he stopped to calculate chances, he must inevitably have failed; for the odds were too great to be combated by sober reason. They were only to be met triumphantly by the spirit of the knight-errant.

After crossing the smooth waters of the Piura, the little army continued to advance over a level district intersected by Streams that descended from the neighbouring Cordilleras. The face of the country was shagged over with forests of gigantic growth, and occasionally traversed by ridges of barren land, that seemed like shoots of the adjacent Andes, breaking up the surface of the region into little sequestered valleys of singular loveliness. The soil, though rarely watered by the rains of heaven, was naturally rich, and wherever it was refreshed with moisture, as on the margins of the streams, it was enamelled with the brightest verdure. The industry of the inhabitants, moreover, had turned these streams to the best account, and canals and aqueducts were seen crossing the low lands in all directions, and spreading over the country, like a vast network, diffusing fertility and beauty around them. The air was scented with the sweet odors of flowers, and everywhere the eye was refreshed by the sight of orchards laden with unknown fruits, and of fields waving with yellow grain and rich in luscious vegetables of every description that teem in the sunny clime of the equator. The Spaniards were among a people who had carried the refinements of husbandry to a greater extent than any yet found on the American continent; and, as they journeyed through this paradise of plenty, their condition formed a pleasing contrast to what they had before endured in the dreary wilderness of the mangroves.

Everywhere, too, they were received with confiding hospitality by the simple people; for which they were no doubt indebted, in a great measure, to their own inoffensive deportment. Every Spaniard seemed to be aware, that his only chance of success lay in conciliating the good opinion of the inhabitants, among whom he had so recklessly cast his fortunes. In most of the hamlets, and in every place of considerable size, some fortress was to be found, or royal caravansary, destined for the Inca on his progresses, the ample halls of which furnished abundant accommodations for the Spaniards; who were thus provided with quarters along their route at the charge of the very government which they were preparing to overturn.[8]

On the fifth day after leaving San Miguel, Pizarro halted in one of these delicious valleys, to give his troops repose, and to make a more complete inspection of them. Their number amounted in all to one hundred and seventy-seven, of which sixty-seven were cavalry. He mustered only three arquebusiers in his whole company, and a few crossbow-men, altogether not exceeding twenty.[9] The troops were tolerably well equipped, and in good condition. But the watchful eye of their commander noticed with uneasiness, that, notwithstanding the general heartiness in the cause manifested by his followers, there were some among them whose countenances lowered with discontent, and who, although they did not give vent to it in open murmurs, were far from moving with their wonted alacrity. He was aware, that, if this spirit became contagious, it would be the ruin of the enterprise; and he thought it best to exterminate the gangrene at once, and at whatever cost, than to wait until it had infected the whole system. He came to an extraordinary resolution.

Calling his men together, he told them that "a crisis had now arrived in their affairs, which it demanded all their courage to meet. No man should think of going forward in the expedition, who could not do so with his whole heart, or who had the least misgiving as to its success. If any repented of his share in it, it was not too late to turn back. San Miguel was but poorly garrisoned, and he should be glad to see it in greater strength. Those who chose might return to this place, and they should be entitled to the same proportion of lands and Indian vassals as the present residents. With the rest, were they few or many, who chose to take their chance with him, he should pursue the adventure to the end."[10]

It was certainly a remarkable proposal for a commander, who was ignorant of the amount of disaffection in his ranks, and who could not safely spare a single man from his force, already far too feeble for the undertaking. Yet, by insisting on the wants of the little colony of San Miguel, he afforded a decent pretext for the secession of the malecontents, and swept away the barrier of shame which might have still held them in the camp. Notwithstanding the fair opening thus afforded, there were but few, nine in all, who availed themselves of the general's permission. Four of these belonged to the infantry, and five to the horse. The rest loudly declared their resolve to go forward with their brave leader; and, if there were some whose voices were faint amidst the general acclamation, they, at least, relinquished the right of complaining hereafter, since they had voluntarily rejected the permission to return.[11] This stroke of policy in their sagacious captain was attended with the best effects. He had winnowed out the few grains of discontent, which, if left to themselves, might have fermented in secret till the whole mass had swelled into mutiny. Cortés had compelled his men to go forward heartily in his enterprise, by burning their vessels, and thus cutting off the only means of retreat. Pizarro, on the other hand, threw open the gates to the disaffected and facilitated their departure. Both judged right, under their peculiar circumstances, and both were perfectly successful.

Feeling himself strengthened, instead of weakened, by his loss, Pizarro now resumed his march, and, on the second day, arrived before a place called Zaran, situated in a fruitful valley among the mountains. Some of the inhabitants had been drawn off to swell the levies of Atahuallpa. The Spaniards had repeated experience on their march of the oppressive exactions of the Inca, who had almost depopulated some of the valleys to obtain reinforcements for his army. The curaca of the Indian town, where Pizarro now arrived, received him with kindness and hospitality, and the troops were quartered as usual in one of the royal *tambos* or caravansaries, which were found in all the principal places.[12]

Yet the Spaniards saw no signs of their approach to the royal encampment, though more time had already elapsed than was originally allowed for reaching it. Shortly before entering Zaran, Pizarro had heard that a Peruvian garrison was established in a place called Caxas, lying among the hills, at no great distance from his present quarters. He immediately despatched a small party under Hernando de Soto in that direction, to reconnoitre the ground, and bring him intelligence of the actual state of things, at Zaran, where he would halt until his officer's return.

Day after day passed on, and a week had elapsed before tidings were received of his companions, and Pizarro was becoming seriously alarmed for their fate, when on the eighth morning Soto appeared, bringing with him an envoy from the Inca himself. He was a person of rank, and was attended by several followers of inferior condition. He had met the Spaniards at Caxas, and now accompanied them on their return, to deliver his sovereign's message, with a present to the Spanish commander. The present consisted of two fountains, made of stone, in the form of fortresses; some fine stuffs of woollen embroidered with gold and silver; and a quantity of goose-flesh, dried and seasoned in a peculiar manner, and much used as a perfume, in a pulverized state, by the Peruvian nobles.[13] The Indian ambassador came charged also with his master's greeting to the strangers, whom Atahuallpa welcomed to his country, and invited to visit him in his camp among the mountains.[14]

Pizarro well understood that the Inca's object in this diplomatic visit was less to do him courtesy, than to inform himself of the strength and condition of the invaders. But he was well pleased with the embassy, and dissembled his consciousness of its real purpose. He caused the Peruvian to be entertained in the best manner the camp could afford, and paid him the respect, says one of the Conquerors, due to the ambassador of so great a monarch.[15] Pizarro urged him to prolong his visit for some days, which the Indian envoy declined, but made the most of his time while there, by gleaning all the information he could in respect to the uses of every strange article which he saw, as well as the object of the white men's visit to the land, and the quarter whence they came.

The Spanish captain satisfied his curiosity in all these particulars. The intercourse with the natives, it may be here remarked, was maintained by means of two of the youths who had accompanied the Conquerors on their return home from their preceding voyage. They had been taken by Pizarro to Spain, and, as much pains had been bestowed on teaching them the Castilian, they now filled the office of interpreters, and opened an easy communication with their countrymen. It was of inestimable service; and well did the Spanish commander reap the fruits of his forecast.[16]

On the departure of the Peruvian messenger, Pizarro presented him with a cap of crimson cloth, some cheap but showy ornaments of glass, and other toys, which he had brought for the purpose from Castile. He charged the envoy to tell his master, that the Spaniards came from a powerful prince, who dwelt far beyond the waters; that they had heard much of the fame of Atahuallpa's victories, and were come to pay their respects to him, and to offer their services by aiding him with their arms against his enemies; and he might be assured, they would not halt on the road, longer than was necessary, before presenting themselves before him.

Pizarro now received from Soto a full account of his late expedition. That chief, on entering Caxas, found the inhabitants mustered in hostile array, as if to dispute his passage. But the cavalier soon convinced them of his pacific intentions, and, laying aside their menacing attitude, they received the Spaniards with the same courtesy which had been shown them in most places on their march.

Here Soto found one of the royal officers, employed in collecting the tribute for the government. From this functionary he learned that the Inca was quartered with a large army at Caxamalca, a place of considerable size on the other side of the Cordillera, where he was enjoying the luxury of the warm baths, supplied by natural springs, for which it was then famous, as it is at the present day. The cavalier gathered, also, much important information in regard to the resources and the general policy of government, the state maintained by the Inca, and the stern severity with which obedience to the law was everywhere enforced. He had some opportunity of observing this for himself, as, on entering the village, he saw several Indians hanging dead by their heels, having been executed for some violence offered to the Virgins of the Sun, of whom there was a convent in the neighbourhood.[17]

From Caxas, De Soto had passed to the adjacent town of Guancabamba, much larger, more populous, and better built than the preceding. The houses, instead of being made of clay baked in the sun, were many of them constructed of solid stone, so nicely put together, that it was impossible to detect the line of junction. A river, which passed through the town, was traversed by a bridge, and the high road of the Incas, which crossed this district, was far superior to that which the Spaniards had seen on the sea-board. It was raised in many places, like a causeway, paved with heavy stone flags, and bordered by trees that afforded a grateful shade to the passenger, while streams of water were conducted through aqueducts along the sides to slake his thirst. At certain distances, also, they noticed small houses, which, they were told, were for the accommodation of the traveller, who might thus pass, without inconvenience, from one end of the kingdom to the other.[18] In another quarter they beheld one of those magazines destined for the army, filled with grain, and with articles of clothing; and at the entrance of the town was a stone building, occupied by a public officer, whose business it was to collect the tolls or duties on various commodities brought into the place, or carried out of it.[19] — These accounts of De Soto not only confirmed all that the Spaniards had heard of the Indian empire, but greatly raised their ideas of its resources and domestic policy. They might well have shaken the confidence of hearts less courageous.

Pizarro, before leaving his present quarters, despatched a messenger to San Miguel with particulars of his movements, sending, at the same time, the articles received from the Inca, as well as those obtained at different places on the route. The skill shown in the execution of some of these fabrics excited great admiration, when sent to Castile. The fine woollen cloths, especially, with their rich embroidery, were pronounced equal to silk, from which it was not easy to distinguish them. It was probably the delicate wool of the vicuña, none of which had then been seen in Europe.[20]

Pizarro, having now acquainted himself with the most direct route to Caxamalca, — the Caxamarca of the present day, — resumed his march, taking a direction nearly south. The first place of any size at which he halted was Motupe, pleasantly situated in a fruitful valley, among hills of no great elevation, which cluster round the base of the Cordilleras. The place was deserted by its curaca, who, with three hundred of its warriors, had gone to join the standard of their Inca. Here the general, notwithstanding his avowed purpose to push forward without delay, halted four days. The tardiness of his movements can be explained only by the hope, which he may have still entertained, of being joined by further reinforcements before crossing the Cordilleras. None such appeared, however; and advancing across a country in which tracts of sandy plain were occasionally relieved by a broad expanse of verdant meadow, watered by natural streams and still more abundantly by those brought through artificial channels, the troops at length arrived at the borders of a river. It was broad and deep, and the rapidity of the current opposed more than ordinary difficulty to the passage. Pizarro, apprehensive lest this might be disputed by the natives on the opposite bank, ordered his brother Hernando to cross over with a small detachment under cover of night, and secure a safe landing for the rest of the troops. At break of day Pizarro made preparations for his own passage, by hewing timber in the neighbouring woods, and constructing a sort of floating bridge, on which before nightfall the whole company passed in safety, the horses swimming, being led by the bridle. It was a day of severe labor, and Pizarro took his own share in it freely, like a common soldier, having ever a word of encouragement to say to his followers.

On reaching the opposite side, they learned from their comrades that the people of the country, instead of offering resistance, had fled in dismay. One of them, having been taken and brought before Hernando Pizarro, refused to answer the questions put to him respecting the Inca and his army; till, being put to the torture, he stated that Atahuallpa was encamped, with his whole force, in three separate divisions, occupying the high grounds and plains of Caxamalca. He further stated, that the Inca was aware of the approach of the white men and of their small number, and that he was purposely decoying them into his own quarters, that he might have them more completely in his power.

This account, when reported by Hernando to his brother, caused the latter much anxiety. As the timidity of the peasantry, however, gradually wore off, some of them mingled with the troops, and among them the curaca or principal person of the village. He had himself visited the royal camp, and he informed the general that Atahuallpa lay at the strong town of Guamachucho, twenty leagues or more south of Caxamalca, with an army of at least fifty thousand men.

These contradictory statements greatly perplexed the chieftain; mid he proposed to one of the Indians who had borne him company during a great part of the march, to go as a spy into the Inca's quarters, and bring him intelligence of his actual position, and, as far as he could learn them, of his intentions towards the Spaniards. But the man positively declined this dangerous service, though he professed his willingness to go as an authorized messenger of the Spanish commander.

Pizarro acquiesced in this proposal, and instructed his envoy to assure the Inca that he was advancing with all convenient speed to meet him. He was to acquaint the monarch with the uniformly considerate conduct of the Spaniards towards his subjects, in their progress through the land, and to assure him that they were now coming in full confidence of finding in him the same amicable feelings towards themselves. The emissary was particularly instructed to observe if the strong passes on the road were defended, or if any preparations of a hostile character were to be discerned. This last intelligence he was to communicate to the general by means of two or three nimble-footed attendants, who were to accompany him on his mission.[21]

Having taken this precaution, the wary commander again resumed his march, and at the end of three days reached the base of the mountain rampart, behind which lay the ancient town of Caxamalca. Before him rose the stupendous Andes, rock piled upon rock, their skirts below dark with evergreen forests, varied here and there by terraced patches of cultivated garden, with the peasant's cottage clinging to their shaggy sides, and their crests of snow glittering high in the heavens,—presenting altogether such a wild chaos of magnificence and beauty as no other mountain scenery in the world can show. Across this tremendous rampart, through a labyrinth of passes, easily capable of defence by a handful of men against an army, the troops were now to march. To the right ran a broad and level road, with its border of friendly shades, and wide enough for two carriages to pass abreast. It was one of the great routes leading to Cuzco, and seemed by its pleasant and easy access to invite the wayworn soldier to choose it in preference to the dangerous mountain defiles. Many were accordingly of opinion that the army should take this course, and abandon the original destination to Caxamalca. But such was not the decision of Pizarro.

The Spaniards had everywhere proclaimed their purpose, he said, to visit the Inca in his camp. This purpose had been communicated to the Inca himself. To take an opposite direction now would only be to draw on them the imputation of cowardice, and to incur Atahuallpa's contempt. No alternative remained but to march straight across the sierra to his quarters. "Let every one of you," said the bold cavalier, "take heart and go forward like a good soldier, nothing daunted by the smallness of your numbers. For in the greatest extremity God ever fights for his own; and doubt not he will humble the pride of the heathen, and bring him to the knowledge of the true faith, the great end and object of the Conquest."[22]

Pizarro, like Cortés, possessed a good share of that frank and manly eloquence which touches the heart of the soldier more than the parade of rhetoric or the finest flow of elocution. He was a soldier himself, and partook in all the feelings of the soldier, his joys, his hopes, and his disappointments. He was not raised by rank and education above sympathy with the humblest of his followers. Every chord in their bosoms vibrated with the same pulsations as his own, and the conviction of this gave him a mastery over them. "Lead on," they shouted, as he finished his brief but animating address, "lead on wherever you think best. We will follow with good-will, and you shall see that we can do our duty in the cause of God and the King!"[23] There was no longer hesitation. All thoughts were now bent on the instant passage of the Cordilleras.

CHAPTER IV

SEVERE PASSAGE OF THE ANDES. — EMBASSIES FROM ATAHUALLPA. — THE SPANIARDS REACH CAXAMALCA. — EMBASSY TO THE INCA. — INTERVIEW WITH THE INCA. — DESPONDENCY OF THE SPANIARDS

1532.

THAT night Pizarro held a council of his principal officers, and it was determined that he should lead the advance, consisting of forty horse and sixty foot, and reconnoitre the ground; while the rest of the company, under his brother Hernando, should occupy their present position till they received further orders.

At early dawn the Spanish general and his detachment were under arms, and prepared to breast the difficulties of the sierra. These proved even greater than had been foreseen. The path had been conducted in the most judicious manner round the rugged and precipitous sides of the mountains, so as best to avoid the natural impediments presented by the ground. But it was necessarily so steep, in many places, that the cavalry were obliged to dismount, and, scrambling up as they could, to lead their horses by the bridle. In many places, too, where some huge crag or eminence overhung the road, this was driven to the very verge of the precipice; and the traveller was compelled to wind along the narrow ledge of rock, scarcely wide enough for his single steed, where a misstep would precipitate him hundreds, nay, thousands, of feet into the dreadful abyss! The wild passes of the sierra, practicable for the half-naked Indian, and even for the sure and circumspect mule, — an animal that seems to have been created for the roads of the Cordilleras, — were formidable to the man-at-arms encumbered with his panoply of mail. The tremendous fissures or *quebradas,* so frightful in this mountain chain, yawned open, as if the Andes had been split asunder by some terrible convulsion, showing a broad expanse of the primitive rock on their sides, partially mantled over with the

154

spontaneous vegetation of ages; while their obscure depths furnished a channel for the torrents, that, rising in the heart of the sierra, worked their way gradually into light, and spread over the savannas and green valleys of the *tierra caliente* on their way to the great ocean.

Many of these passes afforded obvious points of defence; and the Spaniards, as they entered the rocky defiles, looked with apprehension lest they might rouse some foe from his ambush. This apprehension was heightened, as, at the summit of a steep and narrow gorge, in which they were engaged, they beheld a strong work, rising like a fortress, and frowning, as it were, in gloomy defiance on the invaders. As they drew near this building, which was of solid stone, commanding an angle of the road, they almost expected to see the dusky forms of the warriors rise over the battlements, and to receive their tempest of missiles on their bucklers; for it was in so strong a position, that a few resolute men might easily have held there an army at bay. But they had the satisfaction to find the place untenanted, and their spirits were greatly raised by the conviction that the Indian monarch did not intend to dispute their passage, when it would have been easy to do so with success.

Pizarro now sent orders to his brother to follow without delay; and, after refreshing his men, continued his toilsome ascent, and before nightfall reached an eminence crowned by another fortress, of even greater strength than the preceding. It was built of solid masonry, the lower part excavated from the living rock, and the whole work executed with skill not inferior to that of the European architect.[1]

Here Pizarro took up his quarters for the night. Without waiting for the arrival of the rear, on the following morning he resumed his march, leading still deeper into the intricate gorges of the sierra. The climate had gradually changed, and the men and horses, especially the latter, suffered severely from the cold, so long accustomed as they had been to the sultry climate of the tropics.[2] The vegetation also had changed its character; and the magnificent timber which covered the lower level of the country had gradually given way to the funereal forest of pine, and, as they rose still higher, to the stunted growth of numberless Alpine plants, whose hardy natures found a congenial temperature in the icy atmosphere of the more elevated regions. These dreary solitudes seemed to be nearly abandoned by the brute creation as well as by man. The light-footed vicuña, roaming in its native state, might be sometimes seen looking down from some airy cliff, where the foot of the hunter dared not venture. But instead of the feathered tribes whose gay plumage sparkled in the deep glooms of the tropical forests, the adventurers now beheld only the great bird of the Andes, the loathsome condor, who, sailing high above the clouds, followed with doleful cries in the track of the army, as if guided by instinct in the path of blood and carnage.

At length they reached the crest of the Cordillera, where it spreads out into a bold and bleak expanse, with scarce the vestige of vegetation, except what is afforded by the *pajonal,* a dried yellow grass, which, as it is seen from below, encircling the base of the snow-covered peaks, looks, with its brilliant straw-color lighted up in the rays of an ardent sun, like a setting of gold round pinnacles of burnished silver. The land was sterile, as usual in mining districts, and they were drawing near the once famous gold quarries on the way to Caxamalca;

> "Rocks rich in gems, and mountains big with mines,
> That on the high equator ridgy rise."

Here Pizarro halted for the coming up of the rear. The air was sharp and frosty; and the soldiers, spreading their tents, lighted fires, and, huddling round them, endeavoured to find some repose after their laborious march.[3]

They had not been long in these quarters, when a messenger arrived, one of those who had accompanied the Indian envoy sent by Pizarro to Atahuallpa. He informed the general that the road was free from enemies, and that an embassy from the Inca was on its way to the Castilian camp. Pizarro now sent back to quicken the march of the rear, as he was unwilling that the Peruvian envoy should find him with his present diminished numbers. The rest of the army were not far distant, and not long after reached the encampment.

In a short time the Indian embassy also arrived, which consisted of one of the Inca nobles and several attendants, bringing a welcome present of llamas to the Spanish commander. The Peruvian bore, also, the greetings of his master, who wished to know when the Spaniards would arrive at Caxamalca, that he might provide suitable refreshments for them. Pizarro learned that the Inca had left Guamachucho, and was now lying with a small force in the neighbourhood of Caxamalca, at a place celebrated for its natural springs of warm water. The Peruvian was an intelligent person, and the Spanish commander gathered from him many particulars respecting the late contests which had distracted the empire.

As the envoy vaunted in lofty terms the military prowess and resources of his sovereign, Pizarro thought it politic to show that it had no power to overawe him. He expressed his satisfaction at the triumphs of Atahuallpa, who, he acknowledged, had raised himself high in the rank of Indian warriors. But he was as inferior, he added with more policy than politeness, to the monarch who ruled over the white men, as the petty curacas of the country were inferior to him. This was evident from the ease with which a few Spaniards had overrun this great continent, subduing one nation after another, that had offered resistance to their arms. He had been led by the fame of Atahuallpa to visit his dominions, and to offer him his services in his wars; and, if he were received by the Inca in the same friendly spirit with which he came, he was willing, for the aid he could render him, to postpone awhile his passage across the country to the opposite seas. The Indian, according to the Castilian accounts, listened with awe to this strain of glorification from the Spanish commander. Yet it is possible that the envoy was a better diplomatist than they imagined; and that he understood it was only the game of brag at which he was playing with his more civilized antagonist.[4]

On the succeeding morning, at an early hour, the troops were again on their march, and for two days were occupied in threading the airy defiles of the Cordilleras. Soon after beginning their descent on the eastern side, another emissary arrived from the Inca, bearing a message of similar import to the preceding, and a present, in like manner, of Peruvian sheep. This was the same noble that had visited Pizarro in the valley. He now came in more state, quaffing *chicha*—the fermented juice of the maize—from golden goblets borne by his attendants, which sparkled in the eyes of the rapacious adventurers.[5]

While he was in the camp, the Indian messenger, originally sent by Pizarro to the Inca, returned, and no sooner did he behold the Peruvian, and the honorable reception which he met with from the Spaniards, than he was filled with wrath, which would have vented itself in personal violence, but for the interposition of the by-standers. It was hard, he said, that this Peruvian dog should he thus courteously treated, when he himself had nearly lost his life on a similar mission among his countrymen. On reaching the Inca's camp, he had been refused admission to his presence, on the ground that he was keeping a fast and could not be seen. They had paid no respect to his assertion that he came as an envoy from the white men, and would, probably, not have suffered him to escape with life, if he had not assured them that any violence offered to him would be retaliated in full measure on the persons of the Peruvian envoys, now in the Spanish quarters. There was no doubt, he continued, of the hostile intentions of Atahuallpa; for he was surrounded with a powerful army, strongly encamped about a league from Caxamalca, while that city was entirely evacuated by its inhabitants.

To all this the Inca's envoy coolly replied, that Pizarro's messenger might have reckoned on such a reception as he had found, since he seemed to have taken with him no credentials of his mission. As to the Inca's fast, that was true; and, although he would doubtless have seen the messenger, had he known there was one from the strangers, yet it was not safe to disturb him at these solemn seasons, when engaged in his religious duties. The troops by whom he was surrounded were not numerous, considering that the Inca was at that time carrying on an important war; and as to Caxamalca, it was abandoned by the inhabitants in order to make room for the white men, who were so soon to occupy it.[6]

This explanation, however plausible, did not altogether satisfy the general; for he had too deep a conviction of the cunning of Atahuallpa, whose intentions towards the Spaniards he had long greatly distrusted. As he proposed, however, to keep on friendly relations with the monarch for the present, it was obviously not his cue to manifest suspicion. Affecting, therefore, to give full credit to the explanation of the envoy, he dismissed him with reiterated assurances of speedily presenting himself before the Inca.

The descent of the sierra, though the Andes are less precipitous on their eastern side than towards the west, was attended with difficulties almost equal to those of the upward march; and the Spaniards felt no little satisfaction, when, on the seventh day, they arrived in view of the valley of Caxamalca, which, enamelled with all the beauties of cultivation, lay unrolled like a rich and variegated carpet of verdure, in strong contrast with the dark forms of the Andes, that rose up everywhere around it. The valley is of an oval shape, extending about five leagues in length by three in breadth. It was inhabited by a population of a superior character to any which the Spaniards had met on the other side of the mountains, as was argued by the superior style of their attire, and the greater cleanliness and comfort visible both in their persons and dwellings.[7] As far as the eye could reach, the level tract exhibited the show of a diligent and thrifty husbandry. A broad river rolled through the meadows, supplying facilities for copious irrigation by means of the usual canals and subterraneous aqueducts. The land, intersected by verdant hedge-rows, was checkered with patches of various cultivation; for the soil was rich, and the climate, if less stimulating than that of the sultry regions of the coast, was more favorable to the hardy products of the temperate latitudes. Below the adventurers, with its white houses glittering in the sun, lay the little city of Caxamalca, like a sparkling gem on the dark skirts of the sierra. At the distance of about a league farther, across the valley, might be seen columns of vapor rising up towards the heavens, indicating the place of the famous hot baths, much frequented by the Peruvian princes. And here, too, was a spectacle less grateful to the eyes of the Spaniards; for along the slope of the hills a white cloud of pavilions was seen covering the ground, as thick as snow-flakes, for the space, apparently, of several miles. "It filled us all with amazement," exclaims one of the Conquerors, "to behold the Indians occupying so proud a position! So many tents, so well appointed, as were never seen in the Indies till now! The spectacle caused something like confusion and even fear in the stoutest bosom. But it was too late to turn back, or to betray the least sign of weakness, since the natives in our own company would, in such case, have been the first to rise upon us. So, with as bold a countenance as we could, after coolly surveying the ground, we prepared for our entrance into Caxamalca."[8]

What were the feelings of the Peruvian monarch we are not informed, when he gazed on the martial cavalcade of the Christians, as, with banners streaming, and bright panoplies glistening in the rays of the evening sun, it emerged from the dark depths of the sierra, and advanced in hostile array over the fair domain, which, to this period, had never been trodden by other foot than that of the red man. It might be, as several of the reports had stated, that the Inca had purposely decoyed the adventurers into the heart of his populous empire, that he might envelope them with his legions, and the more easily become master of their property and persons.[9] Or was it from a natural feeling of curiosity, and relying on their professions of friendship, that he had thus allowed them, without any attempt at resistance, to come into his presence? At all events, he could hardly have felt such confidence in himself, as not to look with apprehension, mingled with awe, on the mysterious strangers, who, coming from an unknown world, and possessed of such wonderful gifts, had made their way across mountain and valley, in spite of every obstacle which man and nature had opposed to them.

Pizarro, meanwhile, forming his little corps into three divisions, now moved forward, at a more measured pace, and in order of battle, down the slopes that led towards the Indian city. As he drew near, no one came out to welcome him; and he rode through the streets without meeting with a living thing, or hearing a sound, except the echoes, sent back from the deserted dwellings, of the tramp of the soldiery.

It was a place of considerable size, containing about ten thousand inhabitants, somewhat more, probably, than the population assembled at this day within the walls of the modern city of Caxamalca.[10] The houses, for the most part, were built of clay, hardened in the sun; the roofs thatched, or of timber. Some of the more ambitious dwellings were of hewn stone; and there was a convent in the place, occupied by the Virgins of the Sun, and a temple dedicated to the same tutelar deity, which last was hidden in the deep embowering shades of a grove on the skirts of the city. On the quarter towards the Indian camp was a square—if square it might be called, which was almost triangular in form—of an immense size, surrounded by low buildings. These consisted of capacious halls, with wide doors or openings communicating with the square. They were probably intended as a sort of barracks for the Inca's soldiers.[11] At the end of the *plaza,* looking towards the country, was a fortress of stone, with a stairway leading from the city, and a private entrance from the adjoining suburbs. There was still another fortress on the rising ground which commanded the town, built of hewn stone, and encompassed by three circular walls,—or rather one and the same wall, which wound up spirally around it. It was a place of great strength, and the workmanship showed a better knowledge of masonry, and gave a higher impression of the architectural science of the people, than any thing the Spaniards had yet seen.[12]

It was late in the afternoon of the fifteenth of November, 1532, when the Conquerors entered the city of Caxamalca. The weather, which had been fair during the day, now threatened a storm, and some rain mingled with hail— for it was unusually cold—began to fall.[13] Pizarro, however, was so anxious to ascertain the dispositions of the Inca, that he determined to send an embassy, at once, to his quarters. He selected for this, Hernando de Soto with fifteen horse, and, after his departure, conceiving that the number was too small, in case of any unfriendly demonstrations by the Indians, he ordered his brother Hernando to follow with twenty additional troopers. This captain and one other of his party have left us an account of the excursion.[14]

Between the city and the imperial camp was a causeway, built in a substantial manner across the meadow land that intervened. Over this the cavalry galloped at a rapid pace, and, before they had gone a league, they came in front of the Peruvian encampment, where it spread along the gentle slope of the mountains. The lances of the warriors were fixed in the ground before their tents, and the Indian soldiers were loitering without, gazing with silent astonishment at the Christian cavalcade, as with clangor of arms and shrill blast of trumpet it swept by, like some fearful apparition, on the wings of the wind.

The party soon came to a broad but shallow stream, which, winding through the meadow, formed a defence for the Inca's position. Across it was a wooden bridge; but the cavaliers, distrusting its strength, preferred to dash through the waters, and without difficulty gained the opposite bank. A battalion of Indian warriors was drawn up under arms on the farther side of the bridge, but they offered no molestation to the Spaniards; and these latter had strict orders from Pizarro—scarcely necessary in their present circumstances—to treat the natives with courtesy. One of the Indians pointed out the quarter occupied by the Inca.[15]

It was an open court-yard, with a light building or pleasure-house in the centre, having galleries running around it, and opening in the rear on a garden. The walls were covered with a shining plaster, both white and colored, and in the area before the edifice was seen a spacious tank or reservoir of stone, fed by aqueducts that supplied it with both warm and cold water.[16] A basin of hewn stone—it may be of a more recent construction—still bears, on the spot, the name of the "Inca's bath."[17] The court was filled with Indian nobles, dressed in gayly ornamented attire, in attendance on the monarch, and with women of the royal household. Amidst this assembly it was not difficult to distinguish the person of Atahuallpa, though his dress was simpler than that of his attendants. But he wore on his head the crimson *borla* or fringe, which, surrounding the forehead, hung down as low as the eyebrow. This was the well-known badge of Peruvian sovereignty, and had been assumed by the monarch only since the defeat of his brother Huascar. He was seated on a low stool or cushion, somewhat after the Morisco or Turkish fashion, and his nobles and principal officers stood around him, with great ceremony, holding the stations suited to their rank.[18]

The Spaniards gazed with much interest on the prince, of whose cruelty and cunning they had heard so much, and whose valor had secured to him the possession of the empire. But his countenance exhibited neither the fierce passions nor the sagacity which had been ascribed to him; and, though in his bearing he showed a gravity and a calm consciousness of authority well becoming a king, he seemed to discharge all expression from his features, and to discover only the apathy so characteristic of the American races. On the present occasion, this must have been in part, at least, assumed. For it is impossible that the Indian prince should not have contemplated with curious interest a spectacle so strange, and, in some respects, appalling, as that of these mysterious strangers, for which no previous description could have prepared him.

Hernando Pizarro and Soto, with two or three only of their followers, slowly rode up in front of the Inca; and the former, making a respectful obeisance, but without dismounting, informed Atahuallpa that he came as an ambassador from his brother, the commander of the white men, to acquaint the monarch with their arrival in his city of Caxamalca. They were the subjects of a mighty prince across the waters, and had come, he said, drawn thither by the report of his great victories, to offer their services, and to impart to him the doctrines of the true faith which they professed; and he brought an invitation from the general to Atahuallpa that the latter would be pleased to visit the Spaniards in their present quarters.

To all this the Inca answered not a word; nor did he make even a sign of acknowledgment that he comprehended it; though it was translated for him by Felipillo, one of the interpreters already noticed. He remained silent, with his eyes fastened on the ground; but one of his nobles, standing by his side, answered, "It is well."[19] This was an embarrassing situation for the Spaniards, who seemed to be as wide from ascertaining the real disposition of the Peruvian monarch towards themselves, as when the mountains were between them.

In a courteous and respectful manner, Hernando Pizarro again broke the silence by requesting the Inca to speak to them himself, and to inform them what was his pleasure.[20] To this Atahuallpa condescended to reply, while a faint smile passed over his features,—"Tell your captain that I am keeping a fast, which will end to-morrow morning. I will then visit him, with my chieftains. In the mean time, let him occupy the public buildings on the square, and no other, till I come, when I will order what shall be done."[21]

Soto, one of the party present at this interview, as before noticed, was the best mounted and perhaps the best rider in Pizarro's troop. Observing that Atahuallpa looked with some interest on the fiery steed that stood before him, champing the bit and pawing the ground with the natural impatience of a war-horse, the Spaniard gave him the rein, and, striking his iron heel into his side, dashed furiously over the plain; then, wheeling him round and round, displayed all the beautiful movements of his charger, and his own excellent horsemanship. Suddenly checking him in full career, he brought the animal almost on his haunches, so near the person of the Inca, that some of the foam that flecked his horse's sides was thrown on the royal garments. But Atahuallpa maintained the same marble composure as before, though several of his soldiers, whom De Soto passed in the course, were so much disconcerted by it, that they drew back in manifest terror; an act of timidity for which they paid dearly, *if,* as the Spaniards assert, Atahuallpa caused them to be put to death that same evening for betraying such unworthy weakness to the strangers.[22]

Refreshments were now offered by the royal attendants to the Spaniards, which they declined, being unwilling to dismount. They did not refuse, however, to quaff the sparkling chicha from golden vases of extraordinary size, presented to them by the dark-eyed beauties of the harem.[23] Taking then a respectful leave of the Inca, the cavaliers rode back to Caxamalca, with many moody speculations on what they had seen; on the state and opulence of the Indian monarch; on the strength of his military array, their excellent appointments, and the apparent discipline in their ranks, — all arguing a much higher degree of civilization, and consequently of power, than any thing they had witnessed in the lower regions of the country. As they contrasted all this with their own diminutive force, too far advanced, as they now were, for succour to reach them, they felt they had done rashly in throwing themselves into the midst of so formidable an empire, and were filled with gloomy forebodings of the result.[24] Their comrades in the camp soon caught the infectious spirit of despondency, which was not lessened as night came on, and they beheld the watch-fires of the Peruvians lighting up the sides of the mountains, and glittering in the darkness, "as thick," says one who saw them, "as the stars of heaven."[25]

Yet there was one bosom in that little host which was not touched with the feeling either of fear or dejection. That was Pizarro's, who secretly rejoiced that he had now brought matters to the issue for which he had so long panted. He saw the necessity of kindling a similar feeling in his followers, or all would be lost. Without unfolding his plans, he went round among his men, beseeching them not to show faint hearts at this crisis, when they stood face to face with the foe whom they had been so long seeking. "They were to rely on themselves, and on that Providence which had carried them safe through so many fearful trials. It would not now desert them; and if numbers, however great, were on the side of their enemy, it mattered little when theatre of Heaven was on theirs."[26] The Spanish cavalier acted under the combined influence of chivalrous adventure and religious zeal. The latter was the most effective in the hour of peril; and Pizarro, who understood well the characters he had to deal with, by presenting the enterprise as a crusade, kindled the dying embers of enthusiasm in the bosoms of his followers, and restored their faltering courage.

He then summoned a council of his officers, to consider the plan of operations, or rather to propose to them the extraordinary plan on which he had himself decided. This was to lay an ambuscade for the Inca, and take him prisoner in the face of his whole army! It was a project full of peril, — bordering, as it might well seem, on desperation. But the circumstances of the Spaniards were desperate. Whichever way they turned, they were menaced by the most appalling dangers; and better was it bravely to confront the danger, than weakly to shrink from it, when there was no avenue for escape.

To fly was now too late. Whither could they fly? At the first signal of retreat, the whole army of the Inca would be upon them. Their movements would be anticipated by a foe far better acquainted with the intricacies of the sierra than themselves; the passes would be occupied, and they would be hemmed in on all sides; while the mere fact of this retrograde movement would diminish the confidence and with it the effective strength of his own men, while it doubled that of his enemy.

Yet to remain long inactive in his present position seemed almost equally perilous. Even supposing that Atahuallpa should entertain friendly feelings towards the Christians, they could not confide in the continuance of such feelings. Familiarity with the white men would soon destroy the idea of any thing supernatural, or even superior, in their natures. He would feel contempt for their diminutive numbers. Their horses, their arms and showy appointments, would be an attractive bait in the eye of the barbaric monarch, and when conscious that he had the power to crush their possessors, he would not be slow in finding a pretext for it. A sufficient one had already occurred in the highhanded measures of the Conquerors, on their march through his dominions.

But what reason had they to flatter themselves that the Inca cherished such a disposition towards them? He was a crafty and unscrupulous prince, and, if the accounts they had repeatedly received on their march were true, had ever regarded the coming of the Spaniards with an evil eye. It was scarcely possible he should do otherwise. His soft messages had only been intended to decoy them across the mountains, where, with the aid of his warriors, he might readily overpower them. They were entangled in the toils which the cunning monarch had spread for them.

Their only remedy, then, was to turn the Inca's arts against himself; to take him, if possible, in his own snare. There was no time to be lost; for any day might bring back the victorious legions who had recently won his battles at the south, and thus make the odds against the Spaniards far greater than now.

Yet to encounter Atahuallpa in the open field would be attended with great hazard; and even if victorious, there would be little probability that the person of the Inca, of so much importance, would fall into the hands of the victors. The invitation he had so unsuspiciously accepted to visit them in their quarters afforded the best means for securing this desirable prize. Nor was the enterprise so desperate, considering the great advantages afforded by the character and weapons of the invaders, and the unexpectedness of the assault. The mere circumstance of acting on a concerted plan would alone make a small number more than a match for a much larger one. But it was not necessary to admit the whole of the Indian force into the city before the attack; and the person of the Inca once secured, his followers, astounded by so strange an event, were they few or many, would have no heart for further resistance;—and with the Inca once in his power, Pizarro might dictate laws to the empire.

In this daring project of the Spanish chief, it was easy to see that he had the brilliant exploit of Cortés in his mind, when he carried off the Aztec monarch in his capital. But that was not by violence,—at least not by open violence,—and it received the sanction, compulsory though it were, of the monarch himself. It was also true that the results in that case did not altogether justify a repetition of the experiment; since the people rose in a body to sacrifice both the prince and his kidnappers. Yet this was owing, in part, at least, to the indiscretion of the latter. The experiment in the outset was perfectly successful; and, could Pizarro once become master of the person of Atahuallpa, he trusted to

CHAPTER V

DESPERATE PLAN OF PIZARRO. — ATAHUALLPA
VISITS THE SPANIARDS. — HORRIBLE
MASSACRE. — THE INCA A PRISONER. —
CONDUCT OF THE CONQUERORS. — SPLENDID
PROMISES OF THE INCA. — DEATH OF HUASCAR

1532.

THE clouds of the evening had passed away, and the sun rose bright on the following morning, the most memorable epoch in the annals of Peru. It was Saturday, the sixteenth of November, 1532. The loud cry of the trumpet called the Spaniards to arms with the first streak of dawn; and Pizarro, briefly acquainting them with the plan of the assault, made the necessary dispositions.

The *plaza*, as mentioned in the preceding chapter, was defended on its three sides by low ranges of buildings, consisting of spacious halls with wide doors or vomitories opening into the square. In these halls he stationed his cavalry in two divisions, one under his brother Hernando, the other under De Soto. The infantry he placed in another of the buildings, reserving twenty chosen men to act with himself as occasion might require. Pedro de Candia, with a few soldiers and the artillery, — comprehending under this imposing name two small pieces of ordnance, called falconets, — he established in the fortress. All received orders to wait at their posts till the arrival of the Inca. After his entrance into the great square, they were still to remain under cover, withdrawn from observation, till the signal was given by the discharge of a gun, when they were to cry their war-cries, to rush out in a body from their covert, and, putting the Peruvians to the sword, bear off the person of the Inca. The arrangement of the immense halls, opening on a level with the *plaza*, seemed to be contrived on purpose for a *coup de théâtre*. Pizarro particularly inculcated order and implicit obedience, that in the hurry of the moment there should be no confusion. Every thing depended on their acting with concert, coolness, and celerity.[1]

The chief next saw that their arms were in good order; and that the breast-plates of their horses were garnished with bells, to add by their noise to the consternation of the Indians. Refreshments were, also, liberally provided, that the troops should be in condition for the conflict. These arrangements being completed, mass was performed with great solemnity by the ecclesiastics who attended the expedition; the God of battles was invoked to spread his shield over the soldiers who were fighting to extend the empire of the Cross; and all joined with enthusiasm in the chant, "*Exsurge, Domine,*" "Rise, O Lord! and judge thine own cause."[2] One might have supposed them a company of martyrs, about to lay down their lives in defence of their faith, instead of a licentious band of adventurers, meditating one of the most atrocious acts of perfidy on the record of history! Yet, whatever were the vices of the Castilian cavalier, hypocrisy was not among the number. He felt that he was batting for the Cross, and under this conviction, exalted as it was at such a moment as this into the predominant impulse, he was blind to the baser motives which mingled with the enterprise. With feelings thus kindled to a flame of religious ardor, the soldiers of Pizarro looked forward with renovated spirits to the coming conflict; and the chieftain saw with satisfaction, that in the hour of trial his men would be true to their leader and themselves.

It was late in the day before any movement was visible in the Peruvian camp, where much preparation was making to approach the Christian quarters with due state and ceremony. A message was received from Atahuallpa, informing the Spanish commander that he should come with his warriors fully armed, in the same manner as the Spaniards had come to his quarters the night preceding. This was not an agreeable intimation to Pizarro, though he had no reason, probably, to expect the contrary. But to object might imply distrust, or, perhaps, disclose, in some measure, his own designs. He expressed his satisfaction, therefore, at the intelligence, assuring the Inca, that, come as he would, he would be received by him as a friend and brother.[3]

It was noon before the Indian procession was on its march, when it was seen occupying the great causeway for a long extent. In front came a large body of attendants, whose office seemed to be to sweep away every particle of rubbish from the road. High above the crowd appeared the Inca, borne on the shoulders of his principal nobles, while others of the same rank marched by the sides of his litter, displaying such a dazzling show of ornaments on their persons, that, in the language of one of the Conquerors, "they blazed like the sun."[4] But the greater part of the Inca's forces mustered along the fields that lined the road, and were spread over the broad meadows as far as the eye could reach.[5]

When the royal procession had arrived within half a mile of the city, it came to a halt; and Pizarro saw with surprise that Atahuallpa was preparing to pitch his tents, as if to encamp there. A messenger soon after arrived, informing the Spaniards that the Inca would occupy his present station the ensuing night, and enter the city on the following morning.

This intelligence greatly disturbed Pizarro, who had shared in the general impatience of his men at the tardy movements of the Peruvians. The troops had been under arms since daylight, the cavalry mounted, and the infantry at their post, waiting in silence the coming of the Inca. A profound stillness reigned throughout the town, broken only at intervals by the cry of the sentinel from the summit of the fortress, as he proclaimed the movements of the Indian army. Nothing, Pizarro well knew, was so trying to the soldier as prolonged suspense, in a critical situation like the present; and he feared lest his ardor might evaporate, and be succeeded by that nervous feeling natural to the bravest soul at such a crisis, and which, if not fear, is near akin to it.[6] He returned an answer, therefore, to Atahuallpa, deprecating his change of purpose; and adding that he had provided every thing for his entertainment, and expected him that night to sup with him.[7]

This message turned the Inca from his purpose; and, striking his tents again, he resumed his march, first advising the general that he should leave the greater part of his warriors behind, and enter the place with only a few of them, and without arms,[8] as he preferred to pass the night at Caxamalca. At the same time he ordered accommodations to be provided for himself and his retinue in one of the large stone buildings, called, from a serpent sculptured on the walls, "the House of the Serpent."[9] — No tidings could have been more grateful to the Spaniards. It seemed as if the Indian monarch was eager to rush into the snare that had been spread for him! The fanatical cavalier could not fail to discern in it the immediate finger of Providence.

It is difficult to account for this wavering conduct of Atahuallpa, so different from the bold and decided character which history ascribes to him. There is no doubt that he made his visit to the white men in perfect good faith; though Pizarro was probably right in conjecturing that this amiable disposition stood on a very precarious footing. There is as little reason to suppose that he distrusted the sincerity of the strangers; or he would not thus unnecessarily have proposed to visit them unarmed. His original purpose of coming with all his force was doubtless to display his royal state, and perhaps, also, to show greater respect for the Spaniards; but when he consented to accept their hospitality, and pass the night in their quarters, he was willing to dispense with a great part of his armed soldiery, and visit them in a manner that implied entire confidence in their good faith. He was too absolute in his own empire easily to suspect; and he probably could not comprehend the audacity with which a few men, like those now assembled in Caxamalca, meditated an assault on a powerful monarch in the midst of his victorious army. He did not know the character of the Spaniard.

It was not long before sunset, when the van of the royal procession entered the gates of the city. First came some hundreds of the menials, employed to clear the path from every obstacle, and singing songs of triumph as they came, "which, in our ears," says one of the Conquerors, "sounded like the songs of hell"![10] Then followed other bodies of different ranks, and dressed in different liveries. Some wore a showy stuff, checkered white and red, like the squares of a chess-board.[11] Others were clad in pure white, bearing hammers or maces of silver or copper;[12] and the guards, together with those in immediate attendance on the prince, were distinguished by a rich azure livery, and a profusion of gay ornaments, while the large pendants attached to the ears indicated the Peruvian noble.

Elevated high above his vassals came the Inca Atahuallpa, borne on a sedan or open litter, on which was a sort of throne made of massive gold of inestimable value.[13] The palanquin was lined with the richly colored plumes of tropical birds, and studded with shining plates Of gold and silver.[14] The monarch's attire was much richer than on the preceding evening. Round his neck was suspended a collar of emeralds of uncommon size and brilliancy.[15] His short hair was decorated with golden ornaments, and the imperial *borla* encircled his temples. The bearing of the Inca was sedate and dignified; and from his lofty station he looked down on the multitudes below with an air of composure, like one accustomed to command.

As the leading files of the procession entered the great square, larger, says an old chronicler, than any square in Spain, they opened to the right and left for the royal retinue to pass. Every thing was conducted with admirable order. The monarch was permitted to traverse the *plaza* in silence, and not a Spaniard was to be seen. When some five or six thousand of his people had entered the place, Atahuallpa halted, and, turning round with an inquiring look, demanded, "Where are the strangers?"

At this moment Fray Vicente de Valverde, a Dominican friar, Pizarro's chaplain, and afterward Bishop of Cuzco, came forward with his breviary, or, as other accounts say, a Bible, in one hand, and a crucifix in the other, and, approaching the Inca, told him, that he came by order of his commander to expound to him the doctrines of the true faith, for which purpose the Spaniards had come from a great distance to his country. The friar then explained, as clearly as he could, the mysterious doctrine of the Trinity, and, ascending high in his account, began with the creation of man, thence passed to his fall, to his subsequent redemption by Jesus Christ, to the crucifixion, and the ascension, when the Saviour left the Apostle Peter as his Vicegerent upon earth. This power had been transmitted to the successors of the Apostle, good and wise men, who, under the title of Popes, held authority over all powers and potentates on earth. One of the last of these Popes had commissioned the Spanish emperor, the most mighty monarch in the world, to conquer and convert the natives in this western hemisphere; and his general, Francisco Pizarro, had now come to execute this important mission. The friar concluded with beseeching the Peruvian monarch to receive him kindly; to abjure the errors of his own faith, and embrace that of the Christians now proffered to him, the only one by which he could hope for salvation; and, furthermore, to acknowledge himself a tributary of the Emperor Charles the Fifth, who, in that event, would aid and protect him as his loyal vassal.[16]

Whether Atahuallpa possessed himself of every link in the curious chain of argument by which the monk connected Pizarro with St. Peter, may be doubted. It is certain, however, that he must have had very incorrect notions of the Trinity, if, as Garcilasso states, the interpreter Felipillo explained it by saying, that "the Christians believed in three Gods and one God, and that made four."[17] But there is no doubt he perfectly comprehended that the drift of the discourse was to persuade him to resign his sceptre and acknowledge the supremacy of another.

The eyes of the Indian monarch flashed fire, and his dark brow grew darker as he replied, — "I will be no man's tributary. I am greater than any prince upon earth. Your emperor may be a great prince; I do not doubt it, when I see that he has sent his subjects so far across the waters; and I am willing to hold him as a brother. As for the Pope of whom you speak, he must be crazy to talk of giving away countries which do not belong to him. For my faith," he continued, "I will not change it. Your own God, as you say, was put to death by the very men whom he created. But mine," he concluded, pointing to his Deity, — then, alas! sinking in glory behind the mountains, — "my God still lives in the heavens, and looks down on his children."[18]

He then demanded of Valverde by what authority he had said these things. The friar pointed to the book which he held, as his authority. Atahuallpa, taking it, turned over the pages a moment, then, as the insult he had received probably flashed across his mind, he threw it down with vehemence, and exclaimed, — "Tell your comrades that they shall give me an account of their doings in my land. I will not go from here, till they have made me full satisfaction for all the wrongs they have committed."[19]

The friar, greatly scandalized by the indignity offered to the sacred volume, stayed only to pick it up, and, hastening to Pizarro, informed him of what had been done, exclaiming, at the same time, — "Do you not see, that, while we stand here wasting our breath in talking with this dog, full of pride as he is, the fields are filling with Indians? Set on, at once; I absolve you."[20] Pizarro saw that the hour had come. He waved a white scarf in the air, the appointed signal. The fatal gun was fired from the fortress. Then, springing into the square, the Spanish captain and his followers shouted the old war-cry of "St. Jago and at them." It was answered by the battle-cry of every Spaniard in the city, as, rushing from the avenues of the great halls in which they were concealed, they poured into the *plaza,* horse and foot, each in his own dark column, and threw themselves into the midst of the Indian crowd. The latter, taken by surprise, stunned by the report of artillery and muskets, the echoes of which reverberated like thunder from the surrounding buildings, and blinded by the smoke which rolled in sulphurous volumes along the square, were seized with a panic. They knew not whither to fly for refuge from the coming ruin. Nobles and commoners, — all were trampled down under the fierce charge of the cavalry, who dealt their blows, right and left, without sparing; while their swords, flashing through the thick gloom, carried dismay into the hearts of the wretched natives, who now, for the first time, saw the horse and his rider in all their terrors. They made no resistance,—as, indeed, they had no weapons with which to make it. Every avenue to escape was closed, for the entrance to the square was choked up with the dead bodies of men who had perished in vain efforts to fly; and, such was the agony of the survivors under the terrible pressure of their assailants, that a large body of Indians, by their convulsive struggles, burst through the wall of stone and dried clay which formed part of the boundary of the *plaza!* It fell, leaving an opening of more than a hundred paces, through which multitudes now found their way into the country, still hotly pursued by the cavalry, who, leaping the fallen rubbish, hung on the rear of the fugitives, striking them down in all directions.[21]

Meanwhile the fight, or rather massacre, continued hot around the Inca, whose person was the great object of the assault. His faithful nobles, rallying about him, threw themselves in the way of the assailants, and strove, by tearing them from their saddles, or, at least, by offering their own bosoms as a mark for their vengeance, to shield their beloved master. It is said by some authorities, that they carried weapons concealed under their clothes. If so, it availed them little, as it is not pretended that they used them. But the most timid animal will defend itself when at bay. That they did not so in the present instance is proof that they had no weapons to use.[22] Yet they still continued to force back the cavaliers, clinging to their horses with dying grasp, and, as one was cut down, another taking the place of his fallen comrade with a loyalty truly affecting.

The Indian monarch, stunned and bewildered, saw his faithful subjects falling round him without fully comprehending his situation. The litter on which he rode heaved to and fro, as the mighty press swayed backwards and forwards; and he gazed on the overwhelming ruin, like some forlorn mariner, who, tossed about in his bark by the furious elements, sees the lightning's flash and hears the thunder bursting around him with the consciousness that he can do nothing to avert his fate. At length, weary with the work of destruction, the Spaniards, as the shades of evening grew deeper, felt afraid that the royal prize might, after all, elude them; and some of the cavaliers made a desperate attempt to end the affray at once by taking Atahuallpa's life. But Pizarro, who was nearest his person, called out with Stentorian voice, "Let no one, who values his life, strike at the Inca";[23] and, stretching out his arm to shield him, received a wound on the hand from one of his own men,—the only wound received by a Spaniard in the action.[24]

The struggle now became fiercer than ever round the royal litter. It reeled more and more, and at length, several of the nobles who supported it having been slain, it was overturned, and the Indian prince would have come with violence to the ground, had not his fall been broken by the efforts of Pizarro and some other of the cavaliers, who caught him in their arms. The imperial *borla* was instantly snatched from his temples by a soldier named Estete,[25] and the unhappy monarch, strongly secured, was removed to a neighbouring building, where he was carefully guarded.

All attempt at resistance now ceased. The fate of the Inca soon spread over town and country. The charm which might have held the Peruvians together was dissolved. Every man thought only of his own safety. Even the soldiery encamped on the adjacent fields took the alarm, and, learning the fatal tidings, were seen flying in every direction before their pursuers, who in the heat of triumph showed no touch of mercy. At length night, more pitiful than man, threw her friendly mantle over the fugitives, and the scattered troops of Pizarro rallied once more at the sound of the trumpet in the bloody square of Caxamalca.

The number of slain is reported, as usual, with great discrepancy. Pizarro's secretary says two thousand natives fell.[26] A descendant of the Incas—a safer authority than Garcilasso—swells the number to ten thousand.[27] Truth is generally found somewhere between the extremes. The slaughter was incessant, for there was nothing to check it. That there should have been no resistance will not appear strange, when we consider the fact, that the wretched victims were without arms, and that their senses must have been completely overwhelmed by the strange and appalling spectacle which burst on them so unexpectedly. "What wonder was it," said an ancient Inca to a Spaniard, who repeats it, "what wonder that our countrymen lost their wits, seeing blood run like water, and the Inca, whose person we all of us adore, seized and carried off by a handful of men?"[28] Yet though the massacre was incessant, it was short in duration. The whole time consumed by it, the brief twilight of the tropics, did not much exceed half an hour; a short period, indeed,—yet long enough to decide the fate of Peru, and to subvert the dynasty of the Incas.

That night Pizarro kept his engagement with the Inca, since he had Atahuallpa to sup with him. The banquet was served in one of the halls facing the great square, which a few hours before had been the scene of slaughter, and the pavement of which was still encumbered with the dead bodies of the Inca's subjects. The captive monarch was placed next his conqueror. He seemed like one who did not yet fully comprehend the extent of his calamity. If he did, he showed an amazing fortitude. "It is the fortune of war," he said;[29] and, if we may credit the Spaniards, he expressed his admiration of the adroitness with which they had contrived to entrap him in the midst of his own troops.[30] He added, that he had been made acquainted with the progress of the white men from the hour of their landing; but that he had been led to undervalue their strength from the insignificance of their numbers. He had no doubt he should be easily able to overpower them, on their arrival at Caxamalca, by his superior strength; and, as he wished to see for himself what manner of men they were, he had suffered them to cross the mountains, meaning to select such as he chose for his own service, and, getting possession of their wonderful arms and horses, put the rest to death.[31]

That such may have been Atahuallpa's purpose is not improbable. It explains his conduct in not occupying the mountain passes, which afforded such strong points of defence against invasion. But that a prince so astute, as by the general testimony of the Conquerors he is represented to have been, should have made so impolitic a disclosure of his hidden motives is not so probable. The intercourse with the Inca was carried on chiefly by means of the interpreter Felipillo, or *little Philip*, as he was called, from his assumed Christian name,—a malicious youth, as it appears, who bore no good-will to Atahuallpa, and whose interpretations were readily admitted by the Conquerors, eager to find some pretext for their bloody reprisals.

Atahuallpa, as elsewhere noticed, was, at this time, about thirty years of age. He was well made, and more robust than usual with his countrymen. His head was large, and his countenance might have been called handsome, but that his eyes, which were bloodshot, gave a fierce expression to his features. He was deliberate in speech, grave in manner, and towards his own people stern even to severity; though with the Spaniards he showed himself affable, sometimes even indulging in sallies of mirth.[32]

Pizarro paid every attention to his royal captive, and endeavoured to lighten, if he could not dispel, the gloom which, in spite of his assumed equanimity, hung over the monarch's brow. He besought him not to be cast down by his reverses, for his lot had only been that of every prince who had resisted the white men. They had come into the country to proclaim the gospel, the religion of Jesus Christ; and it was no wonder they had prevailed, when his shield was over them. Heaven had permitted that Atahuallpa's pride should be humbled, because of his hostile intentions towards the Spaniards, and the insults he had offered to the sacred volume. But he bade the Inca take courage and confide in him, for the Spaniards were a generous race, warring only against those who made war on them, and showing grace to all who submitted![33]—Atahuallpa may have thought the massacre of that day an indifferent commentary on this vaunted lenity.

Before retiring for the night, Pizarro briefly addressed his troops on their present situation. When he had ascertained that not a man was wounded, he bade them offer up thanksgivings to Providence for so great a miracle; without its care, they could never have prevailed so easily over the host of their enemies; and he trusted their lives had been reserved for still greater things. But if they would succeed, they had much to do for themselves. They were in the heart of a powerful kingdom, encompassed by foes deeply attached to their own sovereign. They must be ever on their guard, therefore, and be prepared at any hour to be roused from their slumbers by the call of the trumpet.[34]— Having then posted his sentinels, placed a strong guard over the apartment of Atahuallpa, and taken all the precautions of a careful commander, Pizarro withdrew to repose; and, if he could really feel, that, in the bloody scenes of the past day, he had been fighting only the good fight of the Cross, he doubtless slept sounder than on the night preceding the seizure of the Inca.

On the following morning, the first commands of the Spanish chief were to have the city cleansed of its impurities; and the prisoners, of whom there were many in the camp, were employed to remove the dead, and give them decent burial. His next care was to despatch a body of about thirty horse to the quarters lately occupied by Atahuallpa at the baths, to take possession of the spoil, and disperse the remnant of the Peruvian forces which still hung about the place.

Before noon, the party which he had detached on this service returned with a large troop of Indians, men and women, among the latter of whom were many of the wives and attendants of the Inca. The Spaniards had met with no resistance; since the Peruvian warriors, though so superior in number, excellent in appointments, and consisting mostly of able-bodied young men, —for the greater part of the veteran forces were with the Inca's generals at the south,—lost all heart from the moment of their sovereign's captivity. There was no leader to take his place; for they recognized no authority but that of the Child of the Sun, and they seemed to be held by a sort of invisible charm near the place of his confinement; while they gazed with superstitious awe on the white men, who could achieve so audacious an enterprise.[35]

The number of Indian prisoners was so great, that some of the Conquerors were for putting them all to death, or, at least, cutting off their hands, to disable them from acts of violence, and to strike terror into their countrymen.[36] The proposition, doubtless, came from the lowest and most ferocious of the soldiery. But that it should have been made at all shows what materials entered into the composition of Pizarro's company. The chief rejected it at once, as no less impolitic than inhuman, and dismissed the Indians to their several homes, with the assurance that none should be harmed who did not offer resistance to the white men. A sufficient number, however, were retained to wait on the Conquerors, who were so well provided, in this respect, that the most common soldier was attended by a retinue of menials that would have better suited the establishment of a noble.[37]

The Spaniards had found immense droves of llamas under the care of their shepherds in the neighbourhood of the baths, destined for the consumption of the Court. Many of them were now suffered to roam abroad among their native mountains; though Pizarro caused a considerable number to be reserved for the use of the army. And this was no small quantity, if, as one of the Conquerors says, a hundred and fifty of the Peruvian sheep were frequently slaughtered in a day.[38] Indeed, the Spaniards were so improvident in their destruction of these animals, that, in a few years, the superb flocks, nurtured with so much care by the Peruvian government, had almost disappeared from the land.[39]

The party sent to pillage the Inca's pleasure-house brought back a rich booty in gold and silver, consisting chiefly of plate for the royal table, which greatly astonished the Spaniards by their size and weight. These, as well as some large emeralds obtained there, together with the precious spoils found on the bodies of the Indian nobles who had perished in the massacre, were placed in safe custody, to be hereafter divided. In the city of Caxamalca, the troops also found magazines stored with goods, both cotton and woollen, far superior to any they had seen, for fineness of texture, and the skill with which the various colors were blended. They were piled from the floors to the very roofs of the buildings, and in such quantity, that, after every soldier had provided himself with what he desired, it made no sensible diminution of the whole amount.[40]

Pizarro would now gladly have directed his march on the Peruvian capital. But the distance was great, and his force was small. This must have been still further crippled by the guard required for the Inca, and the chief feared to involve himself deeper in a hostile empire so populous and powerful, with a prize so precious in his keeping. With much anxiety, therefore, he looked for reinforcements from the colonies; and he despatched a courier to San Miguel, to inform the Spaniards there of his recent successes, and to ascertain if there had been any arrival from Panamá. Meanwhile he employed his men in making Caxamalca a more suitable residence for a Christian host, by erecting a church, or, perhaps, appropriating some Indian edifice to this use, in which mass was regularly performed by the Dominican fathers, with great solemnity. The dilapidated walls of the city were also restored in a more substantial manner than before, and every vestige was soon effaced of the hurricane that had so recently swept over it.

It was not long before Atahuallpa discovered, amidst all the show of religious zeal in his Conquerors, a lurking appetite more potent in most of their bosoms than either religion or ambition. This was the love of gold. He determined to avail himself of it to procure his own freedom. The critical posture of his affairs made it important that this should not be long delayed. His brother Huascar, ever since his defeat, had been detained as a prisoner, subject to the victor's orders. He was now at Andamarca, at no great distance from Caxamalca; and Atahuallpa feared, with good reason, that, when his own imprisonment was known, Huascar would find it easy to corrupt his guards, make his escape, and put himself at the head of the contested empire, without a rival to dispute it.

In the hope, therefore, to effect his purpose by appealing to the avarice of his keepers, he one day told Pizarro, that, if he would set him free, he would engage to cover the floor of the apartment on which they stood with gold. Those present listened with an incredulous smile; and, as the Inca received no answer, he said, with some emphasis, that "he would not merely cover the floor, but would fill the room with gold as high as he could reach"; and, standing on tiptoe, he stretched out his hand against the wall. All stared with amazement; while they regarded it as the insane boast of a man too eager to procure his liberty to weigh the meaning of his words. Yet Pizarro was sorely perplexed. As he had advanced into the country, much that he had seen, and all that he had heard, had confirmed the dazzling reports first received of the riches of Peru. Atahuallpa himself had given him the most glowing picture of the wealth of the capital, where the roofs of the temples were plated with gold, while the walls were hung with tapestry and the floors inlaid with tiles of the same precious metal. There must be some foundation for all this. At all events, it was safe to accede to the Inca's proposition; since, by so doing, he could collect, at once, all the gold at his disposal, and thus prevent its being purloined or secreted by the natives. He therefore acquiesced in Atahuallpa's offer, and, drawing a red line along the wall at the height which the Inca had indicated, he caused the terms of the proposal to be duly recorded by the notary. The apartment was about seventeen feet broad, by twenty-two feet long, and the line round the walls was nine feet from the floor.[41] This space was to be filled with gold; but it was understood that the gold was not to be melted down into ingots, but to retain the original form of the articles into which it was manufactured, that the Inca might have the benefit of the space which they occupied. He further agreed to fill an adjoining room of smaller dimensions twice full with silver, in like manner; and he demanded two months to accomplish all this.[42]

No sooner was this arrangement made, than the Inca despatched couriers to Cuzco and the other principal places in the kingdom, with orders that the gold ornaments and utensils should be removed from the royal palaces, and from the temples and other public buildings, and transported without loss of time to Caxamalca. Meanwhile he continued to live in the Spanish quarters, treated with the respect due to his rank, and enjoying all the freedom that was compatible with the security of his person. Though not permitted to go abroad, his limbs were unshackled, and he had the range of his own apartments under the jealous *surveillance* of a guard, who knew too well the value of the royal captive to be remiss. He was allowed the society of his favorite wives, and Pizarro took care that his domestic privacy should not be violated. His subjects had free access to their sovereign, and every day he received visits from the Indian nobles, who came to bring presents, and offer condolence to their unfortunate master. On such occasions, the most potent of these great vassals never ventured into his presence, without first stripping off their sandals, and bearing a load on their backs in token of reverence. The Spaniards gazed with curious eyes on these acts of homage, or rather of slavish submission, on the one side, and on the air of perfect indifference with which they were received, as a matter of course, on the other; and they conceived high ideas of the character of a prince who, even in his present helpless condition, could inspire such feelings of awe in his subjects. The royal levee was so well attended, and such devotion was shown by his vassals to the captive monarch, as did not fail, in the end, to excite some feelings of distrust in his keepers.[43]

Pizarro did not neglect the opportunity afforded him of communicating the truths of revelation to his prisoner, and both he and his chaplain, Father Valverde, labored in the same good work. Atahuallpa listened with composure and apparent attention. But nothing seemed to move him so much as the argument with which the military polemic closed his discourse,—that it could not be the true God whom Atahuallpa worshipped, since he had suffered him to fall into the hands of his enemies. The unhappy monarch assented to the force of this, acknowledging that his Deity had indeed deserted him in his utmost need.[44]

Yet his conduct towards his brother Huascar, at this time, too clearly proves, that, whatever respect he may have shown for the teachers, the doctrines of Christianity had made little impression on his heart. No sooner had Huascar been informed of the capture of his rival, and of the large ransom he had offered for his deliverance, than, as the latter had foreseen, he made every effort to regain his liberty, and sent, or attempted to send, a message to the Spanish commander, that he would pay a much larger ransom than that promised by Atahuallpa, who, never having dwelt in Cuzco, was ignorant of the quantity of treasure there, and where it was deposited.

Intelligence of all this was secretly communicated to Atahuallpa by the persons who had his brother in charge; and his jealousy, thus roused, was further heightened by Pizarro's declaration, that he intended to have Huascar brought to Caxamalca, where he would himself examine into the controversy, and determine which of the two had best title to the sceptre of the Incas. Pizarro perceived, from the first, the advantages of a competition which would enable him, by throwing his sword into the scale he preferred, to give it a preponderance. The party who held the sceptre by his nomination would henceforth be a tool in his hands, with which to work his pleasure more effectually than he could well do in his own name. It was the game, as every reader knows, played by Edward the First in the affairs of Scotland, and by many a monarch, both before and since,—and though their examples may not have been familiar to the unlettered soldier, Pizarro was too quick in his perceptions to require, in this matter, at least, the teachings of history.

Atahuallpa was much alarmed by the Spanish commander's determination to have the suit between the rival candidates brought before him; for he feared, that, independently of the merits of the case, the decision would be likely to go in favor of Huascar, whose mild and ductile temper would make him a convenient instrument in the hands of his conquerors. Without further hesitation, he determined to remove this cause of jealousy for ever, by the death of his brother.

His orders were immediately executed, and the unhappy prince was drowned, as was commonly reported, in the river of Andamarca, declaring with his dying breath that the white men would avenge his murder, and that his rival would not long survive him.[45]—Thus perished the unfortunate Huascar, the legitimate heir of the throne of the Incas, in the very morning of life, and the commencement of his reign; a reign, however, which had been long enough to call forth the display of many excellent and amiable qualities, though his nature was too gentle to cope with the bold and fiercer temper of his brother. Such is the portrait we have of him from the Indian and Castilian chroniclers, though the former, it should be added, were the kinsmen of Huascar, and the latter certainly bore no goodwill to Atahuallpa.[46]

That prince received the tidings of Huascar's death with every mark of surprise and indignation. He immediately sent for Pizarro, and communicated the event to him with expressions of the deepest sorrow. The Spanish commander refused, at first, to credit the unwelcome news, and bluntly told the Inca, that his brother could not be dead, and that he should be answerable for his life.[47] To this Atahuallpa replied by renewed assurances of the fact, adding that the deed had been perpetrated, without his privity, by Huascar's keepers, fearful that he might take advantage of the troubles of the country to make his escape. Pizarro, on making further inquiries, found that the report of his death was but too true. That it should have been brought about by Atahuallpa's officers, without his express command, would only show, that, by so doing, they had probably anticipated their master's wishes. The crime, which assumes in our eyes a deeper dye from the relation of the parties, had not the same estimation among the Incas, in whose multitudinous families the bonds of brotherhood must have sat loosely, — much too loosely to restrain the arm of the despot from sweeping away any obstacle that lay in his path.

CHAPTER VI

GOLD ARRIVES FOR THE RANSOM. — VISIT TO
PACHACAMAC. — DEMOLITION OF THE IDOL. —
THE INCA'S FAVORITE GENERAL. — THE INCA'S
LIFE IN CONFINEMENT. — ENVOYS' CONDUCT
IN CUZCO. — ARRIVAL OF ALMAGRO

1533.

SEVERAL weeks had now passed since Atahuallpa's emissaries had been
despatched for the gold and silver that were to furnish his ransom to the
Spaniards. But the distances were great, and the returns came in slowly.
They consisted, for the most part, of massive pieces of plate, some of which
weighed two or three *arrobas*, — a Spanish weight of twenty-five pounds. On
some days, articles of the value of thirty or forty thousand *pesos de oro* were
brought in, and, occasionally, of the value of fifty or even sixty thousand
pesos. The greedy eyes of the Conquerors gloated on the shining heaps of
treasure, which were transported on the shoulders of the Indian porters,
and, after being carefully registered, were placed in safe deposit under a
strong guard. They now began to believe that the magnificent promises of
the Inca would be fulfilled. But, as their avarice was sharpened by the rav-
ishing display of wealth, such as they had hardly dared to imagine, they
became more craving and impatient. They made no allowance for the distance and the difficulties of the way, and loudly inveighed against the tardiness with which the royal commands were executed. They even suspected
Atahuallpa of devising this scheme only to gain a pretext for communicating
with his subjects in distant places, and of proceeding as dilatorily as possible,
in order to secure time for the execution of his plans. Rumors of a rising
among the Peruvians were circulated, and the Spaniards were in apprehension of some general and sudden assault on their quarters. Their new acquisitions gave them additional cause for solicitude; like a miser, they trembled
in the midst of their treasures.[1]

Pizarro reported to his captive the rumors that were in circulation among the soldiers, naming, as one of the places pointed out for the rendezvous of the Indians, the neighbouring city of Guamachucho. Atahuallpa listened with undisguised astonishment, and indignantly repelled the charge, as false from beginning to end. "No one of my subjects," said he, "would dare to appear in arms, or to raise his finger, without my orders. You have me," he continued, "in your power. Is not my life at your disposal? And what better security can you have for my fidelity?" He then represented to the Spanish commander, that the distances of many of the places were very great; that to Cuzco, the capital, although a message might be sent by post, through a succession of couriers, in five days from Caxamalca, it would require weeks for a porter to travel over the same ground, with a heavy load on his back. "But that you may be satisfied I am proceeding in good faith," he added, "I desire you will send some of your own people to Cuzco. I will give them a safe-conduct, and, when there, they can superintend the execution of the commission, and see with their own eyes that no hostile movements are intended." It was a fair offer, and Pizarro, anxious to get more precise and authentic information of the state of the country, gladly availed himself of it.[2]

Before the departure of these emissaries, the general had despatched his brother Hernando with about twenty horse and a small body of infantry to the neighbouring town of Guamachucho, in order to reconnoitre the country, and ascertain if there was any truth in the report of an armed force having assembled there. Hernando found every thing quiet, and met with a kind reception from the natives. But before leaving the place, he received further orders from his brother to continue his march to Pachacamac, a town situated on the coast, at least a hundred leagues distant from Caxamalca. It was consecrated as the seat of the great temple of the deity of that name, whom the Peruvians worshipped as the Creator of the world. It is said that they found there altars raised to this god, on their first occupation of the country; and, such was the veneration in which he was held by the natives, that the Incas, instead of attempting to abolish his worship, deemed it more prudent to sanction it conjointly with that of their own deity, the Sun. Side by side, the two temples rose on the heights that overlooked the city of Pachacamac, and prospered in the offerings of their respective votaries. "It was a cunning arrangement," says an ancient writer, "by which the great enemy of man secured to himself a double harvest of souls."[3]

But the temple of Pachacamac continued to maintain its ascendency; and the oracles, delivered from its dark and mysterious shrine, were held in no less repute among the natives of *Tavantinsuyu*, (or "the four quarters of the world," as Peru under the Incas was called,) than the oracles of Delphi obtained among the Greeks. Pilgrimages were made to the hallowed spot from the most distant regions, and the city of Pachacamac became among the Peruvians what Mecca was among the Mahometans, or Cholula with the people of Anahuac. The shrine of the deity, enriched by the tributes of the pilgrims, gradually became one of the most opulent in the land; and Atahuallpa, anxious to collect his ransom as speedily as possible, urged Pizarro to send a detachment in that direction, to secure the treasures before they could be secreted by the priests of the temple.

It was a journey of considerable difficulty. Two thirds of the route lay along the table-land of the Cordilleras, intersected occasionally by crests of the mountain range, that imposed no slight impediment to their progress. Fortunately, much of the way, they had the benefit of the great road to Cuzco, and "nothing in Christendom," exclaims Hernando Pizarro, "equals the magnificence of this road across the sierra."[4] In some places, the rocky ridges were so precipitous, that steps were cut in them for the travellers; and though the sides were protected by heavy stone balustrades or parapets, it was with the greatest difficulty that the horses were enabled to scale them. The road was frequently crossed by streams, over which bridges of wood and sometimes of stone were thrown; though occasionally, along the declivities of the mountains, the waters swept down in such furious torrents, that the only method of passing them was by the swinging bridges of osier, of which, till now, the Spaniards had had little experience. They were secured on either bank to heavy buttresses of stone. But as they were originally designed for nothing heavier than the foot-passenger and the llama, and, as they had something exceedingly fragile in their appearance, the Spaniards hesitated to venture on them with their horses. Experience, however, soon showed they were capable of bearing a much greater weight; and though the traveller, made giddy by the vibration of the long avenue, looked with a reeling brain into the torrent that was tumbling at the depth of a hundred feet or more below him, the whole of the cavalry effected their passage without an accident. At these bridges, it may be remarked, they found persons stationed whose business it was to collect toll for the government from all travellers.[5]

The Spaniards were amazed by the number as well as magnitude of the flocks of llamas which they saw browsing on the stunted herbage that grows in the elevated regions of the Andes. Sometimes they were gathered in inclosures, but more usually were roaming at large under the conduct of their Indian shepherds; and the Conquerors now learned, for the first time, that these animals were tended with as much care, and their migrations as nicely regulated, as those of the vast flocks of merinos in their own country.[6]

The table-land and its declivities were thickly sprinkled with hamlets and towns, some of them of considerable size; and the country in every direction bore the marks of a thrifty husbandry. Fields of Indian corn were to be seen in all its different stages, from the green and tender ear to the yellow ripeness of harvest time. As they descended into the valleys and deep ravines that divided the crests of the Cordilleras, they were surrounded by the vegetation of a warmer climate, which delighted the eye with the gay livery of a thousand bright colors, and intoxicated the senses with its perfumes. Everywhere the natural capacities of the soil were stimulated by a minute system of irrigation, which drew the fertilizing moisture from every stream and rivulet that rolled down the declivities of the Andes; while the terraced sides of the mountains were clothed with gardens and orchards that teemed with fruits of various latitudes. The Spaniards could not sufficiently admire the industry with which the natives had availed themselves of the bounty of Nature, or had supplied the deficiency where she had dealt with a more parsimonious hand.

Whether from the commands of the Inca, or from the awe which their achievements had spread throughout the land, the Conquerors were received, in every place through which they passed, with hospitable kindness. Lodgings were provided for them, with ample refreshments from the well-stored magazines, distributed at intervals along the route. In many of the towns the inhabitants came out to welcome them with singing and dancing; and, when they resumed their march, a number of able-bodied porters were furnished to carry forward their baggage.[7]

At length, after some weeks of travel, severe even with all these appliances, Hernando Pizarro arrived before the city of Pachacamac. It was a place of considerable population, and the edifices were, many of them, substantially built. The temple of the tutelar deity consisted of a vast stone building, or rather pile of buildings, which, clustering around a conical hill, had the air of a fortress rather than a religious establishment. But, though the walls were of stone, the roof was composed of a light thatch, as usual in countries where rain seldom or never falls, and where defence, consequently, is wanted chiefly against the rays of the sun.

Presenting himself at the lower entrance of the temple, Hernando Pizarro was refused admittance by the guardians of the portal. But, exclaiming that "he had come too far to be stayed by the arm of an Indian priest," he forced his way into the passage, and, followed by his men, wound up the gallery which led to an area on the summit of the mount, at one end of which stood a sort of chapel. This was the sanctuary of the dread deity. The door was garnished with ornaments of crystal, and with turquoises and bits of coral.[8] Here again the Indians would have dissuaded Pizarro from violating the consecrated precincts, when, at that moment, the shock of an earthquake, that made the ancient walls tremble to their foundation, so alarmed the natives, both those of Pizarro's own company and the people of the place, that they fled in dismay, nothing doubting that their incensed deity would bury the invaders under the ruins, or consume them with his lightnings. But no such terror found its way into the breast of the Conquerors, who felt that here, at least, they were fighting the good fight of the Faith.

Tearing open the door, Pizarro and his party entered. But instead of a hall blazing, as they had fondly imagined, with gold and precious stones, offerings of the worshippers of Pachacamac, they found themselves in a small and obscure apartment, or rather den, from the floor and sides of which steamed up the most offensive odors,—like those of a slaughter-house. It was the place of sacrifice. A few pieces of gold and some emeralds were discovered on the ground, and, as their eyes became accommodated to the darkness, they discerned in the most retired corner of the room the figure of the deity. It was an uncouth monster, made of wood, with the head resembling that of a man. This was the god, through whose lips Satan had breathed forth the far-famed oracles which had deluded his Indian votaries![9]

Tearing the idol from its recess, the indignant Spaniards dragged it into the open air, and there broke it into a hundred fragments. The place was then purified, and a large cross, made of stone and plaster, was erected on the spot. In a few years the walls of the temple were pulled down by the Spanish settlers, who found there a convenient quarry for their own edifices. But the cross still remained spreading its broad arms over the ruins. It stood where it was planted in the very heart of the stronghold of Heathendom; and, while all was in ruins around it, it proclaimed the permanent triumphs of the Faith.

The simple natives, finding that Heaven had no bolts in store for the Conquerors, and that their god had no power to prevent the profanation of his shrine, came in gradually and tendered their homage to the strangers, whom they now regarded with feelings of superstitious awe. Pizarro profited by this temper to wean them, if possible, from their idolatry; and though no preacher himself, as he tells us, he delivered a discourse as edifying, doubtless, as could be expected from the mouth of a soldier;[10] and, in conclusion, he taught them the sign of the cross, as an inestimable talisman to secure them against the future machinations of the Devil.[11]

But the Spanish commander was not so absorbed in his spiritual labors as not to have an eye to those temporal concerns for which he came into this quarter. He now found, to his chagrin, that he had come somewhat too late; and that the priests of Pachacamac, being advised of his mission, had secured much the greater part of the gold, and decamped with it before his arrival. A quantity was afterwards discovered buried in the grounds adjoining.[12] Still the amount obtained was considerable, falling little short of eighty thousand castellanos, a sum which once would have been deemed a compensation for greater fatigues than they had encountered. But the Spaniards had become familiar with gold; and their imaginations, kindled by the romantic adventures in which they had of late been engaged, indulged in visions which all the gold of Peru would scarcely have realized.

One prize, however, Hernando obtained by his expedition, which went far to console him for the loss of his treasure. While at Pachacamac, he learned that the Indian commander Challcuchima lay with a large force in the neighbourhood of Xauxa, a town of some strength at a considerable distance among the mountains. This man, who was nearly related to Atahuallpa, was his most experienced general, and together with Quizquiz, now at Cuzco, had achieved those victories at the south which placed the Inca on the throne. From his birth, his talents, and his large experience, he was accounted second to no subject in the kingdom. Pizarro was aware of the importance of securing his person. Finding that the Indian noble declined to meet him on his return, he determined to march at once on Xauxa and take the chief in his own quarters. Such a scheme, considering the enormous disparity of numbers, might seem desperate even for Spaniards. But success had given them such confidence, that they hardly condescended to calculate chances.

The road across the mountains presented greater difficulties than those on the former march. To add to the troubles of the cavalry, the shoes of their horses were used up, and their hoofs suffered severely on the rough and stony ground. There was no iron at hand, nothing but gold and silver. In the present emergency they turned even these to account; and Pizarro caused the horses of the whole troop to be shod with silver. The work was done by the Indian smiths, and it answered so well, that in this precious material they found a substitute for iron during the remainder of the march.[13]

Xauxa was a large and populous place; though we shall hardly credit the assertion of the Conquerors, that a hundred thousand persons assembled habitually in the great square of the city.[14] The Peruvian commander was encamped, it was said, with an army of five-and-thirty thousand men at only a few miles' distance from the town. With some difficulty he was persuaded to an interview with Pizarro. The latter addressed him courteously, and urged his return with him to the Castilian quarters in Caxamalca, representing it as the command of the Inca. Ever since the capture of his master, Challcuchima had remained uncertain what course to take. The capture of the Inca in this sudden and mysterious manner by a race of beings who seemed to have dropped from the clouds, and that too in the very hour of his triumph, had entirely bewildered the Peruvian chief. He had concerted no plan for the rescue of Atahuallpa, nor, indeed, did he know whether any such movement would be acceptable to him. He now acquiesced in his commands, and was willing, at all events, to have a personal interview with his sovereign. Pizarro gained his end without being obliged to strike a single blow to effect it. The barbarian, when brought into contact with the white man, would seem to have been rebuked by his superior genius, in the same manner as the wild animal of the forest is said to quail before the steady glance of the hunter.

Challcuchima came attended by a numerous retinue. He was borne in his sedan on the shoulders of his vassals; and, as he accompanied the Spaniards on their return through the country, received everywhere from the inhabitants the homage paid only to the favorite of a monarch. Yet all this pomp vanished on his entering the presence of the Inca, whom he approached with his feet bare, while a light burden, which he had taken from one of the attendants, was laid on his back. As he drew near, the old warrior, raising his hands to heaven, exclaimed, — "Would that I had been here! — this would not then have happened"; then, kneeling down, he kissed the hands and feet of his royal master, and bathed them with his tears. Atahuallpa, on his part, betrayed not the least emotion, and showed no other sign of satisfaction at the presence of his favorite counsellor, than by simply bidding him welcome. The cold demeanour of the monarch contrasted strangely with the loyal sensibility of the subject.[15]

The rank of the Inca placed him at an immeasurable distance above the proudest of his vassals; and the Spaniards had repeated occasion to admire the ascendency which, even in his present fallen fortunes, he maintained over his people, and the awe with which they approached him. Pedro Pizarro records an interview, at which he was present, between Atahuallpa and one of his great nobles, who had obtained leave to visit some remote part of the country on condition of returning by a certain day. He was detained somewhat beyond the appointed time, and, on entering the presence with a small propitiatory gift for his sovereign, his knees shook so violently, that it seemed, says the chronicler, as if he would have fallen to the ground. His master, however, received him kindly, and dismissed him without a word of rebuke.[16]

Atahuallpa in his confinement continued to receive the same respectful treatment from the Spaniards as hitherto. They taught him to play with dice, and the more intricate game of chess, in which the royal captive became expert, and loved to beguile with it the tedious hours of his imprisonment. Towards his own people he maintained as far as possible his wonted state and ceremonial. He was attended by his wives and the girls of his harem, who, as was customary, waited on him at table and discharged the other menial offices about his person. A body of Indian nobles were stationed in the antechamber, but never entered the presence unbidden; and when they did enter it, they submitted to the same humiliating ceremonies imposed on the greatest of his subjects. The service of his table was gold and silver plate. His dress, which he often changed, was composed of the wool of the vicuña wrought into mantles, so fine that it had the appearance of silk. He sometimes exchanged these for a robe made of the skins of bats, as soft and sleek as velvet. Round his head he wore the *llautu*, a woollen turban or shawl of the most delicate texture, wreathed in folds of various bright colors; and he still continued to encircle his temples with the *borla,* the crimson threads of which, mingled with gold, descended so as partly to conceal his eyes. The image of royalty had charms for him, when its substance had departed. No garment or utensil that had once belonged to the Peruvian sovereign could ever be used by another. When he laid it aside, it was carefully deposited in a chest, kept for the purpose, and afterwards burned. It would have been sacrilege to apply to vulgar uses that which had been consecrated by the touch of the Inca.[17]

Not long after the arrival of the party from Pachacamac, in the latter part of May, the three emissaries returned from Cuzco. They had been very successful in their mission. Owing to the Inca's order, and the awe which the white men now inspired throughout the country, the Spaniards had everywhere met with a kind reception. They had been carried on the shoulders of the natives in the *hamacas,* or sedans, of the country; and, as they had travelled all the way to the capital on the great imperial road, along which relays of Indian carriers were established at stated intervals, they performed this journey of more than six hundred miles, not only without inconvenience, but with the most luxurious ease. They passed through many populous towns, and always found the simple natives disposed to venerate them as beings of a superior nature. In Cuzco they were received with public festivities, were sumptuously lodged, and had every want anticipated by the obsequious devotion of the inhabitants.

Their accounts of the capital confirmed all that Pizarro had before heard of the wealth and population of the city. Though they had remained more than a week in this place, the emissaries had not seen the whole of it. The great temple of the Sun they found literally covered with plates of gold. They had entered the interior and beheld the royal mummies, seated each in his gold-embossed chair, and in robes profusely covered with ornaments. The Spaniards had the grace to respect these, as they had been previously enjoined by the Inca; but they required that the plates which garnished the walls should be all removed. The Peruvians most reluctantly acquiesced in the commands of their sovereign to desecrate the national temple, which every inhabitant of the city regarded with peculiar pride and veneration. With less reluctance they assisted the Conquerors in stripping the ornaments from some of the other edifices, where the gold, however, being mixed with a large proportion of alloy, was of much less value.[18]

The number of plates they tore from the temple of the Sun was seven hundred; and though of no great thickness, probably, they are compared in size to the lid of a chest, ten or twelve inches wide.[19] A cornice of pure gold encircled the edifice, but so strongly set in the stone, that it fortunately defied the efforts of the spoilers. The Spaniards complained of the want of alacrity shown by the Indians in the work of destruction, and said that there were other parts of the city containing buildings rich in gold and silver which they had not been allowed to see. In truth, their mission, which, at best, was a most ungrateful one, had been rendered doubly annoying by the manner in which they had executed it. The emissaries were men of a very low stamp, and, puffed up by the honors conceded to them by the natives, they looked on themselves as entitled to these, and contemned the poor Indians as a race immeasurably beneath the European. They not only showed the most disgusting rapacity, but treated the highest nobles with wanton insolence. They even went so far, it is said, as to violate the privacy of the convents, and to outrage the religious sentiments of the Peruvians by their scandalous amours with the Virgins of the Sun. The people of Cuzco were so exasperated, that they would have laid violent hands on them, but for their habitual reverence for the Inca, in whose name the Spaniards had come there. As it was, the Indians collected as much gold as was necessary to satisfy their unworthy visitors, and got rid of them as speedily as possible.[20] It was a great mistake in Pizarro to send such men. There were persons, even in his company, who, as other occasions showed, had some sense of self-respect, if not respect for the natives.

The messengers brought with them, besides silver, full two hundred *cargas* or loads of gold.[21] This was an important accession to the contributions of Atahuallpa; and, although the treasure was still considerably below the mark prescribed, the monarch saw with satisfaction the time drawing nearer for the completion of his ransom.

Not long before this, an event had occurred which changed the condition of the Spaniards, and had an unfavorable influence on the fortunes of the Inca. This was the arrival of Almagro at Caxamalca, with a strong reinforcement. That chief had succeeded, after great efforts, in equipping three vessels, and assembling a body of one hundred and fifty men, with which he sailed from Panamá, the latter part of the preceding year. On his voyage, he was joined by a small additional force from Nicaragua, so that his whole strength amounted to one hundred and fifty foot and fifty horse, well provided with the munitions of war. His vessels were steered by the old pilot Ruiz; but after making the Bay of St. Matthew, he crept slowly along the coast, baffled as usual by winds and currents, and experiencing all the hardships incident to that protracted navigation. From some cause or other, he was not so fortunate as to obtain tidings of Pizarro; and so disheartened were his followers, most of whom were raw adventurers, that, when arrived at Puerto Viejo, they proposed to abandon the expedition, and return at once to Panamá. Fortunately, one of the little squadron which Almagro had sent forward to Tumbez brought intelligence of Pizarro and of the colony he had planted at San Miguel. Cheered by the tidings, the cavalier resumed his voyage, and succeeded, at length, towards the close of December, 1532, in bringing his whole party safe to the Spanish settlement.

He there received the account of Pizarro's march across the mountains, his seizure of the Inca, and, soon afterwards, of the enormous ransom offered for his liberation. Almagro and his companions listened with undisguised amazement to this account of his associate, and of a change in his fortunes so rapid and wonderful that it seemed little less than magic. At the same time, he received a caution from some of the colonists not to trust himself in the power of Pizarro, who was known to bear him no goodwill.

Not long after Almagro's arrival at San Miguel, advices were sent of it to Caxamalca, and a private note from his secretary Perez informed Pizarro that his associate had come with no purpose of coöperating with him, but with the intention to establish an independent government. Both of the Spanish captains seem to have been surrounded by mean and turbulent spirits, who sought to embroil them with each other, trusting, doubtless, to find their own account in the rupture. For once, however, their malicious machinations failed.

Pizarro was overjoyed at the arrival of so considerable a reinforcement, which would enable him to push his fortunes as he had desired, and go forward with the conquest of the country. He laid little stress on the secretary's communication, since, whatever might have been Almagro's original purpose, Pizarro knew that the richness of the vein he had now opened in the land would be certain to secure his coöperation in working it. He had the magnanimity, therefore, — for there is something magnanimous in being able to stifle the suggestions of a petty rivalry in obedience to sound policy, — to send at once to his ancient comrade, and invite him, with many assurances of friendship, to Caxamalca. Almagro, who was of a frank and careless nature, received the communication in the spirit in which it was made, and, after some necessary delay, directed his march into the interior. But before leaving San Miguel, having become acquainted with the treacherous conduct of his secretary, he recompensed his treason by hanging him on the spot.[22]

Almagro reached Caxamalca about the middle of February, 1533. The soldiers of Pizarro came out to welcome their countrymen, and the two captains embraced each other with every mark of cordial satisfaction. All past differences were buried in oblivion, and they seemed only prepared to aid one another in following up the brilliant career now opened to them in the conquest of an empire.

There was one person in Caxamalca on whom this arrival of the Spaniards produced a very different impression from that made on their own countrymen. This was the Inca Atahuallpa. He saw in the new-comers only a new swarm of locusts to devour his unhappy country; and he felt, that, with his enemies thus multiplying around him, the chances were diminished of recovering his freedom, or of maintaining it, if recovered. A little circumstance, insignificant in itself, but magnified by superstition into something formidable, occurred at this time to cast an additional gloom over his situation.

A remarkable appearance, somewhat of the nature of a meteor, or it may have been a comet, was seen in the heavens by some soldiers and pointed out to Atahuallpa. He gazed on it with fixed attention for some minutes, and then exclaimed, with a dejected air, that "a similar sign had been seen in the skies a short time before the death of his father Huayna Capac."[23] From this day a sadness seemed to take possession of him, as he looked with doubt and undefined dread to the future. — Thus it is, that, in seasons of danger, the mind, like the senses, becomes morbidly acute in its perceptions; and the least departure from the regular course of nature, that would have passed unheeded in ordinary times, to the superstitious eye seems pregnant with meaning, as in some way or other connected with the destiny of the individual.

CHAPTER VII

IMMENSE AMOUNT OF TREASURE. — ITS
DIVISION AMONG THE TROOPS. — RUMORS
OF A RISING. — TRIAL OF THE INCA. —
HIS EXECUTION. — REFLECTIONS

1533.

THE arrival of Almagro produced a considerable change in Pizarro's prospects, since it enabled him to resume active operations, and push forward his conquests in the interior. The only obstacle in his way was the Inca's ransom, and the Spaniards had patiently waited, till the return of the emissaries from Cuzco swelled the treasure to a large amount, though still below the stipulated limit. But now their avarice got the better of their forbearance, and they called loudly for the immediate division of the gold. To wait longer would only be to invite the assault of their enemies, allured by a bait so attractive. While the treasure remained uncounted, no man knew its value, nor what was to be his own portion. It was better to distribute it at once, and let every one possess and defend his own. Several, moreover, were now disposed to return home, and take their share of the gold with them, where they could place it in safety. But these were few, while much the larger part were only anxious to leave their present quarters, and march at once to Cuzco. More gold, they thought, awaited them in that capital, than they could get here by prolonging their stay; while every hour was precious, to prevent the inhabitants from secreting their treasures, of which design they had already given indication.

Pizarro was especially moved by the last consideration; and he felt, that, without the capital, he could not hope to become master of the empire. Without further delay, the division of the treasure was agreed upon.

Yet, before making this, it was necessary to reduce the whole to ingots of a uniform standard, for the spoil was composed of an infinite variety of articles, in which the gold was of very different degrees of purity. These articles consisted of goblets, ewers, salvers, vases of every shape and size, ornaments and utensils for the temples and the royal palaces, tiles and plates for the decora-

188

tion of the public edifices, curious imitations of different plants and animals. Among the plants, the most beautiful was the Indian corn, in which the golden ear was sheathed in its broad leaves of silver, from which hung a rich tassel of threads of the same precious metal. A fountain was also much admired, which sent up a sparkling jet of gold, while birds and animals of the same material played in the waters at its base. The delicacy of the workman-ship of some of these, and the beauty and ingenuity of the design, attracted the admiration of better judges than the rude Conquerors of Peru.[1]

Before breaking up these specimens of Indian art, it was determined to send a quantity, which should be deducted from the royal fifth, to the Emperor. It would serve as a sample of the ingenuity of the natives, and would show him the value of his conquests. A number of the most beautiful articles was selected, to the amount of a hundred thousand ducats, and Hernando Pizarro was appointed to be the bearer of them to Spain. He was to obtain an audience of Charles, and, at the same time that he laid the treasures before him, he was to give an account of the proceedings of the Conquerors, and to seek a further augmentation of their powers and dignities.

No man in the army was better qualified for this mission, by his address and knowledge of affairs, than Hernando Pizarro; no one would be so likely to urge his suit with effect at the haughty Castilian court. But other reasons influ-enced the selection of him at the present juncture.

His former jealousy of Almagro still rankled in his bosom, and he had beheld that chief's arrival at the camp with feelings of disgust, which he did not care to conceal. He looked on him as coming to share the spoils of victory, and defraud his brother of his legitimate honors. Instead of exchanging the cordial greeting proffered by Almagro at their first interview, the arrogant cav-alier held back in sullen silence. His brother Francis was greatly displeased at a conduct which threatened to renew their ancient feud, and he induced Hernando to accompany him to Almagro's quarters, and make some acknowl-edgment for his uncourteous behaviour.[2] But, notwithstanding this show of reconciliation, the general thought the present a favorable opportunity to remove his brother from the scene of operations, where his factious spirit more than counterbalanced his eminent services.[3]

The business of melting down the plate was intrusted to the Indian gold-smiths, who were thus required to undo the work of their own hands. They toiled day and night, but such was the quantity to be recast, that it consumed a full month. When the whole was reduced to bars of a uniform standard, they were nicely weighed, under the superintendence of the royal inspec-tors. The total amount of the gold was found to be one million, three hun-dred and twenty-six thousand, five hundred and thirty-nine *pesos de oro,* which, allowing for the greater value of money in the sixteenth century, would be equivalent, probably, at the present time, to near *three millions and a half of pounds sterling,* or somewhat less than *fifteen millions and a half of dol-lars.*[4] The quantity of silver was estimated at fifty-one thousand six hundred and ten marks. History affords no parallel of such a booty—and that, too, in the most convertible form, in ready money, as it were—having fallen to the lot of a little band of military adventurers, like the Conquerors of Peru. The great object of the Spanish expeditions in the New World was gold. It is remarkable that their success should have been so complete. Had they taken the track of the English, the French, or the Dutch, on the shores of the northern continent, how different would have been the result! It is equally worthy of remark, that the wealth thus suddenly acquired, by diverting them from the slow but surer and more permanent sources of national prosperity, has in the end glided from their grasp, and left them among the poorest of the nations of Christendom.

A new difficulty now arose in respect to the division of the treasure. Almagro's followers claimed to be admitted to a share of it; which, as they equalled, and, indeed, somewhat exceeded in number Pizarro's company, would reduce the gains of these last very materially. "We were not here, it is true," said Almagro's soldiers to their comrades, "at the seizure of the Inca, but we have taken our turn in mounting guard over him since his capture, have helped you to defend your treasures, and now give you the means of going forward and securing your conquests. It is a common cause," they urged, "in which all are equally embarked, and the gains should be shared equally between us."

But this way of viewing the matter was not at all palatable to Pizarro's company, who alleged that Atahuallpa's contract had been made exclusively with them; that they had seized the Inca, had secured the ransom, had incurred, in short, all the risk of the enterprise, and were not now disposed to share the fruits of it with every one who came after them.—There was much force, it could not be denied, in this reasoning, and it was finally settled between the leaders, that Almagro's followers should resign their pretensions for a stipulated sum of no great amount, and look to the career now opened to them for carving out their fortunes for themselves.

This delicate affair being thus harmoniously adjusted, Pizarro prepared, with all solemnity, for a division of the imperial spoil. The troops were called together in the great square, and the Spanish commander, "with the fear of God before his eyes," says the record, "invoked the assistance of Heaven to do the work before him conscientiously and justly."[5] The appeal may seem somewhat out of place at the distribution of spoil so unrighteously acquired; yet, in truth, considering the magnitude of the treasure, and the power assumed by Pizarro to distribute it according to the respective deserts of the individuals, there were few acts of his life involving a heavier responsibility. On his present decision might be said to hang the future fortunes of each one of his followers,—poverty or independence during the remainder of his days.

The royal fifth was first deducted, including the remittance already sent to Spain. The share appropriated by Pizarro amounted to fifty-seven thousand two hundred and twenty-two pesos of gold, and two thousand three hundred and fifty marks of silver. He had besides this the great chair or throne of the Inca, of solid gold, and valued at twenty-five thousand *pesos de oro*. To his brother Hernando were paid thirty-one thousand and eighty pesos of gold, and two thousand three hundred and fifty marks of silver. De Soto received seventeen thousand seven hundred and forty pesos of gold, and seven hundred and twenty-four marks of silver. Most of the remaining cavalry, sixty in number, received each eight thousand eight hundred and eighty pesos of gold, and three hundred and sixty-two marks of silver, though some had more, and a few considerably less. The infantry mustered in all one hundred and five men. Almost one fifth of them were allowed, each, four thousand four hundred and forty pesos of gold, and one hundred and eighty marks of silver, half of the compensation of the troopers. The remainder received one fourth part less; though here again there were exceptions, and some were obliged to content themselves with a much smaller share of the spoil.[6]

The new church of San Francisco, the first Christian temple in Peru, was endowed with two thousand two hundred and twenty pesos of gold. The amount assigned to Almagro's company was not excessive, if it was not more than twenty thousand pesos;[7] and that reserved for the colonists of San Miguel, which amounted only to fifteen thousand pesos, was unaccountably small.[8] There were among them certain soldiers, who at an early period of the expedition, as the reader may remember, abandoned the march, and returned to San Miguel. These, certainly, had little claim to be remembered in the division of booty. But the greater part of the colony consisted of invalids, men whose health had been broken by their previous hardships, but who still, with a stout and willing heart, did good service in their military post on the sea-coast. On what grounds they had forfeited their claims to a more ample remuneration, it is not easy to explain.

Nothing is said, in the partition, of Almagro himself, who, by the terms of the original contract, might claim an equal share of the spoil with his associate. As little notice is taken of Luque, the remaining partner. Luque himself, was, indeed, no longer to be benefited by worldly treasure. He had died a short time before Almagro's departure from Panamá;[9] too soon to learn the full success of the enterprise, which, but for his exertions, must have failed; too soon to become acquainted with the achievements and the crimes of Pizarro. But the Licentiate Espinosa, whom he represented, and who, it appears, had advanced the funds for the expedition, was still living at St. Domingo, and Luque's pretensions were explicitly transferred to him. Yet it is unsafe to pronounce, at this distance of time, on the authority of mere negative testimony; and it must be admitted to form a strong presumption in favor of Pizarro's general equity in the distribution, that no complaint of it has reached us from any of the parties present, nor from contemporary chroniclers.[10]

The division of the ransom being completed by the Spaniards, there seemed to be no further obstacle to their resuming active operations, and commencing the march to Cuzco. But what was to be done with Atahuallpa?

In the determination of this question, whatever was expedient was just.[11] To liberate him would be to set at large the very man who might prove their most dangerous enemy; one whose birth and royal station would rally round him the whole nation, place all the machinery of government at his control, and all its resources—, one, in short, whose bare word might concentrate all the energies of his people against the Spaniards, and thus delay for a long period, if not wholly defeat, the conquest of the country. Yet to hold him in captivity was attended with scarcely less difficulty; since to guard so important a prize would require such a division of their force as must greatly cripple its strength, and how could they expect, by any vigilance, to secure their prisoner against rescue in the perilous passes of the mountains?

The Inca himself now loudly demanded his freedom. The proposed amount of the ransom had, indeed, not been fully paid. It may be doubted whether it ever would have been, considering the embarrassments thrown in the way by the guardians of the temples, who seemed disposed to secrete the treasures, rather than despoil these sacred depositories to satisfy the cupidity of the strangers. It was unlucky, too, for the Indian monarch, that much of the gold, and that of the best quality, consisted of flat plates or tiles, which, however valuable, lay in a compact form that did little towards swelling the heap. But an immense amount had been already realized, and it would have been a still greater one, the Inca might allege, but for the impatience of the Spaniards. At all events, it was a magnificent ransom, such as was never paid by prince or potentate before.

These considerations Atahuallpa urged on several of the cavaliers, and especially on Hernando de Soto, who was on terms of more familiarity with him than Pizarro. De Soto reported Atahuallpa's demands to his leader; but the latter evaded a direct reply. He did not disclose the dark purposes over which his mind was brooding.[12] Not long afterward he caused the notary to prepare an instrument, in which he fully acquitted the Inca of further obligation in respect to the ransom. This he commanded to be publicly proclaimed in the camp, while at the same time he openly declared that the safety of the Spaniards required, that the Inca should be detained in confinement until they were strengthened by additional reinforcements.[13]

Meanwhile the old rumors of a meditated attack by the natives began to be current among the soldiers. They were repeated from one to another, gaining something by every repetition. An immense army, it was reported, was mustering at Quito, the land of Atahuallpa's birth, and thirty thousand Caribs were on their way to support it.[14] The Caribs were distributed by the early Spaniards rather indiscriminately over the different parts of America, being invested with peculiar horrors as race of cannibals.

It was not easy to trace the origin of these rumors. There was in the camp a considerable number of Indians, who belonged to the party of Huascar, and who were, of course, hostile to Atahuallpa. But his worst enemy was Felipillo, the interpreter from Tumbez, already mentioned in these pages. This youth had conceived a passion, or, as some say, had been detected in an intrigue with, one of the royal concubines.[15] The circumstance had reached the ears of Atahuallpa, who felt himself deeply outraged by it. "That such an insult should have been offered by so base a person was an indignity," he said, "more difficult to bear than his imprisonment";[16] and he told Pizarro, "that, by the Peruvian law, it could be expiated, not by the criminal's own death alone, but by that of his whole family and kindred."[17] But Felipillo was too important to the Spaniards to be dealt with so summarily; nor did they probably attach such consequence to an offence which, if report be true, they had countenanced by their own example.[18] Felipillo, however, soon learned the state of the Inca's feelings towards himself, and from that moment he regarded him with deadly hatred. Unfortunately, his malignant temper found ready means for its indulgence.

The rumors of a rising among the natives pointed to Atahuallpa as the author of it. Challcuchima was examined on the subject, but avowed his entire ignorance of any such design, which he pronounced a malicious slander. Pizarro next laid the matter before the Inca himself, repeating to him the stories in circulation, with the air of one who believed them. "What treason is this," said the general, "that you have meditated against me,—me, who have ever treated you with honor, confiding in your words, as in those of a brother?" "You jest," replied the Inca, who, perhaps, did not feel the weight of this confidence; "you are always jesting with me. How could I or my people think of conspiring against men so valiant as the Spaniards? Do not jest with me thus, I beseech you."[19] "This," continues Pizarro's secretary, "he said in the most composed and natural manner, smiling all the while to dissemble his falsehood, so that we were all amazed to find such cunning in a barbarian."[20]

But it was not with cunning, but with the consciousness of innocence, as the event afterwards proved, that Atahuallpa thus spoke to Pizarro. He readily discerned, however, the causes, perhaps the consequences, of the accusation. He saw a dark gulf opening beneath his feet; and he was surrounded by strangers, on none of whom he could lean for counsel or protection. The life of the captive monarch is usually short; and Atahuallpa might have learned the truth of this, when he thought of Huascar. Bitterly did he now lament the absence of Hernando Pizarro, for, strange as it may seem, the haughty spirit of this cavalier had been touched by the condition of the royal prisoner, and he had treated him with a deference which won for him the peculiar regard and confidence of the Indian. Yet the latter lost no time in endeavouring to efface the general's suspicions, and to establish his own innocence. "Am I not," said he to Pizarro, "a poor captive in your hands? How could I harbour the designs you impute to me, when I should be the first victim of the outbreak? And you little know my people, if you think that such a movement would be made without my orders; when the very birds in my dominions," said he, with somewhat of an hyperbole, "would scarcely venture to fly contrary to my will."[21]

But these protestations of innocence had little effect on the troops; among whom the story of a general rising of the natives continued to gain credit every hour. A large force, it was said, was already gathered at Guamachucho, not a hundred miles from the camp, and their assault might be hourly expected. The treasure which the Spaniards had acquired afforded a tempting prize, and their own alarm was increased by the apprehension of losing it. The patroles were doubled. The horses were kept saddled and bridled. The soldiers slept on their arms; Pizarro went the rounds regularly to see that every sentinel was on his post. The little army, in short, was in a state of preparation for instant attack.

Men suffering from fear are not likely to be too scrupulous as to the means of removing the cause of it. Murmurs, mingled with gloomy menaces, were now heard against the Inca, the author of these machinations. Many began to demand his life as necessary to the safety of the army. Among these, the most vehement were Almagro and his followers. They had not witnessed the seizure of Atahuallpa. They had no sympathy with him in his fallen state. They regarded him only as an incumbrance, and their desire now was to push their fortunes in the country, since they had got so little of the gold of Caxamalca. They were supported by Riquelme, the treasurer, and by the rest of the royal officers. These men had been left at San Miguel by Pizarro, who did not care to have such official spies on his movements. But they had come to the camp with Almagro, and they loudly demanded the Inca's death, as indispensable to the tranquillity of the country, and the interests of the Crown.[22]

To these dark suggestions Pizarro turned — or seemed to turn — an unwilling ear, showing visible reluctance to proceed to extreme measures with his prisoner.[23] There were some few, and among others Hernando de Soto, who supported him in these views, and who regarded such measures as not at all justified by the evidence of Atahuallpa's guilt. In this state of things, the Spanish commander determined to send a small detachment to Guamachucho, to reconnoitre the country and ascertain what ground there was for the rumors of an insurrection. De Soto was placed at the head of the expedition, which, as the distance was not great, would occupy but a few days.

After that cavalier's departure, the agitation among the soldiers, instead of diminishing, increased to such a degree, that Pizarro, unable to resist their importunities, consented to bring Atahuallpa to instant trial. It was but decent, and certainly safer, to have the forms of a trial. A court was organized, over which the two captains, Pizarro and Almagro, were to preside as judges. An attorney-general was named to prosecute for the Crown, and counsel was assigned to the prisoner.

The charges preferred against the Inca, drawn up in the form of interrogatories, were twelve in number. The most important were, that he had usurped the crown and assassinated his brother Huascar; that he had squandered the public revenues since the conquest of the country by the Spaniards, and lavished them on his kindred and his minions; that he was

guilty of idolatry, and of adulterous practices, indulging openly in a plurality of wives; finally, that he had attempted to excite an insurrection
against the Spaniards.[24]

These charges, most of which had reference to national usages, or to the
personal relations of the Inca, over which the Spanish conquerors had
clearly no jurisdiction, are so absurd, that they might well provoke a smile,
did they not excite a deeper feeling. The last of the charges was the only
one of moment in such a trial; and the weakness of this may be inferred
from the care taken to bolster it up with the others. The mere specification
of the articles must have been sufficient to show that the doom of the Inca
was already sealed.

A number of Indian witnesses were examined, and their testimony, fil-
trated through the interpretation of Felipillo, received, it is said, when necessary, a very different coloring from that of the original. The examination was
soon ended, and "a warm discussion," as we are assured by one of Pizarro's
own secretaries, "took place in respect to the probable good or evil that would
result from the death of Atahuallpa."[25] It was a question of expediency. He was
found guilty,—whether of all the crimes alleged we are not informed,—and
he was sentenced to be burnt alive in the great square of Caxamalca. The sentence was to be carried into execution that very night. They were not even to
wait for the return of De Soto, when the information he would bring would go
far to establish the truth or the falsehood of the reports respecting the insurrection of the natives. It was desirable to obtain the countenance of Father
Valverde to these proceedings, and a copy of the judgment was submitted to
the friar for his signature, which he gave without hesitation, declaring, that,
"in his opinion, the Inca, at all events, deserved death."[26]

Yet there were some few in that martial conclave who resisted these high-
handed measures. They considered them as a poor requital of all the favors
bestowed on them by the Inca, who hitherto had received at their hands nothing but wrong. They objected to the evidence as wholly insufficient; and they
denied the authority of such a tribunal to sit in judgment on a sovereign
prince in the heart of his own dominions. If he were to be tried, he should be
sent to Spain, and his cause brought before the Emperor, who alone had
power to determine it.

But the great majority—and they were ten to one—overruled these objec-
tions, by declaring there was no doubt of Atahuallpa's guilt, and they were
willing to assume the responsibility of his punishment. A full account of the
proceedings would be sent to Castile, and the Emperor should be informed
who were the loyal servants of the Crown, and who were its enemies. The dispute ran so high, that for a time it menaced an open and violent rupture; till,
at length, convinced that resistance was fruitless, the weaker party, silenced,
but not satisfied, contented themselves with entering a written protest against
these proceedings, which would leave an indelible stain on the names of all
concerned in them.[27]

When the sentence was communicated to the Inca, he was greatly over-come by it. He had, indeed, for some time, looked to such an issue as probable, and had been heard to intimate as much to those about him. But the probability of such an event is very different from its certainty, — and that, too, so sudden and speedy. For a moment, the overwhelming conviction of it unmanned him, and he exclaimed, with tears in his eyes, — "What have I done, or my children, that I should meet such a fate? And from your hands, too," said he, addressing Pizarro; "you, who have met with friendship and kindness from my people, with whom I have shared my treasures, who have received nothing but benefits from my hands!" In the most piteous tones, he then implored that his life might be spared, promising any guaranty that might be required for the safety of every Spaniard in the army, — promising double the ransom he had already paid, if time were only given him to obtain it.[28]

An eyewitness assures us that Pizarro was visibly affected, as he turned away from the Inca, to whose appeal he had no power to listen, in opposition to the voice of the army, and to his own sense of what was due to the security of the country.[29] Atahuallpa, finding he had no power to turn his Conqueror from his purpose, recovered his habitual self-possession, and from that moment submitted himself to his fate with the courage of an Indian warrior.

The doom of the Inca was proclaimed by sound of trumqet in the great square of Caxamalca; and, two hours after sunset, the Spanish soldiery assem-bled by torch-light in the *plaza* to witness the execution of the sentence. It was on the twenty-ninth of August, 1533. Atahuallpa was led out chained hand and foot, — for he had been kept in irons ever since the great excitement had prevailed in the army respecting an assault. Father Vicente de Valverde was at his side, striving to administer consolation, and, if possible, to persuade him at this last hour to abjure his superstition and embrace the religion of his Conquerors. He was willing to save the soul of his victim from the terrible expiation in the next world, to which he had so cheerfully consigned his mor-tal part in this.

During Atahuallpa's confinement, the friar had repeatedly expounded to him the Christian doctrines, and the Indian monarch discovered much acuteness in apprehending the discourse of his teacher. But it had not carried conviction to his mind, and though he listened with patience, he had shown no disposition to renounce the faith of his fathers. The Dominican made a last appeal to him in this solemn hour; and, when Atahuallpa was bound to the stake, with the fagots that were to kindle his funeral pile lying around him, Valverde, holding up the cross, besought him to embrace it and be baptized, promising that, by so doing, the painful death to which he had been sentenced should be commuted for the milder form of the *garrote*, — a mode of punishment by strangulation, used for criminals in Spain.[30]

The unhappy monarch asked if this were really so, and, on its being confirmed by Pizarro, he consented to abjure his own religion, and receive baptism. The ceremony was performed by Father Valverde, and the new convert received the name of Juan de Atahuallpa, — the name of Juan being conferred in honor of John the Baptist, on whose day the event took place.[31]

Atahuallpa expressed a desire that his remains might be transported to Quito, the place of his birth, to be preserved with those of his maternal ancestors. Then turning to Pizarro, as a last request, he implored him to take compassion on his young children, and receive them under his protection. Was there no other one in that dark company who stood grimly around him, to whom he could look fort the protection of his offspring? Perhaps he thought there was no other so competent to afford it, and that the wishes so solemnly expressed in that hour might meet with respect even from his Conqueror. Then, recovering his stoical bearing, which for a moment had been shaken, he submitted himself calmly to his fate, — while the Spaniards, gathering around, muttered their *credos* for the salvation of his soul![32] Thus by the death of a vile malefactor perished the last of the Incas!

I have already spoken of the person and the qualities of Atahuallpa. He had a handsome countenance, though with an expression somewhat too fierce to be pleasing. His frame was muscular and well-proportioned; his air commanding; and his deportment in the Spanish quarters had a degree of refinement, the more interesting that it was touched with melancholy. He is accused of having been cruel in his wars, and bloody in his revenge.[33] It may be true, but the pencil of an enemy would be likely to overcharge the shadows of the portrait. He is allowed to have been bold, high-minded, and liberal.[34] All agree that he showed singular penetration and quickness of perception. His exploits as a warrior had placed his valor beyond dispute. The best homage to it is the reluctance shown by the Spaniards to restore him to freedom. They dreaded him as an enemy, and they had done him too many wrongs to think that he could be their friend. Yet his conduct towards them from the first had been most friendly; and they repaid it with imprisonment, robbery, and death.

The body of the Inca remained on the place of execution through the night. The following morning it was removed to the church of San Francisco, where his funeral obsequies were performed with great solemnity. Pizarro and the principal cavaliers went into mourning, and the troops listened with devout attention to the service of the dead from the lips of Father Valverde.[35] The ceremony was interrupted by the sound of loud cries and wailing, as of many voices at the doors of the church. These were suddenly thrown open, and a number of Indian women, the wives and sisters of the deceased, rushing up the great aisle, surrounded the corpse. This was not the way, they cried, to celebrate the funeral rites of an Inca; and they declared their intention to sacrifice themselves on his tomb, and bear him company to the land of spirits. The audience, outraged by this frantic behaviour, told the intruders that

Atahuallpa had died in the faith of a Christian, and that the God of the Christians abhorred such sacrifices. They then caused the women to be excluded from the church, and several, retiring to their own quarters, laid violent hands on themselves, in the vain hope of accompanying their beloved lord to the bright mansions of the Sun.[36]

Atahuallpa's remains, notwithstanding his request, were laid in the cemetery of San Francisco.[37] But from thence, as is reported, after the Spaniards left Caxamalca, they were secretly removed, and carried, as he had desired, to Quito. The colonists of a later time supposed that some treasures might have been buried with the body. But, on excavating the ground, neither treasure nor remains were to be discovered.[38]

A day or two after these tragic events, Hernando de Soto returned from his excursion. Great was his astonishment and indignation at learning what had been done in his absence. He sought out Pizarro at once, and found him, says the chronicler, "with a great felt hat, by way of mourning, slouched over his eyes," and in his dress and demeanour exhibiting all the show of sorrow.[39] "You have acted rashly," said De Soto to him bluntly; "Atahuallpa has been basely slandered. There was no enemy at Guamachucho; no rising among the notives. I have met with nothing on the road but demonstrations of good-will, and all is quiet. If it was necessary to bring the Inca to trial, he should have been taken to Castile and judged by the Emperor. I would have pledged myself to see him safe on board the vessel."[40] Pizarro confessed that he had been precipitate, and said that he had been deceived by Riquelme, Valverde, and the others. These charges soon reached the ears of the treasurer and the Dominican, who, in their turn, exculpated themselves, and upbraided Pizarro to his face, as the only one responsible for the deed. The dispute ran high; and the parties were heard by the by-standers to give one another the lie![41] This vulgar squabble among the leaders, so soon after the event, is the best commentary on the iniquity of their own proceedings and the innocence of the Inca.

The treatment of Atahuallpa, from first to last, forms undoubtedly one of the darkest chapters in Spanish colonial history. There may have been massacres perpetrated on a more extended scale, and executions accompanied with a greater refinement of cruelty. But the blood-stained annals of the Conquest afford no such example of cold-hearted and systematic persecution, not of an enemy, but of one whose whole deportment had been that of a friend and a benefactor.

From the hour that Pizarro and his followers had entered within the sphere of Atahuallpa's influence, the hand of friendship had been extended to them by the natives. Their first act, on crossing the mountains, was to kidnap the monarch and massacre his people. The seizure of his person might be vindicated, by those who considered the end as justifying the means, on the ground that it was indispensable to secure the triumphs of the Cross. But no such apology can be urged for the massacre of the unarmed and helpless population, — as wanton as it was wicked.

The long confinement of the Inca had been used by the Conquerors to wring from him his treasures with the hard gripe of avarice. During the whole of this dismal period, he had conducted himself with singular generosity and good faith. He had opened a free passage to the Spaniards through every part of his empire; and had furnished every facility for the execution of their plans. When these were accomplished, and he remained an encumbrance on their hands, notwithstanding their engagement, expressed or implied, to release him,—and Pizarro, as we have seen, by a formal act, acquitted his captive of any further obligation on the score of the ransom,—he was arraigned before a mock tribunal, and, under pretences equally false and frivolous, was condemned to an excruciating death. From first to last, the policy of the Spanish conquerors towards their unhappy victim is stamped with barbarity and fraud.

It is not easy to acquit Pizarro of being in a great degree responsible for this policy. His partisans have labored to show, that it was forced on him by the necessity of the case, and that in the death of the Inca, especially, he yielded reluctantly to the importunities of others.[42] But weak as is this apology, the historian who has the means of comparing the various testimony of the period will come to a different conclusion. To him it will appear, that Pizarro had probably long felt the removal of Atahuallpa as essential to the success of his enterprise. He foresaw the odium that would be incurred by the death of his royal captive without sufficient grounds; while he labored to establish these, he still shrunk from the responsibility of the deed, and preferred to perpetrate it in obedience to the suggestions of others, rather than his own. Like many an unprincipled politician, he wished to reap the benefit of a bad act, and let others take the blame of it.

Almagro and his followers are reported by Pizarro's secretaries to have first insisted on the Inca's death. They were loudly supported by the treasurer and the royal officers, who considered it as indispensable to the interests of the Crown; and, finally, the rumors of a conspiracy raised the same cry among the soldiers, and Pizarro, with all his tenderness for his prisoner, could not refuse to bring him to trial.—The form of a trial was necessary to give an appearance of fairness to the proceedings. That it was only form is evident from the indecent haste with which it was conducted,—the examination of evidence, the sentence, and the execution, being all on the same day. The multiplication of the charges, designed to place the guilt of the accused on the strongest ground, had, from their very number, the opposite effect, proving only the determination to convict him. If Pizarro had felt the reluctance to his conviction which he pretended, why did he send De Soto, Atahuallpa's best friend, away, when the inquiry was to be instituted? Why was the sentence so summarily executed, as not to afford opportunity, by that cavalier's return, of disproving the truth of the principal charge,—the only one, in fact, with which the Spaniards had any concern? The solemn farce of mourning and deep sorrow affected by Pizarro, who by these honors to the dead would intimate the sincere regard he had entertained for the living, was too thin a veil to impose on the most credulous.

It is not intended by these reflections to exculpate the rest of the army, and especially its officers, from their share in the infamy of the transaction. But Pizarro, as commander of the army, was mainly responsible for its measures. For he was not a man to allow his own authority to be wrested from his grasp, or to yield timidly to the impulses of others. He did not even yield to his own. His whole career shows him, whether for good or for evil, to have acted with a cool and calculating policy.

A story has been often repeated, which refers the motives of Pizarro's conduct, in some degree at least, to personal resentment. The Inca had requested one of the Spanish soldiers to write the name of God on his nail. This the monarch showed to several of his guards successively, and, as they read it, and each pronounced the same word, the sagacious mind of the barbarian was delighted with what seemed to him little short of a miracle, — to which the science of his own nation afforded no analogy. On showing the writing to Pizarro, that chief remained silent; and the Inca, finding he could not read, conceived a contempt for the commander who was even less informed than his soldiers. This he did not wholly conceal, and Pizarro, aware of the cause of it, neither forgot nor forgave it.[43] The anecdote is reported not on the highest authority. It may be true; but it is unnecessary to look for the motives of Pizarro's conduct in personal pique, when so many proofs are to be discerned of a dark and deliberate policy.

Yet the arts of the Spanish chieftain failed to reconcile his countrymen to the atrocity of his proceedings. It is singular to observe the difference between the tone assumed by the first chroniclers of the transaction, while it was yet fresh, and that of those who wrote when the lapse of a few years had shown the tendency of public opinion. The first boldly avow the deed as demanded by expediency, if not necessity; while they deal in no measured terms of reproach with the character of their unfortunate victim.[44] The latter, on the other hand, while they extenuate the errors of the Inca, and do justice to his good faith, are unreserved in their condemnation of the Conquerors, on whose conduct, they say, Heaven set the seal of its own reprobation, by bringing them all to an untimely and miserable end.[45] The sentence of contemporaries has been fully ratified by that of posterity;[46] and the persecution of Atahuallpa is regarded with justice as having left a stain, never to be effaced, on the Spanish arms in the New World.

CHAPTER VIII

DISORDERS IN PERU. — MARCH TO CUZCO. — ENCOUNTER WITH THE NATIVES. — CHALLCUCHIMA BURNT. — ARRIVAL IN CUZCO. — DESCRIPTION OF THE CITY. — TREASURE FOUND THERE

1533-1534.

THE Inca of Peru was its sovereign in a peculiar sense. He received an obedience from his vassals more implicit than that of any despot; for his authority reached to the most secret conduct, to the thoughts of the individual. He was reverenced as more than human.[1] He was not merely the head of the state, but the point to which all its institutions converged, as to a common centre, — the keystone of the political fabric, which must fall to pieces by its own weight when that was withdrawn. So it fared on the death of Atahuallpa.[2] His death not only left the throne vacant, without any certain successor, but the manner of it announced to the Peruvian people that a hand stronger than that of their Incas had now seized the sceptre, and that the dynasty of the Children of the Sun had passed away for ever.

The natural consequences of such a conviction followed. The beautiful order of the ancient institutions was broken up, as the authority which controlled it was withdrawn. The Indians broke out into greater excesses from the uncommon restraint to which they had been before subjected. Villages were burnt, temples and palaces were plundered, and the gold they contained was scattered or secreted. Gold and silver acquired an importance in the eyes of the Peruvian, when he saw the importance attached to them by his conquerors. The precious metals, which before served only for purposes of state or religious decoration, were now hoarded up and buried in caves and forests. The gold and silver concealed by the natives were affirmed greatly to exceed in quantity that which fell into the hands of the Spaniards.[3] The remote provinces now shook off their allegiance to the Incas. Their great captains, at the head of distant armies, set up for themselves. Ruminavi, a commander on

201

the borders of Quito, sought to detach that kingdom from the Peruvian empire, and to reassert its ancient independence. The country, in short, was in that state, in which old things are passing away, and the new order of things has not yet been established. It was in a state of revolution.

The authors of the revolution, Pizarro and his followers, remained meanwhile at Caxamalca. But the first step of the Spanish commander was to name a successor to Atahuallpa. It would be easier to govern under the venerated authority to which the homage of the Indians had been so long paid; and it was not difficult to find a successor. The true heir to the crown was a second son of Huayna Capac, named Manco, a legitimate brother of the unfortunate Huascar. But Pizarro had too little knowledge of the dispositions of this prince; and he made no scruple to prefer a brother of Atahuallpa, and to present him to the Indian nobles as their future Inca. We know nothing of the character of the young Toparca, who probably resigned himself Without reluctance to a destiny which, however humiliating in some points of view, was more exalted than he could have hoped to obtain in the regular course of events. The ceremonies attending a Peruvian coronation were observed, as well as time would allow; the brows of the young Inca were encircled With the imperial *borla* by the hands of his conqueror, and he received the homage of his Indian vassals. They were the less reluctant to pay it, as most of those in the camp belonged to the faction of Quito.

All thoughts were now eagerly turned towards Cuzco, of which the most glowing accounts were circulated among the soldiers, and whose temples and royal palaces were represented as blazing with gold and silver. With imaginations thus excited, Pizarro and his entire company, amounting to almost five hundred men, of whom nearly a third, probably, were cavalry, took their departure early in September from Caxamalca,—a place ever memorable as the theatre of some of the most strange and sanguinary scenes recorded in history. All set forward in high spirits,—the soldiers of Pizarro from the expectation of doubling their present riches, and Almagro's followers from the prospect of sharing equally in the spoil with "the first conquerors."[4] The young Inca and the old chief Challcuchima accompanied the march in their litters, attended by a numerous retinue of vassals, and moving in as much state and ceremony as if in the possession of real power.[5]

Their coarse lay along the great road of the Incas, which stretched across the elevated regions of the Cordilleras, all the way to Cuzco. It was of nearly a uniform breadth, though constructed with different degrees of care, according to the ground.[6] Sometimes it crossed smooth and level valleys, which offered of themselves little impediment to the traveller; at other times, it followed the course of a mountain stream that wound round the base of some beetling cliff, leaving small space for the foothold; at others, again, where the sierra was so precipitous that it seemed to preclude all further progress, the road, accommodated to the natural sinuosities of the ground, wound round the heights which it would have been impossible to scale directly.[7]

But although managed with great address, it was a formidable passage for the cavalry. The mountain was hewn into steps, but the rocky ledges cut up the hoofs of the horses; and, though the troopers dismounted and led them by the bridle, they suffered severely in their efforts to keep their footing.[8] The road was constructed for man and the light-footed llama; and the only heavy beast of burden at all suited to it was the sagacious and sure-footed mule, with which the Spanish adventurers were not then provided. It was a singular chance that Spain was the land of the mule; and thus the country was speedily supplied with the very animal which seems to have been created for the difficult passes of the Cordilleras.

Another obstacle, often occurring, was the deep torrents that rushed down in fury from the Andes. They were traversed by the hanging bridges of osier, whose frail materials were after a time broken up by the heavy tread of the cavalry, and the holes made in them added materially to the dangers of the passage. On such occasions, the Spaniards contrived to work their way across the rivers on rafts, swimming their horses by the bridle.[9]

All along the route they found post-houses for the accommodation of the royal couriers, established at regular intervals; and magazines of grain and other commodities, provided in the principal towns for the Indian armies. The Spaniards profited by the prudent forecast of the Peruvian government.

Passing through several hamlets and towns of some note, the principal of which were Guamachucho and Guanuco, Pizarro, after a tedious march, came in sight of the rich valley of Xauxa. The march, though tedious, had been attended with little suffering, except in crossing the bristling crests of the Cordilleras, which occasionally obstructed their path,—a rough setting to the beautiful valleys, that lay scattered like gems along this elevated region. In the mountain passes they found some inconvenience from the cold; since, to move more quickly, they had disencumbered themselves of all superfluous baggage, and were even unprovided with tents.[10] The bleak winds of the mountains penetrated the thick harness of the soldiers; but the poor Indians, more scantily clothed and accustomed to a tropical climate, suffered most severely. The Spaniard seemed to have a hardihood of body, as of soul, that rendered him almost indifferent to climate.

On the march they had not been molested by enemies. But more than once they had seen vestiges of them in smoking hamlets and ruined bridges. Reports, from time to time, had reached Pizarro of warriors on his track; and small bodies of Indians were occasionally seen like dusky clouds on the verge of the horizon, which vanished as the Spaniards approached. On reaching Xauxa, however, these clouds gathered into one dark mass of warriors, which formed on the opposite bank of the river that flowed through the valley.

The Spaniards advanced to the stream, which, swollen by the melting of the snows, was now of considerable width, though not deep. The bridge had been destroyed; but the Conquerors, without hesitation, dashing boldly in, advanced, swimming and wading, as they best could, to the opposite bank.

The Indians, disconcerted by this decided movement, as they had relied on their watery defences, took to flight, after letting off an impotent volley of missiles. Fear gave wings to the fugitives; but the horse and his rider were swifter, and the victorious pursuers took bloody vengeance on their enemy for having dared even to meditate resistance.

Xauxa was a considerable town. It was the place already noticed as having been visited by Hernando Pizarro. It was seated in the midst of a verdant valley, fertilized by a thousand little rills, which the thrifty Indian husbandman drew from the parent river that rolled sluggishly through the meadows. There were several capacious buildings of rough stone in the town, and a temple of some note in the times of the Incas. But the strong arm of Father Valverde and his countrymen soon tumbled the heathen deities from their pride of place, and established, in their stead, the sacred effigies of the Virgin and Child.

Here Pizarro proposed to halt for some days, and to found a Spanish colony. It was a favorable position, he thought, for holding the Indian mountaineers in check, while, at the same time, it afforded an easy communication with the sea-coast. Meanwhile he determined to send forward De Soto, with a detachment of sixty horse, to reconnoitre the country in advance, and to restore the bridges where demolished by the enemy.[11]

That active cavalier set forward at once, but found considerable impediments to his progress. The traces of an enemy became more frequent as he advanced. The villages were burnt, the bridges destroyed, and heavy rocks and trees strewed in the path to impede the march of the cavalry. As he drew near to Bilcas, once an important place, though now effaced from the map, he had a sharp encounter with the natives, in a mountain defile, which cost him the lives of two or three troopers. The loss was light; but any loss was felt by the Spaniards, so little accustomed, as they had been of late, to resistance.

Still pressing forward, the Spanish captain crossed the river Abancay, and the broad waters of the Apurimac; and, as he drew near the sierra of Vilcaconga, he learned that a considerable body of Indians lay in wait for him in the dangerous passes of the mountains. The sierra was several leagues from Cuzco; and the cavalier, desirous to reach the further side of it before nightfall, incautiously pushed on his wearied horses. When he was fairly entangled in its rocky defiles, a multitude of armed warriors, springing, as it seemed, from every cavern and thicket of the sierra, filled the air with their war-cries, and rushed down, like one of their own mountain torrents, on the invaders, as they were painfully toiling up the steeps. Men and horses were overturned in the fury of the assault, and the foremost files, rolling back on those below, spread ruin and consternation in their ranks. De Soto in vain endeavoured to restore order, and, if possible, to charge the assailants. The horses were blinded and maddened by the missiles, while the desperate natives, clinging to their legs, strove to prevent their ascent up the rocky pathway. De Soto saw, that, unless he gained a level ground which opened at some distance before him, all must be lost. Cheering on his men with the old battle-cry, that always went to the heart of a Spaniard, he struck his spurs deep into the sides of his wearied charger, and, gallantly supported by his troop, broke through the dark array of warriors, and, shaking them off to the right and left, at length succeeded in placing himself on the broad level.

Here both parties paused, as if by mutual consent, for a few moments. A little stream ran through the plain, at which the Spaniards watered their horses;[12] and the animals, having recovered wind, De Soto and his men made a desperate charge on their assailants. The undaunted Indians sustained the shock with firmness; and the result of the combat was still doubtful, when the shades of evening, falling thicker around them, separated the combatants.

Both parties then withdrew from the field, taking up their respective stations within bow-shot of each other, so that the voices of the warriors on either side could be distinctly heard in the stillness of the night. But very different were the reflections of the two hosts. The Indians, exulting in their temporary triumph, looked with confidence to the morrow to complete it. The Spaniards, on the other hand, were proportionably discouraged. They were not prepared for this spirit of resistance in an enemy hitherto so tame. Several cavaliers had fallen; one of them by a blow from a Peruvian battle-axe, which clove his head to the chin, attesting the power of the weapon, and of the arm that used it.[13] Several horses, too, had been killed; and the loss of these was almost as severely felt as that of their riders, considering the great cost and difficulty of transporting them to these distant regions. Few either of the men or horses escaped without wounds, and the Indian allies suffered still more severely.

It seemed probable, from the pertinacity and a certain order maintained in the assault, that it was directed by some leader of military experience; perhaps the Indian commander Quizquiz, who was said to be hanging round the environs of Cuzco with a considerable force.

Notwithstanding the reasonable cause of apprehension for the morrow, De Soto, like a stout-hearted cavalier, as he was, strove to keep up the spirits of his followers. If they had beaten off the enemy when their horses were jaded, and their own strength nearly exhausted, how much easier it would be to come off victorious when both were restored by a night's rest; and he told them to "trust in the Almighty, who would never desert his faithful followers in their extremity." The event justified De Soto's confidence in this seasonable succour.

From time to time, on his march, he had sent advices to Pizarro of the menacing state of the country, till his commander, becoming seriously alarmed, was apprehensive that the cavalier might be overpowered by the superior numbers of the enemy. He accordingly detached Almagro, with nearly all the remaining horse, to his support, — unencumbered by infantry, that he might move the lighter. That efficient leader advanced by forced marches, stimulated by the tidings which met him on the road; and was so fortunate as to reach the foot of the sierra of Vilcaconga the very night of the engagement.

There hearing of the encounter, he pushed forward without halting, though his horses were spent with travel. The night was exceedingly dark, and Almagro, afraid of stumbling on the enemy's bivouac, and desirous to give De Soto information of his approach, commanded his trumpets to sound, till the notes, winding through the defiles of the mountains, broke the slumbers of his countrymen, sounding like blithest music in their ears. They quickly replied with their own bugles, and soon had the satisfaction to embrace their deliverers.[14]

Great was the dismay of the Peruvian host, when the morning light discovered the fresh reinforcement of the ranks of the Spaniards. There was no use in contending with an enemy who gathered strength from the conflict, and who seemed to multiply his numbers at will. Without further attempt to renew the fight, they availed themselves of a thick fog, which hung over the lower slopes of the hills, to effect their retreat, and left the passes open to the invaders. The two cavaliers then continued their march until they extricated their forces from the sierra, when, taking up a secure position, they proposed to await there the arrival of Pizarro.[15]

The commander-in-chief, meanwhile, lay at Xauxa, where he was greatly disturbed by the rumors which reached him of the state of the country. His enterprise, thus far, had gone forward so smoothly, that he was no better prepared than his lieutenant to meet with resistance from the natives. He did not seem to comprehend that the mildest nature might at last be roused by oppression; and that the massacre of their Inca, whom they regarded with such awful veneration, would be likely, if any thing could do it, to wake them from their apathy.

The tidings which he now received of the retreat of the Peruvians were most welcome; and he caused mass to be said, and thanksgivings to be offered up to Heaven, "which had shown itself thus favorable to the Christians throughout this mighty enterprise." The Spaniard was ever a Crusader. He was, in the sixteenth century, what *Cœur de Lion* and his brave knights were in the twelfth, with this difference; the cavalier of that day fought for the Cross and for glory, while gold and the Cross were the watchwords of the Spaniard. The spirit of chivalry had waned somewhat before the spirit of trade; but the fire of religious enthusiasm still burned as bright under the quilted mail of the American Conqueror, as it did of yore under the iron panoply of the soldier of Palestine.

It seemed probable that some man of authority had organized, or at least countenanced, this resistance of the natives, and suspicion fell on the captive chief Challcuchima, who was accused of maintaining a secret correspondence with his confederate, Quiz-quiz. Pizarro waited on the Indian noble, and, charging him with the conspiracy, reproached him, as he had formerly done his royal master, with ingratitude towards the Spaniards, who had dealt with him so liberally. He concluded by the assurance, that, if he did not cause the Peruvians to lay down their arms, and tender their submission at once, he should be burnt alive, so soon as they reached Almagro's quarters.[16]

The Indian chief listened to the terrible menace with the utmost composure. He denied having had any communication with his countrymen, and said, that, in his present state of confinement, at least, he could have no power to bring them to submission. He then remained doggedly silent, and Pizarro did not press the matter further.[17] But he placed a strong guard over his prisoner, and caused him to be put in irons. It was an ominous proceeding, and had been the precursor of the death of Atahuallpa.

Before quitting Xauxa, a misfortune befell the Spaniards in the death of their creature, the young Inca Toparca. Suspicion, of course, fell on Challcuchima, now selected as the scape-goat for all the offences of his nation.[18] It was a disappointment to Pizarro, who hoped to find a convenient shelter for his future proceedings under this shadow of royalty.[19]

The general considered it most prudent not to hazard the loss of his treasures by taking them on the march, and he accordingly left them at Xauxa, under a guard of forty soldiers, who remained there in garrison. No event of importance occurred on the road, and Pizarro, having effected a junction with Almagro, their united forces soon entered the vale of Xaquixaguana, about five leagues from Cuzco. This was one of those bright spots, so often found embosomed amidst the Andes, the more beautiful from contrast with the savage character of the scenery around it. A river flowed through the valley, affording the means of irrigating the soil, and clothing it in perpetual verdure; and the rich and flowering vegetation spread out like a cultivated garden. The beauty of the place and its delicious coolness commended it as a residence for the Peruvian nobles, and the sides of the hills were dotted with their villas, which afforded them a grateful retreat in the heats of summer.[20] Yet the centre of the valley was disfigured by a quagmire of some extent, occasioned by the frequent overflowing of the waters; but the industry of the Indian architects had constructed a solid causeway, faced with heavy stone, and connected with the great road, which traversed the whole breadth of the morass.[21]

In this valley Pizarro halted for several days, while he refreshed his troops from the well-stored magazines of the Incas. His first act was to bring Challcuchima to trial; if trial that could be called, where sentence may be said to have gone hand in hand with accusation. We are not informed of the nature of the evidence. It was sufficient to satisfy the Spanish captains of the chieftain's guilt. Nor is it at all incredible that Challcuchima should have secretly encouraged a movement among the people, designed to secure his country's freedom and his own. He was condemned to be burnt alive on the spot. "Some thought it a hard measure," says Herrera; "but those who are governed by reasons of state policy are apt to shut their eyes against every thing else."[22] Why this cruel mode of execution was so often adopted by the Spanish Conquerors is not obvious; unless it was that the Indian was an infidel, and fire, from ancient date, seems to have been considered the fitting doom of the infidel, as the type of that inextinguishable flame which awaited him in the regions of the damned.

Father Valverde accompanied the Peruvian chieftain to the stake. He seems always to have been present at this dreary moment, anxious to profit by it, if possible, to work the conversion of the victim. He painted in gloomy colors the dreadful doom of the unbeliever, to whom the waters of baptism could alone secure the ineffable glories of paradise.[23] It does not appear that he promised any commutation of punishment in this world. But his arguments fell on a stony heart, and the chief coldly replied, he "did not understand the religion of the white men."[24] He might be pardoned for not comprehending the beauty of a faith which, as it would seem, had borne so bitter fruits to him. In the midst of his tortures, he showed the characteristic courage of the American Indian, whose power of endurance triumphs over the power of persecution in his enemies, and he died with his last breath invoking the name of Pachacamac. His own followers brought the fagots to feed the flames that consumed him.[25]

Soon after this tragic event, Pizarro was surprised by a visit from a Peruvian noble, who came in great state, attended by a numerous and showy retinue. It was the young prince Manco, brother of the unfortunate Huascar, and the rightful successor to the crown. Being brought before the Spanish commander, he announced his pretensions to the throne, and claimed the protection of the strangers. It is said he had meditated resisting them by arms, and had encouraged the assaults made on them on their march; but, finding resistance ineffectual, he had taken this politic course, greatly to the displeasure of his more resolute nobles. However this may be, Pizarro listened to his application with singular contentment, for he saw in this new scion of the true royal stock, a more effectual instrument for his purposes than he could have found in the family of Quito, with whom the Peruvians had but little sympathy. He received the young man, therefore, with great cordiality, and did not hesitate to assure him that he had been sent into the country by his master, the Castilian sovereign, in order to vindicate the claims of Huascar to the crown, and to punish the usurpation of his rival.[26]

Taking with him the Indian prince, Pizarro now resumed his march. It was interrupted for a few hours by a party of the natives, who lay in wait for him in the neighbouring sierra. A sharp skirmish ensued, in which the Indians behaved with great spirit, and inflicted some little injury on the Spaniards; but the latter, at length, shaking them off, made good their passage through the defile, and the enemy did not care to follow them into the open country.

It was late in the afternoon when the Conquerors came in sight of Cuzco.[27] The descending sun was streaming his broad rays full on the imperial city, where many an altar was dedicated to his worship. The low ranges of buildings, showing in his beams like so many lines of silvery light, filled up the bosom of the valley and the lower slopes of the mountains, whose shadowy forms hung darkly over the fair city, as if to shield it from the menaced profanation. It was so late, that Pizarro resolved to defer his entrance till the following morning.

That night vigilant guard was kept in the camp, and the soldiers slept on their arms. But it passed away without annoyance from the enemy, and early on the following day, November 15, 1533, Pizarro prepared for his entrance into the Peruvian capital.[28]

The little army was formed into three divisions, of which the centre, or "battle," as it was called, was led by the general. The suburbs were thronged with a countless multitude of the natives, who had flocked from the city and the surrounding country to witness the showy, and, to them, startling pageant. All looked with eager curiosity on the strangers, the fame of whose terrible exploits had spread to the remotest parts of the empire. They gazed with astonishment on their dazzling arms and fair complexions, which seemed to proclaim them the true Children of the Sun; and they listened with feelings of mysterious dread, as the trumpet sent forth its prolonged notes through the streets of the capital, and the solid ground shook under the heavy tramp of the cavalry.

The Spanish commander rode directly up the great square. It was surrounded by low piles of buildings, among which were several palaces of the Incas. One of these, erected by Huayna Capac, was surmounted by a tower, while the ground-floor was occupied by one or more immense halls, like those described in Caxamalca, where the Peruvian nobles held their *fêtes* in stormy weather. These buildings afforded convenient barracks for the troops, though, during the first few weeks, they remained under their tents in the open *plaza*, with their horses picketed by their side, ready to repulse any insurrection of the inhabitants.[29]

The capital of the Incas, though falling short of the *El Dorado* which had engaged their credulous fancies, astonished the Spaniards by the beauty of its edifices, the length and regularity of its streets, and the good order and appearance of comfort, even luxury, visible in its numerous population. It far surpassed all they had yet seen in the New World. The population of the city is computed by one of the Conquerors at two hundred thousand inhabitants, and that of the suburbs at as many more.[30] This account is not confirmed, as far as I have seen, by any other writer. But however it may be exaggerated, it is certain that Cuzco was the metropolis of a great empire, the residence of the Court and the chief nobility; frequented by the most skilful mechanics and artisans of every description, who found a demand for their ingenuity in the royal precincts; while the place was garrisoned by a numerous soldiery, and was the resort, finally, of emigrants from the most distant provinces. The quarters whence this morley population came were indicated by their peculiar dress, and especially their head-gear, so rarely found at all on the American Indian, which, with its variegated colors, gave a picturesque effect to the groups and masses in the streets. The habitual order and decorum maintained in this multifarious assembly showed the excellent police of the capital, where the only sounds that disturbed the repose of the Spaniards were the noises of feasting and dancing, which the natives, with happy insensibility, constantly prolonged to a late hour of the night.[31]

The edifices of the better sort—and they were very numerous—were of stone, or faced with stone.[32] Among the principal were the royal residences; as each sovereign built a new palace for himself, covering, though low, a large extent of ground. The walls were sometimes stained or painted with gaudy tints, and the gates, we are assured, were sometimes of colored marble.[33] "In the delicacy of the stone-work," says another of the Conquerors, "the natives far excelled the Spaniards, though the roofs of their dwellings, instead of tiles, were only of thatch, but put together with the nicest art."[34] The sunny climate of Cuzco did not require a very substantial material for defence against the weather.

The most important building was the fortress, planted on a solid rock, that rose boldly above the city. It was built of hewn stone, so finely wrought that it was impossible to detect the line of junction between the blocks; and the approaches to it were defended by three semicircular parapets, composed of such heavy masses of rock, that it bore resemblance to the kind of work known to architects as the Cyclopean. The fortress was raised to a height rare in Peruvian architecture; and from the summit of the tower the eye of the spectator ranged over a magnificent prospect, in which the wild features of the mountain scenery, rocks, woods, and waterfalls, were mingled with the rich verdure of the valley, and the shining city filling up the foreground,—all blended in sweet harmony under the deep azure of a tropical sky.

The streets were long and narrow. They were arranged with perfect regularity, crossing one another at right angles; and from the great square diverged four principal streets connecting with the high roads of the empire. The square itself, and many parts of the city, were paved with a fine pebble.[35] Through the heart of the capital ran a river of pure water, if it might not be raffler termed a canal, the banks or sides of which, for the distance of twenty leagues, were faced with stone.[36] Across this stream, bridges, constructed of similar broad flags, were thrown, at intervals, so as to afford an easy communication between the different quarters of the capital.[37]

The most sumptuous edifice in Cuzco, in the times of the Incas, was undoubtedly the great temple dedicated to the Sun, which, studded with gold plates, as already noticed, was surrounded by convents and dormitories for the priests, with their gardens and broad parterres sparkling with gold. The exterior ornaments had been already removed by the Conquerors,—all but the frieze of gold, which, imbedded in the stones, still encircled the principal building. It is probable that the tales of wealth, so greedily circulated among the Spaniards, greatly exceeded the truth. If they did not, the natives must have been very successful in concealing their treasures from the invaders. Yet much still remained, not only in the great House of the Sun, but in the inferior temples which swarmed in the capital.

Pizarro, on entering Cuzco, had issued an order forbidding any soldier to offer violence to the dwellings of the inhabitants.[38] But the palaces were numerous, and the troops lost no time in plundering them of their contents, as well as in despoiling the religious edifices. The interior decorations supplied them with considerable booty. They stripped off the jewels and rich ornaments that garnished the royal mummies in the temple of Coricancha. Indignant at the concealment of their treasures, they put the inhabitants, in some instances, to the torture, and endeavoured to extort from them a confession of their hiding-places.[39] They invaded the repose of the sepulchres, in which the Peruvians often deposited their valuable effects, and compelled the grave to give up its dead. No place was left unexplored by the rapacious Conquerors, and they occasionally stumbled on a mine of wealth that rewarded their labors.

In a cavern near the city they found a number of vases of pure gold, richly embossed with the figures of serpents, locusts, and other animals. Among the spoil were four golden llamas and ten or twelve statues of women, some of gold, others of silver, "which merely to see," says one of the Conquerors, with some *naïveté*, "was truly a great satisfaction." The gold was probably thin, for the figures were all as large as life; and several of them, being reserved for the royal fifth, were not recast, but sent in their original form to Spain.[40] The magazines were stored with curious commodities; richly tinted robes of cotton and feather-work, gold sandals, and slippers of the same material, for the women, and dresses composed entirely of beads of gold.[41] The grain and other articles of food, with which the magazines were filled, were held in contempt by the Conquerors, intent only on gratifying their lust for gold.[42] The time came when the grain would have been of far more value.

Yet the amount of treasure in the capital did not equal the sanguine expectations that had been formed by the Spaniards. But the deficiency was supplied by the plunder which they had collected at various places on their march. In one place, for example, they met with ten planks or bars of solid silver, each piece being twenty feet in length, one foot in breadth, and two or three inches thick. They were intended to decorate the dwelling of an Inca noble.[43]

The whole mass of treasure was brought into a common heap, as in Caxamalca; and after some of the finer specimens had been deducted for the Crown, the remainder was delivered to the Indian goldsmiths to be melted down into ingots of a uniform standard. The division of the spoil was made on the same principle as before. There were four hundred and eighty soldiers, including the garrison of Xauxa, who were each to receive a share, that of the cavalry being double that of the infantry. The amount of booty is stated variously by those present at the division of it. According to some, it considerably exceeded the ransom of Atahuallpa. Others state it as less. Pedro Pizarro says that each horseman got six thousand *pesos de oro,* and each one of the infantry half that sum;[44] though the same discrimination was made by Pizarro as before, in respect to the rank of the parties, and their relative services. But Sancho, the royal notary, and secretary of the commander, estimates the whole amount as far less, — not exceeding five hundred and eighty thousand and two hundred *pesos de oro,* and two hundred and fifteen thousand marks of silver.[45] In the absence of the official returns, it is impossible to determine which is correct. But Sancho's narrative is countersigned, it may be remembered, by Pizarro and the royal treasurer Riquelme, and doubtless, therefore, shows the actual amount for which the Conquerors accounted to the Crown.

Whichever statement we receive, the sum, combined with that obtained at Caxamalca, might well have satisfied the cravings of the most avaricious. The sudden influx of so much wealth, and that, too, in so transferable a form, among a party of reckless adventurers little accustomed to the possession of money, had its natural effect. It supplied them with the means of gaming, so strong and common a passion with the Spaniards, that it may he considered a national vice. Fortunes were lost and won in a single day, sufficient to render the proprietors independent for life; and many a desperate gamester, by an unlucky throw of the dice or turn of the cards, saw himself stripped in a few hours of the fruits of years of toil, and obliged to begin over again the business of rapine. Among these, one in the cavalry service is mentioned, named Leguizano, who had received as his share of the booty the image of the Sun, which, raised on a plate of burnished gold, spread over the walls in a recess of the great temple, and which, for some reason or other,—perhaps because of its superior fineness,—was not recast like the other ornaments. This rich prize the spendthrift lost in a single night; whence it came to be a proverb in Spain, *Juega el Sol antes que amanezca,* "Play away the Sun before sunrise."[46]

The effect of such a surfeit of the precious metals was instantly felt on prices. The most ordinary articles were only to be had for exorbitant sums. A quire of paper sold for ten *pesos de oro;* a bottle of wine, for sixty; a sword, for forty or fifty; a cloak, for a hundred,—sometimes more; a pair of shoes cost thirty or forty *pesos de oro,* and a good horse could not be had for less than twenty-five hundred.[47] Some brought a still higher price. Every article rose in value, as gold and silver, the representatives of all, declined. Gold and silver, in short, seemed to be the only things in Cuzco that were not wealth. Yet there were some few wise enough to return contented with their present gains to their native country. Here their riches brought them consideration and competence, and, while they excited the envy of their countrymen, stimulated them to seek their own fortunes in the like path of adventure.

VOLUME II

BOOK III

CONQUEST OF PERU. — CONTINUED

CHAPTER IX

NEW INCA CROWNED. — MUNICIPAL
REGULATIONS. — TERRIBLE MARCH OF
ALVARADO. — INTERVIEW WITH PIZARRO. —
FOUNDATION OF LIMA. — HERNANDO PIZARRO
REACHES SPAIN. — SENSATION AT COURT. —
FEUDS OF ALMAGRO AND THE PIZARROS

1534-1535.

THE first care of the Spanish general, after the division of the booty, was to place Manco on the throne, and to obtain for him the recognition of his countrymen. He, accordingly, presented the young prince to them as their future sovereign, the legitimate son of Huayna Capac, and the true heir of the Peruvian sceptre. The annunciation was received with enthusiasm by the people, attached to the memory of his illustrious father, and pleased that they were still to have a monarch rule over them of the ancient line of Cuzco.

Every thing was done to maintain the illusion with the Indian population. The ceremonies of a coronation were studiously observed. The young prince kept the prescribed fasts and vigils; and on the appointed day, the nobles and the people, with the whole Spanish soldiery, assembled in the great square of Cuzco to witness the concluding ceremony. Mass was publicly performed by Father Valverde, and the Inca Manco received the fringed diadem of Peru, not from the hand of the high-priest of his nation, but from his Conqueror, Pizarro. The Indian lords then tendered their obeisance in the customary form; after which the royal notary read aloud the instrument asserting the supremacy of the Castilian Crown, and requiring the homage of all present to its authority. This address was explained by an interpreter, and the ceremony of homage was performed by each one of the parties waving the royal banner of Castile twice or thrice with his hands. Manco then pledged the Spanish commander in a golden goblet of the sparkling *chicha;* and, the latter having cordially embraced the new monarch, the trumpets announced the conclusion of the ceremony.[1] But it was not the note of triumph, but of humiliation; for it proclaimed that the armed foot of the stranger was in the halls of the Peruvian Incas; that the ceremony of coronation was a miserable pageant; that their prince himself was but a puppet in the hands of his Conqueror; and that the glory of the Children of the Sun had departed for ever!

Yet the people readily gave in to the illusion, and seemed willing to accept this image of their ancient independence. The accession of the young monarch was greeted by all the usual *fêtes* and rejoicings. The mummies of his royal ancestors, with such ornaments as were still left to them, were paraded in the great square. They were attended each by his own numerous retinue, who performed all the menial offices, as if the object of them were alive and could feel their import. Each ghostly form took its seat at the banquet-table—now, alas! stripped of the magnificent service with which it was wont to blaze at these high festivals—and the guests drank deep to the illustrious dead. Dancing succeeded the carousal, and the festivities, prolonged to a late hour, were continued night after night by the giddy population, as if their conquerors had not been intrenched in the capital![2]—What a contrast to the Aztecs in the conquest of Mexico!

Pizarro's next concern was to organize a municipal government for Cuzco, like those in the cities of the parent country. Two *alcaldes* were appointed, and eight *regidores*, among which last functionaries were his brothers Gonzalo and Juan. The oaths of office were administered with great solemnity, on the twenty-fourth of March, 1534, in presence both of Spaniards and Peruvians, in the public square; as if the general were willing by this ceremony to intimate to the latter, that, while they retained the semblance of their ancient institutions, the real power was henceforth vested in their conquerors.[3] He invited Spaniards to settle in the place by liberal grants of land and houses, for which means were afforded by the numerous palaces and public buildings of the Incas; and many a cavalier, who had been too poor in his own country to find a place to rest in, now saw himself the proprietor of a spacious mansion that might have entertained the retinue of a prince.[4] From this time, says an old chronicler, Pizarro, who had hitherto been distinguished by his military title of "Captain-General," was addressed by that of "Governor."[5] Both had been bestowed on him by the royal grant.

Nor did the chief neglect the interests of religion. Father Valverde, whose nomination as Bishop of Cuzco not long afterwards received the Papal sanction, prepared to enter on the duties of his office. A place was selected for the cathedral of his diocese, facing the *plaza*. A spacious monastery subsequently rose on the ruins of the gorgeous House of the Sun; its walls were constructed of the ancient stones; the altar was raised on the spot where shone the bright image of the Peruvian deity, and the cloisters of the Indian temple were trodden by the friars of St. Dominic.[6] To make the metamorphosis more complete, the House of the Virgins of the Sun was replaced by a Roman Catholic nunnery.[7] Christian churches and monasteries gradually supplanted the ancient edifices, and such of the latter as were suffered to remain, despoiled of their heathen insignia, were placed under the protection of the Cross.

The Fathers of St. Dominic, the Brethren of the Order of Mercy, and other missionaries, now busied themselves in the good work of conversion. We have seen that Pizarro was required by the Crown to bring out a certain number of these holy men in his own vessels; and every succeeding vessel brought an additional reinforcement of ecclesiastics. They were not all like the Bishop of Cuzco, with hearts so seared by fanaticism as to be closed against sympathy with the unfortunate natives.[8] They were, many of them, men of singular humility, who followed in the track of the conqueror to scatter the seeds of spiritual truth, and, with disinterested zeal, devoted themselves to the propagation of the Gospel. Thus did their pious labors prove them the true soldiers of the Cross, and showed that the object so ostentatiously avowed of carrying its banner among the heathen nations was not an empty vaunt.

The effort to Christianize the heathen is an honorable characteristic of the Spanish conquests. The Puritan, with equal religious zeal, did comparatively little for the conversion of the Indian, content, as it would seem, with having secured to himself the inestimable privilege of worshipping God in his own way. Other adventurers who have occupied the New World have often had too little regard for religion themselves, to be very solicitous about spreading it among the savages. But the Spanish missionary, from first to last, has shown a keen interest in the spiritual welfare of the natives. Under his auspices, churches on a magnificent scale have been erected, schools for elementary instruction founded, and every rational means taken to spread the knowledge of religious truth, while he has carried his solitary mission into remote and almost inaccessible regions, or gathered his Indian disciples into communities, like the good Las Casas in Cumaná, or the Jesuits in California and Paraguay. At all times, the courageous ecclesiastic has been ready to lift his voice against the cruelty of the conqueror, and the no less wasting cupidity of the colonist; and when his remonstrances, as was too often the case, have proved unavailing, he has still followed to bind up the broken-hearted, to teach the poor Indian resignation under his lot, and light up his dark intellect with the revelation of a holier and happier existence. — In reviewing the blood-stained records of Spanish colonial history, it is but fair, and at the same time cheering, to reflect, that the same nation which sent forth the hard-hearted conqueror from its bosom sent forth the missionary to do the work of beneficence, and spread the light of Christian civilization over the farthest regions of the New World.

While the governor, as we are henceforth to style him, lay at Cuzco, he received repeated accounts of a considerable force in the neighbourhood, under the command of Atahuallpa's officer, Quizquiz. He accordingly detached Almagro, with a small body of horse and a large Indian force under the Inca Manco, to disperse the enemy, and, if possible, to capture their leader. Manco was the more ready to take part in the expedition, as the enemy were soldiers of Quito, who, with their commander, bore no good-will to himself.

Almagro, moving with his characteristic rapidity, was not long in coming up with the Indian chieftain. Several sharp encounters followed, as the army of Quito fell back on Xauxa, near which a general engagement decided the fate of the war by the total discomfiture of the natives. Quizquiz fled to the ele-vated plains of Quito, where he still held out with undaunted spirit against a Spanish force in that quarter, till at length his own soldiers, wearied by these long and ineffectual hostilities, massacred their commander in cold blood.[9] Thus fell the last of the two great officers of Atahuallpa, who, if their nation had been animated by a spirit equal to their own, might long have successfully maintained their soil against the invader.

Some time before this occurrence, the Spanish governor, while in Cuzco, received tidings of an event much more alarming to him than any Indian hostilities. This was the arrival on the coast of a strong Spanish force, under command of Don Pedro de Alvarado, the gallant officer who had served under Cortés with such renown in the war of Mexico. That cavalier, after forming a brilliant alliance in Spain, to which he was entitled by his birth and military rank, had returned to his government of Guatemala, where his avarice had been roused by the magnificent reports he daily received of Pizarro's conquests. These conquests, he learned, had been confined to Peru; while the northern kingdom of Quito, the ancient residence of Atahuallpa, and, no doubt, the principal depository of his treasures, yet remained untouched. Affecting to consider this country as falling without the governor's jurisdiction, he immediately turned a large fleet, which he had intended for the Spice Islands, in the direction of South America; and in March, 1534, he landed in the bay of Caraques, with five hundred followers, of whom half were mounted, and all admirably provided with arms and ammunition. It was the best equipped and most formidable array that had yet appeared in the southern seas.[10]

Although manifestly an invasion of the territory conceded to Pizarro by the Crown, the reckless cavalier determined to march at once on Quito. With the assistance of an Indian guide, he proposed to take the direct route across the mountains, a passage of exceeding difficulty, even at the most favorable season.

After crossing the Rio Dable, Alvarado's guide deserted him, so that he was soon entangled in the intricate mazes of the sierra; and, as he rose higher and higher into the regions of winter, he became surrounded with ice and snow, for which his men, taken from the warm countries of Guatemala, were but ill prepared. As the cold grew more intense, many of them were so benumbed, that it was with difficulty they could proceed. The infantry, compelled to make exertions, fared best. Many of the troopers were frozen stiff in their saddles. The Indians, still more sensible to the cold, perished by hundreds. As the

Spaniards huddled round their wretched bivouacs, with such scanty fuel as they could glean, and almost without food, they waited in gloomy silence the approach of morning. Yet the morning light, which gleamed coldly on the cheerless waste, brought no joy to them. It only revealed more clearly the extent of their wretchedness. Still struggling on through the winding Puertos Nevados, or Snowy Passes, their track was dismally marked by fragments of dress, broken harness, golden ornaments, and other valuables plundered on their march,—by the dead bodies of men, or by those less fortunate, who were left to die alone in the wilderness. As for the horses, their carcasses were not suffered long to cumber the ground, as they were quickly seized and devoured half raw by the starving soldiers, who, like the famished condors, now hovering in troops above their heads, greedily banqueted on the most offensive offal to satisfy the gnawings of hunger.

Alvarado, anxious to secure the booty which had fallen into his hands at an earlier part of his march, encouraged every man to take what gold he wanted from the common heap, reserving only the royal fifth. But they only answered, with a ghastly smile of derision, "that food was the only gold for them." Yet in this extremity, which might seem to have dissolved the very ties of nature, there are some affecting instances recorded of self-devotion; of comrades who lost their lives in assisting others, and of parents and husbands (for some of the cavaliers were accompanied by their wives) who, instead of seeking their own safety, chose to remain and perish in the snows with the objects of their love.

To add to their distress, the air was filled for several days with thick clouds of earthy particles and cinders, which blinded the men, and made respiration exceedingly difficult.[11] This phenomenon, it seems probable, was caused by an eruption of the distant Cotopaxi, which, about twelve leagues southeast of Quito, rears up its colossal and perfectly symmetrical cone far above the limits of eternal snow,—the most beautiful and the most terrible of the American volcanoes.[12] At the time of Alvarado's expedition, it was in a state of eruption, the earliest instance of the kind on record, though doubtless not the earliest.[13] Since that period, it has been in frequent commotion, sending up its sheets of flame to the height of half a mile, spouting forth cataracts of lava that have overwhelmed towns and villages in their career, and shaking the earth with subterraneous thunders, that, at the distance of more than a hundred leagues, sounded like the reports of artillery![14] Alvarado's followers, unacquainted with the cause of the phenomenon, as they wandered over tracts buried in snow,—the sight of which was strange to them,—in an atmosphere laden with ashes, became bewildered by this confusion of the elements, which Nature seemed to have contrived purposly for their destruction. Some of these men were the soldiers of Cortés, steeled by many a painful march, and many a sharp encounter with the Aztecs. But this war of the elements, they now confessed, was mightier than all.

219

At length, Alvarado, after sufferings, which even the most hardy, probably, could have endured but a few days longer, emerged from the Snowy Pass, and came on the elevated table-land, which spreads out, at the height of more than nine thousand feet above the ocean, in the neighbourhood of Riobamba. But one fourth of his gallant army had been left to feed the condor in the wilderness, besides the greater part, at least two thousand, of his Indian auxiliaries. A great number of his horses, too, had perished; and the men and horses that escaped were all of them more or less injured by the cold and the extremity of suffering. — Such was the terrible passage of the Puertos Nevados, which I have only briefly noticed as an episode to the Peruvian conquest, but the account of which, in all its details, though it occupied but a few weeks in duration, would give one a better idea of the difficulties encountered by the Spanish cavaliers, than volumes of ordinary narrative.[15]

As Alvarado, after halting some time to restore his exhausted troops, began his march across the broad plateau, he was astonished by seeing the prints of horses' hoofs on the soil. Spaniards, then, had been there before him, and, after all his toil and suffering, others had forestalled him in the enterprise against Quito! It is necessary to say a few words in explanation of this.

When Pizarro quitted Caxamalca, being sensible of the growing importance of San Miguel, the only port of entry then in the country, he despatched a person in whom he had great confidence to take charge of it. This person was Sebastian Benalcazar, a cavalier who afterwards placed his name in the first rank of the South American conquerors, for courage, capacity, — and cruelty. But this cavalier had hardly reached his government, when, like Alvarado, he received such accounts of the riches of Quito, that he determined, with the force at his command, though without orders, to undertake its reduction.

At the head of about a hundred and forty soldiers, horse and foot, and a stout body of Indian auxiliaries, he marched up the broad range of the Andes, to where it spreads out into the table-land of Quito, by a road safer and more expeditious than that taken by Alvarado. On the plains of Riobamba, he encountered the Indian general Ruminavi. Several engagements followed, with doubtful success, when, in the end, science prevailed where courage was well matched, and the victorious Benalcazar planted the standard of Castile on the ancient towers of Atahuallpa. The city, in honor of his general, Francis Pizarro, he named San Francisco del Quito. But great was his mortification on finding that either the stories of its riches had been fabricated, or that these riches were secreted by the natives. The city was all that he gained by his victories, — the shell without the pearl of price which gave it its value. While devouring his chagrin, as he best could, the Spanish captain received tidings of the approach of his superior, Almagro.[16]

No sooner had the news of Alvarado's expedition reached Cuzco, than Almagro left the place with a small force for San Miguel, proposing to strengthen himself by a reinforcement from that quarter, and to march at once against the invaders. Greatly was he astonished, on his arrival in that city, to learn the departure of its commander. Doubting the loyalty of his motives, Almagro, with the buoyancy of spirit which belongs to youth, though in truth somewhat enfeebled by the infirmities of age, did not hesitate to follow Benalcazar at once across the mountains.

With his wonted energy, the intrepid veteran, overcoming all the difficulties of his march, in a few weeks placed himself and his little company on the lofty plains which spread around the Indian city of Riobamba; though in his progress he had more than one hot encounter with the natives, whose courage and perseverance formed a contrast sufficiently striking to the apathy of the Peruvians. But the fire only slumbered in the bosom of the Peruvian. His hour had not yet come.

At Riobamba, Almagro was soon joined by the commander of San Miguel, who disclaimed, perhaps sincerely, any disloyal intent in his unauthorized expedition. Thus reinforced, the Spanish captain coolly awaited the coming of Alvarado. The forces of the latter, though in a less serviceable condition, were much superior in number and appointments to those of his rival. As they confronted each other on the broad plains of Riobamba, it seemed probable that a fierce struggle must immediately follow, and the natives of the country have the satisfaction to see their wrongs avenged by the very hands that inflicted them. But it was Almagro's policy to avoid such an issue.

Negotiations were set on foot, in which each party stated his claims to the country. Meanwhile Alvarado's men mingled freely with their countrymen in the opposite army, and heard there such magnificent reports of the wealth and wonders of Cuzco, that many of them were inclined to change their present service for that of Pizarro. Their own leader, too, satisfied that Quito held out no recompense worth the sacrifices he had made, and was like to make, by insisting on his claim, became now more sensible of the rashness of a course which must doubtless incur the censure of his sovereign. In this temper, it was not difficult for them to effect an adjustment of difficulties; and it was agreed, as the basis of it, that the governor should pay one hundred thousand *pesos de oro* to Alvarado, in consideration of which the latter was to resign to him his fleet, his forces, and all his stores and munitions. His vessels, great and small, amounted to twelve in number, and the sum he received, though large, did not cover his expenses. This treaty being settled, Alvarado proposed, before leaving the country, to have an interview with Pizarro.[17]

The governor, meanwhile, had quitted the Peruvian capital for the seacoast, from his desire to repel any invasion that might be attempted in that direction by Alvarado, with whose real movements he was still unacquainted. He left Cuzco in charge of his brother Juan, a cavalier whose manners were such as, he thought, would be likely to gain the good-will of the native population. Pizarro also left ninety of his troops, as the garrison of the capital, and the nucleus of his future colony. Then, taking the Inca Manco with him, he proceeded as far as Xauxa. At this place he was entertained by the Indian prince with the exhibition of a great national hunt, —

such as has been already described in these pages, — in which immense numbers of wild animals were slaughtered, and the vicuñas, and other races of Peruvian sheep, which roam over the mountains, driven into inclosures and relieved of their delicate fleeces.[18]

The Spanish governor then proceeded to Pachacamac, where he received the grateful intelligence of the accommodation with Alvarado; and not long afterward he was visited by that cavalier himself, previously to his embarkation.

The meeting was conducted with courtesy and a show, at least, of good-will, on both sides, as there was no longer real cause for jealousy between the parties; and each, as may be imagined, looked on the other with no little interest, as having achieved such distinction in the bold path of adventure. In the comparison, Alvarado had somewhat the advantage; for Pizarro, though of commanding presence, had not the brilliant exterior, the free and joyous manner, which, no less than his fresh complexion and sunny locks, had won for the conqueror of Guatemala, in his campaigns against the Aztecs, the *sobriquet* of *Tonatiuh,* or "Child of the Sun."

Blithe were the revels that now rang through the ancient city of Pachacamac; where, instead of songs, and of the sacrifices so often seen there in honor of the Indian deity, the walls echoed to the noise of tourneys and Moorish tilts of reeds, with which the martial adventurers loved to recall the sports of their native land. When these were concluded, Alvarado reëmbarked for his government of Guatemala, where his restless spirit soon involved him in other enterprises that cut short his adventurous career. His expedition to Peru was eminently characteristic of the man. It was founded in injustice, conducted with rashness, and ended in disaster.[19]

The reduction of Peru might now be considered as, in a manner, accomplished. Some barbarous tribes in the interior, it is true, still held out, and Alonso de Alvarado, a prudent and able officer, was employed to bring them into subjection. Benalcazar was still at Quito, of which he was subsequently appointed governor by the Crown. There he was laying deeper the foundation of the Spanish power, while he advanced the line of conquest still higher towards the north. But Cuzco, the ancient capital of the Indian monarchy, had submitted. The armies of Atahuallpa had been beaten and scattered. The empire of the Incas was dissolved; and the prince who now wore the Peruvian diadem was but the shadow of a king, who held his commission from his conqueror.

The first act of the governor was to determine on the site of the future capital of this vast colonial empire. Cuzco, withdrawn among the mountains, was altogether too far removed from the sea-coast for a commercial people. The little settlement of San Miguel lay too far to the north. It was desirable to select some more central position, which could be easily found in one of the fruitful valleys that bordered the Pacific. Such was that of Pachacamac, which Pizarro now occupied. But, on further examination, he preferred the neighbouring valley of Rimac, which lay to the north, and which took its name, signifying in the Quichua tongue "one who speaks," from a celebrated idol, whose shrine was much frequented by the Indians for the oracles it delivered. Through the valley flowed a broad stream, which, like a great artery, was made, as usual by the natives, to supply a thousand finer veins that meandered through the beautiful meadows.

On this river Pizarro fixed the site of his new capital, at somewhat less than two leagues' distance from its mouth, which expanded into a commodious haven for the commerce that the prophetic eye of the founder saw would one day—and no very distant one—float on its waters. The central situation of the spot recommended it as a suitable residence for the Peruvian viceroy, whence he might hold easy communication with the different parts of the country, and keep vigilant watch over his Indian vassals. The climate was delightful, and, though only twelve degrees south of the line, was so far tempered by the cool breezes that generally blow from the Pacific, or from the opposite quarter down the frozen sides of the Cordilleras, that the heat was less than in corresponding latitudes on the continent. It never rained on the coast; but this dryness was corrected by a vaporous cloud, which, through the summer months, hung like a curtain over the valley, sheltering it from the rays of a tropical sun, and imperceptibly distilling a refreshing moisture, that clothed the fields in the brightest verdure.

The name bestowed on the infant capital was *Ciudad de los Reyes,* or City of the Kings, in honor of the day, being the sixth of January, 1535,—the festival of Epiphany,—when it was said to have been founded, or more probably when its site was determined, as its actual foundation seems to have been twelve days later.[20] But the Castilian name ceased to be used even within the first generation, and was supplanted by that of Lima, into which the original Indian name of Rimac was corrupted by the Spaniards.[21]

The city was laid out on a very regular plan. The streets were to be much wider than usual in Spanish towns, and perfectly straight, crossing one another at right angles, and so far asunder as to afford ample space for gardens to the dwellings, and for public squares. It was arranged in a triangular form, having the river for its base, the waters of which were to be carried, by means of stone conduits, through all the principal streets, affording facilities for irrigating the grounds around the houses.

No sooner had the governor decided on the site and on the plan of the city, than he commenced operations with his characteristic energy. The Indians were collected from the distance of more than a hundred miles to aid in the work. The Spaniards applied themselves with vigor to the task, under the eye of their chief. The sword was exchanged for the tool of the artisan. The camp was converted into a hive of diligent laborers; and the sounds of war were succeeded by the peaceful hum of a busy population. The *plaza,* which was extensive, was to be surrounded by the cathedral, the palace of the viceroy, that of the municipality, and other public buildings; and their foundations were laid on a scale, and with a solidity, which defied the assaults of time, and, in some instances, even the more formidable shock of earthquakes, that, at different periods, have laid portions of the fair capital in ruins.[22]

While these events were going on, Almagro, the Marshal, as he is usually termed by chroniclers of the time, had gone to Cuzco, whither he was sent by Pizarro to take command of that capital. He received also instructions to undertake, either by himself or by his captains, the conquest of the countries towards the south, forming part of Chili. Almagro, since his arrival at Caxamalca, had seemed willing to smother his ancient feelings of resentment towards his associate, or, at least, to conceal the expression of them, and had consented to take command under him in obedience to the royal mandate. He had even, in his despatches, the magnanimity to make honorable mention of Pizarro, as one anxious to promote the interests of government. Yet he did not so far trust his companion, as to neglect the precaution of sending a confidential agent to represent his own services, when Hernando Pizarro undertook his mission to the mother-country.

That cavalier, after touching at St. Domingo, had arrived without accident at Seville, in January, 1534. Besides the royal fifth, he took with him gold, to the value of half a million of *pesos*, together with a large quantity of silver, the property of private adventurers, some of whom, satisfied with their gains, had returned to Spain in the same vessel with himself. The custom-house was filled with solid ingots, and with vases of different forms, imitations of animals, flowers, fountains, and other objects, executed with more or less skill, and all of pure gold, to the astonishment of the spectators, who flocked from the neighbouring country to gaze on these marvellous productions of Indian art.[23] Most of the manufactured articles were the property of the Crown; and Hernando Pizarro, after a short stay at Seville, selected some of the most gorgeous specimens, and crossed the country to Calatayud, where the emperor was holding the cortes of Aragon.

Hernando was instantly admitted to the royal presence, and obtained a gracious audience. He was more conversant with courts than either of his brothers, and his manners, when in situations that imposed a restraint on the natural arrogance of his temper, were graceful and even attractive. In a respectful tone, he now recited the stirring adventures of his brother and his little troop of followers, the fatigues they had endured, the difficulties they had overcome, their capture of the Peruvian Inca, and his magnificent ransom. He had not to tell of the massacre of the unfortunate prince, for that tragic event, which had occurred since his departure from the country, was still unknown to him. The cavalier expatiated on the productiveness of the soil, and on the civilization of the people, evinced by their proficiency in various mechanic arts; in proof of which he displayed the manufactures of wool and cotton, and the rich ornaments of gold and silver. The monarch's eyes sparkled with delight as he gazed on these last. He was too sagacious not to appreciate the advantages of a conquest which secured to him a country so rich in agricultural resources. But the returns from these must necessarily be gradual and long deferred; and he may be excused for listening with still greater satisfaction to Pizarro's tales of its mineral stores; for his ambitious projects had drained the imperial treasury, and he saw in the golden tide thus unexpectedly poured in upon him the immediate means of replenishing it.

Charles made no difficulty, therefore, in granting the petitions of the fortunate adventurer. All the previous grants to Francis Pizarro and his associates were confirmed in the fullest manner; and the boundaries of the governor's jurisdiction were extended seventy leagues further towards the south. Nor did Almagro's services, this time, go unrequited. He was empowered to discover and occupy the country for the distance of two hundred leagues, beginning at the southern limit of Pizarro's territory.[24] Charles, in proof, still further, of his satisfaction, was graciously pleased to address a letter to the two commanders, in which he complimented them on their prowess, and thanked them for their services. This act of justice to Almagro would have been highly honorable to Hernando Pizarro, considering the unfriendly relations in which they stood to each other, had it not been made necessary by the presence of the marshal's own agents at court, who, as already noticed, stood ready to supply any deficiency in the statements of the emissary.

In this display of the royal bounty, the envoy, as will readily be believed, did not go without his reward. He was lodged as an attendant of the Court; was made a knight of Santiago, the most prized of the chivalric orders in Spain; was empowered to equip an armament, and to take command of it; and the royal officers at Seville were required to aid him in his views and facilitate his embarkation for the Indies.[25]

The arrival of Hernando Pizarro in the country, and the reports spread by him and his followers, created a sensation among the Spaniards such as had not been felt since the first voyage of Columbus. The discovery of the New World had filled the minds of men with indefinite expectations of wealth, of which almost every succeeding expedition had proved the fallacy. The conquest of Mexico, though calling forth general admiration as a brilliant and wonderful exploit, had as yet failed to produce those golden results which had been so fondly anticipated. The splendid promises held out by Francis Pizarro on his recent visit to the country had not revived the confidence of his countrymen, made incredulous by repeated disappointment. All that they were assured of was the difficulties of the enterprise; and their distrust of its results was sufficiently shown by the small number of followers, and those only of the most desperate stamp, who were willing to take their chance in the adventure.

But now these promises were realized. It was no longer the golden reports that they were to trust; but the gold itself, which was displayed in such profusion before them. All eyes were now turned towards the West. The broken spendthrift saw in it the quarter where he was to repair his fortunes as speedily as he had ruined them. The merchant, instead of seeking the precious commodities of the East, looked in the opposite direction, and counted on far higher gains, where the most common articles of life commanded so exorbitant prices. The cavalier, eager to win both gold and glory at the point of his lance, thought to find a fair field for his prowess on the mountain plains of the Andes. Ferdinand Pizarro found that his brother had judged rightly in allowing as many of his company as chose to return home, confident that the display of their wealth would draw ten to his banner for every one that quitted it.

In a short time that cavalier saw himself at the head of one of the most numerous and well-appointed armaments, probably, that had left the shores of Spain since the great fleet of Ovando, in the time of Ferdinand and Isabella. It was scarcely more fortunate than this. Hardly had Ferdinand put to sea, when a violent tempest fell on the squadron, and compelled him to return to port and refit. At length he crossed the ocean, and reached the little harbour of Nombre de Dios in safety. But no preparations had been made for his coming, and, as he was detained here some time before he could pass the mountains, his company suffered greatly from scarcity of food. In their extremity, the most unwholesome articles were greedily devoured, and many a cavalier spent his little savings to procure himself a miserable subsistence. Disease, as usual, trod closely in the track of famine, and numbers of the unfortunate adventurers, sinking under the unaccustomed heats of the climate, perished on the very threshold of discovery.

It was the tale often repeated in the history of Spanish enterprise. A few, more lucky than the rest, stumble on some unexpected prize, and hundreds, attracted by their success, press forward in the same path. But the rich spoil which lay on the surface has been already swept away by the first comers, and those who follow are to win their treasure by long-protracted and painful exertion.—Broken in spirit and in fortune, many returned in disgust to their native shores, while others remained where they were, to die in despair. They thought to dig for gold; but they dug only their graves.

Yet it fared not thus with all Pizarro's company. Many of them, crossing the Isthmus with him to Panamá, came in time to Peru, where, in the desperate chances of its revolutionary struggles, some few arrived at posts of profit and distinction. Among those who first reached the Peruvian shore was an emissary sent by Almagro's agents to inform him of the important grant made to him by the Crown. The tidings reached him just as he was making his entry into Cuzco, where he was received with all respect by Juan and Gonzalo Pizarro, who, in obedience to their brother's commands, instantly resigned the government of the capital into the marshal's hands. But Almagro was greatly elated on finding himself now placed by his sovereign in a command that made him independent of the man who had so deeply wronged him; and he intimated that in the exercise of his present authority he acknowledged no superior. In this lordly humor he was confirmed by several of his followers, who insisted that Cuzco fell to the south of the territory ceded to Pizarro, and consequently came within that now granted to the marshal. Among these followers were several of Alvarado's men, who, though of better condition than the soldiers of Pizarro, were under much worse discipline, and had acquired, indeed, a spirit of unbridled license under that unscrupulous chief.[26] They now evinced little concern for the native population of Cuzco; and, not content with the public edifices, seized on the dwellings of individuals, where it suited their convenience, appropriating their contents without ceremony, — showing as little respect, in short, for person or property, as if the place had been taken by storm.[27]

While these events were passing in the ancient Peruvian capital, the governor was still at Lima, where he was greatly disturbed by the accounts he received of the new honors conferred on his associate. He did not know that his own jurisdiction had been extended seventy leagues further to the south, and he entertained the same suspicion with Almagro, that the capital of the Incas did not rightly come within his present limits. He saw all the mischief likely to result from this opulent city falling into the hands of his rival, who would thus have an almost indefinite means of gratifying his own cupidity, and that of his followers. He felt, that, under the present circumstances, it was not safe to allow Almagro to anticipate the possession of power, to which, as yet, he had no legitimate right; for the despatches containing the warrant for it still remained with Hernando Pizarro, at Panamá, and all that had reached Peru was a copy of a garbled extract.

Without loss of time, therefore, he sent instructions to Cuzco for his brothers to resume the government, while he defended the measure to Almagro on the ground, that, when he should hereafter receive his credentials, it would be unbecoming to be found already in possession of the post. He concluded by urging him to go forward without delay in his expedition to the south.

But neither the marshal nor his friends were pleased with the idea of so soon relinquishing the authority which they now considered as his right. The Pizarros, on the other hand, were pertinacious in reclaiming it. The dispute grew warmer and warmer. Each party had its supporters; the city was split into factions; and the municipality, the soldiers, and even the Indian population, took sides in the struggle for power. Matters were proceeding to extremity, menacing the capital with violence and bloodshed, when Pizarro himself appeared among them.[28]

On receiving tidings of the fatal consequences of his mandates, he had posted in all haste to Cuzco, where he was greeted with undisguised joy by the natives, as well as by the more temperate Spaniards, anxious to avert the impending storm. The governor's first interview was with Almagro, whom he embraced with a seeming cordiality in his manner; and, without any show of resentment, inquired into the cause of the present disturbances. To this the marshal replied, by throwing the blame on Pizarro's brothers; but, although the governor reprimanded them with some asperity for their violence, it was soon evident that his sympathies were on their side, and the dangers of a feud between the two associates seemed greater than ever. Happily, it was postponed by the intervention of some common friends, who showed more discretion than their leaders. With their aid a reconciliation was at length effected, on the grounds substantially of their ancient compact.

It was agreed that their friendship should be maintained inviolate; and, by a stipulation that reflects no great credit on the parties, it was provided that neither should malign nor disparage the other, especially in their despatches to the emperor; and that neither should hold communication with the government without the knowledge of his confederate; lastly, that both the expenditures and the profits of future discovery should be shared equally by the associates. The wrath of Heaven was invoked by the most solemn imprecations on the head of whichever should violate this compact, and the Almighty was implored to visit the offender with loss of property and of life in this world, and with eternal perdition in that to come![29] The parties further bound themselves to the observance of this contract by a solemn oath taken on the sacrament, as it was held in the hands of Father Bartolomé de Segovia, who concluded the ceremony by performing mass. The whole proceeding, and the articles of agreement, were carefully recorded by the notary, in an instrument bearing date June 12, 1535, and attested by a long list of witnesses.[30]

Thus did these two ancient comrades, after trampling on the ties of friendship and honor, hope to knit themselves to each other by the holy bands of religion. That it should have been necessary to resort to so extraordinary a measure might have furnished them with the best proof of its inefficacy.

Not long after this accommodation of their differences, the marshal raised his standard for Chili; and numbers, won by his popular manners, and by his liberal largesses, — liberal to prodigality, — eagerly joined in the enterprise, which they fondly trusted would lead even to greater riches than they had found in Peru. Two Indians, Paullo Topa, a brother of the Inca Manco, and Villac Umu, the high-priest of the nation, were sent in advance, with three Spaniards, to prepare the way for the little army. A detachment of a hundred and fifty men, under an officer named Saavedra, next followed. Almagro remained behind to collect further recruits; but before his levies were completed, he began his march, feeling himself insecure, with his diminished strength, in the neighbourhood of Pizarro![31] The remainder of his forces, when mustered, were to follow him.

Thus relieved of the presence of his rival, the governor returned without further delay to the coast, to resume his labors in the settlement of the country. Besides the principal city of "The Kings," he established others along the Pacific, destined to become hereafter the flourishing marts of commerce. The most important of these, in honor of his birthplace, he named Truxillo, planting it on a site already indicated by Almagro.[32] He made also numerous *repartimientos* both of lands and Indians among his followers, in the usual manner of the Spanish Conquerors;[33] — though here the ignorance of the real resources of the country led to very different results from what he had intended, as the territory smallest in extent, not unfrequently, from the hidden treasures in its bosom, turned out greatest in value.[34]

But nothing claimed so much of Pizarro's care as the rising metropolis of Lima; and, so eagerly did he press forward the work, and so well was he seconded by the multitude of laborers at his command, that he had the satisfaction to see his young capital, with its stately edifices and its pomp of gardens, rapidly advancing towards completion. It is pleasing to contemplate the softer features in the character of the rude soldier, as he was thus occupied with healing up the ravages of war, and laying broad the foundations of an empire more civilized than that which he had overthrown. This peaceful occupation formed a contrast to the life of incessant turmoil in which he had been hitherto engaged. It seemed, too, better suited to his own advancing age, which naturally invited to repose. And, if we may trust his chroniclers, there was no part of his career in which he took greater satisfaction. It is certain there is no part which has been viewed with greater satisfaction by posterity; and, amidst the woe and desolation which Pizarro and his followers brought on the devoted land of the Incas, Lima, the beautiful City of the Kings, still survives as the most glorious work of his creation, the fairest gem on the shores of the Pacific.

CHAPTER X

ESCAPE OF THE INCA. — RETURN OF HERNANDO
PIZARRO. — RISING OF THE PERUVIANS. —
SIEGE AND BURNING OF CUZCO. — DISTRESSES
OF THE SPANIARDS. — STORMING OF THE
FORTRESS. — PIZARRO'S DISMAY. — THE
INCA RAISES THE SIEGE

1535-1536.

WHILE the absence of his rival Almagro relieved Pizarro from all immediate disquietude from that quarter, his authority was menaced in another, where he had least expected it. This was from the native population of the country. Hitherto the Peruvians had shown only a tame and submissive temper, that inspired their conquerors with too much contempt to leave room for apprehension. They had passively acquiesced in the usurpation of the invaders; had seen one monarch butchered, another placed on the vacant throne, their temples despoiled of their treasures, their capital and country appropriated and parcelled out among the Spaniards; but, with the exception of an occasional skirmish in the mountain passes, not a blow had been struck in defence of their rights. Yet this was the warlike nation which had spread its conquests over so large a part of the continent!

In his career, Pizarro, though he scrupled at nothing to effect his object, had not usually countenanced such superfluous acts of cruelty as had too often stained the arms of his countrymen in other parts of the continent, and which, in the course of a few years, had exterminated nearly a whole population in Hispaniola. He had struck one astounding blow, by the seizure of Atahuallpa; and he seemed willing to rely on this to strike terror into the natives. He even affected some respect for the institutions of the country, and had replaced the monarch he had murdered by another of the legitimate line. Yet this was but a pretext. The kingdom had experienced a revolution of the most decisive kind. Its ancient institutions were subverted. Its heaven-descended aristocracy was levelled almost to the condition of the peasant. The people became the serfs of the Conquerors. Their dwellings in the capital—at least, after the arrival of Alvarado's officers—were seized and appropriated. The temples were turned into stables; the royal residences into barracks for the troops. The sanctity of the religious houses was violated. Thousands of matrons and maidens, who, however erroneous their faith, lived in chaste seclusion in the conventual establishments, were now turned abroad, and became the prey of a licentious soldiery.[1] A favorite wife of the young Inca was debauched by the Castilian officers. The Inca, himself treated with contemptuous indifference, found that he was a poor dependant, if not a tool, in the hands of his conquerors.[2]

Yet the Inca Manco was a man of a lofty spirit and a courageous heart; such a one as might have challenged comparison with the bravest of his ancestors in the prouder days of the empire. Stung to the quick by the humiliations to which he was exposed, he repeatedly urged Pizarro to restore him to the real exercise of power, as well as to the show of it. But Pizarro evaded a request so incompatible with his own ambitious schemes, or, indeed, with the policy of Spain, and the young Inca and his nobles were left to brood over their injuries in secret, and await patiently the hour of vengeance.

The dissensions among the Spaniards themselves seemed to afford a favorable opportunity for this. The Peruvian chiefs held many conferences together on the subject, and the high-priest Villac Umu urged the necessity of a rising so soon as Almagro had withdrawn his forces from the city. It would then be comparatively easy, by assaulting the invaders on their several posts, scattered as they were over the country, to overpower them by superior numbers, and shake off their detested yoke before the arrival of fresh reinforcements should rivet it for ever on the necks of his countrymen. A plan for a general rising was formed, and it was in conformity to it that the priest was selected by the Inca to bear Almagro company on the march, that he might secure the coöperation of the natives in the country, and then secretly return —as in fact he did—to take a part in the insurrection.

To carry their plans into effect, it became necessary that the Inca Manco should leave the city and present himself among his people. He found no difficulty in withdrawing from Cuzco, where his presence was scarcely heeded by the Spaniards, as his nominal power was held in little deference by the haughty and confident Conquerors. But in the capital there was a body of Indian allies more jealous of his movements. These were from the tribe of the Cañares, a warlike race of the north, too recently reduced by the Incas to have much sympathy with them or their institutions. There were about a thousand of this people in the place, and, as they had conceived some suspicion of the Inca's purposes, they kept an eye on his movements, and speedily reported his absence to Juan Pizarro.

That cavalier, at the head of a small body of horse, instantly marched in pursuit of the fugitive, whom he was so fortunate as to discover in a thicket of reeds, in which he sought to conceal himself, at no great distance from the city. Manco was arrested, brought back a prisoner to Cuzco, and placed under a strong guard in the fortress. The conspiracy seemed now at an end; and nothing was left to the unfortunate Peruvians but to bewail their ruined hopes, and to give utterance to their disappointment in doleful ballads, which rehearsed the captivity of their Inca, and the downfall of his royal house.[3]

While these things were in progress, Hernando Pizarro returned to Ciudad de los Reyes, bearing with him the royal commission for the extension of his brother's powers, as well as of those conceded to Almagro. The envoy also brought the royal patent conferring on Francisco Pizarro the title of *Marques de los Atavillos,*—a province in Peru. Thus was the fortunate adventurer placed in the ranks of the proud aristocracy of Castile, few of whose members could boast —if they had the courage to boast—their elevation from so humble an origin, as still fewer could justify it by a show of greater services to the Crown.

The new marquess resolved not to forward the commission, at present, to the marshal, whom he designed to engage still deeper in the conquest of Chili, that his attention might be diverted from Cuzco, which, however, his brother assured him, now fell, without doubt, within the newly extended limits of his own territory. To make more sure of this important prize, he despatched Hernando to take the government of the capital into his own hands, as the one of his brothers on whose talents and practical experience he placed greatest reliance.

Hernando, notwithstanding his arrogant bearing towards his countrymen, had ever manifested a more than ordinary sympathy with the Indians. He had been the friend of Atahuallpa; to such a degree, indeed, that it was said, if he had been in the camp at the time, the fate of that unhappy monarch would probably have been averted. He now showed a similar friendly disposition towards his successor, Manco. He caused the Peruvian prince to be liberated from confinement, and gradually admitted him into some intimacy with himself. The crafty Indian availed himself of his freedom to mature his plans for the rising, but with so much caution, that no suspicion of them crossed the mind of Hernando. Secrecy and silence are characteristic of the American, almost as invariably as the peculiar color of his skin. Manco disclosed to his conqueror the existence of several heaps of treasure, and the places where they had been secreted; and, when he had thus won his confidence, he stimulated his cupidity still further by an account of a statue of pure gold of his father Huayna Capac, which the wily Peruvian requested leave to bring from a secret cave in which it was deposited, among the neighbouring Andes. Hernando, blinded by his avarice, consented to the Inca's departure.

He sent with him two Spanish soldiers, less as a guard than to aid him in the object of his expedition. A week elapsed, and yet he did not return, nor were there any tidings to be gathered of him. Hernando now saw his error, especially as his own suspicions were confirmed by the unfavorable reports of his Indian allies. Without further delay, he despatched his brother Juan, at the head of sixty horse, in quest of the Peruvian prince, with orders to bring him back once more a prisoner to his capital.

That cavalier, with his well-armed troops, soon traversed the environs of Cuzco without discovering any vestige of the fugitive. The country was remarkably silent and deserted, until, as he approached the mountain range that hems in the valley of Yucay, about six leagues from the city, he was met by the two Spaniards who had accompanied Manco. They informed Pizarro that it was only at the point of the sword he could recover the Inca, for the country was all in arms, and the Peruvian chief at its head was preparing to march on the capital. Yet he had offered no violence to their persons, but had allowed them to return in safety.

The Spanish captain found this story fully confirmed when he arrived at the river Yucay, on the opposite bank of which were drawn up the Indian battalions to the number of many thousand men, who, with their young monarch at their head, prepared to dispute his passage. It seemed that they could not feel their position sufficiently strong, without placing a river, as usual, between them and their enemy. The Spaniards were not checked by this obstacle. The stream, though deep, was narrow; and plunging in, they swam their horses boldly across, amidst a tempest of stones and arrows that rattled thick as hail on their harness, finding occasionally some crevice or vulnerable point,—although the wounds thus received only goaded them to more desperate efforts. The barbarians fell back as the cavaliers made good their landing; but, without allowing the latter time to form, they returned with a spirit which they had hitherto seldom displayed, and enveloped them on all sides with their greatly superior numbers. The fight now raged fiercely. Many of the Indians were armed with lances headed with copper tempered almost to the hardness of steel, and with huge maces and battle-axes of the same metal. Their defensive armour, also, was in many respects excellent, consisting of stout doublets of quilted cotton, shields covered with skins, and casques richly ornamented with gold and jewels, or sometimes made like those of the Mexicans, in the fantastic shape of the heads of wild animals, garnished with rows of teeth that grinned horribly above the visage of the warrior.[4] The whole army wore an aspect of martial ferocity, under the control of much higher military discipline than the Spaniards had before seen in the country.

The little band of cavaliers, shaken by the fury of the Indian assault, were thrown at first into some disorder, but at length, cheering on one another with the old war-cry of "St. Jago," they formed in solid column, and charged boldly into the thick of the enemy. The latter, incapable of withstanding the shock, gave way, or were trampled down under the feet of the horses, or pierced by the lances of the riders. Yet their flight was conducted with some order; and they turned at intervals, to let off a volley of arrows, or to deal furious blows with their pole-axes and war-clubs. They fought as if conscious that they were under the eye of their Inca.

It was evening before they had entirely quitted the level ground, and withdrawn into the fastnesses of the lofty range of hills which belt round the beautiful valley of Yucay. Juan Pizarro and his little troop encamped on the level at the base of the mountains. He had gained a victory, as usual, over immense odds; but he had never seen a field so well disputed, and his victory had cost him the lives of several men and horses, while many more had been wounded, and were nearly disabled by the fatigues of the day. But he trusted the severe lesson he had inflicted on the enemy, whose slaughter was great, would crush the spirit of resistance. He was deceived.

The following morning, great was his dismay to see the passes of the mountains filled up with dark lines of warriors, stretching as far as the eye could penetrate into the depths of the sierra, while dense masses of the enemy were gathered like thunder-clouds along the slopes and summits, as if ready to pour down in fury on the assailants. The ground, altogether unfavorable to the manœuvres of cavalry, gave every advantage to the Peruvians, who rolled down huge rocks from their elevated position, and sent off incessant showers of missiles on the heads of the Spaniards. Juan Pizarro did not care to entangle himself further in the perilous defile; and, though he repeatedly charged the enemy, and drove them back with considerable loss, the second night found him with men and horses wearied and wounded, and as little advanced in the object of his expedition as on the preceding evening. From this embarrassing position, after a day or two more spent in unprofitable hostilities, he was surprised by a summons from his brother to return with all expedition to Cuzco, which was now besieged by the enemy!

Without delay, he began his retreat, recrossed the valley, the recent scene of slaughter, swam the river Yucay, and, by a rapid countermarch, closely followed by the victorious enemy, who celebrated their success with songs or rather yells of triumph, he arrived before nightfall in sight of the capital.

But very different was the sight which there met his eye from what he had beheld on leaving it a few days before. The extensive environs, as far as the eye could reach, were occupied by a mighty host, which an indefinite computation swelled to the number of two hundred thousand warriors.[5] The dusky lines of the Indian battalions stretched out to the very verge of the mountains; while, all around, the eye saw only the crests and waving banners of chieftains, mingled with rich panoplies of featherwork, which reminded some few who had served under Cortés of the military costume of the Aztecs. Above all rose a forest of long lances and battle-axes edged with copper, which, tossed to and fro in wild confusion, glittered in the rays of the setting sun, like light playing on the surface of a dark and troubled ocean. It was the first time that the Spaniards had beheld an Indian army in all its terrors; such an army as the Incas led to battle, when the banner of the Sun was borne triumphant over the land.

Yet the bold hearts of the cavaliers, if for a moment dismayed by the sight, soon gathered courage as they closed up their files, and prepared to open a way for themselves through the beleaguering host. But the enemy seemed to shun the encounter; and, falling back at their approach, left a free entrance into the capital. The Peruvians were, probably, not unwilling to draw as many victims as they could into the toils, conscious that, the greater the number, the sooner they would become sensible to the approaches of famine.[6]

Hernando Pizarro greeted his brother with no little satisfaction; for he brought an important addition to his force, which now, when all were united, did not exceed two hundred, horse and foot,[7] besides a thousand Indian auxiliaries; an insignificant number, in comparison with the countless multitudes that were swarming at the gates. That night was passed by the Spaniards with feelings of the deepest anxiety, as they looked forward with natural apprehension to the morrow. It was early in February, 1536. when the siege of Cuzco commenced; a siege memorable as calling out the most heroic displays of Indian and European valor, and bringing the two races in deadlier conflict with each other than had yet occurred in the conquest of Peru.

The numbers of the enemy seemed no less formidable during the night than by the light of day; far and wide their watch-fires were to be seen gleaming over valley and hill-top, as thickly scattered, says an eyewitness, as "the stars of heaven in a cloudless summer night."[8] Before these fires had become pale in the light of the morning, the Spaniards were roused by the hideous clamor of conch, trumpet, and atabal, mingled with the fierce war-cries of the barbarians, as they let off volleys of missiles of every description, most of which fell harmless within the city. But others did more serious execution. These were burning arrows, and red-hot stones wrapped in cotton that had been steeped in some bituminous substance, which, scattering long trains of light through the air, fell on the roofs of the buildings, and speedily set them on fire.[9] These roofs, even of the better sort of edifices, were uniformly of thatch, and were ignited as easily as tinder. In a moment the flames burst forth from the most opposite quarters of the city. They quickly communicated to the wood-work in the interior of the buildings, and broad sheets of flame mingled with smoke rose up towards the heavens, throwing a fearful glare over every object. The rarefied atmosphere heightened the previous impetuosity of the wind, which, fanning the rising flames, they rapidly spread from dwelling to dwelling, till the whole fiery mass, swayed to and fro by the tempest, surged and roared with the fury of a volcano. The heat became intense, and clouds of smoke, gathering like a dark pall over the city, produced a sense of suffocation and almost blindness in those quarters where it was driven by the winds.[10]

The Spaniards were encamped in the great square, partly under awnings, and partly in the hall of the Inca Viracocha, on the ground since covered by the cathedral. Three times in the course of that dreadful day, the roof of the building was on fire; but, although no efforts were made to extinguish it, the flames went out without doing much injury. This miracle was ascribed to the Blessed Virgin, who was distinctly seen by several of the Christian combatants, hovering over the spot on which was to be raised the temple dedicated to her worship.[11]

Fortunately, the open space around Hernando's little company separated them from the immediate scene of conflagration. It afforded a means of preservation similar to that employed by the American hunter, who endeavours to surround himself with a belt of wasted land, when overtaken by a conflagration in the prairies. All day the fire continued to rage, and at night the effect was even more appalling; for by the lurid flames the unfortunate Spaniards could read the consternation depicted in each others' ghastly countenances, while in the suburbs, along the slopes of the surrounding hills, might be seen the throng of besiegers, gazing with fiendish exultation on the work of destruction. High above the town to the north, rose the gray fortress, which now showed ruddy in the glare, looking grimly down on the ruins of the fair city which it was no longer able to protect; and in the distance were to be discerned the shadowy forms of the Andes, soaring up in solitary grandeur into the regions of eternal silence, far beyond the wild tumult that raged so fearfully at their base.

Such was the extent of the city, that it was several days before the fury of the fire was spent. Tower and temple, hut, palace, and hall, went down before it. Fortunately, among the buildings that escaped were the magnificent House of the Sun and the neighbouring Convent of the Virgins. Their insulated position afforded the means, of which the Indians from motives of piety were willing to avail themselves, for their preservation.[12] Full one half of the capital, so long the chosen seat of Western civilization, the pride of the Incas, and the bright abode of their tutelar deity, was laid in ashes by the hands of his own children. It was some consolation for them to reflect, that it burned over the heads of its conquerors, — their trophy and their tomb!

During the long period of the conflagration, the Spaniards made no attempt to extinguish the flames. Such an attempt would have availed nothing. Yet they did not tamely submit to the assaults of the enemy, and they sallied forth from time to time to repel them. But the fallen timbers and scattered rubbish of the houses presented serious impediments to the movements of horse; and, when these were partially cleared away by the efforts of the infantry and the Indian allies, the Peruvians planted stakes and threw barricades across the path, which proved equally embarrassing.[13] To remove them was a work of time and no little danger, as the pioneers were exposed to the whole brunt of the enemy's archery, and the aim of the Peruvian was sure. When at length the obstacles were cleared away, and a free course was opened to the cavalry, they rushed with irresistible impetuosity on their foes, who, falling back in confusion, were cut to pieces by the riders, or pierced through with their lances. The slaughter on these occasions was great; but the Indians, nothing disheartened, usually returned with renewed courage to the attack, and, while fresh reinforcements met the Spaniards in front, others, lying in ambush among the ruins, threw the troops into disorder by assailing them on the flanks. The Peruvians were expert both with bow and sling; and these encounters, notwithstanding the superiority of their arms, cost the Spaniards more lives than in their crippled condition they could afford to spare, — a loss poorly compensated by that of tenfold the number of the enemy. One weapon, peculiar to South American warfare, was used with some effect by the Peruvians. This was the *lasso*, — a long rope with a noose at the end, which they adroitly threw over the rider, or entangled with it the legs of his horse, so as to bring them both to the ground. More than one Spaniard fell into the hands of the enemy by this expedient.[14]

236

Thus harassed, sleeping on their arms, with their horses picketed by their side, ready for action at any and every hour, the Spaniards had no rest by night or by day. To add to their troubles, the fortress which overlooked the city, and completely commanded the great square in which they were quartered, had been so feebly garrisoned in their false sense of security, that, on the approach of the Peruvians, it had been abandoned without a blow in its defence. It was now occupied by a strong body of the enemy, who, from his elevated position, sent down showers of missiles, from time to time, which added greatly to the annoyance of the besieged. Bitterly did their captain now repent the improvident security which had led him to neglect a post so important.

Their distresses were still further aggravated by the rumors, which continually reached their ears, of the state of the country. The rising, it was said, was general throughout the land; the Spaniards living on their insulated plantations had all been massacred; Lima and Truxillo and the principal cities were besieged, and must soon fall into the enemy's hands; the Peruvians were in possession of the passes, and all communications were cut off, so that no relief was to be expected from their countrymen on the coast. Such were the dismal stories, (which, however exaggerated, had too much foundation in fact,) that now found their way into the city from the camp of the besiegers. And to give greater credit to the rumors, eight or ten human heads were rolled into the *plaza,* in whose blood-stained visages the Spaniards recognized with horror the lineaments of their companions, who they knew had been dwelling in solitude on their estates![15]

Overcome by these horrors, many were for abandoning the place at once, as no longer tenable, and for opening a passage for themselves to the coast with their own good swords. There was a daring in the enterprise which had a charm for the adventurous spirit of the Castilian. Better, they said, to perish in a manly struggle for life, than to die thus ignominiously, pent up like foxes in their holes, to be suffocated by the hunter!

But the Pizarros, De Rojas, and some other of the principal cavaliers, refused to acquiesce in a measure which, they said, must cover them with dishonor.[16] Cuzco had been the great prize for which they had contended; it was the ancient seat of empire, and, though now in ashes, would again rise from its ruins as glorious as before. All eyes would be turned on them, as its defenders, and their failure, by giving confidence to the enemy, might decide the fate of their countrymen throughout the land. They were placed in that post as the post of honor, and better would it be to die there than to desert it.

There seemed, indeed, no alternative; for every avenue to escape was cut off by an enemy who had perfect knowledge of the country, and possession of all its passes. But this state of things could not last long. The Indian could not, in the long run, contend with the white man. The spirit of insurrection would die out of itself. Their great army would melt away, unaccustomed as the natives were to the privations incident to a protracted campaign. Reinforcements would be daily coming in from the colonies; and, if the

Castilians would be but true to themselves for a season, they would be relieved by their own countrymen, who would never suffer them to die like outcasts among the mountains.

The cheering words and courageous bearing of the cavaliers went to the hearts of their followers; for the soul of the Spaniard readily responded to the call of honor, if not of humanity. All now agreed to stand by their leader to the last. But, if they would remain longer in their present position, it was absolutely necessary to dislodge the enemy from the fortress; and, before venturing on this dangerous service, Hernando Pizarro resolved to strike such a blow as should intimidate the besiegers from further attempt to molest his present quarters.

He communicated his plan of attack to his officers; and, forming his little troop into three divisions, he placed them under command of his brother Gonzalo, of Gabriel de Rojas, an officer in whom he reposed great confidence, and Hernan Ponce de Leon. The Indian pioneers were sent forward to clear away the rubbish, and the several divisions moved simultaneously up the principal avenues towards the camp of the besiegers. Such stragglers as they met in their way were easily cut to pieces, and the three bodies, bursting impetuously on the disordered lines of the Peruvians, took them completely by surprise. For some moments there was little resistance, and the slaughter was terrible. But the Indians gradually rallied, and, coming into something like order, returned to the fight with the courage of men who had long been familiar with danger. They fought hand to hand with their copper-headed war-clubs and pole-axes, while a storm of darts, stones, and arrows rained on the well-defended bodies of the Christians.

The barbarians showed more discipline than was to have been expected; for which, it is said, they were indebted to some Spanish prisoners, from several of whom, the Inca, having generously spared their lives, took occasional lessons in the art of war. The Peruvians had, also, learned to manage with some degree of skill the weapons of their conquerors; and they were seen armed with bucklers, helmets, and swords of European workmanship, and even, in a few instances, mounted on the horses which they had taken from the white men.[17] The young Inca, in particular, accoutred in the European fashion, rode a war-horse which he managed with considerable address, and, with a long lance in his hand, led on his followers to the attack.—This readiness to adopt the superior arms and tactics of the Conquerors intimates a higher civilization than that which belonged to the Aztec, who, in his long collision with the Spaniards, was never so far divested of his terrors for the horse as to venture to mount him.

But a few days or weeks of training were not enough to give familiarity with weapons, still less with tactics, so unlike those to which the Peruvians had been hitherto accustomed. The fight, on the present occasion, though hotly contested, was not of long duration. After a gallant struggle, in which the natives threw themselves fearlessly on the horsemen, endeavouring to tear them from their saddles, they were obliged to give way before the repeated shock of their charges. Many were trampled under foot, others cut down by the Spanish broadswords, while the arquebusiers, supporting the cavalry, kept up a running fire that did terrible execution on the flanks and rear of the fugitives. At length, sated with slaughter, and trusting that the chastisement he had inflicted on the enemy would secure him from further annoyance for the present, the Castilian general drew back his forces to their quarters in the capital.[18]

His next step was the recovery of the citadel. It was an enterprise of danger. The fortress, which overlooked the northern section of the city, stood high on a rocky eminence, so steep as to be inaccessible on this quarter, where it was defended only by a single wall. Towards the open country, it was more easy of approach; but there it was protected by two semicircular walls, each about twelve hundred feet in length, and of great thickness. They were built of massive stones, or rather rocks, put together without cement, so as to form a kind of rustic-work. The level of the ground between these lines of defence was raised up so as to enable the garrison to discharge its arrows at the assailants, while their own persons were protected by the parapet. Within the interior wall was the fortress, consisting of three strong towers, one of great height, which, with a smaller one, was now held by the enemy, under the command of an Inca noble, a warrior of well-tried valor, prepared to defend it to the last extremity.

The perilous enterprise was intrusted by Hernando Pizarro to his brother Juan, a cavalier in whose bosom burned the adventurous spirit of a knight-errant of romance. As the fortress was to be approached through the mountain passes, it became necessary to divert the enemy's attention to another quarter. A little while before sunset Juan Pizarro left the city with a picked corps of horsemen, and took a direction opposite to that of the fortress, that the besieging army might suppose the object was a foraging expedition. But secretly countermarching in the night, he fortunately found the passes unprotected, and arrived before the outer wall of the fortress, without giving the alarm to the garrison.[19]

The entrance was through a narrow opening in the centre of the rampart; but this was now closed up with heavy stones, that seemed to form one solid work with the rest of the masonry. It was an affair of time to dislodge these huge masses, in such a manner as not to rouse the garrison. The Indian nations, who rarely attacked in the night, were not sufficiently acquainted with the art of war even to provide against surprise by posting sentinels. When the task was accomplished, Juan Pizarro and his gallant troop rode through the gateway, and advanced towards the second parapet.

But their movements had not been conducted so secretly as to escape notice, and they now found the interior court swarming with warriors, who, as the Spaniards drew near, let off clouds of missiles that compelled them to come to a halt. Juan Pizarro, aware that no time was to be lost, ordered one half of his corps to dismount, and, putting himself at their head, prepared to make a breach as before in the fortifications. He had been wounded some days previously in the jaw, so that, finding his helmet caused him pain, he rashly dispensed with it, and trusted for protection to his buckler.[20] Leading on his men, he encouraged them in the work of demolition, in the face of such a storm of stones, javelins, and arrows, as might have made the stoutest heart shrink from encountering it. The good mail of the Spaniards did not always protect them; but others took the place of such as fell, until a breach was made, and the cavalry, pouring in, rode down all who opposed them.

The parapet was now abandoned, and the enemy, hurrying with disorderly flight across the inclosure, took refuge on a kind of platform or terrace, commanded by the principal tower. Here rallying, they shot off fresh volleys of missiles against the Spaniards, while the garrison in the fortress hurled down fragments of rock and timber on their heads. Juan Pizarro, still among the foremost, sprang forward on the terrace, cheering on his men by his voice and example; but at this moment he was struck by a large stone on the head, not then protected by his buckler, and was stretched on the ground. The dauntless chief still continued to animate his followers by his voice, till the terrace was carried, and its miserable defenders were put to the sword. His sufferings were then too much for him, and he was removed to the town below, where, notwithstanding every exertion to save him, he survived the injury but a fortnight, and died in great agony.[21]—To say that he was a Pizarro is enough to attest his claim to valor. But it is his praise, that his valor was tempered by courtesy. His own nature appeared mild by contrast with the haughty temper of his brothers, and his manners made him a favorite of the army. He had served in the conquest of Peru from the first, and no name on the roll of its conquerors is less tarnished by the reproach of cruelty, or stands higher in all the attributes of a true and valiant knight.[22]

Though deeply sensible to his brother's disaster, Hernando Pizarro saw that no time was to be lost in profiting by the advantages already gained. Committing the charge of the town to Gonzalo, he put himself at the head of the assailants, and laid vigorous siege to the fortresses. One surrendered after a short resistance. The other and more formidable of the two still held out under the brave Inca noble who commanded it. He was a man of an athletic frame, and might be seen striding along the battlements, armed with a Spanish buckler and cuirass, and in his hand wielding a formidable mace, garnished with points or knobs of copper. With this terrible weapon he struck down all who attempted to force a passage into the fortress. Some of his own followers who proposed a surrender he is said to have slain with his own hand. Hernando prepared to carry the place by escalade. Ladders were planted against the walls, but no sooner did a Spaniard gain the topmost round, than he was hurled to the ground by the strong arm of the Indian warrior. His activity was equal to his strength; and he seemed to be at every point the moment that his presence was needed.

The Spanish commander was filled with admiration at this display of valor; for he could admire valor even in an enemy. He gave orders that the chief should not be injured, but be taken alive, if possible.[23] This was not easy. At length, numerous ladders having been planted against the tower, the Spaniards sealed it on several quarters at the same time, and, leaping into the place, overpowered the few combatants who still made a show of resistance. But the Inca chieftain was not to be taken; and, finding further resistance ineffectual, he sprang to the edge of the battlements, and, casting away his war-club, wrapped his mantle around him and threw himself headlong from the summit.[24] He died like an ancient Roman. He had struck his last stroke for the freedom of his country, and he scorned to survive her dishonor.—The Castilian commander left a small force in garrison to secure his conquest, and returned in triumph to his quarters.

Week after week rolled away, and no relief came to the beleaguered Spaniards. They had long since begun to feel the approaches of famine. Fortunately, they were provided with water from the streams which flowed through the city. But, though they had well husbanded their resources, their provisions were exhausted, and they had for some time depended on such scanty supplies of grain as they could gather from the ruined magazines and dwellings, mostly consumed by the fire, or from the produce of some success-ful foray.[25] This latter resource was attended with no little difficulty; for every expedition led to a fierce encounter with the enemy, which usually cost the lives of several Spaniards, and inflicted a much heavier injury on the Indian allies. Yet it was at least one good result of such loss, that it left fewer to pro-vide for. But the whole number of the besieged was so small, that any loss greatly increased the difficulties of defence by the remainder.

As months passed away without bringing any tidings of their countrymen, their minds were haunted with still gloomier apprehensions as to their fate. They well knew that the governor would make every effort to rescue them from their desperate condition. That he had not succeeded in this made it probable, that his own situation was no better than theirs, or, perhaps, he and his followers had already fallen victims to the fury of the insurgents. It was a dismal thought, that they alone were left in the land, far from all human succour, to perish mis-erably by the hands of the barbarians among the mountains.

Yet the actual state of things, though gloomy in the extreme, was not quite so desperate as their imaginations had painted it. The insurrection, it is true, had been general throughout the country, at least that portion of it occupied by the Spaniards. It had been so well concerted, that it broke out almost simultane-ously, and the Conquerors, who were living in careless security on their estates, had been massacred to the number of several hundreds. An Indian force had sat down before Xauxa, and a considerable army had occupied the valley of Rimac and laid siege to Lima. But the country around that capital was of an open, level character, very favorable to the action of cavalry. Pizarro no sooner saw himself menaced by the hostile array, than he sent such a force against the Peruvians as speedily put them to flight; and, following up his advantage, he inflicted on them such a severe chastisement, that, although they still continued to hover in the distance and cut off his communications with the interior, they did not care to trust themselves on the other side of the Rimac.

The accounts that the Spanish commander now received of the state of the country filled him with the most serious alarm. He was particularly solicitous for the fate of the garrison at Cuzco, and he made repeated efforts to relieve that capital. Four several detachments, amounting to more than four hundred men in all, half of them cavalry, were sent by him at different times, under some of his bravest officers. But none of them reached their place of destination. The wily natives permitted them to march into the interior of the country, until they were fairly entangled in the passes of the Cordilleras. They then enveloped them with greatly superior numbers, and, occupying the heights, showered down their fatal missiles on the heads of the Spaniards, or crushed them under the weight of fragments of rock which they rolled on them from the mountains. In some instances, the whole detachment was cut off to a man. In others, a few stragglers only survived to return and tell the bloody tale to their countrymen at Lima.[26]

Pizarro was now filled with consternation. He had the most dismal forebodings of the fate of the Spaniards dispersed throughout the country, and even doubted the possibility of maintaining his own foothold in it without assistance from abroad. He despatched a vessel to the neighbouring colony at Truxillo, urging them to abandon the place, with all their effects, and to repair to him at Lima. The measure was, fortunately, not adopted. Many of his men were for availing themselves of the vessels which rode at anchor in the port to make their escape from the country at once, and take refuge in Panamá. Pizarro would not hearken to so dastardly a counsel, which involved the desertion of the brave men in the interior who still looked to him for protection. He cut off the hopes of these timid spirits by despatching all the vessels then in port on a very different mission. He sent letters by them to the governors of Panamá, Nicaragua, Guatemala, and Mexico, representing the gloomy state of his affairs, and invoking their aid. His epistle to Alvarado, then established at Guatemala, is preserved. He conjures him by every sentiment of honor and patriotism to come to his assistance, and this before it was too late. Without assistance, the Spaniards could no longer maintain their footing in Peru, and that great empire would be lost to the Castilian Crown. He finally engages to share with him such conquests as they may make with their united arms.[27]—Such concessions, to the very man whose absence from the country, but a few months before, Pizarro would have been willing to secure at almost any price, are sufficient evidence of the extremity of his distress. The succours thus earnestly solicited arrived in time, not to quell the Indian insurrection, but to aid him in a struggle quite as formidable with his own countrymen.

It was now August. More than five months had elapsed since the commencement of the siege of Cuzco, yet the Peruvian legions still lay encamped around the city. The siege had been protracted much beyond what was usual in Indian warfare, and showed the resolution of the natives to exterminate the white men. But the Peruvians themselves had for some time been straitened by the want of provisions. It was no easy matter to feed so numerous a host;

and the obvious resource of the magazines of grain, so providently prepared by the Incas, did them but little service, since their contents had been most prodigally used, and even dissipated, by the Spaniards, on their first occupation of the country.[28] The season for planting had now arrived, and the Inca well knew, that, if his followers were to neglect it, they would be visited by a scourge even more formidable than their invaders. Disbanding the greater part of his forces, therefore, he ordered them to withdraw to their homes, and, after the labors of the field were over, to return and resume the blockade of the capital. The Inca reserved a considerable force to attend on his own person, with which he retired to Tambo, a strongly fortified place south of the valley of Yucay, the favorite residence of his ancestors. He also posted a large body as a corps of observation in the environs of Cuzco, to watch the movements of the enemy, and to intercept supplies.

The Spaniards beheld with joy the mighty host, which had so long encompassed the city, now melting away. They were not slow in profiting by the circumstance, and Hernando Pizarro took advantage of the temporary absence to send out foraging parties to scour the country, and bring back supplies to his famishing soldiers. In this he was so successful that on one occasion no less than two thousand head of cattle — the Peruvian sheep — were swept away from the Indian plantations and brought safely to Cuzco.[29] This placed the army above all apprehensions on the score of want for the present.

Yet these forays were made at the point of the lance, and many a desperate contest ensued, in which the best blood of the Spanish chivalry was shed. The contests, indeed, were not confined to large bodies of troops, but skirmishes took place between smaller parties, which sometimes took the form of personal combats. Nor were the parties so unequally matched as might have been supposed in these single rencontres; and the Peruvian warrior, with his sling, his bow, and his *lasso,* proved no contemptible antagonist for the mailed horseman, whom he sometimes even ventured to encounter, hand to hand, with his formidable battle-axe. The ground around Cuzco became a battle-field, like the *vega* of Granada, in which Christian and Pagan displayed the characteristics of their peculiar warfare; and many a deed of heroism was performed, which wanted only the song of the minstrel to shed around it a glory like that which rested on the last days of the Moslem of Spain.[30]

But Hernando Pizarro was not content to act wholly on the defensive; and he meditated a bold stroke, by which at once to put an end to the war. This was the capture of the Inca Manco, whom he hoped to surprise in his quarters at Tambo.

For this service he selected about eighty of his best-mounted cavalry, with a small body of foot; and, making a large détour through the less frequented mountain defiles, he arrived before Tambo without alarm to the enemy. He found the place more strongly fortified than he had imagined. The palace, or rather fortress, of the Incas stood on a lofty eminence, the steep sides of which, on the quarter where the Spaniards approached, were cut into terraces, defended by strong walls of stone and sunburnt brick.[31] The place was impregnable on this side. On the opposite, it looked towards the Yucay, and the ground descended by a gradual declivity towards the plain through which rolled its deep but narrow current.[32] This was the quarter on which to make the assault.

Crossing the stream without much difficulty, the Spanish commander advanced up the smooth *glacis* with as little noise as possible. The morning light had hardly broken on the mountains; and Pizarro, as he drew near the outer defences, which, as in the fortress of Cuzco, consisted of a stone parapet of great strength drawn round the inclosure, moved quickly forward, confident that the garrison were still buried in sleep. But thousands of eyes were upon him; and as the Spaniards came within bow-shot, a multitude of dark forms suddenly rose above the rampart, while the Inca, with his lance in hand, was seen on horseback in the inclosure, directing the operations of his troops.[33] At the same moment the air was darkened with innumerable missiles, stones, javelins, and arrows, which fell like a hurricane on the troops, and the mountains rang to the wild war-whoop of the enemy. The Spaniards, taken by surprise, and many of them sorely wounded, were staggered; and, though they quickly rallied, and made two attempts to renew the assault, they were at length obliged to fall back, unable to endure the violence of the storm. To add to their confusion, the lower level in their rear was flooded by the waters, which the natives, by opening the sluices, had diverted from the bed of the river, so that their position was no longer tenable.[34] A council of war was then held, and it was decided to abandon the attack as desperate, and to retreat in as good order as possible.

The day had been consumed in these ineffectual operations; and Hernando, under cover of the friendly darkness, sent forward his infantry and baggage, taking command of the centre himself, and trusting the rear to his brother Gonzalo. The river was happily recrossed without accident, although the enemy, now confident in their strength, rushed out of their defences, and followed up the retreating Spaniards, whom they annoyed with repeated discharges of arrows. More than once they pressed so closely on the fugitives, that Gonzalo and his chivalry were compelled to turn and make one of those desperate charges that effectually punished their audacity, and stayed the tide of pursuit. Yet the victorious foe still hung on the rear of the discomfited cavaliers, till they had emerged from the mountain passes, and come within sight of the blackened walls of the capital. It was the last triumph of the Inca.[35]

BOOK IV

CIVIL WARS OF THE CONQUERORS

CHAPTER I

ALMAGRO'S MARCH TO CHILI. — SUFFERING OF THE TROOPS. — HE RETURNS AND SEIZES CUZCO. — ACTION OF ABANCAY. — GASPAR DE ESPINOSA. — ALMAGRO LEAVES CUZCO. — NEGOTIATIONS WITH PIZARRO

1535-1537.

WHILE the events recorded in the preceding chapter were passing, the Marshal Almagro was engaged in his memorable expedition to Chili. He had set out, as we have seen, with only part of his forces, leaving his lieutenant to follow him with the remainder. During the first part of the way, he profited by the great military road of the Incas, which stretched across the table-land far towards the south. But as he drew near to Chili, the Spanish commander became entangled in the defiles of the mountains, where no vestige of a road was to be discerned. Here his progress was impeded by all the obstacles which belong to the wild scenery of the Cordilleras; deep and ragged ravines, round whose sides a slender sheep-path wound up to a dizzy height over the precipices below; rivers rushing in fury down the slopes of the mountains, and throwing themselves in stupendous cataracts into the yawning abyss; dark forests of pine that seemed to have no end, and then again long reaches of desolate table-land, without so much as a bush or shrub to shelter the shivering traveller from the blast that swept down from the frozen summits of the sierra.

The cold was so intense, that many lost the nails of their fingers, their fingers themselves, and sometimes their limbs. Others were blinded by the dazzling waste of snow, reflecting the rays of a sun made intolerably brilliant in the thin atmosphere of these elevated regions. Hunger came, as usual, in the train of woes; for in these dismal solitudes no vegetation that would suffice for the food of man was visible, and no living thing, except only the great bird of the Andes, hovering over their heads in expectation of his banquet. This was too frequently afforded by the number of wretched Indians, who, unable, from the scantiness of their clothing, to encounter the severity of the climate, perished by the way. Such was the pressure of hunger, that the miserable survivors fed on the dead bodies of their countrymen, and the Spaniards forced a similar sustenance from the carcasses of their horses, literally frozen to death in the mountain passes.[1] — Such were the terrible penalties which Nature imposed on those who rashly intruded on these her solitary and most savage haunts.

Yet their own sufferings do not seem to have touched the hearts of the Spaniards with any feeling of compassion for the weaker natives. Their path was everywhere marked by burnt and desolated hamlets, the inhabitants of which were compelled to do them service as beasts of burden. They were chained together in gangs of ten or twelve, and no infirmity or feebleness of body excused the unfortunate captive from his full share of the common toil, till he sometimes dropped dead, in his very chains, from mere exhaustion![2] Alvarado's company are accused of having been more cruel than Pizarro's; and many of Almagro's men, it may be remembered, were recruited from that source. The commander looked with displeasure, it is said, on these enormities, and did what he could to repress them. Yet he did not set a good example in his own conduct, if it be true that he caused no less than thirty Indian chiefs to be burnt alive, for the massacre of three of his followers![3] The heart sickens at the recital of such atrocities perpetrated on an unoffending people, or, at least, guilty of no other crime than that of defending their own soil too well.

There is something in the possession of superior strength most dangerous, in a moral view, to its possessor. Brought in contact with semi-civilized man, the European, with his endowments and effective force so immeasurably superior, holds him as little higher than the brute, and as born equally for his service. He feels that he has a natural right, as it were, to his obedience, and that this obedience is to be measured, not by the powers of the barbarian, but by the will of his conqueror. Resistance becomes a crime to be washed out only in the blood of the victim. The tale of such atrocities is not confined to the Spaniard. Wherever the civilized man and the savage have come in contact, in the East or in the West, the story has been too often written in blood.

From the wild chaos of mountain scenery the Spaniards emerged on the green vale of Coquimbo, about the thirtieth degree of south latitude. Here they halted to refresh themselves in its abundant plains, after their unexampled sufferings and fatigues. Meanwhile Almagro despatched an officer with a strong party in advance, to ascertain the character of the country towards the south. Not long after, he was cheered by the arrival of the remainder of his forces under his lieutenant Rodrigo de Orgoñez. This was a remarkable person, and intimately connected with the subsequent fortunes of Almagro.

He was a native of Oropesa, had been trained in the Italian wars, and held the rank of ensign in the army of the Constable of Bourbon at the famous sack of Rome. It was a good school in which to learn his iron trade, and to steel the heart against any too ready sensibility to human suffering.

Orgoñez was an excellent soldier; true to his commander, prompt, fearless, and unflinching in the execution of his orders. His services attracted the notice of the Crown, and, shortly after this period, he was raised to the rank of Marshal of New Toledo. Yet it may be doubted whether his character did not qualify him for an executive and subordinate station rather than for one of higher responsibility.

Almagro received also the royal warrant, conferring on him his new powers and territorial jurisdiction. The instrument had been detained by the Pizarros to the very last moment. His troops, long since disgusted with their toilsome and unprofitable march, were now clamorous to return. Cuzco, they said, undoubtedly fell within the limits of his government, and it was better to take possession of its comfortable quarters than to wander like outcasts in this dreary wilderness. They reminded their commander that thus only could he provide for the interests of his son Diego. This was an illegitimate son of Almagro, on whom his father doated with extravagant fondness, justified more than usual by the promising character of the youth.

After an absence of about two months, the officer sent on the exploring expedition returned, bringing unpromising accounts of the southern regions of Chili. The only land of promise for the Castilian was one that teemed with gold.[4] He had penetrated to the distance of a hundred leagues, to the limits, probably, of the conquests of the Incas on the river Maule.[5] The Spaniards had fortunately stopped short of the land of Arauco, where the blood of their countrymen was soon after to be poured out like water, and which still maintains a proud independence amidst the general humiliation of the Indian races around it.

Almagro now yielded, with little reluctance, to the renewed importunities of the soldiers, and turned his face towards the North. It is unnecessary to follow his march in detail. Disheartened by the difficulty of the mountain passage, he took the road along the coast, which led him across the great desert of Atacama. In crossing this dreary waste, which stretches for nearly a hundred leagues to the northern borders of Chili, with hardly a green spot in its expanse to relieve the fainting traveller, Almagro and his men experienced as great sufferings, though not of the same kind, as those which they had encountered in the passes of the Cordilleras. Indeed, the captain would not easily be found at this day, who would venture to lead his army across this dreary region. But the Spaniard of the sixteenth century had a strength of limb and a buoyancy of spirit which raised him to a contempt of obstacles, almost justifying the boast of the historian, that "he contended indifferently, at the same time, with man, with the elements, and with famine!"[6]

After traversing the terrible desert, Almagro reached the ancient town of Arequipa, about sixty leagues from Cuzco. Here he learned with astonishment the insurrection of the Peruvians, and further, that the young Inca Manco still lay with a formidable force at no great distance from the capital. He had once been on friendly terms with the Peruvian prince, and he now resolved, before proceeding farther, to send an embassy to his camp, and arrange an interview with him in the neighbourhood of Cuzco

Almagro's emissaries were well received by the Inca, who alleged his grounds of complaint against the Pizarros, and named the vale of Yucay as the place where he would confer with the marshal. The Spanish commander accordingly resumed his march, and, taking one half of his force, whose whole number fell somewhat short of five hundred men, he repaired in person to the place of rendezvous; while the remainder of his army established their quarters at Urcos, about six leagues from the capital.[7]

The Spaniards in Cuzco, startled by the appearance of this fresh body of troops in their neighbourhood, doubted, when they learned the quarter whence they came, whether it betided them good or evil. Hernando Pizarro marched out of the city with a small force, and, drawing near to Urcos, heard with no little uneasiness of Almagro's purpose to insist on his pretensions to Cuzco. Though much inferior in strength to his rival, he determined to resist him.

Meanwhile, the Peruvians, who had witnessed the conference between the soldiers of the opposite camps, suspected some secret understanding between the parties, which would compromise the safety of the Inca. They communicated their distrust to Manco, and the latter, adopting the same sentiments, or perhaps, from the first, meditating a surprise of the Spaniards, suddenly fell upon the latter in the valley of Yucay with a body of fifteen thousand men. But the veterans of Chili were too familiar with Indian tactics to be taken by surprise. And though a sharp engagement ensued, which lasted more than an hour, in which Orgoñez had a horse killed under him, the natives were finally driven back with great slaughter, and the Inca was so far crippled by the blow, that he was not likely for the present to give further molestation.[8]

Almagro, now joining the division left at Urcos, saw no further impediment to his operations on Cuzco. He sent, at once, an embassy to the municipality of the place, requiring the recognition of him as its lawful governor, and presenting at the same time a copy of his credentials from the Crown. But the question of jurisdiction was not one easy to be settled, depending, as it did, on a knowledge of the true parallels of latitude, not very likely to be possessed by the rude followers of Pizarro. The royal grant had placed under his jurisdiction all the country extending two hundred and seventy leagues south of the river of Santiago, situated one degree and twenty minutes north of the equator. Two hundred and seventy leagues on the meridian, by our measurement, would fall more than a degree short of Cuzco, and, indeed, would barely include the city of Lima itself. But the Spanish leagues, of only seventeen and a half to a degree,[9] would remove the southern boundary to nearly half a degree beyond the capital of the Incas, which would thus fall within the jurisdiction of Pizarro.[10] Yet the division-line ran so close to the disputed ground, that the true result might reasonably be doubted, where no careful scientific observations had been made to obtain it; and each party was prompt to assert, as they always are in such cases, that its own claim was clear and unquestionable.[11]

Thus summoned by Almagro, the authorities of Cuzco, unwilling to give umbrage to either of the contending chiefs, decided that they must wait until they could take counsel—which they promised to do at once—with certain pilots better instructed than themselves in the position of the Santiago. Meanwhile, a truce was arranged between the parties, each solemnly engaging to abstain from hostile measures, and to remain quiet in their present quarters.

The weather now set in cold and rainy. Almagro's soldiers, greatly discontented with their position, flooded as it was by the waters, were quick to discover that Hernando Pizarro was busily employed in strengthening himself in the city, contrary to agreement. They also learned with dismay, that a large body of men, sent by the governor from Lima, under command of Alonso de Alvarado, was on the march to relieve Cuzco. They exclaimed that they were betrayed, and that the truce had been only an artifice to secure their inactivity until the arrival of the expected succours. In this state of excitement, it was not very difficult to persuade their commander—too ready to surrender his own judgment to the rash advisers around him—to violate the treaty, and take possession of the capital.[12]

Under cover of a dark and stormy night (April 8th, 1537), he entered the place without opposition, made himself master of the principal church, established strong parties of cavalry at the head of the great avenues to prevent surprise, and detached Orgoñez with a body of infantry to force the dwelling of Hernando Pizarro. That captain was lodged with his brother Gonzalo in one of the large halls built by the Incas for public diversions, with immense doors of entrance that opened on the *plaza*. It was garrisoned by about twenty soldiers, who, as the gates were burst open, stood stoutly to the defence of their leader. A smart struggle ensued, in which some lives were lost, till at length Orgoñez, provoked by the obstinate resistance, set fire to the combustible roof of the building. It was speedily in flames, and the burning rafters falling on the heads of the inmates, they forced their reluctant leader to an unconditional surrender. Scarcely had the Spaniards left the building, when the whole roof fell in with a tremendous crash.[13]

Almagro was now master of Cuzco. He ordered the Pizarros, with fifteen or twenty of the principal cavaliers, to be secured and placed in confinement. Except so far as required for securing his authority, he does not seem to have been guilty of acts of violence to the inhabitants,[14] and he installed one of Pizarro's most able officers, Gabriel de Rojas, in the government of the city. The municipality, whose eyes were now open to the validity of Almagro's pretensions, made no further scruple to recognize his title to Cuzco.

The marshal's first step was to send a message to Alonso de Alvarado's camp, advising that officer of his occupation of the city, and requiring his obedience to him, as its legitimate master. Alvarado was lying, with a body of five hundred men, horse and foot, at Xauxa, about thirteen leagues from the capital. He had been detached several months previously for the relief of Cuzco; but had, most unaccountably, and, as it proved, most unfortunately for the Peruvian capital, remained at Xauxa with the alleged motive of protecting that settlement and the surrounding country against the insurgents.[15] He now showed himself loyal to his commander; and, when Almagro's ambassadors reached his camp, he put them in irons, and sent advice of what had been done to the governor at Lima.

Almagro, offended by the detention of his emissaries, prepared at once to march against Alonso de Alvarado, and take more effectual means to bring him to submission. His lieutenant, Orgoñez, strongly urged him before his departure to strike off the heads of the Pizarros, alleging, "that, while they lived, his commander's life would never be safe"; and concluding with the Spanish proverb, "Dead men never bite."[16] But the marshal, though he detested Hernando in his heart, shrunk from so violent a measure; and, independently of other considerations, he had still an attachment for his old associate, Francis Pizarro, and was unwilling to sever the ties between them for ever. Contenting himself, therefore, with placing his prisoners under strong guard in one of the stone buildings belonging to the House of the Sun, he put himself at the head of his forces, and left the capital in quest of Alvarado.

That officer had now taken up a position on the farther side of the *Rio de Abancay,* where he lay, with the strength of his little army, in front of a bridge, by which its rapid waters are traversed, while a strong detachment occupied a spot commanding a ford lower down the river. But in this detachment was a cavalier of much consideration in the army, Pedro de Lerma, who, from some pique against his commander, had entered into treasonable correspondence with the opposite party. By his advice, Almagro, on reaching the border of the river, established himself against the bridge in face of Alvarado, as if prepared to force a passage, thus concentrating his adversary's attention on that point. But, when darkness had set in, he detached a large body under Orgoñez to pass the ford, and operate in concert with Lerma. Orgoñez executed this commission with his usual promptness. The ford was crossed, though the current ran so swiftly, that several of his men were swept away by it, and perished in the waters. Their leader received a severe wound himself in the mouth, as he was gaining the opposite bank, but, nothing daunted, he cheered on his men, and fell with fury on the enemy. He was speedily joined by Lerma, and such of the soldiers as he had gained over, and, unable to distinguish friend from foe, the enemy's confusion was complete.

Meanwhile, Alvarado, roused by the noise of the attack on this quarter, hastened to the support of his officer, when Almagro, seizing the occasion, pushed across the bridge, dispersed the small body left to defend it, and, falling on Alvarado's rear, that general saw himself hemmed in on all sides. The struggle did not last long; and the unfortunate chief, uncertain on whom he could rely, surrendered with all his force, — those only excepted who had already deserted to the enemy. Such was the battle of Abancay, as it was called, from the river on whose banks it was fought, on the twelfth of July, 1537. Never was a victory more complete, or achieved with less cost of life; and Almagro marched back, with an array of prisoners scarcely inferior to his own army in number, in triumph to Cuzco.[17]

While the events related in the preceding pages were passing, Francisco Pizarro had remained at Lima, anxiously awaiting the arrival of the reinforcements which he had requested, to enable him to march to the relief of the beleaguered capital of the Incas. His appeal had not been unanswered. Among the rest was a corps of two hundred and fifty men, led by the Licentiate Gaspar de Espinosa, one of the three original associates, it may be remembered, who engaged in the conquest of Peru. He had now left his own residence at Panamá, and came in person, for the first time, it would seem, to revive the drooping fortunes of his confederates. Pizarro received also a vessel laden with provisions, military stores, and other necessary supplies, besides a rich wardrobe for himself, from Cortés, the Conqueror of Mexico, who generously stretched forth his hand to aid his kinsman in the hour of need.[18]

With a force amounting to four hundred and fifty men, half of them cavalry, the governor quitted Lima, and began his march on the Inca capital. He had not advanced far, when he received tidings of the return of Almagro, the seizure of Cuzco, and the imprisonment of his brothers; and, before he had time to recover from this astounding intelligence, he learned the total defeat and capture of Alvarado. Filled with consternation at these rapid successes of his rival, he now returned in all haste to Lima, which he put in the best posture of defence, to secure it against the hostile movements, not unlikely, as he thought, to be directed against that capital itself. Meanwhile, far from indulging in impotent sallies of resentment, or in complaints of his ancient comrade, he only lamented that Almagro should have resorted to these violent measures for the settlement of their dispute, and this less—if we may take his word for it—from personal considerations than from the prejudice it might do to the interests of the Crown.[19]

But, while busily occupied with warlike preparations, he did not omit to try the effect of negotiation. He sent an embassy to Cuzco, consisting of several persons in whose discretion he placed the greatest confidence, with Espinosa at their head, as the party most interested in an amicable arrangement.

The licentiate, on his arrival, did not find Almagro in as favorable a mood for an accommodation as he could have wished. Elated by his recent successes, he now aspired not only to the possession of Cuzco, but of Lima itself, as falling within the limits of his jurisdiction. It was in vain that Espinosa urged the propriety, by every argument which prudence could suggest, of moderating his demands. His claims upon Cuzco, at least, were not to be shaken, and he declared himself ready to peril his life in maintaining them. The licentiate coolly replied by quoting the pithy Castilian proverb, *El vencido vencido, y el vencidor perdido;* "The vanquished vanquished, and the victor undone."

What influence the temperate arguments of the licentiate might eventually have had on the heated imagination of the soldier is doubtful; but unfortunately for the negotiation, it was abruptly terminated by the death of Espinosa himself, which took place most unexpectedly, though, strange to say, in those times, without the imputation of poison.[20] He was a great loss to the parties in the existing fermentation of their minds; for he had the weight of character which belongs to wise and moderate counsels, and a deeper interest than any other man in recommending them.

The name of Espinosa is memorable in history from his early connection with the expedition to Peru, which, but for the seasonable, though secret, application of his funds, could not then have been compassed. He had long been a resident in the Spanish colonies of Tierra Firme and Panamá, where he had served in various capacities, sometimes as a legal functionary presiding in the courts of justice,[21] and not unfrequently as an efficient leader in the early expeditions of conquest and discovery. In these manifold vocations he acquired high reputation for probity, intelligence, and courage, and his death at the present crisis was undoubtedly the most unfortunate event that could befall the country.

All attempt at negotiation was now abandoned; and Almagro announced his purpose to descend to the sea-coast, where he could plant a colony and establish a port for himself. This would secure him the means, so essential, of communication with the mother-country, and here he would resume negotiations for the settlement of his dispute with Pizarro. Before quitting Cuzco, he sent Orgoñez with a strong force against the Inca, not caring to leave the capital exposed in his absence to further annoyance from that quarter.

But the Inca, discouraged by his late discomfiture, and unable, perhaps, to rally in sufficient strength for resistance, abandoned his strong-hold at Tambo, and retreated across the mountains. He was hotly pursued by Orgoñez over hill and valley, till, deserted by his followers, and with only one of his wives to bear him company, the royal fugitive took shelter in the remote fastnesses of the Andes.[22]

Before leaving the capital, Orgoñez again urged his commander to strike off the heads of the Pizarros, and then march at once upon Lima. By this decisive step he would bring the war to an issue, and for ever secure himself from the insidious machinations of his enemies. But, in the mean time, a new friend had risen up to the captive brothers. This was Diego de Alvarado, brother of that Pedro, who, as mentioned in a preceding chapter, had conducted the unfortunate expedition to Quito. After his brother's departure, Diego had attached himself to the fortunes of Almagro, had accompanied him to Chili, and, as he was a cavalier of birth, and possessed of some truly noble qualities, he had gained deserved ascendency over his commander. Alvarado had frequently visited Hernando Pizarro in his confinement, where, to beguile the tediousness of captivity, he amused himself with gaming,—the passion of the Spaniard. They played deep, and Alvarado lost the enormous sum of eighty thousand gold castellanos. He was prompt in paying the debt, but Hernando Pizarro peremptorily declined to receive the money. By this politic generosity, he secured an important advocate in the council of Almagro. It stood him now in good stead. Alvarado represented to the marshal, that such a measure as that urged by Orgoñez would not only outrage the feelings of his followers, but would ruin his fortunes by the indignation it must excite at court. When Almagro acquiesced in these views, as in truth most grateful to his own nature, Orgoñez, chagrined at his determination, declared that the day would come when he would repent this mistaken lenity. "A Pizarro," he said, "was never known to forget an injury; and that which they had already received from Almagro was too deep for them to forgive." Prophetic words!

On leaving Cuzco, the marshal gave orders that Gonzalo Pizarro and the other prisoners should be detained in strict custody. Hernando he took with him, closely guarded, on his march. Descending rapidly towards the coast, he reached the pleasant vale of Chincha in the latter part of August. Here he occupied himself with laying the foundations of a town bearing his own name, which might serve as a counterpart to the City of the Kings,—thus bidding defiance, as it were, to his rival on his own borders. While occupied in this manner, he received the unwelcome tidings, that Gonzalo Pizarro, Alonso de Alvarado, and the other prisoners, having tampered with their guards, had effected their escape from Cuzco, and he soon after heard of their safe arrival in the camp of Pizarro.

Chafed by this intelligence, the marshal was not soothed by the insinuations of Orgoñez, that it was owing to his ill-advised lenity; and it might have gone hard with Hernando, but that Almagro's attention was diverted by the negotiation which Francisco Pizarro now proposed to resume.

After some correspondence between the parties, it was agreed to submit the arbitration of the dispute to a single individual, Fray Francisco de Bovadilla, a Brother of the Order of Mercy. Though living in Lima, and, as might be supposed, under the influence of Pizarro, he had a reputation for integrity that disposed Almagro to confide the settlement of the question exclusively to him. In this implicit confidence in the friar's impartiality, Orgoñez, of a less sanguine temper than his chief, did not participate.[23]

An interview was arranged between the rival chiefs. It took place at Mala, November 13th, 1537; but very different was the deportment of the two commanders towards each other from that which they had exhibited at their former meetings. Almagro, indeed, doffing his bonnet, advanced in his usual open manner to salute his ancient comrade; but Pizarro, hardly condescending to return the salute, haughtily demanded why the marshal had seized upon his city of Cuzco, and imprisoned his brothers. This led to a recrimination on the part of his associate. The discussion assumed the tone of an angry altercation, till Almagro, taking a hint—or what he conceived to be such—from an attendant, that some treachery was intended, abruptly quitted the apartment, mounted his horse, and galloped back to his quarters at Chincha.[24] The conference closed, as might have been anticipated from the heated temper of their minds when they began it, by widening the breach it was intended to heal. The friar, now left wholly to himself, after some deliberation, gave his award. He decided that a vessel, with a skilful pilot on board, should be sent to determine the exact latitude of the river of Santiago, the northern boundary of Pizarro's territory, by which all the measurements were to be regulated. In the mean time, Cuzco was to be delivered up by Almagro, and Hernando Pizarro to be set at liberty, on condition of his leaving the country in six weeks for Spain. Both parties were to retire within their undisputed territories, and to abandon all further hostilities.[25]

This award, as may be supposed, highly satisfactory to Pizarro, was received by Almagro's men with indignation and scorn. They had been sold, they cried, by their general, broken, as he was, by age and infirmities. Their enemies were to occupy Cuzco and its pleasant places, while they were to be turned over to the barren wilderness of Charcas. Little did they dream that under this poor exterior were hidden the rich treasures of Potosí. They denounced the umpire as a hireling of the governor, and murmurs were heard among the troops, stimulated by Orgoñez, demanding the head of Hernando. Never was that cavalier in greater danger. But his good genius in the form of Alvarado again interposed to protect him. His life in captivity was a succession of reprieves.[26]

Yet his brother, the governor, was not disposed to abandon him to his fate. On the contrary, he was now prepared to make every concession to secure his freedom. Concessions, that politic chief well knew, cost little to those who are not concerned to abide by them. After some preliminary negotiation, another award, more equitable, or, at all events, more to the satisfaction of the discontented party, was given. The principal articles of it were, that, until the arrival of some definitive instructions on the point from Castile, the city of Cuzco, with its territory, should remain in the hands of Almagro; and that Hernando Pizarro should be set at liberty, on the condition, above stipulated, of leaving the country in six weeks.—When the terms of this agreement were communicated to Orgoñez, that officer intimated his opinion of them, by passing his finger across his throat, and exclaiming, "What has my fidelity to my commander cost me!"[27]

Almagro, in order to do greater honor to his prisoner, visited him in person, and announced to him that he was from that moment free. He expressed a hope, at the same time, that "all past differences would be buried in oblivion, and that henceforth they should live only in the recollection of their ancient friendship." Hernando replied, with apparent cordiality, that "he desired nothing better for himself." He then swore in the most solemn manner, and pledged his knightly honor,—the latter, perhaps, a pledge of quite as much weight in his own mind as the former,—that he would faithfully comply with the terms stipulated in the treaty. He was next conducted by the marshal to his quarters, where he partook of a collation in company with the principal officers; several of whom, together with Diego Almagro, the general's son, afterward escorted the cavalier to his brother's camp, which had been transferred to the neighbouring town of Mala. Here the party received a most cordial greeting from the governor, who entertained them with a courtly hospitality, and lavished many attentions, in particular, on the son of his ancient associate. In short, such, on their return, was the account of their reception, that it left no doubt in the mind of Almagro that all was at length amicably settled.[28] — He did not know Pizarro.

CHAPTER II

FIRST CIVIL WAR. — ALMAGRO RETREATS TO CUZCO. — BATTLE OF LAS SALINAS. — CRUELTY OF THE CONQUERORS. — TRIAL AND EXECUTION OF ALMAGRO. — HIS CHARACTER

1537-1538.

SCARCELY had Almagro's officers left the governor's quarters, when the latter, calling his little army together, briefly recapitulated the many wrongs which had been done him by his rival, the seizure of his capital, the imprisonment of his brothers, the assault and defeat of his troops; and he concluded with the declaration, — heartily echoed back by his military audience, — that the time had now come for revenge. All the while that the negotiations were pending, Pizarro had been busily occupied with military preparations. He had mustered a force considerably larger than that of his rival, drawn from various quarters, but most of them familiar with service. He now declared, that, as he was too old to take charge of the campaign himself, he should devolve that duty on his brothers; and he released Hernando from all his engagements to Almagro, as a measure justified by necessity. That cavalier, with graceful pertinacity, intimated his design to abide by the pledges he had given, but, at length, yielded a reluctant assent to the commands of his brother, as to a measure imperatively demanded by his duty to the Crown.[1]

The governor's next step was to advise Almagro that the treaty was at an end. At the same time, he warned him to relinquish his pretensions to Cuzco, and withdraw into his own territory, or the responsibility of the consequences would lie on his own head.

Reposing in his false security, Almagro was now fully awakened to the consciousness of the error he had committed; and the warning voice of his lieutenant may have risen to his recollection. The first part of the prediction was fulfilled. And what should prevent the latter from being so? To add to his distress, he was laboring at this time under a grievous malady, the result of early excesses, which shattered his constitution, and made him incapable alike of mental and bodily exertion.[2]

In this forlorn condition, he confided the management of his affairs to Orgoñez, on whose loyalty and courage he knew he might implicitly rely. The first step was to secure the passes of the Guaitara, a chain of hills that hemmed in the valley of Zangalla, where Almagro was at present established. But, by some miscalculation, the passes were not secured in season; and the active enemy, threading the dangerous defiles, effected a passage across the sierra, where a much inferior force to his own might have taken him at advantage. The fortunes of Almagro were on the wane.

His thoughts were now turned towards Cuzco, and he was anxious to get possession of this capital before the arrival of the enemy. Too feeble to sit on horseback, he was obliged to be carried in a litter; and, when he reached the ancient town of Bilcas, not far from Guamanga, his indisposition was so severe that he was compelled to halt and remain there three weeks before resuming his march.

The governor and his brothers, in the mean time, after traversing the pass of Guaitara, descended into the valley of Ica, where Pizarro remained a considerable while, to get his troops into order and complete his preparations for the campaign. Then, taking leave of the army, he returned to Lima, committing the prosecution of the war, as he had before announced, to his younger and more active brothers. Hernando, soon after quitting Ica, kept along the coast as far as Nasca, proposing to penetrate the country by a circuitous route in order to elude the enemy, who might have greatly embarrassed him in some of the passes of the Cordilleras. But unhappily for him, this plan of operations, which would have given him such manifest advantage, was not adopted by Almagro; and his adversary, without any other impediment than that arising from the natural difficulties of the march, arrived, in the latter part of April, 1538, in the neighbourhood of Cuzco.

But Almagro was already in possession of that capital, which he had reached ten days before. A council of war was held by him respecting the course to be pursued. Some were for making good the defence of the city. Almagro would have tried what could be done by negotiation. But Orgoñez bluntly replied, — "It is too late; you have liberated Hernando Pizarro, and nothing remains but to fight him." The opinion of Orgoñez finally prevailed, to march out and give the enemy battle on the plains. The marshal, still disabled by illness from taking the command, devolved it on his trusty lieutenant, who, mustering his forces, left the city, and took up a position at Las Salinas, less than a league distant from Cuzco. The place received its name from certain pits or vats in the ground, used for the preparation of salt, that was obtained from a natural spring in the neighbourhood. It was an injudicious choice of ground, since its broken character was most unfavorable to the free action of cavalry, in which the strength of Almagro's force consisted. But, although repeatedly urged by the officers to advance into the open country, Orgoñez persisted in his position, as the most favorable for defence, since the front was protected by a marsh, and by a little stream that flowed over the plain. His forces amounted in all to about five hundred, more than half of them horse. His infantry was deficient in fire-arms, the place of which was supplied by the long pike. He had also six small cannon, or falconets, as they were called, which, with his cavalry, formed into two equal divisions, he disposed on the flanks of his infantry. Thus prepared, he calmly awaited the approach of the enemy.

It was not long before the bright arms and banners of the Spaniards under Hernando Pizarro were seen emerging from the mountain passes. The troops came forward in good order, and like men whose steady step showed that they had been spared in the march, and were now fresh for action. They advanced slowly across the plain and halted on the opposite border of the little stream which covered the front of Orgoñez. Here Hernando, as the sun had set, took up his quarters for the night, proposing to defer the engagement fill daylight.[3]

The rumors of the approaching battle had spread far and wide over the country; and the mountains and rocky heights around were thronged with multitudes of natives, eager to feast their eyes on a spectacle, where, whichever side were victorious, the defeat would fall on their enemies.[4] The Castilian women and children, too, with still deeper anxiety, had thronged out from Cuzco to witness the deadly strife in which brethren and kindred were to contend for mastery.[5] The whole number of the combatants was insignificant; though not as compared with those usually engaged in these American wars. It is not, however, the number of the players, but the magnitude of the stake, that gives importance and interest to the game; and in this bloody game, they were to play for the possession of an empire.

The night passed away in silence, unbroken by the vast assembly which covered the surrounding hill-tops. Nor did the soldiers of the hostile camps, although keeping watch within hearing of one another, and with the same blood flowing in their veins, attempt any communication. So deadly was the hate in their bosoms![6]

The sun rose bright, as usual in this beautiful climate, on Saturday, the twenty-sixth day of April, 1538.[7] But long before his beams were on the plain, the trumpet of Hernando Pizarro had called his men to arms. His forces amounted in all to about seven hundred. They were drawn from various quarters, the veterans of Pizarro, the followers of Alonso de Alvarado,—many of whom, since their defeat, had found their way back to Lima,—and the late reinforcement from the isles, most of them seasoned by many a toilsome march in the Indian campaigns, and many a hard-fought field. His mounted troops were inferior to those of Almagro; but this was more than compensated by the strength of his infantry, comprehending a well-trained corps of arquebusiers, sent from St. Domingo, whose weapons were of the improved construction recently introduced from Flanders. They were of a large calibre, and threw double-headed shot, consisting of bullets linked together by an iron chain. It was doubtless a clumsy weapon compared with modern fire-arms, but, in hands accustomed to wield it, proved a destructive instrument.[8]

Hernando Pizarro drew up his men in the same order of battle as that presented by the enemy,—throwing his infantry into the centre, and disposing his horse on the flanks; one corps of which he placed under command of Alonso de Alvarado, and took charge of the other himself. The infantry was headed by his brother Gonzalo, supported by Pedro de Vadivia; the future hero of Arauco, whose disastrous story forms the burden of romance as well as of chronicle.[9]

Mass was said, as if the Spaniards were about to fight what they deemed the good fight of the faith, instead of imbruing their hands in the blood of their countrymen. Hernando Pizarro then made a brief address to his soldiers. He touched on the personal injuries he and his family had received from Almagro; reminded his brother's veterans that Cuzco had been wrested from their possession; called up the glow of shame on the brows of Alvarado's men as he talked of the rout of Abancay, and, pointing out the Inca metropolis that sparkled in the morning sunshine, he told them that there was the prize of the victor. They answered his appeal with acclamations; and the signal being given, Gonzalo Pizarro, heading his battalion of infantry, led it straight across the river. The water was neither broad nor deep, and the soldiers found no difficulty in gaining a landing, as the enemy's horse was prevented by the marshy ground from approaching the borders. But, as they worked their way across the morass, the heavy guns of Orgoñez played with effect on the leading files, and threw them into disorder. Gonzalo and Valdivia threw themselves into the midst of their followers, menacing some, encouraging others, and at length led them gallantly forward to the firm ground. Here the arquebusiers, detaching themselves from the rest of the infantry, gained a small eminence, whence, in their turn, they opened a galling fire on Orgoñez, scattering his array of spearmen, and sorely annoying the cavalry on the flanks.

Meanwhile, Hernando, forming his two squadrons of horse into one column, crossed under cover of this well-sustained fire, and, reaching the firm ground, rode at once against the enemy. Orgoñez, whose infantry was already much crippled, advancing his horse, formed the two squadrons into one body, like his antagonist, and spurred at full gallop against the assailants. The shock was terrible; and it was hailed by the swarms of Indian spectators on the surrounding heights with a fiendish yell of triumph, that rose far above the din of battle, till it was lost in distant echoes among the mountains.[10]

The struggle was desperate. For it was not that of the white man against the defenceless Indian, but of Spaniard against Spaniard; both parties cheering on their comrades with their battlecries of "*El Rey y Almagro,*" or "*El Rey y Pizarro,*"—while they fought with a hate, to which national antipathy was as nothing; a hate strong in proportion to the strength of the ties that had been rent asunder.

In this bloody field well did Orgoñez do his duty, fighting like one to whom battle was the natural element. Singling out a cavalier, whom, from the color of the sobre-vest on his armour, he erroneously supposed to be Hernando

HISTORY OF THE CONQUEST OF PERU

Pizarro, he charged him in full career, and overthrew him with his lance. Another he ran through in like manner, and a third he struck down with his sword, as he was prematurely shouting "Victory!" But while thus doing the deeds of a paladin of romance, he was hit by a chain-shot from an arquebuse, which, penetrating the bars of his visor, grazed his forehead, and deprived him for a moment of reason. Before he had fully recovered, his horse was killed under him, and though the fallen cavalier succeeded in extricating himself from the stirrups, he was surrounded, and soon overpowered by numbers. Still refusing to deliver up his sword, he asked "if there was no knight to whom he could surrender." One Fuentes, a menial of Pizarro, presenting himself as such, Orgoñez gave his sword into his hands,—and the dastard, drawing his dagger, stabbed his defenceless prisoner to the heart! His head, then struck off, was stuck on a pike, and displayed, a bloody trophy, in the great square of Cuzco, as the head of a traitor.[11] Thus perished as loyal a cavalier, as decided in council, and as bold in action, as ever crossed to the shores of America.

The fight had now lasted more than an hour, and the fortune of the day was turning against the followers of Almagro. Orgoñez being down, their confusion increased. The infantry, unable to endure the fire of the arquebusiers, scattered and took refuge behind the stone-walls, that here and there straggled across the country. Pedro de Lerma, vainly striving to rally the cavalry, spurred his horse against Hernando Pizarro, with whom he had a personal feud. Pizarro did not shrink from the encounter. The lances of both the knights took effect. That of Hernando penetrated the thigh of his opponent, while Lerma's weapon, glancing by his adversary's saddle-bow, struck him with such force above the groin, that it pierced the joints of his mail, slightly wounding the cavalier, and forcing his horse back on his haunches. But the press of the fight soon parted the combatants, and, in the turmoil that ensued, Lerma was unhorsed, and left on the field covered with wounds.[12]

There was no longer order, and scarcely resistance, among the followers of Almagro. They fled, making the best of their way to Cuzco, and happy was the man who obtained quarter when he asked it. Almagro himself, too feeble to sit so long on his horse, reclined on a litter, and from a neighbouring eminence surveyed the battle, watching its fluctuations with all the interest of one who felt that honor, fortune, life itself, hung on the issue. With agony not to be described, he had seen his faithful followers, after their hard struggle, borne down by their opponents, till, convinced that all was lost, he succeeded in mounting a mule, and rode off for a temporary refuge to the fortress of Cuzco. Thither he was speedily followed, taken, and brought in triumph to the capital, where, ill as he was, he was thrown into irons, and confined in the same apartment of the stone building in which he had imprisoned the Pizarros.

The action lasted not quite two hours. The number of killed, variously stated, was probably not less than a hundred and fifty,—one of the combatants calls it two hundred,[13]—a great number, considering the shortness of the time, and the small amount of forces engaged. No account is given of the wounded. Wounds were the portion of the cavalier. Pedro de Lerma is said to have received seventeen, and yet was taken alive from the field! The loss fell chiefly on the followers of Almagro. But the slaughter was not confined to the heat of the action. Such was the deadly animosity of the parties, that several were murdered in cold blood, like Orgoñez, after they had surrendered. Pedro de Lerma himself, while lying on his sick couch in the quarters of a friend in Cuzco, was visited by a soldier, named Samaniego, whom he had once struck for an act of disobedience. This person entered the solitary chamber of the wounded man, took his place by his bed-side, and then, upbraiding him for the insult, told him that he had come to wash it away in his blood! Lerma in vain assured him, that, when restored to health, he would give him the satisfaction he desired. The miscreant, exclaiming "Now is the hour!" plunged his sword into his bosom. He lived several years to vaunt this atrocious exploit, which he proclaimed as a reparation to his honor. It is some satisfaction to know that the insolence of this vaunt cost him his life.[14]—Such anecdotes, revolting as they are, illustrate not merely the spirit of the times, but that peculiarly ferocious spirit which is engendered by civil wars,—the most unforgiving in their character of any, but wars of religion.

In the hurry of the flight of one party, and the pursuit by the other, all pouring towards Cuzco, the field of battle had been deserted. But it soon swarmed with plunderers, as the Indians, descending like vultures from the mountains, took possession of the bloody ground, and, despoiling the dead, even to the minutest article of dress, left their corpses naked on the plain.[15] It has been thought strange that the natives should not have availed themselves of their superior numbers to fall on the victors after they had been exhausted by the battle. But the scattered bodies of the Peruvians were without a leader; they were broken in spirits, moreover, by recent reverses, and the Castilians, although weakened for the moment by the struggle, were in far greater strength in Cuzco than they had ever been before.

Indeed, the number of troops now assembled within its walls, amounting to full thirteen hundred, composed, as they were, of the most discordant materials, gave great uneasiness to Hernando Pizarro. For there were enemies glaring on each other and on him with deadly though smothered rancor, and friends, if not so dangerous, not the less troublesome from their craving and unreasonable demands. He had given the capital up to pillage, and his followers found good booty in the quarters of Almagro's officers. But this did not suffice the more ambitious cavaliers; and they clamorously urged their services, and demanded to be placed in charge of some expedition, nothing doubting that it must prove a golden one. All were in quest of an *El Dorado*. Hernando Pizarro acquiesced as far as possible in these desires, most willing to relieve himself of such importunate creditors. The expeditions, it is true, usually ended in disaster; but the country was explored by them. It was the lottery of adventure; the prizes were few, but they were splendid; and in the excitement of the game, few Spaniards paused to calculate the chances of success.

Among those who left the capital was Diego, the son of Almagro. Hernando was mindful to send him, with a careful escort, to his brother the governor, desirous to remove him at this crisis from the neighbourhood of his father. Meanwhile the marshal himself was pining away in prison under the combined influence of bodily illness and distress of mind. Before the battle of Salinas, it had been told to Hernando Pizarro that Almagro was like to die. "Heaven forbid," he exclaimed, "that this should come to pass before he falls into my hands!"[16] Yet the gods seemed now disposed to grant but half of this pious prayer, since his captive seemed about to escape him just as he had come into his power. To console the unfortunate chief, Hernando paid him a visit in his prison, and cheered him with the assurance that he only waited for the governor's arrival to set him at liberty; adding, "that, if Pizarro did not come soon to the capital, he himself would assume the responsibility of releasing him, and would furnish him with a conveyance to his brother's quarters." At the same time, with considerate attention to his comfort, he inquired of the marshal "what mode of conveyance would be best suited to his state of health." After this he continued to send him delicacies from his own table to revive his faded appetite. Almagro, cheered by these kind attentions, and by the speedy prospect of freedom, gradually mended in health and spirits.[17]

He little dreamed that all this while a process was industriously preparing against him. It had been instituted immediately on his capture, and every one, however humble, who had any cause of complaint against the unfortunate prisoner, was invited to present it. The summons was readily answered; and many an enemy now appeared in the hour of his fallen fortunes, like the base reptiles crawling into light amidst the ruins of some noble edifice; and more than one, who had received benefits from his hands, were willing to court the favor of his enemy by turning on their benefactor. From these loathsome sources a mass of accusations was collected which spread over two thousand folio pages! Yet Almagro was the idol of his soldiers![18]

Having completed the process, (July 8th, 1538,) it was not difficult to obtain a verdict against the prisoner. The principal charges on which he was pronounced guilty were those of levying war against the Crown, and thereby occasioning the death of many of his Majesty's subjects; of entering into conspiracy with the Inca; and finally, of dispossessing the royal governor of the city of Cuzco. On these charges he was condemned to suffer death as a traitor, by being publicly beheaded in the great square of the city. Who were the judges, or what was the tribunal that condemned him, we are not informed. Indeed, the whole trial was a mockery; if that can be called a trial, where the accused himself is not even aware of the accusation.

The sentence was communicated by a friar deputed for the purpose to Almagro. The unhappy man, who all the while had been unconsciously slumbering on the brink of a precipice, could not at first comprehend the nature of his situation. Recovering from the first shock, "It was impossible," he said, "that such wrong could be done him, — he would not believe it." He then besought Hernando Pizarro to grant him an interview. That cavalier, not unwilling, it would seem, to witness the agony of his captive, consented; and Almagro was so humbled by his misfortunes, that he condescended to beg for his life with the most piteous supplications. He reminded Hernando of his ancient relations with his brother, and the good offices he had rendered him and his family in the earlier part of their career. He touched on his acknowledged services to his country, and besought his enemy "to spare his gray hairs, and not to deprive him of the short remnant of an existence from which he had now nothing more to fear." — To this the other coldly replied, that "he was surprised to see Almagro demean himself in a manner so unbecoming a brave cavalier; that his fate was no worse than had befallen many a soldier before him; and that, since God had given him the grace to be a Christian, he should employ his remaining moments in making up his account with Heaven!"[19]

But Almagro was not to be silenced. He urged the service he had rendered Hernando himself. "This was a hard requital," he said, "for having spared his life so recently under similar circumstances, and that, too, when he had been urged again and again by those around him to take it away." And he concluded by menacing his enemy with the vengeance of the emperor, who would never suffer this outrage on one who had rendered such signal services to the Crown to go unrequited. It was all in vain; and Hernando abruptly closed the conference by repeating, that "his doom was inevitable, and he must prepare to meet it."[20]

Almagro, finding that no impression was to he made on his iron-hearted conqueror, now seriously addressed himself to the settlement of his affairs. By the terms of the royal grant he was empowered to name his successor. He accordingly devolved his office on his son, appointing Diego de Alvarado, on whose integrity he had great reliance, administrator of the province during his minority. All his property and possessions in Peru, of whatever kind, he devised to his master the emperor, assuring him that a large balance was still due to him in his unsettled accounts with Pizarro. By this politic bequest, he hoped to secure the monarch's protection for his son, as well as a strict scrutiny into the affairs of his enemy.

The knowledge of Almagro's sentence produced a deep sensation in the community of Cuzco. All were amazed at the presumption with which one, armed with a little brief authority, ventured to sit in judgment on a person of Almagro's station. There were few who did not call to mind some generous or good-natured act of the unfortunate veteran. Even those who had furnished materials for the accusation, now startled by the tragic result to which it was to lead, were heard to denounce Hernando's conduct as that of a tyrant. Some of the principal cavaliers, and among them Diego de Alvarado, to whose intercession, as we have seen, Hernando Pizarro, when a captive, had owed his own life, waited on that commander, and endeavoured to dissuade him from so high-handed and atrocious a proceeding. It was in vain. But it had the effect of changing the mode of execution, which, instead of the public square, was now to take place in prison.[21]

On the day appointed, a strong corps of arquebusiers was drawn up in the *plaza*. The guards were doubled over the houses where dwelt the principal partisans of Almagro. The executioner, attended by a priest, stealthily entered his prison; and the unhappy man, after confessing and receiving the sacrament, submitted without resistance to the *garrote*. Thus obscurely, in the gloomy silence of a dungeon, perished the hero of a hundred battles! His corpse was removed to the great square of the city, where, in obedience to the sentence, the head was severed from the body. A herald proclaimed aloud the nature of the crimes for which he had suffered; and his remains, rolled in their bloody shroud, were borne to the house of his friend Hernan Ponce de Leon, and the next day laid with all due solemnity in the church of Our Lady of Mercy. The Pizarros appeared among the principal mourners. It was remarked, that their brother had paid similar honors to the memory of Atahuallpa.[22]

Almagro, at the time of his death, was probably not far from seventy years of age. But this is somewhat uncertain; for Almagro was a foundling, and his early history is lost in obscurity.[23] He had many excellent qualities by nature; and his defects, which were not few, may reasonably be palliated by the circumstances of his situation. For what extenuation is not authorized by the position of a *foundling*, — without parents, or early friends, or teacher to direct him, — his little bark set adrift on the ocean of life, to take its chance among the rude billows and breakers, without one friendly hand stretched forth to steer or to save it! The name of "foundling" comprehends an apology for much, very much, that is wrong in after life.[24]

He was a man of strong passions, and not too well used to control them.[25] But he was neither vindictive nor habitually cruel. I have mentioned one atrocious outrage which he committed on the natives. But insensibility to the rights of the Indian he shared with many a better-instructed Spaniard. Yet the Indians, after his conviction, bore testimony to his general humanity, by declaring that they had no such friend among the white men.[26] Indeed, far from being vindictive, he was placable, and easily yielded to others. The facility with which he yielded, the result of good-natured credulity, made him too often the dupe of the crafty; and it showed, certainly, a want of that self-reliance which belongs to great strength of character. Yet his facility of temper, and the generosity of his nature, made him popular with his followers. No commander was ever more beloved by his soldiers. His generosity was often carried to prodigality. When he entered on the campaign of Chili, he lent a hundred thousand gold ducats to the poorer cavaliers to equip themselves, and afterwards gave them up the debt.[27] He was profuse to ostentation. But his extravagance did him no harm among the roving spirits of the camp, with whom prodigality is apt to gain more favor than a strict and well-regulated economy.

He was a good soldier, careful and judicious in his plans, patient and intrepid in their execution. His body was covered with the scars of his battles, till the natural plainness of his person was converted almost into deformity. He must not be judged by his closing campaign, when, depressed by disease, he yielded to the superior genius of his rival; but by his numerous expeditions by land and by water for the conquest of Peru and the remote Chili. Yet it may be doubted whether he possessed those uncommon qualities, either as a warrior or as a man, that, in ordinary circumstances, would have raised him to distinction. He was one of the three, or, to speak more strictly, of the two associates, who had the good fortune and the glory to make one of the most splendid discoveries in the Western World. He shares largely in the credit of this with Pizarro; for, when he did not accompany that leader in his perilous expeditions, he contributed no less to their success by his exertions in the colonies.

Yet his connection with that chief can hardly be considered a fortunate circumstance in his career. A partnership between individuals for discovery and conquest is not likely to be very scrupulously observed, especially by men more accustomed to govern others than to govern themselves. If causes for discord do not arise before, they will be sure to spring up on division of the spoil. But this association was particularly ill-assorted. For the free, sanguine, and confiding temper of Almagro was no match for the cool and crafty policy of Pizarro; and he was invariably circumvented by his companion, whenever their respective interests came in collision.

Still the final ruin of Almagro may be fairly imputed to himself. He made two capital blunders. The first was his appeal to arms by the seizure of Cuzco. The determination of a boundary-line was not to be settled by arms. It was a subject for arbitration; and, if arbitrators could not be trusted, it should have been referred to the decision of the Crown. But, having once appealed to arms, he should not then have resorted to negotiation,—above all, to negotiation with Pizarro. This was his second and greatest error. He had seen enough of Pizarro to know that he was not to be trusted. Almagro did trust him, and he paid for it with his life.

CHAPTER III

PIZARRO REVISITS CUZCO. — HERNANDO RETURNS TO CASTILE. — HIS LONG IMPRISONMENT. — COMMISSIONER SENT TO PERU. — HOSTILITIES WITH THE INCA. — PIZARRO'S ACTIVE ADMINISTRATION. — GONZALO PIZARRO

1539-1540.

On the departure of his brother in pursuit of Almagro, the Marquess Francisco Pizarro, as we have seen, returned to Lima. There he anxiously awaited the result of the campaign; and on receiving the welcome tidings of the victory of Las Salinas, he instantly made preparations for his march to Cuzco. At Xauxa, however, he was long detained by the distracted state of the country, and still longer, as it would seem, by a reluctance to enter the Peruvian capital while the trial of Almagro was pending.

He was met at Xauxa by the marshal's son Diego, who had been sent to the coast by Hernando Pizarro. The young man was filled with the most gloomy apprehensions respecting his father's fate, and he besought the governor not to allow his brother to do him any violence. Pizarro, who received Diego with much apparent kindness, bade him take heart, as no harm should come to his father;[1] adding, that he trusted their ancient friendship would soon be renewed. The youth, comforted by these assurances, took his way to Lima, where, by Pizarro's orders, he was received into his house, and treated as a son.

The same assurances respecting the marshal's safety were given by the governor to Bishop Valverde, and some of the principal cavaliers who interested themselves in behalf of the prisoner.[2] Still Pizarro delayed his march to the capital; and when he resumed it, he had advanced no farther than the *Rio de Abancay* when he received tidings of the death of his rival. He appeared greatly shocked by the intelligence, his whole frame was agitated, and he remained for some time with his eyes bent on the ground, showing signs of strong emotion.[3]

Such is the account given by his friends. A more probable version of the matter represents him to have been perfectly aware of the state of things at Cuzco. When the trial was concluded, it is said he received a message from Hernando, inquiring what was to be done with the prisoner. He answered in a few words: — "Deal with him so that he shall give us no more trouble."[4] It is also stated that Hernando, afterwards, when laboring under the obloquy caused by Almagro's death, shielded himself under instructions affirmed to have been received from the governor.[5] It is quite certain, that, during his long residence at Xauxa, the latter was in constant communication with Cuzco; and that had he, as Valverde repeatedly urged him,[6] quickened his march to that capital, he might easily have prevented the consummation of the tragedy. As commander-in-chief, Almagro's fate was in his hands; and, whatever his own partisans may affirm of his innocence, the impartial judgment of history must hold him equally accountable with Hernando for the death of his associate.

Neither did his subsequent conduct show any remorse for these proceedings. He entered Cuzco, says one who was present there to witness it, amidst the flourish of clarions and trumpets, at the head of his martial cavalcade, and dressed in the rich suit presented him by Cortés, with the proud bearing and joyous mien of a conqueror.[7] When Diego de Alvarado applied to him for the government of the southern provinces, in the name of the young Almagro, whom his father, as we have seen, had consigned to his protection, Pizarro answered, that "the marshal, by his rebellion, had forfeited all claims to the government." And, when he was still further urged by the cavalier, he bluntly broke off the conversation by declaring that "his own territory covered all on this side of Flanders"![8] — intimating, no doubt, by this magnificent vaunt, that he would endure no rival on this side of the water.

In the same spirit, he had recently sent to supersede Benalcazar, the conqueror of Quito, who, he was informed, aspired to an independent government. Pizarro's emissary had orders to send the offending captain to Lima; but Benalcazar, after pushing his victorious career far into the north, had returned to Castile to solicit his guerdon from the emperor.

To the complaints of the injured natives, who invoked his protection, he showed himself strangely insensible, while the followers of Almagro he treated with undisguised contempt. The estates of the leaders were confiscated, and transferred without ceremony to his own partisans. Hernando had made attempts to conciliate some of the opposite faction by acts of liberality, but they had refused to accept any thing from the man whose hands were stained with the blood of their commander.[9] The governor held to them no such encouragement; and many were reduced to such abject poverty, that, too proud to expose their wretchedness to the eyes of their conquerors, they withdrew from the city, and sought a retreat among the neighbouring mountains.[10]

For his own brothers he provided by such ample *repartimientos,* as excited the murmurs of his adherents. He appointed Gonzalo to the command of a strong force destined to act against the natives of Charcas, a hardy people occupying the territory assigned by the Crown to Almagro. Gonzalo met with a sturdy resistance, but, after some severe fighting, succeeded in reducing the province to obedience. He was recompensed, together with Hernando, who aided him in the conquest, by a large grant in the neighbourhood of Porco, the productive mines of which had been partially wrought under the Incas. The territory, thus situated, embraced part of those silver hills of Potosí which have since supplied Europe with such stores of the precious metals. Hernando comprehended the capabilities of the ground, and he began working the mines on a more extensive scale than that hitherto adopted, though it does not appear that any attempt was then made to penetrate the rich crust of Potosí.[11] A few years more were to elapse before the Spaniards were to bring to light the silver quarries that lay hidden in the bosom of its mountains.[12]

It was now the great business of Hernando to collect a sufficient quantity of treasure to take with him to Castile. Nearly a year had elapsed since Almagro's death; and it was full time that he should return and present himself at court, where Diego de Alvarado and other friends of the marshal, who had long since left Peru, were industriously maintaining the claims of the younger Almagro, as well as demanding redress for the wrongs done to his father. But Hernando looked confidently to his gold to dispel the accusations against him.

Before his departure, he counselled his brother to beware of the "men of Chili," as Almagro's followers were called; desperate men, who would stick at nothing, he said, for revenge. He besought the governor not to allow them to consort together in any number within fifty miles of his person; if he did, it would be fatal to him. And he concluded by recommending a strong bodyguard; "for I," he added, "shall not be here to watch over you." But the governor laughed at the idle fears, as he termed them, of his brother, bidding the latter take no thought of him, "as every hair in the heads of Almagro's followers was a guaranty for his safety."[13] He did not know the character of his enemies so well as Hernando.

The latter soon after embarked at Lima in the summer of 1539. He did not take the route of Panamá, for he had heard that it was the intention of the authorities there to detain him. He made a circuitous passage, therefore, by way of Mexico, landed in the Bay of Tecoantepec, and was making his way across the narrow strip that divides the great oceans, when he was arrested and taken to the capital. But the Viceroy Mendoza did not consider that he had a right to detain him, and he was suffered to embark at Vera Cruz, and to proceed on his voyage. Still he did not deem it safe to trust himself in Spain without further advices. He accordingly put in at one of the Azores, where he remained until he could communicate with home. He had some powerful friends at court, and by them he was encouraged to present himself before the emperor. He took their advice, and, shortly after, reached the Spanish coast in safety.[14]

The Court was at Valladolid; but Hernando, who made his entrance into that city, with great pomp and a display of his Indian riches, met with a reception colder than he had anticipated.[15] For this he was mainly indebted to Diego de Alvarado, who was then residing there, and who, as a cavalier of honorable standing, and of high connections, had considerable influence. He had formerly, as we have seen, by his timely interposition, more than once saved the life of Hernando; and he had consented to receive a pecuniary obligation from him to a large amount. But all were now forgotten in the recollection of the wrong done to his commander; and, true to the trust reposed in him by that chief in his dying hour, he had come to Spain to vindicate the claims of the young Almagro.

But although coldly received at first, Hernando's presence, and his own version of the dispute with Almagro, aided by the golden arguments which he dealt with no stinted hand, checked the current of indignation, and the opinion of his judges seemed for a time suspended. Alvarado, a cavalier more accustomed to the prompt and decisive action of a camp than to the tortuous intrigues of a court, chafed at the delay, and challenged Hernando to settle their quarrel by single combat. But his prudent adversary had no desire to leave the issue to such an ordeal; and the affair was speedily terminated by the death of Alvarado himself, which happened five days after the challenge. An event so opportune naturally suggested the suspicion of poison.[16]

But his accusations had not wholly fallen to the ground; and Hernando Pizarro had carried measures with too high a hand, and too grossly outraged public sentiment, to be permitted to escape. He received no formal sentence, but he was imprisoned in the strong fortress of Medina del Campo, where he was allowed to remain for twenty years, when in 1560, after a generation had nearly passed away, and time had, in some measure, thrown its softening veil over the past, he was suffered to regain his liberty.[17] But he came forth an aged man, bent down with infirmities and broken in spirit, — an object of pity, rather than indignation. Rarely has retributive justice been meted out in fuller measure to offenders so high in authority, — most rarely in Castile.[18]

Yet Hernando bore this long imprisonment with an equanimity which, had it been founded on principle, might command our respect. He saw brothers and kindred, all on whom he leaned for support, cut off one after another; his fortune, in part, confiscated, while he was involved in expensive litigation for the remainder;[19] his fame blighted, his career closed in an untimely hour, himself an exile in the heart of his own country; — yet he bore it all with the constancy of a courageous spirit. Though very old when released, he still survived several years, and continued to the extraordinary age of a hundred.[20] He lived long enough to see friends, rivals, and foes all called away to their account before him.

Hernando Pizarro was in many respects a remarkable character. He was the eldest of the brothers, to whom he was related only by the father's side, for he was born in wedlock, of honorable parentage on both sides of his house. In his early years, he received a good education, — good for the time. He was taken by his father, while quite young, to Italy, and there learned the art of war under the Great Captain. Little is known of his history after his return to Spain; but, when his brother had struck out for himself his brilliant career of discovery in Peru, Hernando consented to take part in his adventures.

He was much deferred to by Francisco, not only as his elder brother, but from his superior education and his knowledge of affairs. He was ready in his perceptions, fruitful in resources, and possessed of great vigor in action. Though courageous, he was cautious; and his counsels, when not warped by passion, were wise and wary. But he had other qualities, which more than counterbalanced the good resulting from excellent parts and attainments. His ambition and avarice were insatiable. He was supercilious even to his equals; and he had a vindictive temper, which nothing could appease. Thus, instead of aiding his brother in the Conquest, he was the evil genius that blighted his path. He conceived from the first an unwarrantable contempt for Almagro, whom he regarded as his brother's rival, instead of what he then was, the faithful partner of his fortunes. He treated him with personal indignity, and, by his intrigues at court, had the means of doing him sensible injury. He fell into Almagro's hands, and had nearly paid for these wrongs with his life. This was not to be forgiven by Hernando, and he coolly waited for the hour of revenge. Yet the execution of Almagro was a most impolitic act; for an evil passion can rarely be gratified with impunity. Hernando thought to buy off justice with the gold of Peru. He had studied human nature on its weak and wicked side, and he expected to profit by it. Fortunately, he was deceived. He had, indeed, his revenge; but the hour of his revenge was that of his ruin.

The disorderly state of Peru was such as to demand the immediate interposition of government. In the general license that prevailed there, the rights of the Indian and of the Spaniard were equally trampled under foot. Yet the subject was one of great difficulty; for Pizarro's authority was now firmly established over the country, which itself was too remote from Castile to be readily controlled at home. Pizarro, moreover, was a man not easy to be approached, confident in his own strength, jealous of interference, and possessed of a fiery temper, which would kindle into a flame at the least distrust of the government. It would not answer to send out a commission to suspend him from the exercise of his authority until his conduct could be investigated, as was done with Cortés, and other great colonial officers, on whose rooted loyalty the Crown could confidently rely. Pizarro's loyalty sat, it was feared, too lightly on him to be a powerful restraint on his movements; and there were not wanting those among his reckless followers, who, in case of extremity, would be prompt to urge him to throw off his allegiance altogether, and set up an independent government for himself.

Some one was to be sent out, therefore, who should possess, in some sort, a controlling, or, at least, concurrent power with the dangerous chief, while ostensibly he should act only in subordination to him. The person selected for this delicate mission, was the Licentiate Vaca de Castro, a member of the Royal Audience of Valladolid. He was a learned judge, a man of integrity and wisdom, and, though not bred to arms, had so much address, and such knowledge of character, as would enable him readily to turn the resources of others to his own account.

His commission was guarded in a way which showed the embarrassment of the government. He was to appear before Pizarro in the capacity of a royal judge; to consult with him on the redress of grievances, especially with reference to the unfortunate natives; to concert measures for the prevention of future evils; and above all, to possess himself faithfully of the condition of the country in all its details, and to transmit intelligence of it to the Court of Castile. But, in case of Pizarro's death, he was to produce his warrant as royal governor, and as such to claim the obedience of the authorities throughout the land. — Events showed the wisdom of providing for this latter contingency.[21]

The licentiate, thus commissioned, quitted his quiet residence at Valladolid, embarked at Seville, in the autumn of 1540, and, after a tedious voyage across the Atlantic, he traversed the Isthmus, and, encountering a succession of tempests on the Pacific, that had nearly sent his frail bark to the bottom, put in with her, a mere wreck, at the northerly port of Buenaventura.[22] The affairs of the country were in a state to require his presence.

The civil war which had lately distracted the land had left it in so unsettled a state, that the agitation continued long after the immediate cause had ceased. This was especially the case among the natives. In the violent transfer of *repartimientos,* the poor Indian hardly knew to whom he was to look as his master. The fierce struggles between the rival chieftains left him equally in doubt whom he was to regard as the rulers of the land. As to the authority of a common sovereign, across the waters, paramount over all, he held that in still greater distrust; for what was the authority which could not command the obedience even of its own vassals?[23] The Inca Manco was not slow in taking advantage of this state of feeling. He left his obscure fastnesses in the depths of the Andes, and established himself with a strong body of followers in the mountain country lying between Cuzco and the coast. From this retreat, he made descents on the neighbouring plantations, destroying the houses, sweeping off the cattle, and massacring the people. He fell on travellers, as they were journeying singly or in caravans from the coast, and put them to death — it is told by his enemies — with cruel tortures. Single detachments were sent against him, from time to time, but without effect. Some he eluded, others he defeated; and, on one occasion, cut off a party of thirty troopers, to a man.[24]

At length, Pizarro found it necessary to send a considerable force under his brother Gonzalo against the Inca. The hardy Indian encountered his enemy several times in the rough passes of the Cordilleras. He was usually beaten, and sometimes with heavy loss, which he repaired with astonishing facility; for he always contrived to make his escape, and so true were his followers, that, in defiance of pursuit and ambuscade, he found a safe shelter in the secret haunts of the sierra.

Thus baffled, Pizarro determined to try the effect of pacific overtures. He sent to the Inca, both in his own name, and in that of the Bishop of Cuzco, whom the Peruvian prince held in reverence, to invite him to enter into negotiation.[25] Manco acquiesced, and indicated, as he had formerly done with Almagro, the valley of Yucay, as the scene of it. The governor repaired thither, at the appointed time, well guarded, and, to propitiate the barbarian monarch, sent him a rich present by the hands of an African slave. The slave was met on the route by a party of the Inca's men, who, whether with or without their master's orders, cruelly murdered him, and bore off the spoil to their quarters. Pizarro resented this outrage by another yet more atrocious.

Among the Indian prisoners was one of the Inca's wives, a young and beautiful woman, to whom he was said to be fondly attached. The governor ordered her to be stripped naked, bound to a tree, and, in presence of the camp, to be scourged with rods, and then shot to death with arrows. The wretched victim bore the execution of the sentence with surprising fortitude. She did not beg for mercy, where none was to be found. Not a complaint, scarcely a groan, escaped her under the infliction of these terrible torments. The iron Conquerors were amazed at this power of endurance in a delicate woman, and they expressed their admiration, while they condemned the cruelty of their commander,—in their hearts.[26] Yet constancy under the most excruciating tortures that human cruelty can inflict is almost the universal characteristic of the American Indian.

Pizarro now prepared, as the most effectual means of checking these disorders among the natives, to establish settlements in the heart of the disaffected country. These settlements, which received the dignified name of cities, might be regarded in the light of military colonies. The houses were usually built of stone, to which were added the various public offices, and sometimes a fortress. A municipal corporation was organized. Settlers were invited by the distribution of large tracts of land in the neighbourhood, with a stipulated number of Indian vassals to each. The soldiers then gathered there, sometimes accompanied by their wives and families; for the women of Castile seem to have disdained the impediments of sex, in the ardor of conjugal attachment, or, it may be, of romantic adventure. A populous settlement rapidly grew up in the wilderness, affording protection to the surrounding territory, and furnishing a commercial *dépôt* for the country, and an armed force ready at all times to maintain public order.

Such a settlement was that now made at Guamanga, midway between Cuzco and Lima, which effectually answered its purpose by guarding the communications with the coast.[27] Another town was founded in the mining district of Charcas, under the appropriate name of the Villa de la Plata, the "City of

Silver." And Pizarro, as he journeyed by a circuitous route along the shores of the southern sea towards Lima, planted there the city of Arequipa, since arisen to such commercial celebrity.

Once more in his favorite capital of Lima, the governor found abundant occupation in attending to its municipal concerns, and in providing for the expansive growth of its population. Nor was he unmindful of the other rising settlements on the Pacific. He encouraged commerce with the remoter colonies north of Peru, and took measures for facilitating internal intercourse. He stimulated industry in all its branches, paying great attention to husbandry, and importing seeds of the different European grains, which he had the satisfaction, in a short time, to see thriving luxuriantly in a country where the variety of soil and climate afforded a home for almost every product.[28] Above all, he promoted the working of the mines, which already began to make such returns, that the most common articles of life rose to exorbitant prices, while the precious metals themselves seemed the only things of little value. But they soon changed hands, and found their way to the mother-country, where they rose to their true level as they mingled with the general currency of Europe. The Spaniards found that they had at length reached the land of which they had been so long in search,—the land of gold and silver. Emigrants came in greater numbers to the country, and, spreading over its surface, formed in the increasing population the most effectual barrier against the rightful owners of the soil.[29]

Pizarro, strengthened by the arrival of fresh adventurers, now turned his attention to the remoter quarters of the country. Pedro de Valdivia was sent on his memorable expedition to Chili; and to his own brother Gonzalo the governor assigned the territory of Quito, with instructions to explore the unknown country towards the east, where, as report said, grew the cinnamon. As this chief, who has hitherto acted but a subordinate part in the Conquest, is henceforth to take the most conspicuous, it may be well to give some account of him.

Little is known of his early life, for he sprang from the same obscure origin with Francisco, and seems to have been as little indebted as his elder brother to the fostering care of his parents. He entered early on the career of a soldier; a career to which every man in that iron age, whether cavalier or vagabond, seems, if left to himself, to have most readily inclined. Here he soon distinguished himself by his skill in martial exercises, was an excellent horseman, and, when he came to the New World, was esteemed the best lance in Peru.[30]

In talent and in expansion of views, he was inferior to his brothers. Neither did he discover the same cool and crafty policy; but he was equally courageous, and in the execution of his measures quite as unscrupulous. He had a handsome person, with open, engaging features, a free, soldier-like address, and a confiding temper, which endeared him to his followers. His spirit was high and adventurous, and, what was equally important, he could inspire others with the same spirit, and thus do much to insure the success of his enterprises. He was an excellent captain in *guerilla* warfare, an admirable leader in doubtful and difficult expeditions; but he had not the enlarged capacity for a great military chief, still less for a civil ruler. It was his misfortune to be called to fill both situations.

CHAPTER IV

GONZALO PIZARRO'S EXPEDITION. — PASSAGE ACROSS THE MOUNTAINS. — DISCOVERS THE NAPO. — INCREDIBLE SUFFERINGS. — ORELLANA SAILS DOWN THE AMAZON. — DESPAIR OF THE SPANIARDS. — THE SURVIVORS RETURN TO QUITO

1540-1542.

GONZALO Pizarro received the news of his appointment to the government of Quito with undisguised pleasure; not so much for the possession that it gave him of this ancient Indian province, as for the field that it opened for discovery towards the east, — the fabled land of Oriental spices, which had long captivated the imagination of the Conquerors. He repaired to his government without delay, and found no difficulty in awakening a kindred enthusiasm to his own in the bosoms of his followers. In a short time, he mustered three hundred and fifty Spaniards, and four thousand Indians. One hundred and fifty of his company were mounted, and all were equipped in the most thorough manner for the undertaking. He provided, moreover, against famine by a large stock of provisions, and an immense drove of swine which followed in the rear.[1]

It was the beginning of 1540, when he set out on this celebrated expedition. The first part of the journey was attended with comparatively little difficulty, while the Spaniards were yet in the land of the Incas; for the distractions of Peru had not been felt in this distant province, where the simple people still lived as under the primitive sway of the Children of the Sun. But the scene changed as they entered the territory of Quixos, where the character of the inhabitants, as well as of the climate, seemed to be of another description. The country was traversed by lofty ranges of the Andes, and the adventurers were soon entangled in their deep and intricate passes. As they rose into the more elevated regions, the icy winds that swept down the sides of the Cordilleras benumbed their limbs, and many of the natives found a wintry grave in the wilderness. While crossing this formidable barrier, they experienced one of those tremendous earthquakes which, in these volcanic regions, so often shake the mountains to their base. In one place, the earth was rent asunder by the terrible throes of Nature, while streams of sulphurous vapor issued from the cavity, and a village with some hundreds of houses was precipitated into the frightful abyss![2]

On descending the eastern slopes, the climate changed; and, as they came on the lower level, the fierce cold was succeeded by a suffocating heat, while tempests of thunder and lightning, rushing from out the gorges of the sierra, poured on their heads with scarcely any intermission day or night, as if the offended deities of the place were willing to take vengeance on the invaders of their mountain solitudes. For more than six weeks the deluge continued unabated, and the forlorn wanderers, wet, and weary with incessant toil, were scarcely able to drag their limbs along the soil broken up and saturated with the moisture. After some months of toilsome travel, in which they had to cross many a morass and mountain stream, they at length reached *Canelas*, the Land of Cinnamon.[3] They saw the trees bearing the precious bark, spreading out into broad forests; yet, however valuable an article for commerce it might have proved in accessible situations, in these remote regions it was of little worth to them. But, from the wandering tribes of savages whom they had occasionally met in their path, they learned that at ten days' distance was a rich and fruitful land abounding with gold, and inhabited by populous nations. Gonzalo Pizarro had already reached the limits originally proposed for the expedition. But this intelligence renewed his hopes, and he resolved to push the adventure farther. It would have been well for him and his followers, had they been content to return on their footsteps.

Continuing their march, the country now spread out into broad savannas terminated by forests, which, as they drew near, seemed to stretch on every side to the very verge of the horizon. Here they beheld trees of that stupendous growth seen only in the equinoctial regions. Some were so large, that sixteen men could hardly encompass them with extended arms![4] The wood was thickly matted with creepers and parasitical vines, which hung in gaudy-colored festoons from tree to tree, clothing them in a drapery beautiful to the eye, but forming an impenetrable network. At every step of their way, they were obliged to hew open a passage with their axes, while their garments, rotting from the effects of the drenching rains to which they had been exposed, caught in every bush and bramble, and hung about them in shreds.[5] Their provisions, spoiled by the weather, had long since failed, and the live stock which they had taken with them had either been consumed or made their escape in the woods and mountain passes. They had set out with nearly a thousand dogs, many of them of the ferocious breed used in hunting down the unfortunate natives. These they now gladly killed, but their miserable carcasses furnished a lean banquet for the famishing travellers; and, when these were gone, they had only such herbs and dangerous roots as they could gather in the forest.[6]

At length the way-worn company came on a broad expanse of water formed by the Napo, one of the great tributaries of the Amazon, and which, though only a third or fourth rate river in America, would pass for one of the first magnitude in the Old World. The sight gladdened their hearts, as, by winding along its banks, they hoped to find a safer and more practicable route. After traversing its borders for a considerable distance, closely beset with thickets which it taxed their strength to the utmost to overcome, Gonzalo and his party came within hearing of a rushing noise that sounded like subterranean thunder. The river, lashed into fury, tumbled along over rapids with frightful velocity, and conducted them to the brink of a magnificent cataract, which, to their wondering fancies, rushed down in one vast volume of foam to the depth of twelve hundred feet![7] The appalling sounds which they had heard for the distance of six leagues were rendered yet more oppressive to the spirits by the gloomy stillness of the surrounding forests. The rude warriors were filled with sentiments of awe. Not a bark dimpled the waters. No living thing was to be seen but the wild tenants of the wilderness, the unwieldy boa, and the loathsome alligator basking on the borders of the stream. The trees towering in wide-spread magnificence towards the heavens, the river rolling on in its rocky bed as it had rolled for ages, the solitude and silence of the scene, broken only by the hoarse fall of waters, or the faint rustling of the woods,—all seemed to spread out around them in the same wild and primitive state as when they came from the hands of the Creator.

For some distance above and below the falls, the bed of the river contracted so that its width did not exceed twenty feet. Sorely pressed by hunger, the adventurers determined, at all hazards, to cross to the opposite side, in hopes of finding a country that might afford them sustenance. A frail bridge was constructed by throwing the huge trunks of trees across the chasm, where the cliffs, as if split asunder by some convulsion of nature, descended sheer down a perpendicular depth of several hundred feet. Over this airy causeway the men and horses succeeded in effecting their passage with the loss of a single Spaniard, who, made giddy by heedlessly looking down, lost his footing and fell into the boiling surges below.

Yet they gained little by the exchange. The country wore the same unpromising aspect, and the river-banks were studded with gigantic trees, or fringed with impenetrable thickets. The tribes of Indians, whom they occasionally met in the pathless wilderness, were fierce and unfriendly, and they were engaged in perpetual skirmishes with them. From these they learned that a fruitful country was to be found down the river at the distance of only a few days' journey, and the Spaniards held on their weary way, still hoping and still deceived, as the promised land flitted before them, like the rainbow, receding as they advanced.

At length, spent with toil and suffering, Gonzalo resolved to construct a bark large enough to transport the weaker part of his company and his baggage. The forests furnished him with timber; the shoes of the horses which had died on the road or been slaughtered for food, were converted into nails; gum distilled from the trees took the place of pitch; and the tattered garments of the soldiers supplied a substitute for oakum. It was a work of difficulty; but Gonzalo cheered his men in the task, and set an example by taking part in their labors. At the end of two months a brigantine was completed, rudely put together, but strong and of sufficient burden to carry half the company,—the first European vessel that ever floated on these inland waters.

Gonzalo gave the command to Francisco de Orellana, a cavalier from Truxillo, on whose courage and devotion to himself he thought he could rely. The troops now moved forward, still following the descending course of the river, while the brigantine kept alongside; and when a bold promontory or more impracticable country intervened, it furnished timely aid by the transportation of the feebler soldiers. In this way they journeyed, for many a wearisome week, through the dreary wilderness on the borders of the Napo. Every scrap of provisions had been long since consumed. The last of their horses had been devoured. To appease the gnawings of hunger, they were fain to eat the leather of their saddles and belts. The woods supplied them with scanty sustenance, and they greedily fed upon toads, serpents, and such other reptiles as they occasionally found.[8]

They were now told of a rich district, inhabited by a populous nation, where the Napo emptied into a still greater river that flowed towards the east. It was, as usual, at the distance of several days' journey; and Gonzalo Pizarro resolved to halt where he was and send Orellana down in his brigantine to the confluence of the waters to procure a stock of provisions, with which he might return and put them in condition to resume their march. That cavalier, accordingly, taking with him fifty of the adventurers, pushed off into the middle of the river, where the stream ran swiftly, and his bark, taken by the current, shot forward with the speed of an arrow, and was soon out of sight.

Days and weeks passed away, yet the vessel did not return; and no speck was to be seen on the waters, as the Spaniards strained their eyes to the farthest point, where the line of light faded away in the dark shadows of the foliage on the borders. Detachments were sent out, and, though absent several days, came back without intelligence of their comrades. Unable longer to endure this suspense, or, indeed, to maintain themselves in their present quarters, Gonzalo and his famishing followers now determined to proceed towards the junction of the rivers. Two months elapsed before they accomplished this terrible journey,—those of them who did not perish on the way,—although the distance probably did not exceed two hundred leagues; and they at length reached the spot so long desired, where the Napo pours its tide into the Amazon, that mighty stream, which, fed by its thousand tributaries, rolls on towards the ocean, for many hundred miles, through the heart of the great continent,—the most majestic of American rivers.

But the Spaniards gathered no tidings of Orellana, while the country, though more populous than the region they had left, was as little inviting in its aspect, and was tenanted by a race yet more ferocious. They now abandoned the hope of recovering their comrades, who they supposed must have miserably perished by famine or by the hands of the natives. But their doubts were at length dispelled by the appearance of a white man wandering half—naked in the woods, in whose famine-stricken countenance they recognized the features of one of their countrymen. It was Sanchez de Vargas, a cavalier of good descent, and much esteemed in the army. He had a dismal tale to tell.

Orellana, borne swiftly down the current of the Napo, had reached the point of its confluence with the Amazon in less than three days; accomplishing in this brief space of time what had cost Pizarro and his company two months. He had found the country altogether different from what had been represented; and, so far from supplies for his countrymen, he could barely obtain sustenance for himself. Nor was it possible for him to return as he had come, and make head against the current of the river; while the attempt to journey by land was an alternative scarcely less formidable. In this dilemma, an idea flashed across his mind. It was to launch his bark at once on the bosom of the Amazon, and descend its waters to its mouth. He would then visit the rich and populous nations that, as report said, lined its borders, sail out on the great ocean, cross to the neighbouring isles, and return to Spain to claim the glory and the guerdon of discovery. The suggestion was eagerly taken up by his reckless companions, welcoming any course that would rescue them from the wretchedness of their present existence, and fired with the prospect of new and stirring adventure,—for the love of adventure was the last feeling to become extinct in the bosom of the Castilian cavalier. They heeded little their unfortunate comrades, whom they were to abandon in the wilderness![9]

This is not the place to record the circumstances of Orellana's extraordinary expedition. He succeeded in his enterprise. But it is marvellous that he should have escaped shipwreck in the perilous and unknown navigation of that river. Many times his vessel was nearly dashed to pieces on its rocks and in its furious rapids;[10] and he was in still greater peril from the warlike tribes on its borders, who fell on his little troop whenever he attempted to land, and followed in his wake for miles in their canoes. He at length emerged from the great river; and, once upon the sea, Orellana made for the isle of Cubagua; thence passing over to Spain, he repaired to court, and told the circumstances of his voyage,—of the nations of Amazons whom he had found on the banks of the river, the El Dorado which report assured him existed in the neighbourhood, and other marvels,—the exaggeration rather than the coinage of a credulous fancy. His audience listened with willing ears to the tales of the traveller; and in an age of wonders, when the mysteries of the East and the West were hourly coming to light, they might be excused for not discerning the true line between romance and reality.[11]

He found no difficulty in obtaining a commission to conquer and colonize the realms he had discovered. He soon saw himself at the head of five hundred followers, prepared to share the perils and the profits of his expedition. But neither he, nor his country, was destined to realize these profits. He died on his outward passage, and the lands washed by the Amazon fell within the territories of Portugal. The unfortunate navigator did not even enjoy the undivided honor of giving his name to the waters he had discovered. He enjoyed only the barren glory of the discovery, surely not balanced by the iniquitous circumstances which attended it.[12]

One of Orellana's party maintained a stout opposition to his proceedings, as repugnant both to humanity and honor. This was Sanchez de Vargas; and the cruel commander was revenged on him by abandoning him to his fate in the desolate region where he was now found by his countrymen.[13]

The Spaniards listened with horror to the recital of Vargas, and their blood almost froze in their veins as they saw themselves thus deserted in the heart of this remote wilderness, and deprived of their only means of escape from it. They made an effort to prosecute their journey along the banks, but, after some toilsome days, strength and spirits failed, and they gave up in despair!

Then it was that the qualities of Gonzalo Pizarro, as a fit leader in the hour of despondency and danger, shone out conspicuous. To advance farther was hopeless. To stay where they were, without food or raiment, without defence from the fierce animals of the forest and the fiercer natives, was impossible. One only course remained; it was to return to Quito. But this brought with it the recollection of the past, of sufferings which they could too well estimate,—hardly to be endured even in imagination. They were now at least four hundred leagues from Quito, and more than a year had elapsed since they had set out on their painful pilgrimage. How could they encounter these perils again![14]

Yet there was no alternative. Gonzalo endeavoured to reassure his followers by dwelling on the invincible constancy they had hitherto displayed; adjuring them to show themselves still worthy of the name of Castilians. He reminded them of the glory they would for ever acquire by their heroic achievement, when they should reach their own country. He would lead them back, he said, by another route, and it could not be but that they should meet somewhere with those abundant regions of which they had so often heard. It was something, at least, that every step would take them nearer home; and as, at all events, it was clearly the only course now left, they should prepare to meet it like men. The spirit would sustain the body; and difficulties encountered in the right spirit were half vanquished already!

The soldiers listened eagerly to his words of promise and encouragement. The confidence of their leader gave life to the desponding. They felt the force of his reasoning, and, as they lent a willing ear to his assurances, the pride of the old Castilian honor revived in their bosoms, and every one caught somewhat of the generous enthusiasm of their commander. He was, in truth, entitled to their devotion. From the first hour of the expedition, he had freely borne his part in its privations. Far from claiming the advantage of his position, he had taken his lot with the poorest soldier; ministering to the wants of the sick, cheering up the spirits of the desponding, sharing his stinted allowance with his famished followers, bearing his full part in the toil and burden of the march, ever showing himself their faithful comrade, no less than their captain. He found the benefit of this conduct in a trying hour like the present.

I will spare the reader the recapitulation of the sufferings endured by the Spaniards on their retrograde march to Quito. They took a more northerly route than that by which they had approached the Amazon; and, if it was attended with fewer difficulties, they experienced yet greater distresses from their greater inability to overcome them. Their only nourishment was such scanty fare as they could pick up in the forest, or happily meet with in some forsaken Indian settlement, or wring by violence from the natives. Some sickened and sank down by the way, for there was none to help them. Intense misery had made them selfish; and many a poor wretch was abandoned to his fate, to die alone in the wilderness, or, more probably, to be devoured, while living, by the wild animals which roamed over it.

At length, in June, 1542, after somewhat more than a year consumed in their homeward march, the way-worn company came on the elevated plains in the neighbourhood of Quito. But how different their aspect from that which they had exhibited on issuing from the gates of the same capital, two years and a half before, with high romantic hope and in all the pride of military array! Their horses gone, their arms broken and rusted, the skins of wild animals instead of clothes hanging loosely about their limbs, their long and matted locks streaming wildly down their shoulders, their faces burned and blackened by the tropical sun, their bodies wasted by famine and sorely disfigured by scars,—it seemed as if the charnel-house had given up its dead, as, with uncertain step, they glided slowly onwards like a troop of dismal spectres! More than half of the four thousand Indians who had accompanied the expedition had perished, and of the Spaniards only eighty, and many of these irretrievably broken in constitution, returned to Quito.[15]

The few Christian inhabitants of the place, with their wives and children, came out to welcome their countrymen. They ministered to them all the relief and refreshment in their power; and, as they listened to the sad recital of their sufferings, they mingled their tears with those of the wanderers. The whole company then entered the capital, where their first act—to their credit be it mentioned—was to go in a body to the church, and offer up thanksgivings to the Almighty for their miraculous preservation through their long and perilous pilgrimage.[16] Such was the end of the expedition to the Amazon; an expedition which, for its dangers and hardships, the length of their duration, and the constancy with which they were endured, stands, perhaps, unmatched in the annals of American discovery.

CHAPTER V

THE ALMAGRO FACTION. — THEIR DESPERATE CONDITION. — CONSPIRACY AGAINST FRANCISCO PIZARRO. — ASSASSINATION OF PIZARRO. — ACTS OF THE CONSPIRATORS. — PIZARRO'S CHARACTER

1541.

WHEN Gonzalo Pizarro reached Quito, he received tidings of an event which showed that his expedition to the Amazon had been even more fatal to his interests than he had imagined. A revolution had taken place during his absence, which had changed the whole condition of things in Peru.

In a preceding chapter we have seen, that, when Hernando Pizarro returned to Spain, his brother the marquess repaired to Lima, where he continued to occupy himself with building up his infant capital, and watching over the general interests of the country. While thus employed, he gave little heed to a danger that hourly beset his path, and this, too, in despite of repeated warnings from more circumspect friends.

After the execution of Almagro, his followers, to the number of several hundred, remained scattered through the country; but, however scattered, still united by a common sentiment of indignation against the Pizarros, the murderers, as they regarded them, of their leader. The governor was less the object of these feelings than his brother Hernando, as having been less instrumental in the perpetration of the deed. Under these circumstances, it was clearly Pizarro's policy to do one of two things; to treat the opposite faction either as friends, or as open enemies. He might conciliate the most factious by acts of kindness, efface the remembrance of past injury, if he could, by present benefits; in short, prove to them that his quarrel had been with their leader, not with themselves, and that it was plainly for their interest to come again under his banner. This would have been the most politic, as well as the most magnanimous course; and, by augmenting the number of his adherents, would have greatly strengthened his power in the land. But, unhappily, he had not the magnanimity to pursue it. It was not in the nature of a Pizarro to forgive an injury, or the man whom he had injured. As he would not, therefore, try to conciliate Almagro's adherents, it was clearly the governor's policy to regard them as enemies,—not the less so for being in disguise,—and to take such measures as should disqualify them for doing mischief. He should have followed the counsel of his more prudent brother Hernando, and distributed them in different quarters, taking care that no great number should assemble at any one point, or, above all, in the neighbourhood of his own residence.

But the governor despised the broken followers of Almagro too heartily to stoop to precautionary measures. He suffered the son of his rival to remain in Lima, where his quarters soon became the resort of the disaffected cavaliers. The young man was well known to most of Almagro's soldiers, having been trained along with them in the camp under his father's eye, and, now that his parent was removed, they naturally transferred their allegiance to the son who survived him.

That the young Almagro, however, might be less able to maintain this retinue of unprofitable followers, he was deprived by Pizarro of a great part of his Indians and lands, while he was excluded from the government of New Toledo, which had been settled on him by his father's testament.[1] Stripped of all means of support, without office or employment of any kind, the men of Chili, for so Almagro's adherents continued to be called, were reduced to the utmost distress. So poor were they, as is the story of the time, that twelve cavaliers, who lodged in the same house, could muster only one cloak among them all; and, with the usual feeling of pride that belongs to the poor *hidalgo*, unwilling to expose their poverty, they wore this cloak by turns, those who had no right to it remaining at home.[2] Whether true or not, the anecdote well illustrates the extremity to which Almagro's faction was reduced. And this distress was rendered yet more galling by the effrontery of their enemies, who, enriched by their forfeitures, displayed before their eyes all the insolent bravery of equipage and apparel that could annoy their feelings.

Men thus goaded by insult and injury were too dangerous to be lightly regarded. But, although Pizarro received various intimations intended to put him on his guard, he gave no heed to them. "Poor devils!" he would exclaim, speaking with contemptuous pity of the men of Chili; "they have had bad luck enough. We will not trouble them further."[3] And so little did he consider them, that he went freely about, as usual, tiding without attendants to all parts of the town and to its immediate environs.[4]

News now reached the colony of the appointment of a judge by the Crown to take cognizance of the affairs of Peru. Pizarro, although alarmed by the intelligence, sent orders to have him well entertained on his landing, and suitable accommodations prepared for him on the route. The spirits of Almagro's followers were greatly raised by the tidings. They confidently looked to this high functionary for the redress of their wrongs; and two of their body, clad in suits of mourning, were chosen to go to the north, where the judge was expected to land, and to lay their grievances before him.

But months elapsed, and no tidings came of his arrival, till, at length, a vessel, coming into port, announced that most of the squadron had foundered in the heavy storms on the coast, and that the commissioner had probably perished with them. This was disheartening intelligence to the men of Chili, whose "miseries," to use the words of their young leader, "had become too grievous to be borne."[5] Symptoms of disaffection had already begun openly to manifest themselves. The haughty cavaliers did not always doff their bonnets, on meeting the governor in the street; and on one occasion, three ropes were found suspended from the public gallows, with labels attached to them, bearing the names of Pizarro, Velasquez the judge, and Picado the governor's secretary.[6] This last functionary was peculiarly odious to Almagro and his followers. As his master knew neither how to read nor write, all his communications passed through Picado's hands; and, as the latter was of a hard and arrogant nature, greatly elated by the consequence which his position gave him, he exercised a mischievous influence on the governor's measures. Almagro's poverty-stricken followers were the objects of his open ridicule, and he revenged the insult now offered him by riding before their young leader's residence, displaying a tawdry magnificence in his dress, sparkling with gold and silver, and with the inscription, "For the Men of Chili," set in his bonnet. It was a foolish taunt; but the poor cavaliers who were the object of it, made morbidly sensitive by their sufferings, had not the philosophy to despise it.[7]

At length, disheartened by the long protracted coming of Vaca de Castro, and still more by the recent reports of his loss, Almagro's faction, despairing of redress from a legitimate authority, determined to take it into their own hands. They came to the desperate resolution of assassinating Pizarro. The day named for this was Sunday, the twenty-sixth of June, 1541. The conspirators, eighteen or twenty in number, were to assemble in Almagro's house, which stood in the great square next to the cathedral, and, when the governor was returning from mass, they were to issue forth and fall on him in the street. A white flag, unfurled at the same time from an upper window in the house, was to be the signal for the rest of their comrades to move to the support of those immediately engaged in the execution of the deed.[8]

These arrangements could hardly have been concealed from Almagro, since his own quarters were to be the place of rendezvous. Yet there is no good evidence of his having taken part in the conspiracy.[9] He was, indeed, too young to make it probable that he took a leading part in it. He is represented by contemporary writers to have given promise of many good qualities, though, unhappily, he was not placed in a situation favorable for their development. He was the son of an Indian woman of Panamá; but from early years had followed the troubled fortunes of his father, to whom he bore much resemblance in his free and generous nature, as well as in the violence of his passions. His youth and inexperience disqualified him from taking the lead in the perplexing circumstances in which he was placed, and made him little more than a puppet in the hands of others.[10]

The most conspicuous of his advisers was Juan de Herrada, or Rada, as his name is more usually spelt,—a cavalier of respectable family, but who, having early enlisted as a common soldier, had gradually risen to the highest posts in the army by his military talents. At this time he was well advanced in years; but the fires of youth were not quenched in his bosom, and he burned with desire to avenge the wrongs done to his ancient commander. The attachment which he had ever felt for the elder Almagro he seems to have transferred in full measure to his son; and it was apparently with reference to him, even more than to himself, that he devised this audacious plot, and prepared to take the lead in the execution of it.

There was one, however, in the band of conspirators who felt some compunctions of conscience at the part he was acting, and who relieved his bosom by revealing the whole plot to his confessor. The latter lost no time in reporting it to Picado, by whom in turn it was communicated to Pizarro. But, strange to say, it made little more impression on the governor's mind than the vague warnings he had so frequently received. "It is a device of the priest," said he; "he wants a mitre."[11] Yet he repeated the story to the judge Velasquez, who, instead of ordering the conspirators to be seized, and the proper steps taken for learning the truth of the accusation, seemed to be possessed with the same infatuation as Pizarro; and he bade the governor be under no apprehension, "for no harm should come to him, while the rod of justice," not a metaphorical badge of authority in Castile, "was in his hands."[12] Still, to obviate every possibility of danger, it was deemed prudent for Pizarro to abstain from going to mass on Sunday, and to remain at home on pretence of illness.

On the day appointed, Rada and his companions met in Almagro's house, and waited with anxiety for the hour when the governor should issue from the church. But great was their consternation, when they learned that he was not there, but was detained at home, as currently reported, by illness. Little doubting that their design was discovered, they felt their own ruin to be the inevitable consequence, and that, too, without enjoying the melancholy consolation of having struck the blow for which they had incurred it. Greatly perplexed, some were for disbanding, in the hope that Pizarro might, after all, be ignorant of their design. But most were for carrying it into execution at once, by assaulting him in his own house. The question was summarily decided by one of the party, who felt that in this latter course lay their only chance of safety. Throwing open the doors, he rushed out, calling on his comrades "to follow him, or he would proclaim the purpose for which they had met." There was no longer hesitation, and the cavaliers issued forth, with Rada at their head, shouting, as they went, "Long live the king! Death to the tyrant!"[13]

It was the hour of dinner, which, in this primitive age of the Spanish colonies, was at noon. Yet numbers, roused by the cries of the assailants, came out into the square to inquire the cause. "They are going to kill the marquess," some said very coolly; others replied, "It is Picado." No one stirred in their defence. The power of Pizarro was not seated in the hearts of his people.

As the conspirators traversed the *plaza*, one of the party made a circuit to avoid a little pool of water that lay in their path. "What!" exclaimed Rada, "afraid of wetting your feet, when you are to wade up to your knees in blood!" And he ordered the man to give up the enterprise and go home to his quarters. The anecdote is characteristic.[14]

The governor's palace stood on the opposite side of the square. It was approached by two courtyards. The entrance to the outer one was protected by a massive gate, capable of being made good against a hundred men or more. But it was left open, and the assailants, hurrying through to the inner court, still shouting their fearful battle-cry, were met by two domestics loitering in the yard. One of these they struck down. The other, flying in all haste towards the house, called out, "Help, help! the men of Chili are all coming to murder the marquess!"

Pizarro at this time was at dinner, or, more probably, had just dined. He was surrounded by a party of friends, who had dropped in, it seems, after mass, to inquire after the state of his health, some of whom had remained to partake of his repast. Among these was Don Martinez de Alcantara, Pizarro's half-brother by the mother's side, the judge Velasquez, the bishop elect of Quito, and several of the principal cavaliers in the place, to the number of fifteen or twenty. Some of them, alarmed by the uproar in the court-yard, left the saloon, and, running down to the first landing on the stairway, inquired into the cause of the disturbance. No sooner were they informed of it by the cries of the servant, than they retreated with precipitation into the house; and, as they had no mind to abide the storm unarmed, or at best imperfectly armed, as most of them were, they made their way to a corridor that overlooked the gardens, into which they easily let themselves down without injury. Velasquez, the judge, the better to have the use of his hands in the descent, held his rod of office in his mouth, thus taking care, says a caustic old chronicler, not to falsify his assurance, that "no harm should come to Pizarro while the rod of justice was in his hands"![15]

Meanwhile, the marquess, learning the nature of the tumult, called out to Francisco de Chaves, an officer high in his confidence, and who was in the outer apartment opening on the staircase, to secure the door, while he and his brother Alcantara buckled on their armour. Had this order, coolly given, been as coolly obeyed, it would have saved them all, since the entrance could easily have been maintained against a much larger force, till the report of the cavaliers who had fled had brought support to Pizarro. But unfortunately, Chaves, disobeying his commander, half opened the door, and attempted to enter into a parley with the conspirators. The latter had now reached the head of the stairs, and cut short the debate by running Chaves through the body, and tumbling his corpse down into the area below. For a moment they were kept at bay by the attendants of the slaughtered cavalier, but these, too, were quickly despatched; and Rada and his companions, entering the apartment, hurried across it, shouting out, "Where is the marquess? Death to the tyrant!"

Martinez de Alcantara, who in the adjoining room was assisting his brother to buckle on his mail, no sooner saw that the entrance to the antechamber had been gained, than he sprang to the doorway of the apartment, and, assisted by two young men, pages of Pizarro, and by one or two cavaliers in attendance, endeavoured to resist the approach of the assailants. A desperate struggle now ensued. Blows were given on both sides, some of which proved fatal, and two of the conspirators were slain, while Alcantara and his brave companions were repeatedly wounded.

At length, Pizarro, unable, in the hurry of the moment, to adjust the fastenings of his cuirass, threw it away, and, enveloping one arm in his cloak, with the other seized his sword, and sprang to his brother's assistance. It was too late; for Alcantara was already staggering under the loss of blood, and soon fell to the ground. Pizarro threw himself on his invaders, like a lion roused in his lair, and dealt his blows with as much rapidity and force, as if age had no power to stiffen his limbs. "What ho!" he cried, "traitors! have you come to kill me in my own house?" The conspirators drew back for a moment, as two of their body fell under Pizarro's sword; but they quickly rallied, and, from their superior numbers, fought at great advantage by relieving one another in the assault. Still the passage was narrow, and the struggle lasted for some minutes, till both of Pizarro's pages were stretched by his side, when Rada, impatient of the delay, called out, "Why are we so long about it? Down with the tyrant!" and taking one of his companions, Narvaez, in his arms, he thrust him against the marquess. Pizarro, instantly grappling with his opponent, ran him through with his sword. But at that moment he received a wound in the throat, and reeling, he sank on the floor, while the swords of Rada and several of the conspirators were plunged into his body. "Jesu!" exclaimed the dying man, and, tracing a cross with his finger on the bloody floor, he bent down his head to kiss it, when a stroke, more friendly than the rest, put an end to his existence.[16]

The conspirators, having accomplished their bloody deed, rushed into the street, and, brandishing their dripping weapons, shouted out, "The tyrant is dead! The laws are restored! Long live our master the emperor, and his governor, Almagro!" The men of Chili, roused by the cheering cry, now flocked in from every side to join the banner of Rada, who soon found himself at the head of nearly three hundred followers, all armed and prepared to support his authority. A guard was placed over the houses of the principal partisans of the late governor, and their persons were taken into custody. Pizarro's house, and that of his secretary Picado, were delivered up to pillage, and a large booty in gold and silver was found in the former. Picado himself took refuge in the dwelling of Riquelme, the treasurer; but his hiding-place was detected, —betrayed, according to some accounts, by the looks, though not the words, of the treasurer himself, —and he was dragged forth and committed to a secure prison.[17] The whole city was thrown into consternation, as armed bodies hurried to and fro on their several errands, and all who were not in the faction of Almagro trembled lest they should be involved in the proscription of their enemies. So great was the disorder, that the Brothers of Mercy, turning out in a body, paraded the streets in solemn procession, with the host elevated in the air, in hopes by the presence of the sacred symbol to calm the passions of the multitude.

But no other violence was offered by Rada and his followers than to apprehend a few suspected persons, and to seize upon horses and arms wherever they were to be found. The municipality was then summoned to recognize the authority of Almagro; the refractory were ejected without ceremony from their offices, and others of the Chili faction were substituted. The claims of the new aspirant were fully recognized; and young Almagro, parading the streets on horseback, and escorted by a well-armed body of cavaliers, was proclaimed by sound of trumpet governor and captain-general of Peru.

Meanwhile, the mangled bodies of Pizarro and his faithful adherents were left weltering in their blood. Some were for dragging forth the governor's corpse to the market-place, and fixing his head upon a gibbet. But Almagro was secretly prevailed on to grant the entreaties of Pizarro's friends, and allow his interment. This was stealthily and hastily performed, in the fear of momentary interruption. A faithful attendant and his wife, with a few black domestics, wrapped the body in a cotton cloth and removed it to the cathedral. A grave was hastily dug in an obscure corner, the services were hurried through, and, in secrecy, and in darkness dispelled only by the feeble glimmering of a few tapers furnished by these humble menials, the remains of Pizarro, rolled in their bloody shroud, were consigned to their kindred dust. Such was the miserable end of the Conqueror of Peru, —of the man who but a few hours before had lorded it over the land with as absolute a sway as was possessed by its hereditary Incas. Cut off in the broad light of day, in the heart of his own capital, in the very midst of those who had been his companions in arms and shared with him his triumphs and his spoils, he perished like a wretched outcast. "There was none, even," in the expressive language of the chronicler, "to say, God forgive him!"[18]

A few years later, when tranquillity was restored to the country, Pizarro's remains were placed in a sumptuous coffin and deposited under a monument in a conspicuous part of the cathedral. And in 1607, when time had thrown its friendly mantle over the past, and the memory of his errors and his crimes was merged in the consideration of the great services he had rendered to the Crown by the extension of her colonial empire, his bones were removed to the new cathedral, and allowed to repose side by side with those of Mendoza, the wise and good viceroy of Peru.[19]

Pizarro was, probably, not far from sixty-five years of age at the time of his death; though this, it must be added, is but loose conjecture, since there exists no authentic record of the date of his birth.[20] He was never married; but by an Indian princess of the Inca blood, daughter of Atahuallpa and granddaughter of the great Huayna Capac, he had two children, a son and a daughter. Both survived him; but the son did not live to manhood. Their mother, after Pizarro's death, wedded a Spanish cavalier, named Ampuero, and removed with him to Spain. Her daughter Francisca accompanied her, and was there subsequently married to her uncle Hernando Pizarro, then a prisoner in the Mota del Medina. Neither the title nor estates of the Marquess Francisco descended to his illegitimate offspring. But in the third generation, in the reign of Philip the Fourth, the title was revived in favor of Don Juan Hernando Pizarro, who, out of gratitude for the services of his ancestor, was created Marquess of the Conquest, *Marques de la Conquista,* with a liberal pension from government. His descendants, bearing the same title of nobility, are still to be found, it is said, at Truxillo, in the ancient province of Estremadura, the original birthplace of the Pizarros.[21]

Pizarro's person has been already described. He was tall in stature, well-proportioned, and with a countenance not unpleasing. Bred in camps, with nothing of the polish of a court, he had a soldier-like bearing, and the air of one accustomed to command. But though not polished, there was no embarrassment or rusticity in his address, which, where it served his purpose, could be plausible and even insinuating. The proof of it is the favorable impression made by him, on presenting himself, after his second expedition—stranger as he was to all its forms and usages—at the punctilious court of Castile.

Unlike many of his countrymen, he had no passion for ostentatious dress, which he regarded as an incumbrance. The costume which he most affected on public occasions was a black cloak, with a white hat, and shoes of the same color; the last, it is said, being in imitation of the Great Captain, whose character he had early learned to admire in Italy, but to which his own, certainly, bore very faint resemblance.[22]

He was temperate in eating, drank sparingly, and usually rose an hour before dawn. He was punctual in attendance to business, and shrunk from no toil. He had, indeed, great powers of patient endurance. Like most of his nation, he was fond of play, and cared little for the quality of those with whom he played; though, when his antagonist could not afford to lose, he would allow himself, it is said, to be the loser; a mode of conferring an obligation much commended by a Castilian writer, for its delicacy.[23]

Though avaricious, it was in order to spend and not to hoard. His ample treasures, more ample than those, probably, that ever before fell to the lot of an adventurer,[24] were mostly dissipated in his enterprises, his architectural works, and schemes of public improvement, which, in a country where gold and silver might be said to have lost their value from their abundance, absorbed an incredible amount of money. While he regarded the whole country, in a manner, as his own, and distributed it freely among his captains, it is certain that the princely grant of a territory with twenty thousand vassals, made to him by the Crown, was never carried into effect; nor did his heirs ever reap the benefit of it.[25]

To a man possessed of the active energies of Pizarro, sloth was the greatest evil. The excitement of play was in a manner necessary to a spirit accustomed to the habitual stimulants of war and adventure. His uneducated mind had no relish for more refined, intellectual recreation. The deserted foundling had neither been taught to read nor write. This has been disputed by some, but it is attested by unexceptionable authorities.[26] Montesinos says, indeed, that Pizarro, on his first voyage, tried to learn to read; but the impatience of his temper prevented it, and he contented himself with learning to sign his name.[27] But Montesinos was not a contemporary historian. Pedro Pizarro, his companion in arms, expressly tells us he could neither read nor write;[28] and Zarate, another contemporary, well acquainted with the Conquerors, confirms this statement, and adds, that Pizarro could not so much as sign his name.[29] This was done by his secretary—Picado, in his latter years—while the governor merely made the customary *rúbrica* or flourish at the sides of his name. This is the case with the instruments I have examined, in which his signature, written probably by his secretary, or his title of *Marques,* in later life substituted for his name, is garnished with a flourish at the ends, executed in as bungling a manner as if done by the hand of a ploughman. Yet we must not estimate this deficiency as we should in this period of general illumination,—general, at least, in our own fortunate country. Reading and writing, so universal now, in the beginning of the sixteenth century might be regarded in the light of accomplishments; and all who have occasion to consult the autograph memorials of that time will find the execution of them, even by persons of the highest rank, too often such as would do little credit to a schoolboy of the present day.

Though bold in action and not easily turned from his purpose, Pizarro was slow in arriving at a decision. This gave him an appearance of irresolution foreign to his character.[30] Perhaps the consciousness of this led him to adopt the custom of saying "No," at first, to applicants for favor; and afterwards, at leisure, to revise his judgment, and grant what seemed to him expedient. He took the opposite course from his comrade Almagro, who, it was observed, generally said "Yes," but too often failed to keep his promise. This was characteristic of the careless and easy nature of the latter, governed by impulse rather than principle.[31]

It is hardly necessary to speak of the courage of a man pledged to such a career as that of Pizarro. Courage, indeed, was a cheap quality among the Spanish adventurers, for danger was their element. But he possessed something higher than mere animal courage, in that constancy of purpose which was rooted too deeply in his nature to be shaken by the wildest storms of fortune. It was this inflexible constancy which formed the key to his character, and constituted the secret of his success. A remarkable evidence of it was given in his first expedition, among the mangroves and dreary marshes of Choco. He saw his followers pining around him under the blighting malaria, wasting before an invisible enemy, and unable to strike a stroke in their own defence. Yet his spirit did not yield, nor did he falter in his enterprise.

There is something oppressive to the imagination in this war against nature. In the struggle of man against man, the spirits are raised by a contest conducted on equal terms; but in a war with the elements, we feel, that, however bravely we may contend, we can have no power to control. Nor are we cheered on by the prospect of glory in such a contest; for, in the capricious estimate of human glory, the silent endurance of privations, however painful, is little, in comparison with the ostentatious trophies of victory. The laurel of the hero—alas for humanity that it should be so!—grows best on the battle-field.

This inflexible spirit of Pizarro was shown still more strongly, when, in the little island of Gallo, he drew the line on the sand, which was to separate him and his handful of followers from their country and from civilized man. He trusted that his own constancy would give strength to the feeble, and rally brave hearts around him for the prosecution of his enterprise. He looked with confidence to the future, and he did not miscalculate. This was heroic, and wanted only a nobler motive for its object to constitute the true moral sublime.

Yet the same feature in his character was displayed in a manner scarcely less remarkable, when, landing on the coast and ascertaining the real strength and civilization of the Incas, he persisted in marching into the interior at the head of a force of less than two hundred men. In this he undoubtedly proposed to himself the example of Cortés, so contagious to the adventurous spirits of that day, and especially to Pizarro, engaged, as he was, in a similar enterprise. Yet the hazard assumed by Pizarro was far greater than that of the Conqueror of Mexico, whose force was nearly three times as large, while the terrors of the Inca name—however justified by the result—were as widely spread as those of the Aztecs.

It was doubtless in imitation of the same captivating model, that Pizarro planned the seizure of Atahuallpa. But the situations of the two Spanish captains were as dissimilar as the manner in which their acts of violence were conducted. The wanton massacre of the Peruvians resembled that perpetrated by Alvarado in Mexico, and might have been attended with consequences as disastrous, if the Peruvian character had been as fierce as that of the Aztecs.[32] But the blow which roused the latter to madness broke the tamer spirits of the Peruvians. It was a bold stroke, which left so much to chance, that it scarcely merits the name of policy.

When Pizarro landed in the country, he found it distracted by a contest for the crown. It would seem to have been for his interest to play off one party against the other, throwing his own weight into the scale that suited him. Instead of this, he resorted to an act of audacious violence which crushed them both at a blow. His subsequent career afforded no scope for the profound policy displayed by Cortés, when he gathered conflicting nations under his banner, and directed them against a common foe. Still less did he have the opportunity of displaying the tactics and admirable strategy of his rival. Cortés conducted his military operations on the scientific principles of a great captain at the head of a powerful host. Pizarro appears only as an adventurer, a fortunate knight-errant. By one bold stroke, he broke the spell which had so long held the land under the dominion of the Incas. The spell was broken, and the airy fabric of their empire, built on the superstition of ages, vanished at a touch. This was good fortune, rather than the result of policy.

Pizarro was eminently perfidious. Yet nothing is more opposed to sound policy. One act of perfidy fully established becomes the ruin of its author. The man who relinquishes confidence in his good faith gives up the best basis for future operations. Who will knowingly build on a quicksand? By his perfidious treatment of Almagro, Pizarro alienated the minds of the Spaniards. By his perfidious treatment of Atahuallpa, and subsequently of the Inca Manco, he disgusted the Peruvians. The name of Pizarro became a by-word for perfidy. Almagro took his revenge in a civil war; Manco in an insurrection which nearly cost Pizarro his dominion. The civil war terminated in a conspiracy which cost him his life. Such were the fruits of his policy. Pizarro may be regarded as a cunning man; but not, as he has been often eulogized by his countrymen, as a politic one.

When Pizarro obtained possession of Cuzco, he found a country well advanced in the arts of civilization; institutions under which the people lived in tranquillity and personal safety; the mountains and the uplands whitened with flocks; the valleys teeming with the fruits of a scientific husbandry; the granaries and warehouses filled to overflowing; the whole land rejoicing in its abundance; and the character of the nation, softened under the influence of the mildest and most innocent form of superstition, well prepared for the reception of a higher and a Christian civilization. But, far from introducing this, Pizarro delivered up the conquered races to his brutal soldiery; the sacred cloisters were abandoned to their lust; the towns and villages were given up to pillage; the wretched natives were parcelled out like slaves, to toil for their conquerors in the mines; the flocks were scattered, and wantonly destroyed; the granaries were dissipated; the beautiful contrivances for the more perfect culture of the soil were suffered to fall into decay; the paradise was converted into a desert. Instead of profiting by the ancient forms of civilization, Pizarro preferred to efface every vestige of them from the land, and on their ruin to erect the institutions of his own country. Yet these institutions did little for the poor Indian, held in iron bondage. It was little to him that the shores of the Pacific were studded with rising communities and cities, the marts of a flourishing commerce. He had no share in the goodly heritage. He was an alien in the land of his fathers.

The religion of the Peruvian, which directed him to the worship of that glorious luminary which is the best representative of the might and beneficence of the Creator, is perhaps the purest form of superstition that has existed among men. Yet it was much, that, under the new order of things, and through the benevolent zeal of the missionaries, some glimmerings of a nobler faith were permitted to dawn on his darkened soul. Pizarro, himself, cannot be charged with manifesting any overweening solicitude for the propagation of the Faith. He was no bigot, like Cortés. Bigotry is the perversion of the religious principle; but the principle itself was wanting in Pizarro. The conversion of the heathen was a predominant motive with Cortés in his expedition. It was not a vain boast. He would have sacrificed his life for it at any time; and more than once, by his indiscreet zeal, he actually did place his life and the success of his enterprise in jeopardy. It was his great purpose to purify the land from the brutish abominations of the Aztecs, by substituting the religion of Jesus. This gave to his expedition the character of a crusade. It furnished the best apology for the Conquest, and does more than all other considerations towards enlisting our sympathies on the side of the conquerors.

But Pizarro's ruling motives, so far as they can be scanned by human judgment, were avarice and ambition. The good missionaries, indeed, followed in his train to scatter the seeds of spiritual truth, and the Spanish government, as usual, directed its beneficent legislation to the conversion of the natives. But the moving power with Pizarro and his followers was the lust of gold. This was the real stimulus to their toil, the price of perfidy, the true guerdon of their victories. This gave a base and mercenary character to their enterprise; and when we contrast the ferocious cupidity of the conquerors with the mild and inoffensive manners of the conquered, our sympathies, the sympathies even of the Spaniard, are necessarily thrown into the scale of the Indian.[33]

But as no picture is without its lights, we must not, in justice to Pizarro, dwell exclusively on the darker features of his portrait. There was no one of her sons to whom Spain was under larger obligations for extent of empire; for his hand won for her the richest of the Indian jewels that once sparkled in her imperial diadem. When we contemplate the perils he braved, the sufferings he patiently endured, the incredible obstacles he overcame, the magnificent results he effected with his single arm, as it were, unaided by the government, —though neither a good, nor a great man in the highest sense of that term, it is impossible not to regard him as a very extraordinary one.

Nor can we fairly omit to notice, in extenuation of his errors, the circumstances of his early life; for, like Almagro, he was the son of sin and sorrow, early cast upon the world to seek his fortunes as he might. In his young and tender age he was to take the impression of those into whose society he was thrown. And when was it the lot of the needy outcast to fall into that of the

CHAPTER VI

MOVEMENTS OF THE CONSPIRATORS. — ADVANCE OF VACA DE CASTRO. — PROCEEDINGS OF ALMAGRO. — PROGRESS OF THE GOVERNOR. — THE FORCES APPROACH EACH OTHER. — BLOODY PLAINS OF CHUPAS. — CONDUCT OF VACA DE CASTRO

1541-1543.

THE first step of the conspirators, after securing possession of the capital, was to send to the different cities, proclaiming the revolution which had taken place, and demanding the recognition of the young Almagro as governor of Peru. Where the summons was accompanied by a military force, as at Truxillo and Arequipa, it was obeyed without much cavil. But in other cities a colder assent was given, and in some the requisition was treated with contempt. In Cuzco, the place of most importance next to Lima, a considerable number of the Almagro faction secured the ascendency of their party; and such of the magistracy as resisted were ejected from their offices to make room for others of a more accommodating temper. But the loyal inhabitants of the city, dissatisfied with this proceeding, privately sent to one of Pizarro's captains, named Alvarez de Holguin, who lay with a considerable force in the neighbourhood; and that officer, entering the place, soon dispossessed the new dignitaries of their honors, and restored the ancient capital to its allegiance.

The conspirators experienced a still more determined opposition from Alonso de Alvarado, one of the principal captains of Pizarro, — defeated, as the reader will remember, by the elder Almagro at the bridge of Abancay, — and now lying in the north with a corps of about two hundred men, as good troops as any in the land. That officer, on receiving tidings of his general's assassination, instantly wrote to the Licentiate Vaca de Castro, advising him of the state of affairs in Peru, and urging him to quicken his march towards the south.[1]

This functionary had been sent out by the Spanish Crown, as noticed in a preceding chapter, to coöperate with Pizarro in restoring tranquillity to the country, with authority to assume the government himself, in case of that commander's death. After a long and tempestuous voyage, he had landed, in the spring of 1541, at the port of Buena Ventura, and, disgusted with the dangers of the sea, preferred to continue his wearisome journey by land. But so enfeebled was he by the hardships he had undergone, that it was full three months before he reached Popayan, where he received the astounding tidings of the death of Pizarro. This was the contingency which had been provided for, with such judicious forecast, in his instructions. Yet he was sorely perplexed by the difficulties of his situation. He was a stranger in the land, with a very imperfect knowledge of the country, without an armed force to support him, without even the military science which might be supposed necessary to avail himself of it. He knew nothing of the degree of Almagro's influence, or of the extent to which the insurrection had spread,—nothing, in short, of the dispositions of the people among whom he was cast.

In such an emergency, a feebler spirit might have listened to the counsels of those who advised to return to Panamá, and stay there until he had mustered a sufficient force to enable him to take the field against the insurgents with advantage. But the courageous heart of Vaca de Castro shrunk from a step which would proclaim his incompetency to the task assigned him. He had confidence in his own resources, and in the virtue of the commission under which he acted. He relied, too, on the habitual loyalty of the Spaniards; and, after mature deliberation, he determined to go forward, and trust to events for accomplishing the objects of his mission.

He was confirmed in this purpose by the advices he now received from Alvarado; and without longer delay, he continued his march towards Quito. Here he was well received by Gonzalo Pizarro's lieutenant, who had charge of the place during his commander's absence on his expedition to the Amazon. The licentiate was also joined by Benalcazar, the conqueror of Quito, who brought a small reinforcement, and offered personally to assist him in the prosecution of his enterprise. He now displayed the royal commission, empowering him, on Pizarro's death, to assume the government. That contingency had arrived, and Vaca de Castro declared his purpose to exercise the authority conferred on him. At the same time, he sent emissaries to the principal cities, requiring their obedience to him as the lawful representative of the Crown,—taking care to employ discreet persons on the mission, whose character would have weight with the citizens. He then continued his march slowly towards the south.[2]

He was willing by his deliberate movements to give time for his summons to take effect, and for the fermentation caused by the late extraordinary events to subside. He reckoned confidently on the loyalty which made the Spaniard unwilling, unless in cases of the last extremity, to come into collision with the royal authority; and, however much this popular sentiment might be disturbed by temporary gusts of passion, he trusted to the habitual current of their feelings for giving the people a right direction. In this he did not miscalculate; for so deep-rooted was the principle of loyalty in the ancient Spaniard, that ages of oppression and misrule could alone have induced him to shake off his allegiance. Sad it is, but not strange, that the length of time passed under a bad government has not qualified him for devising a good one.

While these events were passing in the north, Almagro's faction at Lima was daily receiving new accessions of strength. For, in addition to those who, from the first, had been avowedly of his father's party, there were many others who, from some cause or other, had conceived a disgust for Pizarro, and who now willingly enlisted under the banner of the chief that had overthrown him.

The first step of the young general, or rather of Rada, who directed his movements, was to secure the necessary supplies for the troops, most of whom, having long been in indigent circumstances, were wholly unprepared for service. Funds to a considerable amount were raised, by seizing on the moneys of the Crown in the hands of the treasurer. Pizarro's secretary, Picado, was also drawn from his prison, and interrogated as to the place where his master's treasures were deposited. But, although put to the torture, he would not—or, as is probable, could not—give information on the subject; and the conspirators, who had a long arrear of injuries to settle with him, closed their proceedings by publicly beheading him in the great square of Lima.[3]

Valverde, Bishop of Cuzco, as he himself assures us, vainly interposed in his behalf. It is singular, that, the last time this fanatical prelate appears on the stage, it should be in the benevolent character of a supplicant for mercy.[4] Soon afterwards, he was permitted, with the judge, Velasquez, and some other adherents of Pizarro, to embark from the port of Lima. We have a letter from him, dated at Tumbez, in November, 1541; almost immediately after which he fell into the hands of the Indians, and with his companions was massacred at Puná. A violent death not unfrequently closed the stormy career of the American adventurer. Valverde was a Dominican friar, and, like Father Olmedo in the suite of Cortés, had been by his commander's side throughout the whole of his expedition. But he did not always, like the good Olmedo, use his influence to stay the uplifted hand of the warrior. At least, this was not the mild aspect in which he presented himself at the terrible massacre of Caxamalca. Yet some contemporary accounts represent him, after he had been installed in his episcopal office, as unwearied in his labors to convert the natives, and to ameliorate their condition; and his own correspondence with the government, after that period, shows great solicitude for these praiseworthy objects. Trained in the severest school of monastic discipline, which too often closes the heart against the common charities of life, he could not, like the benevolent Las Casas, rise so far above its fanatical tenets as to regard the heathen as his brother, while in the state of infidelity; and, in the true spirit of that school, he doubtless conceived that the sanctity of the end justified the means, however revolting in themselves. Yet the same man, who thus freely shed the blood of the poor native to secure the triumph of his faith, would doubtless have as freely poured out his own in its defence. The character was no uncommon one in the sixteenth century.[5]

Almagro's followers, having supplied themselves with funds, made as little scruple to appropriate to their own use such horses and arms, of every description, as they could find in the city. And this they did with the less reluctance, as the inhabitants for the most part testified no good-will to their cause. While thus employed, Almagro received intelligence that Holguin had left Cuzco with a force of near three hundred men, with which he was preparing to effect a junction with Alvarado in the north. It was important to Almagro's success that he should defeat this junction. If to procrastinate was the policy of Vaca de Castro, it was clearly that of Almagro to quicken operations, and to bring matters to as speedy an issue as possible; to march at once against Holguin, whom he might expect easily to overcome with his superior numbers; then to follow up the stroke by the still easier defeat of Alvarado, when the new governor would be, in a manner, at his mercy. It would be easy to beat these several bodies in detail, which, once united, would present formidable odds. Almagro and his party had already arrayed themselves against the government by a proceeding too atrocious, and which struck too directly at the royal authority, for its perpetrators to flatter themselves with the hopes of pardon. Their only chance was boldly to follow up the blow, and, by success, to place themselves in so formidable an attitude as to excite the apprehensions of government. The dread of its too potent vassal might extort terms that would never be conceded to his prayers.

But Almagro and his followers shrunk from this open collision with the Crown. They had taken up rebellion because it lay in their path, not because they had wished it. They had meant only to avenge their personal wrongs on Pizarro, and not to defy the royal authority. When, therefore, some of the more resolute, who followed things fearlessly to their consequences, proposed to march at once against Vaca de Castro, and, by striking at the head, settle the contest by a blow, it was almost universally rejected; and it was not till after long debate that it was finally determined to move against Holguin, and cut off his communication with Alonso de Alvarado.

Scarcely had Almagro commenced his march on Xauxa, where he proposed to give battle to his enemy, than he met with a severe misfortune in the death of Juan de Rada. He was a man somewhat advanced in years; and the late exciting scenes, in which he had taken the principal part, had been too much for a frame greatly shattered by a life of extraordinary hardship. He was thrown into a fever, of which he soon after died. By his death, Almagro sustained an inestimable loss; for, besides his devoted attachment to his young leader, he was, by his large experience, and his cautious though courageous character, better qualified than any other cavalier in the army to conduct him safely through the stormy sea on which he had led him to embark.

Among the cavaliers of highest consideration after Rada's death, the two most aspiring were Christoval de Sotelo, and Garcia de Alvarado; both possessed of considerable military talent, but the latter marked by a bold, presumptuous manner, which might remind one of his illustrious namesake, who achieved much higher renown under the banner of Cortés. Unhappily, a jealousy grew up between these two officers; that jealousy, so common among the Spaniards, that it may seem a national characteristic; an impatience of equality, founded on a false principle of honor, which has ever been the fruitful source of faction among them, whether under a monarchy or a republic.

This was peculiarly unfortunate for Almagro, whose inexperience led him to lean for support on others, and who, in the present distracted state of his council, knew scarcely where to turn for it. In the delay occasioned by these dissensions, his little army did not reach the valley of Xauxa till after the enemy had passed it. Almagro followed close, leaving behind his baggage and artillery that he might move the lighter. But the golden opportunity was lost. The rivers, swollen by autumnal rains, impeded his pursuit; and, though his light troops came up with a few stragglers of the rear-guard, Holguin succeeded in conducting his forces through the dangerous passes of the mountains, and in effecting a junction with Alonso de Alvarado, near the northern seaport of Huaura.

Disappointed in his object, Almagro prepared to march on Cuzco,—the capital, as he regarded it, of his own jurisdiction,—to get possession of that city, and there make preparations to meet his adversary in the field. Sotelo was sent forward with a small corps in advance. He experienced no opposition from the now defenceless citizens; the government of the place was again restored to the hands of the men of Chili, and their young leader soon appeared at the head of his battalions, and established his winter-quarters in the Inca capital.

Here, the jealousy of the rival captains broke out into an open feud. It was ended by the death of Sotelo, treacherously assassinated in his own apartment by Garcia de Alvarado. Almagro, greatly outraged by this atrocity, was the more indignant, as he felt himself too weak to punish the offender. He smothered his resentment for the present, affecting to treat the dangerous officer with more distinguished favor. But Alvarado was not the dupe of this specious behaviour. He felt that he had forfeited the confidence of his commander. In revenge, he laid a plot to betray him; and Almagro, driven to the necessity of self-defence, imitated the example of his officer, by entering his house with a party of armed men, who, laying violent hands on the insurgent, slew him on the spot.[6]

This irregular proceeding was followed by the best consequences. The seditious schemes of Alvarado perished with him. The seeds of insubordination were eradicated, and from that moment Almagro experienced only implicit obedience and the most loyal support from his followers. From that hour, too, his own character seemed to be changed; he relied far less on others than on himself, and developed resources not to have been anticipated in one of his years; for he had hardly reached the age of twenty-two.[7] From this time he displayed an energy and forecast, which proved him, in despite of his youth, not unequal to the trying emergencies of the situation in which it was his unhappy lot to be placed.

He instantly set about providing for the wants of his men, and strained every nerve to get them in good fighting order for the approaching campaign. He replenished his treasury with a large amount of silver which he drew from the mines of La Plata. Saltpetre, obtained in abundance in the neighbourhood of Cuzco, furnished the material for gunpowder. He caused cannon, some of large dimensions, to be cast under the superintendence of Pedro de Candia, the Greek, who, it may be remembered, had first come into the country with Pizarro, and who, with a number of his countrymen,—Levantines, as they were called,—was well acquainted with this manufacture. Under their care, fire-arms were made, together with cuirasses and helmets, in which silver was mingled with copper,[8] and of so excellent a quality, that they might vie, says an old soldier of the time, with those from the workshops of Milan.[9] Almagro received a seasonable supply, moreover, from a source scarcely to have been expected. This was from Manco, the wandering Inca, who, detesting the memory of Pizarro, transferred to the young Almagro the same friendly feelings which he had formerly borne to his father; heightened, it may be, by the consideration that Indian blood flowed in the veins of the young commander. From this quarter Almagro obtained a liberal supply of swords, spears, shields, and arms and armour of every description, chiefly taken by the Inca at the memorable siege of Cuzco. He also received the gratifying assurance, that the latter would support him with a detachment of native troops when he opened the campaign.

Before making a final appeal to arms, however, Almagro resolved to try the effect of negotiation with the new governor. In the spring, or early in the summer, of 1542, he sent an embassy to the latter, then at Lima, in which he deprecated the necessity of taking arms against an officer of the Crown. His only desire, he said, was to vindicate his own rights; to secure the possession of New Toledo, the province bequeathed to him by his father, and from which he had been most unjustly excluded by Pizarro. He did not dispute the governor's authority over New Castile, as the country was designated which had been assigned to the marquess; and he concluded by proposing that each party should remain within his respective territory until the determination of the Court of Castile could be made known to them. To this application, couched in respectful terms, Almagro received no answer.

Frustrated in his hopes of a peaceful accommodation, the young captain now saw that nothing was left but the arbitrament of arms. Assembling his troops, preparatory to his departure from the capital, he made them a brief address. He protested that the step which he and his brave companions were about to take was not an act of rebellion against the Crown. It was forced on them by the conduct of the governor himself. The commission of that officer gave him no authority over the territory of New Toledo, settled on Almagro's father, and by his father bequeathed to him. If Vaca de Castro, by exceeding the limits of his authority, drove him to hostilities, the blood spilt in the quarrel would lie on the head of that commander, not on his. "In the assassination of Pizarro," he continued, "we took that justice into our own hands which elsewhere was denied us. It is the same now, in our contest with the royal governor. We are as true-hearted and loyal subjects of the Crown as he is." And he concluded by invoking his soldiers to stand by him heart and hand in the approaching contest, in which they were all equally interested with himself.

The appeal was not made to an insensible audience. There were few among them who did not feel that their fortunes were indissolubly connected with those of their commander; and while they had little to expect from the austere character of the governor, they were warmly attached to the person of their young chief, who, with all the popular qualities of his father, excited additional sympathy from the circumstances of his age and his forlorn condition. Laying their hands on the cross, placed on an altar raised for the purpose, the officers and soldiers severally swore to brave every peril with Almagro, and remain true to him to the last.

In point of numbers, his forces had not greatly strengthened since his departure from Lima. He mustered but little more than five hundred in all; but among them were his father's veterans, well seasoned by many an Indian campaign. He had about two hundred horse, many of them clad in complete mail, a circumstance not too common in these wars, where a stuffed doublet of cotton was often the only panoply of the warrior. His infantry, formed of pikemen and arquebusiers, was excellently armed. But his strength lay in his heavy ordnance, consisting of sixteen pieces, eight large and eight smaller guns, or falconets, as they were called, forming, says one who saw it, a beautiful park of artillery, that would have made a brave show on the citadel of Burgos.[10] The little army, in short, though not imposing from its numbers, was under as good discipline, and as well appointed, as any that ever fought on the fields of Peru; much better than any which Almagro's own father or Pizarro ever led into the field and won their conquests with. Putting himself at the head of his gallant company, the chieftain sallied forth from the walls of Cuzco about midsummer, in 1542, and directed his march towards the coast in expectation of meeting the enemy.[11]

While the events detailed in the preceding pages were passing, Vaca de Castro, whom we left at Quito in the preceding year, was advancing slowly towards the south. His first act, after leaving that city, showed his resolution to enter into no compromise with the assassins of Pizarro. Benalcazar, the distinguished officer whom I have mentioned as having early given in his adherence to him, had protected one of the principal conspirators, his personal friend, who had come into his power, and had facilitated his escape.

The governor, indignant at the proceeding, would listen to no explanation, but ordered the offending officer to return to his own district of Popayan. It was a bold step, in the precarious state of his own fortunes.

As the governor pursued his march, he was well received by the people on the way; and when he entered the cities of San Miguel and of Truxillo, he was welcomed with loyal enthusiasm by the inhabitants, who readily acknowledged his authority, though they showed little alacrity to take their chance with him in the coming struggle.

After lingering a long time in each of these places, he resumed his march and reached the camp of Alonso de Alvarado at Huaura, early in 1542. Holguin had established his quarters at some little distance from his rival; for a jealousy had sprung up, as usual, between these two captains, who both aspired to the supreme command of Captain-General of the army. The office of governor, conferred on Vaca de Castro, might seem to include that of commander-in-chief of the forces. But De Castro was a scholar, bred to the law; and, whatever authority he might arrogate to himself in civil matters, the two captains imagined that the military department he would resign into the hands of others. They little knew the character of the man.

Though possessed of no more military science than belonged to every cavalier in that martial age, the governor knew that to avow his ignorance, and to resign the management of affairs into the hands of others, would greatly impair his authority, if not bring him into contempt with the turbulent spirits among whom he was now thrown. He had both sagacity and spirit, and trusted to be able to supply his own deficiencies by the experience of others. His position placed the services of the ablest men in the country at his disposal, and with the aid of their counsels he felt quite competent to decide on his plan of operations, and to enforce the execution of it. He knew, moreover, that the only way to allay the jealousy of the two parties in the present crisis was to assume himself the office which was the cause of their dissension.

Still he approached his ambitious officers with great caution; and the representations, which he made through some judicious persons who had the most intimate access to them, were so successful, that both were in a short time prevailed on to relinquish their pretensions in his favor. Holguin, the more unreasonable of the two, then waited on him in his rival's quarters, where the governor had the further satisfaction to reconcile him to Alonso de Alvarado. It required some address, as their jealousy of each other had proceeded to such lengths that a challenge had passed between them.

Harmony being thus restored, the licentiate passed over to Holguin's camp, where he was greeted with salvoes of artillery, and loud acclamations of "Viva el Rey" from the loyal soldiery. Ascending a platform covered with velvet, he made an animated harangue to the troops; his commission was read aloud by the secretary; and the little army tendered their obedience to him as the representative of the Crown.

Vaca de Castro's next step was to send off the greater part of his force, in the direction of Xauxa, while, at the head of a small corps, he directed his march towards Lima. Here he was received with lively demonstrations of joy by the citizens, who were generally attached to the cause of Pizarro, the founder and constant patron of their capital. Indeed, the citizens had lost no time after Almagro's departure in expelling his creatures from the municipality, and reasserting their allegiance. With these favorable dispositions towards himself, the governor found no difficulty in obtaining a considerable loan of money from the wealthier inhabitants. But he was less successful, at first, in his application for horses and arms, since the harvest had been too faithfully gleaned, already, by the men of Chili. As, however, he prolonged his stay some time in the capital, he obtained important supplies, before he left it, both of arms and ammunition, while he added to his force by a considerable body of recruits.[12]

As he was thus employed, he received tidings that the enemy had left Cuzco, and was on his march towards the coast. Quitting Los Reyes, therefore, with his trusty followers, Vaca de Castro marched at once to Xauxa, the appointed place of rendezvous. Here he mustered his forces, and found that they amounted to about seven hundred men. The cavalry, in which lay his strength, was superior in numbers to that of his antagonist, but neither so well mounted or armed. It included many cavaliers of birth, and well-tried soldiers, besides a number who, having great interests at stake, as possessed of large estates in the country, had left them at the call of government, to enlist under its banners.[13] His infantry, besides pikes, was indifferently well supplied with fire-arms; but he had nothing to show in the way of artillery except three or four ill-mounted falconets. Yet, notwithstanding these deficiencies, the royal army, if so insignificant a force can deserve that name, was so far superior in numbers to that of his rival, that the one might be thought, on the whole, to be no unequal match for the other.[14]

The reader, familiar with the large masses employed in European warfare, may smile at the paltry forces of the Spaniards. But in the New World, where a countless host of natives went for little, five hundred well-trained Europeans were regarded as a formidable body. No army, up to the period before us, had ever risen to a thousand. Yet it is not numbers, as I have already been led to remark, that give importance to a conflict; but the consequences that depend on it,—the magnitude of the stake, and the skill and courage of the players. The more limited the means, even, the greater may be the science shown in the use of them; until, forgetting the poverty of the materials, we fix our attention on the conduct of the actors, and the greatness of the results.

While at Xauxa, Vaca de Castro received an embassy from Gonzalo Pizarro, returned from his expedition from the "Land of Cinnamon," in which that chief made an offer of his services in the approaching contest. The governor's answer showed that he was not wholly averse to an accommodation with Almagro, provided it could be effected without compromising the royal authority. He was willing, perhaps, to avoid the final trial by battle, when he considered, that, from the equality of the contending forces, the issue must be extremely doubtful. He knew that the presence of Pizarro in the camp, the detested enemy of the Almagrians, would excite distrust in their bosoms that would probably baffle every effort at accommodation. Nor is it likely that the governor cared to have so restless a spirit introduced into his own councils. He accordingly sent to Gonzalo, thanking him for the promptness of his support, but courteously declined it, while he advised him to remain in his province, and repose after the fatigues of his wearisome expedition. At the same time, he assured him that he would not fail to call for his services when occasion required it.—The haughty cavalier was greatly disgusted by the repulse.[15]

The governor now received such an account of Almagro's movements as led him to suppose that he was preparing to occupy Guamanga, a fortified place of considerable strength, about thirty leagues from Xauxa.[16] Anxious to secure this post, he broke up his encampment, and by forced marches, conducted in so irregular a manner as must have placed him in great danger if his enemy had been near to profit by it, he succeeded in anticipating Almagro, and threw himself into the place while his antagonist was at Bilcas, some ten leagues distant.

At Guamanga, Vaca de Castro received another embassy from Almagro, of similar import with the former. The young chief again deprecated the existence of hostilities between brethren of the same family, and proposed an accommodation of the quarrel on the same basis as before. To these proposals the governor now condescended to reply. It might be thought, from his answer, that he felt some compassion for the youth and inexperience of Almagro, and that he was willing to distinguish between him and the principal conspirators, provided he could detach him from their interests. But it is more probable that he intended only to amuse his enemy by a show of negotiation, while he gained time for tampering with the fidelity of his troops.

He insisted that Almagro should deliver up to him all those immediately implicated in the death of Pizarro, and should then disband his forces. On these conditions the government would pass over his treasonable practices, and he should be reinstated in the royal favor. Together with this mission, Vaca de Castro, it is reported, sent a Spaniard, disguised as an Indian, who was instructed to communicate with certain officers in Almagro's camp, and prevail on them, if possible, to abandon his cause and return to their allegiance. Unfortunately, the disguise of the emissary was detected. He was seized, put to the torture, and, having confessed the whole of the transaction, was hanged as a spy.

Almagro laid the proceeding before his captains. The terms proffered by the governor were such as no man with a particle of honor in his nature could entertain for a moment; and Almagro's indignation, as well as that of his companions, was heightened by the duplicity of their enemy, who could practise such insidious arts, while ostensibly engaged in a fair and open negotiation. Fearful, perhaps, lest the tempting offers of their antagonist might yet prevail over the constancy of some of the weaker spirits among them, they demanded that all negotiation should be broken off, and that they should be led at once against the enemy.[17]

The governor, meanwhile, finding the broken country around Guamanga unfavorable for his cavalry, on which he mainly relied, drew off his forces to the neighbouring lowlands, known as the Plains of Chupas. It was the tempestuous season of the year, and for several days the storm raged wildly among the hills, and, sweeping along their sides into the valley, poured down rain, sleet, and snow on the miserable bivouacs of the soldiers, till they were drenched to the skin and nearly stiffened by the cold.[18] At length, on the sixteenth of September, 1542, the scouts brought in tidings that Almagro's troops were advancing, with the intention, apparently, of occupying the highlands around Chupas. The war of the elements had at last subsided, and was succeeded by one of those brilliant days which are found only in the tropics. The royal camp was early in motion, as Vaca de Castro, desirous to secure the heights that commanded the valley, detached a body of arquebusiers on that service, supported by a corps of cavalry, which he soon followed with the rest of the forces. On reaching the eminence, news was brought that the enemy had come to a halt, and established himself in a strong position at less than a league's distance.

It was now late in the afternoon, and the sun was not more than two hours above the horizon. The governor hesitated to begin the action when they must so soon be overtaken by night. But Alonso de Alvarado assured him that "now was the time; for the spirits of his men were hot for fight, and it was better to take the benefit of it than to damp their ardor by delay." The governor acquiesced, exclaiming at the same time, — "O for the might of Joshua, to stay the sun in his course!"[19] He then drew up his little army in order of battle, and made his dispositions for the attack.

In the centre he placed his infantry, consisting of arquebusiers and pikemen, constituting the *battle*, as it was called. On the flanks, he established his cavalry, placing the right wing, together with the royal standard, under charge of Alonso de Alvarado, and the left under Holguin, supported by a gallant body of cavaliers. His artillery, too insignificant to be of much account, was also in the centre. He proposed himself to lead the van, and to break the first lance with the enemy; but from this chivalrous display he was dissuaded by his officers, who reminded him that too much depended on his life to have it thus wantonly exposed. The governor contented himself, therefore, with heading a body of reserve, consisting of forty horse, to act on any quarter as occasion might require. This corps, comprising the flower of his chivalry, was chiefly drawn from Alvarado's troop, greatly to the discontent of that captain. The governor himself rode a coal-black charger, and wore a rich surcoat of brocade over his mail, through which the habit and emblems of the knightly order of St. James, conferred on him just before his departure from Castile, were conspicuous.[20] It was a point of honor with the chivalry of the period to court danger by displaying their rank in the splendor of their military attire and the caparisons of their horses.

Before commencing the assault, Vaca de Castro addressed a few remarks to his soldiers, in order to remove any hesitation that some might yet feel, who recollected the displeasure shown by the emperor to the victors as well as the vanquished after the battle of Salinas. He told them that their enemies were rebels. They were in arms against him, the representative of the Crown, and it was his duty to quell this rebellion and punish the authors of it. He then caused the law to be read aloud, proclaiming the doom of traitors. By this law, Almagro and his followers had forfeited their lives and property, and the governor promised to distribute the latter among such of his men as showed the best claim to it by their conduct in the battle. This last politic promise vanquished the scruples of the most fastidious; and, having completed his dispositions in the most judicious and soldier-like manner, Vaca de Castro gave the order to advance.[21]

As the forces turned a spur of the hills which had hitherto screened them from their enemies, they came in sight of the latter, formed along the crest of a gentle eminence, with their snow-white banners, the distinguishing color of the Almagrians, floating above their heads, and their bright arms flinging back the broad rays of the evening sun. Almagro's disposition of his troops was not unlike that of his adversary. In the centre was his excellent artillery, covered by his arquebusiers and spearmen; while his cavalry rode on the flanks. The troops on the left he proposed to lead in person. He had chosen his position with judgment, as the character of the ground gave full play to his guns, which opened an effective fire on the assailants as they drew near. Shaken by the storm of shot, Vaca de Castro saw the difficulty of advancing in open view of the hostile battery. He took the counsel, therefore, of Francisco de Carbajal, who undertook to lead the forces by a circuitous, but safer, route. This is the first occasion on which the name of this veteran appears in these American wars, where it was afterwards to acquire a melancholy notoriety. He had come to the country after the campaigns of forty years in Europe, where he had studied the art of war under the Great Captain, Gonsalvo de Cordova. Though now far advanced in age, he possessed all the courage and indomitable energy of youth, and well exemplified the lessons he had studied under his great commander.

Taking advantage of a winding route that sloped round the declivity of the hills, he conducted the troops in such a manner, that, until they approached quite near the enemy, they were protected by the intervening ground. While thus advancing, they were assailed on the left flank by the Indian battalions under Paullo, the Inca Manco's brother; but a corps of musketeers, directing a scattering fire among them, soon rid the Spaniards of this annoyance. When, at length, the royal troops, rising above the hill, again came into view of Almagro's lines, the artillery opened on them with fatal effect. It was but for a moment, however, as, from some unaccountable cause, the guns were pointed at such an angle, that, although presenting an obvious mark, by far the greater part of the shot passed over their heads. Whether this was the result of treachery, or merely of awkwardness, is uncertain. The artillery was under charge of the engineer, Pedro de Candia. This man, who, it may be remembered, was one of the thirteen that so gallantly stood by Pizarro in the island of Gallo, had fought side by side with his leader through the whole of the Conquest. He had lately, however, conceived some disgust with him, and had taken part with the faction of Almagro. The death of his old commander, he may perhaps have thought, had settled all their differences, and he was now willing to return to his former allegiance. At least, it is said, that, at this very time, he was in correspondence with Vaca de Castro. Almagro himself seems to have had no doubt of his treachery. For, after remonstrating in vain with him on his present conduct, he ran him through the body, and the unfortunate cavalier fell lifeless on the field. Then, throwing himself on one of the guns, Almagro gave it a new direction, and that so successfully, that, when it was discharged, it struck down several of the cavalry.[22]

The firing now took better effect, and by one volley a whole file of the royal infantry was swept off, and though others quickly stepped in to fill up the ranks, the men, impatient of their sufferings, loudly called on the troopers, who had halted for a moment, to quicken their advance.[23] This delay had been caused by Carbajal's desire to bring his own guns to bear on the opposite columns. But the design was quickly abandoned; the clumsy ordnance was left on the field, and orders were given to the cavalry to charge; the trumpets sounded, and, crying their war-cries, the bold cavaliers struck their spurs into their steeds, and rode at full speed against the enemy.

Well had it been for Almagro, if he had remained firm on the post which gave him such advantage. But from a false point of honor, he thought it derogatory to a brave knight passively to await the assault, and, ordering his own men to charge, the hostile squadrons, rapidly advancing against each other, met midway on the plain. The shock was terrible. Horse and rider reeled under the force of it. The spears flew into shivers;[24] and the cavaliers, drawing their swords, or wielding their maces and battle-axes, — though some of the royal troopers were armed only with a common axe, — dealt their blows with all the fury of civil hate. It was a fearful struggle, not merely of man against man, but, to use the words of an eyewitness, of brother against brother, and friend against friend.[25] No quarter was asked; for the wrench that had been strong enough to tear asunder the dearest ties of kindred left no hold for humanity. The excellent arms of the Almagrians counterbalanced the odds of numbers; but the royal partisans gained some advantage by striking at the horses instead of the mailed bodies of their antagonists.

The infantry, meanwhile, on both sides, kept up a sharp cross-fire from their arquebuses, which did execution on the ranks of the cavaliers, as well as on one another. But Almagro's battery of heavy guns, now well directed, mowed down the advancing columns of foot. The latter, staggering, began to fall back from the terrible fire, when Francisco de Carbajal, throwing himself before them, cried out, "Shame on you, my men! Do you give way now? I am twice as good a mark for the enemy as any of you!" He was a very large man; and, throwing off his steel helmet and cuirass, that he might have no advantage over his followers, he remained lightly attired in his cotton doublet, when, swinging his partisan over his head, he sprang boldly forward through blinding volumes of smoke and a tempest of musket-balls, and, supported by the bravest of his troops, overpowered the gunners, and made himself master of their pieces.

The shades of night had now, for some time, been coming thicker and thicker over the field. But still the deadly struggle went on in the darkness, as the red and white badges intimated the respective parties, and their war-cries rose above the din, — "Vaca de Castro y el Rey," — "Almagro y el Rey," — while both invoked the aid of their military apostle St. James. Holguin, who commanded the royalists on the left, pierced through by two musket-balls, had been slain early in the action. He had made himself conspicuous by a rich sobrevest of white velvet over his armour. Still a gallant band of cavaliers maintained the fight so valiantly on that quarter, that the Almagrians found it difficult to keep their ground.[26]

It fared differently on the right, where Alonso de Alvarado commanded. He was there encountered by Almagro in person, who fought worthy of his name. By repeated charges on his opponent, he endeavoured to bear down his squadrons, so much worse mounted and worse armed than his own. Alvarado resisted with undiminished courage; but his numbers had been thinned, as we have seen, before the battle, to supply the governor's reserve, and, fairly overpowered by the superior strength of his adversary, who had already won two of the royal banners, he was slowly giving ground. "Take, but kill not!" shouted the generous young chief, who felt himself sure of victory.[27]

But at this crisis, Vaca de Castro, who, with his reserve, had occupied a rising ground that commanded the field of action, was fully aware that the time had now come for him to take part in the struggle. He had long strained his eyes through the gloom to watch the movements of the combatants, and received constant tidings how the fight was going. He no longer hesitated, but, calling on his men to follow, led off boldly into the thickest of the *mêlée* to the support of his stout-hearted officer. The arrival of a new corps on the field, all fresh for action, gave another turn to the tide.[28] Alvarado's men took heart and rallied. Almagro's, though driven back by the fury of the assault, quickly returned against their assailants. Thirteen of Vaca de Castro's cavaliers fell dead from their saddles. But it was the last effort of the Almagrians. Their strength, though not their spirit, failed them. They gave way in all directions, and, mingling together in the darkness, horse, foot, and artillery, they trampled one another down, as they made the best of their way from the press of their pursuers. Almagro used every effort to stay them. He performed miracles of valor, says one who witnessed them; but he was borne along by the tide, and, though he seemed to court death, by the freedom with which he exposed his person to danger, yet he escaped without a wound.

Others there were of his company, and among them a young cavalier named Gerónimo de Alvarado, who obstinately refused to quit the field; and shouting out,— "We slew Pizarro! we killed the tyrant!" they threw themselves on the lances of their conquerors, preferring death on the battle-field to the ignominious doom of the gibbet.[29]

It was nine o'clock when the battle ceased, though the firing was heard at intervals over the field at a much later hour, as some straggling party of fugitives were overtaken by their pursuers. Yet many succeeded in escaping in the obscurity of night, while some, it is said, contrived to elude pursuit in a more singular way; tearing off the badges from the corpses of their enemies, they assumed them for themselves, and, mingling in the ranks as followers of Vaca de Castro, joined in the pursuit.

That commander, at length, fearing some untoward accident, and that the fugitives, should they rally again under cover of the darkness, might inflict some loss on their pursuers, caused his trumpets to sound, and recalled his scattered forces under their banners. All night they remained under arms on the field, which, so lately the scene of noisy strife, was now hushed in silence, broken only by the groans of the wounded and the dying. The natives, who had hung, during the fight, like a dark cloud, round the skirts of the mountains, contemplating with gloomy satisfaction the destruction of their enemies, now availed themselves of the obscurity to descend, like a pack of famished wolves, upon the plains, where they stripped the bodies of the slain, and even of the living, but disabled wretches, who had in vain dragged themselves into the bushes for concealment. The following morning, Vaca de Castro gave orders that the wounded—those who had not perished in the cold damps of the night—should be committed to the care of the surgeons, while the priests were occupied with administering confession and absolution to the dying. Four large graves or pits were dug, in which the bodies of the slain—the conquerors and the conquered—were heaped indiscriminately together. But the remains of Alvarez de Holguin and several other cavaliers of distinction were transported to Guamanga, where they were buried with the solemnities suited to their rank; and the tattered banners won from their vanquished countrymen waved over their monuments, the melancholy trophies of their victory.

The number of killed is variously reported,—from three hundred to five hundred on both sides.[30] The mortality was greatest among the conquerors, who suffered more from the cannon of the enemy before the action, than the latter suffered in the rout that followed it. The number of wounded was still greater; and full half of the survivors of Almagro's party were made prisoners. Many, indeed, escaped from the field to the neighbouring town of Guamanga, where they took refuge in the churches and monasteries. But their asylum was not respected, and they were dragged forth and thrown into prison. Their brave young commander fled with a few followers only to Cuzco, where he was instantly arrested by the magistrates whom he had himself placed over the city.[31]

At Guamanga, Vaca de Castro appointed a commission, with the Licentiate de la Gama at its head, for the trial of the prisoners; and *justice* was not satisfied, till forty had been condemned to death, and thirty others—some of them with the loss of one or more of their members—sent into banishment.[32] Such severe reprisals have been too common with the Spaniards in their civil feuds. Strange that they should so blindly plunge into these, with this dreadful doom for the vanquished!

From the scene of this bloody tragedy, the governor proceeded to Cuzco, which he entered at the head of his victorious battalions, with all the pomp and military display of a conqueror. He maintained a corresponding state in his way of living, at the expense of a sneer from some, who sarcastically contrasted this ostentatious profusion with the economical reforms he subsequently introduced into the finances.[33] But Vaca de Castro was sensible of the effect of this outward show on the people generally, and disdained no means of giving authority to his office. His first act was to determine the fate of his prisoner, Almagro. A council of war was held. Some were for sparing the unfortunate chief, in consideration of his youth, and the strong cause of provocation he had received. But the majority were of opinion that such mercy could not be extended to the leader of the rebels, and that his death was indispensable to the permanent tranquillity of the country.

When led to execution in the great square of Cuzco,—the same spot where his father had suffered but a few years before,—Almagro exhibited the most perfect composure, though, as the herald proclaimed aloud the doom of the traitor, he indignantly denied that he was one. He made no appeal for mercy to his judges, but simply requested that his bones might be laid by the side of his father's. He objected to having his eyes bandaged, as was customary on such occasions, and, after confession, he devoutly embraced the cross, and submitted his neck to the stroke of the executioner. His remains, agreeably to his request, were transported to the monastery of La Merced, where they were deposited side by side with those of his unfortunate parent.[34]

There have been few names, indeed, in the page of history, more unfortunate than that of Almagro. Yet the fate of the son excites a deeper sympathy than that of the father; and this, not merely on account of his youth, and the peculiar circumstances of his situation. He possessed many of the good qualifies of the elder Almagro, with a frank and manly nature, in which the bearing of the soldier was somewhat softened by the refinement of a better education than is to be found in the license of a camp. His career, though short, gave promise of considerable talent, which required only a fair field for its development. But he was the child of misfortune, and his morning of life was overcast by clouds and tempests. If his character, naturally benignant, sometimes showed the fiery sparkles of the vindictive Indian temper, some apology may be found, not merely in his blood, but in the circumstances of his situation. He was more sinned against than sinning; and, if conspiracy could ever find a justification, it must be in a case like his, where, borne down by injuries heaped on his parent and himself, he could obtain no redress from the only quarter whence he had a right to look for it. With him, the name of Almagro became extinct, and the faction of Chili, so long the terror of the land, passed away for ever.

While these events were occurring in Cuzco, the governor learned that Gonzalo Pizarro had arrived at Lima, where he showed himself greatly discontented with the state of things in Peru. He loudly complained that the government of the country, after his brother's death, had not been placed in his hands; and, as reported by some, he was now meditating schemes for getting possession of it. Vaca de Castro well knew that there would be no lack of evil counsellors to urge Gonzalo to this desperate step; and, anxious to extinguish the spark of insurrection before it had been fanned by these turbulent spirits into a flame, he detached a strong body to Lima to secure that capital. At the same time he commanded the presence of Gonzalo Pizarro in Cuzco.

That chief did not think it prudent to disregard the summons; and shortly after entered the Inca capital, at the head of a well-armed body of cavaliers. He was at once admitted into the governor's presence, when the latter dismissed his guard, remarking that he had nothing to fear from a brave and loyal knight like Pizarro. He then questioned him as to his late adventures in Canelas, and showed great sympathy for his extraordinary sufferings. He took care not to alarm his jealousy by any allusion to his ambitious schemes, and concluded by recommending him, now that the tranquillity of the country was reëstablished, to retire and seek the repose he so much needed, on his valuable estates at Charcas. Gonzalo Pizarro, finding no ground opened for a quarrel with the cool and politic governor, and probably feeling that he was, at least not now, in sufficient strength to warrant it, thought it prudent to take the advice, and withdrew to La Plata, where he busied himself in working those rich mines of silver that soon put him in condition for a more momentous enterprise than any he had yet attempted.[35]

Thus rid of his formidable competitor, Vaca de Castro occupied himself with measures for the settlement of the country. He began with his army, a part of which he had disbanded. But many cavaliers still remained, pressing their demands for a suitable recompense for their services. These they were not disposed to undervalue, and the governor was happy to rid himself of their importunities by employing them on distant expeditions, among which was the exploration of the country watered by the great Rio de la Plata. The boiling spirits of the high-mettled cavaliers, without some such vent, would soon have thrown the whole country again into a state of fermentation.

His next concern was to provide laws for the better government of the colony. He gave especial care to the state of the Indian population; and established schools for teaching them Christianity. By various provisions, he endeavoured to secure them from the exactions of their conquerors, and he encouraged the poor natives to transfer their own residence to the communities of the white men. He commanded the caciques to provide supplies for the *tambos,* or houses for the accommodation of travellers, which lay in their neighbourhood, by which regulation he took away from the Spaniards a plausible apology for rapine, and greatly promoted facility of intercourse. He was watchful over the finances, much dilapidated in the late troubles, and in several instances retrenched what he deemed excessive *repartimientos* among the Conquerors. This last act exposed him to much odium from the objects of it. But his measures were so just and impartial, that he was supported by public opinion.[36]

Indeed, Vaca de Castro's conduct, from the hour of his arrival in the country, had been such as to command respect, and prove him competent to the difficult post for which he had been selected. Without funds, without troops, he had found the country, on his landing, in a state of anarchy; yet, by courage and address, he had gradually acquired sufficient strength to quell the insurrection. Though no soldier, he had shown undaunted spirit and presence of mind in the hour of action, and made his military preparations with a forecast and discretion that excited the admiration of the most experienced veterans.

If he may be thought to have abused the advantages of victory by cruelty towards the conquered, it must be allowed that he was not influenced by any motives of a personal nature. He was a lawyer, bred in high notions of royal prerogative. Rebellion he looked upon as an unpardonable crime; and, if his austere nature was unrelenting in the exaction of justice, he lived in an iron age, when justice was rarely tempered by mercy.

In his subsequent regulations for the settlement of the country, he showed equal impartiality and wisdom. The colonists were deeply sensible of the benefits of his administration, and afforded the best commentary on his services by petitioning the Court of Castile to continue him in the government of Peru.[37] Unfortunately, such was not the policy of the Crown.

CHAPTER VII

ABUSES BY THE CONQUERORS. — CODE FOR
THE COLONIES. — GREAT EXCITEMENT IN
PERU. — BLASCO NUÑEZ THE VICEROY. —
HIS SEVERE POLICY. — OPPOSED
BY GONZALO PIZARRO

1543-1544.

BEFORE continuing the narrative of events in Peru, we must turn to the
mother-country, where important changes were in progress in respect to the
administration of the colonies.

Since his accession to the Crown, Charles the Fifth had been chiefly
engrossed by the politics of Europe, where a theatre was opened more stimulating to his ambition than could be found in a struggle with the barbarian
princes of the New World. In this quarter, therefore, an empire almost
unheeded, as it were, had been suffered to grow up, until it had expanded
into dimensions greater than those of his European dominions, and destined
soon to become far more opulent. A scheme of government had, it is true,
been devised, and laws enacted from time to time for the regulation of the
colonies. But these laws were often accommodated less to the interests of the
colonies themselves, than to those of the parent country; and, when contrived
in a better spirit, they were but imperfectly executed; for the voice of authority, however loudly proclaimed at home, too often died away in feeble echoes
before it had crossed the waters.

This state of things, and, indeed, the manner in which the Spanish territories in the New World had been originally acquired, were most unfortunate
both for the conquered races and their masters. Had the provinces gained by
the Spaniards been the fruit of peaceful acquisition, — of barter and negotiation, — or had their conquest been achieved under the immediate direction of
government, the interests of the natives would have been more carefully protected. From the superior civilization of the Indians in the Spanish American
colonies, they still continued after the Conquest to remain on the ground,

and to mingle in the same communities, with the white men; in this forming an obvious contrast to the condition of our own aborigines, who, shrinking from the contact of civilization, have withdrawn, as the latter has advanced, deeper and deeper into the heart of the wilderness. But the South American Indian was qualified by his previous institutions for a more refined legislation than could be adapted to the wild hunters of the forest; and, had the sovereign been there in person to superintend his conquests, he could never have suffered so large a portion of his vassals to be wantonly sacrificed to the cupidity and cruelty of the handful of adventurers who subdued them.

But, as it was, the affair of reducing the country was committed to the hands of irresponsible individuals, soldiers of fortune, desperate adventurers, who entered on conquest as a game, which they were to play in the most unscrupulous manner, with little care but to win it. Receiving small encouragement from the government, they were indebted to their own valor for success; and the right of conquest, they conceived, extinguished every existing right in the unfortunate natives. The lands, the persons, of the conquered races were parcelled out and appropriated by the victors as the legitimate spoils of victory; and outrages were perpetrated every day, at the contemplation of which humanity shudders.

These outrages, though nowhere perpetrated on so terrific a scale as in the islands, where, in a few years, they had nearly annihilated the native population, were yet of sufficient magnitude in Peru to call down the vengeance of Heaven on the heads of their authors; and the Indian might feel that this vengeance was not long delayed, when he beheld his oppressors, wrangling over their miserable spoil, and turning their swords against each other. Peru, as already mentioned, was subdued by adventurers, for the most part, of a lower and more ferocious stamp than those who followed the banner of Cortés. The character of the followers partook, in some measure, of that of the leaders in their respective enterprises. It was a sad fatality for the Incas; for the reckless soldiers of Pizarro were better suited to contend with the fierce Aztec than with the more refined and effeminate Peruvian. Intoxicated by the unaccustomed possession of power, and without the least notion of the responsibilities which attached to their situation as masters of the land, they too often abandoned themselves to the indulgence of every whim which cruelty or caprice could dictate. Not unfrequently, says an unsuspicious witness, I have seen the Spaniards, long after the Conquest, amuse themselves by hunting down the natives with bloodhounds for mere sport, or in order to train their dogs to the game![1] The most unbounded scope was given to licentiousness. The young maiden was torn without remorse from the arms of her family to gratify the passion of her brutal conqueror.[2] The sacred houses of the Virgins of the Sun were broken open and violated, and the cavalier swelled his harem with a troop of Indian girls, making it seem that the Crescent would have been a much more fitting symbol for his banner than the immaculate Cross.[3]

But the dominant passion of the Spaniard was the lust of gold. For this he shrunk from no toil himself, and was merciless in his exactions of labor from his Indian slave. Unfortunately, Peru abounded in mines which too well repaid this labor; and human life was the item of least account in the estimate of the Conquerors. Under his Incas, the Peruvian was never suffered to be idle; but the task imposed on him was always proportioned to his strength. He had his seasons of rest and refreshment, and was well protected against the inclemency of the weather. Every care was shown for his personal safety. But the Spaniards, while they taxed the strength of the native to the utmost, deprived him of the means of repairing it, when exhausted. They suffered the provident arrangements of the Incas to fall into decay. The granaries were emptied; the flocks were wasted in riotous living. They were slaughtered to gratify a mere epicurean whim, and many a llama was destroyed solely for the sake of the brains, — a dainty morsel, much coveted by the Spaniards.[4] So reckless was the spirit of destruction after the Conquest, says Ondegardo, the wise governor of Cuzco, that in four years more of these animals perished than in four hundred, in the times of the Incas.[5] The flocks, once so numerous over the broad table-lands, were now thinned to a scanty number, that sought shelter in the fastnesses of the Andes. The poor Indian, without food, without the warm fleece which furnished him a defence against the cold, now wandered half-starved and naked over the plateau. Even those who had aided the Spaniards in the conquest fared no better; and many an Inca noble roamed a mendicant over the lands where he once held rule, and if driven, perchance, by his necessities, to purloin something from the superfluity of his conquerors, he expiated it by a miserable death.[6]

It is true, there were good men, missionaries, faithful to their calling, who wrought hard in the spiritual conversion of the native, and who, touched by his misfortunes, would gladly have interposed their arm to shield him from his oppressors.[7] But too often the ecclesiastic became infected by the general spirit of licentiousness; and the religious fraternities, who led a life of easy indulgence on the lands cultivated by their Indian slaves, were apt to think less of the salvation of their souls than of profiting by the labor of their bodies.[8]

Yet still there were not wanting good and wise men in the colonies, who, from time to time, raised the voice of remonstrance against these abuses, and who carried their complaints to the foot of the throne. To the credit of the government, it must also be confessed, that it was solicitous to obtain such information as it could, both from its own officers, and from commissioners deputed expressly for the purpose, whose voluminous communications throw a flood of light on the internal condition of the country, and furnish the best materials for the historian.[9] But it was found much easier to get this information than to profit by it.

In 1541, Charles the Fifth, who had been much occupied by the affairs of Germany, revisited his ancestral dominions, where his attention was imperatively called to the state of the colonies. Several memorials in relation to it were laid before him; but no one pressed the matter so strongly on the royal conscience as Las Casas, afterwards Bishop of Chiapa. This good ecclesiastic, whose long life had been devoted to those benevolent labors which gained him the honorable title of Protector of the Indians, had just completed his celebrated treatise on the Destruction of the Indies, the most remarkable record, probably, to be found, of human wickedness, but which, unfortunately, loses much of its effect from the credulity of the writer, and his obvious tendency to exaggerate.

In 1542, Las Casas placed his manuscript in the hands of his royal master. That same year, a council was called at Valladolid, composed chiefly of jurists and theologians, to devise a system of laws for the regulation of the American colonies.

Las Casas appeared before this body, and made an elaborate argument, of which a part only has been given to the public. He there assumes, as a fundamental proposition, that the Indians were by the law of nature free; that, as vassals of the Crown, they had a right to its protection, and should be declared free from that time, without exception and for ever.[10] He sustains this proposition by a great variety of arguments, comprehending the substance of most that has been since urged in the same cause by the friends of humanity. He touches on the ground of expediency, showing, that, without the interference of government, the Indian race must be gradually exterminated by the systematic oppression of the Spaniards. In conclusion, he maintains, that, if the Indians, as it was pretended, would not labor unless compelled, the white man would still find it for his interest to cultivate the soil; and that if he should not be able to do so, that circumstance would give him no right over the Indian, since *God does not allow evil that good may come of it.*[11] — This lofty morality, it will be remembered, was from the lips of a Dominican, in the sixteenth century, one of the order that founded the Inquisition, and in the very country where the fiery tribunal was then in most active operation![12]

The arguments of Las Casas encountered all the opposition naturally to be expected from indifference, selfishness, and bigotry. They were also resisted by some persons of just and benevolent views in his audience, who, while they admitted the general correctness of his reasoning, and felt deep sympathy for the wrongs of the natives, yet doubted whether his scheme of reform was not fraught with greater evils than those it was intended to correct. For Las Casas was the uncompromising friend of freedom. He intrenched himself strongly on the ground of natural right; and, like some of the reformers of our own day, disdained to calculate the consequences of carrying out the principle to its full and unqualified extent. His earnest eloquence, instinct with the generous love of humanity, and fortified by a host of facts, which it was not easy to assail, prevailed over his auditors. The result of their deliberations was a code of ordinances, which, however, far from being limited to the wants of the natives, had particular reference to the European population, and the distractions of the country. It was of general application to all the American colonies. It will be necessary here only to point out some of the provisions having immediate reference to Peru.

The Indians were declared true and loyal vassals of the Crown, and their freedom as such was fully recognized. Yet, to maintain inviolate the guaranty of the government to the Conquerors, it was decided, that those lawfully possessed of slaves might still retain them; but, at the death of the present proprietors, they were to revert to the Crown.

It was provided, however, that slaves, in any event, should be forfeited by all those who had shown themselves unworthy to hold them by neglect or ill-usage; by all public functionaries, or such as had held offices under the government; by ecclesiastics and religious corporations; and lastly, — a sweeping clause, — by all who had taken a criminal part in the feuds of Almagro and Pizarro.

It was further ordered, that the Indians should be moderately taxed; that they should not be compelled to labor where they did not choose, and that where, from particular circumstances, this was made necessary, they should receive a fair compensation. It was also decreed, that, as the *repartimientos* of land were often excessive, they should in such cases be reduced; and that, where proprietors had been guilty of a notorious abuse of their slaves, their estates should be forfeited altogether.

As Peru had always shown a spirit of insubordination, which required a more vigorous interposition of authority than was necessary in the other colonies, it was resolved to send a viceroy to that country, who should display a state, and be armed with powers, that might make him a more fitting representative of the sovereign. He was to be accompanied by a Royal Audience, consisting of four judges, with extensive powers of jurisdiction, both criminal and civil, who, besides a court of justice, should constitute a sort of council to advise with and aid the viceroy. The Audience of Panamá was to be dissolved, and the new tribunal, with the vice-king's court, was to be established at Los Reyes, or Lima, as it now began to be called, — henceforth the metropolis of the Spanish empire on the Pacific.[13]

Such were some of the principal features of this remarkable code, which, touching on the most delicate relations of society, broke up the very foundations of property, and, by a stroke of the pen, as it were, converted a nation of slaves into freemen. It would have required, we may suppose, but little forecast to divine, that in the remote regions of America, and especially in Peru, where the colonists had been hitherto accustomed to unbounded license, a reform, so salutary in essential points, could be enforced thus summarily only at the price of a revolution. — Yet the ordinances received the sanction of the emperor that same year, and in November, 1543, were published at Madrid.[14]

No sooner was their import known than it was conveyed by numerous letters to the colonists, from their friends in Spain. The tidings flew like wildfire over the land, from Mexico to Chili. Men were astounded at the prospect of the ruin that awaited them. In Peru, particularly, there was scarcely one that could hope to escape the operation of the law. Few there were who had not taken part, at some time or other, in the civil feuds of

Almagro and Pizarro; and still fewer of those that remained that would not be entangled in some one or other of the insidious clauses that seemed spread out, like a web, to ensnare them.

The whole country was thrown into commotion. Men assembled tumultuously in the squares and public places, and, as the regulations were made known, they were received with universal groans and hisses. "Is this the fruit," they cried, "of all our toil? Is it for this that we have poured out our blood like water? Now that we are broken down by hardships and sufferings, to be left at the end of our campaigns as poor as at the beginning! Is this the way government rewards our services in winning for it an empire? The government has done little to aid us in making the conquest, and for what we have we may thank our own good swords; and with these same swords," they continued, warming into menace, "we know how to defend it." Then, stripping up his sleeve, the war-worn veteran bared his arm, or, exposing his naked bosom, pointed to his scars, as the best title to his estates.[15]

The governor, Vaca de Castro, watched the storm thus gathering from all quarters, with the deepest concern. He was himself in the very heart of disaffection; for Cuzco, tenanted by a mixed and lawless population, was so far removed into the depths of the mountains, that it had much less intercourse with the parent country, and was consequently much less under her influence, than the great towns on the coast. The people now invoked the governor to protect them against the tyranny of the Court; but he endeavoured to calm the agitation by representing, that by these violent measures they would only defeat their own object. He counselled them to name deputies to lay their petition before the Crown, stating the impracticability of the present scheme of reform, and praying for the repeal of it; and he conjured them to wait patiently for the arrival of the viceroy, who might be prevailed on to suspend the ordinances till further advices could be received from Castile.

But it was not easy to still the tempest; and the people now eagerly looked for some one whose interests and sympathies might lie with theirs, and whose position in the community might afford them protection. The person to whom they naturally turned in this crisis was Gonzalo Pizarro, the last in the land of that family who had led the armies of the Conquest, — a cavalier whose gallantry and popular manners had made him always a favorite with the people. He was now beset with applications to interpose in their behalf with the government, and shield them from the oppressive ordinances.

But Gonzalo Pizarro was at Charcas, busily occupied in exploring the rich veins of Potosí, whose silver fountains, just brought into light, were soon to pour such streams of wealth over Europe. Though gratified with this appeal to his protection, the cautious cavalier was more intent on providing for the means of enterprise than on plunging prematurely into it; and, while he secretly encouraged the malecontents, he did not commit himself by taking part in any revolutionary movement. At the same period, he received letters from Vaca de Castro, — whose vigilant eye watched all the aspects of the time, — cautioning Gonzalo and his friends not to be seduced, by any wild schemes of reform, from their allegiance. And, to check still further these disorderly movements, he ordered his alcaldes to arrest every man guilty of seditious language, and bring him at once to punishment. By this firm yet temperate conduct the minds of the populace were overawed, and there was a temporary lull in the troubled waters, while all looked anxiously for the coming of the viceroy.[16]

The person selected for this critical post was a knight of Avila, named Blasco Nuñez Vela. He was a cavalier of ancient family, handsome in person, though now somewhat advanced in years, and reputed brave and devout. He had filled some offices of responsibility to the satisfaction of Charles the Fifth, by whom he was now appointed to this post in Peru. The selection did no credit to the monarch's discernment.

It may seem strange that this important place should not have been bestowed on Vaca de Castro, already on the spot, and who had shown himself so well qualified to fill it. But ever since that officer's mission to Peru, there had been a series of assassinations, insurrections, and civil wars, that menaced the wretched colony with ruin; and, though his wise administration had now brought things into order, the communication with the Indies was so tardy, that the results of his policy were not yet fully disclosed. As it was designed, moreover, to make important innovations in the government, it was thought better to send some one who would have no personal prejudices to encounter, from the part he had already taken, and who, coming directly from the Court, and clothed with extraordinary powers, might present himself with greater authority than could one who had become familiar to the people in an inferior capacity. The monarch, however, wrote a letter with his own hand to Vaca de Castro, in which he thanked that officer for his past services, and directed him, after aiding the new viceroy with the fruits of his large experience, to return to Castile, and take his seat in the Royal Council. Letters of a similar complimentary kind were sent to the loyal colonists who had stood by the governor in the late troubles of the country. Freighted with these testimonials, and with the ill-starred ordinances, Blasco Nuñez embarked at San Lucar, on the 3d of November, 1543. He was attended by the four judges of the Audience, and by a numerous retinue, that he might appear in the state befitting his distinguished rank.[17]

About the middle of the following January, 1544, the viceroy, after a favorable passage, landed at Nombre de Dios. He found there a vessel laden with silver from the Peruvian mines, ready to sail for Spain. His first act was to lay an embargo on it for the government, as containing the proceeds of slave labor. After this extraordinary measure, taken in opposition to the advice of the Audience, he crossed the Isthmus to Panamá. Here he gave sure token of his future policy, by causing more than three hundred Indians, who had been brought by their owners from Peru, to be liberated and sent back to their own country. This high-handed measure created the greatest sensation in the city, and was strongly resisted by the judges of the Audience. They besought him not to begin thus precipitately to execute his commission, but to wait till his arrival in the colony, when he should have taken time to acquaint himself somewhat with the country, and with the temper of the people. But Blasco Nuñez coldly replied, that "he had come, not to tamper with the laws, nor to discuss their merits, but to execute them,—and execute them he would, to the letter, whatever might be the consequence."[18] This answer, and the peremptory tone in which it was delivered, promptly adjourned the debate; for the judges saw that debate was useless with one who seemed to consider all remonstrance as an attempt to turn him from his duty, and whose ideas of duty precluded all discretionary exercise of authority, even where the public good demanded it.

Leaving the Audience, as one of its body was ill, at Panamá, the viceroy proceeded on his way, and, coasting down the shores of the Pacific, on the fourth of March he disembarked at Tumbez. He was well received by the loyal inhabitants; his authority was publicly proclaimed, and the people were overawed by the display of a magnificence and state such as had not till then been seen in Peru. He took an early occasion to intimate his future line of policy by liberating a number of Indian slaves on the application of their caciques. He then proceeded by land towards the south, and showed his determination to conform in his own person to the strict letter of the ordinances, by causing his baggage to be carried by mules, where it was practicable; and where absolutely necessary to make use of Indians, he paid them fairly for their services.[19]

The whole country was thrown into consternation by reports of the proceedings of the viceroy, and of his conversations, most unguarded, which were eagerly circulated, and, no doubt, often exaggerated. Meetings were again called in the cities. Discussions were held on the expediency of resisting his further progress, and a deputation of citizens from Cuzco, who were then in Lima, strongly urged the people to close the gates of that capital against him. But Vaca de Castro had also left Cuzco for the latter city, on the earliest intimation of the viceroy's approach, and, with some difficulty, he prevailed on the inhabitants not to swerve from their loyalty, but to receive their new ruler with suitable honors, and trust to his calmer judgment for postponing the execution of the law till the case could be laid before the throne.

But the great body of the Spaniards, after what they had heard, had slender confidence in the relief to be obtained from this quarter. They now turned with more eagerness than ever towards Gonzalo Pizarro; and letters and addresses poured in upon him from all parts of the country, inviting him to take on himself the office of their protector. These applications found a more favorable response than on the former occasion.

There were, indeed, many motives at work to call Gonzalo into action. It was to his family, mainly, that Spain was indebted for this extension of her colonial empire; and he had felt deeply aggrieved that the government of the colony should be trusted to other hands than his. He had felt this on the arrival of Vaca de Castro, and much more so when the appointment of a viceroy proved it to be the settled policy of the Crown to exclude his family from the management of affairs. His brother Hernando still languished in prison, and he himself was now to be sacrificed as the principal victim of the fatal ordinances. For who had taken so prominent a part in the civil war with the elder Almagro? And the viceroy was currently reported—it may have been scandal—to have intimated that Pizarro would be dealt with accordingly.[20] Yet there was no one in the country who had so great a stake, who had so much to lose by the revolution. Abandoned thus by the government, he conceived that it was now time to take care of himself.

Assembling together some eighteen or twenty cavaliers in whom he most trusted, and taking a large amount of silver, drawn from the mines, he accepted the invitation to repair to Cuzco. As he approached this capital, he was met by a numerous body of the citizens, who came out to welcome him, making the air ring with their shouts, as they saluted him with the title of Procurator-General of Peru. The title was speedily confirmed by the municipality of the city, who invited him to head a deputation to Lima, in order to state their grievances to the viceroy, and solicit the present suspension of the ordinances.

But the spark of ambition was kindled in the bosom of Pizarro. He felt strong in the affections of the people; and, from the more elevated position in which he now stood, his desires took a loftier and more unbounded range. Yet, if he harboured a criminal ambition in his breast, he skilfully veiled it from others,—perhaps from himself. The only object he professed to have in view was the good of the people;[21] a suspicious phrase, usually meaning the good of the individual. He now demanded permission to raise and organize an armed force, with the further title of Captain-General. His views were entirely pacific; but it was not safe, unless strongly protected, to urge them on a person of the viceroy's impatient and arbitrary temper. It was further contended by Pizarro's friends, that such a force was demanded, to rid the country of their old enemy, the Inca Manco, who hovered in the neighbouring mountains with a body of warriors, ready, at the first opportunity, to descend on the Spaniards. The municipality of Cuzco hesitated, as well it might, to confer powers so far beyond its legitimate authority. But Pizarro avowed his purpose, in case of refusal, to decline the office of Procurator; and the efforts of his partisans, backed by those of the people, at length silenced the scruples of the magistrates, who bestowed on the ambitious chief the military command to which he aspired. Pizarro accepted it with the modest assurance, that he did so "purely from regard to the interests of the king, of the Indies, and, above all, of Peru"![22]

CHAPTER VIII

THE VICEROY ARRIVES AT LIMA. — GONZALO PIZARRO MARCHES FROM CUZCO. — DEATH OF THE INCA MANCO. — RASH CONDUCT OF THE VICEROY. — SEIZED AND DEPOSED BY THE AUDIENCE. — GONZALO PROCLAIMED GOVERNOR OF PERU

1544.

WHILE the events recorded in the preceding pages were in progress, Blasco Nuñez had been journeying towards Lima. But the alienation which his conduct had already caused in the minds of the colonists was shown in the cold reception which he occasionally experienced on the route, and in the scanty accommodations provided for him and his retinue. In one place where he took up his quarters, he found an ominous inscription over the door: — "He that takes my property must expect to pay for it with his life."[1] Neither daunted, nor diverted from his purpose, the inflexible viceroy held on his way towards the capital, where the inhabitants, preceded by Vaca de Castro and the municipal authorities, came out to receive him. He entered in great state, under a canopy of crimson cloth, embroidered with the arms of Spain, and supported by stout poles or staves of solid silver, which were borne by the members of the municipality. A cavalier, holding a mace, the emblem of authority, rode before him; and after the oaths of office were administered in the council-chamber, the procession moved towards the cathedral, where *Te Deum* was sung, and Blasco Nuñez was installed in his new dignity of viceroy of Peru.[2]

His first act was to proclaim his determination in respect to the ordinances. He had no warrant to suspend their execution. He should fulfil his commission; but he offered to join the colonists in a memorial to the emperor, soliciting the repeal of a code which he now believed would be for the interests neither of the country nor of the Crown.[3] With this avowed view of the subject, it may seem strange that Blasco Nuñez should not have taken the responsibility of suspending the law until his sovereign could be assured of the inevitable consequences of enforcing it. The pacha of a Turkish despot, who had allowed himself this latitude for the interests of his master, might, indeed, have reckoned on the bowstring. But the example of Mendoza, the prudent viceroy of Mexico, who adopted this course in a similar crisis, and precisely at the same period, showed its propriety under existing circumstances. The ordinances were suspended by him till the Crown could be warned of the consequences of enforcing them, — and Mexico was saved from revolution.[4] But Blasco Nuñez had not the wisdom of Mendoza.

The public apprehension was now far from being allayed. Secret cabals were formed in Lima, and communications held with the different towns. No distrust, however, was raised in the breast of the viceroy, and, when informed of the preparations of Gonzalo Pizarro, he took no other step than to send a message to his camp, announcing the extraordinary powers with which he was himself invested, and requiring that chief to disband his forces. He seemed to think that a mere word from him would be sufficient to dissipate rebellion. But it required more than a breath to scatter the iron soldiery of Peru.

Gonzalo Pizarro, meanwhile, was busily occupied in mustering his army. His first step was to order from Guamanga sixteen pieces of artillery, sent there by Vaca de Castro, who, in the present state of excitement, was unwilling to trust the volatile people of Cuzco with these implements of destruction. Gonzalo, who had no scruples as to Indian labor, appropriated six thousand of the natives to the service of transporting this train of ordnance across the mountains.[5]

By his exertions and those of his friends, the active chief soon mustered a force of nearly four hundred men, which, if not very imposing in the outset, he conceived would be swelled, in his descent to the coast, by tributary levies from the towns and villages on the way. All his own funds were expended in equipping his men and providing for the march; and, to supply deficiencies, he made no scruple — since, to use his words, it was for the public interest — to appropriate the moneys in the royal treasury. With this seasonable aid, his troops, well mounted and thoroughly equipped, were put in excellent fighting order; and, after making them a brief harangue, in which he was careful to insist on the pacific character of his enterprise, somewhat at variance with its military preparations, Gonzalo Pizarro sallied forth from the gates of the capital.

Before leaving it, he received an important accession of strength in the person of Francisco de Carbajal, the veteran who performed so conspicuous a part in the battle of Chupas. He was at Charcas when the news of the ordinances reached Peru; and he instantly resolved to quit the country and return to Spain, convinced that the New World would be no longer the land for him, — no longer the golden Indies. Turning his effects into money, he prepared to embark them on board the first ship that offered. But no opportunity occurred, and he could have little expectation now of escaping the vigilant eye of the viceroy. Yet, though solicited by Pizarro to take command under him in the present expedition, the veteran declined, saying, he was eighty years old, and had no wish but to return home, and spend his few remaining days in quiet.[6] Well had it been for him, had he persisted in his refusal. But he yielded to the importunities of his friend; and the short space that yet remained to him of life proved long enough to brand his memory with perpetual infamy.

Soon after quitting Cuzco, Pizarro learned the death of the Inca Manco. He was massacred by a party of Spaniards, of the faction of Almagro, who, on the defeat of their young leader, had taken refuge in the Indian camp. They, in turn, were all slain by the Peruvians. It is impossible to determine on whom the blame of the quarrel should rest, since no one present at the time has recorded it.[7]

The death of Manco Inca, as he was commonly called, is an event not to be silently passed over in Peruvian history; for he was the last of his race that may be said to have been animated by the heroic spirit of the ancient Incas. Though placed on the throne by Pizarro, far from remaining a mere puppet in his hands, Manco soon showed that his lot was not to be cast with that of his conquerors. With the ancient institutions of his country lying a wreck around him, he yet struggled bravely, like Guatemozin, the last of the Aztecs, to uphold her tottering fortunes, or to bury his oppressors under her ruins. By the assault on his own capital of Cuzco, in which so large a portion of it was demolished, he gave a check to the arms of Pizarro, and, for a season, the fate of the Conquerors trembled in the balance. Though foiled, in the end, by the superior science of his adversary, the young barbarian still showed the same unconquerable spirit as before. He withdrew into the fastnesses of his native mountains, whence sallying forth as occasion offered, he fell on the caravan of the traveller, or on some scattered party of the military; and, in the event of a civil war, was sure to throw his own weight into the weaker scale, thus prolonging the contest of his enemies, and feeding his revenge by the sight of their calamities. Moving lightly from spot to spot, he eluded pursuit amidst the wilds of the Cordilleras; and, hovering in the neighbourhood of the towns, or lying in ambush on the great thoroughfares of the country, the Inca Manco made his name a terror to the Spaniards. Often did they hold out to him terms of accommodation; and every succeeding ruler, down to Blasco Nuñez, bore instructions from the Crown to employ every art to conciliate the formidable warrior. But Manco did not trust the promises of the white man; and he chose rather to maintain his savage independence in the mountains, with the few brave spirits around him, than to live a slave in the land which had once owned the sway of his ancestors.

The death of the Inca removed one of the great pretexts for Gonzalo Pizarro's military preparations; but it had little influence on him, as may be readily imagined. He was much more sensible to the desertion of some of his followers, which took place early on the march. Several of the cavaliers of Cuzco, startled by his unceremonious appropriation of the public moneys, and by the belligerent aspect of affairs, now for the first time seemed to realize that they were in the path of rebellion. A number of these, including some principal men of the city, secretly withdrew from the army, and, hastening to Lima, offered their services to the viceroy. The troops were disheartened by this desertion, and even Pizarro for a moment faltered in his purpose, and thought of retiring with some fifty followers to Charcas, and there making his composition with government. But a little reflection, aided by the remonstrances of the courageous Carbajal, who never turned his back on an enterprise which he had once assumed, convinced him that he had gone too far to recede, — that his only safety was to advance.

He was reassured by more decided manifestations, which he soon after received, of the public opinion. An officer named Puelles, who commanded at Guanuco, joined him, with a body of horse with which he had been intrusted by the viceroy. This defection was followed by that of others, and Gonzalo, as he descended the sides of the table-land, found his numbers gradually swelled to nearly double the amount with which he had left the Indian capital.

As he traversed with a freer step the bloody field of Chupas, Carbajal pointed out the various localities of the battle-ground, and Pizarro might have found food for anxious reflection, as he meditated on the fortunes of a rebel. At Guamanga he was received with open arms by the inhabitants, many of whom eagerly enlisted under his banner; for they trembled for their property, as they heard from all quarters of the inflexible temper of the viceroy.[8]

That functionary began now to be convinced that he was in a critical position. Before Puelles's treachery, above noticed, had been consummated, the viceroy had received some vague intimation of his purpose. Though scarcely crediting it, he detached one of his company, named Diaz, with a force to intercept him. But, although that cavalier undertook the mission with alacrity, he was soon after prevailed on to follow the example of his comrade, and, with the greater part of the men under his command, went over to the enemy. In the civil feuds of this unhappy land, parties changed sides so lightly, that treachery to a commander had almost ceased to be a stain on the honor of a cavalier. Yet all, on whichever side they cast their fortunes, loudly proclaimed their loyalty to the Crown.

Thus betrayed by his own men, by those apparently most devoted to his service, Blasco Nuñez became suspicious of every one around him. Unfortunately, his suspicions fell on some who were most deserving of his confidence. Among these was his predecessor, Vaca de Castro. That officer had conducted himself, in the delicate situation in which he had been placed, with his usual discretion, and with perfect integrity and honor. He had frankly communicated with the viceroy, and well had it been for Blasco Nuñez, if he had known how to profit by it. But he was too much puffed up by the arrogance of office, and by the conceit of his own superior wisdom, to defer much to the counsels of his experienced predecessor. The latter was now suspected by the viceroy of maintaining a secret correspondence with his enemies at Cuzco,—a suspicion which seems to have had no better foundation than the personal friendship which Vaca de Castro was known to entertain for these individuals. But, with Blasco Nuñez, to suspect was to be convinced; and he ordered De Castro to be placed under arrest, and confined on board of a vessel lying in the harbour. This high-handed measure was followed by the arrest and imprisonment of several other cavaliers, probably on grounds equally frivolous.[9]

He now turned his attention towards the enemy. Notwithstanding his former failure, he still did not altogether despair of effecting something by negotiation, and he sent another embassy, having the bishop of Lima at its head, to Gonzalo Pizarro's camp, with promises of a general amnesty, and some proposals of a more tempting character to the commander. But this step, while it proclaimed his own weakness, had no better success than the preceding.[10]

The viceroy now vigorously prepared for war. His first care was to put the capital in a posture of defence, by strengthening its fortifications, and throwing barricades across the streets. He ordered a general enrolment of the citizens, and called in levies from the neighbouring towns,—a call not very promptly answered. A squadron of eight or ten vessels was got ready in the port to act in concert with the land forces. The bells were taken from the churches, and used in the manufacture of muskets;[11] and funds were procured from the fifths which had accumulated in the royal treasury. The most extravagant bounty was offered to the soldiers, and prices were paid for mules and horses, which showed that gold, or rather silver, was the commodity of least value in Peru.[12] By these efforts, the active commander soon assembled a force considerably larger than that of his adversary. But how could he confide in it?

While these preparations were going forward, the judges of the Audience arrived at Lima. They had shown, throughout their progress, no great respect either for the ordinances, or the will of the viceroy; for they had taxed the poor natives as freely and unscrupulously as any of the Conquerors. We have seen the entire want of cordiality subsisting between them and their principal in Panamá. It became more apparent, on their landing at Lima. They disapproved of his proceedings in every particular; of his refusal to suspend the ordinances,—although, in fact, he had found no opportunity, of late, to enforce them; of his preparations for defence, declaring that he ought rather trust to the effect of negotiation; and, finally, of his imprisonment of so many loyal cavaliers, which they pronounced an arbitrary act, altogether beyond the bounds of his authority; and they did not scruple to visit the prison in person, and discharge the captives from their confinement.[13]

This bold proceeding, while it conciliated the good-will of the people, severed, at once, all relations with the viceroy. There was in the Audience a lawyer, named Cepeda, a cunning, ambitious man, with considerable knowledge in the way of his profession, and with still greater talent for intrigue. He did not disdain the low arts of a demagogue to gain the favor of the populace, and trusted to find his own account in fomenting a misunderstanding with Blasco Nuñez. The latter, it must be confessed, did all in his power to aid his counsellor in this laudable design.

A certain cavalier in the place, named Suarez de Carbajal, who had long held an office under government, fell under the viceroy's displeasure, on suspicion of conniving at the secession of some of his kinsmen, who had lately taken part with the malecontents. The viceroy summoned Carbajal to attend him at his palace, late at night; and when conducted to his presence, he bluntly charged him with treason. The latter stoutly denied the accusation, in tones as haughty as those of his accuser. The altercation grew warm, until, in the heat of passion, Blasco Nuñez struck him with his poniard. In an instant, the attendants, taking this as a signal, plunged their swords into the body of the unfortunate man, who fell lifeless on the floor.[14]

Greatly alarmed for the consequences of his rash act, — for Carbajal was much beloved in Lima, — Blasco Nuñez ordered the corpse of the murdered man to be removed by a private stairway from the house, and carried to the cathedral, where, rolled in his bloody cloak, it was laid in a grave hastily dug to receive it. So tragic a proceeding, known to so many witnesses, could not long be kept secret. Vague rumors of the fact explained the mysterious disappearance of Carbajal. The grave was opened, and the mangled remains of the slaughtered cavalier established the guilt of the viceroy.[15]

From this hour Blasco Nuñez was held in universal abhorrence; and his crime, in this instance, assumed the deeper dye of ingratitude, since the deceased was known to have had the greatest influence in reconciling the citizens early to his government. No one knew where the blow would fall next, or how soon he might himself become the victim of the ungovernable passions of the viceroy. In this state of things, some looked to the Audience, and yet more to Gonzalo Pizarro, to protect them.

That chief was slowly advancing towards Lima, from which, indeed, he was removed but a few days' march. Greatly perplexed, Blasco Nuñez now felt the loneliness of his condition. Standing aloof, as it were, from his own followers, thwarted by the Audience, betrayed by his soldiers, he might well feel the consequences of his misconduct. Yet there seemed no other course for him, but either to march out and meet the enemy, or to remain in Lima and defend it. He had placed the town in a posture of defence, which argued this last to have been his original purpose. But he felt he could no longer rely on his troops, and he decided on a third course, most unexpected.

This was to abandon the capital, and withdraw to Truxillo, about eighty leagues distant. The women would embark on board the squadron, and, with the effects of the citizens, be transported by water. The troops, with the rest of

the inhabitants, would march by land, laying waste the country as they proceeded. Gonzalo Pizarro, when he arrived at Lima, would find it without supplies for his army, and, thus straitened, he would not care to take a long march
across a desert in search of his enemy.[16]

What the viceroy proposed to effect by this movement is not clear, unless it
were to gain time; and yet the more time he had gained, thus far, the worse it
had proved for him. But he was destined to encounter a decided opposition
from the judges. They contended that he had no warrant for such an act, and
that the Audience could not lawfully hold its sessions out of the capital. Blasco
Nuñez persisted in his determination, menacing that body with force, if necessary. The judges appealed to the citizens to support them in resisting such
an arbitrary measure. They mustered a force for their own protection, and
that same day passed a decree that the viceroy should be arrested.

Late at night, Blasco Nuñez was informed of the hostile preparations of
the judges. He instantly summoned his followers, to the number of more than
two hundred, put on his armour, and prepared to march out at the head of his
troops against the Audience. This was the true course; for in a crisis like that
in which he was placed, requiring promptness and decision, the presence of
the leader is essential to insure success. But, unluckily, he yielded to the
remonstrances of his brother and other friends, who dissuaded him from
rashly exposing his life in such a venture.

What Blasco Nuñez neglected to do was done by the judges. They sallied
forth at the head of their followers, whose number, though small at first, they
felt confident would be swelled by volunteers as they advanced. Rushing forward, they cried out, — "Liberty! Liberty! Long live the king and the
Audience!" It was early dawn, and the inhabitants, startled from their slumbers, ran to the windows and balconies, and, learning the object of the movement, some snatched up their arms and joined in it, while the women, waving
their scarfs and kerchiefs, cheered on the assault.

When the mob arrived before the viceroy's palace, they halted for a
moment, uncertain what to do. Orders were given to fire on them from the
windows, and a volley passed over their heads. No one was injured; and the
greater part of the viceroy's men, with most of the officers, — including some
of those who had been so anxious for his personal safety, — now openly joined
the populace. The palace was then entered, and abandoned to pillage. Blasco
Nuñez, deserted by all but a few faithful adherents, made no resistance. He
surrendered to the assailants, was led before the judges, and by them was
placed in strict confinement. The citizens, delighted with the result, provided
a collation for the soldiers; and the affair ended without the loss of a single
life. Never was there so bloodless a revolution.[17]

The first business of the judges was to dispose of the prisoner. He was sent,
under a strong guard, to a neighbouring island, till some measures could be
taken respecting him. He was declared to be deposed from his office; a provi-
sional government was established, consisting of their own body, with Cepeda

at its head, as president; and its first act was to pronounce the detested ordinances suspended, till instructions could be received from Court. It was also decided to send Blasco Nuñez back to Spain with one of their own body, who should explain to the emperor the nature of the late disturbances, and vindicate the measures of the Audience. This was soon put in execution. The Licentiate Alvarez was the person selected to bear the viceroy company; and the unfortunate commander, after passing several days on the desolate island, with scarcely any food, and exposed to all the inclemencies of the weather, took his departure for Panamá.[18]

A more formidable adversary yet remained in Gonzalo Pizarro, who had now advanced to Xauxa, about ninety miles from Lima. Here he halted, while numbers of the citizens prepared to join his banner, choosing rather to take service under him than to remain under the self-constituted authority of the Audience. The judges, meanwhile, who had tasted the sweets of office too short a time to be content to resign them, after considerable delay, sent an embassy to the Procurator. They announced to him the revolution that had taken place, and the suspension of the ordinances. The great object of his mission had been thus accomplished; and, as a new government was now organized, they called on him to show his obedience to it, by disbanding his forces, and withdrawing to the unmolested enjoyment of his estates. It was a bold demand, — though couched in the most courteous and complimentary phrase, — to make of one in Pizarro's position. It was attempting to scare away the eagle just ready to stoop on his prey. If the chief had faltered, however, he would have been reassured by his lion-hearted lieutenant. "Never show faint heart," exclaimed the latter, "when you are so near the goal. Success has followed every step of your path. You have now only to stretch forth your hand, and seize the government. Every thing else will follow." — The envoy who brought the message from the judges was sent back with the answer, that "the people had called Gonzalo Pizarro to the government of the country, and, if the Audience did not at once invest him with it, the city should be delivered up to pillage."[19]

The bewildered magistrates were thrown into dismay by this decisive answer. Yet loth to resign, they took counsel in their perplexity of Vaca de Castro, still detained on board of one of the vessels. But that commander had received too little favor at the hands of his successors to think it necessary to peril his life on their account by thwarting the plans of Pizarro. He maintained a discreet silence, therefore, and left the matter to the wisdom of the Audience.

Meanwhile, Carbajal was sent into the city to quicken their deliberations. He came at night, attended only by a small party of soldiers, intimating his contempt of the power of the judges. His first act was to seize a number of cavaliers, whom he dragged from their beds, and placed under arrest. They were men of Cuzco, the same already noticed as having left Pizarro's ranks soon after his departure from that capital. While the Audience still hesitated as to the course they should pursue, Carbajal caused three of his prisoners, persons of consideration and property, to be placed on the backs of mules, and escorted out of town to the suburbs, where, with brief space allowed for confession, he hung them all on the branches of a tree. He superintended the execution himself, and tauntingly complimented one of his victims, by telling him, that, "in consideration of his higher rank, he should have the privilege of selecting the bough on which to be hanged!"[20] The ferocious officer would have proceeded still further in his executions, it is said, had it not been for orders received from his leader. But enough was done to quicken the perceptions of the Audience as to their course, for they felt their own lives suspended by a thread in such unscrupulous hands. Without further delay, therefore, they sent to invite Gonzalo Pizarro to enter the city, declaring that the security of the country and the general good required the government to be placed in his hands.[21]

That chief had now advanced within half a league of the capital, which soon after, on the twenty-eighth of October, 1544, he entered in battle-array. His whole force was little short of twelve hundred Spaniards, besides several thousand Indians, who dragged his heavy guns in the advance.[22] Then came the files of spearmen and arquebusiers, making a formidable corps of infantry for a colonial army; and lastly, the cavalry, at the head of which rode Pizarro himself, on a powerful charger, gayly caparisoned. The rider was in complete mail, over which floated a richly embroidered surcoat, and his head was protected by a crimson cap, highly ornamented,—his showy livery setting off his handsome, soldierlike person to advantage.[23] Before him was borne the royal standard of Castile; for every one, royalist or rebel, was careful to fight under that sign. This emblem of loyalty was supported on the right by a banner, emblazoned with the arms of Cuzco, and by another on the left, displaying the armorial bearings granted by the Crown to the Pizarros. As the martial pageant swept through the streets of Lima, the air was rent with acclamations from the populace, and from the spectators in the balconies. The cannon sounded at intervals, and the bells of the city—those that the viceroy had spared—rang out a joyous peal, as if in honor of a victory!

The oaths of office were duly administered by the judges of the Royal Audience, and Gonzalo Pizarro was proclaimed Governor and Captain-General of Peru, till his Majesty's pleasure could be known in respect to the government. The new ruler then took up his quarters in the palace of his brother,—where the stains of that brother's blood were not yet effaced. *Fêtes,* bull-fights, and tournaments graced the ceremony of inauguration, and were prolonged for several days, while the giddy populace of the capital abandoned themselves to jubilee, as if a new and more auspicious order of things had commenced for Peru![24]

CHAPTER IX

MEASURES OF GONZALO PIZARRO. — ESCAPE OF
VACA DE CASTRO. — REAPPEARANCE OF THE
VICEROY. — HIS DISASTROUS RETREAT. —
DEFEAT AND DEATH OF THE VICEROY. —
GONZALO PIZARRO LORD OF PERU

1544-1546.

THE first act of Gonzalo Pizarro was to cause those persons to be appre-
hended who had taken the most active part against him in the late troubles.
Several he condemned to death; but afterwards commuted the sentence, and
contented himself with driving them into banishment and confiscating their
estates.[1] His next concern was to establish his authority on a firm basis. He
filled the municipal government of Lima with his own partisans. He sent his
lieutenants to take charge of the principal cities. He caused galleys to be built
at Arequipa to secure the command of the seas; and brought his forces into
the best possible condition, to prepare for future emergencies.

The Royal Audience existed only in name; for its powers were speedily
absorbed by the new ruler, who desired to place the government on the
same footing as under the marquess, his brother. Indeed, the Audience necessarily fell to pieces, from the position of its several members. Alvarez had
been sent with the viceroy to Castile. Cepeda, the most aspiring of the court,
now that he had failed in his own schemes of ambition, was content to
become a tool in the hands of the military chief who had displaced him.
Zarate, a third judge, who had, from the first, protested against the violent
measures of his colleagues, was confined to his house by a mortal illness;[2]
and Tepeda, the remaining magistrate, Gonzalo now proposed to send back
to Castile with such an account of the late transactions as should vindicate
his own conduct in the eyes of the emperor. This step was opposed by
Carbajal, who bluntly told his commander that "he had gone too far to
expect favor from the Crown; and that he had better rely for his vindication
on his pikes and muskets!"[3]

But the ship which was to transport Tepeda was found to have suddenly disappeared from the port. It was the same in which Vaca de Castro was confined; and that officer, not caring to trust to the forbearance of one whose advances, on a former occasion, he had so unceremoniously repulsed, and convinced, moreover, that his own presence could profit nothing in a land where he held no legitimate authority, had prevailed on the captain to sail with him to Panamá. He then crossed the Isthmus, and embarked for Spain. The rumors of his coming had already preceded him, and charges were not wanting against him from some of those whom he had offended by his administration. He was accused of having carried measures with a high hand, regardless of the rights, both of the colonist and of the native; and, above all, of having embezzled the public moneys, and of returning with his coffers richly freighted to Castile. This last was an unpardonable crime.

No sooner had the governor set foot in his own country than he was arrested, and hurried to the fortress of Arevalo; and, though he was afterwards removed to better quarters, where he was treated with the indulgence due to his rank, he was still kept a prisoner of state for twelve years, when the tardy tribunals of Castile pronounced a judgment in his favor. He was acquitted of every charge that had been brought against him, and, so far from peculation, was proved to have returned home no richer than he went. He was released from confinement, reinstated in his honors and dignities, took his seat anew in the royal council, and Vaca de Castro enjoyed, during the remainder of his days, the consideration to which he was entitled by his deserts.[4] The best eulogium on the wisdom of his administration was afforded by the troubles brought on the colonies by that of his successor. The nation became gradually sensible of the value of his services; though the manner in which they were requited by the government must be allowed to form a cold commentary on the gratitude of princes.

Gonzalo Pizarro was doomed to experience a still greater disappointment than that caused by the escape of Vaca de Castro, in the return of Blasco Nuñez. The vessel which bore him from the country had hardly left the shore, when Alvarez, the judge, whether from remorse at the part which he had taken, or apprehensive of the consequences of carrying back the viceroy to Spain, presented himself before that dignitary, and announced that he was no longer a prisoner. At the same time he excused himself for the part he had taken, by his desire to save the life of Blasco Nuñez, and extricate him from his perilous situation. He now placed the vessel at his disposal, and assured him it should take him wherever he chose.

The viceroy, whatever faith he may have placed in the judge's explanation, eagerly availed himself of his offer. His proud spirit revolted at the idea of returning home in disgrace, foiled, as he had been, in every object of his mission. He determined to try his fortune again in the land, and his only doubt was, on what point to attempt to rally his partisans around him. At Panamá he might remain in safety, while he invoked assistance from Nicaragua, and other colonies at the north. But this would be to abandon his government at once; and such a confession of weakness would have a bad effect on his followers in Peru. He determined, therefore, to direct his steps towards Quito, which, while it was within his jurisdiction, was still removed far enough from the theatre of the late troubles to give him time to rally, and make head against his enemies.

In pursuance of this purpose, the viceroy and his suite disembarked at Tumbez, about the middle of October, 1544. On landing, he issued a manifesto setting forth the violent proceedings of Gonzalo Pizarro and his followers, whom he denounced as traitors to their prince, and he called on all true subjects in the colony to support him in maintaining the royal authority. The call was not unheeded; and volunteers came in, though tardily, from San Miguel, Puerto Viejo, and other places on the coast, cheering the heart of the viceroy with the conviction that the sentiment of loyalty was not yet extinct in the bosoms of the Spaniards.

But, while thus occupied, he received tidings of the arrival of one of Pizarro's captains on the coast, with a force superior to his own. Their number was exaggerated; but Blasco Nuñez, without waiting to ascertain the truth, abandoned his position at Tumbez, and, with as much expedition as he could make across a wild and mountainous country half-buried in snow, he marched to Quito. But this capital, situated at the northern extremity of his province, was not a favorable point for the rendezvous of his followers; and, after prolonging his stay till he had received assurance from Benalcazar, the loyal commander at Popayan, that he would support him with all his strength in the coming conflict, he made a rapid countermarch to the coast, and took up his position at the town of San Miguel. This was a spot well suited to his purposes, as lying on the great high road along the shores of the Pacific, besides being the chief mart for commercial intercourse with Panamá and the north.

Here the viceroy erected his standard, and in a few weeks found himself at the head of a force amounting to nearly five hundred in all, horse and foot, ill provided with arms and ammunition, but apparently zealous in the cause. Finding himself in sufficient strength to commence active operations, he now sallied forth against several of Pizarro's captains in the neighbourhood, over whom he obtained some decided advantages, which renewed his confidence, and flattered him with the hopes of reëstablishing his ascendency in the country.[5]

During this time, Gonzalo Pizarro was not idle. He had watched with anxiety the viceroy's movements; and was now convinced that it was time to act, and that, if he would not be unseated himself, he must dislodge his formidable rival. He accordingly placed a strong garrison under a faithful officer in Lima, and, after sending forward a force of some six hundred men by land to Truxillo, he embarked for the same port himself, on the 4th of March, 1545, the very day on which the viceroy had marched from Quito.

At Truxillo, Pizarro put himself at the head of his little army, and moved without loss of time against San Miguel. His rival, eager to bring their quarrel to an issue, would fain have marched out to give him battle; but his soldiers, mostly young and inexperienced levies, hastily brought together, were intimidated by the name of Pizarro. They loudly insisted on being led into the upper country, where they would be reinforced by Benalcazar; and their unfortunate commander, like the rider of some unmanageable steed, to whose humors he is obliged to submit, was hurried away in a direction contrary to his wishes. It was the fate of Blasco Nuñez to have his purposes baffled alike by his friends and his enemies.

On arriving before San Miguel, Gonzalo Pizarro found, to his great mortification, that his antagonist had left it. Without entering the town, he quickened his pace, and, after traversing a valley of some extent, reached the skirts of a mountain chain, into which Blasco Nuñez had entered but a few hours before. It was late in the evening; but Pizarro, knowing the importance of despatch, sent forward Carbajal with a party of light troops to overtake the fugitives. That captain succeeded in coming up with their lonely bivouac among the mountains at midnight, when the weary troops were buried in slumber. Startled from their repose by the blast of the trumpet, which, strange to say, their enemy had incautiously sounded,[6] the viceroy and his men sprang to their feet, mounted their horses, grasped their arquebuses, and poured such a volley into the ranks of their assailants, that Carbajal, disconcerted by his reception, found it prudent, with his inferior force, to retreat. The viceroy followed, till, fearing an ambuscade in the darkness of the night, he withdrew, and allowed, his adversary to rejoin the main body of the army under Pizarro.

This conduct of Carbajal, by which he allowed the game to slip through his hands, from mere carelessness, is inexplicable. It forms a singular exception to the habitual caution and vigilance displayed in his military career. Had it been the act of any other captain, it would have cost him his head. But Pizarro, although greatly incensed, set too high a value on the services and well-tried attachment of his lieutenant, to quarrel with him. Still it was considered of the last importance to overtake the enemy, before he had advanced much farther to the north, where the difficulties of the ground would greatly embarrass the pursuit. Carbajal, anxious to retrieve his error, was accordingly again placed at the head of a corps of light troops, with instructions to harass the enemy's march, cut off his stores, and keep him in check, if possible, till the arrival of Pizarro.[7]

But the viceroy had profited by the recent delay to gain considerably on his pursuers. His road led across the valley of Caxas, a broad, uncultivated district, affording little sustenance for man or beast. Day after day, his troops held on their march through this dreary region, intersected with *barrancas* and rocky ravines that added incredibly to their toil. Their principal food was the parched corn, which usually formed the nourishment of the travelling Indians, though held of much less account by the Spaniards; and this meagre fare was reinforced by such herbs as they found on the way-side, which, for want of better utensils, the soldiers were fain to boil in their helmets.[8] Carbajal, meanwhile, pressed on them so close, that their baggage, ammunition, and sometimes their mules, fell into his hands. The indefatigable warrior was always on their track, by day and by night, allowing them scarcely any repose. They spread no tent, and lay down in their arms, with their steeds standing saddled beside them; and hardly had the weary soldier closed his eyes, when he was startled by the cry that the enemy was upon him.[9]

At length, the harassed followers of Blasco Nuñez reached the *depoblado*, or desert of Paltos, which stretches towards the north for many a dreary league. The ground, intersected by numerous streams, has the character of a great quagmire, and men and horses floundered about in the stagnant waters, or with difficulty worked their way over the marsh, or opened a passage through the tangled underwood that shot up in rank luxuriance from the surface. The wayworn horses, without food, except such as they could pick up in the wilderness, were often spent with travel, and, becoming unserviceable, were left to die on the road, with their hamstrings cut, that they might be of no use to the enemy; though more frequently they were despatched to afford a miserable banquet to their masters.[10] Many of the men now fainted by the way from mere exhaustion, or loitered in the woods, unable to keep up with the march. And woe to the straggler who fell into the hands of Carbajal, at least if he had once belonged to the party of Pizarro. The mere suspicion of treason sealed his doom with the unrelenting soldier.[11]

The sufferings of Pizarro and his troop were scarcely less than those of the viceroy; though they were somewhat mitigated by the natives of the country, who, with ready instinct, discerned which party was the strongest, and, of course, the most to be feared. But, with every alleviation, the chieftain's sufferings were terrible. It was repeating the dismal scenes of the expedition to the Amazon. The soldiers of the Conquest must be admitted to have purchased their triumphs dearly.

Yet the viceroy had one source of disquietude, greater, perhaps, than any arising from physical suffering. This was the distrust of his own followers. There were several of the principal cavaliers in his suite whom he suspected of being in correspondence with the enemy, and even of designing to betray him into their hands. He was so well convinced of this, that he caused two of these officers to be put to death on the march; and their dead bodies, as they lay by the roadside, meeting the eye of the soldier, told him that there were others to be feared in these frightful solitudes besides the enemy in his rear.[12]

Another cavalier, who held the chief command under the viceroy, was executed, after a more formal investigation of his case, at the first place where the army halted. At this distance of time, it is impossible to determine how far the suspicions of Blasco Nuñez were founded on truth. The judgments of contemporaries are at variance.[13] In times of political ferment, the opinion of the writer is generally determined by the complexion of his party. To judge from the character of Blasco Nuñez, jealous and irritable, we might suppose him to have acted without sufficient cause. But this consideration is counterbalanced by that of the facility with which his followers swerved from their allegiance to their commander, who seems to have had so light a hold on their affections, that they were shaken off by the least reverse of fortune. Whether his suspicions were well or ill founded, the effect was the same on the mind of the viceroy. With an enemy in his rear whom he dared not fight, and followers whom he dared not trust, the cup of his calamities was nearly full.

At length, he issued forth on firm ground, and, passing through Tomebamba, Blasco Nuñez reëntered his northern capital of Quito. But his reception was not so cordial as that which he had before experienced. He now came as a fugitive, with a formidable enemy in pursuit; and he was soon made to feel that the surest way to receive support is not to need it.

Shaking from his feet the dust of the disloyal city, whose superstitious people were alive to many an omen that boded his approaching ruin,[14] the unfortunate commander held on his way towards Pastos, in the jurisdiction of Benalcazar. Pizarro and his forces entered Quito not long after, disappointed, that, with all his diligence, the enemy still eluded his pursuit. He halted only to breathe his men, and, declaring that "he would follow up the viceroy to the North Sea but he would overtake him,"[15] he resumed his march. At Pastos, he nearly accomplished his object. His advance-guard came up with Blasco Nuñez as the latter was halting on the opposite bank of a rivulet. Pizarro's men, fainting from toil and heat, staggered feebly to the water-side, to slake their burning thirst, and it would have been easy for the viceroy's troops, refreshed by repose, and superior in number to their foes, to have routed them. But Blasco Nuñez could not bring his soldiers to the charge. They had fled so long before their enemy, that the mere sight of him filled their hearts with panic, and they would have no more thought of turning against him than the hare would turn against the hound that pursues her. Their safety, they felt, was to fly, not to fight, and they profited by the exhaustion of their pursuers only to quicken their retreat.

Gonzalo Pizarro continued the chase some leagues beyond Pastos; when, finding himself carried farther than he desired into the territories of Benalcazar, and not caring to encounter this formidable captain at disadvantage, he came to a halt, and, notwithstanding his magnificent vaunt about the North Sea, ordered a retreat, and made a rapid countermarch on Quito. Here he found occupation in repairing the wasted spirits of his troops, and in strengthening himself with fresh reinforcements, which much increased his numbers; though these were again diminished by a body that he detached under Carbajal to suppress an insurrection, which he now learned had broken out in the south. It was headed by Diego Centeno, one of his own officers, whom he had established in La Plata, the inhabitants of which place had joined in the revolt and raised the standard for the Crown. With the rest of his forces, Pizarro resolved to remain at Quito, waiting the hour when the viceroy would reënter his dominions; as the tiger crouches by some spring in the wilderness, patiently waiting the return of his victims.

Meanwhile Blasco Nuñez had pushed forward his retreat to Popayan, the capital of Benalcazar's province. Here he was kindly received by the people; and his soldiers, reduced by desertion and disease to one fifth of their original number, rested from the unparalleled fatigues of a march which had continued for more than two hundred leagues.[16] It was not long before he was joined by Cabrera, Benalcazar's lieutenant, with a stout reinforcement, and, soon after, by that chieftain himself. His whole force now amounted to near four hundred men, most of them in good condition, and well trained in the school of American warfare. His own men were sorely deficient both in arms and ammunition; and he set about repairing the want by building furnaces for manufacturing arquebuses and pikes.[17]—One familiar with the history of these times is surprised to see the readiness with which the Spanish adventurers turned their hands to various trades and handicrafts usually requiring a long apprenticeship. They displayed the dexterity so necessary to settlers in a new country, where every man must become in some degree his own artisan. But this state of things, however favorable to the ingenuity of the artist, is not very propitious to the advancement of the art; and there can be little doubt that the weapons thus made by the soldiers of Blasco Nuñez were of the most rude and imperfect construction.

As week after week rolled away, Gonzalo Pizarro, though fortified with the patience of a Spanish soldier, felt uneasy at the protracted stay of Blasco Nuñez in the north, and he resorted to stratagem to decoy him from his retreat. He marched out of Quito with the greater part of his forces, pretending that he was going to support his lieutenant in the south, while he left a garrison in the city under the command of Puelles, the same officer who had formerly deserted from the viceroy. These tidings he took care should be conveyed to the enemy's camp. The artifice succeeded as he wished. Blasco Nuñez and his followers, confident in their superiority over Puelles, did not hesitate for a moment to profit by the supposed absence of Pizarro. Abandoning Popayan, the viceroy, early in January, 1546, moved by rapid marches towards the south. But before he reached the place of his destination, he became apprised of the snare into which he had been drawn. He communicated the fact to his officers; but he had already suffered so much from suspense, that his only desire now was, to bring his quarrel with Pizarro to the final arbitrament of arms.

That chief, meanwhile, had been well informed, through his spies, of the viceroy's movements. On learning the departure of the latter from Popayan, he had reëntered Quito, joined his forces with those of Puelles, and, issuing from the capital, had taken up a strong position about three leagues to the north, on a high ground that commanded a stream, across which the enemy must pass. It was not long before the latter came in sight, and Blasco Nuñez, as night began to fall, established himself on the opposite bank of the rivulet. It was so near to the enemy's quarters, that the voices of the sentinels could be distinctly heard in the opposite camps, and they did not fail to salute one another with the epithet of "traitors." In these civil wars, as we have seen, each party claimed for itself the exclusive merit of loyalty.[18]

But Benalcazar soon saw that Pizarro's position was too strong to be assailed with any chance of success. He proposed, therefore, to the viceroy, to draw off his forces secretly in the night; and, making a détour round the hills, to fall on the enemy's rear, where he would be least prepared to receive them. The counsel was approved; and, no sooner were the two hosts shrouded from each other's eyes by the darkness, than, leaving his camp-fires burning to deceive the enemy, Blasco Nuñez broke up his quarters, and began his circuitous march in the direction of Quito. But either he had been misinformed, or his guides misled him; for the roads proved so impractica-ble, that he was compelled to make a circuit of such extent, that dawn broke before he drew near the point of attack. Finding that he must now abandon the advantage of a surprise, he pressed forward to Quito, where he arrived with men and horses sorely fatigued by a nightmarch of eight leagues, from a point which, by the direct route, would not have exceeded three. It was a fatal error on the eve of an engagement.[19]

He found the capital nearly deserted by the men. They had all joined the standard of Pizarro; for they had now caught the general spirit of disaffection, and looked upon that chief as their protector from the oppressive ordinances. Pizarro was the representative of the people. Greatly moved at this desertion, the unhappy viceroy, lifting his hands to heaven, exclaimed,—"Is it thus, Lord, that thou abandonest thy servants?" The women and children came out, and in vain offered him food, of which he stood obviously in need, asking him, at the same time, "Why he had come there to die?" His followers, with more indifference than their commander, entered the houses of the inhabi-tants, and unceremoniously appropriated whatever they could find to appease the cravings of appetite.

Benalcazar, who saw the temerity of giving battle, in their present condi-tion, recommended the viceroy to try the effect of negotiation, and offered himself to go to the enemy's camp, and arrange, if possible, terms of accommodation with Pizarro. But Blasco Nuñez, if he had desponded for a moment, had now recovered his wonted constancy, and he proudly replied, —"There is no faith to be kept with traitors. We have come to fight, not to parley; and we must do our duty like good and loyal cavaliers. I will do mine," he continued, "and be assured I will be the first man to break a lance with the enemy."[20]

He then called his troops together, and addressed to them a few words preparatory to marching. "You are all brave men," he said, "and loyal to your sovereign. For my own part, I hold life as little in comparison with my duty to my prince. Yet let us not distrust our success; the Spaniard, in a good cause, has often overcome greater odds than these. And we are fighting for the right; it is the cause of God,—the cause of God,"[21] he concluded, and the soldiers, kindled by his generous ardor, answered him with huzzas that went to the heart of the unfortunate commander, little accustomed of late to this display of enthusiasm.

It was the eighteenth of January, 1546, when Blasco Nuñez marched out at the head of his array, from the ancient city of Quito. He had proceeded but a mile,[22] when he came in view of the enemy, formed along the crest of some high lands, which, by a gentle swell, rose gradually from the plains of Añaquito. Gonzalo Pizarro, greatly chagrined on ascertaining the departure of the viceroy, early in the morning, had broken up his camp, and directed his march on the capital, fully resolved that his enemy should not escape him.

The viceroy's troops, now coming to a halt, were formed in order of battle. A small body of arquebusiers was stationed in the advance to begin the fight. The remainder of that corps was distributed among the spearmen, who occupied the centre, protected on the flanks by the horse drawn up in two nearly equal squadrons. The cavalry amounted to about one hundred and forty, being little inferior to that on the other side, though the whole number of the viceroy's forces, being less than four hundred, did not much exceed the half of his rival's. On the right, and in front of the royal banner, Blasco Nuñez, supported by thirteen chosen cavaliers, took his station, prepared to head the attack.

Pizarro had formed his troops in a corresponding manner with that of his adversary. They mustered about seven hundred in all, well appointed, in good condition, and officered by the best knights in Peru.[23] As, notwithstanding his superiority of numbers, Pizarro did not seem inclined to abandon his advantageous position, Blasco Nuñez gave orders to advance. The action commenced with the arquebusiers, and in a few moments the dense clouds of smoke, rolling over the field, obscured every object; for it was late in the day when the action began, and the light was rapidly fading.

The infantry, now levelling their pikes, advanced under cover of the smoke, and were soon hotly engaged with the opposite files of spearmen. Then came the charge of the cavalry, which—notwithstanding they were thrown into some disorder by the fire of Pizarro's arquebusiers, far superior in number to their own—was conducted with such spirit that the enemy's horse were compelled to reel and fall back before it. But it was only to recoil with greater violence, as, like an overwhelming wave, Pizarro's troopers rushed on their foes, driving them along the slope, and bearing down man and horse in indiscriminate ruin. Yet these, in turn, at length rallied, cheered on by the cries and desperate efforts of their officers. The lances were shivered, and they fought hand to hand with swords and battle-axes mingled together in wild confusion. But the struggle was of no long duration; for, though the numbers were nearly equal, the viceroy's cavalry, jaded by the severe march of the previous night,[24] were no match for their antagonists. The ground was strewn with the wreck of their bodies; and horses and riders, the dead and the dying, lay heaped on one another. Cabrera, the brave lieutenant of Benalcazar, was slain, and that commander was thrown under his horse's feet, covered with wounds, and left for dead on the field. Alvarez, the judge, was mortally wounded. Both he and his colleague Cepeda were in the action, though ranged on opposite sides, fighting as if they had been bred to arms, not to the peaceful profession of the law.

Yet Blasco Nuñez and his companions maintained a brave struggle on the right of the field. The viceroy had kept his word by being the first to break his lance against the enemy, and by a well-directed blow had borne a cavalier, named Alonso de Montalvo, clean out of his saddle. But he was at length overwhelmed by numbers, and, as his companions, one after another, fell by his side, he was left nearly unprotected. He was already wounded, when a blow on the head from the battle-axe of a soldier struck him from his horse, and he fell stunned on the ground. Had his person been known, he might have been taken alive, but he wore a sobre-vest of Indian cotton over his armour, which concealed the military order of St. James, and the other badges of his rank.[25]

His person, however, was soon recognized by one of Pizarro's followers, who, not improbably, had once followed the viceroy's banner. The soldier immediately pointed him out to the Licentiate Carbajal. This person was the brother of the cavalier whom, as the reader may remember, Blasco Nuñez had so rashly put to death in his palace at Lima. The licentiate had afterwards taken service under Pizarro, and, with several of his kindred, was pledged to take vengeance on the viceroy. Instantly riding up, he taunted the fallen commander with the murder of his brother, and was in the act of dismounting to despatch him with his own hand, when Puelles remonstrating on this, as an act of degradation, commanded one of his attendants, a black slave, to cut off the viceroy's head. This the fellow executed with a single stroke of his sabre, while the wretched man, perhaps then dying of his wounds, uttered no word, but with eyes imploringly turned up towards heaven, received the fatal blow.[26] The head was then borne aloft on a pike, and some were brutal enough to pluck out the grey hairs from the beard and set them in their caps, as grisly trophies of their victory.[27] The fate of the day was now decided. Yet still the infantry made a brave stand, keeping Pizarro's horse at bay with their bristling array of pikes. But their numbers were thinned by the arquebusiers; and, thrown into disorder, they could no longer resist the onset of the horse, who broke into their column, and soon scattered and drove them off the ground. The pursuit was neither long nor bloody; for darkness came on, and Pizarro bade his trumpets sound, to call his men together under their banners.

Though the action lasted but a short time, nearly one third of the viceroy's troops had perished. The loss of their opponents was inconsiderable.[28] Several of the vanquished cavaliers took refuge in the churches of Quito. But they were dragged from the sanctuary, and some—probably those who had once espoused the cause of Pizarro—were led to execution, and others banished to Chili. The greater part were pardoned by the conqueror. Benalcazar, who recovered from his wounds, was permitted to return to his government, on condition of no more bearing arms against Pizarro. His troops were invited to take service under the banner of the victor, who, however, never treated them with the confidence shown to his ancient partisans. He was greatly displeased at the indignities offered to the viceroy; whose mangled remains he caused to be buried with the honors due to his rank in the cathedral of Quito. Gonzalo Pizarro, attired in black, walked as chief mourner in the procession. —It was usual with the Pizarros, as we have seen, to pay these obituary honors to their victims.[29]

Such was the sad end of Blasco Nuñez Vela, first viceroy of Peru. It was less than two years since he had set foot in the country, a period of unmitigated disaster and disgrace. His misfortunes may be imputed partly to circumstances, and partly to his own character. The minister of an odious and oppressive law, he was intrusted with no discretionary power in the execution of it.[30] Yet every man may, to a certain extent, claim the right to such a power; since, to execute a commission, which circumstances show must certainly defeat the object for which it was designed, would be absurd. But it requires sagacity to determine the existence of such a contingency, and moral courage to assume the responsibility of acting on it. Such a crisis is the severest test of character. To dare to disobey from a paramount sense of duty, is a paradox that a little soul can hardly comprehend. Unfortunately, Blasco Nuñez was a pedantic martinet, a man of narrow views, who could not feel himself authorized under any circumstances to swerve from the letter of the law. Puffed up by his brief authority, moreover, he considered opposition to the ordinances as treason to himself; and thus, identifying himself with his commission, he was prompted by personal feelings, quite as much as by those of a public and patriotic nature.

Neither was the viceroy's character of a kind that tended to mitigate the odium of his measures, and reconcile the people to their execution. It afforded a strong contrast to that of his rival, Pizarro, whose frank, chivalrous bearing, and generous confidence in his followers, made him universally popular, blinding their judgments, and giving to the worse the semblance of the better cause. Blasco Nuñez, on the contrary, irritable and suspicious, placed himself in a false position with all whom he approached; for a suspicious temper creates an atmosphere of distrust around it that kills every kindly affection. His first step was to alienate the members of the Audience who were sent to act in concert with him. But this was their fault as well as his, since they were as much too lax, as he was too severe, in the interpretation of the law.[31] He next alienated and outraged the people whom he was appointed to govern. And, lastly, he disgusted his own friends, and too often turned them into enemies; so that, in his final struggle for power and for existence, he was obliged to rely on the arm of the stranger. Yet in the catalogue of his qualities we must not pass insilence over his virtues. There are two to the credit of which he is undeniably entitled,—a loyalty, which shone the brighter amidst the general defection around him, and a constancy under misfortune, which might challenge the respect even of his enemies. But with the most liberal allowance for his merits, it can scarcely be doubted that a person more incompetent to the task assigned him could not have been found in Castile.[32]

The victory of Añaquito was received with general joy in the neighbouring capital; all the cities of Peru looked on it as sealing the downfall of the detested ordinances, and the name of Gonzalo Pizarro was sounded from one end of the country to the other as that of its deliverer. That chief continued to prolong his stay in Quito during the wet season, dividing his time between the licentious pleasures of the reckless adventurer and the cares of business that now pressed on him as ruler of the state. His administration was stained with fewer acts of violence than might have been expected from the circumstances of his situation. So long as Carbajal, the counsellor in whom he unfortunately placed greatest reliance, was absent, Gonzalo sanctioned no execution, it was observed, but according to the forms of law.[33] He rewarded his followers by new grants of land, and detached several on expeditions, to no greater distance, however, than would leave it in his power readily to recall them. He made various provisions for the welfare of the natives, and some, in particular, for instructing them in the Christian faith. He paid attention to the faithful collection of the royal dues, urging on the colonists that they should deport themselves so as to conciliate the good-will of the Crown, and induce a revocation of the ordinances. His administration, in short, was so conducted, that even the austere Gasca, his successor, allowed "it was a good government,—for a tyrant."[34]

At length, in July, 1546, the new governor bade adieu to Quito, and, leaving there a sufficient garrison under his officer Puelles, began his journey to the south. It was a triumphal progress, and everywhere he was received on the road with enthusiasm by the people. At Truxillo, the citizens came out in a body to welcome him, and the clergy chanted anthems in his honor, extolling him as the "victorious prince," and imploring the Almighty "to lengthen his days, and give him honor."[35] At Lima, it was proposed to clear away some of the buildings, and open a new street for his entrance, which might ever after bear the name of the victor. But the politic chieftain declined this flattering tribute, and modestly preferred to enter the city by the usual way. A procession was formed of the citizens, the soldiers, and the clergy, and Pizarro made his entry into the capital with two of his principal captains on foot, holding the reins of his charger, while the archbishop of Lima, and the bishops of Cuzco, Quito, and Bogotá, the last of whom had lately come to the city to be consecrated, rode by his side. The streets were strewn with boughs, the walls of the houses hung with showy tapestries, and triumphal arches were thrown over the way in honor of the victor. Every balcony, veranda, and house-top was crowded with spectators, who sent up huzzas, loud and long, saluting the victorious soldier with the titles of "Liberator, and Protector of the people." The bells rang out their joyous peal, as on his former entrance into the capital; and amidst strains of enlivening music, and the blithe sounds of jubilee, Gonzalo held on his way to the palace of his brother. Peru was once more placed under the dynasty of the Pizarros.[36]

Deputies came from different parts of the country, tendering the congratulations of their respective cities; and every one eagerly urged his own claims to consideration for the services he had rendered in the revolution. Pizarro, at the same time, received the welcome intelligence of the success of his arms in the south. Diego Centeno, as before stated, had there raised the standard of rebellion, or rather, of loyalty to his sovereign. He had made himself master of La Plata, and the spirit of insurrection had spread over the broad province of Charcas. Carbajal, who had been sent against him from Quito, after repairing to Lima, had passed at once to Cuzco, and there, strengthening his forces, had descended by rapid marches on the refractory district. Centeno did not trust himself in the field against this formidable champion. He retreated with his troops into the fastnesses of the sierra. Carbajal pursued, following on his track with the pertinacity of a bloodhound; over mountain and moor, through forests and dangerous ravines, allowing him no respite, by day or by night. Eating, drinking, sleeping in his saddle, the veteran, eighty years of age, saw his own followers tire one after another, while he urged on the chase, like the wild huntsman of Bürger, as if endowed with an unearthly frame, incapable of fatigue! During this terrible pursuit, which continued for more than two hundred leagues over a savage country, Centeno found himself abandoned by most of his followers. Such of them as fell into Carbajal's hands were sent to speedy execution; for that inexorable chief had no mercy on those who had been false to their party.[37] At length, Centeno, with a handful of men, arrived on the borders of the Pacific, and there, separating from one another, they provided, each in the best way he could, for their own safety. Their leader found an asylum in a cave in the mountains, where he was secretly fed by an Indian curaca, till the time again came for him to unfurl the standard of revolt.[38]

Carbajal, after some further, decisive movements, which fully established the ascendency of Pizarro over the south, returned in triumph to La Plata. There he occupied himself with working the silver mines of Potosí, in which a vein, recently opened, promised to make richer returns than any yet discovered in Mexico or Peru;[39] and he was soon enabled to send large remittances to Lima, deducting no stinted commission for himself,—for the cupidity of the lieutenant was equal to his cruelty.

Gonzalo Pizarro was now undisputed master of Peru. From Quito to the northern confines of Chili, the whole country acknowledged his authority. His fleet rode triumphant on the Pacific, and gave him the command of every city and hamlet on its borders. His admiral, Hinojosa, a discreet and gallant officer, had secured him Panamá, and, marching across the Isthmus, had since obtained for him the possession of Nombre de Dios,—the principal key of communication with Europe. His forces were on an excellent footing, including the flower of the warriors who had fought under his brother, and who now eagerly rallied under the name of Pizarro; while the tide of wealth that flowed in from the mines of Potosí supplied him with the resources of an European monarch.

The new governor now began to assume a state correspondent with his full-blown fortunes. He was attended by a body-guard of eighty soldiers. He dined always in public, and usually with not less than a hundred guests at table. He even affected, it was said, the more decided etiquette of royalty, giving his hand to be kissed, and allowing no one, of whatever rank, to be seated in his presence.[40] But this is denied by others. It would not be strange that a vain man like Pizarro, with a superficial, undisciplined mind, when he saw himself thus raised from an humble condition to the highest post in the land, should be somewhat intoxicated by the possession of power, and treat with superciliousness those whom he had once approached with deference. But one who had often seen him in his prosperity assures us, that it was not so, and that the governor continued to show the same frank and soldierlike bearing as before his elevation, mingling on familiar terms with his comrades, and displaying the same qualities which had hitherto endeared him to the people.[41]

However this may be, it is certain there were not wanting those who urged him to throw off his allegiance to the Crown, and set up an independent government for himself. Among these was his lieutenant, Carbajal, whose daring spirit never shrunk from following things to their consequences. He plainly counselled Pizarro to renounce his allegiance at once. "In fact, you have already done so," he said. "You have been in arms against a viceroy, have driven him from the country, beaten and slain him in battle. What favor, or even mercy, can you expect from the Crown? You have gone too far either to halt, or to recede. You must go boldly on, proclaim yourself king; the troops, the people, will support you." And he concluded, it is said, by advising him to marry the Coya, the female representative of the Incas, that the two races might henceforth repose in quiet under a common sceptre![42]

The advice of the bold counsellor was, perhaps, the most politic that could have been given to Pizarro under existing circumstances. For he was like one who had heedlessly climbed far up a dizzy precipice,—too far to descend safely, while he had no sure hold where he was. His only chance was to climb still higher, till he had gained the summit. But Gonzalo Pizarro shrunk from the attitude, in which this placed him, of avowed rebellion. Notwithstanding the criminal course into which he had been, of late, seduced, the sentiment of loyalty was too deeply implanted in his bosom to be wholly eradicated. Though in arms against the measures and ministers of his sovereign, he was not prepared to raise the sword against that sovereign himself. He, doubtless, had conflicting emotions in his bosom; like Macbeth, and many a less noble nature,

> "Would not play false,
> And yet would wrongly win."

And however grateful to his vanity might be the picture of the air-drawn sceptre thus painted to his imagination, he had not the audacity—we may, perhaps, say, the criminal ambition—to attempt to grasp it.

Even at this very moment, when urged to this desperate extremity, he was preparing a mission to Spain, in order to vindicate the course he had taken, and to solicit an amnesty for the past, with a full confirmation of his authority, as successor to his brother in the government of Peru.—Pizarro did not read the future with the calm, prophetic eye of Carbajal.

BOOK V

SETTLEMENT OF THE COUNTRY

CHAPTER I

GREAT SENSATION IN SPAIN. — PEDRO DE
LA GASCA. — HIS EARLY LIFE. — HIS MISSION
TO PERU. — HIS POLITIC CONDUCT. — HIS
OFFERS TO PIZARRO. — GAINS THE FLEET

1545-1547.

WHILE the important revolution detailed in the preceding pages was going forward in Peru, rumors of it, from time to time, found their way to the mother-country; but the distance was so great, and opportunities for communication so rare, that the tidings were usually very long behind the occurrence of the events to which they related. The government heard with dismay of the troubles caused by the ordinances and the intemperate conduct of the viceroy; and it was not long before it learned that this functionary was deposed and driven from his capital, while the whole country, under Gonzalo Pizarro, was arrayed in arms against him. All classes were filled with consternation at this alarming intelligence; and many that had before approved the ordinances now loudly condemned the ministers, who, without considering the inflammable temper of the people, had thus rashly fired a train which menaced a general explosion throughout the colonies.[1] No such rebellion, within the memory of man, had occurred in the Spanish empire. It was compared with the famous war of the *comunidades,* in the beginning of Charles the Filth's reign. But the Peruvian insurrection seemed the more formidable of the two. The troubles of Castile, being under the eye of the Court, might be the more easily managed; while it was difficult to make the same power felt on the remote shores of the Indies. Lying along the distant Pacific, the principle of attraction which held Peru to the parent country was so feeble, that this colony might, at any time, with a less impulse than that now given to it, fly from its political orbit. It seemed as if the fairest of its jewels was about to fall from the imperial diadem!

Such was the state of things in the summer of 1545, when Charles the Fifth was absent in Germany, occupied with the religious troubles of the empire. The government was in the hands of his son, who, under the name of Philip the Second, was soon to sway the sceptre over the largest portion of his father's dominions, and who was then holding his court at Valladolid. He called together a council of prelates, jurists, and military men of greatest experience, to deliberate on the measures to be pursued for restoring order in the colonies. All agreed in regarding Pizarro's movement in the light of an audacious rebellion; and there were few, at first, who were not willing to employ the whole strength of government to vindicate the honor of the Crown,—to quell the insurrection, and bring the authors of it to punishment.[2]

But, however desirable this might appear, a very little reflection showed that it was not easy to be done, if, indeed, it were practicable. The great distance of Peru required troops to be transported not merely across the ocean, but over the broad extent of the great continent. And how was this to be effected, when the principal posts, the keys of communication with the country, were in the hands of the rebels, while their fleet rode in the Pacific, the mistress of its waters, cutting off all approach to the coast? Even if a Spanish force could be landed in Peru, what chance would it have, unaccustomed, as it would be, to the country and the climate, of coping with the veterans of Pizarro, trained to war in the Indies and warmly attached to the person of their commander? The new levies thus sent out might become themselves infected with the spirit of insurrection, and cast off their own allegiance.[3]

Nothing remained, therefore, but to try conciliatory measures. The government, however mortifying to its pride, must reface its steps. A free grace must be extended to those who submitted, and such persuasive arguments should be used, and such politic concessions made, as would convince the refractory colonists that it was their interest, as well as their duty, to return to their allegiance.

But to approach the people in their present state of excitement, and to make those concessions without too far compromising the dignity and permanent authority of the Crown, was a delicate matter, for the success of which they must rely wholly on the character of the agent. After much deliberation, a competent person, as it was thought, was found in an ecclesiastic, by the name of Pedro de la Gasca,—a name which, brighter by contrast with the gloomy times in which it first appeared, still shines with undiminished splendor after the lapse of ages.

Pedro de la Gasca was born, probably, towards the close of the fifteenth century, in a small village in Castile, named Barco de Avila. He came, both by father and mother's side, from an ancient and noble lineage; ancient indeed, if, as his biographers contend, he derived his descent from Casca, one of the conspirators against Julius Cæsar![4] Having the misfortune to lose his father early in life, he was placed by his uncle in the famous seminary of Alcalá de Henares, founded by the great Ximénes. Here he made rapid proficiency in liberal studies, especially in those connected with his profession, and at length received the degree of Master of Theology.

The young man, however, discovered other talents than those demanded by his sacred calling. The war of the *comunidades* was then raging in the country; and the authorities of his college showed a disposition to take the popular side. But Gasca, putting himself at the head of an armed force, seized one of the gates of the city, and, with assistance from the royal troops, secured the place to the interests of the Crown. This early display of loyalty was probably not lost on his vigilant sovereign.[5]

From Alcalá, Gasca was afterwards removed to Salamanca; where he distinguished himself by his skill in scholastic disputation, and obtained the highest academic honors in that ancient university, the fruitful nursery of scholarship and genius. He was subsequently intrusted with the management of some important affairs of an ecclesiastical nature, and made a member of the Council of the Inquisition.

In this latter capacity he was sent to Valencia, about 1540, to examine into certain alleged cases of heresy in that quarter of the country. These were involved in great obscurity; and, although Gasca had the assistance of several eminent jurists in the investigation, it occupied him nearly two years. In the conduct of this difficult matter, he showed so much penetration, and such perfect impartiality, that he was appointed by the Cortes of Valencia to the office of *visitador* of that kingdom; a highly responsible post, requiring great discretion in the person who filled it, since it was his province to inspect the condition of the courts of justice and of finance, throughout the land, with authority to reform abuses. It was proof of extraordinary consideration, that it should have been bestowed on Gasca; since it was a departure from the established usage — and that in a nation most wedded to usage — to confer the office on any but a subject of the Aragonese crown.[6]

Gasca executed the task assigned to him with independence and ability. While he was thus occupied, the people of Valencia were thrown into consternation by a meditated invasion of the French and the Turks, who, under the redoubtable Barbarossa, menaced the coast and the neighbouring Balearic isles. Fears were generally entertained of a rising of the Morisco population; and the Spanish officers who had command in that quarter, being left without the protection of a navy, despaired of making head against the enemy. In this season of general panic, Gasca alone appeared calm and self-possessed. He remonstrated with the Spanish commanders on their unsoldierlike despondency; encouraged them to confide in the loyalty of the Moriscos; and advised the immediate erection of fortifications along the shores for their protection. He was, in consequence, named one of a commission to superintend these works, and to raise levies for defending the sea-coast; and so faithfully was the task performed, that Barbarossa, after some ineffectual attempts to make good his landing, was baffled at all points, and compelled to abandon the enterprise as hopeless. The chief credit of this resistance must be assigned to Gasca, who superintended the construction of the defences, and who was enabled to contribute a large part of the requisite funds by the economical reforms he had introduced into the administration of Valencia.[7]

It was at this time, the latter part of the year 1545, that the council of Philip selected Gasca as the person most competent to undertake the perilous mission to Peru.[8] His character, indeed, seemed especially suited to it. His loyalty had been shown through his whole life. With great suavity of manners he combined the most intrepid resolution. Though his demeanour was humble, as be seemed his calling, it was far from abject; for he was sustained by a conscious rectitude of purpose, that impressed respect on all with whom he had intercourse. He was acute in his perceptions, had a shrewd knowledge of character, and, though bred to the cloister, possessed an acquaintance with affairs, and even with military science, such as was to have been expected only from one reared in courts and camps.

Without hesitation, therefore, the council unanimously recommended him to the emperor, and requested his approbation of their proceedings. Charles had not been an inattentive observer of Gasca's course. His attention had been particularly called to the able manner in which he had conducted the judicial process against the heretics of Valencia.[9] The monarch saw, at once, that he was the man for the present emergency; and he immediately wrote to him, with his own hand, expressing his entire satisfaction at the appointment, and intimating his purpose to testify his sense of his worth by preferring him to one of the principal sees then vacant.

Gasca accepted the important mission now tendered to him without hesitation; and, repairing to Madrid, received the instructions of the government as to the course to be pursued. They were expressed in the most benign and conciliatory tone, perfectly in accordance with the suggestions of his own benevolent temper.[10] But, while he commended the tone of the instructions, he considered the powers with which he was to be intrusted as wholly incompetent to their object. They were conceived in the jealous spirit with which the Spanish government usually limited the authority of its great colonial officers, whose distance from home gave peculiar cause for distrust. On every strange and unexpected emergency, Gasca saw that he should be obliged to send back for instructions. This must cause delay, where promptitude was essential to success. The Court, moreover, as he represented to the council, was, from its remoteness from the scene of action, utterly incompetent to pronounce as to the expediency of the measures to be pursued. Some one should be sent out in whom the king could implicitly confide, and who should be invested with powers competent to every emergency; powers not merely to decide on what was best, but to carry that decision into execution; and he boldly demanded that he should go not only as the representative of the sovereign, but clothed with all the authority of the sovereign himself. Less than this would defeat the very object for which he was to be sent. "For myself," he concluded, "I ask neither salary nor compensation of any kind. I covet no display of state or military array. With my stole and breviary I trust to do the work that is committed to me.[11] Infirm as I am in body, the repose of my own home would have been more grateful to me than this dangerous mission; but I will not shrink from it at the bidding of my sovereign, and if, as is very probable, I may not be permitted again to see my native land, I shall, at least, be cheered by the consciousness of having done my best to serve its interests."[12]

The members of the council, while they listened with admiration to the disinterested avowal of Gasca, were astounded by the boldness of his demands. Not that they distrusted the purity of his motives, for these were above suspicion. But the powers for which he stipulated were so far beyond those hitherto delegated to a colonial viceroy, that they felt they had no warrant to grant them. They even shrank from soliciting them from the emperor, and required that Gasca himself should address the monarch, and state precisely the grounds on which demands so extraordinary were founded.

Gasca readily adopted the suggestion, and wrote in the most full and explicit manner to his sovereign, who had then transferred his residence to Flanders. But Charles was not so tenacious, or, at least, so jealous, of authority, as his ministers. He had been too long in possession of it to feel that jealousy; and, indeed, many years were not to elapse, before, oppressed by its weight, he was to resign it altogether into the hands of his son. His sagacious mind, moreover, readily comprehended the difficulties of Gasca's position. He felt that the present extraordinary crisis was to be met only by extraordinary measures. He assented to the force of his vassal's arguments, and, on the sixteenth of February, 1546, wrote him another letter expressive of his approbation, and intimated his willingness to grant him powers as absolute as those he had requested.

Gasca was to be styled President of the Royal Audience. But, under this simple title, he was placed at the head of every department in the colony, civil, military, and judicial. He was empowered to make new *repartimientos,* and to confirm those already made. He might declare war, levy troops, appoint to all offices, or remove from them, at pleasure. He might exercise the royal prerogative of pardoning offences, and was especially authorized to grant an amnesty to all, without exception, implicated in the present rebellion. He was, moreover, to proclaim at once the revocation of the odious ordinances. These two last provisions might be said to form the basis of all his operations.

Since ecclesiastics were not to be reached by the secular arm, and yet were often found fomenting troubles in the colonies, Gasca was permitted to banish from Peru such as he thought fit. He might even send home the viceroy, if the good of the country required it. Agreeably to his own suggestion, he was to receive no specified stipend; but he had unlimited orders on the treasuries both of Panamá and Peru. He was furnished with letters from the emperor to the principal authorities, not only in Peru, but in Mexico and the neighbour-

ing colonies, requiring their countenance and support; and, lastly, blank letters, bearing the royal signature, were delivered to him, which he was to fill
up at his pleasure.[13]

While the grant of such unbounded powers excited the warmest sentiments of gratitude in Gasca towards the sovereign who could repose in him so
much confidence, it seems—which is more extraordinary—not to have raised
corresponding feelings of envy in the courtiers. They knew well that it was not
for himself that the good ecclesiastic had solicited them. On the contrary,
some of the council were desirous that he should be preferred to the bishopric, as already promised him, before his departure; conceiving that he
would thus go with greater authority than as an humble ecclesiastic, and fearing, moreover, that Gasca himself, were it omitted, might feel some natural
disappointment. But the president hastened to remove these impressions.
"The honor would avail me little," he said, "where I am going; and it would be
manifestly wrong to appoint me to an office in the Church, while I remain at
such a distance that I cannot discharge the duties of it. The consciousness of
my insufficiency," he continued, "should I never return, would lie heavy on my
soul in my last moments."[14] The politic reluctance to accept the mitre has
passed into a proverb. But there was no affectation here; and Gasca's friends,
yielding to his arguments, forbore to urge the matter further.

The new president now went forward with his preparations. They were
few and simple; for he was to be accompanied by a slender train of followers, among whom the most conspicuous was Alonso de Alvarado, the gallant officer who, as the reader may remember, long commanded under
Francisco Pizarro. He had resided of late years at court; and now at Gasca's
request accompanied him to Peru, where his presence might facilitate
negotiations with the insurgents, while his military experience would
prove no less valuable in case of an appeal to arms.[15] Some delay necessarily occurred in getting ready his little squadron, and it was not till the 26th
of May, 1546, that the president and his suite embarked at San Lucar for
the New World.

After a prosperous voyage, and not a long one for that day, he landed,
about the middle of July, at the port of Santa Martha. Here he received the
astounding intelligence of the battle of Añaquito, of the defeat and death of
the viceroy, and of the manner in which Gonzalo Pizarro had since established
his absolute rule over the land. Although these events had occurred several
months before Gasca's departure from Spain, yet, so imperfect was the intercourse, no tidings of them had then reached that country.

They now filled the president with great anxiety; as he reflected that the
insurgents, after so atrocious an act as the slaughter of the viceroy, might well
despair of grace, and become reckless of consequences. He was careful, therefore, to have it understood, that the date of his commission was subsequent to
that of the fatal battle, and that it authorized an entire amnesty of all offences
hitherto committed against the government.[16]

Yet, in some points of view, the death of Blasco Nuñez might be regarded as an auspicious circumstance for the settlement of the country. Had he lived till Gasca's arrival, the latter would have been greatly embarrassed by the necessity of acting in concert with a person so generally detested in the colony, or by the unwelcome alternative of sending him back to Castile. The insurgents, moreover, would, in all probability, be now more amenable to reason, since all personal animosity might naturally be buried in the grave of their enemy.

The president was much embarrassed by deciding in what quarter he should attempt to enter Peru. Every port was in the hands of Pizarro, and was placed under the care of his officers, with strict charge to intercept any communications from Spain, and to detain such persons as bore a commission from that country until his pleasure could be known respecting them. Gasca, at length, decided on crossing over to Nombre de Dios, then held with a strong force by Hernan Mexia, an officer to whose charge Gonzalo had committed this strong gate to his dominions, as to a person on whose attachment to his cause he could confidently rely.

Had Gasca appeared off this place in a menacing attitude, with a military array, or, indeed, with any display of official pomp that might have awakened distrust in the commander, he would doubtless have found it no easy matter to effect a landing. But Mexia saw nothing to apprehend in the approach of a poor ecclesiastic, without an armed force, with hardly even a retinue to support him, coming solely, as it seemed, on an errand of mercy. No sooner, therefore, was he acquainted with the character of the envoy and his mission, than he prepared to receive him with the honors due to his rank, and marched out at the head of his soldiers, together with a considerable body of ecclesiastics resident in the place. There was nothing in the person of Gasca, still less in his humble clerical attire and modest retinue, to impress the vulgar spectator with feelings of awe or reverence. Indeed, the poverty-stricken aspect, as it seemed, of himself and his followers, so different from the usual state affected by the Indian viceroys, excited some merriment among the rude soldiery, who did not scruple to break their coarse jests on his appearance, in hearing of the president himself.[17] "If this is the sort of governor his Majesty sends over to us," they exclaimed, "Pizarro need not trouble his head much about it."

Yet the president, far from being ruffled by this ribaldry, or from showing resentment to its authors, submitted to it with the utmost humility, and only seemed the more grateful to his own brethren, who, by their respectful demeanour, appeared anxious to do him honor.

But, however plain and unpretending the manners of Gasca, Mexia, on his first interview with him, soon discovered that he had no common man to deal with. The president, after briefly explaining the nature of his commission, told him that he had come as a messenger of peace; and that it was on peaceful measures he relied for his success. He then stated the general scope of his commission, his authority to grant a free pardon to all, without exception, who at once submitted to government, and, finally, his purpose to proclaim the revocation of the ordinances. The objects of the revolution were thus attained. To contend longer would be manifest rebellion, and that without a motive; and he urged the commander by every principle of loyalty and patriotism to support him in settling the distractions of the country, and bringing it back to its allegiance.

The candid and conciliatory language of the president, so different from the arrogance of Blasco Nuñez, and the austere demeanour of Vaca de Castro, made a sensible impression on Mexia. He admitted the force of Gasca's reasoning, and flattered himself that Gonzalo Pizarro would not be insensible to it. Though attached to the fortunes of that leader, he was loyal in heart, and, like most of the party, had been led by accident, rather than by design, into rebellion; and now that so good an opportunity occurred to do it with safety, he was not unwilling to retrace his steps, and secure the royal favor by thus early returning to his allegiance. This he signified to the president, assuring him of his hearty coöperation in the good work of reform.[18]

This was an important step for Gasca. It was yet more important for him to secure the obedience of Hinojosa, the governor of Panamá, in the harbour of which city lay Pizarro's navy, consisting of two-and-twenty vessels. But it was not easy to approach this officer. He was a person of much higher character than was usually found among the reckless adventurers in the New World. He was attached to the interests of Pizarro, and the latter had requited him by placing him in command of his armada and of Panamá, the key to his territories on the Pacific.

The president first sent Mexia and Alonso de Alvarado to prepare the way for his own coming, by advising Hinojosa of the purport of his mission. He soon after followed, and was received by that commander with every show of outward respect. But while the latter listened with deference to the representations of Gasca, they failed to work the change in him which they had wrought in Mexia; and he concluded by asking the president to show him his powers, and by inquiring whether they gave him authority to confirm Pizarro in his present post, to which he was entitled no less by his own services than by the general voice of the people.

This was an embarrassing question. Such a concession would have been altogether too humiliating to the Crown; but to have openly avowed this at the present juncture to so stanch an adherent of Pizarro might have precluded all further negotiation. The president evaded the question, therefore, by simply stating, that the time had not yet come for him to produce his powers, but that Hinojosa might be assured they were such as to secure an ample recompense to every loyal servant of his country.[19]

Hinojosa was not satisfied; and he immediately wrote to Pizarro, acquainting him with Gasca's arrival and with the object of his mission, at the same time plainly intimating his own conviction that the president had no authority to confirm him in the government. But before the departure of the ship, Gasca secured the services of a Dominican friar, who had taken his passage on board for one of the towns on the coast. This man he intrusted with manifestoes, setting forth the purport of his visit, and proclaiming the abolition of the ordinances, with a free pardon to all who returned to their obedience. He wrote, also, to the prelates and to the corporations of the different cities. The former he requested to coöperate with him in introducing a spirit of loyalty and subordination among the people, while he intimated to the towns his purpose to confer with them hereafter, in order to devise some effectual measures for the welfare of the country. These papers the Dominican engaged to distribute, himself, among the principal cities of the colony; and he faithfully kept his word, though, as it proved, at no little hazard of his life. The seeds thus scattered might many of them fall on barren ground. But the greater part, the president trusted, would take root in the hearts of the people; and he patiently waited for the harvest.

Meanwhile, though he failed to remove the scruples of Hinojosa, the courteous manners of Gasca, and his mild, persuasive discourse, had a visible effect on other individuals with whom he had daily intercourse. Several of these, and among them some of the principal cavaliers in Panamá, as well as in the squadron, expressed their willingness to join the royal cause, and aid the president in maintaining it. Gasca profited by their assistance to open a communication with the authorities of Guatemala and Mexico, whom he advised of his mission, while he admonished them to allow no intercourse to be carried on with the insurgents on the coast of Peru. He, at length, also prevailed on the governor of Panamá to furnish him with the means of entering into communication with Gonzalo Pizarro himself; and a ship was despatched to Lima, bearing a letter from Charles the Fifth, addressed to that chief, with an epistle also from Gasca.

The emperor's communication was couched in the most condescending and even conciliatory terms. Far from taxing Gonzalo with rebellion, his royal master affected to regard his conduct as in a manner imposed on him by circumstances, especially by the obduracy of the viceroy Nuñez in denying the colonists the inalienable right of petition. He gave no intimation of an intent to confirm Pizarro in the government, or, indeed, to remove him from it; but simply referred him to Gasca as one who would acquaint him with the royal pleasure, and with whom he was to coöperate in restoring tranquillity to the country.

Gasca's own letter was pitched on the same politic key. He remarked, however, that the exigencies which had hitherto determined Gonzalo's line of conduct existed no longer. All that had been asked was conceded. There was nothing now to contend for; and it only remained for Pizarro and his followers to show their loyalty and the sincerity of their principles by obedience to the Crown. Hitherto, the president said, Pizarro had been in arms against the viceroy; and the people had supported him as against a common enemy. If he prolonged the contest, that enemy must be his sovereign. In such a struggle, the people would be sure to desert him; and Gasca conjured him, by his honor as a cavalier, and his duty as a loyal vassal, to respect the royal authority, and not rashly provoke a contest which must prove to the world that his conduct hitherto had been dictated less by patriotic motives than by selfish ambition.

This letter, which was conveyed in language the most courteous and complimentary to the subject of it, was of great length. It was accompanied by another much more concise, to Cepeda, the intriguing lawyer, who, as Gasca knew, had the greatest influence over Pizarro, in the absence of Carbajal, then employed in reaping the silver harvest from the newly discovered mines of Potosí.[20] In this epistle, Gasca affected to defer to the cunning politician as a member of the Royal Audience, and he conferred with him on the best manner of supplying a vacancy in that body. These several despatches were committed to a cavalier, named Paniagua, a faithful adherent of the president, and one of those who had accompanied him from Castile. To this same emissary he also gave manifestoes and letters, like those intrusted to the Dominican, with orders secretly to distribute them in Lima, before he quitted that capital.[21]

Weeks and months rolled away, while the president still remained at Panamá, where, indeed, as his communications were jealously cut off with Peru, he might be said to be detained as a sort of prisoner of state. Meanwhile, both he and Hinojosa were looking with anxiety for the arrival of some messenger from Pizarro, who should indicate the manner in which the president's mission was to be received by that chief. The governor of Panamá was not blind to the perilous position in which he was himself placed, nor to the madness of provoking a contest with the Court of Castile. But he had a reluctance —not too often shared by the cavaliers of Peru—to abandon the fortunes of the commander who had reposed in him so great confidence. Yet he trusted that this commander would embrace the opportunity now offered, of placing himself and the country in a state of permanent security.

Several of the cavaliers who had given in their adhesion to Gasca, displeased by this obstinacy, as they termed it, of Hinojosa, proposed to seize his person and then get possession of the armada. But the president at once rejected this offer. His mission, he said, was one of peace, and he would not stain it at the outset by an act of violence. He even respected the scruples of Hinojosa; and a cavalier of so honorable a nature, he conceived, if once he could be gained by fair means, would be much more likely to be true to his interests, than if overcome either by force or fraud. Gasca thought he might safely abide his time. There was policy, as well as honesty, in this; indeed, they always go together.

Meantime, persons were occasionally arriving from Lima and the neighbouring places, who gave accounts of Pizarro, varying according to the character and situation of the parties. Some represented him as winning all hearts by his open temper and the politic profusion with which, though covetous of wealth, he distributed *repartimientos* and favors among his followers. Others spoke of him as carrying matters with a high hand, while the greatest timidity and distrust prevailed among the citizens of Lima. All agreed that his power rested on too secure a basis to be shaken; and that, if the president should go to Lima, he must either consent to become Pizarro's instrument and confirm him in the government, or forfeit his own life.[22]

It was undoubtedly true, that Gonzalo, while he gave attention, as his friends say, to the public business, found time for free indulgence in those pleasures which wait on the soldier of fortune in his hour of triumph. He was the object of flattery and homage; courted even by those who hated him. For such as did not love the successful chieftain had good cause to fear him; and his exploits were commemorated in *romances* or ballads, as rivalling—it was not far from truth—those of the most doughty paladins of chivalry.[23]

Amidst this burst of adulation, the cup of joy commended to Pizarro's lips had one drop of bitterness in it that gave its flavor to all the rest; for, notwithstanding his show of confidence, he looked with unceasing anxiety to the arrival of tidings that might assure him in what light his conduct was regarded by the government at home. This was proved by his jealous precautions to guard the approaches to the coast, and to detain the persons of the royal emissaries. He learned, therefore, with no little uneasiness, from Hinojosa, the landing of President Gasca, and the purport of his mission. But his discontent was mitigated, when he understood that the new envoy had come without military array, without any of the ostentatious trappings of office to impose on the minds of the vulgar, but alone, as it were, in the plain garb of an humble missionary.[24] Pizarro could not discern, that under this modest exterior lay a moral power, stronger than his own steel-clad battalions, which, operating silently on public opinion,—the more sure that it was silent,—was even now undermining his strength, like a subterraneous channel eating away the foundations of some stately edifice, that stands secure in its pride of place!

But, although Gonzalo Pizarro could not foresee this result, he saw enough to satisfy him that it would be safest to exclude the president from Peru. The tidings of his arrival, moreover, quickened his former purpose of sending an embassy to Spain to vindicate his late proceedings, and request the royal confirmation of his authority. The person placed at the head of this mission was Lorenzo de Aldana, a cavalier of discretion as well as courage, and high in the confidence of Pizarro, as one of his most devoted partisans. He had occupied some important posts under that chief, one secret of whose successes was the sagacity he showed in the selection of his agents.

Besides Aldana and one or two cavaliers, the bishop of Lima was joined in the commission, as likely, from his position, to have a favorable influence on Gonzalo's fortunes at court. Together with the despatches for the government, the envoys were intrusted with a letter to Gasca from the inhabitants of Lima; in which, after civilly congratulating the president on his arrival, they announce their regret that he had come too late. The troubles of the country were now settled by the overthrow of the viceroy, and the nation was reposing in quiet under the nile of Pizarro. An embassy, they stated, was on its way to Castile, *not to solicit pardon,* for they had committed no crime,[25] but to petition the emperor to confirm their leader in the government, as the man in Peru best entitled to it by his virtues.[26] They expressed the conviction that Gasca's presence would only serve to renew the distractions of the country, and they darkly intimated that his attempt to land would probably cost him his life. — The language of this singular document was more respectful than might be inferred from its import. It was dated the 14th of October, 1546, and was subscribed by seventy of the principal cavaliers in the city. It was not improbably dictated by Cepeda, whose hand is visible in most of the intrigues of Pizarro's little court. It is also said, — the authority is somewhat questionable, — that Aldana received instructions from Gonzalo secretly to offer a bribe of fifty thousand *pesos de oro* to the president, to prevail on him to return to Castile; and in case of his refusal, some darker and more effectual way was to be devised to rid the country of his presence.[27]

Aldana, fortified with his despatches, sped swiftly on his voyage to Panamá. Through him the governor learned the actual state of feeling in the councils of Pizarro; and he listened with regret to the envoy's conviction, that no terms would be admitted by that chief or his companions, that did not confirm him in the possession of Peru.[28]

Aldana was soon admitted to an audience by the president. It was attended with very different results from what had followed from the conferences with Hinojosa; for Pizarro's envoy was not armed by nature with that stubborn panoply which had hitherto made the other proof against all argument. He now learned with surprise the nature of Gasca's powers, and the extent of the royal concessions to the insurgents. He had embarked with Gonzalo Pizarro on a desperate venture, and he found that it had proved successful. The colony had nothing more, in reason, to demand; and, though devoted in heart to his leader, he did not feel bound by any principle of honor to take part with him, solely to gratify his ambition, in a wild contest with the Crown that must end in inevitable ruin. He consequently abandoned his mission to Castile, probably never very palatable to him, and announced his purpose to accept the pardon proffered by government, and support the president in settling the affairs of Peru. He subsequently wrote, it should be added, to his former commander in Lima, stating the course he had taken, and earnestly recommending the latter to follow his example.

The influence of this precedent: in so important a person as Aldana, aided, doubtless, by the conviction that no change was now to be expected in Pizarro, while delay would be fatal to himself, at length prevailed over Hinojosa's scruples, and he intimated to Gasca his willingness to place the fleet under his command. The act was performed with great pomp and ceremony. Some of Pizarro's stanchest partisans were previously removed from the vessels; and on the nineteenth of November, 1546, Hinojosa and his captains resigned their commissions into the hands of the president. They next took the oaths of allegiance to Castile; a free pardon for all past offences was proclaimed by the herald from a scaffold erected in the great square of the city; and the president, greeting them as true and loyal vassals of the Crown, restored their several commissions to the cavaliers. The royal standard of Spain was then unfurled on board the squadron, and proclaimed that this strong-hold of Pizarro's power had passed away from him for ever.[29]

The return of their commissions to the insurgent captains was a politic act in Gasca. It secured the services of the ablest officers in the country, and turned against Pizarro the very arm on which he had most leaned for support. Thus was this great step achieved, without force or fraud, by Gasca's patience and judicious forecast. He was content to bide his time; and he now might rely with well-grounded confidence on the ultimate success of his mission.

CHAPTER II

GASCA ASSEMBLES HIS FORCES. — DEFECTION OF PIZARRO'S FOLLOWERS. — HE MUSTERS HIS LEVIES. — AGITATION IN LIMA. — HE ABANDONS THE CITY. — GASCA SAILS FROM PANAMÁ. — BLOODY BATTLE OF HUARINA

1547.

No sooner was Gasca placed in possession of Panamá and the fleet, than he entered on a more decisive course of policy than he had been hitherto allowed to pursue. He raised levies of men, and drew together supplies from all quarters. He took care to discharge the arrears already due to the soldiers, and promised liberal pay for the future; for, though mindful that his personal charges should cost little to the Crown, he did not stint his expenditure when the public good required it. As the funds in the treasury were exhausted, he obtained loans on the credit of the government from the wealthy citizens of Panamá, who, relying on his good faith, readily made the necessary advances. He next sent letters to the authorities of Guatemala and Mexico, requiring their assistance in carrying on hostilities, if necessary, against the insurgents; and he despatched a summons, in like manner, to Benalcazar, in the provinces north of Peru, to meet him, on his landing in that country, with his whole available force.

The greatest enthusiasm was shown by the people of Panamá in getting the little navy in order for his intended voyage; and prelates and commanders did not disdain to prove their loyalty by taking part in the good work, along with the soldiers and sailors.[1] Before his own departure, however, Gasca proposed to send a small squadron of four ships under Aldana, to cruise off the port of Lima, with instructions to give protection to those well affected to the royal cause, and receive them, if need be, on board his vessels. He was also intrusted with authenticated copies of the president's commission, to be delivered to Gonzalo Pizarro, that the chief might feel, there was yet time to return before the gates of mercy were closed against him.[2]

362

While these events were going on, Gasca's proclamations and letters were doing their work in Peru. It required but little sagacity to perceive that the nation at large, secured in the protection of person and property, had nothing to gain by revolution. Interest and duty, fortunately, now lay on the same side; and the ancient sentiment of loyalty, smothered for a time, but not extinquished, revived in the breasts of the people. Still this was not manifested, at once, by any overt act; for, under a strong military rule, men dared hardly think for themselves, much less communicate their thoughts to one another. But changes of public opinion, like changes in the atmosphere that come on slowly and imperceptibly, make themselves more and more widely felt, till, by a sort of silent sympathy, they spread to the remotest corners of the land. Some intimations of such a change of sentiment at length found their way to Lima, although all accounts of the president's mission had been jealously excluded from that capital. Gonzalo Pizarro himself became sensible of these symptoms of disaffection, though almost too faint and feeble, as yet, for the most experienced eye to descry in them the coming tempest.

Several of the president's proclamations had been forwarded to Gonzalo by his faithful partisans; and Carbajal, who had been summoned from Potosí, declared they were "more to be dreaded than the lances of Castile."[3] Yet Pizarro did not, for a moment, lose his confidence in his own strength; and with a navy like that now in Panamá at his command, he felt he might bid defiance to any enemy on his coasts. He had implicit confidence in the fidelity of Hinojosa.

It was at this period that Paniagua arrived off the port with Gasca's despatches to Pizarro, consisting of the emperor's letter and his own. They were instantly submitted by that chieftain to his trusty counsellors, Carbajal and Cepeda, and their opinions asked as to the course to be pursued. It was the crisis of Pizarro's fate.

Carbajal, whose sagacious eye fully comprehended the position in which they stood, was in favor of accepting the royal grace on the terms proposed; and he intimated his sense of their importance by declaring, that "he would pave the way for the bearer of them into the capital with ingots of gold and silver."[4] Cepeda was of a different way of thinking. He was a judge of the Royal Audience; and had been sent to Peru as the immediate counsellor of Blasco Nuñez. But he had turned against the viceroy, had encountered him in battle, and his garments might be said to be yet wet with his blood! What grace was there, then, for him? Whatever respect might be shown to the letter of the royal provisions, in point of fact, he must ever live under the Castilian rule a ruined man. He accordingly strongly urged the rejection of Gasca's offers. "They will cost you your government," he said to Pizarro; "the smooth-tongued priest is not so simple a person as you take him to be. He is deep and politic.[5] He knows well what promises to make; and, once master of the country, he will know, too, how to keep them."

Carbajal was not shaken by the arguments or the sneers of his companions; and as the discussion waxed warm, Cepeda taxed his opponent with giving counsel suggested by fears for his own safety, — a foolish taunt, sufficiently disproved by the whole life of the doughty old warrior. Carbajal did not insist further on his own views, however, as he found them unwelcome to Pizarro, and contented himself with coolly remarking, that "he had, indeed, no relish for rebellion; but he had as long a neck for a halter, he believed, as any of his companions; and as he could hardly expect to live much longer, at any rate, it was, after all, of little moment to him."[6]

Pizarro, spurred on by a fiery ambition that overleaped every obstacle,[7] did not condescend to count the desperate chances of a contest with the Crown. He threw his own weight into the scale with Cepeda. The offer of grace was rejected; and he thus cast away the last tie which held him to his country, and, by the act, proclaimed himself a rebel.[8]

It was not long after the departure of Paniagua, that Pizarro received tidings of the defection of Aldana and Hinojosa, and of the surrender of the fleet, on which he had expended an immense sum, as the chief bulwark of his power. This unwelcome intelligence was followed by accounts of the further defection of some of the principal towns in the north, and of the assassination of Puelles, the faithful lieutenant to whom he had confided the government of Quito. It was not very long, also, before he found his authority assailed in the opposite quarter at Cuzco; for Centeno, the loyal chieftain who, as the reader may remember, had been driven by Carbajal to take refuge in a cave near Arequipa, had issued from his concealment after remaining there a year, and, on learning the arrival of Gasca, had again raised the royal standard. Then collecting a small body of followers, and falling on Cuzco by night, he made himself master of that capital, defeated the garrison who held it, and secured it for the Crown. Marching soon after into the province of Charcas, the bold chief allied himself with the officer who commanded for Pizarro in La Plata; and their combined forces, to the number of a thousand, took up a position on the borders of Lake Titicaca, where the two cavaliers coolly waited an opportunity to take the field against their ancient commander.

Gonzalo Pizarro, touched to the heart by the desertion of those in whom he most confided, was stunned by the dismal tidings of his losses coming so thick upon him. Yet he did not waste his time in idle crimination or complaint; but immediately set about making preparations to meet the storm with all his characteristic energy. He wrote, at once, to such of his captains as he believed still faithful, commanding them to be ready with their troops to march to his assistance at the shortest notice. He reminded them of their obligations to him, and that their interests were identical with his own. The president's commission, he added, had been made out before the news had reached Spain of the battle of Añaquito, and could never cover a pardon to those concerned in the death of the viceroy.[9]

Pizarro was equally active in enforcing his levies in the capital, and in putting them in the best fighting order. He soon saw himself at the head of a thousand men, beautifully equipped, and complete in all their appointments; "as gallant an array," says an old writer, "though so small in number, as ever trod the plains of Italy," — displaying in the excellence of their arms, their gorgeous uniforms, and the caparisons of their horses, a magnificence that could be furnished only by the silver of Peru.[10] Each company was provided with a new stand of colors, emblazoned with its peculiar device. Some bore the initials and arms of Pizarro, and one or two of these were audaciously surmounted by a crown, as if to intimate the rank to which their commander might aspire.[11]

Among the leaders most conspicuous on this occasion was Cepeda, "who," in the words of a writer of his time, "had exchanged the robe of the licentiate for the plumed casque and mailed harness of the warrior."[12] But the cavalier to whom Pizarro confided the chief care of organizing his battalions was the veteran Carbajal, who had studied the art of war under the best captains of Europe, and whose life of adventure had been a practical commentary on their early lessons. It was on his arm that Gonzalo most leaned in the hour of danger; and well had it been for him, if he had profited by his counsels at an earlier period.

It gives one some idea of the luxurious accommodations of Pizarro's forces, that he endeavoured to provide each of his musketeers with a horse. The expenses incurred by him were enormous. The immediate cost of his preparations, we are told, was not less than half a million of *pesos de oro;* and his pay to the cavaliers, and, indeed, to the common soldiers, in his little army, was on an extravagant scale, nowhere to be met with but on the silver soil of Peru.[13]

When his own funds were exhausted, he supplied the deficiency by fines imposed on the rich citizens of Lima as the price of exemption from service, by forced loans, and various other schemes of military exaction.[14] From this time, it is said, the chieftain's temper underwent a visible change.[15] He became more violent in his passions, more impatient of control, and indulged more freely in acts of cruelty and license. The desperate cause in which he was involved made him reckless of consequences. Though naturally frank and confiding, the frequent defection of his followers filled him with suspicion. He knew not in whom to confide. Every one who showed himself indifferent to his cause, or was suspected of being so, was dealt with as an open enemy. The greatest distrust prevailed in Lima. No man dared confide in his neighbour. Some concealed their effects; others contrived to dude the vigilance of the sentinels, and hid themselves in the neighbouring woods and mountains.[16] No one was allowed to enter or leave the city without a license. All commerce, all intercourse, with other places was cut off. It was long since the fifths belonging to the Crown had been remitted to Castile; as Pizarro had appropriated them to his own use. He now took possession of the mints, broke up the royal stamps, and issued a debased coin, emblazoned with his own cipher.[17] It was the most decisive act of sovereignty.

At this gloomy period, the lawyer Cepeda contrived a solemn farce, the intent of which was to give a sort of legal sanction to the rebel cause in the eyes of the populace. He caused a process to be prepared against Gasca, Hinojosa, and Aldana, in which they were accused of treason against the existing government of Peru, were convicted, and condemned to death. This instrument he submitted to a number of jurists in the capital, requiring their signatures. But they had no mind thus inevitably to implicate themselves, by affixing their names to such a paper; and they evaded it by representing, that it would only serve to cut off all chance, should any of the accused be so disposed, of their again embracing the cause they had deserted. Cepeda was the only man who signed the document. Carbajal treated the whole thing with ridicule. "What is the object of your process?" said he to Cepeda. "Its object," replied the latter, "is to prevent delay, that, if taken at any time, the guilty party may be at once led to execution." "I cry you mercy," retorted Carbajal; "I thought there must be some virtue in the instrument, that would have killed them outright. Let but one of these same traitors fall into my hands, and I will march him off to execution, without waiting for the sentence of a court, I promise you!"[18]

While this paper war was going on, news was brought that Aldana's squadron was off the port of Callao. That commander had sailed from Panamá, the middle of February, 1547. On his passage down the coast he had landed at Truxillo, where the citizens welcomed him with enthusiasm, and eagerly proclaimed their submission to the royal authority. He received, at the same time, messages from several of Pizarro's officers in the interior, intimating their return to their duty, and their readiness to support the president. Aldana named Caxamalca as a place of rendezvous, where they should concentrate their forces, and wait the landing of Gasca. He then continued his voyage towards Lima.

No sooner was Pizarro informed of his approach, than, fearful lest it might have a disastrous effect in seducing his followers from their fidelity, he marched them about a league out of the city, and there encamped. He was two leagues from the coast, and he posted a guard on the shore, to intercept all communication with the vessels. Before leaving the capital, Cepeda resorted to an expedient for securing the inhabitants more firmly, as he conceived, in Pizarro's interests. He caused the citizens to be assembled, and made them a studied harangue, in which he expatiated on the services of their governor, and the security which the country had enjoyed under his rule. He then told them that every man was at liberty to choose for himself; to remain under the protection of their present ruler, or, if they preferred, to transfer their allegiance to his enemy. He invited them to speak their minds, but required every one who would still continue under Pizarro to take an oath of fidelity to his cause, with the assurance, that, if any should be so false hereafter as to violate this pledge, he should pay for it with his life.[19] There was no one found bold enough—with his head thus in the lion's mouth—to swerve from his obedience to Pizarro; and every man took the oath prescribed, which was administered in the most solemn and imposing form by the licentiate. Carbajal, as usual, made a jest of the whole proceeding. "How long," he asked his companion, "do you think these same oaths will stand? The first wind that blows off the coast after we are gone will scatter them in air!" His prediction was soon verified.

Meantime, Aldana anchored off the port, where there was no vessel of the insurgents to molest him. By Cepeda's advice, some four or five had been burnt a short time before, during the absence of Carbajal, in order to cut off all means by which the inhabitants could leave the place. This was deeply deplored by the veteran soldier on his return. "It was destroying," he said, "the guardian angels of Lima."[20] And certainly, under such a commander, they might now have stood Pizarro in good stead; but his star was on the wane.

The first act of Aldana was to cause the copy of Gasca's powers, with which he had been intrusted, to be conveyed to his ancient commander, by whom it was indignantly torn in pieces. Aldana next contrived, by means of his agents, to circulate among the citizens, and even the soldiers of the camp, the president's manifestoes. They were not long in producing their effect. Few had been at all aware of the real purport of Gasca's mission, of the extent of his powers, or of the generous terms offered by government. They shrunk from the desperate course into which they had been thus unwarily seduced, and they sought only in what way they could, with least danger, extricate themselves from their present position, and return to their allegiance. Some escaped by night from the camp, eluded the vigilance of the sentinels, and effected their retreat on board the vessels. Some were taken, and found no quarter at the hands of Carbajal and his merciless ministers. But, where the spirit of disaffection was abroad, means of escape were not wanting.

As the fugitives were cut off from Lima and the neighbouring coast, they secreted themselves in the forests and mountains, and watched their opportunity for making their way to Truxillo and other ports at a distance; and so contagious was the example, that it not unfrequently happened that the very soldiers sent in pursuit of the deserters joined with them. Among those that fled was the Licentiate Carbajal, who must not be confounded with his military namesake. He was the same cavalier whose brother had been put to death in Lima by Blasco Nuñez, and who revenged himself, as we have seen, by imbruing his own hands in the blood of the viceroy. That a person thus implicated should trust to the royal pardon showed that no one need despair of it; and the example proved most disastrous to Pizarro.[21]

Carbajal, Who made a jest of every thing, even of the misfortunes which pinched him the sharpest, when told of the desertion of his comrades, amused himself by humming the words of a popular ditty: —

"The wind blows the hairs off my head, mother;
Two at a time, it blows them away!"[22]

But the defection of his followers made a deeper impression on Pizarro, and he was sorely distressed as he beheld the gallant array, to which he had so confidently looked for gaining his battles, thus melting away like a morning mist. Bewildered by the treachery of those in whom he had most trusted, he knew not where to turn, nor what course to take. It was evident that he must leave his present dangerous quarters without loss of time. But whither should he direct his steps? In the north, the great towns had abandoned his cause, and the president was already marching against him; while Centeno held the passes of the south, with a force double his own. In this emergency, he at length resolved to occupy Arequipa, a seaport still true to him, where he might remain till he had decided on some future course of operations.

After a painful but rapid march, Gonzalo arrived at this place, where he was speedily joined by a reinforcement that he had detached for the recovery of Cuzco. But so frequent had been the desertions from both companies, — though in Pizarro's corps these had greatly lessened since the departure from the neighbourhood of Lima, — that his whole number did not exceed five hundred men, less than half of the force which he had so recently mustered in the capital. To such humble circumstances was the man now reduced, who had so lately lorded it over the land with unlimited sway! Still the chief did not despond. He had gathered new spirit from the excitement of his march and his distance from Lima; and he seemed to recover his former confidence, as he exclaimed, — "It is misfortune that teaches us who are our friends. If but ten only remain true to me, fear not but I will again be master of Peru!"[23]

No sooner had the rebel forces withdrawn from the neighbourhood of Lima, than the inhabitants of that city, little troubled, as Carbajal had predicted, by their compulsory oaths of allegiance to Pizarro, threw open their gates to Aldana, who took possession of this important place in the name of the president. That commander, meanwhile, had sailed with his whole fleet from Panamá, on the tenth of April, 1547. The first part of his voyage was prosperous; but he was soon perplexed by contrary currents, and the weather became rough and tempestuous. The violence of the storm continuing day after day, the sea was lashed into fury, and the fleet was tossed about on the billows, which ran mountain high, as if emulating the wild character of the region they bounded. The rain descended in torrents, and the lightning was so incessant, that the vessels, to quote the lively language of the chronicler, "seemed to be driving through seas of flame!"[24] The hearts of the stoutest mariners were filled with dismay. They considered it hopeless to struggle against the elements, and they loudly demanded to return to the continent, and postpone the voyage till a more favorable season of the year.

But the president saw in this the ruin of his cause, as well as of the loyal vassals who had engaged, on his landing, to support it. "I am willing to die," he said, "but not to return"; and, regardless of the remonstrances of his more timid followers, he insisted on carrying as much sail as the ships could possibly bear, at every interval of the storm.[25] Meanwhile, to divert the minds of the seamen from their present danger, Gasca amused them by explaining some of the strange phenomena exhibited by the ocean in the tempest, which had filled their superstitious minds with mysterious dread.[26]

Signals had been given for the ships to make the best of their way, each for itself, to the island of Gorgona. Here they arrived, one after another, with but a single exception, though all more or less shattered by the weather. The president waited only for the fury of the elements to spend itself, when he again embarked, and, on smoother waters, crossed over to Manta. From this place he soon after continued his voyage to Tumbez, and landed at that port on the thirteenth of June. He was everywhere received with enthusiasm, and all seemed anxious to efface the remembrance of the past by professions of future fidelity to the Crown. Gasca received, also, numerous letters of congratulation from cavaliers in the interior, most of whom had formerly taken service under Pizarro. He made courteous acknowledgments for their offers of assistance, and commanded them to repair to Caxamalca, the general place of rendezvous.

To this same spot he sent Hinojosa, so soon as that officer had disembarked with the land forces from the fleet, ordering him to take command of the levies assembled there, and then join him at Xauxa. Here he determined to establish his head-quarters. It lay in a rich and abundant territory, and by its central position afforded a point for acting with greatest advantage against the enemy.

He then moved forward, at the head of a small detachment of cavalry, along the level road on the coast towards Truxillo. After halting for a short time in that loyal city, he traversed the mountain range on the southeast, and soon entered the fruitful valley of Xauxa. There he was presently joined by reinforcements from the north, as well as from the principal places on the coast; and, not long after his arrival, received a message from Centeno, informing him that he held the passes by which Gonzalo Pizarro was preparing to make his escape from the country, and that the insurgent chief must soon fall into his hands.

The royal camp was greatly elated by these tidings. The war, then, was at length terminated, and that without the president having been called upon so much as to lift his sword against a Spaniard. Several of his counsellors now advised him to disband the greater part of his forces, as burdensome and no longer necessary. But the president was too wise to weaken his strength before he had secured the victory. He consented, however, to countermand the requisition for levies from Mexico and the adjoining colonies, as now feeling sufficiently strong in the general loyalty of the country. But, concentrating his forces at Xauxa, he established his quarters in that town, as he had first intended, resolved to await there tidings of the operations in the south. The result was different from what he had expected.[27]

Pizarro, meanwhile, whom we left at Arequipa, had decided, after much deliberation, to evacuate Peru, and pass into Chili. In this territory, beyond the president's jurisdiction, he might find a safe retreat. The fickle people, he thought, would soon weary of their new ruler; and he would then rally in sufficient strength to resume active operations for the recovery of his domain. Such were the calculations of the rebel chieftain. But how was he to effect his object, while the passes among the mountains, where his route lay, were held by Centeno with a force more than double his own? He resolved to try negotiation; for that captain had once served under him, and had, indeed, been most active in persuading Pizarro to take on himself the office of procurator. Advancing, accordingly, in the direction of Lake Titicaca, in the neighbourhood of which Centeno had pitched his camp, Gonzalo despatched as emissary to his quarters to open a negotiation. He called to his adversary's recollection the friendly relations that had once subsisted between them; and reminded him of one occasion in particular, in which he had spared his life, when convicted of a conspiracy against himself. He harboured no sentiments of unkindness, he said, for Centeno's recent conduct, and had not now come to seek a quarrel with him. His purpose was to abandon Peru; and the only favor he had to request of his former associate was to leave him a free passage across the mountains.

To this communication Centeno made answer in terms as courtly as those of Pizarro himself, that he was not unmindful of their ancient friendship. He was now ready to serve his former commander in any way not inconsistent with honor, or obedience to his sovereign. But he was there in arms for the royal cause, and he could not swerve from his duty. If Pizarro would but rely on his faith, and surrender himself up, he pledged his knightly word to use all his interest with the government, to secure as favorable terms for him and his followers as had been granted to the rest of their countrymen. — Gonzalo listened to the smooth promises of his ancient comrade with bitter scorn depicted in his countenance, and, snatching the letter from his secretary, cast it away from him with indignation. There was nothing left but an appeal to arms.[28]

He at once broke up his encampment, and directed his march on the borders of Lake Titicaca, near which lay his rival. He resorted, however, to stratagem, that he might still, if possible, avoid an encounter. He sent forward his scouts in a different direction from that which he intended to take, and then quickened his march on Huarina. This was a small town situated on the south-

370

eastern extremity of Lake Titicaca, the shores of which, the seat of the primitive civilization of the Incas, were soon to resound with the murderous strife of their more civilized conquerors!

But Pizarro's movements had been secretly communicated to Centeno, and that commander, accordingly, changing his ground, took up a position not far from Huarina, on the same day on which Gonzalo reached this place. The videttes of the two camps came in sight of each other that evening, and the rival forces, lying on their arms, prepared for action on the following morning.

It was the twenty-sixth of October, 1547, when the two commanders, having formed their troops in order of battle, advanced to the encounter on the plains of Huarina. The ground, defended on one side by a bold spur of the Andes, and not far removed on the other from the waters of Titicaca, was an open and level plain, well suited to military manœuvres. It seemed as if prepared by Nature as the lists for an encounter.

Centeno's army amounted to about a thousand men. His cavalry consisted of near two hundred and fifty, well equipped and mounted. Among them were several gentlemen of family, some of whom had once followed the banners of Pizarro, the whole forming an efficient corps, in which rode some of the best lances of Peru. His arquebusiers were less numerous, not exceeding a hundred and fifty, indifferently provided with ammunition. The remainder, and much the larger part of Centeno's army, consisted of spearmen, irregular levies hastily drawn together, and possessed of little discipline.[29]

This corps of infantry formed the centre of his line, flanked by the arquebusiers in two nearly equal divisions, while his cavalry were also disposed in two bodies on the right and left wings. Unfortunately, Centeno had been for the past week ill of a pleurisy, — so ill, indeed, that on the preceding day he had been bled several times. He was now too feeble to keep his saddle, but was carried in a litter, and when he had seen his men formed in order, he withdrew to a distance from the field, unable to take part in the action. But Solano, the militant bishop of Cuzco, who, with several of his followers, took part in the engagement, — a circumstance, indeed, of no strange occurrence, — rode along the ranks with the crucifix in his hand, bestowing his benediction on the soldiers, and exhorting each man to do his duty.

Pizarro's forces were less than half of his rival's, not amounting to more than four hundred and eighty men. The horse did not muster above eighty-five in all, and he posted them in a single body on the right of his battalion. The strength of his army lay in his arquebusiers, about three hundred and fifty in number. It was an admirable corps, commanded by Carbajal, by whom it had been carefully drilled. Considering the excellence of its arms, and its thorough discipline, this little body of infantry might be considered as the flower of the Peruvian soldiery, and on it Pizarro mainly relied for the success of the day.[30] The remainder of his force, consisting of pikemen, not formidable for their numbers, though, like the rest of the infantry, under excellent discipline, he distributed on the left of his musketeers, so as to repel the enemy's horse.

Pizarro himself had charge of the cavalry, taking his place, as usual, in the foremost rank. He was superbly accoutred. Over his shining mail he wore a sobre-vest of slashed velvet of a rich crimson color; and he rode a high-mettled charger, whose gaudy caparisons, with the showy livery of his rider, made the fearless commander the most conspicuous object in the field.

His lieutenant, Carbajal, was equipped in a very different style. He wore armour of proof of the most homely appearance, but strong and serviceable; and his steel bonnet, with its closely barred visor of the same material, protected his head from more than one desperate blow on that day. Over his arms he wore a surcoat of a greenish color, and he rode an active, strong-boned jennet, which, though capable of enduring fatigue, possessed neither grace nor beauty. It would not have been easy to distinguish the veteran from the most ordinary cavalier.

The two hosts arrived within six hundred paces of each other, when they both halted. Carbajal preferred to receive the attack of the enemy, rather than advance further; for the ground he now occupied afforded a free range for his musketry, unobstructed by the trees or bushes that were sprinkled over some other parts of the field. There was a singular motive, in addition, for retaining his present position. The soldiers were encumbered, some with two, some with three, arquebuses each, being the arms left by those who, from time to time, had deserted the camp. This uncommon supply of muskets, however serious an impediment on a march, might afford great advantage to troops waiting an assault; since, from the imperfect knowledge as well as construction of fire-arms at that day, much time was wasted in loading them.[31]

Preferring, therefore, that the enemy should begin the attack, Carbajal came to a halt, while the opposite squadron, after a short respite, continued their advance a hundred paces farther. Seeing that they then remained immovable, Carbajal detached a small party of skirmishers to the front, in order to provoke them; but it was soon encountered by a similar party of the enemy, and some shots were exchanged, though with little damage to either side. Finding this manœuvre fail, the veteran ordered his men to advance a few paces, still hoping to provoke his antagonist to the charge. This succeeded. "We lose honor," exclaimed Centeno's soldiers; who, with a bastard sort of chivalry, belonging to undisciplined troops, felt it a disgrace to await an assault. In vain their officers called out to them to remain at their post. Their commander was absent, and they were urged on by the cries of a frantic friar, named Domingo Ruiz, who, believing the Philistines were delivered into their hands, called out,—"Now is the time! Onward, onward, fall on the enemy!"[32] There needed nothing further, and the men rushed forward in tumultuous haste, the pikemen carrying their levelled weapons so heedlessly as to interfere with one another, and in some instances to wound their comrades. The musketeers, at the same time, kept up a disorderly fire as they advanced, which, from their rapid motion and the distance, did no execution.

Carbajal was well pleased to see his enemies thus wasting their ammunition. Though he allowed a few muskets to be discharged, in order to stimulate his opponents the more, he commanded the great body of his infantry to reserve their fire till every shot could take effect. As he knew the tendency of marksmen to shoot above the mark, he directed his men to aim at the girdle, or even a little below it; adding, that a shot that fell short might still do damage, while one that passed a hair's breadth above the head was wasted.[33]

The veteran's company stood calm and unmoved, as Centeno's rapidly advanced; but when the latter had arrived within a hundred paces of their antagonists, Carbajal gave the word to fire. An instantaneous volley ran along the line, and a tempest of balls was poured into the ranks of the assailants, with such unerring aim, that more than a hundred fell dead on the field, while a still greater number were wounded. Before they could recover from their disorder, Carbajal's men, snatching up their remaining pieces, discharged them with the like dreadful effect into the thick of the enemy. The confusion of the latter was now complete. Unable to sustain the incessant shower of balls which fell on them from the scattering fire kept up by the arquebusiers, they were seized with a panic, and fled, scarcely making a show of further fight, from the field.

But very different was the fortune of the day in the cavalry combat. Gonzalo Pizarro had drawn up his troop somewhat in the rear of Carbajal's right, in order to give the latter a freer range for the play of his musketry. When the enemy's horse on the left galloped briskly against him, Pizarro, still favoring Carbajal,—whose fire, moreover, inflicted some loss on the assailants,—advanced but a few rods to receive the charge. Centeno's squadron, accordingly, came thundering on in full career, and, notwithstanding the mischief sustained from their enemy's musketry, fell with such fury on their adversaries as to overturn them, man and horse, in the dust; "riding over their prostrate bodies," says the historian, "as if they had been a flock of sheep!"[34] The latter, with great difficulty recovering from the first shock, attempted to rally and sustain the fight on more equal terms.

Yet the chief could not regain the ground he had lost. His men were driven back at all points. Many were slain, many more wounded, on both sides, and the ground was covered with the dead bodies of men and horses. But the loss fell much the most heavily on Pizarro's troop; and the greater part of those who escaped with life were obliged to surrender as prisoners. Cepeda, who fought with the fury of despair, received a severe cut from a sabre across the face, which disabled him and forced him to yield.[35] Pizarro, after seeing his best and bravest fall around him, was set upon by three or four cavaliers at once. Disentangling himself from the *mêlée*, he put spurs to his horse, and the noble animal, bleeding from a severe wound across the back, outstripped all his pursuers except one, who stayed him by seizing the bridle. It would have gone hard with Gonzalo, but, grasping a light battle-axe, which hung by his side, he dealt such a blow on the head of his enemy's horse that he plunged violently, and compelled his rider to release his hold. A number of arquebusiers, in the mean time, seeing Pizarro's distress, sprang forward to his rescue, slew two of his assailants who had now come up with him, and forced the others to fly in their turn.[36]

The rout of the cavalry was complete; and Pizarro considered the day as lost, as he heard the enemy's trumpet sending forth the note of victory. But the sounds had scarcely died away, when they were taken up by the opposite side. Centeno's infantry had been discomfited, as we have seen, and driven off the ground. But his cavalry on the right had charged Carbajal's left, consisting of spearmen mingled with arquebusiers. The horse rode straight against this formidable phalanx. But they were unable to break through the dense array of pikes, held by the steady hands of troops who stood firm and fearless on their post; while, at the same time, the assailants were greatly annoyed by the galling fire of the arquebusiers in the rear of the spearmen. Finding it impracticable to make a breach, the horsemen rode round the flanks in much disorder, and finally joined themselves with the victorious squadron of Centeno's cavalry in the rear. Both parties now attempted another charge on Carbajal's battalion. But his men facing about with the promptness and discipline of well-trained soldiers, the rear was converted into the front. The same forest of spears was presented to the attack; while an incessant discharge of bails punished the audacity of the cavaliers, who, broken and completely dispirited by their ineffectual attempt, at length imitated the example of the panic-struck foot, and abandoned the field.

Pizarro and a few of his comrades still fit for action followed up the pursuit for a short distance only, as, indeed, they were in no condition themselves, nor sufficiently strong in numbers, long to continue it. The victory was complete, and the insurgent chief took possession of the deserted tents of the enemy, where an immense booty was obtained in silver;[37] and where he also found the tables spread for the refreshment of Centeno's soldiers after their return from the field. So confident were they of success! The repast now served the necessities of their conquerors. Such is the fortune of war! It was, indeed, a most decisive action; and Gonzalo Pizarro, as he rode over the field strewed with the corpses of his enemies, was observed several times to cross himself and exclaim, — "Jesu! what a victory!"

No less than three hundred and fifty of Centeno's followers were killed, and the number of wounded was even greater. More than a hundred of these are computed to have perished from exposure during the following night; for, although the climate in this elevated region is temperate, yet the night winds blowing over the mountains are sharp and piercing, and many a wounded wretch, who might have been restored by careful treatment, was chilled by the damps, and found a stiffened corpse at sunrise. The victory was not purchased without a heavy loss on the part of the conquerors, a hundred or more of whom were left on the field. Their bodies lay thick on that part of the ground occupied by Pizarro's cavalry, where the fight raged hottest. In this narrow space were found, also, the bodies of more than a hundred horses, the greater part of which, as well as those of their riders, usually slain with them, belonged to the victorious army. It was the most fatal battle that had yet been fought on the blood-stained soil of Peru.[38]

The glory of the day—the melancholy glory—must be referred almost wholly to Carbajal and his valiant squadron. The judicious arrangements of the old warrior, with the thorough discipline and unflinching courage of his followers, retrieved the fortunes of the fight, when it was nearly lost by the cavalry, and secured the victory.

Carbajal, proof against all fatigue, followed up the pursuit with those of his men that were in condition to join him. Such of the unhappy fugitives as fell into his hands—most of whom had been traitors to the cause of Pizarro—were sent to instant execution. The laurels he had won in the field against brave men in arms, like himself, were tarnished by cruelty towards his defenceless captives. Their commander, Centeno, more fortunate, made his escape. Finding the battle lost, he quitted his litter, threw himself upon his horse, and, notwithstanding his illness, urged on by the dreadful doom that awaited him, if taken, he succeeded in making his way into the neighbouring sierra. Here he vanished from his pursuers, and, like a wounded stag, with the chase close upon his track, he still contrived to elude it, by plunging into the depths of the forests, till, by a circuitous route, he miraculously succeeded in effecting his escape to Lima. The bishop of Cuzco, who went off in a different direction, was no less fortunate. Happy for him that he did not fall into the hands of the ruthless Carbajal, who, as the bishop had once been a partisan of Pizarro, would, to judge from the little respect he usually showed those of his cloth, have felt as little compunction in sentencing him to the gibbet as if he had been the meanest of the common file.[39]

On the day following the action, Gonzalo Pizarro caused the bodies of the soldiers, still lying side by side on the field where they had been so lately engaged together in mortal strife, to be deposited in a common sepulchre. Those of higher rank—for distinctions of rank were not to be forgotten in the grave—were removed to the church of the village of Huarina, which gave its name to the battle. There they were interred with all fitting solemnity. But in later times they were transported to the cathedral church of La Paz, "The City of Peace," and laid under a mausoleum erected by general subscription in that quarter. For few there were who had not to mourn the loss of some friend or relative on that fatal day.

The victor now profited by his success to send detachments to Arequipa, La Plata, and other cities in that part of the country, to raise funds and reinforcements for the war. His own losses were more than compensated by the number of the vanquished party who were content to take service under his banner. Mustering his forces, he directed his march to Cuzco, which capital, though occasionally seduced into a display of loyalty to the Crown, had early manifested an attachment to his cause.

Here the inhabitants were prepared to receive him in triumph, under arches thrown across the streets, with bands of music, and minstrelsy commemorating his successes. But Pizarro, with more discretion, declined the honors of an ovation while the country remained in the hands of his enemies. Sending forward the main body of his troops, he followed on foot, attended by a slender retinue of friends and citizens, and proceeded at once to the cathedral, where thanksgivings were offered up, and *Te Deum* was chanted in honor of his victory. He then withdrew to his residence, announcing his purpose to establish his quarters, for the present, in the venerable capital of the Incas.[40]

All thoughts of a retreat into Chili were abandoned; for his recent success had kindled new hopes in his bosom, and revived his ancient confidence. He trusted that it would have a similar effect on the vacillating temper of those whose fidelity had been shaken by fears for their own safety, and their distrust of his ability to cope with the president. They would now see that his star was still in the ascendant. Without further apprehensions for the event, he resolved to remain in Cuzco, and there quietly await the hour when a last appeal to arms should decide which of the two was to remain master of Peru.

CHAPTER III

DISMAY IN GASCA'S CAMP. — HIS WINTER
QUARTERS. — RESUMES HIS MARCH. — CROSSES
THE APURIMAC. — PIZARRO'S CONDUCT IN
CUZCO. — HE ENCAMPS NEAR THE CITY. —
ROUT OF XAQUIXAGUANA

1547-1548.

WHILE the events recorded in the preceding chapter were passing, President Gasca had remained at Xauxa, awaiting further tidings from Centeno, little doubting that they would inform him of the total discomfiture of the rebels. Great was his dismay, therefore, on learning the issue of the fatal conflict at Huarina, — that the royalists had been scattered far and wide before the sword of Pizarro, while their commander had vanished like an apparition,[1] leaving the greatest uncertainty as to his fate.

The intelligence spread general consternation among the soldiers, proportioned to their former confidence; and they felt it was almost hopeless to contend with a man who seemed protected by a charm that made him invincible against the greatest odds. The president, however sore his disappointment, was careful to conceal it, while he endeavoured to restore the spirits of his followers. "They had been too sanguine," he said, "and it was in this way that Heaven rebuked their presumption. Yet it was but in the usual course of events, that Providence, when it designed to humble the guilty, should allow him to reach as high an elevation as possible, that his fall might be the greater!"

But while Gasca thus strove to reassure the superstitious and the timid, he bent his mind, with his usual energy, to repair the injury which the cause had sustained by the defeat at Huarina. He sent a detachment under Alvarado to Lima, to collect such of the royalists as had fled thither from the field of battle, and to dismantle the ships of their cannon, and bring them to the camp. Another body was sent to Guamanga, about sixty leagues from Cuzco, for the similar purpose of protecting the fugitives, and also of preventing the Indian caciques from forwarding supplies to the insurgent army in Cuzco. As his own forces now amounted to considerably more than any his opponent could bring against him, Gasca determined to break up his camp without further delay, and march on the Inca capital.[2]

Quitting Xauxa, December 29, 1547, he passed through Guamanga, and after a severe march, rendered particularly fatiguing by the inclement state of the weather and the badness of the roads, he entered the province of Andaguaylas. It was a fair and fruitful country, and since the road beyond would take him into the depths of a gloomy sierra, scarcely passable in the winter snows, Gasca resolved to remain in his present quarters until the severity of the season was mitigated. As many of the troops had already contracted diseases from exposure to the incessant rains, he established a camp hospital; and the good president personally visited the quarters of the sick, ministering to their wants, and winning their hearts by his sympathy.[3]

Meanwhile, the royal camp was strengthened by the continual arrival of reinforcements; for notwithstanding the shock that was caused throughout the country by the first tidings of Pizarro's victory, a little reflection convinced the people that the right was the strongest, and must eventually prevail. There came, also, with these levies, several of the most distinguished captains in the country. Centeno, burning to retrieve his late disgrace, after recovering from his illness, joined the camp with his followers from Lima. Benalcazar, the conqueror of Quito, who, as the reader will remember, had shared in the defeat of Blasco Nuñez in the north, came with another detachment; and was soon after followed by Valdivia, the famous conqueror of Chili, who, having returned to Peru to gather recruits for his expedition, had learned the state of the country, mid had thrown himself, without hesitation, into the same scale with the president, though it brought him into collision with his old friend and comrade, Gonzalo Pizarro. The arrival of this last ally was greeted with general rejoicing by the camp; for Valdivia, schooled in the Italian wars, was esteemed the most accomplished soldier in Peru; and Gasca complimented him by declaring "he would rather see him than a reinforcement of eight hundred men!"[4]

Besides these warlike auxiliaries, the president was attended by a train of ecclesiastics and civilians, such as was rarely found in the martial fields of Peru. Among them were the bishops of Quito, Cuzco, and Lima, the four judges of the new Audience, and a considerable number of churchmen and monkish missionaries.[5] However little they might serve to strengthen his arm in battle, their presence gave authority and something of a sacred character to the cause, which had their effect on the minds of the soldiers.

The wintry season now began to give way before the mild influence of spring, which makes itself early felt in these tropical, but from their elevation temperate, regions; and Gasca, after nearly three months' detention in Andaguaylas, mustered his levies for the final march upon Cuzco.[6] Their whole number fell little short of two thousand, — the largest European force yet assembled in Peru. Nearly half were provided with fire-arms; and infantry was more available than horse in the mountain countries which they were to traverse. But his cavalry was also numerous, and he carried with him a train of eleven heavy guns. The equipment and discipline of the troops were good; they were well provided with ammunition and military stores; and were led by officers whose names were associated with the most memorable achievements in the New World. All who had any real interest in the weal of the country were to be found, in short, under the president's banner, making a striking contrast to the wild and reckless adventurers who now swelled the ranks of Pizarro.

Gasca, who did not affect a greater knowledge of military affairs than he really possessed, had given the charge of his forces to Hinojosa, naming the Marshal Alvarado as second in command. Valdivia, who came after these dispositions had been made, accepted a colonel's commission, with the understanding that he was to be consulted and employed in all matters of moment.[7] — Having completed his arrangements, the president broke up his camp in March, 1548, and moved upon Cuzco.

The first obstacle to his progress was the river Abancay, the bridge over which had been broken down by the enemy. But as there was no force to annoy them on the opposite bank, the army was not long in preparing a new bridge, and throwing it across the stream, which in this place had nothing formidable in its character. The road now struck into the heart of a mountain region, where woods, precipices, and ravines were mingled together in a sort of chaotic confusion, with here and there a green and sheltered valley, glittering like an island of verdure amidst the wild breakers of a troubled ocean! The bold peaks of the Andes, rising far above the clouds, were enveloped in snow, which, descending far down their sides, gave a piercing coldness to the winds that swept over their surface, until men and horses were benumbed and stiffened under their influence. The roads, in these regions, were in some places so narrow and broken, as to be nearly impracticable for cavalry. The cavaliers were compelled to dismount; and the president, with the rest, performed the journey on foot, so hazardous, that, even in later times, it has been no uncommon thing for the sure-footed mule to be precipitated, with its cargo of silver, thousands of feet down the sheer sides of a precipice.[8]

By these impediments of the ground, the march was so retarded, that the troops seldom accomplished more than two leagues a day.[9] Fortunately, the distance was not great; and the president looked with more apprehension to the passage of the Apurimac, which he was now approaching. This river, one of the most formidable tributaries of the Amazon, rolls its broad waters through the gorges of the Cordilleras, that rise up like an immense rampart of rock on either side, presenting a natural barrier which it would be easy for an enemy to make good against a force much superior to his own. The bridges over this river, as Gasca learned before his departure from Andaguaylas, had been all destroyed by Pizarro. The president, accordingly, had sent to explore the banks of the stream, and determine the most eligible spot for reëstablishing communications with the opposite side.

The place selected was near the Indian village of Cotapampa, about nine leagues from Cuzco; for the river, though rapid and turbulent from being compressed within more narrow limits, was here less than two hundred paces in width; a distance, however, not inconsiderable. Directions had been given to collect materials in large quantities in the neighbourhood of this spot as soon as possible; and at the same time, in order to perplex the enemy and compel him to divide his forces, should he be disposed to resist, materials in smaller quantities were assembled on three other points of the river. The officer stationed in the neighbourhood of Cotapampa was instructed not to begin to lay the bridge, till the arrival of a sufficient force should accelerate the work, and insure its success.

The structure in question, it should be remembered, was one of those suspension bridges formerly employed by the Incas, and still used in crossing the deep and turbulent rivers of South America. They are made of osier withes, twisted into enormous cables, which, when stretched across the water, are attached to heavy blocks of masonry, or, where it will serve, to the natural rock. Planks are laid transversely across these cables, and a passage is thus secured, which, notwithstanding the light and fragile appearance of the bridge, as it swings at an elevation sometimes of several hundred feet above the abyss, affords a tolerably safe means of conveyance for men, and even for such heavy burdens as artillery.[10]

Notwithstanding the peremptory commands of Gasca, the officer intrusted with collecting the materials for the bridge was so anxious to have the honor of completing the work himself, that he commenced it at once. The president, greatly displeased at learning this, quickened his march, in order to cover the work with his whole force. But, while toiling through the mountain labyrinth, tidings were brought him that a party of the enemy had demolished the small portion of the bridge already made, by cutting the cables on the opposite bank. Valdivia, accordingly, hastened forward at the head of two hundred arquebusiers, while the main body of the army followed with as much speed as practicable.

That officer, on reaching the spot, found that the interruption had been caused by a small party of Pizarro's followers, not exceeding twenty in number, assisted by a stronger body of Indians. He at once caused *balsas,* broad and clumsy barks, or rather rafts, of the country, to be provided, and by this means passed his men over, without opposition, to the other side of the river. The enemy, disconcerted by the arrival of such a force, retreated and made the best of their way to report the affair to their commander at Cuzco. Meanwhile, Valdivia, who saw the importance of every moment in the present crisis, pushed forward the work with the greatest vigor. Through all that night his weary troops continued the labor, which was already well advanced, when the president and his battalions, emerging from the passes of the Cordilleras, presented themselves at sunrise on the opposite bank.

Little time was given for repose, as all felt assured that the success of their enterprise hung on the short respite now given them by the improvident enemy. The president, with his principal officers, took part in the labor with the common soldiers;[11] and before ten o'clock in the evening, Gasca had the satisfaction to see the bridge so well secured, that the leading files of the army, unencumbered by their baggage, might venture to cross it. A short time sufficed to place several hundred men on the other bank. But here a new difficulty, not less formidable than that of the river, presented itself to the troops. The ground rose up with an abrupt, almost precipitous, swell from the riverside, till, in the highest peaks, it reached an elevation of several thousand feet. This steep ascent, though not to its full height, indeed, was now to be surmounted. The difficulties of the ground, broken up into fearful chasms and water-courses, and tangled with thickets, were greatly increased by the darkness of the night; and the soldiers, as they toiled slowly upward, were filled with apprehension, akin to fear, from the uncertainty whether each successive step might not bring them into an ambuscade, for which the ground was so favorable. More than once, the Spaniards were thrown into a panic by false reports that the enemy were upon them. But Hinojosa and Valdivia were at hand to rally their men, and cheer them on, until, at length, before dawn broke, the bold cavaliers and their followers placed themselves on the highest point traversed by the road, where they waited the arrival of the president. This was not long delayed; and in the course of the following morning, the royalists were already in sufficient strength to bid defiance to their enemy.

The passage of the river had been effected with less loss than might have been expected, considering the darkness of the night, and the numbers that crowded over the aërial causeway. Some few, indeed, fell into the water, and were drowned; and more than sixty horses, in the attempt to swim them across the river, were hurried down the current, and dashed against the rocks below.[12] It still required time to bring up the heavy train of ordnance and the military wagons; and the president encamped on the strong ground which he now occupied, to await their arrival, and to breathe his troops after their extraordinary efforts. In these quarters we must leave him, to acquaint the reader with the state of things in the insurgent army, and with the cause of its strange remissness in guarding the passes of the Apurimac.[13]

From the time of Pizarro's occupation of Cuzco, he had lived in careless luxury in the midst of his followers, like a soldier of fortune in the hour of prosperity; enjoying the present, with as little concern for the future as if the crown of Peru were already fixed irrevocably upon his head. It was otherwise with Carbajal. He looked on the victory at Huarina as the commencement, not the close, of the struggle for empire; and he was indefatigable in placing his troops in the best condition for maintaining their present advantage. At the first streak of dawn, the veteran might be seen mounted on his mule, with the garb and air of a common soldier, riding about in the different quarters of the capital, sometimes superintending the manufacture of arms, or providing military stores, and sometimes drilling his men, for he was most careful always to maintain the strictest discipline.[14] His restless spirit seemed to find no pleasure but in incessant action; living, as he had always done, in the turmoil of military adventure, he had no relish for any thing unconnected with war, and in the city saw only the materials for a well-organized camp.

With these feelings, he was much dissatisfied at the course taken by his younger leader, who now professed his intention to abide where he was, and, when the enemy advanced, to give him battle. Carbajal advised a very different policy. He had not that full confidence, it would seem, in the loyalty of Pizarro's partisans, at least, not of those who had once followed the banner of Centeno. These men, some three hundred in number, had been in a manner compelled to take service under Pizarro. They showed no heartiness in the cause, and the veteran strongly urged his commander to disband them at once; since it was far better to go to battle with a few faithful followers than with a host of the false and faint-hearted.

But Carbajal thought, also, that his leader was not sufficiently strong in numbers to encounter his opponent, supported as he was by the best captains of Peru. He advised, accordingly, that he should abandon Cuzco, carrying off all the treasure, provisions, and stores of every kind from the city, which might, in any way, serve the necessities of the royalists. The latter, on their arrival, disappointed by the poverty of a place where they had expected to find so much booty, would become disgusted with the service. Pizarro, meanwhile, might take refuge with his men in the neighbouring fastnesses, where, familiar with the ground, it would be easy to elude the enemy; and if the latter persevered in the pursuit, with numbers diminished by desertion, it would not be difficult in the mountain passes to find an opportunity for assailing him at advantage.—Such was the wary counsel of the old warrior. But it was not to the taste of his fiery commander, who preferred to risk the chances of a battle, rather than turn his back on a foe.

Neither did Pizarro show more favor to a proposition, said to have been made by the Licentiate Cepeda,—that he should avail himself of his late success to enter into negotiations with Gasca. Such advice, from the man who had so recently resisted all overtures of the president, could only have proceeded from a conviction, that the late victory placed Pizarro on a vantage-ground for demanding terms far better than would have been before conceded to him. It may be that subsequent experience had also led him to distrust the fidelity of Gonzalo's followers, or, possibly, the capacity of their chief to conduct them through the present crisis. Whatever may have been the motives of the slippery counsellor, Pizarro gave little heed to the suggestion, and even showed some resentment, as the matter was pressed on him. In every contest, with Indian or European, whatever had been the odds, he had come off victorious. He was not now for the first time to despond; and he resolved to remain in Cuzco, and hazard all on the chances of a battle. There was something in the hazard itself captivating to his bold and chivalrous temper. In this, too, he was confirmed by some of the cavaliers who had followed him through all his fortunes; reckless young adventurers, who, like himself, would rather risk all on a single throw of the dice, than adopt the cautious, and, as it seemed to them, timid, policy of graver counsellors. It was by such advisers, then, that Pizarro's future course was to be shaped.[15]

Such was the state of affairs in Cuzco, when Pizarro's soldiers returned with the tidings, that a detachment of the enemy had crossed the Apurimac, and were busy in reëstablishing the bridge. Carbajal saw at once the absolute necessity of maintaining this pass. "It is my affair," he said; "I claim to be employed on this service. Give me but a hundred picked men, and I will engage to defend the pass against an army, and bring back the *chaplain*—the name by which the president was known in the rebel camp—a prisoner to Cuzco."[16] "I cannot spare you, father," said Gonzalo, addressing him by this affectionate epithet, which he usually applied to his aged follower,[17] "I cannot spare you so far from my own person"; and he gave the commission to Juan de Acosta, a young cavalier warmly attached to his commander, and who had given undoubted evidence of his valor on more than one occasion, but who, as the event proved, was signally deficient in the qualities demanded for so critical an undertaking as the present. Acosta, accordingly, was placed at the head of two hundred mounted musketeers, and, after much wholesome counsel from Carbajal, set out on his expedition.

But he soon forgot the veteran's advice, and moved at so dull a pace over the difficult roads, that, although the distance was not more than nine leagues, he found, on his arrival, the bridge completed, and so large a body of the enemy already crossed, that he was in no strength to attack them. Acosta did, indeed, meditate an ambuscade by night; but the design was betrayed by a deserter, and he contented himself with retreating to a safe distance, and sending for a further reinforcement from Cuzco. Three hundred men were promptly detached to his support; but when they arrived, the enemy was already planted in full force on the crest of the eminence. The golden opportunity was irrecoverably lost; and the disconsolate cavalier rode back in all haste to report the failure of his enterprise to his commander in Cuzco.[18]

The only question now to be decided was as to the spot where Gonzalo Pizarro should give battle to his enemies. He determined at once to abandon the capital, and wait for his opponents in the neighbouring valley of Xaquixaguana. It was about five leagues distant, and the reader may remember it as the place where Francis Pizarro burned the Peruvian general Challcuchima, on his first occupation of Cuzco. The valley, fenced round by the lofty rampart of the Andes, was, for the most part, green and luxuriant, affording many picturesque points of view; and, from the genial temperature of the climate, had been a favorite summer residence of the Indian nobles, many of whose pleasure-houses still dotted the sides of the mountains. A river, or rather stream, of no great volume, flowed through one end of this inclosure, and the neighbouring soil was so wet and miry as to have the character of a morass.

Here the rebel commander arrived, after a tedious march over roads not easily traversed by his train of heavy wagons and artillery. His forces amounted in all to about nine hundred men, with some half-dozen pieces of ordnance. It was a well-appointed body, and under excellent discipline, for it had been schooled by the strictest martinet in the Peruvian service. But it was the misfortune of Pizarro that his army was composed, in part, at least, of men on whose attachment to his cause he could not confidently rely. This was a deficiency which no courage nor skill in the leader could supply.

On entering the valley, Pizarro selected the eastern quarter of it, towards Cuzco, as the most favorable spot for his encampment. It was crossed by the stream above mentioned, and he stationed his army in such a manner, that, while one extremity of the camp rested on a natural barrier formed by the mountain cliffs that here rose up almost perpendicularly, the other was protected by the river. While it was scarcely possible, therefore, to assail his flanks, the approaches in front were so extremely narrowed by these obstacles, that it would not be easy to overpower him by numbers in that direction. In the rear, his communications remained open with Cuzco, furnishing a ready means for obtaining supplies. Having secured this strong position, he resolved patiently to wait the assault of the enemy.[19]

Meanwhile, the royal army had been toiling up the steep sides of the Cordilleras, until, at the close of the third day, the president had the satisfaction to find himself surrounded by his whole force, with their guns and military stores. Having now sufficiently refreshed his men, he resumed his march, and all went forward with the buoyant confidence of bringing their quarrel with the *tyrant*, as Pizarro was called, to a speedy issue.

Their advance was slow, as in the previous part of the march, for the ground was equally embarrassing. It was not long, however, before the president learned that his antagonist had pitched his camp in the neighbouring valley of Xaquixaguana. Soon afterward, two friars, sent by Gonzalo himself, appeared in the army, for the ostensible purpose of demanding a sight of the powers with which Gasca was intrusted. But as their conduct gave reason to suspect they were spies, the president caused the holy men to be seized, and refused to allow them to return to Pizarro. By an emissary of his own, whom he despatched to the rebel chief, he renewed the assurance of pardon already given him, in case he would lay down his arms and submit. Such an act of generosity, at this late hour, must be allowed to be highly creditable to Gasca, believing, as he probably did, that the game was in his own hands.—It is a pity that the anecdote does not rest on the best authority.[20]

After a march of a couple of days, the advanced guard of the royalists came suddenly on the outposts of the insurgents, from whom they had been concealed by a thick mist, and a slight skirmish took place between them. At length, on the morning of the eighth of April, the royal army, turning the crest of the lofty range that belts round the lovely valley of Xaquixaguana, beheld far below on the opposite side the glittering lines of the enemy, with their white pavilions, looking like clusters of wild fowl nestling among the cliffs of the mountains. And still further off might be descried a host of Indian warriors, showing gaudily in their variegated costumes; for the natives, in this part of the country, with little perception of their true interests, manifested great zeal in the cause of Pizarro.

Quickening their step, the royal army now hastily descended the steep sides of the sierra; and notwithstanding every effort of their officers, they moved in so little order, each man picking his way as he could, that the straggling column presented many a vulnerable point to the enemy; and the descent would not have been accomplished without considerable loss, had Pizarro's cannon been planted on any of the favorable positions which the ground afforded. But that commander, far from attempting to check the president's approach, remained doggedly in the strong position he had occupied, with the full confidence that his adversaries would not hesitate to assail it, strong as it was, in the same manner as they had done at Huarina.[21]

Yet he did not omit to detach a corps of arquebusiers to secure a neighbouring eminence or spur of the Cordilleras, which in the hands of the enemy might cause some annoyance to his own camp, while it commanded still more effectually the ground soon to be occupied by the assailants. But his manœuvre was noticed by Hinojosa; and he defeated it by sending a stronger detachment of the royal musketeers, who repulsed the rebels, and, after a short skirmish, got possession of the heights. Gasca's general profited by this success to plant a small battery of cannon on the eminence, from which, although the distance was too great for him to do much execution, he threw some shot into the hostile camp. One ball, indeed, struck down two men, one of them Pizarro's page, killing a horse, at the same time, which he held by the bridle; and the chief instantly ordered the tents to be struck, considering that they afforded too obvious a mark for the artillery.[22]

Meanwhile, the president's forces had descended into the valley, and as they came on the plain were formed into line by their officers. The ground occupied by the army was somewhat lower than that of their enemy, whose shot, as discharged, from time to time, from his batteries, passed over their heads. Information was now brought by a deserter, one of Centeno's old followers, that Pizarro was getting ready for a night attack. The president, in consequence, commanded his whole force to be drawn up in battle array, prepared, at any instant, to repulse the assault. But if such were meditated by the insurgent chief, he abandoned it, — and, as it is said, from a distrust of the fidelity of some of the troops, who, under cover of the darkness, he feared, would go over to the opposite side. If this be true, he must have felt the full force of Carbajal's admonition, when too late to profit by it. The unfortunate commander was in the situation of some bold, high-mettled cavalier, rushing to battle on a war-horse whose tottering joints threaten to give way under him at every step, and leave his rider to the mercy of his enemies!

The president's troops stood to their arms the greater part of the night, although the air from the mountains was so keen, that it was with difficulty they could hold their lances in their hands.[23] But before the rising sun had kindled into a glow the highest peaks of the sierra, both camps were in motion, and busily engaged in preparations for the combat. The royal army was formed into two battalions of infantry, one to attack the enemy in front, and the other, if possible, to operate on his flank. These battalions were protected by squadrons of horse on the wings and ill the rear, while reserves both of horse and arquebusiers were stationed to act as occasion might require. The dispositions were made in so masterly a manner, as to draw forth a hearty eulogium from old Carbajal, who exclaimed, "Surely the Devil or Valdivia must be among them!" an undeniable compliment to the latter, since the speaker was ignorant of that commander's presence in the camp.[24]

Gasca, leaving the conduct of the battle to his officers, withdrew to the rear with his train of clergy and licentiates, the last of whom did not share in the ambition of their rebel brother, Cepeda, to break a lance in the field.

Gonzalo Pizarro formed his squadron in the same manner as he had done on the plains of Huarina; except that the increased number of his horse now enabled him to cover both flanks of his infantry. It was still on his fire-arms, however, that he chiefly relied. As the ranks were formed, he rode among them, encouraging his men to do their duty like brave cavaliers, and true soldiers of the Conquest. Pizarro was superbly armed, as usual, and wore a complete suit of mail, of the finest manufacture, which, as well as his helmet, was richly inlaid with gold.[25] He rode a chestnut horse of great strength and spirit, and as he galloped along the line, brandishing his lance, and displaying his easy horsemanship, he might be thought to form no bad personification of the Genius of Chivalry. To complete his dispositions, he ordered Cepeda to lead up the infantry; for the licentiate seems to have had a larger share in the conduct of his affairs of late, or at least in the present military arrangements, than Carbajal. The latter, indeed, whether from disgust at the course taken by his leader, or from a distrust, which, it is said, he did not affect to conceal, of the success of the present operations, disclaimed all responsibility for them, and chose to serve rather as a private cavalier than as a commander.[26] Yet Cepeda, as the event showed, was no less shrewd in detecting the coming ruin.

When he had received his orders from Pizarro, he rode forward as if to select the ground for his troops to occupy; and in doing so disappeared for a few moments behind a projecting cliff. He soon reappeared, however, and was seen galloping at full speed across the plain. His men looked with astonishment, yet not distrusting his motives, till, as he continued his course direct towards the enemy's lines, his treachery became apparent. Several pushed forward to overtake him, and among them a cavalier, better mounted than

Cepeda. The latter rode a horse of no great strength or speed, quite unfit for this critical manœuvre of his master. The animal, was, moreover, encumbered by the weight of the caparisons with which his ambitious rider had loaded him, so that, on reaching a piece of miry ground that lay between the armies, his pace was greatly retarded.[27] Cepeda's pursuers rapidly gained on him, and the cavalier above noticed came, at length, so near as to throw a lance at the fugitive, which, wounding him in the thigh, pierced his horse's flank, and they both came headlong to the ground. It would have fared ill with the licentiate, in this emergency, but fortunately a small party of troopers on the other side, who had watched the chase, now galloped briskly forward to the rescue, and, beating off his pursuers, they recovered Cepeda from the mire, and bore him to the president's quarters.

He was received by Gasca with the greatest satisfaction,—so great, that, according to one chronicler, he did not disdain to show it by saluting the licentiate on the cheek.[28] The anecdote is scarcely reconcilable with the characters and relations of the parties, or with the president's subsequent conduct. Gasca, however, recognized the full value of his prize, and the effect which his desertion at such a time must have on the spirits of the rebels. Cepeda's movement, so unexpected by his own party, was the result of previous deliberation, as he had secretly given assurance, it is said, to the prior of Arequipa, then in the royal camp, that, if Gonzalo Pizarro could not be induced to accept the pardon offered him, he would renounce his cause.[29] The time selected by the crafty counsellor for doing so was that most fatal to the interests of his commander.

The example of Cepeda was contagious. Garcilasso de la Vega, father of the historian, a cavalier of old family, and probably of higher consideration than any other in Pizarro's party, put spurs to his horse, at the same time with the licentiate, and rode over to the enemy. Ten or a dozen of the arquebusiers followed in the same direction, and succeeded in placing themselves under the protection of the advanced guard of the royalists.

Pizarro stood aghast at this desertion, in so critical a juncture, of those in whom he had most trusted. He was, for a moment, bewildered. The very ground on which he stood seemed to be crumbling beneath him. With this state of feeling among his soldiers, he saw that every minute of delay was fatal. He dared not wait for the assault, as he had intended, in his strong position, but instantly gave the word to advance. Gasca's general, Hinojosa, seeing the enemy in motion, gave similar orders to his own troops. Instantly the skirmishers and arquebusiers on the flanks moved rapidly forward, the artillery prepared to open their fire, and "the whole army," says the president in his own account of the affair, "advanced with steady step and perfect determination."[30]

But before a shot was fired, a column of arquebusiers, composed chiefly of Centeno's followers, abandoned their post, and marched directly over to the enemy. A squadron of horse, sent in pursuit of them, followed their example. The president instantly commanded his men to halt, unwilling to spill blood unnecessarily, as the rebel host was like to fall to pieces of itself.

Pizarro's faithful adherents were seized with a panic, as they saw themselves and their leader thus betrayed into the enemy's hands. Further resistance was useless. Some threw down their arms, and fled in the direction of Cuzco. Others sought to escape to the mountains; and some crossed to the opposite side, and surrendered themselves prisoners, hoping it was not too late to profit by the promises of grace. The Indian allies, on seeing the Spaniards falter, had been the first to go off the ground.[31]

Pizarro, amidst the general wreck, found himself left with only a few cavaliers who disdained to fly. Stunned by the unexpected reverse of fortune, the unhappy chief could hardly comprehend his situation. "What remains for us?" said he to Acosta, one of those who still adhered to him. "Fail on the enemy, since nothing else is left," answered the lion-hearted soldier, "and die like Romans!" "Better to die like Christians," replied his commander; and, slowly turning his horse, he rode off in the direction of the royal army.[32]

He had not proceeded far, when he was met by an officer, to whom, after ascertaining his name and rank, Pizarro delivered up his sword, and yielded himself prisoner. The officer, overjoyed at his prize, conducted him, at once, to the president's quarters. Gasca was on horseback, surrounded by his captains, some of whom, when they recognized the person of the captive, had the grace to withdraw, that they might not witness his humiliation.[33] Even the best of them, with a sense of right on their side, may have felt some touch of compunction at the thought that their desertion had brought their benefactor to this condition.

Pizarro kept his seat in his saddle, but, as he approached, made a respectful obeisance to the president, which the latter acknowledged by a cold salute. Then, addressing his prisoner in a tone of severity, Gasca abruptly inquired, — "Why he had thrown the country into such confusion; — raising the banner of revolt; killing the viceroy; usurping the government; and obstinately refusing the offers of grace that had been repeatedly made him?"

Gonzalo attempted to justify himself by referring the fate of the viceroy to his misconduct, and his own usurpation, as it was styled, to the free election of the people, as well as that of the Royal Audience. "It was my family," he said, "who conquered the country; and, as their representative here, I felt I had a right to the government." To this Gasca replied, in a still severer tone, "Your brother did, indeed, conquer the land; and for this the emperor was pleased to raise both him and you from the dust. He lived and died a true and loyal subject; and it only makes your ingratitude to your sovereign the more heinous." Then, seeing his prisoner about to reply, the president cut short the conference, ordering him into close confinement. He was committed to the charge of Centeno, who had sought the office, not from any unworthy desire to gratify his revenge, — for he seems to have had a generous nature, — but for the honorable purpose of ministering to the comfort of the captive. Though held in strict custody by this officer, therefore, Pizarro was treated with the deference due to his rank, and allowed every indulgence by his keeper, except his freedom.[34]

In this general wreck of their fortunes, Francisco de Carbajal fared no better than his chief. As he saw the soldiers deserting their posts and going over to the enemy, one after another, he coolly hummed the words of his favorite old ballad, —

"The wind blows the hairs off my head, mother!"

But when he found the field nearly empty, and his stout-hearted followers vanished like a wreath of smoke, he felt it was time to provide for his own safety. He knew there could be no favor for him; and, putting spurs to his horse, he betook himself to flight with all the speed he could make. He crossed the stream that flowed, as already mentioned, by the camp, but, in scaling the opposite bank, which was steep and stony, his horse, somewhat old, and oppressed by the weight of his rider, who was large and corpulent, lost his footing and fell with him into the water. Before he could extricate himself, Carbajal was seized by some of his own followers, who hoped, by such a prize, to make their peace with the victor, and hurried off towards the president's quarters.

The convoy was soon swelled by a number of the common file from the royal army, some of whom had long arrears to settle with the prisoner; and, not content with heaping reproaches and imprecations on his head, they now threatened to proceed to acts of personal violence, which Carbajal, far from deprecating, seemed rather to court, as the speediest way of ridding himself of life.[35] When he approached the president's quarters, Centeno, who was near, rebuked the disorderly rabble, and compelled them to give way. Carbajal, on seeing this, with a respectful air demanded to whom he was indebted for this courteous protection. To which his ancient comrade replied, "Do you not know me?—Diego Centeno!:" "I crave your pardon," said the veteran, sarcastically alluding to his long flight in the Charcas, and his recent defeat at Huarina; "it is so long since I have seen any thing but your back, that I had forgotten your face!"[36]

Among the president's suite was the martial bishop of Cuzco, who, it will be remembered, had shared with Centeno in the disgrace of his defeat. His brother had been taken by Carbajal, in his flight from the field, and instantly hung up by that fierce chief, who, as we have had more than one occasion to see, was no respecter of persons. The bishop now reproached him with his brother's murder, and, incensed by his cool replies, was ungenerous enough to strike the prisoner on the face. Carbajal made no attempt at resistance. Nor would he return a word to the queries put to him by Gasca; but, looking haughtily round on the circle, maintained a contemptuous silence. The president, seeing that nothing further was to be gained from his captive, ordered him, together with Acosta, and the other cavaliers who had surrendered, into strict custody, until their fate should be decided.[37]

Gasca's next concern was to send an officer to Cuzco, to restrain his partisans from committing excesses in consequence of the late victory,—if victory that could be called, where not a blow had been struck. Every thing belonging to the vanquished, their tents, arms, ammunition, and military stores, became the property of the victors. Their camp was well victualled, furnishing a seasonable supply to the royalists, who had nearly expended their own stock of provisions. There was, moreover, considerable booty in the way of plate and money; for Pizarro's men, as was not uncommon in those turbulent times, went, many of them, to the war with the whole of their worldly wealth, not knowing of any safe place in which to bestow it. An anecdote is told of one of Gasca's soldiers, who, seeing a mule running over the field, with a large pack on his back, seized the animal, and mounted him, having first thrown away the burden, supposing it to contain armour, or something of little worth. Another soldier, more shrewd, picked up the parcel, as his share of the spoil, and found it contained several thousand gold ducats! It was the fortune of war.[38]

Thus terminated the battle, or rather rout, of Xaquixaguana. The number of killed and wounded—for some few perished in the pursuit—was not great; according to most accounts, not exceeding fifteen killed on the rebel side, and one only on that of the royalists! and that one, by the carelessness of a comrade.[39] Never was there a cheaper victory; so bloodless a termination of a fierce and bloody rebellion! It was gained not so much by the strength of the victors as by the weakness of the vanquished. They fell to pieces of their own accord, because they had no sure ground to stand on. The arm, not nerved by the sense of right, became powerless in the hour of battle. It was better that they should thus be overcome by moral force than by a brutal appeal to arms. Such a victory was more in harmony with the beneficent character of the conqueror and of his cause. It was the triumph of order; the best homage to law and justice.

CHAPTER IV

EXECUTION OF CARBAJAL. — GONZALO PIZARRO BEHEADED. — SPOILS OF VICTORY. — WISE REFORMS BY GASCA. — HE RETURNS TO SPAIN. — HIS DEATH AND CHARACTER

1548-1550.

IT was now necessary to decide on the fate of the prisoners; and Alonso de Alvarado, with the Licentiate Cianca, one of the new Royal Audience, was instructed to prepare the process. It did not require a long time. The guilt of the prisoners was too manifest, taken, as they had been, with arms in their hands. They were all sentenced to be executed, and their estates were confiscated to the use of the Crown. Gonzalo Pizarro was to be beheaded, and Carbajal to be drawn and quartered. No mercy was shown to him who had shown none to others. There was some talk of deferring the execution till the arrival of the troops in Cuzco; but the fear of disturbances from those friendly to Pizarro determined the president to carry the sentence into effect the following day, on the field of battle.[1]

When his doom was communicated to Carbajal, he heard it with his usual indifference. "They can but kill me," he said, as if he had already settled the matter in his own mind.[2] During the day, many came to see him in his confinement; some to upbraid him with his cruelties; but most, from curiosity to see the fierce warrior who had made his name so terrible through the land. He showed no unwillingness to talk with them, though it was in those sallies of caustic humor in which he usually indulged at the expense of his hearer. Among these visitors was a cavalier of no note, whose life, it appears, Carbajal had formerly spared, when in his power. This person expressed to the prisoner his strong desire to serve him; and as he reiterated his professions, Carbajal cut them short by exclaiming, — "And what service can you do me? Can you set me free? If you cannot do that, you can do nothing. If I spared your life, as you say, it was probably because I did not think it worth while to take it."

Some piously disposed persons urged him to see a priest, if it were only to unburden his conscience before leaving the world. "But of what use would that be?" asked Carbajal. "I have nothing that lies heavy on my conscience, unless it be, indeed, the debt of half a real to a shopkeeper in Seville, which I forgot to pay before leaving the country!"[3]

He was carried to execution on a hurdle, or rather in a basket, drawn by two mules. His arms were pinioned, and, as they forced his bulky body into this miserable conveyance, he exclaimed, — "Cradles for infants, and a cradle for the old man too, it seems!"[4] Notwithstanding the disinclination he had manifested to a confessor, he was attended by several ecclesiastics on his way to the gallows; and one of them repeatedly urged him to give some token of penitence at this solemn hour, if it were only by repeating the *Pater Noster* and *Ave Maria*. Carbajal, to rid himself of the ghostly father's importunity, replied by coolly repeating the words, "*Pater Noster*," "*Ave Maria*"! He then remained obstinately silent. He died, as he had lived, with a jest, or rather a scoff, upon his lips.[5]

Francisco de Carbajal was one of the most extraordinary characters of these dark and turbulent times; the more extraordinary from his great age; for, at the period of his death, he was in his eighty-fourth year; — an age when the bodily powers, and, fortunately, the passions, are usually blunted; when, in the witty words of the French moralist, "We flatter ourselves we are leaving our vices, whereas it is our vices that are leaving us."[6] But the fires of youth glowed fierce and unquenchable in the bosom of Carbajal.

The date of his birth carries us back towards the middle of the fifteenth century, before the times of Ferdinand and Isabella. He was of obscure parentage, and born, as it is said, at Arevalo. For forty years he served in the Italian wars, under the most illustrious captains of the day, Gonsalvo de Córdora, Navarro, and the Colonnas. He was an ensign at the battle of Ravenna; witnessed the capture of Francis the First at Pavia; and followed the banner of the ill-starred Bourbon at the sack of Rome. He got no gold for his share of the booty, on this occasion, but simply the papers of a notary's office, which, Carbajal shrewdly thought, would be worth gold to him. And so it proved; for the notary was fain to redeem them at a price which enabled the adventurer to cross the seas to Mexico, and seek his fortune in the New World. On the insurrection of the Peruvians, he was sent to the support of Francis Pizarro, and was rewarded by that chief with a grant of land in Cuzco. Here he remained for several years, busily employed in increasing his substance; for the love of lucre was a ruling passion in his bosom. On the arrival of Vaca de Castro, we find him doing good service under the royal banner; and at the breaking out of the great rebellion under Gonzalo Pizarro, he converted his property into gold, and prepared to return to Castile. He seemed to have a presentiment that to remain where he was would be fatal. But, although he made every effort to leave Peru, he was unsuccessful, for the viceroy had laid an embargo on the shipping.[7] He remained in the country, therefore, and took service, as we have seen, though reluctantly, under Pizarro. It was his destiny.

The tumultuous life on which he now entered roused all the slumbering passions of his soul, which lay there, perhaps unconsciously to himself; cruelty, avarice, revenge. He found ample exercise for them in the war with his countrymen; for civil war is proverbially the most sanguinary and ferocious of all. The atrocities recorded of Carbajal, in his new career, and the number of his victims, are scarcely credible. For the honor of humanity, we may trust the accounts are greatly exaggerated; but that he should have given rise to them at all is sufficient to consign his name to infamy.[8]

He even took a diabolical pleasure, it is said, in amusing himself with the sufferings of his victims, and in the hour of execution would give utterance to frightful jests, that made them taste more keenly the bitterness of death! He had a sportive vein, if such it could be called, which he freely indulged on every occasion. Many of his sallies were preserved by the soldiery; but they are, for the most part, of a coarse, repulsive character, flowing from a mind familiar with the weak and wicked side of humanity, and distrusting every other. He had his jest for every thing,—for the misfortunes of others, and for his own. He looked on life as a farce,—though he too often made it a tragedy.

Carbajal must be allowed one virtue; that of fidelity to his party. This made him less tolerant of perfidy in others. He was never known to show mercy to a renegade. This undeviating fidelity, though to a bad cause, may challenge something like a feeling of respect, where fidelity was so rare.[9]

As a military man, Carbajal takes a high rank among the soldiers of the New World. He was strict, even severe, in enforcing discipline, so that he was little loved by his followers. Whether he had the genius for military combinations requisite for conducting war on an extended scale may be doubted; but in the shifts and turns of guerilla warfare he was unrivalled. Prompt, active, and persevering, he was insensible to danger or fatigue, and, after days spent in the saddle, seemed to attach little value to the luxury of a bed.[10]

He knew familiarly every mountain pass, and, such were the sagacity and the resources displayed in his roving expeditions, that he was vulgarly believed to be attended by a *familiar*,[11] With a character so extraordinary, with powers prolonged so far beyond the usual term of humanity, and passions so fierce in one tottering on the verge of the grave, it was not surprising that many fabulous stories should be eagerly circulated respecting him, and that Carbajal should be clothed with mysterious terrors as a sort of supernatural being,— the demon of the Andes!

Very different were the circumstances attending the closing scene of Gonzalo Pizarro. At his request, no one had been allowed to visit him in his confinement. He was heard pacing his tent during the greater part of the day, and when night came, having ascertained from Centeno that his execution was to take place on the following noon, he laid himself down to rest. He did not sleep long, however, but soon rose, and continued to traverse his apartment, as if buried in meditation, till dawn. He then sent for a confessor, and remained with him till after the hour of noon, taking little or no refreshment.

The officers of justice became impatient; but their eagerness was sternly rebuked by the soldiery, many of whom, having served under Gonzalo's banner, were touched with pity for his misfortunes.

When the chieftain came forth to execution, he showed in his dress the same love of magnificence and display as in happier days. Over his doublet he wore a superb cloak of yellow velvet, stiff with gold embroidery, while his head was protected by a cap of the same materials, richly decorated, in like manner, with ornaments of gold.[12] In this gaudy attire he mounted his mule, and the sentence was so far relaxed that his arms were suffered to remain unshackled. He was escorted by a goodly number of priests and friars, who held up the crucifix before his eyes, while he carried in his own hand an image of the Virgin. She had ever been the peculiar object of Pizarro's devotion; so much so, that those who knew him best in the hour of his prosperity were careful, when they had a petition, to prefer it in the name of the blessed Mary.

Pizarro's lips were frequently pressed to the emblem of his divinity, while his eyes were bent on the crucifix in apparent devotion, heedless of the objects around him. On reaching the scaffold, he ascended it with a firm step, and asked leave to address a few words to the soldiery gathered round it. "There are many among you," said he, "who have grown rich on my brother's bounty, and my own. Yet, of all my riches, nothing remains to me but the garments I have on; and even these are not mine, but the property of the executioner. I am without means, therefore, to purchase a mass for the welfare of my soul; and I implore you, by the remembrance of past benefits, to extend this charity to me when I am gone, that it may be well with you in the hour of death." A profound silence reigned throughout the martial multitude, broken only by sighs and groans, as they listened to Pizarro's request; and it was faithfully responded to, since, after his death, masses were said in many of the towns for the welfare of the departed chieftain.

Then, kneeling down before a crucifix placed on a table, Pizarro remained for some minutes absorbed in prayer; after which, addressing the soldier who was to act as the minister of justice, he calmly bade him "do his duty with a steady hand." He refused to have his eyes bandaged, and, bending forward his neck, submitted it to the sword of the executioner, who struck off the head with a single blow, so true that the body remained for some moments in the same erect posture as in life.[13] The head was taken to Lima, where it was set in a cage or frame, and then fixed on a gibbet by the side of Carbajal's. On it was placed a label, bearing, — "This is the head of the traitor Gonzalo Pizarro, who rebelled in Peru against his sovereign, and battled in the cause of tyranny and treason against the royal standard in the valley of Xaquixaguana."[14] His large estates, including the rich mines in Potosí, were confiscated; his mansion in Lima was razed to the ground, the place strewed with salt, and a stone pillar set up, with an inscription interdicting any one from building on a spot which had been profaned by the residence of a traitor.

Gonzalo's remains were not exposed to the indignities inflicted on Carbajal's, whose quarters were hung in chains on the four great roads leading to Cuzco. Centeno saved Pizarro's body from being stripped, by redeeming his costly raiment from the executioner, and in this sumptuous shroud it was laid in the chapel of the convent of Our Lady of Mercy in Cuzco. It was the same spot where, side by side, lay the bloody remains of the Almagros, father and son, who in like manner had perished by the hand of justice, and were indebted to private charity for their burial. All these were now consigned "to the same grave," says the historian, with some bitterness, "as if Peru could not afford land enough for a burial-place to its conquerors."[15]

Gonzalo Pizarro had reached only his forty-second year at the time of his death,—being just half the space allotted to his follower Carbajal. He was the youngest of the remarkable family to whom Spain was indebted for the acquisition of Peru. He came over to the country with his brother Francisco, on the return of the latter from his visit to Castile. Gonzalo was present in all the remarkable passages of the Conquest. He witnessed the seizure of Atahuallpa, took an active part in suppressing the insurrection of the Incas, and especially in the reduction of Charcas. He afterwards led the disastrous expedition to the Amazon; and, finally, headed the memorable rebellion which ended so fatally to himself. There are but few men whose lives abound in such wild and romantic adventure, and, for the most part, crowned with success. The space which he occupies in the page of history is altogether disproportioned to his talents. It may be in some measure ascribed to fortune, but still more to those showy qualities which form a sort of substitute for mental talent, and which secured his popularity with the vulgar.

He had a brilliant exterior; excelled in all martial exercises; rode well, fenced well, managed his lance to perfection, was a first-rate marksman with the arquebuse, and added the accomplishment of being an excellent draughtsman. He was bold and chivalrous, even to temerity; courted adventure, and was always in the front of danger. He was a knight-errant, in short, in the most extravagant sense of the term, and, "mounted on his favorite charger," says one who had often seen him, "made no more account of a squadron of Indians than of a swarm of flies."[16]

While thus, by his brilliant exploits and showy manners, he captivated the imaginations of his countrymen, he won their hearts no less by his soldier-like frankness, his trust in their fidelity,—too often abused,—and his liberal largesses; for Pizarro, though avaricious of the property of others, was, like the Roman conspirator, prodigal of his own. This was his portrait in happier days, when his heart had not been corrupted by success; for that some change was wrought on him by his prosperity is well attested. His head was made giddy by his elevation; and it is proof of a want of talent equal to his success, that he knew not how to profit by it. Obeying the dictates of his own rash judgment, he rejected the warnings of his wisest counsellors, and relied with blind confidence on his destiny. Garcilasso imputes this to the malignant influence of the stars.[17] But the superstitious chronicler might have better explained it by a common principle of human nature; by the presumption nourished by success; the insanity, as the Roman, or rather Grecian, proverb calls it, with which the gods afflict men when they design to ruin them.[18]

Gonzalo was without education, except such as he had picked up in the rough school of war. He had little even of that wisdom which springs from natural shrewdness and insight into character. In all this he was inferior to his elder brothers, although he fully equalled them in ambition. Had he possessed a tithe of their sagacity, he would not have madly persisted in rebellion, after the coming of the president. Before this period, he represented the people. Their interests and his were united. He had their support, for he was contending for the redress of their wrongs. When these were redressed by the government, there was nothing to contend for. From that time, he was battling only for himself. The people had no part nor interest in the contest. Without a common sympathy to bind them together, was it strange that they should fall off from him, like leaves in winter, and leave him exposed, a bare and sapless trunk, to the fury of the tempest?

Cepeda, more criminal than Pizarro, since he had both superior education and intelligence, which he employed only to mislead his commander, did not long survive him. He had come to the country in an office of high responsibility. His first step was to betray the viceroy whom he was sent to support; his next was to betray the Audience with whom he should have acted; and lastly, he betrayed the leader whom he most affected to serve. His whole career was treachery to his own government. His life was one long perfidy.

After his surrender, several of the cavaliers, disgusted at his cold-blooded apostasy, would have persuaded Gasca to send him to execution along with his commander; but the president refused, in consideration of the signal service he had rendered the Crown by his defection. He was put under arrest, however, and sent to Castle. There he was arraigned for high-treason. He made a plausible defence, and as he had friends at court, it is not improbable he would have been acquitted; but, before the trial was terminated, he died in prison. It was the retributive justice not always to be found in the affairs of this world.[19]

Indeed, it so happened, that several of those who had been most forward to abandon the cause of Pizarro survived their commander but a short time. The gallant Centeno, and the Licentiate Carbajal, who deserted him near Lima, and bore the royal standard on the field of Xaquixaguana, both died within a year after Pizarro. Hinojosa was assassinated but two years later in La Plata; and his old comrade Valdivia, after a series of brilliant exploits in Chili, which furnished her most glorious theme to the epic Muse of Castile, was cut off by the invincible warriors of Arauco. The Manes of Pizarro were amply avenged.

Acosta, and three or four other cavaliers who surrendered with Gonzalo, were sent to execution on the same day with their chief; and Gasca, on the morning following the dismal tragedy, broke up his quarters and marched with his whole army to Cuzco, where he was received by the politic people with the same enthusiasm which they had so recently shown to his rival. He found there a number of the rebel army who had taken refuge in the city after their late defeat, where they were immediately placed under arrest. Proceedings, by Gasca's command, were instituted against them. The principal cavaliers, to the number of ten or twelve, were executed; others were banished or sent to the galleys. The same rigorous decrees were passed against such as had fled and were not yet taken; and the estates of all were confiscated. The estates of the rebels supplied a fund for the recompense of the loyal.[20] The execution of justice may seem to have been severe; but Gasca was willing that the rod should fall heavily on those who had so often rejected his proffers of grace. Lenity was wasted on a rude, licentious soldiery, who hardly recognized the existence of government, unless they felt its rigor.

A new duty now devolved on the president,—that of rewarding his faithful followers,—not less difficult, as it proved, than that of punishing the guilty. The applicants were numerous; since every one who had raised a finger in behalf of the government claimed his reward. They urged their demands with a clamorous importunity which perplexed the good president, and consumed every moment of his time.

Disgusted with this unprofitable state of things, Gasca resolved to rid himself of the annoyance at once, by retiring to the valley of Guaynarima, about twelve leagues distant from the city, and there digesting, in quiet, a scheme of compensation, adjusted to the merits of the parties. He was accompanied only by his secretary, and by Loaysa, now archbishop of Lima, a man of sense, and well acquainted with the affairs of the country. In this seclusion the president remained three months, making a careful examination into the conflicting claims, and apportioning the forfeitures among the parties according to their respective services. The *repartimientos,* it should be remarked, were usually granted only for life, and, on the death of the incumbent, reverted to the Crown, to be reassigned or retained at its pleasure.

When his arduous task was completed, Gasca determined to withdraw to Lima, leaving the instrument of partition with the archbishop, to be communicated to the army. Notwithstanding all the care that had been taken for an equitable adjustment, Gasca was aware that it was impossible to satisfy the demands of a jealous and irritable soldiery, where each man would be likely to exaggerate his own deserts, while he underrated those of his comrades; and he did not care to expose himself to importunities and complaints that could serve no other purpose than to annoy him.

On his departure, the troops were called together by the archbishop in the cathedral, to learn the contents of the schedule intrusted to him. A discourse was first preached by a worthy Dominican, the prior of Arequipa, in which the

reverend father expatiated on the virtue of contentment, the duty of obedience, and the folly, as well as wickedness, of an attempt to resist the constituted authorities, — topics, in short, which he conceived might best conciliate
the good-will and conformity of his audience.

A letter from the president was then read from the pulpit. It was addressed
to the officers and soldiers of the army. The writer began with briefly exposing
the difficulties of his task, owing to the limited amount of the gratuities, and
the great number and services of the claimants. He had given the matter the
most careful consideration, he said, and endeavoured to assign to each his
share, according to his deserts, without prejudice or partiality. He had, no
doubt, fallen into errors, but he trusted his followers would excuse them,
when they reflected that he had done according to the best of his poor abilities; and all, he believed, would do him the justice to acknowledge he had not
been influenced by motives of personal interest. He bore emphatic testimony
to the services they had rendered to the good cause, and concluded with the
most affectionate wishes for their future prosperity and happiness. The letter
was dated at Guaynarima, August 17, 1548, and bore the simple signature of
the Licentiate Gasca.[21]

The archbishop next read the paper containing the president's award. The
annual rent of the estates to be distributed amounted to a hundred and thirty
thousand *pesos ensayados*;[22] a large amount, considering the worth of money in
that day, — in any other country than Peru, where money was a drug.[23]

The *repartimientos* thus distributed varied in value from one hundred to
thirty-five hundred *pesos* of yearly rent; all, apparently, graduated with the
nicest precision to the merits of the parties. The number of pensioners was
about two hundred and fifty; for the fund would not have sufficed for general
distribution, nor were the services of the greater part deemed worthy of such
a mark of consideration.[24]

The effect produced by the document, on men whose minds were filled
with the most indefinite expectations, was just such as had been anticipated by
the president. It was received with a general murmur of disapprobation. Even
those who had got more than they expected were discontented, on comparing their condition with that of their comrades, whom they thought still better
remunerated in proportion to their deserts. They especially inveighed against
the preference shown to the old partisans of Gonzalo Pizarro—as Hinojosa,
Centeno, and Aldana—over those who had always remained loyal to the
Crown. There was some ground for such a preference; for none had rendered
so essential services in crushing the rebellion; and it was these services that
Gasca proposed to recompense. To reward every man who had proved himself
loyal, simply for his loyalty, would, have frittered away the donative into frac-
tions that would be of little value to any.[25]

It was in vain, however, that the archbishop, seconded by some of the principal cavaliers, endeavoured to infuse a more contented spirit into the multitude. They insisted that the award should be rescinded, and a new one made

on more equitable principles; threatening, moreover, that, if this were not done by the president, they would take the redress of the matter into their own hands. Their discontent, fomented by some mischievous persons who thought to find their account in it, at length proceeded so far as to menace a mutiny; and it was not suppressed till the commander of Cuzco sentenced one of the ringleaders to death, and several others to banishment. The iron soldiery of the Conquest required an iron hand to rule them.

Meanwhile, the president had continued his journey towards Lima; and on the way was everywhere received by the people with an enthusiasm, the more grateful to his heart that he felt he had deserved it. As he drew near the capital, the loyal inhabitants prepared to give him a magnificent reception. The whole population came forth from the gates, led by the authorities of the city, with Aldana as corregidor at their head. Gasca rode on a mule, dressed in his ecclesiastical robes. On his right, borne on a horse richly caparisoned, was the royal seal, in a box curiously chased and ornamented. A gorgeous canopy of brocade was supported above his head by the officers of the municipality, who, in their robes of crimson velvet, walked bareheaded by his side. Gay troops of dancers, clothed in fantastic dresses of gaudy-colored silk, followed the procession, strewing flowers and chanting verses as they went, in honor of the president. They were designed as emblematical of the different cities of the colony; and they bore legends or mottoes in rhyme on their caps, intimating their loyal devotion to the Crown, and evincing much more loyalty in their composition, it may be added, than poetical merit.[26] In this way, without beat of drum, or noise of artillery, or any of the rude accompaniments of war, the good president made his peaceful entry into the City of the Kings, while the air was rent with the acclamations of the people, who hailed him as their "Father and Deliverer, the Saviour of their country!"[27]

But, however grateful was this homage to Gasca's heart, he was not a man to waste his time in idle vanities. He now thought only by what means he could eradicate the seeds of disorder which shot up so readily in this fruitful soil, and how he could place the authority of the government on a permanent basis. By virtue of his office, he presided over the Royal Audience, the great judicial, and, indeed, executive tribunal of the colony; and he gave great despatch to the business, which had much accumulated during the late disturbances. In the unsettled state of property, there was abundant subject for litigation; but, fortunately, the new Audience was composed of able, upright judges, who labored diligently with their chief to correct the mischief caused by the misrule of their predecessors

Neither was Gasca unmindful of the unfortunate natives; and he occupied himself earnestly with that difficult problem,—the best means practicable of ameliorating their condition. He sent a number of commissioners, as visitors, into different parts of the country, whose business it was to inspect the *encomiendas,* and ascertain the manner in which the Indians were treated, by conversing not only with the proprietors, but with the natives themselves. They were also to learn the nature and extent of the tributes paid in former times by the vassals of the Incas.[28]

In this way, a large amount of valuable information was obtained, which enabled Gasca, with the aid of a council of ecclesiastics and jurists, to digest a uniform system of taxation for the natives, lighter even than that imposed on them by the Peruvian princes. The president would gladly have relieved the conquered races from the obligations of personal service; but, on mature consideration, this was judged impracticable in the present state of the country, since the colonists, more especially in the tropical regions, looked to the natives for the performance of labor, and the latter, it was found from experience, would not work at all, unless compelled to do so. The president, however, limited the amount of service to be exacted with great precision, so that it was in the nature of a moderate personal tax. No Peruvian was to be required to change his place of residence, from the climate to which he had been accustomed, to another; a fruitful source of discomfort, as well as of disease, in past times. By these various regulations, the condition of the natives, though not such as had been contemplated by the sanguine philanthropy of Las Casas, was improved far more than was compatible with the craving demands of the colonists; and all the firmness of the Audience was required to enforce provisions so unpalatable to the latter. Still they were enforced. Slavery, in its most odious sense, was no longer tolerated in Peru. The term "slave" was not recognized as having relation to her institutions; and the historian of the Indies makes the proud boast,—it should have been qualified by the limitations I have noticed,—that every Indian vassal might aspire to the rank of a freeman.[29]

Besides these reforms, Gasca introduced several in the municipal government of the cities, and others yet more important in the management of the finances, and in the mode of keeping the accounts. By these and other changes in the internal economy of the colony, he placed the administration on a new basis, and greatly facilitated the way for a more sure and orderly government by his successors. As a final step, to secure the repose of the country after he was gone, he detached some of the more aspiring cavaliers on distant expeditions, trusting that they would draw off the light and restless spirits, who might otherwise gather together and disturb the public tranquillity; as we sometimes see the mists which have been scattered by the genial influence of the sun become condensed, and settle into a storm, on his departure.[30]

Gasca had been now more than fifteen months in Lima, and nearly three years had elapsed since his first entrance into Peru. In that time, he had accomplished the great objects of his mission. When he landed, he found the colony in a state of anarchy, or rather organized rebellion under a powerful and popular chief. He came without funds or forces to support him. The former he procured through the credit which he established in his good faith; the latter he won over by argument and persuasion from the very persons to whom they had been confided by his rival. Thus he turned the arms of that rival against himself. By a calm appeal to reason he wrought a change in the hearts of the people; and, without costing a drop of blood to a single loyal subject, he suppressed a rebellion which had menaced Spain with the loss of the wealthiest of her provinces. He had punished the guilty, and in their spoils found the means to recompense the faithful. He had, moreover, so well husbanded the resources of the country, that he was enabled to pay off the large loan he had negotiated with the merchants of the colony, for the expenses of the war, exceeding nine hundred thousand *pesos de oro*.[31] Nay, more, by his economy he had saved a million and a half of ducats for the government, which for some years had received nothing from Peru; and he now proposed to carry back this acceptable treasure to swell the royal coffers.[32] All this had been accomplished without the cost of outfit or salary, or any charge to the Crown except that of his own frugal expenditure.[33] The country was now in a state of tranquillity. Gasca felt that his work was done; and that he was free to gratify his natural longing to return to his native land.

Before his departure, he arranged a distribution of those *repartimientos* which had lapsed to the Crown during the past year by the death of the incumbents. Life was short in Peru; since those who lived by the sword, if they did not die by the sword, too often fell early victims to the hardships incident to their adventurous career. Many were the applicants for the new bounty of government; and, as among them were some of those who had been discontented with the former partition, Gasca was assailed by remonstrances, and sometimes by reproaches couched in no very decorous or respectful language. But they had no power to disturb his equanimity; he patiently listened, and replied to all in the mild tone of expostulation best calculated to turn away wrath; "by this victory over himself," says an old writer, "acquiring more real glory, than by all his victories over his enemies."[34]

An incident occurred on the eve of his departure, touching in itself, and honorable to the parties concerned. The Indian caciques of the neighbouring country, mindful of the great benefits he had rendered their people, presented him with a considerable quantity of plate in token of their gratitude. But Gasca refused to receive it, though in doing so he gave much concern to the Peruvians, who feared they had unwittingly fallen under his displeasure.

Many of the principal colonists, also, from the same wish to show their sense of his important services, sent to him, after he had embarked, a magnificent donative of fifty thousand gold *castellanos*. "As he had taken leave of Peru," they said, "there could be no longer any ground for declining it." But Gasca was as decided in his rejection of this present, as he had been of the other. "He had come to the country," he remarked, "to serve the king, and to secure the blessings of peace to the inhabitants; and now that, by the favor of Heaven, he had been permitted to accomplish this, he would not dishonor the cause by any act that might throw suspicion on the purity of his motives." Notwithstanding his refusal, the colonists contrived to secrete the sum of twenty thousand *castellanos* on board of his vessel, with the idea, that, once in his own country, with his mission concluded, the president's scruples would be removed. Gasca did, indeed, accept the donative; for he felt that it would be ungracious to send it back; but it was only till he could ascertain the relatives of the donors, when he distributed it among the most needy.[35]

Having now settled all his affairs, the president committed the government, until the arrival of a viceroy, to his faithful partners of the Royal Audience; and in January, 1550, he embarked with the royal treasure on board of a squadron for Panamá. He was accompanied to the shore by a numerous crowd of the inhabitants, cavaliers and common people, persons of all ages and conditions, who followed to take their last look of their benefactor, and watch with straining eyes the vessel that bore him away from their land.

His voyage was prosperous, and early in March the president reached his destined port. He stayed there only till he could muster horses and mules sufficient to carry the treasure across the mountains; for he knew that this part of the country abounded in wild, predatory spirits, who would be sorely tempted to some act of violence by a knowledge of the wealth which he had with him. Pushing forward, therefore, he crossed the rugged Isthmus, and, after a painful march, arrived in safety at Nombre de Dios.

The event justified his apprehensions. He had been gone but three days, when a ruffian horde, after murdering the bishop of Guatemala, broke into Panamá with the design of inflicting the same fate on the president, and of seizing the booty. No sooner were the tidings communicated to Gasca, than, with his usual energy, he levied a force and prepared to march to the relief of the invaded capital. But Fortune — or, to speak more correctly, Providence — favored him here, as usual; and, on the eve of his departure, he learned that the marauders had been met by the citizens, and discomfited with great slaughter. Disbanding his forces, therefore, he equipped a fleet of nineteen vessels to transport himself and the royal treasure to Spain, where he arrived in safety, entering the harbour of Seville after a little more than four years from the period when he had sailed from the same port.[36]

Great was the sensation throughout the country caused by his arrival. Men could hardly believe that results so momentous had been accomplished in so short a time by a single individual, — a poor ecclesiastic, who, unaided by government, had, by his own strength, as it were, put down a rebellion which had so long set the arms of Spain at defiance!

The emperor was absent in Flanders. He was overjoyed on learning the complete success of Gasca's mission; and not less satisfied with the tidings of the treasure he had brought with him; for the exchequer, rarely filled to overflowing, had been exhausted by the recent troubles in Germany. Charles instantly wrote to the president, requiring his presence at court, that he might learn from his own lips the particulars of his expedition. Gasca, accordingly, attended by a numerous retinue of nobles and cavaliers,—for who does not pay homage to him whom the king delighteth to honor?—embarked at Barcelona, and, after a favorable voyage, joined the Court in Flanders.

He was received by his royal master, who fully appreciated his services, in a manner most grateful to his feelings; and not long afterward he was raised to the bishopric of Palencia,—a mode of acknowledgment best suited to his character and deserts. Here he remained till 1561, when he was promoted to the vacant see of Siguenza. The rest of his days he passed peacefully in the discharge of his episcopal functions; honored by his sovereign, and enjoying the admiration and respect of his countrymen.[37]

In his retirement, he was still consulted by the government in matters of importance relating to the Indies. The disturbances of that unhappy land were renewed, though on a much smaller scale than before, soon after the president's departure. They were chiefly caused by discontent with the *repartimientos,* and with the constancy of the Audience in enforcing the benevolent restrictions as to the personal services of the natives. But these troubles subsided, after a very few years, under the wise rule of the Mendozas,—two successive viceroys of that illustrious house which has given so many of its sons to the service of Spain. Under their rule, the mild yet determined policy was pursued, of which Gasca had set the example. The ancient distractions of the country were permanently healed. With peace, prosperity returned within the borders of Peru; and the consciousness of the beneficent results of his labors may have shed a ray of satisfaction, as it did of glory, over the evening of the president's life.

That life was brought to a close in November, 1567, at an age, probably, not far from the one fixed by the sacred writer as the term of human existence.[38] He died at Valladolid, and was buried in the church of Santa Maria Magdalena, in that city, which he had built and liberally endowed. His monument, surmounted by the sculptured effigy of a priest in his sacerdotal robes, is still to be seen there, attracting the admiration of the traveller by the beauty of its execution. The banners taken from Gonzalo Pizarro on the field of Xaquixaguana were suspended over his tomb, as the trophies of his memorable mission to Peru.[39] The banners have long since mouldered into dust, with the remains of him who slept beneath them; but the memory of his good deeds will endure for ever.[40]

Gasca was plain in person, and his countenance was far from comely. He was awkward and ill-proportioned; for his limbs were too long for his body,— so that when he rode, he appeared to he much shorter than he really was.[41] His dress was humble, his manners simple, and there was nothing imposing in his presence. But, on a nearer intercourse, there was a charm in his discourse that effaced every unfavorable impression produced by his exterior, and won the hearts of his hearers.

The president's character may be thought to have been sufficiently portrayed in the history already given of his life. It presented a combination of qualities which generally serve to neutralize each other, but which were mixed in such proportions in him as to give it additional strength. He was gentle, yet resolute; by nature intrepid, yet preferring to rely on the softer arts of policy. He was frugal in his personal expenditure, and economical in the public; yet caring nothing for riches on his own account, and never stinting his bounty when the public good required it. He was benevolent and placable, yet could deal sternly with the impenitent offender; lowly in his deportment, yet with a full measure of that self-respect which springs from conscious rectitude of purpose; modest and unpretending, yet not shrinking from the most difficult enterprises; deferring greatly to others, yet, in the last resort, relying mainly on himself; moving with deliberation,—patiently waiting his time; but, when that came, bold, prompt, and decisive.

Gasca was not a man of genius, in the vulgar sense of that term. At least, no one of his intellectual powers seems to have received an extraordinary development, beyond what is found in others. He was not a great writer, nor a great orator, nor a great general. He did not affect to be either. He committed the care of his military matters to military men; of ecclesiastical, to the clergy; and his civil and judicial concerns he reposed on the members of the Audience. He was not one of those little great men who aspire to do every thing themselves, under the conviction that nothing can be done so well by others. But the president was a keen judge of character. Whatever might be the office, he selected the best man for it. He did more. He assured himself of the fidelity of his agents, presided at their deliberations; dictated a general line of policy, and thus infused a spirit of unity into their plans, which made all move in concert to the accomplishment of one grand result.

A distinguishing feature of his mind was his common sense,—the best substitute for genius in a ruler who has the destinies of his fellow-men at his disposal, and more indispensable than genius itself. In Gasca, the different qualities were blended in such harmony, that there was no room for excess. They seemed to regulate each other. While his sympathy with mankind taught him the nature of their wants, his reason suggested to what extent these were capable of relief, as well as the best mode of effecting it. He did not waste his strength on illusory schemes of benevolence, like Las Casas, on the one hand; nor did he countenance the selfish policy of the colonists, on the other. He aimed at the practicable,—the greatest good practicable.

In accomplishing his objects, he disclaimed force equally with fraud. He trusted for success to his power over the convictions of his hearers; and the source of this power was the confidence he inspired in his own integrity. Amidst all the calumnies of faction, no imputation was ever cast on the integrity of Gasca.[42] No wonder that a virtue so rare should be of high price in Peru.

There are some men whose characters have been so wonderfully adapted to the peculiar crisis in which they appeared, that they seem to have been specially designed for it by Providence. Such was Washington in our own country, and Gasca in Peru. We can conceive of individuals with higher qualities, at least with higher intellectual qualities, than belonged to either of these great men. But it was the wonderful conformity of their characters to the exigencies of their situation, the perfect adaptation of the means to the end, that constituted the secret of their success; that enabled Gasca so gloriously to crush revolution, and Washington still more gloriously to achieve it.

Gasca's conduct on his first coming to the colonies affords the best illustration of his character. Had he come backed by a military array, or even clothed in the paraphernalia of authority, every heart and hand would have been closed against him. But the humble ecclesiastic excited no apprehension; and his enemies were already disarmed, before he had begun his approaches. Had Gasca, impatient of Hinojosa's tardiness, listened to the suggestions of those who advised his seizure, he would have brought his cause into jeopardy by this early display of violence. But he wisely chose to win over his enemy by operating on his conviction.

In like manner, he waited his time for making his entry into Peru. He suffered his communications to do their work in the minds of the people, and was careful not to thrust in the sickle before the harvest was ripe. In this way, wherever he went, every thing was prepared for his coming; and when he set foot in Peru, the country was already his own.

After the dark and turbulent spirits with which we have been hitherto occupied, it is refreshing to dwell on a character like that of Gasca. In the long procession which has passed in review before us, we have seen only the mail-clad cavalier, brandishing his bloody lance, and mounted on his warhorse, riding over the helpless natives, or battling with his own friends and brothers; fierce, arrogant, and cruel, urged on by the lust of gold, or the scarce more honorable love of a bastard glory. Mingled with these qualities, indeed, we have seen sparkles of the chivalrous and romantic temper which belongs to the heroic age of Spain. But, with some honorable exceptions, it was the scum of her chivalry that resorted to Peru, and took service under the banner of the Pizarros. At the close of this long array of iron warriors, we behold the poor and humble missionary coming into the land on an errand of mercy, and everywhere proclaiming the glad tidings of peace. No warlike trumpet heralds his approach, nor is his course to be tracked by the groans of the wounded and the dying. The means he employs are in perfect harmony with his end. His weapons are argument and mild persuasion. It is the reason he would conquer, not the body. He wins his way by conviction, not by violence. It is a moral victory to which he aspires, more potent, and happily more permanent, than that of the blood-stained conqueror. As he thus calmly, and imperceptibly, as it were, comes to his great results, he may remind us of the slow, insensible manner in which Nature works out her great changes in the material world, that are to endure when the ravages of the hurricane are passed away and forgotten.

With the mission of Gasca terminates the history of the Conquest of Peru. The Conquest, indeed, strictly terminates with the suppression of the Peruvian revolt, when the strength, if not the spirit, of the Inca race was crushed for ever. The reader, however, might feel a natural curiosity to follow to its close the fate of the remarkable family who achieved the Conquest. Nor would the story of the invasion itself be complete without some account of the civil wars which grew out of it; which serve, moreover, as a moral commentary on preceding events, by showing that the indulgence of fierce, unbridled passions is sure to recoil, sooner or later, even in this life, on the heads of the guilty.

It is true, indeed, that the troubles of the country were renewed on the departure of Gasca. The waters had been too fearfully agitated to be stilled, at once, into a calm; but they gradually subsided, under the temperate rule of his successors, who wisely profited by his policy and example. Thus the influence of the good president remained after he was withdrawn from the scene of his labors; and Peru, hitherto so distracted, continued to enjoy as large a share of repose as any portion of the colonial empire of Spain. With the benevolent mission of Gasca, then, the historian of the Conquest may be permitted to terminate his labors,—with feelings not unlike those of the traveller, who, having long journeyed among the dreary forests and dangerous defiles of the mountains, at length emerges on some pleasant landscape smiling in tranquillity and peace.

APPENDIX

No. I.—See Vol. I., p. 28.

DESCRIPTION OF THE ROYAL PROGRESSES OF THE INCAS;
EXTRACTED FROM SARMIENTO'S RELACION, MS.

[The original manuscript, which was copied for Lord Kingsborough's valuable collection, is in the Library of the Escurial.]

Quando en tiempo de paz salian los Yngas a visitar su Reyno, cuentan que iban por el con gran majestad, sentados en ricas andas armadas sobre unos palos lisos largos, de manera escelente, engastadas en oro y argenteria, y de las andas salian dos arcos altos hechos de oro, engastados en piedras preciosas: caian unas mantas algo largas por todas las andas, de tal manera que las cubrian todas, y sino era queriendo el que iba dentro, no podia ser visto, ni alzaban las mantas si no era cuando entraba y salia, tanta era su estimacion; y para que le entrase aire, y el pudiese ver el camino, havia en las mantas hechos algunos agujeros hechos por todas partes. En estas andas habia riqueza, y en algunas estaba esculpido el Sol y la luna, y en otras unas culebras grandes ondadas y unos como bastones que las atravesaban. Esto trahian por encima por armas, y estas andas las llevaban en ombros de los Señores, los mayores y mas principales del Reyno, y aquel que mas con ellas andaba, aquel se tenia por mas onrado y por mas faborecido. En rededor de las andas, a la ila, iba la guardia del Rey con los arqueros y alabarderos, y delante iban cinco mil honderos, y detras venian otros tantos Lanceros con sus Capitanes, y por los lados del camino y por el mesmo camino iban corredores fides, descubriendo lo que habia, y avisando la ida del Señor; y acudia tanta gente por lo ver, que parecia que todos los cerros y laderas estaba lleno de ella, y todos le davan las vendiciones, alzando alaridos, y grita grande á su usanza, llamandole, *Ancha atunapo indichiri campa capalla apatuco pacha camba bolla Yulley*, que en nuestra lengua dirá "Muy grande y poderoso Señor, hijo del Sol, tu solo eres Señor, todo el mundo te oya en verdad," y sin esto le decian otras cosas mas altas, tanto que poco faltaba para le adorar por Dios. Todo el camino iban Yndios llimpiandolo, de tal manera que ni yerba ni piedra no parecia, sino todo limpio y barrido. Andaba cada dia cuatro leguas, o lo que el queria, paraba lo que era servido, para enterder el estado de su Reyno, oia alegremente a los que con quejas le venian, remediando, y castigando a quien hacia injusticias; los que con ellos iban no se desmandaban a nada ni salian un paso del camino. Los naturales proveian a lo necesario, sin lo cual lo havia tan cumplido en los depositos, que sobraba, y ninguna cosa faltaba. Por donde iba, salian muchos hombres y mujeres y muchachos a servir personalmente en lo que les era mandado, y para llebar las cargas, los de un pueblo las llebaban hasta otro, de donde los unos las tomaban y los otros las dejaban, y como era un dia, y cuando mucho dos, no lo sentian, ni de ello recivian agravio ninguno. Pues yendo el Señor de esta manera, caminaba por su tierra el tiempo que le placia, viendo por sus ojos lo que pasaba, y proveyendo lo que entendia que convenia, que todo era cosas grandes e importantes; lo cual hecho, daba la buelta al Cuzco, principal Ciudad de todo su imperio.

No. II.—See Vol. I., p. 64.

ACCOUNT OF THE GREAT ROAD MADE BY THE INCAS OVER THE PLATEAU, FROM QUITO TO CUZCO; EXTRACTED FROM SARMIENTO'S RELACION, MS.

Una de las cosas de que yo mas me admiré, contemplando y notando las cosas de estos Reynos, fue pensar como y de que manera se pudieron hacer caminos tan grandes y sovervios como por el vemos, y que fuerzas de hombres bastaran á lo hacer, y con que herramientas y instrumentos pudieron allanar los montes y quebrantar las peñas para hacerlos tan anchos y buenos como estan; por que me parece que si el Emperador quisiese mandar hacer otro camino Real como el que bá del Quito al Cuzco ó sale del Cuzco para ir á Chile, ciertam^te creo, con todo su poder, para ello no fuese poderoso, ni fuerzas de hombres lo pudiesen hacer, sino fuese con la orden tan grande que para ello los Yngas mandaron que hubiese: por que si fuera Camino de cinquenta leguas, ó de ciento, ó de doscientas, es de creer que aunque la tierra fuera mas aspera, no se tubiera en mucho con buena diligencia hacerlo; mas estos eran tan largos que havia alguno que tenia mas de mil y cien leguas, todo hechado por sierras tan grandes y espantosas que por algunas partes mirando abajo so quitaba la vista, y algunas de estas Sierras derechas y llenas de piedras, tanto que era menester cavar por las laderas en peña viva para hacer el camino ancho y llano, todo lo qual hacian con fuego y con sus picos; por otras lugares havia subidas tan altas y asperas, que hacian desde lo bajo escalones para poder subir por ellos á lo mas alto, haciendo entre medias de ellos algunos descansos anchos para el reposo de la gente; en otros lugares havia montones de nieve que eran mas de temer, y estos no en un lugar sino en muchas partes, y no asi como quiera sino que no bá ponderado ni encarecido como ello és, ni como lo bemos, y por estas nieves y por donde havia montañas, de arboles y cespedes lo hacian llano y empedrado si menester fuese. Los que leyeren este Libro y hubieren estado en el Peru, miren el Camino que bá desde Lima á Xauxa por las Sierras tan asperas de Guayacoire y por las montañas nevadas de Pavacaca, y entenderán los que á ellos lo oyeren si es mas lo que ellos vieron que no lo que yo escrivo.

No. III.—See Vol. I., p. 79.

POLICY OBSERVED BY THE INCAS IN THEIR CONQUESTS; TAKEN FROM SARMIENTO'S RELACION, MS.

Una de las cosas de que mas se tiene embidia á estos Señores, és entender quan bien supieron conquistar tan grandes tierras y ponerlas con su prudencia en tanta razon como los Españoles las hallaron quando por ellos fué descubierto este Reyno, y de que esto sea asi muchas vezes me acuerdo yo estando en alguna Provincia indomita fuera de estos Reynos oir luego á los mesmos Españoles yo aseguro que si los Yngas anduvieran por aqui que otra cosa fuera esto, es decir no conquistaran los Yngas esto como lo otro porque supieran servir y tributar, por manera que quanto á esto, conozida está la ventaja que nos hacen pues con su orden las gentes vivian con ella y crecian en multiplicacion, y de las Provincias esteriles hacian fertiles y abundantes en tanta manera y por tan galana orden como se dirá, siempre procuraron de hacer por bien las cosas y no por mal en el comienzo de los negocios, despues algunos Yngas hicieron grandes castigos en muchas partes, pero antes todos afirman que fue grande con la benevolencia y amicicia que procuraban el atraer á su servicio estas gentes, ellos salian del Cuzco con su gente y aparato de guerra y caminaban con gran concierto hasta cerca de donde havian de ir, y querian conquistar, donde muy bastantemente se informaban del poder que tenian los enemigos y de las ayudas que podrian tener y de que parte les podrian venir favores y por que Camino, y esto entendido por ellos, procuraban por las vias á ellos posibles estorvar que no fuesen socorridos ora con dones grandes que hacian ora con resistencias que ponian, entendiendo sin esto de mandar hacer sus fuertes, los quales eran en Cerro ó ladera hechos en ellos ciertas Cercas altas y largas, con su puerta cada una, porque perdida la una pudiesen pasarse a la otra y de la otra hasta lo mas alto, y embiaban esanchas de los Confederados para marcar la tierra y ver los caminos y conocer del arte q^e estaban aguardando y por donde havia mas mantenimiento, saviendo por el camino que havian de llevar y la orden con que havian de ir, embiabales mensageros propios con los quales les embiaba á decir, que él los queria tener por parientes y aliados, por tanto que con buen animo y corazon alegre se saliesen á lo recevir y recevirlo an su Provincia, para que an ella le sea dada la obediencia como en las demas, y porq^e lo hagan con voluntad, embiaba presentes á los Señores naturales, y con esto y con otras buenas maneras que tenia entraron en muchas tierras sin guerra, en las quales mandaban á la gente de guerra que con él iba que no hiciesen daño ni injuria ninguna ni robo ni fuerza, y si en tal

Provincia no havia mantenimiento mandaba que de otra parte se proveyese, porque á los nuebamente venidos á su servicio no les pareciese desde luego pesado su mando y conocimiento, y el conocerle y aborrecerle fuese en un tiempo, y si en alguna de estas Provincias no havia ganado mandaba luego que les diese por quenta tantas mil Cavezas, lo qual mandaban que mirasen mucho y con ello multiplicasen para proberse de Lana para sus Ropas, y que no fuesen osados de comer ni matar ninguna cria por los años y tiempo que les señalaba, y si havia ganado y tenian de otra cosa falta era lo mismo, y si estaban en Collados y arenales bien les hacian entender con buenas palabras que hiciesen Pueblos y Casas en lo mas llano de las Sierras y laderas, y como muchos no eran diestros en cultibar las tierras abecavanles como lo havian de hacer imponiendoles en que supiesen sacar acequias y regar con ellas los Campos, en todo los havian de proveer tan concertadamente que quando entraba por amistad alguno de los Yngas en Provincias de estas, en brebe tiempo quedaba tal que parecia otra y los naturales le daban la obediencia consintiendo que sus delegados quedasen en ellos, y lo mismo los Mitimaes; en otras muchas que entraron de guerra y por fuerza de armas mandabase que en los mantenimientos y Casas de los enemigos se hiciese poco daño, diciendoles el Señor, presto serán estos nuestros como los que ya lo son; como esto tenian conocido, procuraban q̃. la guerra fuese la mas liviana que ser pudiese, no embargante que en muchos lugares se dieron grandes batallas, porque todavia los naturales de ellos querian conservarse en la livertad antigua sin perder sus costumbres y Religion por tomar otras estrañas, mas durando la guerra siempre havian los Yngas lo mejor, y vencidos no los destruian de nuebo, antes mandaban restituhir los Presos si algunos havia y el despojo y ponerlos en posesion de sus haciendas y señorio, amonestandoles que no quieran ser locos en tener contra su Persona Real competencias ni dejar su amistad, antes querian ser sus amigos como lo son los Comarcanos suyos, y diciendoles esto, dabanles algunas mugeres hermosas y presas ricas de Lana ó de metal de oro, con estas dadivas y buenas palabras havia las voluntades de todos, de tal manera que sin ningun temor los huidos á los montes se bolvian á sus Casas y todos dejaban las armas y el que mas veces veia al Ynga se tenia por mas bien aventurado y dichoso. Los señorios nunca los tiraban a los naturales, á todos mandaban unos y otros que por Dios adorasen el Sol; sus demas religiones y costumbres no se las prohivian, pero mandabanles que se governasen por las Leyes y costumbres que se governaban en el Cuzco y que todos hablasen en la Lengua general, y puesto Governador por el Señor con guarniciones de gente de guerra, parten para lo de adelante; y si estas Provincias eran grandes, luego se entendia en edificar Temple del Sol y colocar las mugeres que ponian en los demas y hacer Palacios para los Señores, y cobraban para los tributos que havian de pagar sin llevarles nada demasiado ni agraviarles en cosa ninguna, encaminandoles en su policia y en que supiesen hacer edificios y traer ropas largas y vivir concertadamente en sus Pueblos, á los quales si algo les faltaba de que tubiesen necesidad eran provehidos y enseñados como lo havian de sembrar y beneficiar, de tal manera se hacia esto que sabemos en muchos Lugares que no havia maiz, tenello despues sobrado, y en todo lo demas andaban como salvages mal vestidos y descalsos, y desde que conocieron á estos Señores usaron de Camisetas lares y mantas y las mugeres lo mismo y de otras buenas cosas, tanto que para siempre habra memoria de todo ello; y en el Collao y en otras partes mandó pasar Mitimaes á la Sierra de los Andes para que sembrasen maiz y coca y otras frutas y raizes de todos los Pueblos la cantidad combeniente, los quales con sus mugeres vivian siempre en aquella parte donde sembraban y cojian tanto de lo que digo que se sentia poco la falta por traer mucho de estas partes y no haver Pueblo ninguno por pequeño que fuese que no tubiese de estos Mitimaes. Adelante trataremos quantas suertes havia de estos Mitimaes y hacian los unos y entendian los otros.

No. IV.—See Vol. I., p. 171.

EXTRACT FROM THE LAST WILL AND TESTAMENT
OF MANCIO SIERRA LEJESEMA, MS.

[The following is the preamble of the testament of a soldier of the Conquest, named Lejesema. It is in the nature of a death-bed confession; and seems intended to relieve the writer's mind, who sought to expiate his own sins by this sincere though tardy tribute to the merits of the vanquished. As the work in which it appears is rarely to be met with, I have extracted the whole of the preamble.]

Verdadera confesion y protestacion en articulo de muerte hecha por uno de los primeros españoles conquistadores del Peru, nombrado Mancio Sierra Lejesema, con su testamento otorgado en la ciudad del Cuzco el dia 15 de Setiembre de 1589 ante Geronimo Sanchez de Quesada escribano publico: la qual la trae el P. Fr. Antonio Calancha del orden de hermitanos de San Agustin en la cronica de su religion en el lib. 1, cap. 15, folio 98, y es del tenor siguiente.

"Primeramente antes de empezar dicho mi testamento, declaro que ha muchos años que yo he deseado tener orden de advertir a la Catolica Majestad del Rey Don Felipe, nuestro Señor, viendo cuan catolico y cristianisimoes, y cuan zeloso del servicio de Dios nuestro Señor, por lo que toca al descargo de mi anima, à causa de haber sido yo mucho parte en descubrimiento, conquista, y poblacion de estos Reynos, cuando los quitamos a los que eran Señores Ingas, y los poseian, y regian como suyos propios, y los pusimos debajo de la real corona, que entienda su Majestad Catolica que los dichos Ingas los tenian gobernados de tal manera, que en todos ellos no habia un Ladron ni hombre vicioso, ni hombre holgazán, ni una muger adúltera ni mala; ni se permitia entre ellos ni gente de mal vivir en lo moral; que los hombres tenian sus ocupaciones honestas y provechosas; y que los montes y minas, pastos, caza y madera, y todo genero de aprovechamientos estaba gobernado y repartido de suerte que cada uno conocia y tenia su hacienda sin que otro ninguno se la ocupase ò tomase, ni sobre ello habian pleytos; y que las cosas de guerra, aunque eran muchas, no impedian à las del Comercio, ni estas a las cosas de labranza, ò cultivar de las tierras, ni otra cosa alguna, y que en todo, desde lo mayor hasta lo mas menudo, tenia su orden y concierto con mucho acierto: y que los Ingas eran tenidos y obecidos y respetados de sus subditos como gente muy capaz y de mucho Gobierno, y que lo mismo eran sus Gobernadores y Capitanes, y que como en estos hallamos la fuerza y el mando y la resistencia para poderlos sugetar é oprimir al servicio de Dios nuestro Señor y quitarles su tierra y ponerla debaxo de la real corona, fue necesario quitarles totalmente el poder y mando y los bienes, como se los quitamos á fuerza de armas: y que mediante haberlo permitido Dios nuestro Señor nos fue posible sujetar este reyno de tanta multitud de gente y riqueza, y de Señores los hicimos Siervos tan sujetos, como se ve: y que entienda su Magestad que el intento que me mueve à hacer esta relacion, es por descargo de mi conciencia, y por hallarme culpado en ello, pues habemos destruido con nuestro mal exemplo gente de tanto gobierno como eran estos naturales, y tan quitados de cometer delitos ni excesos asi hombres como mugeres, tanto por el Indio que tenia cien mil pesos de oro y plata en su casa, y otros indios dejaban abierta y puesta una escoba ò un palo pequeño atravesado en la puerta para señal de que no estaba alli su dueño, y con esto segun su costumbre no podia entrar nadie adentro, ni tomar cosa de las que alli habia, y cuando ellos vieron que nosotros poniamos puertas y llaves en nuestras casas entendieron que era de miedo de ellos, porque no nos matasen, pero no porque creyesen que ninguno tomase ni hurtase á otro su hacienda; y asi cuando vieron que habia entre nosotros ladrones, y hombres que incitaban á pecado á sus mugeres y hijas nos tubieron en poco, y han venido á tal rotura en ofensa de Dios estos naturales por el mal exemplo que les hemos dado en todo, que aquel extremo de no hacer cosa mala se ha convertido en que hoy ninguna ò pocas hacen buenas, y requieren remedio, y esto toca à su Magestad, para que descargue su conciencia, y se lo advierte, pues no soy parte para mas; y con esto suplico à mi Dios me perdone; y mueveme à decirlo porque soy el postrero que mueve de todos los descubridores y conquistadores, que como es notorio ya no hay ninguno, sino yo solo en este reyno, ni fuera de el, y con esto hago lo que puedo para descargo de mi conciencia."

No. V.—See Vol. I., p. 233.

TRANSLATION FROM OVIEDO'S HISTORIA GENERAL DE LAS INDIAS, MS., PARTE II., CAP. 23.

[This chapter of the gossiping old chronicler describes a conversation between the governor of Tierra Firme and Almagro, at which the writer was present. It is told with much spirit; and is altogether so curious, from the light it throws on the characters of the parties, that I have thought the following translation, which has been prepared for me, might not be uninteresting to the English reader.]

The Interview Between Almagro and Pedrarias, in which the Latter Relinquished his Share of the Profits Arising from the Discovery of Peru. Translated from Oviedo, Historia General, MS., Parte II., Cap. 23.

In February, 1527, I had some accounts to settle with Pedrarias, and was frequently at his house for the purpose. While there one day, Almagro came in and said to him, — "Your Excellency is of course aware that you contracted with Francisco Pizarro, Don Fernando de Luque, the schoolmaster, and myself, to fit out an expedition for the discovery of Peru. You have contributed nothing for the enterprise, while we have sunk both fortune and credit; for our expenses have already amounted to about fifteen thousand *castellanos de oro*. Pizarro and his followers are now in the greatest distress, and require a supply of provisions, with a reinforcement of brave recruits. Unless these are promptly raised, we shall be wholly ruined, and our glorious enterprise, from which the most brilliant results have been justly anticipated, will fall to the ground. An exact account will be kept of our expenses, that each may share the profits of the discovery in proportion to the amount of his contribution towards the outfit. You have connected yourself with us in the adventure, and, from the terms of our contract, have no right to waste our time and involve us in ruin. But if you no longer wish to be a member of the partnership, pay down your share of what has already been advanced, and leave the affair to us."

To this proposal Pedrarias replied with indignation: — "One would really think, from the lofty tone you take, that my power was at an end; but if I have not been degraded from my office, you shall be punished for your insolence. You shall be made to answer for the lives of the Christians who have perished through Pizarro's obstinacy and your own. A day of reckoning will come for all these disturbances and murders, as you shall see, and that before you leave Panamá."

"I grant," returned Almagro, "that, as there is an almighty Judge, before whose tribunal we must appear, it is proper that all should render account of the living as well as the dead. And, Sir, I shall not shrink from doing so, when I have received an account from you, to be immediately sent to Pizarro, of the gratitude which our sovereign, the emperor, has been pleased to express for our services. Pay, — if you wish to enjoy the fruits of this enterprise; for you neither sweat nor toil for them, and have not contributed even a third of the sum you promised when the contract was drawn up, — your whole expenditure not exceeding two or three paltry *pesos*. But if you prefer to leave the partnership at once, we will remit one half of what you owe us, for our past outlays."

Pedrarias, with a bitter smile, replied, — "It would not ruin you, if you were to give me four thousand *pesos* to dissolve our connection."

"To forward so happy an event," said Almagro, "we will release you from your whole debt, although it may prove our ruin; but we will trust our fortunes in the hand of God."

Although Pedrarias found himself relieved from the debt incurred for the outfit of the expedition, which could not be less than four or five thousand *pesos*, he was not satisfied, but asked, "What more will you give me?"

Almagro, much chagrined, said, "I will give three hundred *pesos*, though I swear by God, I have not so much money in the world; but I will borrow it to be rid of such an incubus."

"You must give me two thousand."

"Five hundred is the most I will offer."

"You must pay me more than a thousand."

"A thousand *pesos*, then," cried the captain in a rage, "I will give you, though I do not own them; but I will find sufficient security for their future payment."

Pedrarias declared himself satisfied with this arrangement; and a contract was accordingly drawn up, in which it was agreed, that, on the receipt of a thousand *pesos*, the governor should abandon the partnership, and give up his share in the profits of the expedition. I was one of the witnesses who signed this instrument, in which Pedrarias released and assigned over all his interest in Peru to Almagro and his associates, — by this act deserting the enterprise, and, by his littleness of soul, forfeiting the rich treasures which it is well known he might have acquired from the golden empire of the Incas.

No. VI. — See Vol. I., p. 236.

CONTRACT BETWEEN PIZARRO, ALMAGRO, AND LUQUE; EXTRACTED FROM MONTESINOS, ANNALES, MS., AÑO 1526.

[This memorable contract between three adventurers for the discovery and partition of an empire is to be found entire in the manuscript history of Montesinos, whose work derives more value from the insertion in it of this, and of other original documents, than from any merit of its own. This instrument, which may be considered as the basis of the operations of Pizarro, seems to form a necessary appendage to a history of the Conquest of Peru.]

En el nombre de la santisima Trinidad, Padre, Hijo y Espíritu-Santo, tres personas distintas y un solo Dios verdadero, y de la santísima Vírgen nuestra Señora hacemos esta compañía. —

Sepan cuantos esta carta de compañía vieren como yo don Fernando de Luque, clérigo presbítero, vicario de la santa iglesia de Panamá, de la una parte; y de la otra el capitan Francisco Pizarro y Diego de Almagro, vecinos que somos en esta ciudad de Panamá, decimos: que somos concertados y convenidos de hacer y formar compañia la cual sea firme y valedera para siempre jamas en esta manera: — Que por cuanto nos los dichos capitan Francisco Pizarro y Diego de Almagro, tenemos licencia del señor gobernador Pedro Arias de Avila para descubrir y conquistar las tierras y provincias de los reinos llamados del Peru, que está, por noticia que hay, pasado el golfo y travesía del mar de la otra parte; y porque para hacer la dicha conquista y jornada y navios y gente y bastimento y otras cosas que son necesarias, no lo podemos hacer por no tener dinero y posibilidad tanta cuanta es menester; y vos el dicho don Fernando de Luque nos los dais porque esta compañia la hagamos por iguales partes: somos contentos y convenidos de que todos tres hermanablemente, sin que hagan de haber ventaja ninguna mas el uno que el otro, ni el otro que el otro de todo lo que se descubriere, ganare y conquistare, y poblar en los dichos reinos y provincias del Perú. Y por cuanto vos el dicho D. Fernando de Luque nos disteis, y poneis de puesto por vuestra parte en esta dicha compañia para gastos de la armada y gente que se hace para la dicha jornada y conquista del dicho reino del Perú, veinte mil pesos en barras de oro y de á cuatrocientos y cincuenta maravedis el peso, los cuales los recibimos luego en las dichas barras de oro que pasaron de vuestro poder al nuestro en presencia del escribano de esta carta, que lo valió y monto; y yo Hernando del Castillo doy fé que los vide pesar los dichos veinte mil pesos en las dichas barras de oro y lo recibieron en mi presencia los dichos capitan Francisco Pizarro y Diego de Almagro, y se dieron por contentos y pagados de ella. Y nos los dichos capitan Francisco Pizarro y Diego de Almagro ponemos de nuestra parte en esta dicha compañia la merced que tenemos del dicho señor gobernador, y que la dicha conquista y reino que descubriremos de la tierra del dicho Perú, que en nombre de S. M. nos ha hecho, y las demas mercedes que nos hiciere y acrescentare S. M., y los de su consejo de las Indias de aqui adelante, para que de todo goceis y hayais vuestra tercera parte, sin que en cosa alguna hayamos de tener mas parte cada uno de nos, el uno que el otro, sino que hayamos de todo ello partes iguales. Y mas ponemos en esta dicha compañia nuestras personas y el haber de hacer la dicha conquista y descubrimiento con asistir con ellas en la guerra todo el tiempo que se tardare en conquistar y ganar y poblar el dicho reino del Perú, sin que por ello hayamos de llevar ninguno ventaja y parte mas de la que vos el dicho don Fernando de Luque llevaredes, que ha de ser por iguales partes todos tres, asi de los aprovechamientos que con nuestras personas tuvieremos, y ventajas de las partes que nos cupieren en la guerra y en los despojos y ganancias y suertes que en la dicha tierra del Perú hubiéremos y gozáremos, y nos cupieren por cualquier via y forma que sea, asi á mi el dicho capitan Francisco Pizarro como á mi Diego de Almagro, habeis de haber de todo ello, y es vuestro, y os lo daremos bien y fielmente, sin desfraudaros en cosa alguna de ello, la tercera parte, porque desde ahora en lo que Dios nuestro Señor nos diere, decimos y confesamos que es vuestro y de vuestros herederos y succesores, de quien en esta dicha compañia succediere y lo hubiere de haber, en vuestro nombre se lo daremos, y le daremos cuenta de todo ello á vos, y á vuestros succesores, quieta y pacificamente, sin llevar mas parte cada uno de nos, que vos el dicho don Fernando de Luque, y quien vuestro poder hubiere y le perteneciere; y asi de cualquier dictado y estado de señorio perpetuo, ó por tiempo señalado que S. M. nos hiciere merced en el dicho reino del Perú, así á mí el dicho capitan Francisco Pizarro, ó á mí el dicho Diego de Almagro, ó á cualquiera de nos, sea vuestro el tercio de toda la renta y estado y vasallos que á cada uno de nos se nos diere y hiciere merced en cualquiera manera ó forma que sea en el dicho reino del Perú por via de estado, ó renta, repartimiento de indios, situaciones, vasallos, seais señor y goceis de la tercia parte de ello como nosotros mismos, sin adicion ni condicion ninguna, y si la hubiere y alegáremos, yo el dicho capitan Francisco Pizarro y Diego de Almagro, y en nuestros nombres nuestros herederos, que no seamos oidos en juicio ni fuera dél, y nos damos por condenados en todo y por todo como en esta escriptura se contiene para lo pagar y que haya efecto; y yo el dicho D. Fernando de Luque hago la dicha compañia en la forma y manera que de suso está declarado, y doy los veinte mil pesos de buen oro para el dicho descubrimiento y conquista del dicho reino del Perú, á perdida ó ganancia, como Dios nuestro Señor sea servido, y de lo sucedido en el dicho descubrimiento de la dicha gobernacion y tierra, he yo de gozar y haber la tercera parte, y la otra tercera para el capitan Francisco Pizarro, y la otra tercera para Diego de Almagro, sin que el uno lleve mas que el otro, asi de estado de señor, como de repartimiento de indios perpétuos, como de tierras y solares y heredades; como de tesoros, y escondijos encubiertos, como de cualquier riqueza ó aprovechamiento de oro, plata, perlas, esmeraldas, diamantes y rubíes, y de cualquier estado y condicion que sea, que los dichos capitan Francisco Pizarro y Diego de Almagro hayais y tengais en el dicho reino del Perú, me habeis de dar la tercera parte. Y nos el dicho capitan Francisco Pizarro y Diego de Almagro decimos que aceptamos la dicha compañía y la hacemos con el dicho don Fernando de Luque de la forma y manera que lo pide él, y lo declara para que todos por iguales partes hayamos en todo y por todo, asi de estados perpetuos que S. M. nos hiciese mercedes en vasallos ó indios ó en otras cualesquiera rentas, goce el derecho don Fernando de Luque, y haya la dicha tercia parte de todo ello enteramente, y goce de ello como cosa suya desde el dia que S. M. nos hiciere cualesquiera mercedes como dicho es. Y para mayor verdad y seguridad de esta escriptura de compañia, y de todo lo en ella contenido, y que os acudirémos y pagarémos nos los dichos capitan Francisco Pizarro y Diego de Almagro á vos el dicho Fernando de Luque con la tercia parte de todo lo que se hubiere y descubriere, y nosotros hubiéremos por cualquiera via y forma que sea; para mayor fuerza de que lo cumpliremos como en esta escriptura se contiene, juramos a Dios nuestro señor y á los Santos Evangelios donde mas largamente son escritos y estan en este libro Misal, donde pusieron sus manos el dicho capitan Francisco Pizarro, y Diego de Almagro, hicieron la señal de la cruz en semejanza de esta † con sus dedos de la mano en presencia de mí el presente escribano, y dijeron que guardarán y cumplirán esta dicha compañia y escriptura en todo y por todo, como en ello se contiene, sopena de infames y malos cristianos, y caer en caso de menos valer, y que Dios se lo demande mal y caramente; y dijeron el dicho capitan Francisco Pizarro y Diego de Almagro, amen; y asi lo juramos y le daremos el tercio de todo lo que descubriéremos y conquistáremos y pobláremos en el dicho reino y tierra del Perú, y que goce de ello como nuestras personas, de todo aquello en que fuere nuestro y tuviéremos parte como dicho es en esta dicha escriptura; y nos obligamos de acudir con ello á vos el dicho don Fernando de Luque, y á quien en vuestro nombre le perteneciere y hubiere de haber, y les daremos cuenta con pago de todo ello cada y cuando que se nos pidiere, hecho el dicho descubrimiento y conquista y poblacion del dicho reino y tierra del Perú; y prometemos que en la dicha conquista y descubrimiento nos ocuparémos y trabajarémos con nuestras personas sin ocuparnos en otra cosa hasta que se conquiste la tierra y se ganáre, y si no lo hiciéremos seamos castigados por todo rigor de justicia por infames y perjuros, seamos obligados á volver á vos el dicho don Fernando de Luque los dichos veinte mil pesos de oro que de vos recibimos. Y para lo cumplir y pagar y haber por firme todo lo en esta escriptura contenido, cada uno por lo que le toca, renunciaron todas y cualesquier leyes y ordenamientos, y pramáticas, y otras cualesquier constituciones, ordenanzas que estén fechas en su favor, y cualesquiera de ellos para que aunque las pidan y aleguen, que no les valga. Y valga esta escriptura dicha, y todo lo en ella contenido, y traiga aparejada y debida ejecucion asi en sus personas come en sus bienes, muebles y raices habidos y por haber; y para lo cumplir y pagar, cada uno por lo que le toca, obligaron sus personas y bienes habidos y por haber segun dicho es, y dieron poder cumplido á cualesquier justicias y jueces de S. M. para que por todo rigor y mas breve remedio de derecho les compelan y apremien á lo asi cumplir y pagar, como si lo que dicho es fuese sentencia difinitiva de juez competente pasada en cosa juzgada; y renunciaron cualesquier leyes y derechos que en su favor hablan, especialmente la ley que dice: Que general renunciacion de leyes no vala: Que es fecha en la ciudad de Panamá á diez dias del mes de marzo, año del nacimiento de nuestro Salvador Jesucristo de mil quinientos veinte y seis años: testigos que fueron presentes á lo que dicho es Juan de Panés, y Alvaro del Quiro y Juan de Vallejo, vecinos de la ciudad de Panamá, y firmó el dicho D. Fernando de Luque; y porque no saben firmar el dicho capitan Francisco Pizarro y Diego de Almagro, firmaron por ellos en el registro de esta carta Juan de Panés y Alvaro del Quiro, á los cuales otorgantes yo el presente escribano doy fé que conozco. Don Fernando de Luque.—A su ruego de Francisco Pizarro—Juan de Panés; y á su ruego de Diego de Almagro—Alvaro del Quiro: E yo Hernando del Castillo, escribano de S. M. y escribano publico y del numero de esta ciudad de Panamá, presente fui al otorgamiento de esta carta, y la fice escribir en estas cuatro fojas con esta, y por ende fice aquí este mi signo á tal en testimonio de verdad. Hernando del Castillo, escribano publico.

No. VII.—See Vol. I., pp. 211, 307.

CAPITULATION MADE BY FRANCIS PIZARRO WITH THE QUEEN,
MS., DATED TOLEDO, JULY 26, 1529.

[For a copy of this document, I am indebted to Don Martin Fernandez de
Navarrete, late Director of the Royal Academy of History at Madrid. Though
sufficiently long, it is of no less importance than the preceding contract, forming, like that, the foundation on which the enterprise of Pizarro and his associates may be said to have rested.]

La Reina:—Por cuanto vos el capitan Francisco Pizarro, vecino de Tierra
firme, llamada Castilla del Oro, por vos y en nombre del venerable padre D.
Fernando de Luque, maestre escuela y provisor de la iglesia del Darien, *sede
vacante,* que es en la dicha Castilla del Oro, y el capitan Diego de Almagro,
vecino de la ciudad de Panamá, nos hicísteis relacion, que vos e los dichos vuestros compañeros con deseo de nos servir e del bien e acrecentamiento de
nuestra corona real, puede haber cinco años, poco mas o menos, que con
licencia e parecer de Pedrarias Dávila, nuestro gobernador e capitan general
que fue de la dicha Tierra firme, tomastes cargo de ir a conquistar, descubrir
e pacificar e poblar por la costa del mar del Sur, de la dicha tierra a la parte de
Levante, a vuestra costa e de los dichos vuestros compañeros, todo lo mas que
por aquella parte pudiéredes, e hicísteis para ello dos navíos e un bergantin
en la dicha costa, en que asi en esto por se haber de pasar la jarcia e aparejos
necesarios al dicho viaje e armada desde el Nombre de Dios, que es la costa
del Norte, a la otra costa del Sur, como con la gente e otras cosas necesarias al
dicho viaje, e tornar a rehacer la dicha armada, gastásteis mucha suma de
pesos de oro, e fuistes a hacer e hicísteis el dicho descubrimiento, donde
pasastes muchos peligros e trabajo, a causa de lo cual os dejó toda la gente
que con vos iba en una isla despoblada con solos trece hombres que no vos
quisieron dejar, y que con ellos y con el socorro que de navíos e gente vos hizo
el dicho capitan Diego de Almagro, pasastes de la dicha isla e descubristes las
tierras e provincias del Pirú e ciudad de Tumbes, en que habeis gastado vos e
los dichos vuestros compañeros mas de treinta mil pesos de oro, e que con el
deseo que teneis de nos servir querríades continuar la dicha conquista e
poblacion a vuestra costa e mision, sin que en ningun tiempo seamos obligados a vos pagar ni satisfacer los gastos que en ello hiciéredes, mas de lo que en
esta capitulacion vos fuese otorgado, e me suplicasteis e pedistes por merced
vos mandase encomendar la conquista de las dichas tierras, e vos concediese e
otorgase las mercedes, e con las condiciones que de suso serán contenidas;
sobre lo cual yo mandé tomar con vos el asiento y capitulacion siguiente.

Primeramente doy licencia y facultad a vos el dicho capitan Francisco
Pizarro, para que por nos y en nuestro nombre e de la corona real de Castilla,
podais continuar el dicho descubrimiento, conquista y poblacion de la dicha
provincia del Perú, fasta ducientas leguas de tierra por la misma costa, las

cuales dichas ducientas leguas comienzan desde el pueblo que en lengua de indios se dice Tenumpuela, e despues le llamásteis Santiago, hasta llegar al pueblo de Chincha, que puede haber las dichas ducientas leguas de costa, poco mas o menos.

ITEM: Entendiendo ser cumplidero al servicio de Dios nuestro Señor y nuestro, y por honrar vuestra persona, e por vos hacer merced, prometemos de vos hacer nuestro gobernador e capitan general de toda la dicha provincia del Pirú, e tierras y pueblos que al presente hay e adelante hubiere en todas las dichas ducientas leguas, por todos los dias de vuestra vida, con salario de setecientos e veinte y cinco mill maravedís cada año, contados desde el dia que vos hiciésedes a la vela destos nuestros reinos para continuar la dicha poblacion e conquista, los cuales vos han de ser pagados de las rentas y derechos a nos pertenecientes en la dicha tierra que ansi habeis de poblar; del cual salario habeis de pagar en cada un año un alcalde mayor, diez escuderos, e treinta peones, e un médico, e un boticario, el cual salario vos ha de ser pagado por los nuestros oficiales de la dicha tierra.

OTROSI: Vos hacemos merced de título de nuestro Adelantado de la dicha provincia del Perú, e ansimismo del oficio de alguacil mayor della, todo ello por los dias de vuestra vida.

OTROSI: Vos doy licencia para que con parecer y acuerdo de los dichos nuestros oficiales podais hacer en las dichas tierras e provincias del Perú, hasta cuatro fortalezas, en las partes y lugares que mas convengan, paresciendo a vos e a los dichos nuestros oficiales ser necesarias para guarda e pacificacion de la dicha tierra, e vos haré merced de las tenencias dellas, para vos, e para los herederos, e subcesores vuestros, uno en pos de otro, con salario de setenta y cinco mill maravedís en cada un año por cada una de las dichas fortalezas, que ansi estuvieren hechas, las cuales habeis de hacer a vuestra costa, sin que nos, ni los reyes que despues de nos vinieren, seamos obligado a vos lo pagar al tiempo que asi lo gastáredes, salvo dende en cinco años despues de acabada la fortaleza, pagándoos en cada un año de los dichos cinco años la quinta parte de lo que se montare el dicho gasto, de los frutos de la dicha tierra.

OTROSI: Vos hacemos merced para ayuda a vuestra costa de mill ducados en cada un año por los dias de vuestra vida de las rentas de las dichas tierras.

OTROSI: Es nuestra merced, acatando la buena vida e doctrina de la persona del dicho don Fernando de Luque de le presentar a nuestro muy Sancto Padre por obispo de la ciudad de Tumbes, que es en la dicha provincia y gobernacion del Perú, con límites e diciones que por nos con autoridad apostólica serán señalados; y entretanto que vienen las bulas del dicho obispado, le hacemos protector universal de todos los indios de dicha provincia, con salario de mill ducados en cada un año, pagado de nuestras rentas de la dicha tierra, entretanto que hay diezmos eclesiásticos de que se pueda pagar.

OTROSI: Por cuanto nos habedes suplicado por vos en el dicho nombre vos hiciese merced de algunos vasallos en las dichas tierras, e al presente lo dejamos de hacer por no tener entera relacion de ellas, es nuestra merced que, entretanto que informados proveamos en ello lo que a nuestro servicio e a la enmienda e satisfaccion de vuestros trabajos e servicios conviene, tengais la veintena parte de los pechos que nos tuviéremos en cada un año en la dicha tierra, con tanto que no exceda de mill y quinientos ducados, los mill para vos el dicho capitan Pizarro, e los quinientos para el dicho Diego de Almagro.

OTROSI: Hacemos merced al dicho capitan Diego de Almagro de la tenencia de la fortaleza que hay u obiere en la dicha ciudad de Tumbes, que es en la dicha provincia del Perú, con salario de cien mill maravedís cada un año, con mas ducientos mill maravedís cada un año de ayuda de costa, todo pagado de las rentas de la dicha tierra, de las cuales ha de gozar desde el dia que vos el dicho Francisco Pizarro llegáredes a la dicha tierra, aunque el dicho capitan Almagro se quede en Panamá, e en otra parte que le convenga; e le haremos home hijodalgo, para que goce de las honras e preminencias que los homes hijodalgo pueden y deben gozar en todas las Indias, islas e tierra firme del mar Océano.

OTROSI: Mandamos que las dichas haciendas, e tierras, e solares que teneis en tierra firme, llamada Castilla del Oro, e vos estan dadas como a vecino de ella, las tengais e goceis, e hagais de ello lo que quisiéredes e por bien tuviéredes, conforme a lo que tenemos concedido y otorgado a los vecinos de la dicha tierra firme; e en lo que toca a los indios e naborias que teneis e vos estan encomendados, es nuestra merced e voluntad e mandamos que los tengais e goceis e sirvais de ellos, e que no vos serán quitados ni removidos por el tiempo que nuestra voluntad fuere.

OTROSI: Concedemos a los que fueren a poblar la dicha tierra que en los seis años primeros siguientes desde el dia de la data de esta en adelante, que del oro que se cogiere de las minas nos paguen el diezmo, y cumplidos los dichos seis años paguen el noveno, e ansi decendiendo en cada un año hasta llegar al quinto: pero del oro e otras cosas que se obieren de rescatar, o cabalgadas, o en otra cualquier manera, desde luego nos han de pagar el quinto de todo ello.

OTROSI: Franqueamos a los vecinos de la dicha tierra por los dichos seis años, y mas, y cuanto fuere nuestra voluntad, de almojarifazgo de todo lo que llevaren para proveimiento e provision de sus casas, con tanto que no sea para lo vender; e de lo que vendieren ellos, e otras cualesquier personas, mercaderes e tratantes, ansimesmo los franqueamos por dos años tan solamente.

ITEM: Prometemos que por término de diez años, e mas adelante hasta que otra cosa mandemos en contrario, no impornemos a los vecinos de las dichas tierras alcabalas ni otro tributo alguno.

ITEM: Concedemos a los dichos vecinos e pobladores que les sean dados por vos los solares y tierras convenientes a sus personas, conforme a lo que se ha hecho e hace en la dicha Isla Española; e ansimismo os daremos poder para que en nuestro nombre, durante el tiempo de vuestra gobernacion, hagais la encomienda de los indios de la dicha tierra, guardando en ella las instrucciones e ordenanzas que vos serán dadas.

ITEM: A suplicacion vuestra hacemos nuestro piloto mayor de la mar del Sur a Bartolomé Ruiz, con setenta y cinco mill maravedís de salario en cada un año, pagados de la renta de la dicha tierra, de los cuales ha de gozar desde el dia que le fuere entregado el título que de ello le mandaremos dar, e en las espaldas se asentará el juramento e solenidad que ha de hacer ante vos, e otorgado ante escribano. Asimismo daremos título de escribano de número e del consejo de la dicha ciudad de Tumbes, a un hijo de dicho Bartolomé Ruiz, siendo habil e suficiente para ello.

OTROSI: Somos contentos e nos place que vos el dicho capitan Pizarro, cuanto nuestra merced e voluntad fuere, tengais la gobernacion e administracion de los indios de la nuestra isla de Flores, que es cerca de Panamá, e goceis para vos e para quien vos quisiéredes, de todos los aprovechamientos que hobiere en la dicha isla, asi de tierras como de solares, e montes, e árboles, e mineros, e pesquería de perlas, con tanto que seais obligado por razon de ello a dar a nos e a los nuestros oficiales de Castilla del Oro en cada un año de los que ansi fuere nuestra voluntad que vos la tengais, ducientos mill maravedís, e mas el quinto de todo el oro e perlas que en cualquier manera e por cualesquier personas se sacare en la dicha isla de Flores, sin descuento alguno, con tanto que los dichos indios de la dicha isla de Flores no los podais ocupar en la pesquería de las perlas, ni en las minas del oro, ni en otros metales, sino en las otras granjerías e aprovechamientos de la dicha tierra, para provision e mantenimiento de la dicha vuestra armada, e de las que adelante obiéredes de hacer para la dicha tierra; e permitimos que si vos el dicho Francisco Pizarro llegado a Castilla del Oro, dentro de dos meses luego siguientes, declarades ante el dicho nuestro gobernador e juez de residencia que alli estuviere, que no vos querais encargar de la dicha isla de Flores, que en tal caso no seais tenudo e obligado a nos pagar por razon de ello las dichas ducientas mill maravedís, e que se quede para nos la dicha isla, como agora la tenemos.

ITEM: Acatando lo mucho que han servido en el dicho viaje e descubrimiento Bartolomé Ruiz, Cristoval de Peralta, e Pedro de Candia, e Domingo de Soria Luce, e Nicolas de Ribera, e Francisco de Cuellar, e Alonso de Molina, e Pedro Alcon, e García de Jerez, e Anton de Carrion, e Alonso Briceño, e Martin de Paz, e Joan de la Torre, e porque vos me lo suplicásteis e pedistes por merced, es nuestra merced e voluntad de les hacer merced, como por la presente vos la hacemos a los que de ellos no son idalgos, que sean idalgos notorios de solar conocido en aquellas partes, e que en ellas e en todas las nuestras Indias, islas y tierra firme del mar Océano, gocen de las preeminencias e libertades, e otras cosas de que gozan, y deben ser guardadas a los hijosdalgo notorios de solar conocido dentro nuestros reinos, e a los que de los susodichos son idalgos, que sean caballeros de espuelas doradas, dando primero la informacion que en tal caso se requiere.

ITEM: Vos hacemos merced de veinte y cinco veguas e otros tantos caballos de los que nos tenemos en la isla de Jamaica, e no las abiendo cuando las pidiéredes, no seamos tenudos al precio de ellas, ni de otra cosa por razon de ellas.

OTROSI: Os hacemos merced de trescientos mill maravedís pagados en Castilla del Oro para el artillería e municion que habeis de llevar a la dicha provincia del Perú, llevando fe de los nuestros oficiales de la casa de Sevilla de las cosas que ansi comprastes, e de lo que vos costó, contando el interese e cambio de ello, e mas os haré merced de otros ducientos ducados pagados en Castilla del Oro para ayuda al acarreto de la dicha artillería e municiones e otras cosas vuestras desde el Nombre de Dios so la dicha mar del Sur.

OTROSI: Vos daremos licencia, como por la presente vos la damos, para que destos nuestros reinos, e del reino de Portugal e islas de Cabo Verde, e dende, vos, e quien vuestro poder hubiere, quisiéredes e por bien tuviéredes, podais pasar e paseis a la dicha tierra de vuestra gobernacion cincuenta esclavos negros en que haya a lo menos el tercio de hembras, libres de todos derechos a nos pertenecientes, con tanto que si los dejáredes e parte de ellos en la isla Española, San Joan, Cuba, Santiago e en Castilla del Oro, e en otra parte alguna los que de ellos ansi dejáredes, sean perdidos e aplicados, e por la presente los aplicamos a nuestra cámara e fisco.

OTROSI: Que hacemos merced y limosna al hospital que se hiciese en la dicha tierra, para ayuda al remedio de los pobres que allá fueren, de cien mill maravedís librados en las penas aplicadas de la cámara de la dicha tierra. Ansimismo a vuestro pedimento e consentimiento de los primeros pobladores de la dicha tierra, decimos que haremos merced, como por la presente la hacemos, á los hospitales de la dicha tierra de los derechos de la escubilla e relaves que hubiere en las fundiciones que en ella se hicieren, e de ello mandaremos dar nuestra provision en forma.

OTROSI: Decimos que mandaremos, e por la presente mandamos, que hayan e residan en la ciudad de Panamá, e donde vos fuere mandado, un carpintero e un calafate, e cada uno de ellos tenga de salario treinta mill maravedís en cada un año dende que comenzaren a residir en la dicha ciudad, o donde, como dicho es, vos les mandáredes; a los cuales les mandaremos pagar por los nuestros oficiales de la dicha tierra de vuestra gobernacion cuando nuestra merced y voluntad fuere.

ITEM: Que vos mandaremos dar nuestra provision en forma para que en la dicha costa del mar del Sur podais tomar cualesquier navíos que hubiéredes menester, de consentimiento de sus dueños, para los viajes que hobiéredes de hacer a la dicha tierra, pagando a los dueños de los tales navíos el flete que justo sea, no embargante que otras personas los tengan fletados para otras partes.

Ansimismo que mandaremos, e por la presente mandamos e defendemos, que destos nuestros reinos no vayan ni pasen a las dichas tierras ningunas personas de las prohibidas que no puedan pasar a aquellas partes, so las penas contenidas en las leyes e ordenanzas e cartas nuestras, que cerca de esto por nos e por los reyes católicos están dadas; ni letrados ni procuradores para usar de sus oficios.

Lo cual que dicho es, e cada cosa e parte de ello vos concedemos, con tanto que vos el dicho capitan Pizarro seais tenudo e obligado de salir destos nuestros reinos con los navíos e aparejos e mantenimientos e otras cosas que fueren menester para el dicho viaje y poblacion, con ducientos e cincuenta hombres, los ciento y cincuenta destos nuestros reinos e otras partes no prohibidas, e los ciento restantes podais llevar de las islas e tierra firme del mar Océano, con tanto que de la dicha tierra firme llamada Castilla del Oro no saqueis mas de veinte hombres, sino fuere de los que en el primero e segundo viaje que vos hicísteis a la dicha tierra del Perú se hallaron con vos, porque a estos damos licencia que puedan ir con vos libremente; lo cual hayais de cumplir desde el dia de la data de esta hasta seis meses primeros siguientes: allegado a la dicha Castilla del Oro, e allegado a Panamá, seais tenudo de proseguir el dicho viaje, e hacer el dicho descubrimiento e poblacion dentro de otros seis meses luego siguientes.

ITEM: Con condicion que cuando saliéredes destos nuestros reinos e llegáredes a las dichas provincias del Perú hayais de llevar y tener con vos a los oficiales de nuestra hacienda, que por nos estan e fueren nombrados; e asimismo las personas religiosas o eclesiásticas que por nos serán señaladas para instruccion de los indios e naturales de aquella provincia a nuestra santa fé católica, con cuyo parecer e no sin ellos habeis de hacer la conquista, descubrimiento e poblacion de la dicha tierra; a los cuales religiosos habeis de dar e pagar el flete e matalotaje, e los otros mantenimientos necesarios conforme a sus personas, todo a vuestra costa, sin por ello les llevar cosa alguna durante la dicha navegacion, lo cual mucho vos lo encargamos que ansi hagais e cumplais, como cosa de servicio de Dios e nuestro, porque de lo contrario nos terníamos de vos por deservidos.

OTROSI: Con condicion que en la dicha pacificacion, conquista y poblacion e tratamiento de dichos indios en sus personas y bienes, seais tenudos e obligados de guardar en todo e por todo lo contenido en las ordenanzas e instrucciones que para esto tenemos fechas, e se hicieren, e vos seran dadas en la nuestra carta e provision que vos mandaremos dar para la encomienda de los dichos indios. E cumpliendo vos el dicho capitan Francisco Pizarro lo contenido en este asiento, en todo lo que a vos toca e incumbe de guardar e cumplir, prometemos, e vos aseguramos por nuestra palabra real que agora e de aqui adelante vos mandaremos guardar e vos será guardado todo lo que ansi vos concedemos, e facemos merced, a vos e a los pobladores e tratantes en la dicha tierra; e para ejecucion y cumplimiento dello, vos mandaremos dar nuestras cartas e provisiones particulares que convengan e menester sean, obligándoos vos el dicho capitan Pizarro primeramente ante escribano público de guardar e cumplir lo contenido en este asiento que a vos toca como dicho es. Fecha en Toledo a 26 de jullio de 1529 años.—YO LA. REINA.—Por mandado de S. M.—Juan Vazquez.

No. VIII.—See Vol. I., p. 417.

CONTEMPORARY ACCOUNTS OF ATAHUALLPA'S SEIZURE.

[As the seizure of the Inca was one of the most memorable, as well as foulest, transactions of the Conquest, I have thought it might be well to put on record the testimony, fortunately in my possession, of several of the parties present on the occasion.]

Relacion del Primer Descubrimiento de la Costa y Mar del Sur, MS.

A la hora de las cuatro comienzan á caminar por su calzada adelante derecho a donde nosotros estabamos, y á las cinco o poco mas llegó á la puerta de la ciudad, quedando todos los campos cubiertos de gente, y asi comenzaron á entrar por la plaza hasta trescientos hombres como mozos despuelas con sus arcos y flechas en las manos, cantando un cantar no nada gracioso para los que lo oyamos, antes espantoso porque parecia cosa infernal, y dieron una vuelta á aquella mezquita amagando al suelo con las manos á limpiar lo que por el estaba, de lo cual habia poca necesidad, porque los del pueblo le tenian bien barrido para cuando entrase. Acabada de dar su vuelta pararon todos juntos, y entró otro escuadron de hasta mil hombres con picas sin yerros tostadas las puntas, todos de una librea de colores, digo que la de los primeros era blanca y colorada, como las casas de un axedrez. Entrado el segundo escuadron entró el tercero de otra librea, todos con martillos en las manos de cobre y plata, que es una arma que ellos tienen, y ansi desta manera entraron en la dicha plaza muchos Señores principales que venian en medio de los delanteros y de la persona de Atabalipa. Detras destos en una litera muy rica, los cabos de los maderos cubiertos de plata, venia la persona de Atabalipa, la cual traian ochenta Señores en hombros todos vestidos de una librea azul muy rica, y él vestido su persona muy ricamente con su corona en la cabeza, y al cuello un collar de esmeraldas grandes, y sentado en la litera en una silla muy pequeña con un coxin muy rico. En llegando al medio de la plaza paró, llevando descubierto el medio cuerpo de fuera; y toda la gente de guerra que estaba en la plaza le tenian en medio, estando dentro hasta seis ó siete mil hombres. Como el vió que ninguna persona salia á el, ni parecia, tubo creido, y asi lo confesó el despues de preso, que nos habiamos escondido de miedo de ver su poder; y dió una voz y dixo: Donde estan estos? A la cual salió del aposento del dicho Gobernador Pizarro el Padre Fray Vicente de Valverde de la orden de los Predicadores, que despues fué obispo de aquella tierra con la bribia en la mano y con él una lengua, y asi juntos llegaron por entre la gente á poder hablar con Atabalipa, al cual le comenzó á decir cosas de la sagrada escriptura, y que nuestro Señor Jesu-Christo mandaba que entre los suyos no hubiese guerra, ni discordia, sino todo paz, y que él en su nombre ansi se lo pedia y requeria; pues habia quedado de tratar della el dia antes, y de venir solo sin gente de guerra. A las cuales palabras y otras muchas que el Frayle le dixo, el estubo callando sin volver respuesta; y tornandole á decir que mirase lo que Dios mandaba, lo cual estaba en aquel libro que llevaba en la mano escripto, admirandose á mi parecer mas de la escriptura, que de lo escripto en ella: le pidió el libro, y le abrió y ojeó, mirando el molde y la orden dél, y despues de visto, le arrojó por entre la gente con mucha ira, el rostro muy encarnizado, diciendo: Decildes á esos, que vengan acá, que no pasaré de aqui hasta que me dén cuenta y satisfagan y paguen lo que han hecho en la tierra. Visto esto por el Frayle y lo poco que aprovechaban sus palabras, tomó su libro, y abajó su cabeza, y fuese para donde estaba el dicho Pizarro, casi corriendo, y dijole: No veis lo que pasa: para que estais en comedimientos y requerimientos con este perro lleno de soberbia, que vienen los campos llenos de Indios? Salid á el, — que yo os absuelvo. Y ansi acabadas de decir estas palabras que fué todo en un instante, tocan las trompetas, y parte de su posada con toda la gente de pie, que con él estaba, diciendo: Santiago á ellos; y asi salimos todos á aquella voz á una, porque todas aquellas casas que salian á la plaza tenian muchas puertas, y parece que se habian fecho á aquel proposito. En arremetiendo los de caballo y rompiendo por ellos todo fué uno, que sin matar sino solo un negro de nuestra parte, fueron todos desbaratados y Atabalipa preso, y la gente puesta en huida, aunque no pudieron huir del tropel, porque la puerta por dó habian entrado era pequeña y con la turbacion no podian salir; y visto los traseros cuan lejos tenian la acoxida y remedio de huir, arri-maronse dos ó tres mil dellos á un lienso de pared, y dieron con él a tierra, el cual salia al campo porque por aquella parte no habia casas, y ansi tubieron camino ancho para huir; y los escuadrones de gente que habian quedado en el campo sin entrar en el pueblo, como vieron huir y dar alaridos, los mas dellos fueron desbaratados y se pusieron en huida, que era cosa harto de ver, que un valle de cuatro ó cinco leguas todo iba cuaxado de gente. En este vino la noche muy presto, y la gente se recogió, y Atabalipa se puso en una casa de piedra, que era el templo del sol, y asi se pasó aquella noche con grand rego-cijo y placer de la vitoria que nuestro Señor nos habia dado, poniendo mucho recabdo en hacer guardia á la persona de Atabalipa para que no volviesen á tomarnosle. Cierto fué permision de Dios y grand acertamiento guiado por su mano, porque si este dia no se prendiera, con la soberbia que trahia, aquella noche fueramos todos asolados por ser tan pocos, como tengo dicho, y ellos tantos.

Pedro Pizarro, Descubrimiento y Conquista de los Reynos del Peru, MS.

Pues despues de aver comido, que acavaria á hora de missa mayor, enpeço á levantar su gente y á venirse hazia Caxamalca. Hechos sus esquadrones, que cubrian los campos, y el metido en vnas ándas enpeço á caminar, viniendo delante del dos mil yndios que le barrian el camino por donde venia cami-nando, y la gente de guerra la mitad de vn lado y la mitad de otro por los cam-pos sin entrar en camino: traia ansi mesmo al señor de Chincha consigo en vnas andas, que parescia á los suyos cossa de admiracion, porque ningun yndio, por señor principal que fuese, avia de parescer delante del sino fuese con vna carga á cuestas y descalzo: pues hera tanta la pateneria que traian d' oro y plata, que hera cossa estraña lo que reluzia con el sol: venian ansi mesmo delante de Atabalipa muchos yndios cantando y danzando. Tardose ste señor en ándar esta media legua que ay dende los baños á donde el estava hasta Caxamalca, dende ora de missa mayor, como digo, hasta tres oras antes que anochesciese. Pues llegada la gente á la puerta de la plaza, enpeçaron á entrar los esquadrones con grandes cantares, y ansi entrando ocuparon toda la plaza por todas partes. Visto el marquez don Francisco Piçarro que Atabalipa venia ya junto á la plaza, embio al padre fr. Vicente de Balverde primero obispo del Cuzco, y á Hernando de Aldana vn buen soldado, y á don Martinillo lengua, que fuesen á hablar á Atabalipa y á requerille de parte de dios y del Rey se subjetase á la ley de nuestro Señor Jesucristo y al servicio de S. Mag., y que el Marquez le tendria en lugar de hermano, y no consintiria le hiziesen enojo ni daño en su tierra. Pues llegado que fue el padre á las andas donde Atabalipa venia, le hablo y le dixo á lo que yva, y le predico cossas de nuestra sancta ffee, declarandoselas la lengua. Llevava el padre vn breviario en las manos donde leya lo que le predicaba: el Atabalipa se lo pidio, y el cerrado se lo dio, y como le tuvo en las manos y no supo abrille arrojole al suelo. Llamo al Aldana que se llegase á el y le diese la espada, y el Aldana la saco y se la mostro, pero no se la quiso dar. Pues pasado lo dicho, el Atabalipa les dixo que se fuesen para Vellacos ladrones, y que los avia de matar á todos. Pues oydo esto, el padre se bolvio y conto al marquez lo que lo avia pasado; y el Atabalipa entro en la plaza con todo su trono que traya, y el señor de Chincha tras del. Desque ovieron entrado y vieron que no parescia español ninguno, pregunto á sus capitanes, Donde estan estos cristianos que no parescen? Ellos le dixeron, Señor, estan escondidos de miedo. Pues visto el marquez don Francisco Piçarro las dos andas, no conosciendo qual hera la de Atabalipa, mando a Joan Piçarro su hermano fuese con los peones que tenia á la vna, y el yria á la otra. Pues mandado esto, hizieron la seña al Candia, el qual solto el tiro, y en soltandolo tocaron las trompetas, y salieron los de acavallo de tropel, y el marquez con los de á pie, como esta dicho, tras dellos, de manera que con el estruendo del tiro y las trompetas y el tropel de los cavallos con los cascaveles los yndios se embararon y se cortaron. Los españoles dieron en ellos y empeçaron á matar, y fue tanto el miedo que los yndios ovieron, que por huir, no pudiendo salir por la puerta, derribaron vn lienzo de vna pared de la çerca de la plaza de largo de mas de dos mil passos y de alto de mas de vn estado. Los de acavallo fueron en su seguimiento hasta los baños, donde hizieron grande estrago, y hizieran mas sino les anochesciera. Pues bolviendo á don Francisco Piçarro y á su hermano, salieron, como estava dicho, con la gente de á pie: el marquez fue á dar con las andas de Atabalipa, y el hermano con el señor de Chincha, al qual mataron alli en las ándas; y lo mismo fuera del Atabalipa sino se hallara el marquez alli, porque no podian derivalle de las andas, que aunque matavan los yndios que las tenian, se metian luego otros de Reffresco á sustentallas, y desta manera estuvieron vn gran rrato fforcejando y matando indios, y de cansados vn español tiro vna cuchillada para matalle, y el marquez don Francisco Piçarro se la rreparo, y del rreparo le hirio en la mano al marquez el español, queriendo dar al Atabalipa, á cuya caussa el marquez dio bozes diciendo: Nadie hiera al indio so pena de la vida. Entendido esto, aguijaron siete ó ocho españoles y asieron de vn bordo de las andas y haziendo fuerça las trastornaron á vn lado, y ansi fue preso el Atabalipa, y el marquez le llevo á su aposento, y alli le puso guardas que le guardavan de dia y de noche. Pues venida la noche, los españoles se recoxieron todos y dieron muchas gracias á nuestro señor por las Mercedes que les avia hecho, y muy contentos en tener presso al señor, porque á no prendelle no se ganara la tierra como se gano.

Carta de Hernando Pizarro, ap. Oviedo, Historia General de las Indias,
MS., lib. 46, cap. 15.

Venia en unas handas, é delante de él hasta trecientos o cuatrocientos Yndios con Camisetas de librea limpiando las pajas del camino, é cantando, é el en medio de la otra gente que eran Caciques é principales, é los mas principales Caciques le traian en los hombros; é entrando en la Plaza subieron doce ó quince Yndios en una fortaleza que alli estaba, é tomaronla a manera de posesion con vandera puesta en una lanza: entrando hasta la mitad de la Plaza reparó alli: é salió un Fraile Dominico que estaba con el Gobernador á hablarle de su parte, que el Gobernador le esperaba en su aposento, que le fuese á hablar, é dijole como era Sacerdote, é que era embiado por el Emperador para que le enseñase las cosas de la fe si quisiesen ser Cristianos, é mostroles un libro que llevaba en las manos, é dijole que aquel libro era de las cosas de Dios; é el Atabaliva pidió el libro, é arrojole en el suelo é dijo: Yo no pasaré de aqui hasta que me deis todo lo que habeis tomado en mi tierra, que yo bien se quien sois vosotros, y en lo que andais: è levantose en las andas, é habló á su gente, é obo murmullo entre ellos llamando á la gente que tenian las armas: é el fraile fué al Gobernador é dijole que que hacia, que ya no estaba la cosa en tiempo de esperar mas: el Gobernador me lo embió a decir: yo tenia concertado con el Capitan de la artilleria, que haciendole una seña disparasen los tiros, é con la gente que oyendolos saliesen todos á un tiempo; é como asi se hizo é como los Yndios estaban sin armas fueron desbaratados sin peligro de ningun Cristiano. Los que traian las andas, é los Caciques que venian al rededor del, nunca lo desampararon hasta que todos murieron al rededor del: el Gobernador salio é tomó á Atabaliva, é por defenderle le dió un cristiano una cuchillada en una mano. La gente siguió el alcance hasta donde estaban los Yndios con armas; no se halló en ellos resistencia alguna, porque ya era noche: recogieronse todos al Pueblo donde el Gobernador quedaba.

No. IX.—See Vol. I., p. 455.

ACCOUNT OF THE PERSONAL HABITS OF ATAHUALLPA;
EXTRACTED FROM THE MS. OF PEDRO PIZARRO.

[This minute account of the appearance and habits of the captive Inca is of the most authentic character, coming, as it does, from the pen of one who had the best opportunities of personal observation, during the monarch's imprisonment by his Conquerors. Pizarro's MS. is among those recently given to the world by the learned Academicians Salvá and Baranda.]

Este Atabalipa ya dicho hera indio bien dispuesto, de buena persona, de medianas carnes, no grueso demasiado, hermosso de Rostro y grave en el, los ojos encarnizados, muy temido de los suyos. (Acuérdome que el Señor de Guaylas le pidió licencia para yr á ver su tierra, y se la dió, dándole tiempo en que fuese y viniese limitado. Tardose algo mas, y cuando bolvio, estando yo presente, llegó con vn presente de fruta de la tierra, y llegado que fue á su presencia empeço á temblar en tanta manera que no se podia tener en los pies. El Atabalipa alço la caveza vn poquito y sonrriendose le hizo seña que se ffuese.) Quando le sacaron á matar, toda la gente que avia en la plaza de los naturales, que avia harto, se prostraron por tierra, dexandose caer en el suelo como Borrachos. Este indio se servia de sus mugeres por la horden que tengo ya dicha, sirviendole vna hermana diez dias ó ocho con mucha cantidad de hijas de señores que á estas hermanas servian, mudandose de ocho á ocho dias. Estas estavan siempre con el para serville, que yndio no entrava dond' el estava. Tenia muchos caciques consigo: estos estavan afuera en vn patio, y en llamando alguno entrava descalzo y donde el estava; y si venia de fuera parte, avia de entrar descalzo y cargado con vna carga; y quando su capitan Challicuchima vino con Hernando Piçarro y le entro á ver, entro asi como digo con vna carga y descalzo y se hecho á sus pies, y llorando se los beso. El Atabalipa con Rostro sereno le dixo: Seas bien venido alli, Challicuchima; queriendo dezir, Seas bien venido, Challicuchima. Este yndio se ponia en la caveza vnos llautos que son vnas trenças hechas de lanas de colores, de grosor de medio dedo y de anchor de vno, hecho desto vna manera de corona y no con puntas, sino redonda, de anchor de vna mano, que encaxava en la caveza, y en la frente vna borla cossida en este llauto, de anchor de vna mano, poco mas, de lana muy ffina de grana, cortada muy ygual, metida por vnos cañutitos de oro muy sotilmente hasta la mitad: esta lana hera hilada, y de los cañutos abaxo destorcida, que hera lo que caya en la frente; que los cañutillos de oro hera quanto tomavan todo el llauto ya dicho. Cayale esta borla hasta encima de las cejas, de vn dedo de grosor, que le tomava toda la frente; y todos estos señores andavan tresquilados y los orejones como á sobre peine. Vestian Ropa muy delgada y muy blanda ellos y sus hermanas que tenian por mugeres, y sus deudos, orejones principales, que se la davan los señores, y todos los demas vestian Ropa basta. Poniase este señor la manta por encima de la caveça y atabasela debajo de la barva, tapandose las orejas: esto traia el por tapar vna oreja que tenia rompida, que quando le prendieron los de Guascar se la quebraron. Bestiase este señor Ropas muy delicadas. Estando vn dia comiendo, questas señoras ya dichas le llevavan la comida y se la ponian delante en vnos juncos verdes muy delgados y pequeños, estaba sentado este señor en vn duo de madera de altor de poco mas de un palmo: este duo hera de madera colorada muy linda, y tenianle siempre tapado con vna manta muy delgada, aunque stuviese el sentado en el: estos juncos ya dichos le tendian siempre delante quando queria comer, y alli le ponian todos los manjares en oro, plata y Barro, y el que á el apetescia señalava se lo truxesen, y tomandolo vna señora destas dichas se lo tenia en la mano mientras comia. Pues estando vn dia desta manera comiendo y yo presente, llevando vna tajada del manjar á la boca le cayo vna gota en el vestido que tenia puesto, y dando de mano á la yndia se levanto y se entro á su aposento á vestir otro vestido, y buelto saco vestido vna camiseta y vna manta (pardo escuro). Llegandome yo pues á el le tente la manta que hera mas blanda que seda, y dixele: Ynga, de que es este vestido tan blando? El me dixo, Es de vnos pajaros que andan de noche en Puerto Viejo y en Tumbez, que muerden á los indios. Venido á aclararse dixo, que hera de pelo de murcielagos. Diziendole, que de donde se podria juntar tanto murcielago? dixo, Aquellos perros de Tumbez y Puerto Viejo que avian de hazer sino tomar destos para hazer Ropa á mi padre? Y es ansi questos murcielagos de aquellas partes muerden de noche á los indios y á españoles y á cavallos, y sacan tanta sangre ques cossa de misterio, y ansi se averiguo ser este vestido de lana de murcielagos, y ansi hera la color como dellos del vestido, que en Puerto Viejo y en Tumbez y sus comarcas ay gran cantidad dellos. Pues acontescio vn dia que viniendose á quexar en indio que en español tomava vnos bestidos de Atabalipa, el marquez me mando fuesse yo á saver quien hera y llamar al español para castigallo. El indio me llevo á vn buhio donde avia gran cantidad de petacas, porquel español ya hera ydo, diciendome que de alli avia tomado vn bestido del señor; e yo preguntandole que que tenian aquellas petacas, me mostro algunas en que tenian todo aquello que Atabalipa avia tocado con las manos, y avia estado de pies, y vestidos que el avia deshechado; en vnas los junquillos que le hechavan delante á los pies quando comia; en otras los guessos de las carnes ó aves que comia, que el avia tocado con las manos; en otras los maslos de las mazorcas de mahiz que avia tomado en sus manos; en otras las rropas que havia deshechado: finalmente todo aquello que el avia tocado. Preguntelee, que para que tenian aquello alli? Respondieronme, que para quemallo, porque cada año quemavan todo esto, porque lo que tocavan los señores que heran hijos del sol, se avia de quemar y hazer seniza y hechallo por el ayre, que nadie avia de tocar á ello; y en guarda desto estava vn prencipal con indios que lo guardava y rrecoxia de las mugeres que les servian. Estos señores dormian en el suelo en vnos colchones grandes de algodon: tenian vnas ffrecadas grandes de lana con que se cubijaban: y no e visto en todo este Piru indio semejante á este Atabalipa ni de su ferocidad ni autoridad.

No. X.—See Vol. I., p. 491.

CONTEMPORARY ACCOUNTS OF THE EXECUTION OF ATAHUALLPA.

[The following notices of the execution of the Inca are from the hands of eyewitnesses; for Oviedo, though not present himself, collected his particulars from those who were. I give the notices here in the original, as the best authority for the account of this dismal tragedy.]

Pedro Pizarro, Descubrimiento y Conquista de los Reynos del Peru, MS.

Acordaron pues los officiales y Almagro que Atabalipa muriese, tratando entre si que muerto Atabalipa se acababa el auto hecho acerca del tesoro. Pues dixeron al Marquez don Francisco Piçarro que no convenia que Atabalipa biviese; porque si se soltava, S. Mag. perderia la tierra y todos los españoles serian muertos; y á la verdad, si esto no fuera tratado con malicia, como esta dicho, tenian Razon, porque hera imposible soltandose poder ganar la tierra. Pues el marquez no quiso venir en ello. Visto esto los oficiales hizieronle muchos rrequerimientos, poniendole el servicio de S. Mag. per delante. Pues estando asi atravesose vn demonio de vna lengua que se dezia ffelipillo, vno de los muchachos que el marquez avia llevado á España, que al presente hera lengua, y andava enamordo de vna muger de Atabalipa, y por avella hizo entender al marquez que Atabalipa hazia gran junta de gente para matar los españoles en Caxas. Pues sabido el marquez esto prendio á Challicuchima que estava suelto y preguntandole per esta gente que dezia la lengua se juntavan, aunque negava y dezia que no, el ffelipillo dezia á la contra trastornando las palabras dezian á quien se preguntava este casso. Pues el marquez don Francisco Piçarro acordo embiar á Soto á Caxas á saver si se hazia alli alguna junta de gente, porque cierto el marquez no quisiera matalle. Pues visto Almagro y los oficiales la yda de Soto apretaron al marquez con muchos rrequirimientos, y la lengua por su parte que ayudava con sus rretruecos, vinieron á convencer al marquez que muriese Atabalipa, porque el marquez hera muy zeloso del servicio de S. Mag. y ansi le hizieron temer, y contra su veluntad sentenecio á muerte á Atabalipa mandando le diesen garrote, y despues de muerto le quemasen porque tenia las hermanas por mugeres. Cierto pocas leyes avian leido estos señores ni entendido, pues al infiel sin aver sido predicado le davan esta sentencia. Pues el Atabalipa llorava y dezia que no le matasen, que no abria yndio on la tierra que se meneasse sin su mandado, y que presso le tenian, que de que temian? y que si lo avian por oro y plata, que el daria dos tanto de lo que avia mandado. Yo vide llorar al marques de pesar por no podelle dar la vida, porque cierto temio los requirimientos y el rriezgo que avia en la tierra si se soltava. Este Atabalipa avia hecho entender á sus mugeres é yndios que si no le quemavan el cuerpo, aunque le matassen avia de bolver á ellos, que el sol su padre le rresucitaria. Pues sacandole á dar garrote á la plaza el padre fray Vicente de Balverde ya dicho le predico dizien-dole se tornase cristiano: y el dixo que si el se tornava christiano, si le que-marian, y dixeronle que no: y dixo que pues no le avian de quemar que queria ser baptizado, y ansi fray Vicente le baptizo y le dieron garrote, y otro dia le enterrarron en la yglesia que en Caxamalca teniamos los españoles. Esto se hizo antes que Soto bolviese á dar aviso de lo que le hera mandado; y quando vino truxo por nueva no aver visto nada ni aver nada, de que al marquez le peso mucho de avelle muerto, y al Soto mucho mas, porque dezia el, y tenia rrazon, que mejor ffuera embialle á España, y que el se obligara á ponello en la mar: y cierto esto fuera lo mejor que con este indio se pudiera hazer, porque quedar en la tierra no convenia: tambien se entendio que no biviera muchos dias, aunque le embiara, porque el hera muy regalado y muy señor.

Relacion del Primer Descubrimiento de la Costa y Mar del Sur, MS.

Dando forma como se llevaria Atabalipa de camino, y que guardia se le pondria, y consultando y tratando si seriamos parte para defenderle en aquellos pasos malos y rios si nos le quisiesen tomar los suyos: comenzóse á decir y á certificar entre los Indios, que el mandaba venir grand multitud de gente sobre nosotros: esta nueva se fué encendiendo tanto, que se tomó informacion de muchos señores de la tierra, que todos á una dijeron que era verdad, que el mandaba venir sobre nosotros para que le salvasen, y nos matasen si pudiesen, y que estaba toda la gente en cierta provincia ayuntada que ya venia de camino. Tomada esta informacion, juntáronse el dicho Gobernador, y Almagro, y los Oficiales de S. Mag. no estando ahi Hernando Pizarro, porque ya era partido para España con alguna parte del quinto de S. Mag. y á darle noticia y nueva de lo acaecido; y resumieronse, aunque contra voluntad del dicho Gobernador, que nunca estubo bien en ello, que Atabalipa, pues quebrantaba la paz, y queria hacer traicion y traher gentes para matar los cristianos, muriese, porque con su muerte cesaria todo, y se allanaria la tierra: á lo cual hubo contraíos pareceres, y la mas de la gente se puso en defender que no muriese; al cabo insistiendo muncho en su muerte el dicho Capitan Almagro, y dando muchas razones por qué debia morir, el fué muerto, aunque para él no fué muerte, sino vida, porque murió cristiano, y es de creer que se fué al cielo. Publicado per toda la tierra su muerte, la gente comun, y de pueblos venian donde el dicho Gobernador estaba á dar la obediencia á S. Mag.; pero los capitanes y gente de guerra que estaban en Xauxa y en el Cuzco, antes se rehicieron, y no quisieron venir de paz. Aqui acaeció la cosa mas estraña que se ha visto en el mundo, que yo vi por mis ojos, y fué; que estando en la iglesia cantando los oficios de difuntos á Atabalipa, presente el cuerpo, llegaron ciertas señoras hermanas y mugeres suyas, y otros privados con grand estruendo, tal que impidieron el oficio, y dijeron que les hiciesen aquella fiesta muy mayor, porque era costumbre cuando el grand señor moria, que todos aquellos que bien le querian, se enterrasen vivos con el: á los cuales se les respondio, que Atabalipa habia muerto como cristiano, y como tal le hacian aquel oficio, que no se habia de hacer lo que ellos pedian, que era muy mal hecho y contra cristianidad; que se fuesen de alli, y no les estorbasen, y se le dejasen enterrar, y ansi se fueron á sus aposentos, y se ahorcaron todos ellos y ellos. Las cosas que pasaron en estos dias, y los extremos y llantos de la gente son muy largas y prolijas, y por eso no se dirán aqui.

Oviedo, Historia General de las Indias, MS., lib. 46, *cap.* 22.

Cuando el Marques Don Francisco Pizarro tubo preso al gran Rey Atabaliva le aconsejaron hombres faltos de buen entendimiento, que le matase, ó el obo gana, porque como se vieron cargados de oro parecioles que muerto aquel Señor lo podian poner mas á su salvo en España donde quisiesen, é dejando la tierra, y que asimismo serian mas parte para se sustener en ella sin aquel escrupuloso impedimento, que no conservandose la vida de un Principe tan grande, é tan temido é acatado de sus naturales, y en todas aquellas partes; é la esperiencia ha mostrado cuan mal acordado é peor fecho fue todo lo que contra Atabaliva se hizo despues de su prision en le quitar la vida, con la cual demas de deservirse Dios quitaron al Emperador nuestro Señor, é á los mismos Españoles que en aquellas partes se hallaron, y á los que en España quedaron, que entonces vivian y a los que aora viven é nacerán innumerables tesoros, que aquel Principe les diera; é ninguno de sus vasallos se mobiera ni alterara como se alteraron é revelaron en faltando su Persona. Notorio es que el Gobernador le aseguró la vida, y sin que le diese tal seguro el se le tenia, pues ningun Capitan puede disponer sin licencia de su Rey y Señor de la Persona del Principe que tiene preso, cuyo es de derecho, cuanto mas que Atabaliva dijo al Marques, que si algun Cristiano matasen los Yndios, ó le hiciesen el menor daño del mundo, que creyese que por su mandado lo hacia, y que cuando eso fuese le matase ó hiciese del lo que quisiese; é que tratandelo bien él le chaparia las paredes de plata, é le allanaria las Sierras é los montes, é le dariá á el, é á los Cristianos cuanto oro quisiesen, é que desto no tubiese duda alguna; y en pago de sus ofrecimientos encendidas pajas se las ponian en los pies ardiendo, porque digese que traicion era la que tenia ordenada contra los Cristianos, é inventando é fabricando contra el falsedades, le levantaron que los queria matar, é todo aquello fue rodeado por malos e por la inadvertencia é mal Consejo del Gobernador, é comenzaron á le hacer proceso mal compuesto y peor escrito, seyendo uno de los Adalides un inquieto, desasosegado é deshonesto Clerigo, y un Escribano falto de conciencia, é de mala habilidad, y otros tales que la maldad concurrieron, é asi mal fundado el libelo se concluyo á sabor de dañados paladares, como se dijo en el Capitulo catorce, no acordandose que les habian enchido las casas de oro é plata, é le habian tomado sus mugeres é repartidolas en su presencia é usaban de ellas en sus adulterios, é en lo que les placia á aquellos aquien las dieron; y como les pareció á los culpados que tales ofensas no eran de olvidar, é que merecian que el Atabaliva les diese la recompensa como sus obras eran, asentoselés en el animo un temor é enemistad con él entrañable; é por salir de tal cuidado é sospecha le ordenaron la muerte por aquello que él no hizo ni pensó; y de ver aquesto algunos Españoles comedidos aquien pesaba que tan grande deservicio se hiciese á

Dios y al Emperador nuestro Señor; y aunque tan grande ingratitud se perpetraba é tan señalada maldad se cometia como matar a un Principe tan grande sin culpa. E viendo que le traian á colacion sus delitos é crueldades pasadas, que el habia usado entre sus Yndios y enemigos en el tiempo pasado, de lo cual ninguno era Juez, sino Dios; queriendo saber la verdad é por excusar tan notorios danos como se esperaban que habian de proceder matando aquel Señor se ofrecieron cinco hidalgos de ir en persona á saber y ver si venia aquella gente de guerra que los falsos inventores é sus mentirosas espias publicaban, á dar en los Cristianos; en fin el Gobernador (que tambien so puede creer que era engañado) lo obo por bien; é fueron el Capitan Hernando de Soto, el Capitan Rodrigo Orgaiz, é Pedro Ortiz, é Miguel de Estete, é Lope Velez a ver esos enemigos que decian que venian; é el Gobernador les dió una Guia ó Espia, que decia que sabia donde estaban; é á dos dias de camino se despeño la guia de un risco, que lo supo muy bien hacer el Diablo para que el daño fuese mayor; pero aquellos cinco de caballo que he dicho pasaron adelante hasta que llegaron al lugar donde se decian que habian de hallar el egercito contrario, é no hallaron hombre de guerra, ni con armas algunas, sino todos de paz; é aunque no iban sino esos pocos cristianos que es dicho les hicieron mucha fiesta por donde andubieron, é les dieron todo lo que les pidieron de lo que tenian para ellos é sus criados, é Yndios de servicio que llevaban; por manera que viendo que era burla, é muy notoria mentira é falsedad palpable, se tornaron á Cajamalca donde el Gobernador estaba; el cual ya habia fecho morir al Principe Atabaliva se que la historia lo ha contado; é como llegaron al Gobernador hallaronle mostrando mucho sentimiento con un gran sombrero de fieltro puesto en la cabeza por luto é muy calado sobre los ojos, é le digeron: Señor, muy mal lo ha fecho V. Sª, y fuera justo que fueramos atendidos para que supierades que es muy gran traicion la que se le levantó á Atabaliva, porque ningun hombre de guerra hay en el Campo, ni le hallamos, sino todo de paz, é muy buen tratamiento que no se nos hizo en todo lo que habemos andado. El Gobernador respondió é les dijo: Ya veo que me han engañado: desde á pocos dias sabida esta verdad, e murmurandose de la crueldad que con aquel Principe se usó, vinieron á malas palabras el Gobernador y fray Vicente de Valverde, y el Tesorere Riqualme, é á cada uno de ellos decia que el otro lo habia fecho, é se desmintieron unos á otros muchas veces, oyendo muchos su rencilla.

No. XI.—See Vol. II., p. 35.

CONTRACT BETWEEN PIZARRO AND ALMAGRO, MS.; DATED AT CUZCO,
JUNE 12, 1535.

[This agreement between these two celebrated captains, in which they bind themselves by solemn oaths to the observance of what would seem to be required by the most common principles of honesty and honor, is too characteristic of the men and the times to be omitted. The original exists in the archives at Simancas.]

Nos Dⁿ Francisco Pizarro, Adelantado, Capitan General y Governador por S. M. en estos Reynos de la Nueva Castilla, é Dⁿ Diego de Almagro, asimismo Governador por S. M. en la provincia de Toledo, decimos: que por que mediante la intima amistad y compañia que entre nosotros con tanto amor ha permanecido, y queriendolo Dios Nuestro Señor hacer, ha sido parte y cabsa que el Emperador é Rey nuestro Señor haya recevido señalados servicios con la conquista, sujecion é poblacion destas provincias y tierras, é atrayendo á la conversion y camino de nuestra Santa Fee Catolica tanta muchedumbre de infieles, é confiando S. M. que durante nuestra amistad y compañia su real patrimonio sera acrecentado, é asi por tener este intento como por los servicios pasados, S. M. Catolica tubo por bien de conceder á mi el dicho Dⁿ Francisco Pizarro la governacion de estos nuebos Reynos, y á mi el dicho DⁿDiego de Almagro la governacion de la provincia de Toledo, de las quales mercedes que de su Real liberalidad hemos recevido, resulta tan nueba obligacion, que perpetuamente nuestras vidas y patrimonios, y de los que de nos decendieren en su Real servicio se gasten y consuman, y para que esto mas seguro y mejor efecto haya y la confianza de S. M. por nuestra parte no fallezca Renunciando la Ley que cerca de los tales juramentos dispone, prometemos é juramos en presencia de Dios Nuestro Señor, ante cuyo acatamiento estamos, de guardar y cumplir bien y enteramente, y sin cabtela ni otro entendimiento alguno lo espresado y contenido en los capitulos siguientes, é suplicamos á su infinita bondad que á qualquier de nos que fuere en contrario de lo asi convenido, con todo rigor de justicia permita la perdicion de su anima, fin y mal acavamiento de su vida, destruicion y perdimiento de su familia, honrras y hacienda, porque como quebrantador de su fee, la qual el uno al otro y el otro nos damos, y no temerosos de su acatamiento, reciva del tal justa venganza: y lo que por parte de cada uno de nosotros juramos y prometemos es lo siguiente.

Primeramente que nuestra amistad é compañia se conserve mantenga para en adelante con aquel amor y voluntad que hasta el dia presente entre nosotros ha habido, no la alterando ni quebrantando por algunos intereses, cobdicias, ni ambicion de qualesquiera honrras é oficios, sino que hermanablemente entre nosotros se comunique é seamos parcioneros en todo el bien que Dios Nuestro Señor nos quiera hacer.

Otrosi, decimos so cargo del juramento é promesa que hacemos, que ninguno de nosotros calumniara ni procurara cosa alguna que en daño o menos cabo de su honrra, vida y hacienda al otro pueda subceder ni venir, ni dello sera cabsa por vias directas ni indirectas por si propio ni por otra persona tacita ni espresamente cabsandolo ni permitiendolo, antes procurará todo bien y honrra y trabajará de se lo llegar y adquirir, y evitando todas perdidas y daños que se le puedan recrecer, no siendo de la otra parte avisado.

Otrosi: juramos de mantener, guardar y cumplir lo que entre nosotros esta capitulado, á lo qual al presente nos referimos, é que por via, causa ni maña alguna ninguno de nosotros verná en contrario ni en quevrantamiento dello, ni hará diligencía, protestacion ni Reclamacion alguna, é que si alguna oviere fecha, se aparta ó desiste de ella é la renuncia so cargo del dicho juramento.

Otrosi: juramos que juntamente ambos á dos, y no el uno sin el otro, informaremos y escriviremos á S. M. las cosas que segun nuestro parecer mejor á su Real servicio convengan, suplicandole, informandole de todo aquello con que mas su catolica conciencia se descargue, y estas provincias y Reynos mas y mejor se conserven y goviernen, y que no habrá relacion particular por ninguno de nosotros hecha en fraude é cabtela y con intento de dañar y enpecer al otro, procurando para si, posponiendo el servicio de Nuestro Señor Dios y de S. M., y en quebrantamiento de nuestra amistad y compañia, y asimismo no permitira que sea hecho por otra qualquier persona, dicho ni comunicado, ni lo permita ni consienta, sino que todo se haga manifiestamente entre ambos, porque se conozca mejor el celo que de servir á S. M. tenemos, pues de nuestra amistad é compañia, tanta confianza ha mostrado.

Yten: juramos que todos los provechos é intereses que se nos recrecieren asi de los que yo D^n Francisco Pizarro oviere y adquiriere en esta governacion por qualquier vias y cabsas, como los otros que yo D^n Diego de Almagro he de haber en la conquista y descubrimiento que en nombre y por mandado de S. M. hago, lo traeremos manifiestamente á monton y collacion, por manera que la compañia que en este caso tenemos hecha permanezca, y en ella no haya fraude, cabtela ni engaño alguno, é que los gastos que por ambos é qualquier de nos se obieren de hacer se haga moderada y discretamente conforme, y proveyendo á la necesidad que se ofreciere evitando lo escesivo y superfluo socorriendo y proveyendo á lo necesario.

Todo lo qual segun en la forma que dicho esta, es nuestra voluntad de lo asi guardar y cumplir se cargo del juramento que asi tenemos fecho, poniendo á Nuestro Señor Dios por juez y á su gloriosa Madre Santa Maria con todos los Santos por testigos, y por que sea notorio á todos los que aqui juramos y prometemos, lo firmamos de nuestros nombres, siendo presentes por testigos el Licenciado Hernando Caldera Teniente General de Governador en estos Reynos por el dicho Señor Governador, é Francisco Pineda Capellan de su Señoria, é Antonio Picado su Secretario, é Antonio Tellez de Guzman y el Doctor Diego de Loaisa, el qual dicho juramento fue fecho en la gran Cibdad del Cuzco en la casa del dicho Governador D^n Diego Dalmagro, estando diciendo misa el Padre Bartolome de Segovia Clerigo, despues de dicho el pater noster, poniendo los dichos Governadores las manos derechas encima del Ara consagrada á 12 de Junio de 1535 años.—Francisco Pizarro.—El Adelantado Diego Dalmagro.—Testigos el Licenciado Hernando Caldera—Antonio Tellez de Guzman.

Yo Antonio Picado Escrivano de S. M. doy fee que fui testígo y me halle presente al dicho juramento é solenidad fecho por los dichos Governadores, y yo saqué este traslado del original que queda en mi poder como secretario del Señor Governador D[n] Francisco Pizarro, en fee de lo qual firmé aqui nombre. Fecho en la gran Cibdad del Cuzco á 12 dias del mes de Julio de 1535 años. Antonio Picado Escribano de

No. XII.—See Vol. II., p. 177.

LETTER FROM THE YOUNGER ALMAGRO TO THE ROYAL AUDIENCE OF PANAMÁ, MS.; DATED AT LOS REYES [LIMA], JULY 14, 1541.

[This document, coming from Almagro himself, is valuable as exhibiting the best apology for his conduct, and, with due allowance for the writer's position, the best account of his proceedings. The original—which was transcribed by Muñoz for his collection—is preserved in the archives at Simancas.]

Mui magnificos Señores,—Ya V[s] Mrds. havran sabido el estado en que he estado despues que fué desta vida el Adelantado Don Diego de Almagro mi padre que Dios tenga en el Cielo, i como quedé debajo de la vara del Marqués Don Francisco Pizarro, i creo yo que pues son notorias las molestias i malos tratamientos que me hicieron i la necesidad en que me tenian á vn rincon de mi casa sin tener otro remedio sino el de S. M. á quien ocurri que me lo diese como Señor agradecido de quien yo lo esperava pagando los servicios tan grandes que mi padre le hizo de tan gran ganancia é acrecentamiento para su Real Corona, no hay necesidad de contarlas, i por eso no las contaré, i dejaré lo pasado i vendré á dar á V[s] Mrds. cuenta de lo presente, é diré que aunque me llegava al alma verme tan afligido, acordandome del mandamiento que mi padre me dejó que amase el servicio de S. M. i questava en poder de mis enemigos; sufria mas de lo que mi juicio bastava, en especial ser cada dia quien á mi padre quitó la vida, i havian escurecido sus servicios por manera que dél ni de mi no havia memoria; i como la Enemistad quel Marques me tenia é á todos mis amigos é criados fuese tan cruel i mortal, i sobre mi sucedieso, quiso efetualla por la medida con que la usó con mi padre, estando siguro en mi casa, gimiendo mi necesidad, esperando el remedio i Mercades que de S. M. era razon que yo alcanzase, mui confiado de gozarlas, haciendo á S. M. servicios como yo lo deseo; fui informado quel Marques trataba mi prendimiento i fin, determinado que no quedase en el mundo quien la muerte de mi padre le pidiese, y acordandome que para darsela hallaron testigos á su voluntad, asi mismo los hallaron para mi, por manera que padre i hijo fueran por vn juicio juzgados. Por no dejar mi vida en alvedrio tan diabolico i desatinado, temiendo la muerte, determinado de morir defendiendo mi vida i honra, con los criados de mi padre i amigos, acordé de entrar en su casa i prenderle para escusar mayores daños, pues el Juez de S. M. ya venia i á cada uno hiciera justicia, i el Marques como persona culpada en la defensa de su prision é persona armada para ello hizo tanto que por desdicha suya fué herido de vna herida de que murió luego, i puesto que como hijo de padre á quien el havia muerto lo podia recibir por venganza, me pesó tan estrañamente que todos conocieron en mi mui gran diferencia, i por ver que estava tan poderoso i acatado como era razon no hovo hombre viendolo en mitad del dia que echase mano á espada para ayuda suya ni despues hay hombre que por el responda: parece que se hizo por juicio de Dios i por su voluntad, porque mi deseo no era tan largo que se estendiese á mas de conservar mi vida en tanto aquel juez llegava; é como vi el hecho procuré antes que la cosa mas se encendiese en el pueblo i que cesasen esecucion de prisiones de personas que ambas opiniones havian seguido questaban afrontadas, i cesasen crueldades, é huviese justicia que lo estorvase é castigase, é se tomase cabeza que en nombre de S. M. hiciese justicia é governase la tierra, pareciendo á la republica é comunidad de su Cibdad é oficiales de S. M. que por los servicios de mi padre é por haver él descubierto é ganado esta tierra me pertenecia mas justamente que á otro la governacion della, me pidieron por Governador i dentro de dos horas consultado é negociado con el Cabildo, fui recibido en amor i conformidad de toda la republica: Asi quedó todo en paz i tan asentados i serenos los animos de todos, que no hovo mudanza, i todo está pacifico, i los pueblos en la misma conformidad i justicia que han estado, i con el ayuda de Dios se asentará cada dia la paz tan bien que de todos sea obedecida por señora, i S. M. será tambien servido como es razon, como se deve: porque acabadas son las opiniones é parcialidades, é yo é todos pretendemos la poblacion de la tierra i el descubrimiento della, porque los tiempos pasados que se han gastado tan mal con alborotos que se han ofrecido, é descuidos que ha habido, agora se ganen é se alcancen i cobren, i con este presupuesto esten Vs Mrcds. ciertos que está el Perú en Sosiego, i que las riquezas se descubrirán é irán á poder de S. M. mas acrecentadas i multiplicadas que hasta aqui, ni havrá mas pasion ni movimiento sino toda quietud, amando el servicio de S. M. i su obidiencia, aprovechando sus Reales rentas: Suplico á Vs Mrds. pues el caso parece que lo hizo Dios i no los hombres, ni yo lo quise asi como Dios lo hizo por su juicio secreto, é como tengo dicho la tierra está sosegada, i todos en paz; Vs Mrds. por el presente manden suspender qualquiera novedad, pues la tierra se conservará como está, é será S. M. mui servido; é despues que toda la gente que no tienen vecindades las tengan, é otros vayan á poblar é descubrir, podrán proveer lo que conviniere, i es tiempo que la tierra Españoles i naturales no reciban mas alteracion, pues no pretenden sino sosiego i quietud, i poblar la tierra i servir á S. M. porque con este deseo todos estamos i estaremos, i de otra manera crean Vs Mrds. que de nuevo la tierra se rebuelve é inquieta, porque de las cosas pasadas vnos i otros han pretendido cada vno su fin, é sino descansan de los trabajos que han padecido con tantas persecuciones de buena ni de mala perdiendose no terná S. M. della cuenta, é los naturales se destruirían é no asentarán en sus casas é

Lope Ydiaquez i á Diego de Mercado Fator de la nueva Toledo, para ver si los podian reducir i atraer al servicio de V. M. i fueron tan mal rescibidos que quando escaparon con las vidas se tuvieron por bien librados. La respuesta que les dieron fué que no querian obedecer las provisiones reales de V. M. sino darle la batalla, i luego alzaron su Real i caminaron para nosotros. Visto esto el Governador sacó su Real deste pueblo i caminó contra ellos dos leguas, donde supo, que los traidores estavan á tres, en un asiento fuerte i comodo para su artilleria. El governador acordó de los guardar alli, donde le tomó la voz, porque era llano i lugar fuerte al nuestro proposito. Como esto vieron los traidores, sabado que se contaron diez i seis de setiembre, se levantaron de donde estavan, i caminaron por lo alto de la sierra i vinieron una legua de nosotros, i sus corredores vinieron á ver nuestro asiento. Luego el Governador provio que por una media loma fuese un Capitan con cinquenta arcabuceros, i otro con cinquenta lanzas á tomar lo alto, i sucedió tambien que sin ningun riesgo se tomó, i luego todo el exercito de V. M. lo subió. Visto esto, los enemigos que estarian tres quartos de legua, procuraron de buscar campo donde nos dar la batalla, i asi le tomaron á su proposito i asentaron su artilleria i concertaron sus esquadrones, que eran ducientos i treinta de cavallo, en que venian cinquenta hombres de armas: la infanteria eran ducientos arcabuzeros i ciento i cinquenta piqueros, todos tan lucidos é bien armados, que de Milan no pudieran salir mejor aderezados: el artilleria eran seis medias culebrinas de diez á doze pies de largo, que echavan de bateria una naranja: tenian mas otros seis tiros medianos todos de fruslera, tan bien aderezados i con tanta municion, que mas parecia artilleria de Ytalia que no de Yndias. El Governador vista su desverguenza, la gente mui en orden, despues de haver hecho los razonamientos que convenian, diciendonos que viesemos la desverguenza que los traidores tenian i el gran desacato á la corona Real, caminó á ellos, i llegando á tiro donde su artilleria podia alcanzar, jugo luego en nosotros, que la nuestra por ser mui pequeña é ir caminando, no nos podimos aprovechar della de ninguna cosa, i asi la dexamos por popa: matarnos hian antes que llegasemos á romper con ellos mas de 30 hombres, i siempre con este daño que rescebiamos, caminamos hasta nos poner á tiro de arcabuz, donde de una parte i de otra jugaron i se hizo de a mas partes arto daño, i lo mas presto que nos fué posible porque su artilleria aun nos echava algunas pelotas ea nuestros esquadrones, cerramos con ellos, donde duró la battalla de lanzas, porras i espadas mas de una grande hora; fué tan reñida i porfiada que despues de la de Rebena no se ha visto entre tan poca gente mas cruel batalla, donde hermanos á hermanos, ni deudos á deudos, ni amigos á amigos no se davan vida uno á otro. Finalmente como llevasemos la justicia de nuestra parte, nuestro Señor en ventura de V. M. nos dió vitoria, i en el denuedo con que acometió el Governador Baca de Castro el qual estava sobresaliente con treinta de cavallo, armado en blanco con una ropilla de brocado sobre las armas con su encomienda descubierta en los pechos, contra el qual estavan conjurados muchos de los traidores, pero él como cavallero se les mostró i defendió tan bien, que para hombre de su edad i profesion, estamos espantados de lo que hizo i trabajo, i como rompió con sus sobresalientes, luego desampararon el campo i conseguimos gloriosa vitoria, la qual estuvo harto dudosa, porque si eramos en numero ciento mas que ellos, en escoger el campo i artilleria i hombres de armas i arcabuzes, nos tenian doblada ventaja. Fué bien sangrienta de entramas partes, i si la noche no cerrara tan presto, V. M. quedara bien satisfecho destos traidores, pero lo que no se pudo entonses hacer, ahora el Governador lo hace, desquartizando cada dia á los que se escaparon: murieron en la batalla de los nuestros el capitan Per Alvarez Holguin i otros sesenta cavalleros i Hidalgos; i están eridos de muerte Gomez de Tordoya i el Capitan Peranzures i otros mas de ciento. De los traidores murieron ciento é cinquenta, i mas de otros tantos eridos; presos están mas de ciento i cinquenta: Don Diego i otros tres capitanes se escaparon: cada ora se traen presos, esperamos que un dia se habrá Don Diego á las manos, porque los Yndios como villanos de Ytalia los matan i traen presos. V. M. tenga esta vitoria en gran servicio, porque puede creer que agora se acabó de ganar esta tierra i ponerla debaxo del cetro Real de V. M. i que esta ha sido verdadera conquista i pacificacion della, i asi es justo que V. M. como gratisimo Principe gratifique i haga mercedes á los que se la dieron; i al Governador Baca de Castro perpetuarle en ella en entramas governaciones no dividiendo nada dellas porque no hai otra batalla, i á los soldados i vecinos que en ella se hallaron, remunerarles sus trabajos i perdidas, que han rescibido por reducir estos Reinos á la Corona Real de V. M. i mandando castigar á los vecinos que oyendo la voz Real de V. M. se quedaron en sus casas grangeando sus repartimientos i haciendas, porque gran sin justicia seria, Sacra M. que bolviendo nosotros á nuestras casas pobres i mancos de guerra de mas de un año, hallasemos á los que se quedaron sanos i salvos i ricos, i que á ellos no se les diese pena ni á nosotros premio ni galardon, i esto seria ocasion para que si otra vez oviese otra rebelion en esta tierra ó en otra, no acudiesen al servicio de V. M. como seria razon i somos obligados. Todos tenemos por cierto, quel Governador Baca de Castro lo hará asi, i que en nombre de V. M. á los que le han servido hará mercedes, i á los que no acudieron á servir á V. M. castigará. S. C. C. M. Dios todo poderoso acreciente la vida de V. M. dandole vitoria contra sus enemigos, porque sea acrescentada su santa fee, amen. De San Joan de la Frontera á 24 de septiembre de 1542 años.—Besan las manos i pies de V. M. sus leales Vasallos,—Hernando de Silva,—Pedro Piçarro,—Lucas Martinez,—Gomez de Leon,—Hernando de Torre,—Lope de Alarcon,—Juan de Arves,—Juan Flores,—Juan Ramirez,—Alonso Buelte,—Melchior de Cervantes,—Martin Lopez,—Juan Crespo,—Francisco Pinto,—Alonso Rodriguez Picado.

No. XIV.—See Vol. II., p. 433.

PROCESS CONTAINING THE SENTENCE OF DEATH PASSED ON GONZALO PIZARRO, AT XAQUIXAGUANA, APRIL 9, 1548.

[This instrument is taken from the original manuscript of Zarate's Chronicle, which is still preserved at Simancas. Muñoz has made several extracts from this MS., showing that Zarate's history, in its printed form, underwent considerable alteration, both in regard to its facts, and the style of its execution. The printed copy is prepared with more consideration; various circumstances, too frankly detailed in the original, are suppressed; and the style and disposition of the work show altogether a more fastidious and practised hand. These circumstances have led Muñoz to suppose that the Chronicle was submitted to the revision of some more experienced writer, before its publication; and a correspondence which the critic afterwards found in the Escurial, between Zarate and Florian d' Ocampo, leads to the inference that the latter historian did this kind office for the former. But whatever the published work may have gained as a literary composition, as a book of reference and authority it falls behind its predecessor, which seems to have come without much premeditation from the author, or, at least, without much calculation of consequences. Indeed, its obvious value for historical uses led Muñoz, in a note indorsed on the fragments, to intimate his purpose of copying the whole manuscript at some future time.]

Vista é entendida por Nos el Mariscal Francisco de Albarado, Maestre de Campo deste Real exercito, el Licenciado Andres de Cianca, Oidor de S. M. destos Reinos, é subdelegados por el mui Ilustre Señor el Licenciado Pedro de la Gazca del Consejo de S. M. de la Santa Inquisicion, Presidente destos Reinos é provincias del Perú, para lo infra escripto, la notoriedad de los muchos graves é atroces delitos que Gonzalo Pizarro ha cometido é consentido cometer á los que le han seguido, despues que á estos Reinos ha venido el Visorrey Blasco Nuñez Vela, en deservicio é desacato de S. M. é de su preminencia é corona Real, é contra la natural obligacion é fidelidad que como su vasallo tenia é devia á su Rei é señor natural é de personas particulares, los quales por ser tan notorios del dicho no se requiere orden ni tela de juicio, mayormente que muchos de los dichos delitos consta por confesion del dicho Gonzalo Pizarro é la notoriedad por la informacion que se ha tomado, é que combiene para la pacificacion destos Reinos é exemplo con brevedad hacer justicia del dicho Gonzalo Pizarro.

Fallamos atento lo susodicho junta la dispusicion del derecho, que devemos declarar é declaramos el dicho Gonzalo Pizarro haver cometido crimen laesae Majestatis contra la corona Real Despaña en todos los grados é causas en derecho contenidas despues que á estos Reinos vino el Virrey Blasco Nuñez Vela, é asi le declaramos é condenamos al dicho Gonzalo Pizarro por traidor, é haver incurrido él é sus descendientes nacidos despues quel cometió este dicho crimen é traicion los por linea masculina hasta la segunda generacion, é por la femenina hasta la primera, en la infamia é inabilidad é inabilidades, é como á tal condenamos al dicho Gonzalo Pizarro en pena de muerte natural, la qual le mandamos que sea dada en la forma siguiente: que sea sacado de la prision en questá cavallero en una mula de silla atados pies é manos é traido publicamente por este Real de S. M. con voz de pregonero que manifieste su delito, sea llevado al tablado que por nuestro mandado esta fecho en este Real, é alli sea apeado é cortada la cabeza por el pescueso, é despues de muerta naturalmente, mandamos que la dicha cabeza sea llevada á la Ciudad de los Reyes como ciudad mas principal destos Reinos, é sea puesta é clavada en el rollo de la dicha Ciudad con un retulo de letra gruesa que diga, Esta es la cabeza del traidor de Gonzalo Pizarro que se hizo justicia del en el valle de Aquixaguan, donde dió la batalla campal contra el estandarte Real queriendo defender su traicion é tirania; ninguno sea osado de la quitar de aqui so pena de muerte natural: é mandamos que las casas quel dicho Pizarro tiene en la Cibdad del Cuzco. . . . . sean derribadas por los cimientos é aradas de sal, é á donde agora es la puerta sea puesto un letrero en un pilar que diga: Estas casas eran de Gonzalo Pizarro las quales fueron mandadas derrocar por traidor, é ninguna persona sea osado dellas tornar á hacer i edificar sin licencia expresa de S. M. so pena de muerte natural: e condenamosle mas en perdimiento de todos sus bienes de qualquier calidad que sean é le pertenezcan, los quales aplicamos á la Camara é Fisco de S. M. é en todas las otras penas que contra los tales están instituidas: é por esta nuestra sentencia definitiva juzgamos é asi lo pronunciamos é mandamos en estos escritos é por ellos. —Alonso de Albarado; el Lic^{do} Cianca.

relation, in which it is more familiarly employed by most of the nations of Europe. Nor was the use of it limited to modern times, being applied in the same way both by Greeks and Romans; "Πάππα φίλε," says Nausikaa, addressing her father, in the simple language which the modern versifiers have thought too simple to render literally.

[9] *Inca* signified *king* or *lord*. Capac meant *great* or *powerful*. It was applied to several of the successors of Manco, in the same manner as the epithet *Yupanqui,* signifying *rich in all virtues,* was added to the names of several Incas. (Cieza de Leon, Cronica, cap. 41.— Garcilasso, Com. Real., Parte 1, lib. 2, cap. 17.) The good qualities commemorated by the cognomens of most of the Peruvian princes afford an honorable, though not altogether unsuspicious, tribute to the excellence of their characters.

[10] Com. Real., Parte 1, lib. 1, cap. 9-16.

[11] These several traditions, all of a very puerile character, are to be found in Ondegardo, Relacion Segunda, MS.,—Sarmiento, Relacion, MS., cap. 1,—Cieza de Leon, Cronica, cap. 105,—Conquista i Poblacion del Piru, MS.,—Declaracion de los Presidente é Oydores de la Audiencia Reale del Peru, MS.,—all of them authorities contemporary with the Conquest. The story of the bearded white men finds its place in most of their legends.

[12] Some writers carry back the date 500, or even 550, years before the Spanish invasion. (Balboa, Histoire du Perou, chap. 1.—Velasco, Histoire du Royaume de Quito, tom. I. p. 81.—Ambo auct. ap. Relations et Mémoires Originaux pour servir à l'Histoire de la Découverte de l'Amérique, par Ternaux-Compans, (Paris, 1840.)) In the Report of the Royal Audience of Peru, the epoch is more modestly fixed at 200 years before the Conquest. Dec. de la Aud. Real., MS.

[13] "Otras cosas ay mas que dezir deste Tiaguanaco, que passo por no detenerme: concluyŏdo que yo para mi tengo esta antigualla por la mas antigua de todo el Peru. Y assi so tiene que antes q̃ los Ingas reynassen con muchos tiempos estavan hechos algunos edificios destos: porque yo he oydo afirmar a Indios, que los Ingas hizieron los edificios grandes del Cuzco por la forma que vieron tener la muralla o pared que se vee en este pueblo." (Cieza de Leon, Cronica, cap. 105.) See also Garcilasso, (Com. Real., Parte 1, lib. 3, cap. 1,) who gives an account of these remains, on the authority of a Spanish ecclesiastic, which might compare, for the marvellous, with any of the legends of his order. Other ruins of similar traditional antiquity are noticed by Herrera, (Histeria General de los Hechos de los Castellanos en las Islas y Tierra Firme del Mar Océano, (Madrid, 1730,) dec. 6, lib. 6, cap. 9.) McCulloh, in some sensible reflections on the origin of the Peruvian civilization, adduces, on the authority of Garcilasso de la Vega, the famous temple of Pachacamac, not far from Lima, as an example of architecture more ancient than that of the Incas. (Researches, Philosophical and Antiquarian, concerning the Aboriginal History of America, (Baltimore, 1829,) p. 405.) This, if true, would do much to confirm the views in our text. But McCulloh is led into an error by his blind guide, Rycaut, the translator of Garcilasso, for the latter does not speak of the temple as existing before the time of the Incas, but before the time when the country was conquered by the Incas. Com. Real., Parte 1, lib. 6, cap. 30.

[14] Among other authorities for this tradition, see Sarmiento, Relacion, MS., cap. 3, 4,— Herrera, Hist. General, dec. 5, lib. 3, cap. 6,—Conq. i Pob. del Piru, MS.,—Zarate, Historia del Descubrimiento y de la Conquista del Peru, lib. 1, cap. 10, ap. Barcia, Historiadores Primitivos de las Indias Occidentales, (Madrid, 1749,) tom. 3.

In most, not all, of the traditions, Manco Capac is recognized as the name of the founder of the Peruvian monarchy, though his history and character are related with sufficient discrepancy.

[15] Mr. Ranking,

> "Who can deep mysteries unriddle,
> As easily as thread a needle,"

finds it "highly probable that the first Inca of Peru was a son of the Grand Khan Kublai"! (Historical Researches on the Conquest of Peru, &c., by the Moguls, (London, 1827,) p. 170.) The coincidences are curious, though we shall hardly jump at the conclusion of the adventurous author. Every scholar will agree with Humboldt, in the wish that "some learned traveller would visit the borders of the lake of Titicaca, the district of Callao, and the high plains of Tiahuanaco, the theatre of the ancient American civilization." (Vues des Cordillères, p. 199.) And yet the architectural monuments of the aborigines, hitherto brought to light, have furnished few materials for a bridge of communication across the dark gulf that still separates the Old World from the New.

[16] A good deal within a century, to say truth. Garcilasso and Sarmiento, for example, the two ancient authorities in highest repute, have scarcely a point of contact in their accounts of the earlier Peruvian princes; the former representing the sceptre as gliding down in peaceful succession from hand to hand, through an unbroken dynasty, while the latter garnishes his tale with as many conspiracies, depositions, and revolutions, as belong to most barbarous, and, unhappily, most civilized communities. When to these two are added the various writers, contemporary and of the succeeding age, who have treated of the Peruvian annals, we shall find ourselves in such a conflict of traditions, that criticism is lost in conjecture. Yet this uncertainty as to historical events fortunately does not extend to the history of arts and institutions, which were in existence on the arrival of the Spaniards.

[17] Sarmiento, Relacion, MS., cap. 57, 64.—Conq. i Pob. del Piru, MS.—Velasco, Hist. de Quito, p. 59.—Dec. de la Aud. Real., MS.—Garcilasso, Com. Real., Parte 1, lib. 7, cap. 18, 19; lib. 8, cap. 5-8.

The last historian, and, indeed, some others, refer the conquest of Chili to Yupanqui, the father of Topa Inca. The exploits of the two monarchs are so blended together by the different annalists, as in a manner to confound their personal identity.

[18] Garcilasso, Com. Real., lib. 7, cap. 8-11.—Cieza de Leon, Cronica, cap. 92.

"El Cuzco tuuo gran manera y calidad, deuio set fundada por gente de gran ser. Auia grandes calles, saluo q̃ erã angostas, y las casas hechas de piedra pura cõ tan lindas junturas, q̃ illustra el antiguedad del edificio, pues estauan piedras tan grâdes muy bien assentadas." (Ibid., ubi supra.) Compare with this Miller's account of the city, as existing at the present day. "The walls of many of the houses have remained unaltered for centuries. The great size of the stones, the variety of their shapes, and the inimitable workmanship they display, give to the city that interesting air of antiquity and romance, which fills the mind with pleasing though painful veneration." Memoirs of Gen. Miller in the Service of the Republic of Peru, (London, 1829, 2d ed.) vol. II. p. 225.

[19] "La Imperial Ciudad de Cozco, que la adoravan los Indios, como á Cosa Sagrada." Garcilasso, Com. Real., Parte 1, lib. 3, cap. 20.—Also Ondegardo, Rel. Seg., MS.

[20] See, among others, the Memoirs, above cited, of Gen. Miller, which contain a minute and very interesting notice of modern Cuzco. (Vol. II. p. 223, et seq.) Ulloa, who visited the country in the middle of the last century, is unbounded in his expressions of admiration. Voyage to South America, Eng. trans., (London, 1806,) book VII. ch. 12.

[21] Betanzos, Suma y Narracion de los Yngas, MS., cap. 12.—Garcilasso, Com. Real., Parte 1, iib. 7, cap. 27-29.

The demolition of the fortress, begun immediately after the Conquest, provoked the remonstrance of more than one enlightened Spaniard, whose voice, however, was impotent against the spirit of cupidity and violence. See Sarmiento, Relacion, MS., cap. 48.

[22] Ibid., ubi supra.—Inscripciones, Medallas, Templos, Edificios, Antiguedades, y Monumentos del Peru, MS. This manuscript, which formerly belonged to Dr. Robertson, and which is now in the British Museum, is the work of some unknown author, somewhere probably about the time of Charles III.; a period when, as the sagacious scholar to whom I am indebted for a copy of it remarks, a spirit of sounder criticism was visible in the Castilian historians.

[23] Acosta, Naturall and Morall Historie of the East and West Indies, Eng. trans., (London, 1604,) lib. 6, cap. 14.—He measured the stones himself.—See also Garcilasso, Com. Real., loc. cit.

[24] Cieza de Leon, Cronica, cap. 93.—Ondegardo, Rel. Seg., MS.

Many hundred blocks of granite may still be seen, it is said, in an unfinished state, in a quarry near Cuzco.

[25] Sarmiento, Relacion, MS., cap. 48.—Ondegardo, Rel. Seg., MS.—Garcilasso, Com. Real., Parte 1, lib. 7, cap. 27, 28.

The Spaniards, puzzled by the execution of so great a work with such apparently inadequate means, referred it all, in their summary way, to the Devil; an opinion which Garcilasso seems willing to indorse. The author of the Antig. y Monumentos del Peru, MS., rejects this notion with becoming gravity.

[26] Sarmiento, Relacion, MS., cap. 7.—Garcilasso, Com. Real., Parte 1, lib. 1, cap. 26.

Acosta speaks of the eldest brother of the Inca as succeeding in preference to the son. (lib. 6, cap. 12.) He may have confounded the Peruvian with the Aztec usage. The Report of the Royal Audience states that a brother succeeded in default of a son. Dec. de la Aud. Real., MS.

[27] "*Et soror et conjux.*"—According to Garcilasso, the heir-apparent *always* married a sister. (Com. Real., Parte 1, lib. 4, cap. 9.) Ondegardo notices this as an innovation at the close of the fifteenth century. (Relacion Primera, MS.) The historian of the Incas, however, is confirmed in his extraordinary statement by Sarmiento. Relacion, MS., cap. 7.

[28] Garcilasso, Com. Real., Parte 1, lib. 1, cap. 26.

[29] From *oreja* "ear."—"Los caballeros de la sangre Real tenian orejas horadadas, y de ellas colgando grandes rodetes de plata y oro: llamaronles por esto los *orejones* los Castellaños la primera vez que los vieron." (Montesinos, Memorias Antiguas Historiales del Peru, MS., lib. 2, cap. 6.) The ornament, which was in the form of a wheel, did not depend from the ear, but was inserted in the gristle of it, and was as large as an orange. "La hacen tan ancha como una gran rosca de naranja; los Señores i Principales traian aquellas roscas de oro fino en las orejas." (Conq. i Pob. del Piru, MS.—Also Garcilasso, Com. Real., Parte 1, lib. 1, cap. 22.) "The larger the hole," says one of the old Conquerors, "the more of a gentleman!" Pedro Pizarro, Descub. y Conq., MS.

[30] Garcilasso, Com. Real., Parte 1, lib. 6, cap. 27.

[31] Ibid., Parte 1, lib. 6, cap. 24-28.

According to Fernandez, the candidates wore white shirts, with something like a cross embroidered in front! (Historia del Peru, (Sevilla, 1571,) Parte 2, lib. 3, cap. 6.) We may fancy ourselves occupied with some chivalrous ceremonial of the Middle Ages.

[32] Zarate, Conq. del Peru, lib. 1, cap. 11.—Sarmiento, Relacion, MS., cap. 7.

"Porque verdaderamente á lo que yo he averiguado toda la pretension de los Ingas fue una subjeccion en toda la gente, qual yo nunca he oido decir de ninguna otra nacion en tanto grado, que por muy principal que un Señor fuese, dende que entrava cerca del Cuzco en cierta señal que estava puesta en cada camino de quatro que hay, havia dende alli de venir cargado hasta la presencia del Inga, y alli dejava la carga y hacia su obediencia." Ondegardo, Rel. Prim., MS.

[33] It was only at one of these festivals, and hardly authorizes the sweeping assertion of Carli, that the royal and sacerdotal authority were blended together in Peru. We shall see, hereafter, the important and independent position occupied by the high-priest. "La Sacerdoce et l'Empire étoient divisés au Mexique; au lieu qu'ils étoient réunis au Pérou, comme au Tibet et à la Chine, et comme il le fut à Rome, lorsqu' Auguste jetta les fondemens de l'Empire, en y réunissant le Sacerdoce ou la dignité de Souverain Pontife." Lettres Américaines, (Paris, 1788,) trad. Franç., tom I. let. 7.

[34] "Porque el Inga dava á entender que era hijo del Sol, con este titulo se hacia adorar, i governava principalmente en tanto grado que nadie se le atrevia, i su palabra era ley, i nadie osaba ir contra su palabra ni voluntad; aunque obiese de matar cient mill Indios, no havia ninguno en su Reino que le osase decir que no lo hiciese." Conq. i Pob. del Piru, MS.

[35] Cieza de Leon, Cronica, cap. 114.—Garcilasso, Com. Real., Parte 1, lib. 1, cap. 22; lib. 6, cap. 28.—Acosta, lib. 6, cap. 12.

[36] One would hardly expect to find among the American Indians this social and kindly custom of our Saxon ancestors,—now fallen somewhat out of use, in the capricious innovations of modern fashion. Garcilasso is diffuse in his account of the forms observed at the royal table. (Com. Real., Parte 1, lib. 6, cap. 23.) The only hours of eating were at eight or nine in the morning, and at sunset, which took place at nearly the same time, in all seasons, in the latitude of Cuzco. The historian of the Incas admits that, though temperate in eating, they indulged freely in their cups, frequently prolonging their revelry to a late hour of the night. Ibid., Parte 1, lib. 6, cap. 1.

[37] "In lecticâ, aureo tabulato constratâ, humeris ferebant; in ummâ, ea erat observantia, vt vultum ejus intueri maxime incivile putarent, et inter baiulos, quicunque vel leviter pede offenso hæsitaret, e vestigio interficerent." Levinus Apollonius, De Peruviæ Regionis Inventione, et Rebus in eâdem gestis, (Antverpiæ, 1567,) fol. 37.—Zarate, Conq. del Peru, lib. 1, cap. 11.

According to this writer, the litter was carried by the nobles; one thousand of whom were specially reserved for the humiliating honor. Ubi supra.

[38] The acclamations must have been potent indeed, if, as Sarmiento tells us, they sometimes brought the birds down from the sky! "De esta manera eran tan temidos los Reyes que si salian por el Reyno y permitian alzar algun paño de los que iban en las andas para dejarse ver de sus vasallos, alzaban tan gran alarido que hacian caer las aves de lo alto donde iban volando á ser tomadas á manos." (Relacion, MS., cap. 10.) The same author has given in another place a more credible account of the royal progresses, which the Spanish reader will find extracted in *Appendix, No. 1.*

[39] Garcilasso, Com. Real., Parte 1, lib. 3, cap. 14; lib. 6, cap. 3.—Zarate, Conq. del Peru, lib. 1, cap. 11.

[40] Velasco has given some account of several of these palaces situated in different places in the kingdom of Quito. Hist. de Quito, tom. I. pp. 195-197.

[41] Cieza de Leon, Cronica, cap. 44.—Antig. y Monumentos del Peru, MS.—See, among others, the description of the remains still existing of the royal buildings at Callo, about ten leagues south of Quito, by Ulloa, Voyage to S. America, book 6, ch. 11, and since, more carefully, by Humboldt, Vues des Cordillères, p. 197.

[42] Garcilasso, Com. Real., Parte 1, lib. 6, cap. 1.

"Tanto que todo el servicio de la Casa del Rey así de cantaras para su vino, *como de cozina*, todo era oro y plata, y esto no en un lugar y en una parte lo tenia, sino en muchas." (Sarmiento, Relacion, MS., cap. 11.) See also the flaming accounts of the palaces of Bilcas, to the west of Cuzco, by Cieza de Leon, as reported to him by Spaniards who had seen them in their glory. (Cronica, cap. 89.) The niches are still described by modern travellers as to be found in the walls. (Humboldt, Vues des Cerdillères, p. 197.)

[43] "La ropa de la cama toda era de mantas, y freçadas de lana de Vicuña, que es tan fina, y tan regalada, que entre otras cosas preciadas de aquellas Tierras, se las han traìdo para la cama del Rey Don Phelipe Segundo." Garcilasso, Com. Real., Parte 1, lib. 6, cap. 1.

[44] Garcilasso, Com. Real., Parte 1, lib. 5, cap. 26; lib. 6, cap. 2.—Sarmiento, Relacion, MS., cap. 24.—Cieza de Leon, Cronica, cap. 94.

The last writer speaks of a cement, made in part of liquid gold, as used in the royal buildings of Tambo, a valley not far from Yucay! (Ubi supra.) We may excuse the Spaniards for demolishing such edifices,—if they ever met with them.

[45] Acosta, lib. 6, cap. 12.—Garcilasso, Com. Real., Parte 1, lib. 6, cap. 4.

[46] The Aztecs, also, believed that the soul of the warrior who fell in battle went to accompany the Sun in his bright progress through the heavens. (See Conquest of Mexico, book 1, chap. 3.)

[47] Conq. i Pob. del Piru, MS.—Acosta, lib. 5, cap. 6.

Four thousand of these victims, according to Sarmiento,—we may hope it is an exaggeration,—graced the funeral obsequies of Huayna Capac, the last of the Incas before the coming of the Spaniards. Ralacion, MS., cap. 65

[48] Cieza de Leon, Cronica, cap. 62.—Garcilasso, Com. Real., Parte 1, lib. 6, cap. 5.—Sarmiento, Relacion, MS., cap. 8.

[49] Ondegardo, Rel. Prim., MS.—Garcilasso, Com. Real., Parte 1, lib. 5, cap. 29.

The Peruvians secreted these mummies of their sovereigns after the Conquest, that they might not be profaned by the insults of the Spaniards. Ondegardo, when *corregidor* of Cuzco, discovered five of them, three male and two female. The former were the bodies of Viracocha, of the great Tupac Inca Yupanqui, and of his son Huayna Capac. Garcilasso saw them in 1560. They were dressed in their regal robes, with no insignia but the *llautu* on their heads. They were in a sitting posture, and, to use his own expression, "perfect as life, without so much as a hair or an eyebrow wanting." As they were carried through the streets, decently shrouded with a mantle, the Indians threw themselves on their knees, in sign of reverence, with many tears and groans, and were still more touched as they beheld some of the Spaniards themselves doffing their caps, in token of respect to departed royalty. (Ibid., ubi supra.) The bodies were subsequently removed to Lima; and Father Acosta, who saw them there some twenty years later, speaks of them as still in perfect preservation.

[50] "Tenemos por muy cierto que ni en Jerusalem, Roma, ni en Persia, ni en ninguna parte del mundo por ninguna Republica ni Rey de el, se juntaba en un lugar tanta riqueza de Metales de oro y Plata y Pedreria como en esta Plaza del Cuzco; quando estas fiestas y otras semejantes se hacian." Sarmiento, Relacion, MS., cap. 27.

[51] Idem, Relacion, MS., cap. 8, 27.—Ondegardo, Rel. Seg., MS.

It was only, however, the great and good princes that were thus honored, according to Sarmiento, "whose souls the silly people fondly believed, on account of their virtues, were in heaven, although, in truth," as the same writer assures us, "they were all the time burning in the flames of hell"! "Digo los que haviendo sido en vida buenos y valerosos, generosos con los Indios en les hacer mercedes, perdonadores de injurias, porque á estos tales canonizaban en su ceguedad por Santos y honrraban sus huesos, sin entender que las animas ardian en los Ynfiernos y creian que estaban en el Cielo." Ibid., ubi supra.

[52] Garcilasso says over three hundred! (Com. Real., Parte 1, lib. 3, cap. 19.) The fact, though rather startling, is not incredible, if, like Huayna Capac, they counted seven hundred wives in their seraglio. See Sarmiento, Relacion, MS., cap. 7.

[53] Garcilasso mentions a class of Incas *por privilegio,* who were allowed to possess the name and many of the immunities of the blood royal, though only descended from the great vassals that first served under the banner of Manco Capac. (Com. Real., Parte 1, lib. 1, cap. 22.) This important fact, to which he often refers, one would be glad to see confirmed by a single authority.

[54] "Los Incas tuvieron otra Lengua particular, que hablavan entre ellos, que no la entendian los demàs Indios, ni les era licito aprenderla, como Lenguage Divino. Esta me escriven del Per, que se ha perdido totalmente; porque como pereciò la Republica particular de los Incas, pereciò tambien el Lenguage dellos." Garcilasso, Com. Real., Parte 1, lib. 7, cap. 1.

[55] "Una sola gente hallo yo que era exenta, que eran los Ingas del Cuzco y por alli al rededor de ambas parcialidades, porque estos no solo no pagavan tributo, pero aun comian de lo que traian al Inga de todo el reino, y estos eran por la mayor parte los Governadores en todo el reino, y por donde quiera que iban se les hacia mucha honrra." Ondegardo, Rel. Prim., MS.

[56] Garcilasso, Com. Real., Parte 1, lib. 2, cap. 15.

[57] In this event, it seems, the successor named was usually presented to the Inca for confirmation. (Dec. de la Aud. Real., MS.) At other times, the Inca himself selected the heir from among the children of the deceased Curaca. "In short," says Ondegardo, "there was no rule of succession so sure, but it might be set aside by the supreme will of the sovereign." Rel. Prim., MS.

[58] Garcilasso, Com. Real., Parte 1, lib. 4, cap. 10.—Sarmiento, Relacion, MS., cap. 11.— Dec. de la Aud. Real., MS.—Cieza de Leon, Cronica, cap. 93.—Conq. i Pob. del Piru, MS.

[59] Dr. Morton's valuable work contains several engravings of both the Inca and the common Peruvian skull, showing that the facial angle in the former, though by no means great, was much larger than that in the latter, which was singularly flat and deficient in intellectual character. Crania Americana, (Philadelphia, 1829.)

CHAPTER II

[1] Pelu, according to Garcilasso, was the Indian name for "river," and was given by one of the natives in answer to a question put to him by the Spaniards, who conceived it to be the name of the country. (Com. Real., Parte 1, lib. 1, cap. 6.) Such blunders have led to the names of many places both in North and South America. Montesinos, however, denies that there is such an Indian term for "river." (Mem. Antiguas, MS., lib. 1, cap. 2.) According to this writer, Peru was the ancient *Ophir*, whence Solomon drew such stores of wealth; and which, by a very *natural* transition, has in time been corrupted into *Phiru, Piru, Peru!* The first book of the Memorias, consisting of thirty-two chapters, is devoted to this precious discovery.

[2] Ondegardo, Rel. Prim., MS.—Garcilasso, Com. Real., Parte 1, lib. 2, cap. 11.

[3] Yet an *American* may find food for his vanity in the reflection, that the name of a quarter of the globe, inhabited by so many civilized nations, has been exclusively conceded to him.—Was it conceded or assumed?

[4] Ibid., parte 1, cap. 9, 10.—Cieza de Leon, Cronica, cap. 93.

The capital was further divided into two parts, the Upper and Lower town, founded, as pretended, on the different origin of the population; a division recognized also in the inferior cities. Ondegardo, Rel. Seg., MS.

[5] Dec. de la Aud. Real., MS.—Garcilasso, Com. Real., Parte 1, lib. 2, cap. 15.

For this account of the councils I am indebted to Garcilasso, who frequently fills up gaps that have been left by his fellow-laborers. Whether the filling up will, in all cases, bear the touch of time, as well as the rest of his work, one may doubt.

[6] Dec. de la Aud. Real., MS.—Montesinos, Mem. Antiguas, MS., lib. 2, cap. 6.—Ondegardo, Rel. Prim., MS.

How analogous is the Peruvian to the Anglo-Saxon division into hundreds and tithings! But the Saxon law was more humane, which imposed only a fine on the district, in case of a criminal's escape.

[7] Dec. de la Aud. Real., MS.—Ondegardo, Rel. Prim. et Seg., MSS.—Garcilasso, Com. Real., Parte 1, lib. 2, cap. 11-14.—Montesinos, Mem. Antiguas, MS., lib. 2, cap. 6.

The accounts of the Peruvian tribunals by the early authorities are very meagre and unsatisfactory. Even the lively imagination of Garcilasso has failed to supply the blank.

[8] Ondegardo, Rel. Prim., MS.—Herrera, Hist. General, dec. 5, lib. 4, cap. 3.

Theft was punished less severely, if the offender had been really guilty of it to supply the necessities of life. It is a singular circumstance, that the Peruvian law made no distinction between fornication and adultery, both being equally punished with death. Yet the law could hardly have been enforced, since prostitutes were assigned, or at least allowed, a residence in the suburbs of the cities. See Garcilasso, Com. Real., Parte 1, lib. 4, cap. 34.

[9] Sarmiento, Relacion, MS., cap. 23.

"I los traidores entre ellos llamava *aucaes,* i esta palabra es la mas abiltada de todas quantas pueden decir aun Indio del Pirú, que quiere decir traidor á su Señor." (Conq. i Pob. del Pirú, MS.) "En las rebeliones y alzamientos se hicieron los castigos tan asperos, que algunas veces asolaron las provincias de todos los varones de edad sin quedar ninguno." Ondegardo, Rel. Prim., MS.

[10] "El castigo era riguroso, que por la mayor parte era de muerte, por liviano que fuese el delito; porque decian, que no los castigavan por el delito que avian hecho, ni por la ofensa agena, sino por aver quebrantado el mandamiento, y rompido la palabra del Inca, que lo respetavan como á Dios." Garcilasso, Com. Real., Parte 1, lib. 2, cap. 12.

[11] One of the punishments most frequent for minor offences was to carry a stone on the back. A punishment attended with no suffering but what arises from the disgrace attached to it is very justly characterized by McCulloh as a proof of sensibility and refinement. Researches, p. 361.

[12] The Royal Audience of Peru under Philip II.—there cannot be a higher authority—bears emphatic testimony to the cheap and efficient administration of justice under the Incas. "De suerte que los vicios eran bien castigados y la gente estaba bien sujeta y obediente; y aunque en las dichas penas havia esceso, redundaba en buen govierno y policia suya, y mediante ella eran aumentados. . . . . . Porque los Yndios alababan la governacion del Ynga, y aun los Españoles que algo alcanzan de ella, es porque todas las cosas susodichas se determinaban sin hacerles costas." Dec. de la Aud. Real., MS.

[13] Acosta, lib. 6, cap. 15.—Garcilasso, Com. Real., Parte 1, lib. 5, cap. 1.

"Si estas partes fuesen iguales, o qual fuese mayor, yo lo he procurado averiguar, y en unas es diferente de otras, y finalm^te yo tengo entendido que se hacia conforme á la disposicion de la tierra y a la calidad de los Indies." Ondegardo, Rel. Prim., MS.

[14] Ondegardo, Rel. Prim., MS.—Garcilasso, Com. Real., Parte 1, lib. 5, cap. 2.

The portion granted to each new-married couple, according to Garcilasso, was a *fanega* and a half of land. A similar quantity was added for each male child that was born; and half of the quantity for each female. The *fanega* was as much land as could be planted with a hundred weight of Indian corn. In the fruitful soil of Peru, this was a liberal allowance for a family.

[15] Ibid., Parte 1, lib. 5, cap. 3.

It is singular, that while so much is said of the Inca sovereign, so little should be said of the Inca nobility, of their estates, or the tenure by which they held them. Their historian tells us, that they had the best of the lands, wherever they resided, besides the interest which they had in those of the Sun and the Inca, as children of the one, and kinsmen of the other. He informs us, also, that they were supplied from the royal table, when living at court. (lib. 6, cap. 3.) But this is very loose language. The student of history will learn, on the threshold, that he is not to expect precise, or even very consistent, accounts of the institutions of a barbarous age and people, from contemporary annalists.

[16] Garcilasso relates that an Indian was hanged by Huayna Capac for tilling a curaca's ground, his near relation, before that of the poor. The gallows was erected on the curaca's own land. Ibid., Parte 1, lib. 5, cap. 2.

[17] Ibid., Parte 1, lib. 5, cap. 1-3.—Ondegardo, Rel. Seg., MS.

[18] Ondegardo, Rel. Prim., MS.

Yet sometimes the sovereign would recompense some great chief, or even some one among the people, who had rendered him a service, by the grant of a small number of llamas,—never many. These were not to be disposed of or killed by their owners, but descended as common property to their heirs. This strange arrangement proved a fruitful source of litigation after the Conquest. Ibid., ubi supra.

451

[19] See especially the account of the Licentiate Ondegardo, who goes into more detail than any contemporary writer, concerning the management of the Peruvian flocks. Rel. Seg., MS.

[20] Ondegardo, Rel. Prim. et Seg., MSS.

The manufacture of cloths for the Inca included those for the numerous persons of the blood royal, who wore garments of a finer texture than was permitted to any other Peruvian. Garcilasso, Com. Real., Parte 1, lib. 5, cap. 6.

[21] Ondegardo, Rel. Seg., MS.—Acosta, lib. 6, cap. 15.

[22] Ondegardo, Rel. Seg., MS.—Garcilasso, Com, Real., Parte 1, lib. 5, cap. 11.

[23] Garcilasso would have us believe that the Inca was indebted to the curacas for his gold and silver, which were furnished by the great vassals as presents. (Com. Real., Parte 1, lib. 5, cap. 7.) This improbable statement is contradicted by the Report of the Royal Audience, MS., by Sarmiento, (Relacion, MS., cap. 15,) and by Ondegardo, (Rel. Prim., MS.) who all speak of the mines as the property of the government, and wrought exclusively for its benefit. From this reservoir the proceeds were liberally dispensed in the form of presents among the great lords, and still more for the embellishment of the temples.

[24] Garcilasso, Com. Real., Parte 1, lib. 5, cap. 13-16.—Ondegardo, Rel. Prim. et Seg., MSS.

[25] Montesinos, Mem. Antiguas, MS., lib. 2, cap. 6.—Pedro Pizarro, Relacion del Descubrimiento y Conquista de los Reynos del Perú, MS.

"Cada provincia, en fin del año, mandava asentar en los quipos, por la cuenta de sus nudos, todos los hombres que habian muerto en ella en aquel año, y por el consiguiente los que habian nacido, y por principio del año que entraba, venian con los quipos al Cuzco." Sarmiento, Relacion, MS., cap. 16.

[26] Garcilasso, Com. Real., Parte 1, lib. 2, cap. 14.

[27] Ondegardo, Rel. Prim., MS.—Sarmiento, Rel., MS., cap. 15.

"Presupuesta y entendida la dicha division que el Inga tenia hecha de su gente, y orden que tenia puesta en el govierno de ella, era muy facil haverla en la division y cobranza de los dichos tributos; porque era claro y cierto lo que á cada uno cabia sin que hubiese desigualdad ni engaño." Dec. de la Aud. Real., MS.

[28] Sarmiento, Relacion, MS., cap. 15.—Ondegardo, Rel. Seg., MS.

[29] Ondegardo, Rel. Prim., MS.—Garcilasso, Com. Real., Parte 1, lib. 5, cap. 5.

[30] "Y tambien se tenia cuenta que el trabajo que pasavan fuese moderado, y con el menos riesgo que fuese posible. . . . . . Era tanta la orden que tuvieron estos Indios, que a mi parecer aunque mucho se piense en ello seria dificultoso mejorarla conocida su condicion y costumbres." Ondegardo, Rel. Prim., MS.

[31] "The working of the mines," says the President of the Council of the Indies, "was so regulated that no one felt it a hardship, much less was his life shortened by it." (Sarmiento, Relacion, MS., cap. 15.) It is a frank admission for a Spaniard.

[32] Garcilasso, Com. Real., Parte 1, lib. 5, cap. 34.—Ondegardo, Rel. Prim., MS.

"E asi esta parte del Inga no hay duda sino que de todas tres era la mayor, y en los depositos se parece bien que yó visité muchos en diferentes partes, é son mayores é mas largos que nó los de su religion sin comparasion." Idem, Rel. Seg., MS.

[33] "Todos los dichos tributos y servicios que el Inga imponia y llevaba como dicho es eran con color y para efecto del govierno y pro comun de todos asi como lo que se ponia en depositos todo se combertia y distribuia entre los mismos naturales." Dec. de la Aud. Real., MS.

[34] Acosta, lib. 6, cap. 15.

"No podre decir," says one of the Conquerors, "los depositos. Vide de rropas y de todos generos de rropas y vestidos que en este reino se hacian y vsavan que faltava tiempo para vello y entendimiento para comprender tanta cosa, muchos depositos de barretas de cobre para las minas y de costales y sogas de vasos de palo y platos del oro y plata que aqui se hallo hera cosa despanto." Pedro Pizarro, Descub. y Conq., MS.

[35] For ten years, sometimes, if we may credit Ondegardo, who had every means of knowing. "É ansi cuando nó era menester se estaba en los depositos é habia algunas vezes comida de diez años. . . . . . Los cuales todos se hallaron llenos cuando llegaron los Españoles desto y de todas las cosas necesarias para la vida humana." Rel. Seg., MS.

[36] Ondegardo, Rel. Prim., MS. "Por tanta orden é cuenta que seria dificultoso creerlo ni darlo á entender como ellos lo tienen en su cuenta é por registros é por menudo lo manifestaron que se pudiera por estenso." Idem, Rel. Seg., MS.

[37] Garcilasso, Com. Real., Parte 1, lib. 5, cap. 15.

[38] "Solo el trabajo de las personas era el tributo que se dava, porque ellos no poseian otra cosa." Ondegardo, Rel. Prim., MS.

[39] "Era tanta la orden que tenia en todos sus Reinos y provincias, que no consentia haver ningun Indio pobre ni menesteroso, porque havia orden i formas para ello sin que los pueblos reciviesen vexacion ni molestia, porque el Inga lo suplia de sus tributos." (Conq. i Pob. del Piru, MS.) The Licentiate Ondegardo sees only a device of Satan in these provisions of the Peruvian law, by which the old, the infirm, and the poor were rendered, in a manner, independent of their children, and those nearest of kin, on whom they would naturally have leaned for support; no surer way to harden the heart, he considers, than by thus disengaging it from the sympathies of humanity; and no circumstance has done more, he concludes, to counteract the influence and spread of Christianity among the natives. (Rel. Seg., MS.) The views are ingenious; but, in a country where the people had no property, as in Peru, there would seem to be no alternative for the supernumeraries, but to receive support from government or to starve.

[40] Acosta, lib. 6, cap. 12, 15.—Sarmiento, Relacion, MS., cap. 10.

[41] Dec. de la Aud. Real., MS. "Este camino hecho por valles ondos y por sierras altas, por montes de nieve, por tremedales de agua y por peña viva y junto á rios furiosos por estas partes y ballano y empedrado por las laderas, bien sacado por las sierras, deshechado, por las peñas socavado, por junto á los Rios sus paredes, entre nieves con escalones y descanso, por todas partes limpio barrido descombrado, lleno de aposentos, de depositos de tesoros, de Templos del Sol, de Postas que havia en este camino." Sarmiento, Relacion, MS., cap. 60.

[42] "On avait comblé les vides et les ravins par de grandes masses de maçonnerie. Les torrents qui descendent des hauteurs après des pluies abondantes, avaient creusé les endroits les moins solides, et s'etaient frayé une voie sous le chemin, le laissant ainsi suspendu en l'air comme un pont fait d'une seule pièce." (Velasco, Hist. de Quito, tom. I. p. 206.) This writer speaks from personal observation, having examined and measured different parts of the road, in the latter part of the last century. The Spanish scholar will find in *Appendix, No. 2.*, an animated description of this magnificent work, and of the obstacles encountered in the execution of it, in a passage borrowed from Sarmiento, who saw it in the days of the Incas.

[43] Garcilasso, Com. Real., Parte 1, lib. 3, cap. 7.

A particular account of these bridges, as they are still to be seen in different parts of Peru, may be found in Humboldt. (Vues des Cordillères, p. 230, et seq.) The *balsas* are described with equal minuteness by Stevenson. Residence in America, vol. II. p. 222, et seq.

[44] Cieza de Leon, Cronica, cap. 60.—Relacion del Primer Descubrimiento de la Costa y Mar del Sur, MS.

This anonymous document of one of the early Conquerors contains a minute and probably trustworthy account of both the high roads, which the writer saw in their glory, and which he ranks among the greatest wonders of the world.

[45] Relacion del Primer Descub., MS.—Cieza de Leon, Cronica, cap. 37.—Zarate, Conq. del Peru, lib. 1, cap. 11.—Garcilasso, Com. Real., Parte 1, lib. 9, cap. 13.

[46] "Cette chaussée, bordée de grandes pierres de taille, peut être comparée aux plus belles routes des Romains que j'aie vues en Italie, en France et en Espagne. . . . . . Le grand chemin de l'Inca, un des ouvrages les plus utiles, et en même temps des plus gigantesques que les hommes aient exécuté." Humboldt, Vues des Cordillères, p. 294.

[47] The distance between the posthouses is variously stated; most writers not estimating it at more than three fourths of a league. I have preferred the authority of Ondegardo, who usually writes with more conscientiousness and knowledge of his ground than most of his contemporaries.

[48] The term *chasqui,* according to Montesinos, signifies "one that receives a thing." (Mem. Antiguas, MS., cap. 7.) But Garcilasso, a better authority for his own tongue, says it meant "one who makes an exchange." Com. Real., Parte 1, lib. 6, cap. 8.

[49] "Con vn hilo de esta Borla, entregado á uno de aquellos Orejones, governaban la Tierra, i proveian lo que querian con maior obediencia, que en ninguna Provincia del Mundo se ha visto tener á las Provissiones de su Rei." Zarate, Conq. del Peru, lib. 1, cap. 9.

[50] Sarmiento, Relacion, MS., cap. 18.—Dec. de la Aud. Real., MS.

If we may trust Montesinos, the royal table was served with fish, taken a hundred leagues from the capital, in twenty-four hours after it was drawn from the ocean! (Mem. Antiguas, MS., lib. 2, cap. 7.) This is rather too expeditious for any thing but rail-cars.

[51] The institution of the Peruvian posts seems to have made a great impression on the minds of the Spaniards who first visited the country; and ample notices of it may be found in Sarmiento, Relacion, MS., cap. 15.—Dec. de la Aud. Real., MS.—Fernandez, Hist. del Peru, Parte 2, lib. 3, cap. 5.—Conq. i Pob. del Piru, MS., et auct. plurimis.

The establishment of posts is of old date among the Chinese, and, probably, still older among the Persians. (See Herodotus, Hist., Urania, sec. 98.) It is singular, that an invention designed for the uses of a despotic government should have received its full application only under a free one. For in it we have the germ of that beautiful system of intercommunication, which binds all the nations of Christendom together as one vast commonwealth.

[52] "Mas se hicieron Señores al principio por maña, que por fuerza." Ondegardo, Rel. Prim., MS.

[53] Idem, Rel. Prim., MS.—Dec. de la Aud. Real., MS.

[54] Gomara, Cronica, cap. 195.—Conq. i Pob. del Piru, MS.

[55] Gomara, Cronica, ubi supra.—Sarmiento, Relacion, MS., cap. 20.—Velasco, Hist. de Quito, tom. I. pp. 176-179.

This last writer gives a minute catalogue of the ancient Peruvian arms, comprehending nearly every thing familiar to the European soldier, except fire-arms.—It was judicious in him to omit these.

[56] Zarate, Conq. del Peru, lib. 1, cap. 11.—Sarmiento, Relacion, MS., cap. 60.

Condamine speaks of the great number of these fortified places, scattered over the country between Quito and Lima, which he saw in his visit to South America in 1737; some of which he has described with great minuteness. Mémoire sur Quelques Anciens Monumens du Pérou, du Tems des Incas, ap. Historie de l'Académie Royale des Sciences et de Belles Lettres, (Berlin, 1748,) tom. II. p. 438.

[57] "E ansi cuando," says Ondegardo, speaking from his own personal knowledge, "el Señor Presidente Gasca passó con la gente de castigo de Gonzalo Pizarro por el valle de Jauja, estuvo alli siete semanas á lo que me acuerdo, se hallaron en deposito maiz de cuatro y de tres y de dos años mas de 15 ᴢ. hanegas junto al camino, é alli comió la gente, y se entendió que si fuera menester muchas mas nó faltaran en el valle en aquellos depositos, conforme á la orden antigua, porque á mi cargo estubo el repartirlas y hacer la cuenta para pagarlas." Rel. Seg., MS.

[58] Pedro Pizarro, Descub. y Conq., MS.—Cieza de Leon, Cronica, cap. 44.—Sarmiento, Relacion, MS., cap. 14.

[59] "Mandabase que en los mantenimientos y casas de los enemigos se hiciese poco daño, diciendoles el Señor, presto serán estos nuestros como los que ya lo son; como esto tenian conocido, procuraban que la guerra fuese la mas liviana que ser pudiese." Sarmiento, Relacion, MS., cap. 14.

[60] "Plus pene parcendo victis, quàm vincendo imperium auxisse." Livy, lib. 30, cap. 42.

[61] Garcilasso, Com. Real., Parte 1, lib. 6, cap. 18.

[62] Sarmiento, Relacion, MS., cap. 14.

[63] Acosta, lib. 5, cap. 12.—Garcilasso, Com. Real., Parte 1, lib. 5, cap. 12.

[64] Ibid., Parte 1, lib. 5, cap. 13, 14.—Sarmiento, Relacion, MS., cap. 15.

[65] Sarmiento, Relacion, MS., cap. 19.

[66] Fernandez, Hist. del Peru, Parte 2, lib. 3, cap. 11.

[67] Sarmiento has given a very full and interesting account of the singularly humane policy observed by the Incas in their conquests, forming a striking contrast with the usual course of those scourges of mankind, whom mankind are wise enough to requite with higher admiration, even, than it bestows on its benefactors. As Sarmiento, who was President of the Royal Council of the Indies, and came into the country soon after the Conquest, is a high authority, and as his work, lodged in the dark recesses of the Escurial, is almost unknown, I have transferred the whole chapter to *Appendix, No. 3.*

[68] According to Velasco, even the powerful state of Quito, sufficiently advanced in civilization to have the law of property well recognized by its people, admitted the institutions of the Incas "not only without repugnance, but with joy." (Hist. de Quito, tom. II. p. 183.) But Velasco, a modern authority, believed easily,—or reckoned on his readers' doing so.

[69] Garcilasso, Com. Real., Parte 1, lib. 5, cap. 12; lib. 7, cap. 2.

[70] Ibid., Parte 1, lib. 6, cap. 35; lib. 7, cap. 1, 2.—Ondegardo, Rel. Seg., MS.—Sarmiento, Relacion, MS., cap. 55.

"Aun la Criatura no hubiese dejado el Pecho de su Madre quando le comenzasen á mostrar la Lengua que havia de saber; y aunque al principio fué dificultoso, é muchos se pusieron en no querer deprender mas lenguas de las suyas propias, los Reyes pudieron tanto que salieron con su intencion y ellos tubieron por bien de cumplir su mandado y tan de veras se entendió en ello que en tiempo de pocos años se savia y usaba una lengua en mas de mil y doscientas leguas." Ibid., cap. 21.

[71] Ondegardo, Rel. Prim., MS.—Fernandez, Hist. del Peru, Parte 2, lib. 3, cap. 11.

[72] "This regulation," says Father Acosta, "the Incas held to be of great importance to the order and right government of the realm." lib. 6, cap. 16.

[73] Conq. i Pob. del Piru, MS.

[74] "Trasmutaban de las tales Provincias la cantidad de gente de que de ella parecia convenir que saliese, á los cuales mandaban pasar a poblar otra tierra del temple y manera de donde salian, si fria fria, si caliente caliente, en donde les daban tierras, y campos, y casas, tanto, y mas como dejaron." Sarmiento, Relacion, MS., cap. 19.

[75] Ondegardo, Rel. Prim., MS.

[76] The descendants of these *mitimaes* are still to be found in Quito, or were so at the close of the last century, according to Velasco, distinguished by this name from the rest of the population. Hist. de Quito, tom. I. p. 175.

[77] Sarmiento, Relacion, MS., cap. 55.—Garcilasso, Com. Real., Parte 1, lib. 3, cap. 11, 17; lib. 6, cap. 16.

CHAPTER III

[1] They related, that, after the deluge, seven persons issued from a cave where they had saved themselves, and by them the earth was repeopled. One of the traditions of the Mexicans deduced their descent, and that of the kindred tribes, in like manner, from seven persons who came from as many caves in Aztlan. (Conf. Acosta, lib. 6, cap. 19; lib. 7, cap. 2.—Ondegardo, Rel. Prim., MS.) The story of the deluge is told by different writers with many variations, in some of which it is not difficult to detect the plastic hand of the Christian convert.

[2] Ondegardo, Rel. Seg., MS.—Gomara, Hist. de las Ind., cap. 123.—Garcilasso, Com. Real., Parte 1, lib. 2, cap. 2, 7.

One might suppose that the educated Peruvians—if I may so speak—imagined the common people had no souls, so little is said of their opinions as to the condition of these latter in a future life, while they are diffuse on the prospects of the higher orders, which they fondly believed were to keep pace with their condition here.

[3] Such, indeed, seems to be the opinion of Garcilasso, though some writers speak of resinous and other applications for embalming the body. The appearance of the royal mummies found at Cuzco, as reported both by Ondegardo and Garcilasso, makes it probable that no foreign substance was employed for their preservation.

[4] Ondegardo, Rel. Seg., MS.

The Licentiate says, that this usage continued even after the Conquest; and that he had saved the life of more than one favorite domestic, who had fled to him for protection, as they were about to be sacrificed to the Manes of their deceased lords. Ibid., ubi supra.

[5] Yet these sepulchral mines have sometimes proved worth the digging. Sarmiento speaks of gold to the value of 100,000 *castellanos*, as occasionally buried with the Indian lords; (Relacion, MS., cap. 57;) and Las Casas—not the best authority in numerical estimates— says that treasures worth more than half a million of ducats had been found, within twenty years after the Conquest, in the tombs near Truxillo. (Œuvres, ed. par Llorente, (Paris, 1822,) tom. II. p. 192.) Baron Humboldt visited the sepulchre of a Peruvian prince in the same quarter of the country, whence a Spaniard in 1576 drew forth a mass of gold worth a million of dollars! Vues des Cordillères, p. 29.

[6] *Pachacamac* signifies "He who sustains or gives life to the universe." The name of the great deity is sometimes expressed by both Pachacamac and Viracocha combined. (See Balboa, Hist. du Pérou, chap. 6.—Acosta, lib. 6, cap. 21.) An old Spaniard finds in the popular meaning of *Viracocha,* "foam of the sea," an argument for deriving the Peruvian civilization from some voyager from the Old World. Conq. i Pob. del Piru, MS.

[7] Pedro Pizarro, Descub. y Conq., MS.—Sarmiento, Relacion, MS., cap. 27.

Ulloa notices the extensive ruins of brick, which mark the probable site of the temple of Pachacamac, attesting by their present appearance its ancient magnificence and strength. Mémoires Philosophiques, Historiques, Physiques, (Paris, 1787,) trad. Fr., p. 78.

[8] At least, so says Dr. McCulloh; and no better authority can be required on American antiquities. (Researches, p. 392.) Might he not have added *barbarous* nations, also?

[9] Thunder, Lightning, and Thunderbolt, could be all expressed by the Peruvians in one word, *Illapa.* Hence some Spaniards have inferred a knowledge of the Trinity in the natives! "The Devil stole all he could," exclaims Herrera, with righteous indignation. (Hist. General, dec. 5, lib. 4, cap. 5.) These, and even rasher conclusions, (see Acosta, lib. 5, cap. 28,) are scouted by Garcilasso, as inventions of Indian converts, willing to please the imaginations of their Christian teachers. (Com. Real., Parte 1, lib. 2, cap. 5, 6; lib. 3, cap. 21.) Imposture, on the one hand, and credulity on the other, have furnished a plentiful harvest of absurdities, which has been diligently gathered in by the pious antiquary of a later generation.

[10] Garcilasso's assertion, that these heavenly bodies were objects of reverence as holy things, but not of worship, (Com. Real., Parte 1, lib. 2, cap. 1, 23,) is contradicted by Ondegardo, Rel. Seg., MS.,—Dec. de la Aud. Real., MS.,—Herrera, Hist. General, dec. 5, lib. 4, cap. 4, —Gomara, Hist. de las Ind., cap. 121,—and, I might add, by almost every writer of authority whom I have consulted. It is contradicted, in a manner, by the admission of Garcilasso himself, that these several objects were all personified by the Indians as living beings, and had temples dedicated to them as such, with their effigies delineated in the same manner as was that of the Sun in his dwelling. Indeed, the effort of the historian to reduce the worship of the Incas to that of the Sun alone is not very reconcilable with what he elsewhere says of the homage paid to Pachacamac, above all, and to Rimac, the great oracle of the common people. The Peruvian mythology was, probably, not unlike that of Hindostan, where, under two, or at most three, principal deities, were assembled a host of inferior ones, to whom the nation paid religious homage, as personifications of the different objects in nature.

[11] Ondegardo, Rel. Seg., MS.

These consecrated objects were termed *huacas,*—a word of most prolific import; since it signified a temple, a tomb, any natural object remarkable for its size or shape, in short, a cloud of meanings, which by their contradictory sense have thrown incalculable confusion over the writings of historians and travellers.

[12] "La orden por donde fundavan sus huacas que ellos llamavan á las Idolatrias hera porque decian que todas criava el sol i que les dava madre por madre que mostravan á la tierra, porque decian que tenia madre, i tenian lé echo su vulto i sus adoratorios, i al fuego decian que tambien tenia madre i al mais i á las otras sementeras i á las ovejas iganado decian que tenian madre, i a la chocha ques el brevaje que ellos usan decian que el vinagre della hera la madre i lo reverenciavan i llamavan mama agua madre del vinagre, i á cada cosa adoravan destas de su manera." Conq. i Pob. del Piru, MS.

[13] Pedro Pizarro, Descub. y Conq., MS.

So it seems to have been regarded by the Licentiate Ondegardo. "E los Idolos estaban en aq¹ *galpon* grande de la casa del Sol, y cada Idolo destos tenia su servicio y gastos y mugeres, y en la casa del Sol le iban á hacer reverencia los que venian de su provincia, para lo qual é sacrificios que se hacian proveian de su misma tierra ordinaria é muy abundantemente por la misma orden que lo hacian quando estaba en la misma provincia, que daba gran autoridad á mi parecer é aun fuerza á estos Ingas que cierto me causó gran admiracion." Rel. Seg., MS.

[14] Garcilasso, Com. Real., Parte 1, lib. 3, cap. 25.

[15] "Tenia este Templo en circuito mas de quatro cientos pasos, todo cercado de una muralla fuerte, labrado todo el edificio de cantera muy excelente de fina piedra, muy bien puesta y asentada, y algunas piedras eran muy grandes y soberbias, no tenian mezcla de tierra ni cal, sino con el betun que ellos suelen hacer sus edificios, y estan tan bien labradas estas piedras que no se les parece mezcla ni juntura ninguna. En toda España no he visto cosa que pueda comparar á estas paredes y postura de piedra, sino a la torre que llaman la Calahorra que está junto con la puente de Cordoba, y á una obra que vi en Toledo, cuando fui a presentar la primera parte de mi Cronica al Principe Dⁿ Felipe." Sarmiento, Relacion, MS., cap. 24.

[16] Conq. i Pob. del Piru, MS.—Cieza de Leon, Cronica, cap. 44, 92.

"La figura del Sol, muy grande, hecha de oro obrada muy primamente engastonada en muchas piedras ricas." Sarmiento, Relacion, MS., cap. 24.

[17] "I al oro asimismo decian que era lagrimas que el Sol llorava." Conq. i Pob. del Piru, MS.

[18] Sarmiento, Relacion, MS., cap. 24.—Antig. y Monumentos del Peru, MS.

"Cercada junto á la techumbre de una plancha de oro de palmo i medio de ancho i lo mismo tenian por de dentro en cada bohio ó casa i aposento." (Conq. i Pob. del Piru, MS.) "Tenia una cinta de planchas de oro de anchor de mas de un palmo enlazadas en las piedras." Pedro Pizarro, Descub. y Conq., MS.

[19] Sarmiento, Relacion, MS., cap. 24.—Garcilasso, Com. Real., Parte 1, lib. 3, cap. 21.—Pedro Pizarro, Descub. y Conq., MS.

[20] "El bulto del Sol tenian mui grande de oro, i todo el servicio desta casa era de plata i oro, i tenian doze horones de plata blanca que dos hombres no abrazarian cada uno quadrados, i eran mas altos que una buena pica donde hechavan el maiz que havian de dar al Sol, segun ellos decian que comiese." Conq. i Pob. del Piru, MS.

The original, as the Spanish reader perceives, says each of these silver vases or bins was as high as a good lance, and so large that two men with outspread arms could barely encompass them! As this might, perhaps, embarrass even the most accommodating faith, I have preferred not to become responsible for any particular dimensions.

[21] Levinus Apollonius, fol. 38.—Garcilasso, Com. Real., Parte 1, lib. 3, cap. 24.—Pedro Pizarro, Descub. y Conq., MS.

"Tenian un Jardin que los Terrones eran pedazos de oro fino y estaban artificiosamente sembrado de maizales los quales eran oro asi las Cañas de ello como las ojas y mazorcas, y estaban tan bien plantados que aunque hiciesen recios bientos no se arrancaban. Sin todo esto tenian hechas mas de veinte obejas de oro con sus Corderos y los Pastores con sus ondas y cayados que las guardaban hecho de este metal; havia mucha cantidad de Tinajas de oro y de Plata y esmeraldas, vasos, ollas y todo genero de vasijas todo de oro fino; por otras Paredes tenian esculpidas y pintadas otras mayores cosas, en fin era uno de los ricos Templos que hubo en el mundo." Sarmiento, Relacion, MS., cap. 24.

[22] Miller's Memoirs, vol. II. pp. 223, 224.

[23] Herrera, Hist. General, dec 5, lib. 4, cap. 8.

"Havia en aquella ciudad y legua y media de la redonda, quatrocientos y tantos lugares, donde se hacian sacrificios, y se gastava mucha suma de hacienda en ellos." Ondegardo, Rel. Prim., MS.

[24] "Que aquella ciudad del Cuzco era casa y morada de Dioses, é ansi nó habia en toda ella fuente ni paso ni pared que nó dixesen que tenia misterio." Ondegardo, Rel. Seg., MS.

[25] Conq. i Pob. del Piru, MS.

An army, indeed, if, as Cieza de Leon states, the number of priests and menials employed in the famous temple of Bilcas, on the route to Chili, amounted to 40,000! (Cronica, cap. 89.) Every thing relating to these Houses of the Sun appears to have been on a grand scale. But we may easily believe this a clerical error for 4,000.

[26] Sarmiento, Relacion, MS., cap. 27.—Conq. i Pob. del Piru, MS.

It was only while the priests were engaged in the service of the temples, that they were maintained, according to Garcilasso, from the estates of the Sun. At other times, they were to get their support from their own lands, which, if he is correct, were assigned to them in the same manner as to the other orders of the nation. Com. Real., Parte 1, lib. 5, cap. 8.

[27] Dec. de la Aud. Real., MS.—Sarmiento, Relacion, MS., cap. 27.

The reader will find a brilliant, and not very extravagant, account of the Peruvian festivals in Marmontel's romance of *Les Incas*. The French author saw in their gorgeous ceremonial a fitting introduction to his own literary pageant. Tom. I. chap. 1-4.

[28] "Ningun Indio comun osaba pasar por la calle del Sol calzado; ni ninguno, aunque fuese mui grand Señor, entrava en las casas del Sol con zapatos." Conq. i Pob. del Piru, MS.

[29] Garcillaso de la Vega flatly denies that the Incas were guilty of human sacrifices; and maintains, on the other hand, that they uniformly abolished them in every country they subdued, where they had previously existed. (Com. Real., Parte 1, lib. 2, cap. 9, et alibi.) But in this material fact he is unequivocally contradicted by Sarmiento, Relacion, MS., cap. 22,—Dec. de la Aud. Real., MS.,—Montesinos, Mem. Antiguas, MS., lib. 2, cap. 8,—Balboa, Hist. du Perou, chap. 5, 8,—Cieza de Leon, Cronica, cap. 72,—Ondegardo, Rel. Seg., MS.,—Acosta, lib. 5, cap. 19,—and I might add, I suspect, were I to pursue the inquiry, by nearly every ancient writer of authority; some of whom, having come into the country soon after the Conquest, while its primitive institutions were in vigor, are entitled to more deference in a matter of this kind than Garcilasso himself. It was natural that the descendant of the Incas should desire to relieve his race from so odious an imputation; and we must have charity for him, if he does show himself, on some occasions, where the honor of his country is at stake, "high gravel blind." It should be added, in justice to the Peruvian government, that the best authorities concur in the admission, that the sacrifices were few, both in number and in magnitude, being reserved for such extraordinary occasions as those mentioned in the text.

[30] "Augurque cum esset, dicere ausus est, optimis auspiciis ea geri, quæ pro reipublicæ salute gererentur." Cicero, De Senectute.

This inspection of the entrails of animals for the purposes of divination is worthy of note, as a most rare, if not a solitary, instance of the kind among the nations of the New World, though so familiar in the ceremonial of sacrifice among the pagan nations of the Old.

[31] "Vigilemque sacraverat ignem, Excubias divûm æternas."

Plutarch, in his life of Numa, describes the reflectors used by the Romans for kindling the sacred fire, as concave instruments of brass, though not spherical like the Peruvian, but of a triangular form.

[32] Acosta, lib. 5, cap. 28, 29.—Garcilasso, Com. Real., Parte 1, lib. 6, cap. 23.

[33] "That which is most admirable in the hatred and presumption of Sathan is, that he not onely counterfeited in idolatry and sacrifices, but also in certain ceremonies, our sacraments, which Jesus Christ our Lord instituted, and the holy Church uses, having especially pretended to imitate, in some sort, the sacrament of the communion, which is the most high and divine of all others." Acosta, lib. 5, cap. 23.

[34] Herrera, Hist. General, dec. 5, lib. 4, cap. 4.—Ondegardo, Rel. Prim., MS.

"The father of lies would likewise counterfeit the sacrament of Confession, and in his idolatries sought to be honored with ceremonies very like to the manner of Christians." Acosta, lib. 5, cap. 25.

[35] Cieza de Leon, not content with many marvellous accounts of the influence and real apparition of Satan in the Indian ceremonies, has garnished his volume with numerous wood-cuts representing the Prince of Evil in bodily presence with the usual accompaniments of tail, claws, &c., as if to reënforce the homilies in his text! The Peruvian saw in his idol a god. His Christian conqueror saw in it the Devil. One may be puzzled to decide which of the two might lay claim to the grossest superstition.

[36] Piedrahita, the historian of the Muyscas, is satisfied that this apostle must have been St. Bartholomew, whose travels were known to have been extensive. (Conq. de Granada, Parte 1, lib. 1, cap. 3.) The Mexican antiquaries consider St. Thomas as having had charge of the mission to the people of Anahuac. These two apostles, then, would seem to have divided the New World, at least the civilized portions of it, between them. How they came, whether by Behring's Straits, or directly across the Atlantic, we are not informed. Velasco—a writer of the eighteenth century!—has little doubt that they did really come. Hist. de Quito, tom. I. pp. 89, 90.

[37] The subject is illustrated by some examples in the "History of the Conquest of Mexico," vol. III., *Appendix, No.* 1.; since the same usages in that country led to precisely the same rash conclusions among the Conquerors.

[38] Llamavase Casa de Escogidas; porque las escogian, ó por Linage, ó por Hermosura." Garcilasso, Com. Real., Parte 1, lib. 4, cap. 1.

[39] Ondegardo, Rel. Prim., MS.

The word *mamacona* signified "matron"; *mama*, the first half of this compound word, as already noticed, meaning "mother." See Garcilasso, Com. Real., Parte 1, lib. 4, cap. 1.

[40] Pedro Pizarro, Descub. y Conq., MS.

[41] Dec. de la Aud. Real., MS.

[42] Balboa, Hist. du Pérou, chap. 9.—Fernandez, Hist. del Peru, Parte 2, lib. 3, cap. 11.—Garcilasso, Com. Real., Parte 1, lib. 4, cap. 3.

According to the historian of the Incas, the terrible penalty was never incurred by a single lapse on the part of the fair sisterhood; though, if it had been, the sovereign, he assures us, would have "exacted it to the letter, with as little compunction as he would have drowned a puppy." (Com. Real., Parte 1, lib. 4, cap. 3.) Other writers contend, on the contrary, that these Virgins had very little claim to the reputation of Vestals. (See Pedro Pizarro, Descub. y Conq., MS.—Gomara, Hist. de las Ind., cap. 121.) Such imputations are common enough on the inhabitants of religions houses, whether pagan or Christian. They are contradicted in the present instance by the concurrent testimony of most of those who had the best opportunity of arriving at truth, and are made particularly improbable by the superstitious reverence entertained for the Incas.

[43] Pedro Pizarro, Descub. y Conq., MS.—Garcilasso, Com. Real., Parte 1, lib. 4, cap. 1.

[44] Ibid., Parte 1, lib. 4, cap. 5.—Cieza de Leon, Cronica, cap. 44.

[45] Dec. de la Aud. Real., MS.—Garcilasso, Com. Real., Parte 1, lib. 4, cap. 4.—Montesinos, Mem. Antiguas, MS., lib. 2, cap. 19.

[46] By the strict letter of the law, according to Garcilasso, no one was to marry out of his own lineage. But this narrow rule had a most liberal interpretation, since all of the same town, and even province, he assures us, were reckoned of kin to one another. Com. Real., Parte 1, lib. 4, cap. 8.

[47] Fernandez, Hist. del Peru, Parte 2, lib. 3, cap. 9.

This practice, so revolting to our feelings that it might well be deemed to violate the law of nature, must not, however, be regarded as altogether peculiar to the Incas, since it was countenanced by some of the most polished nations of antiquity.

[48] Ondegardo, Rel. Seg., MS.—Garcilasso, Com. Real., Parte 1, lib. 6, cap. 36.—Dec. de la Aud Real., MS.—Montesinos, Mem. Antiguas, MS., lib. 2, cap. 6.

CHAPTER IV

[1] "No es licito, que enseñen à los hijos de los Plebeios, las Ciencias, que pertenescen à los Generosos, y no mas; porque como Gente baja, no se eleven, y ensobervezcan, y menoscaben, y apoquen la Republica: bastales, que aprendan los Oficios de sus Padres; que el Mandar, y Governar no es de Plebeios, que es hacer agravio al Oficio, y à la Republica, encomendarsela à Gente comun." Garcilasso, Com. Real., Parte 1, lib. 8, cap. 8.

[2] Ibid., Parte 1, lib 7, cap. 10.

The descendant of the Incas notices the remains, visible in his day, of two of the palaces of his royal ancestors, which had been built in the vicinity of the schools, for more easy access to them.

[3] Ibid., Parte 1, lib. 4, cap. 19.

[4] Conq. i Pob. del Piru, MS.—Sarmiento, Relacion, MS., cap. 9.—Acosta, lib. 6, cap. 8.—Garcilasso, Parte 1, lib. 6, cap. 8.

[5] Ondegardo expresses his astonishment at the variety of objects embraced by these simple records, "hardly credible by one who had not seen them." "En aquella ciudad se hallaron muchos viejos oficiales antiguos del Inga, asi de la religion, como del Govierno, y otra cosa que no pudiera creer sino la viera, que por hilos y nudos se hallan figuradas las leyes, y estatutos asi de lo uno como de lo otro, y las sucesiones de los Reyes y tiempo que governaron: y hallose lo que todo esto tenian a su cargo que no fue poco, y aun tube alguna claridad de los estatutos que en tiempo de cada uno se havian puesto." (Rel. Prim., MS.) (See also Sarmiento, Relacion, MS., cap. 9.—Acosta, lib. 6, cap. 8.—

Garcillasso, Parte 1, lib. 6, cap. 8, 9.) A vestige of the quipus is still to be found in some parts of Peru, where the shepherds keep the tallies of their numerous flocks by means of this ancient arithmetic.

[6] Ibid., ubi supra.

[7] Ibid., ubi supra.—Dec. de la Aud. Real., MS.—Sarmiento, Relacion, MS., cap. 9.

Yet the quipus must be allowed to bear some resemblance to the belts of wampum—made of colored beads strung together—in familiar use among the North American tribes, for commemorating treaties, and for other purposes.

[8] Dec. de la Aud. Real., MS.—Garcilasso, Com. Real., Parte 1, lib. 2, cap. 27.

The word *haravec* signified "inventor" or "finder"; and in his title, as well as in his functions, the minstrel-poet may remind us of the Norman *trouvère*. Garcilasso has translated one of the little lyrical pieces of his countrymen. It is light and lively; but one short specimen affords no basis for general criticism.

[9] Ondegardo, Rel. Prim., MS. Sarmiento justly laments that his countrymen should have suffered this dialect, which might have proved so serviceable in their intercourse with the motley tribes of the empire, to fall so much out of use as it has done. "Y con tanto digo que fué harto beneficio para los Españoles haver esta lengua pues podian con ella andar por todas partes en algunas de las quales ya se vá perdiendo." Relacion, MS., cap. 21.

According to Velasco, the Incas, on arriving with their conquering legions at Quito, were astonished to find a dialect of the Quichua spoken there, although it was unknown over much of the intermediate country; a singular fact, if true. (Hist. de Quito, tom. I. p. 185.) The author, a native of that country, had access to some rare sources of information; and his curious volumes show an intimate analogy between the science and social institutions of the people of Quito and Peru. Yet his book betrays an obvious anxiety to set the pretensions of his own country in the most imposing point of view, and he frequently hazards assertions with a confidence that is not well calculated to secure that of his readers.

[10] Garcillasso, Com. Real., ubi supra.

[11] Ondegardo, Rel. Prim., MS. Fernandez, who differs from most authorities in dating the commencement of the year from June, gives the names of the several months, with their appropriate occupations. Hist. del Peru, Parte 2, lib. 3, cap. 10.

[12] Garcillasso, Com. Real., Parte 1, lib. 2, cap. 22-26.

The Spanish conquerors threw down these pillars, as savouring of idolatry in the Indians. Which of the two were best entitled to the name of barbarians?

[13] Betanzos, Nar. de los Ingas, MS., cap. 16.—Sarmiento, Relacion, MS., cap. 23.—Acosta, lib. 6, cap. 3.

The most celebrated gnomon in Europe, that raised on the dome of the metropolitan church of Florence, was erected by the famous Toscanelli,—for the purpose of determining the solstices, and regulating the festivals of the Church,—about the year 1468; perhaps at no very distant date from that of the similar astronomical contrivance of the American Indian. See Tiraboschi, Historia della Letteratura Italiana, tom. VI. lib. 2, cap. 2, sec. 38.

[14] A tolerably meagre account—yet as full, probably, as authorities could warrant—of this interesting people has been given by Piedrahita, Bishop of Panamá, in the first two Books of his Historia General de las Conquistas del Nuevo Regno de Granada, (Madrid, 1688.)

—M. de Humboldt was fortunate in obtaining a MS., composed by a Spanish ecclesiastic resident in Santa Fé de Bogota, in relation to the Muysca calendar, of which the Prussian philosopher has given a large and luminous analysis. Vues des Cordillères, p. 244.

[15] Montesinos, Mem. Antiguas, MS., lib. 2, cap. 7.

"Renovó la computacion de los tiempos, que se iba perdiendo, y se contaron en su Reynado los años por 365 dias y seis horas; á los años añadió decadas de diez años, á cada diez decadas una centuria de 100 años, y á cada diez centurias una capachoata ó Jutiphuacan, que son 1000 años, que quiere decir el grande año del Sol; asi contaban los siglos y los sucesos memorables de sus Reyes." Ibid., loc. cit.

[16] "Ansi mismo les hicieron señalar gente para hechizeros que tambien es entre ellos, oficio publico y conoscido en todos,. . . . .los diputados para ello no lo tenian por travajo, por que ninguno podia tener semejante oficio como los dichos sino fuesen viejos é viejas, y personas inaviles para travajar, como mancos, cojos ó contrechos, y gente asi á quien faltava las fuerzas para ello." Ondegardo, Rel. Seg., MS.

[17] See Codex Tel.-Remensis, Part 4, Pl. 22, ap. Antiquities of Mexico, vol. I. London, 1829.

[18] Sarmiento, Relacion, MS., cap. 16.

The nobles, also, it seems, at this high festival, imitated the example of their master. "Pasadas todas las fiestas, en la ultima llevavan muchos arados de manos, los quales antiguamente heran de oro; i échos los oficios, tomava el Inga un arado i comenzava con el a romper la tierra, i lo mismo los demas señores, para que de alli adelante en todo su señorio hiciesen lo mismo, i sin que el Inga hiciese esto no avia Indio que osase romper la tierra, ni pensavan que produjese si el Inga no la rompia primero i esto vaste quanto á las fiestas." Conq. i Pob. del Piru, MS.

[19] Sarmiento, Relacion, MS., cap. 21.—Garcilasso, Com. Real., Parte 1, lib. 5, cap. 24.—Stevenson, Narrative of a Twenty Years' Residence in S. America, (London, 1829,) vol. I. p. 412; II. pp. 173, 174.

"Sacauan acequias en cabos y por partes que es cosa estraña afirmar lo: purque las echauan por lugares altos y baxos: y por laderas de los cabeços y haldas de sierras q estan en los valles: y por ellos mismos atrauiessan muchas: unas por una parte, y otras por otra, que es gran delectació caminar por aquellos valles: porque parece que se anda entre huertas y florestas llenas de frescuras." Cieza de Leon, Cronica, cap. 66.

[20] Pedro Pizarro, Descub. y Conq., MS.—Memoirs of Gen. Miller, vol. II. p. 220.

[21] Miller supposes that it was from these *andenes* that the Spaniards gave the name of Andes to the South American Cordilleras. (Memoirs of Gen. Miller, vol. II. p. 219.) But the name is older than the Conquest, according to Garcillaso, who traces it to *Anti*, the name of a province that lay east of Cuzco. (Com. Real., Parte 1, lib. 2, cap. 11.) *Anta*, the word for copper, which was found abundant in certain quarters of the country, may have suggested the name of the province, if not immediately that of the mountains.

[22] Memoirs of Gen. Miller, ubi supra.—Garcilasso, Com. Real., Parte 1, lib. 5, cap. 1.

[23] Cieza de Leon, Cronica, cap. 73.

The remains of these ancient excavations still excite the wonder of the modern traveller. See Stevenson, Residence in S. America, vol. I. p. 359.—Also McCulloh, Researches, p. 358.

[24] Acosta, lib. 4, cap. 36.—Garcilasso, Com. Real., Parte 1, lib. 5, cap. 3.

[25] Ibid., Parte 1, lib. 5, cap. 2.

[26] Sarmiento, Relacion, MS., cap. 19.—Garcilasso, Com. Real., Parte 1, lib. 6, cap. 36; lib. 7, cap. 1.—Herrera, Hist. General, dec. 5, lib. 4, cap. 3.

[27] The prolific properties of the banana are shown by M. de Humboldt, who states that its productiveness, as compared with that of wheat, is as 133 to 1, and with that of the potato, as 44 to 1. (Essai Politique sur le Royaume de la Nouvelle Espagne, Paris, 1827, tom. II. p. 389.) It is a mistake to suppose that this plant was not indigenous to South America. The banana-leaf has been frequently found in ancient Peruvian tombs.

[28] The misnomer of *blé de Turquie* shows the popular error. Yet the rapidity of its diffusion through Europe and Asia, after the discovery of America, is of itself sufficient to show that it could not have been indigenous to the Old World, and have so long remained generally unknown there.

[29] Acosta, lib. 4, cap. 16.

The saccharine matter contained in the maize-stalk is much greater in tropical countries than in more northern latitudes; so that the natives in the former may be seen sometimes sucking it like the sugarcane. One kind of the fermented liquors, *sora,* made from the corn, was of such strength, that the use of it was forbidden by the Incas, at least to the common people. Their injunctions do not seem to have been obeyed so implicitly in this instance as usual.

[30] Garcilasso, Com. Real., Parte 1, lib. 2, cap. 25.

[31] The pungent leaf of the *betel* was in like manner mixed with lime when chewed. (Elphinstone, History of India, London, 1841, vol. I. p. 331.) The similarity of this social indulgence, in the remote East and West, is singular.

[32] Ondegardo, Rel. Seg., MS.—Acosta, lib. 4, cap. 22.—Stevenson, Residence in S. America, vol. II. p. 63.—Cieza de Leon, Cronica, cap. 96.

[33] A traveller (Poeppig) noticed in the Foreign Quarterly Review, (No. 33,) expatiates on the malignant effects of the habitual use of the *cuca,* as very similar to those produced on the chewer of opium. Strange that such baneful properties should not be the subject of more frequent comment with other writers! I do not remember to have seen them even adverted to.

[34] Malte-Brun, book 86.

The potato, found by the early discoverers in Chili, Peru, New Granada, and all along the Cordilleras of South America, was unknown in Mexico,—an additional proof of the entire ignorance in which the respective nations of the two continents remained of one another. M. de Humboldt, who has bestowed much attention on the early history of this vegetable, which has exerted so important an influence on European society, supposes that the cultivation of it in Virginia, where it was known to the early planters, must have been originally derived from the Southern Spanish colonies. Essai Politique, tom. II. p. 462.

[35] While Peru, under the Incas, could boast these indigenous products, and many others less familiar to the European, it was unacquainted with several of great importance, which, since the Conquest, have thriven there as on their natural soil. Such are the olive, the grape, the fig, the apple, the orange, the sugar-cane. None of the cereal grains of the Old World were found there. The first wheat was introduced by a Spanish lady of Trujillo, who took great pains to disseminate it among the colonists, of which the government, to its credit, was not unmindful. Her name was Maria de Escobar. History, which is so much occupied with celebrating the scourges of humanity, should take pleasure in commemorating one of its real benefactors.

CHAPTER V

[1] Walton, Historical and Descriptive Account of the Peruvian Sheep, (London, 1811,) p. 115. This writer's comparison is directed to the wool of the vicuña, the most esteemed of the genus for its fleece.

[2] Ibid., p. 23, et seq. — Garcilasso, Com. Real., Parte 1, lib. 8, cap. 16. — Acosta, lib. 4, cap. 41.

Llama, according to Garcilasso de la Vega, is a Peruvian word signifying "flock." (Ibid., ubi supra.) The natives got no milk from their domesticated animals; nor was milk used, I believe, by any tribe on the American continent.

[3] Ganado maior, ganado menor.

[4] The judicious Ondegardo emphatically recommends the adoption of many of these regulations by the Spanish government, as peculiarly suited to the exigencies of the natives. "En esto de los ganados paresció haber hecho muchas constituciones en diferentes tiempos é algunas tan utiles é provechosas para su conservacion que convendria que tambien guardasen agora." Rel. Seg., MS.

[5] Malte-Brun book 86.

[6] Ychu, called in the Flora Peruana Jarava; Class, Monandria Digynia. See Walton, p. 17.

[7] Ondegardo, Rel. Prim., MS.

[8] Sometimes even a hundred thousand mustered, when the Inca hunted in person, if we may credit Sarmiento. "De donde haviendose ya juntado cinquenta ó sesenta mil Personas ó cien mil si mandado les era." Relacion, MS, cap. 13.

[9] Ibid., ubi supra.

Charqui; hence, probably, says McCulloh, the term "jerked," applied to the dried beef of South America. Researches, p. 377.

[10] Sarmiento, Relacion, MS., loc. cit. — Cieza de Leon, Cronica, cap. 81. — Garcilasso, Com. Real., Parte 1, lib. 6, cap. 6.

[11] Acosta, lib. 4, cap. 41.

[12] "Ropas finisimas para los Reyes, que lo eran tanto que parecian de sarga de seda y con colores tan perfectos quanto se puede afirmar." Sarmiento, Relacion, MS., cap. 13.

[13] Pedro Pizarro, Descub. y Conq., MS.

"Ropa finissima para los señores Ingas de lana de las Vicunias. Y cierto fuetan prima esta ropa, como auran visto en España: por alguna que alla fue luego que se gano este reyno. Los vestidos destos Ingas eran camisetas desta ropa: vnas pobladas de argenteria de oro, otras de esmeraldas y piedras preciosas: y algunas de plumas de aues: otras de solamente la manta. Para hazer estas ropas, tuuieró y tienen tan perfetas colores de carmesi, azul, amarillo, negro, y de otras suertes: que verdaderamente tienen ventaja a las de España." Cieza de Leon, Cronica, cap. 114.

[14] Ondegardo, Rel. Prim. et Seg., MSS. — Garcilasso, Com. Real., Parte 1, lib. 5, cap. 7, 9, 13.

[15] At least, such was the opinion of the Egyptians, who referred to this arrangement of castes as the source of their own peculiar dexterity in the arts. See Diodorus Sic., lib. 1, sec. 74.

[16] Ulloa, Not. Amer., ent. 21. — Pedro Pizarro, Descub. y Conq., MS. — Cieza de Leon, Cronica, cap. 114. — Condamine, Mem. ap. Hist. de l'Acad. Royale de Berlin, tom. II. p. 454-456.

The last writer says, that a large collection of massive gold ornaments of very rich workmanship was long preserved in the royal treasury of Quito. But on his going there to examine them, he learned that they had just been melted down into ingots to send to Carthagena, then besieged by the English! The art of war can flourish only at the expense of all the other arts.

[17] They had turquoises, also, and might have had pearls, but for the tenderness of the Incas, who were unwilling to risk the lives of their people in this perilous fishery! At least, so we are assured by Garcilasso, Com. Real., Parte 1, lib. 8, cap. 23.

[18] "No tenian herramientas de hierro ni azero." Ondegardo, Rel. Seg., MS.—Herrera, Hist. General, dec. 5, lib. 4, cap. 4.

[19] M. de Humboldt brought with him back to Europe one of these metallic tools, a chisel, found in a silver mine opened by the Incas not far from Cuzco. On an analysis, it was found to contain 0·94 of copper, and 0·06 of tin. See Vues des Cordillères, p. 117.

[20] "Quoiqu'il en soit," says M. de la Condamine, "nous avons vû en quelques autres ruïnes des ornemens du même granit, qui représentoient des mufles d'animaux, dont les narines percées portoient des anneaux mobiles de la même pierre." Mem. ap. Hist. de l'Acad. Royale de Berlin, tom. II. p. 452.

[21] See the History of the Conquest of Mexico, Book 1, chap. 5.

[22] Garcillasso, Com. Real., Parte 1, lib. 8, cap. 25.

[23] Ibid., Parte 1, lib. 5, cap. 7; lib. 6, cap. 8.—Ondegardo, Rel. Seg., MS.

This, which Bonaparte thought so incredible of the little island of Loo Choo, was still more extraordinary in a great and flourishing empire like Peru;—the country, too, which contained within its bowels the treasures that were one day to furnish Europe with the basis of its vast metallic currency.

[24] Ulloa, Not. Amer., ent. 21.

[25] It is the observation of Humboldt. "Il est impossible d'examiner attentivement un seul édifice du temps des Incas, sans reconnoître le même type dans tous les autres qui couvrent le dos des Andes, sur une longueur de plus de quatre cent cinquante lieues, depuis mille jusqu'à quatre mille mêtres d'élévation au-dessus du niveau de l'Océan. On dirait qu'un seul architecte a construit ce grand nombre de monumens." Vues des Cordilléres, p. 197.

[26] Ulloa, who carefully examined these bricks, suggests that there must have been some secret in their composition,—so superior in many respects to our own manufacture,—now lost. Not. Amer., ent. 20.

[27] Ibid., ubi supra.

[28] Among others, see Acosta, lib. 6, cap. 15.—Robertson, History of America, (London, 1796,) vol. III. p. 213.

[29] Ondegardo, Rel. Seg., MS.—Ulloa, Not. Amer., ent. 21.

Humboldt, who analyzed the cement of the ancient structures at Cannar, says that it is a true mortar, formed of a mixture of pebbles and a clayey marl. (Vues des Cordillères, p. 116.) Father Velasco is in raptures with an "almost imperceptible kind of cement" made of lime and a bituminous substance resembling glue, which incorporated with the stones so as to hold them firmly together like one solid mass, yet left nothing visible to the eye of the common observer. This glutinous composition, mixed with pebbles, made a sort of *Macadamized* road much used by the Incas, as hard and almost as smooth as marble. Hist. de Quito, tom. I. pp. 126-128.

[30] Condamine, Mem. ap. Hist. de l'Acad. Royale de Berlin, tom. II. p. 448.—Antig. y Monumentos del Peru, MS.—Herrera, Hist. General, dec. 5, lib. 4, cap. 4.—Acosta, lib. 6, cap. 14.—Ulloa, Voyage to S. America, vol. I. p. 469.—Ondegardo, Rel. Seg., MS.

[31] "Simplicité, symétrie, et solidité, voilà les trois caractères par lesquels se distinguent avantageusement tous les édifices péruviens." Humboldt, Vues des Cordillées, p. 115.

[32] The anonymous author of the Antig. y Monumentos del Peru, MS., gives us, at second hand, one of those golden traditions which, in early times, fostered the spirit of adventure. The tradition, in this instance, he thinks well entitled to credit. The reader will judge for himself.

"It is a well-authenticated report, and generally received, that there is a secret hall in the fortress of Cuzco, where an immense treasure is concealed, consisting of the statues of all the Incas, wrought in gold. A lady is still living, Doña Maria de Esquivel, the wife of the last Inca, who has visited this hall, and I have heard her relate the way in which she was carried to see it.

"Don Carlos, the lady's husband, did not maintain a style of living becoming his high rank. Doña Maria sometimes reproached him, declaring that she had been deceived into marrying a poor Indian under the lofty title of Lord or Inca. She said this so frequently, that Don Carlos one night exclaimed, 'Lady! do you wish to know whether I am rich or poor? You shall see that no lord nor king in the world has a larger treasure than I have.' Then covering her eyes with a handkerchief, he made her turn round two or three times, and, taking her by the hand, led her a short distance before he removed the bandage. On opening her eyes, what was her amazement! She had gone not more than two hundred paces, and descended a short flight of steps, and she now found herself in a large quadrangular hall, where, ranged on benches round the walls, she beheld the statues of the Incas, each of the size of a boy twelve years old, all of massive gold! She saw also many vessels of gold and silver, 'In fact,' she said, 'it was one of the most magnificent treasures in the whole world!'"

[33] Ante, chap. 1.

[34] Count Carli has amused himself with tracing out the different points of resemblance between the Chinese and the Peruvians. The emperor of China was styled the son of Heaven or of the Sun. He also held a plough once a year in presence of his people, to show his respect for agriculture. And the solstices and equinoxes were noted, to determine the periods of their religious festivals. The coincidences are curious. Lettres Américaines, tom. II. pp. 7, 8.

[35] "Era muy principal intento que la gente no holgase, que dava causa a que despues que los Ingas estuvieron en paz hacer traer de Quito al Cuzco piedra que venia de provincia en provincia para hacer casas para si ó p^a el Sol en gran cantidad, y del Cuzco llevalla a Quito p^a el mismo efecto, ... y asi destas cosas hacian los Ingas muchas de poco provecho y de escesivo travajo en que traian ocupadas las provincias ordinariam^{te}, y en fin el travajo era causa de su conservacion." Ondegardo, Rel. Prim., MS.—Also Antig. y Monumentos del Peru, MS.

[36] This was literally gold dust; for Ondegardo states, that, when governor of Cuzco, he caused great quantities of gold vessels and ornaments to be disinterred from the sand in which they had been secreted by the natives. "Que toda aquella plaza del Cuzco le sacaron la tierra propia, y se llevó á otras partes por cosa de gran estima, é la hincheron de arena

de la costa de la mar, como hasta dos palmos y medio en algunas partes, mas sembraron por toda ella muchos vasos de oro é plata, y hovejuelas y hombrecillos pequeños de lo mismo, lo cual se ha sacado en mucha cantidad, que todo lo hemos visto; desta arena estaba toda la plaza, quando yo fui á governar aquella Ciudad; é si fue verdad que aquella se trajo de ellos, afirman é tienen puestos en sus registros, paresceme que sea ansi, que toda la tierra junta tubo necesidad de entender en ello, por que la plaza es grande, y no tiene numero las cargas que en ella entraron; y la costa por lo mas cerca esta mas de nobenta leguas á lo que creo, y cierto yo me satisfice, porque todos dicen, que aquel genero de arena, no lo hay hasta la costa." Rel. Seg., MS.

[37] "Y si Dios permitiera que tubieran quien con celo de Cristiandad, y no con ramo de codicia, en lo pasado, les dieran entera noticia de nuestra sagrada Religion, era gente en que bien imprimiera, segun vemos por lo que ahora con la buena orden que hay se obra." Sarmiento, Relacion, MS., cap. 22.

But the most emphatic testimony to the merits of the people is that afforded by Mancio Sierra Lejesema the last survivor of the early Spanish Conquerors, who settled in Peru. In the preamble to his testament, made, as he states, to relieve his conscience, at the time of his death, he declares that the whole population, under the Incas, was distinguished by sobriety and industry; that such things as robbery and theft were unknown; that, far from licentiousness, there was not even a prostitute in the country; and that every thing was conducted with the greatest order, and entire submission to authority. The panegyric is somewhat too unqualified for a whole nation, and may lead one to suspect that the stings of remorse for his own treatment of the natives goaded the dying veteran into a higher estimate of their deserts than was strictly warranted by facts. Yet this testimony by such a man at such a time is too remarkable, as well as too honorable to the Peruvians, to be passed over in silence by the historian; and I have transferred the document in the original to *Appendix, No. 4.*

[38] "Sans doute l'homme moral du Pérou étoit infiniment plus perfectionné que l'Européen." Carli, Lettres Américaines, tom. I. p, 215.

[39] "Heran muy dados á la lujuria y al bever, tenian acceso carnal con las hermanas y las mugeres de sus padres como no fuesen sus mismas madres, y aun algunos avia que con ellas mismas lo hacian y ansi mismo con sus hijas. Estando borrachos tocavan algunos en el pecado nefando, emborrachavanse muy á menudo, y estando borrachos todo lo que el demonio les traia á la voluntad hacian. Heran estos orejones muy seberbios y presuntuosos. . . . . . Tenian otras muchas maldades que por ser muchas no las digo." Pedro Pizarro, Descub. y Conq., MS.

These random aspersions of the hard conqueror show too gross an ignorance of the institutions of the people to merit much confidence as to what is said of their character.

NOTE. I have not thought it necessary to swell this Introduction by an inquiry into the origin of Peruvian civilization, like that appended to the history of the Mexican. The Peruvian history doubtless suggests analogies with more than one nation in the East, some of which have been briefly adverted to in the preceding pages; although these analogies are adduced there not as evidence of a common origin, but as showing the coincidences which might naturally spring up among different nations under the same phase of civilization. Such coincidences are neither so numerous nor so striking as those afforded by the Aztec history. The correspondence presented by the astronomical science of the Mexicans is alone of more importance than all the rest. Yet the light of analogy, afforded by the institutions of the Incas, seems to point, as far as it goes, towards the same direction; and as the investigation could present but little substantially to confirm, and still less to confute, the views taken in the former disquisition, I have not thought it best to fatigue the reader with it.

Two of the prominent authorities on whom I have relied in this Introductory portion of the work, are Juan de Sarmiento and the Licentiate Ondegardo. Of the former I have been able to collect no information beyond what is afforded by his own writings. In the title prefixed to his manuscript, he is styled President of the Council of the Indies, a post of high authority, which infers a weight of character in the party, and means of information, that entitle his opinions on colonial topics to great deference.

These means of information were much enlarged by Sarmiento's visit to the colonies, during the administration of Gasca. Having conceived the design of compiling a history of the ancient Peruvian institutions, he visited Cuzco, as he tells us, in 1550, and there drew from the natives themselves the materials for his narrative. His position gave him access to the most authentic sources of knowledge, and from the lips of the Inca nobles, the best instructed of the conquered race, he gathered the traditions of their national history and institutions. The quipus formed, as we have seen, an imperfect system of mnemonics, requiring constant attention, and much inferior to the Mexican hieroglyphics. It was only by diligent instruction that they were made available to historical purposes; and this instruction was so far neglected after the Conquest, that the ancient annals of the country would have perished with the generation which was the sole depositary of them, had it not been for the efforts of a few intelligent scholars, like Sarmiento, who saw the importance, at this critical period, of cultivating an intercourse with the natives, and drawing from them their hidden stores of information.

To give still further authenticity to his work, Sarmiento travelled over the country, examined the principal objects of interest with his own eyes, and thus verified the accounts of the natives as far as possible by personal observation. The result of these labors was his work entitled, "Relacion de la sucesion y govierno de las Yngas Señores naturales que fueron de las Provincias del Peru y otras cosas tocantes á aquel Reyno, para el Iltmo. Señor Dⁿ Juan Sarmiento, Presidente del Consejo Rˡ de Indias."

It is divided into chapters, and embraces about four hundred folio pages in manuscript. The introductory portion of the work is occupied with the traditionary tales of the origin and early period of the Incas; teeming, as usual, in the antiquities of a barbarous people, with legendary fables of the most wild and monstrous character. Yet these puerile conceptions afford an inexhaustible mine for the labors of the antiquarian, who endeavours to unravel the allegorical web which a cunning priesthood had devised as symbolical of those mysteries of creation that it was beyond their power to comprehend. But Sarmiento happily confines himself to the mere statement of traditional fables, without the chimerical ambition to explain them.

From this region of romance, Sarmiento passes to the institutions of the Peruvians, describes their ancient polity, their religion, their progress in the arts, especially agriculture; and presents, in short, an elaborate picture of the civilization which they reached under the Inca dynasty. This part of his work, resting, as it does, on the best authority, confirmed in many instances by his own observation, is of unquestionable value, and is written with an apparent respect for truth, that engages the confidence of the reader. The concluding portion of the manuscript is occupied with the civil history of the country. The reigns of the early Incas, which lie beyond the sober province of history, he despatches with commendable brevity. But on the three last reigns, and fortunately of the greatest princes who occupied the Peruvian throne, he is more diffuse. This was comparatively firm ground for the chronicler, for the events were too recent to be obscured by the vulgar legends that gather like moss round every incident of the older time. His account stops with the Spanish invasion; for this story, Sarmiento felt, might be safely left to his contemporaries who acted a part in it, but whose taste and education had qualified them but indifferently for exploring the antiquities and social institutions of the natives.

Sarmiento's work is composed in a simple, perspicuous style, without that ambition of rhetorical display too common with his countrymen. He writes with honest candor, and while he does ample justice to the merits and capacity of the conquered races, he notices with indignation the atrocities of the Spaniards and the demoralizing tendency of the Conquest. It may be thought, indeed, that he forms too high an estimate of the attainments of the nation under the Incas. And it is not improbable, that, astonished by the vestiges it afforded of an original civilization, he became enamoured of his subject, and thus exhibited it in colors somewhat too glowing to the eye of the European. But this was an amiable failing, not too largely shared by the stern Conquerors, who subverted the institutions of the country, and saw little to admire in it, save its gold. It must be further admitted, that Sarmiento has no design to impose on his reader, and that he is careful to distinguish between what he reports on hearsay, and what on personal experience. The Father of History himself does not discriminate between these two things more carefully.

Neither is the Spanish historian to be altogether vindicated from the superstition which belongs to his time; and we often find him referring to the immediate interposition of Satan those effects which might quite as well be charged on the perverseness of man. But this was common to the age, and to the wisest men in it; and it is too much to demand of a man to be wiser than his generation. It is sufficient praise of Sarmiento, that, in an age when superstition was too often allied with fanaticism, he seems to have had no tincture of bigotry in his nature. His heart opens with benevolent fulness to the unfortunate native; and his language, while it is not kindled into the religious glow of the missionary, is warmed by a generous ray of philanthropy that embraces the conquered, no less than the conquerors, as his brethren.

Notwithstanding the great value of Sarmiento's work for the information it affords of Peru under the Incas, it is but little known, has been rarely consulted by historians, and still remains among the unpublished manuscripts which lie, like uncoined bullion, in the secret chambers of the Escurial.

The other authority to whom I have alluded, the Licentiate Polo de Ondegardo, was a highly respectable jurist, whose name appears frequently in the affairs of Peru. I find no account of the period when he first came into the country. But he was there on the arrival of Gasca, and resided at Lima under the usurpation of Gonzalo Pizarro. When the artful Cepeda endeavoured to secure the signatures of the inhabitants to the instrument proclaiming the sovereignty of his chief, we find Ondegardo taking the lead among those of his profession in resisting it. On Gasca's arrival, he consented to take a commission in his army. At the close of the rebellion he was made corregidor of La Plata, and subsequently of Cuzco, in which honorable station he seems to have remained several years. In the exercise of his magisterial functions, he was brought into familiar intercourse with the natives, and had ample opportunity for studying their laws and ancient customs. He conducted himself with such prudence and moderation, that he seems to have won the confidence not only of his countrymen but of the Indians; while the administration was careful to profit by his large experience in devising measures for the better government of the colony.

The *Relaciones,* so often cited in this History, were prepared at the suggestion of the viceroys, the first being addressed to the Marques de Cañete, in 1561, and the second, ten years later, to the Conde de Nieva. The two cover about as much ground as Sarmiento's manuscript; and the second memorial, written so long after the first, may be thought to intimate the advancing age of the author, in the greater carelessness and diffuseness of the composition.

As these documents are in the nature of answers to the interrogatories propounded by government, the range of topics might seem to be limited within narrower bounds than the modern historian would desire. These queries, indeed, had particular reference to the revenues, tributes, — the financial administration, in short, of the Incas; and on these obscure topics the communication of Ondegardo is particularly full. But the enlightened curiosity of government embraced a far wider range; and the answers necessarily implied an acquaintance with the domestic policy of the Incas, with their laws, social habits, their religion, science, and arts, in short, with all that make up the elements of civilization. Ondegardo's memoirs, therefore, cover the whole ground of inquiry for the philosophic historian.

In the management of these various subjects, Ondegardo displays both acuteness and erudition. He never shrinks from the discussion, however difficult; and while he gives his conclusions with an air of modesty, it is evident that he feels conscious of having derived his information through the most authentic channels. He rejects the fabulous with disdain; decides on the probabilities of such facts as he relates, and candidly exposes the deficiency of evidence. Far from displaying the simple enthusiasm of the well-meaning but credulous missionary, he proceeds with the cool and cautious step of a lawyer accustomed to the conflict of testimony and the uncertainty of oral tradition. This circumspect manner of proceeding, and the temperate character of his judgments, entitle Ondegardo to much higher consideration as an authority than most of his countrymen who have treated of Indian antiquities.

There runs through his writings a vein of humanity, shown particularly in his tenderness to the unfortunate natives, to whose ancient civilization he does entire, but not extravagant, justice; while, like Sarmiento, he fearlessly denounces the excesses of his own countrymen, and admits the dark reproach they had brought on the honor of the nation. But while this censure forms the strongest ground for condemnation of the Conquerors, since it comes from the lips of a Spaniard like themselves, it proves, also, that Spain in this age of violence could send forth from her bosom wise and good men who refused to make common cause with the licentious rabble around them. Indeed, proof enough is given in these very memorials of the unceasing efforts of the colonial government, from the good viceroy Mendoza downwards, to secure protection and the benefit of a mild legislation to the unfortunate natives. But the iron Conquerors, and the colonist whose heart softened only to the touch of gold, presented a formidable barrier to improvement.

Ondegardo's writings are honorably distinguished by freedom from that superstition which is the debasing characteristic of the times; a superstition shown in the easy credit given to the marvellous, and this equally whether in heathen or in Christian story; for in the former the eye of credulity could discern as readily the direct interposition of Satan, as in the latter the hand of the Almighty. It is this ready belief in a spiritual agency, whether for good or for evil, which forms one of the most prominent features in the writings of the sixteenth century. Nothing could be more repugnant to the true spirit of philosophical inquiry, or more irreconcilable with rational criticism. Far from betraying such weakness, Ondegardo writes in a direct and business-like manner, estimating things for what they are worth by the plain rule of common-sense. He keeps the main object of his argument ever in view, without allowing himself, like the garrulous chroniclers of the period, to be led astray into a thousand rambling episodes that bewilder the reader and lead to nothing.

Ondegardo's memoirs deal not only with the antiquities of the nation, but with its actual condition, and with the best means for redressing the manifold evils to which it was subjected under the stern rule of its conquerors. His suggestions are replete with wisdom, and a merciful policy, that would reconcile the interests of government with the prosperity and happiness of its humblest vassal. Thus, while his contemporaries gathered light from his suggestions as to the present condition of affairs, the historian of later times is no less indebted to him for information in respect to the past. His manuscript was freely consulted by Herrera, and the reader, as he peruses the pages of the learned historian of the Indies, is unconsciously enjoying the benefit of the researches of Ondegardo. His valuable *Relaciones* thus had their uses for future generations, though they have never been admitted to the honors of the press. The copy in my possession, like that of Sarmiento's manuscript, for which I am indebted to that industrious bibliographer, Mr. Rich, formed part of the magnificent collection of Lord Kingsborough,—a name ever to be held in honor by the scholar for his indefatigable efforts to illustrate the antiquities of America.

Ondegardo's manuscripts, it should be remarked, do not bear his signature. But they contain allusions to several actions of the writer's life, which identify them, beyond any reasonable doubt, as his production. In the archives of Simancas is a duplicate copy of the first memorial, *Relacion Primera*, though, like the one in the Escurial, without its author's name. Muñoz assigns it to the pen of Gabriel de Rojas, a distinguished cavalier of the Conquest. This is clearly an error; for the author of the manuscript identifies himself with Ondegardo, by declaring, in his reply to the fifth interrogatory, that he was the person who discovered the mummies of the Incas in Cuzco; an act expressly referred, both by Acosta and Garcilasso, to the Licentiate Polo de Ondegardo, when corregidor of that city. —Should the *savans* of Madrid hereafter embrace among the publications of valuable manuscripts these *Relaciones*, they should be careful not to be led into an error here, by the authority of a critic like Muñoz, whose criticism is rarely at fault.

BOOK II

CHAPTER I

[1] Seneca's well-known prediction, in his Medea, is, perhaps, the most remarkable random prophecy on record. For it is not a simple extension of the boundaries of the known parts of the globe that is so confidently announced, but the existence of a *New World* across the waters, to be revealed in coming ages.

"Quibus Oceanus Vincula rerum laxet, et ingens Pateat tellus, Typhisque Novos Detegat Orbes."

It was the lucky hit of the philosopher rather than the poet.

[2] The Venetian ambassador, Andrea Navagiero, who travelled through Spain in 1525, near the period of the commencement of our narrative, notices the general fever of emigration. Seville, in particular, the great port of embarkation, was so stripped of its inhabitants, he says, "that the city was left almost to the women." Viaggio fatto in Spagna, (Vinegia, 1563,) fol. 15.

[3] Herrera, Hist. General, dec. 1, lib. 10, cap. 2.—Quintana, Vidas de Españoles Celebres, (Madrid, 1830,) tom. II. p. 44.

[4] The memorable adventures of Vasco Nuñez de Balboa have been recorded by Quintana, (Españoles Celebres, tom. II.) and by Irving in his Companions of Columbus.—It is rare that the life of an individual has formed the subject of two such elegant memorials, produced at nearly the same time, and in different languages, without any communication between the authors.

[5] The Court gave positive instructions to Pedrarias to make a settlement in the Gulf of St. Michael, in obedience to the suggestion of Vasco Nuñez, that it would be the most eligible site for discovery and traffic in the South Sea. "El asiento que se oviere de hacer en el golfo de S. Miguel en la mar del sur debe ser en el puerto que mejor se hallare y mas convenible para la contratacion de aquel golfo, porque segund lo que Vasco Nuñez escribe, seria muy necesario que allí haya algunos navíos, así para descubrir las cosas del golfo; y de la comarca dél, como para la contratacion de rescates de las otras cosas necesarias al buen proveimiento de aquello; é para que estos naviós aprovechen es menester que se hagan allá." Capítulo de Carta escrita por el Rey Católico á Pedrarias Dávila, ap. Navarrete, Coleccion de los Viages y Descubrimientos, (Madrid, 1829,) tom. III. No. 3.

[6] According to Montesinos, Andagoya received a severe injury by a fall from his horse, while showing off the high-mettled animal to the wondering eyes of the natives. (Annales del Peru, MS., año 1524.) But the Adelantado, in a memorial of his own discoveries, drawn up by himself, says nothing of this unlucky feat of horsemanship, but imputes his illness to his having fallen into the water, an accident by which he was near being drowned, so that it was some years before he recovered from the effects of it; a mode of accounting for his premature return, more soothing to his vanity, probably, than the one usually received. This document, important as coming from the pen of one of the primitive discoverers, is preserved in the Indian Archives of Seville, and was published by Navarrete, Coleccion, tom. III. No 7.

CHAPTER II

[1] The few writers who venture to assign the date of Pizarro's birth do it in so vague and contradictory a manner as to inspire us with but little confidence in their accounts. Herrera, it is true, says positively, that he was sixty-three years old at the time of his death, in 1541. (Hist. General, dec. 6, lib. 10, cap. 6.) This would carry back the date of his birth only to 1478. But Garcilasso de la Vega affirms that he was more than fifty years old in 1525. (Com. Real., Parte 2, lib. 1, cap. 1.) This would place his birth before 1475. Pizarro y Orellana, who, as a kinsman of the Conqueror, may be supposed to have had better means of information, says he was fifty-four years of age at the same date of 1525. (Varones Ilustres del Nuevo Mundo, (Madrid, 1639,) p. 128.) But at the period of his death he calls him nearly eighty years old! (p. 185.) Taking this latter as a round exaggeration for effect in the particular connection in which it is used, and admitting the accuracy of the former statement, the epoch of his birth will conform to that given in the text. This makes him somewhat late in life to set about the conquest of an empire. But Columbus, when he entered on his career, was still older.

[2] Xerez, Conquista del Peru, ap. Barcia, tom. III. p. 179.—Zarate, Conq. del Peru, lib. 1, cap. 1.—Pizarro y Orellana, Varones Ilustres, p. 128.

[3] "Nació en Truxillo, i echaronlo à la puerta de la Iglesia, mamò una Puerca ciertos Dias, no se hallando quien le quisiese dàr leche." Gomara, Hist. de las Ind., cap. 144.

[4] According to the Comendador Pizarro y Orellana, Francis Pizarro served, while quite a stripling, with his father, in the Italian wars; and afterwards, under Columbus and other illustrious discoverers, in the New World, whose successes the author modestly attributes to his kinsman's valor, as a principal cause! Varones Ilustres, p. 187.

[5] Pizarro y Orellana, Varones Ilustres, pp. 121, 128.—Herrera, Hist. Gen., dec. 1, lib. 7, cap. 14.—Montesinos, Annales, MS., año 1510.

[6] "Teniendo su casa, i Hacienda, i Repartimiento de Indios como uno de los Principales de la Tierra; porque siempre lo fue." Xerez, Conq. del Peru, ap. Barcia, tom. III. p. 79.

[7] Andagoya says that he obtained, while at Birú, very minute accounts of the empire of the Incas, from certain itinerant traders who frequented that country. "En esta provincia supe y hube relacion, ansí de los señores como de mercaderes é intérpretes que ellos tenian, de toda la costa de todo lo que despues se ha visto hasta el Cuzco, particularmente de cada provincia la manera y gente della, porque estos alcanzaban por via de mercaduria mucha tierra." Navarrete, Coleccion, tom. III. No. 7.

[8] "Decia el que hera de *Almagro*," says Pedro Pizarro, who knew him well. Relacion del Descubrimiento y Conquista de los Reynos del Peru, MS.—See also Zarate, Conq. del Peru, lib. 1, cap. 1.—Gomara, Hist. de las Ind., cap. 141.—Pizarro y Orellana, Varones Ilustres, p. 211.

The last writer admits that Almagro's parentage is unknown; but adds that the character of his early exploits infers an illustrious descent.—This would scarcely pass for evidence with the College of Heralds.

[9] "Asi que estos tres compañeros ya dichos Acordaron de yr á conquistar esta provincia ya dicha. Pues consultandolo con Pedro Arias de Avila que a la sazon hera governador en tierra firme. Vino en ello haziendo compañia con los dichos compañeros con condicion que Pedro Arias no havia de contribuir entonces con ningun dinero ni otra cosa sino de lo que se hallase en la tierra de lo que á el le cupiese por virtud de la compañia de alli se

pagasen los gastos que á el le cupiesen. Los tres compañeros vinieron en ello por aver esta licencia porque de otra manera no la alcanzaran." (Pedro Pizarro, Descub. y Conq., MS.) Andagoya, however, affirms that the governor was interested equally with the other associates in the adventure, each taking a fourth part on himself. (Navarrete, Coleccion, tom. III. No. 7.) But whatever was the original interest of Pedrarias, it mattered little, as it was surrendered before any profits were realized from the expedition.

[10] Herrera the most popular historian of these transactions, estimates the number of Pizarro's followers only at eighty. But every other authority which I have consulted raises them to over a hundred. Father Naharro, a contemporary, and resident at Lima, even allows a hundred and twenty-nine. Relacion sumaria de la entrada de los Españoles en el Peru, MS.

[11] There is the usual discrepancy among authors about the date of this expedition. Most fix it at 1525. I have conformed to Xerez, Pizarro's secretary, whose narrative was published ten years after the voyage, and who could hardly have forgotten the date of so memorable an event, in so short an interval of time. (See his Conquista del Peru, ap. Barcia, tom. III. p. 179.)

The year seems to be settled by Pizarro's *Capitulacion* with the Crown, which I had not examined till after the above was written. This instrument, dated July, 1529, speaks of his first expedition as having taken place about five years previous. (See *Appendix, No.* VII.)

[12] Zarate, Conq. del Peru, lib. 1, cap. 1.—Herrera, Hist. General, dec. 3, lib. 6, cap. 13.

[13] Xerez, Conq. del Peru, ap. Barcia, tom. III. p. 180.—Relacion del Primer. Descub., MS.— Montesinos, Annales, MS., año 1515.—Zarate, Conq. del Peru, lib. 1, cap. 1.—Garcilasso, Com. Real., Parte 2, lib. 1, cap. 7.—Herrera, Hist. General, dec. 3, lib. 6, cap. 13.

[14] Ibid., ubi supra.—Relacion del Primer. Descub., MS.—Xerez, Conq. del Peru, ubi supra.

[15] "Porque decian à los Castellanos, que por què no sembraban, i cogian, sin andar tomando los Bastimentos agenos, pasando tantos trabajos?" Herrera, Hist. General, loc. cit.

[16] "Dioles noticia el viejo por medio del lengua, como diez soles de alli habia un Rey muy poderoso yendo por espesas montañas, y que otro mas poderoso hijo del sol habia venido de milagro á quitarle el Reino sobre que tenian mui sangrientas batallas." (Montesinos, Annales, MS., año 1525.) The conquest of Quito by Huayna Capac took place more than thirty years before this period in our history.

But the particulars of this revolution, its time or precise theatre, were, probably, but very vaguely comprehended by the rude nations in the neighbourhood of Panamá; and their allusion to it in an unknown dialect was as little comprehended by the Spanish voyagers, who must have collected their information from signs much more than words.

[17] "I en las Ollas de la comida, que estaban al Fuego, entre la Carne, que sacaban, havia Pies i Manos de Hembres, de donde conocieron, que aquellos Indios eran Caribes." Herrera, Hist. General, dec. 3, lib. 8, cap. 11.

[18] Naharro, Relacion Sumaria, MS.—Xerez, Conq. del Peru, ap. Barcia, tom. III. p. 180.— Zarate, Conq. del Peru, lib. 1, cap. 1.—Balboa, Hist. du Perou, chap. 15.

[19] Herrera, Hist. General, dec. 3, lib. 8, cap. 11.—Xerez, ubi supra.

[20] Xerez, ubi supra.—Naharro, Relacion Sumaria, MS.—Zarate, Conq. del Peru, loc. cit.— Balboa, Hist. du Perou, chap. 15.—Relacion del Primer. Descub., MS.—Herrera, Hist. General, dec. 3, lib. 8, cap. 13.—Levinus Apollonius, fol. 12.—Gomara, Hist. de las Ind., cap. 108.

CHAPTER III

[1] Xerez, Conq. del Peru, ap. Barcia, tom. III. p. 180.—Montesinos, Annales, MS., año 1526.—Herrera, Hist. General, dec. 3, lib. 8, cap. 12.

[2] Such is Oviedo's account, who was present at the interview between the governor and Almagro, when the terms of compensation were discussed. The dialogue, which is amusing enough, and well told by the old Chronicler, may be found translated in *Appendix, No. 5.* Another version of the affair is given in the *Relacion,* often quoted by me, of one of the Peruvian conquerors, in which Pedrarias is said to have gone out of the partnership voluntarily, from his disgust at the unpromising state of affairs. "Vueltos con la dicha gente á Panamá, destrozados y gastados que ya no tenian haciendas para tornar con provisiones y gentes que todo lo habian gastado, el dicho Pedrarias de Avila les dijo, que ya el no queria mas hacer compañia con ellos en los gastos de la armada, que si ellos querian volver á su costa, que lo hiciesen; y ansi como gente que habia perdido todo lo que tenia y tanto habia trabajado, acordaron de tornar á proseguir su jornada y dar fin á las vidas y haciendas que les quedaba, ó descubrir aquella tierra, y ciertamente ellos tubieron grande constancia y animo." Relacion del Primer. Descub., MS.

[3] This policy is noticed by the sagacious Martyr. "De mutandis namque plærisque gubernatoribus, ne longa nimis imperii assuetudine insolescant, cogitatur, qui præcipue non fuerint prouinciarum domitores, de hisce ducibus namque alia ratio ponderatur." (De Orbe Novo, (Parisiis, 1587,) p. 498.) One cannot but regret that the philosopher, who took so keen an interest in the successive revelations of the different portions of the New World, should have died before the empire of the Incas was disclosed to Europeans. He lived to learn and to record the wonders of

"Rich Mexico, the seat of Montezuma; *Not* Cuzco in Peru, the richer seat of Atabalipa."

[4] In opposition to most authorities,—but not to the judicious Quintana,—I have conformed to Montesinos, in placing the execution of the contract at the commencement of the second, instead of the first, expedition. This arrangement coincides with the date of the instrument itself, which, moreover, is reported *in extenso* by no ancient writer whom I have consulted except Montesinos.

[5] This singular instrument is given at length by Montesinos. (Annales, MS., año 1526.) It may be found in the original in *Appendix, No. 6.*

[6] For some investigation of the fact, which has been disputed by more than one, of Pizarro's ignorance of the art of writing, see Book 4, chap. 5, of this History.

[7] The epithet of *loco* or "madman" was *punningly* bestowed on Father Luque, for his spirited exertions in behalf of the enterprise; *Padre Luque ò loco,* says Oviedo of him, as if it were synonymous. Historia de las Indias Islas e Tierra Firme del Mar Oceano, MS., Parte 3, lib. 8, cap. 1.

[8] Robertson, America, vol. III. p. 5.

[9] "A perfect judge will read each work of wit
    With the same spirit that its author writ,"
    says the great bard of Reason. A fair criticism will apply the same rule to action as to writing, and, in the moral estimate of conduct, will take largely into account the spirit of the age which prompted it.

[10] The instrument making this extraordinary disclosure is cited at length in a manuscript entitled Noticia General del Perú, Tierra Firme y Chili, by Francisco Lopez de Caravantes, a fiscal officer in these colonies. The MS., formerly preserved in the library of the great college of Cuença at Salamanca, is now to be found in her Majesty's library at Madrid. The passage is extracted by Quintana, Españoles Célebres, tom. II. Apend. No. 2, nota.

[11] "Con ciento i diez Hombres saliò de Panamà, i fue donde estaba el Capitan Piçarro con otros cinquenta de los primeros ciento i diez, que con èl salieron, i de los setenta, que el Capitan Almagro llevò, quando le fue à buscar, que los ciento i treinta ià eran muertos." Xerez, Conq. del Peru, ap. Barcia, tom. III. p. 180.

[12] Ibid., pp. 180, 181.—Naharro, Relacion Sumaria, MS.—Zarate, Conq. del Peru, lib. 1, cap. 1.—Herrera, Hist. General, dec. 3, lib. 8, cap. 13.

[13] "Traia sus manteles y antenas de muy fina madera y velas de algodon del mismo talle de manera que los nuestros navios." Relacion de los Primeros Descubrimientos de F. Pizarro y Diego de Almagro, sacada del Codice, No. 120 de la Biblioteca Imperial de Vienna, MS.

[14] In a short notice of this expedition, written apparently at the time of it, or soon after, a minute specification is given of the several articles found in the balsa; among them are mentioned vases and mirrors of burnished silver, and curious fabrics both cotton and woollen. "Espejos guarnecidos de la dicha plata, y tasas y otras vasijas para beber, trahian muchas mantas de lana y de algodon, y camisas y aljubas y alcaçeres y alaremes, y otras muchas ropas, todo lo mas de ello muy labrado de labores muy ricas de colores de grana y carmisi y azul y amarillo, y de todas otras colores de diversas maneras de labores y figuras de aves y animales, y Pescados, y arbolesas y trahian unos pesos chiquitos de pesar oro como hechura de Romana, y otras muchas cosas." Relacion sacada de la Biblioteca Imperial de Vienna, MS.

[15] Xerez, Conq. del Peru, ap. Barcia, tom. III. p. 181.—Relacion sacada de la Biblioteca Imperial de Vienna, MS.—Herrera, Hist. General, dec. 3, lib. 8, cap. 13.

One of the authorities speaks of his having been sixty days on this cruise. I regret not to be able to give precise dates of the events in these early expeditions. But chronology is a thing beneath the notice of these ancient chroniclers, who seem to think that the date of events, so fresh in their own memory, must be so in that of every one else.

[16] "Todo era montañas, con arboles hasta el cielo!" Herrera, Hist. General, ubi supra.

[17] Ibid., ubi supra.

[18] Ibid., loc. cit.—Gomara, Hist. de las Ind., cap. 108.—Naharro, Relacion Sumaria, MS.

[19] Xerez, Conq. del Peru, ap. Barcia, tom. III. p. 181.—Relacion sacada de la Biblioteca Imperial de Vienna, MS.—Naharro, Relacion Sumaria, MS.—Montesinos, Annales, MS., año 1526.—Zarate, Conq. del Peru, lib. 1, cap. 1.—Relation del Primer. Descub., MS.

[20] Pizarro's secretary speaks of one of the towns as containing 3,000 houses. "En esta Tierra havia muchos Mantenimientos, i la Gente tenia mui buena orden de vivir, los Pueblos con sus Calles, i Plaças: Pueblo havia que tenia mas de tres mil Casas, i otros havia menores." Conq. del Peru, ap. Barcia, tom. III. p. 181.

[21] Stevenson, who visited this part of the coast early in the present century, is profuse in his description of its mineral and vegetable treasures. The emerald mine in the neighbourhood of Las Esmeraldas, once so famous, is now placed under the ban of a superstition,

more befitting the times of the Incas. "I never visited it," says the traveller, "owing to the superstitious dread of the natives, who assured me that it was enchanted, and guarded by an enormous dragon, which poured forth thunder and lightning on those who dared to ascend the river," Residence in South America, vol. II. p. 406.

[22] "Salieron á los dichos navios quatorce canoas grandes con muchos Indios dos armados de oro y plata, y trahian en la una canoa ó en estandarte y encima de él un bolto de un mucho desio de oro, y dieron una suelta á los navios por avisarlos en manera que no los pudiese enojar, y asi dieron vuelta acia á su pueblo, y los navios no los pudieron tomar porque se metieron en los baxos junto á la tierra." Relacion sacada de la Biblioteca Imperial de Vienna, MS.

[23] "Al tiempo del romper los unos con los otros, uno de aquellos de caballo cayó del caballo abajo; y como los Indios vieron dividirse aquel animal en dos partes, teniendo por cierto que todo era una cosa, fué tanto el miedo que tubieron que volvieron las espaldas dando voces á los suyos, diciendo, que se habia hecho dos haciendo admiracion dello: lo cual no fué sin misterio; porque á no acaecer esto se presume, que mataran todos los cristianos." (Relacion del Primer. Descub., MS.) This way of accounting for the panic of the barbarians is certainly quite as credible as the explanation, under similar circumstances, afforded by the apparition of the militant apostle St. James, so often noticed by the historians of these wars.

[24] "No era bien bolver pobres, á pedir limosna, i morir en las Carceles, los que tenian deudas." Herrera, Hist. General, dec. 3, lib. 10, cap. 2.

[25] "Como iba, i venia en los Navios, adonde no le faltaba Vitualla, no padecia la miseria de la hambre, i otras angustias que tenian, i ponian á todos en estrema congoja." (Herrera, Hist. General, dec. 3, lib. 10, cap. 2.) The cavaliers of Cortés and Pizarro however doughty their achievements, certainly fell short of those knights-errant, commemorated by Hudibras, who,

"As some think, Of old did neither eat nor drink; Because, when thorough deserts vast And regions desolate they past, Unless they grazed, there's not one word Of their provision on record; Which made some confidently write, They had no stomachs but to fight."

[26] Pedro Pizarro, Descub. y Conq., MS.—Relacion sacada de la Biblioteca Imperial de Vienna, MS.—Naharro, Relacion Sumaria, MS.—Zarate, Conq. del Peru, lib. 1, cap. 1.— Herrera, Hist. General, dec. 3, lib. 10, cap. 2.

It was singularly unfortunate, that Pizarro, instead of striking farther south, should have so long clung to the northern shores of the continent. Dampier notices them as afflicted with incessant rain; while the inhospitable forests and the particularly ferocious character of the natives continued to make these regions but little known down to his time. See his Voyages and Adventures, (London, 1776,) vol. I. chap. 14.

[27] "Miserablemente morir adonde aun no havia lugar Sagrado, para sepultura de sus cuerpos." Herrera, Hist. General, dec. 3, lib. 10, cap. 3.

[28] "Metieron en un ovillo de algodon una carta firmada de muchos en que sumariamente daban cuenta de las hambres, muertes y desnudez que padecian, y que era cosa de risa todo, pues las riquezas se habian convertido en flechas, y no havia otra cosa." Montesinos, Annales, MS., año 1527.

[29] Xerez, Conq. del Peru, ap. Barcia, tom. III. p. 181.—Naharro, Relacion Sumaria, MS.— Balboa, Hist. du Perou, chap. 15.

"Al fin de la peticion que hacian en la carta al Governador puso Juan de Sarabia, natural de Trujillo, esta cuarteta: —

Pues Señor Gobernador, Mirelo bien por entero que alla va el recogedor, y acá queda el carnicero."

Montesinos, Annales, MS., año 1527.

CHAPTER IV

[1] Xerez, Conq. del Peru, ap. Barcia, tom. III. p. 182.—Zarate, Conq. del Peru, lib. 1, cap. 2.
—Montesinos, Annales, MS., año 1527.—Herrera, Hist. General, dec. 3, lib. 10, cap. 3.—
Naharro, Relacion Sumaria, MS.

[2] "Obedeciola Pizarro y antes que se egecutase sacó un Puñal, y con notable animo hizo con la punta una raya de Oriente á Poniente; y señalando al medio dia, que era la parte de su noticia, y derrotero dijo: camaradas y amigos esta parte es la de la muerte, de los trabajos, de las hambres, de la desnudez, de los aguaceros, y desamparos; la otra la del gusto: Por aqui se ba à Panama à ser pobres, por alla al Peru à ser ricos. Escoja el que fuere buen Castellano lo que mas bien le estubiere. Diciendo esto pasó la raya: siguieronle Barthome Ruiz natural de Moguer, Pedro de Candi Griego, natural de Candia." Montesinos, Annales, MS., año 1527.

[3] The names of these thirteen faithful companions are preserved in the convention made with the Crown two years later, where they are suitably commemorated for their loyalty. Their names should not be omitted in a history of the Conquest of Peru. They were "Bartolomé Ruiz, Cristoval de Peralta, Pedro de Candia, Domingo de Soria Luce, Nícolas de Ribera, Francisco de Cuellar, Alonso de Molina, Pedro Alcon, Garcia de Jerez, Anton de Carrion, Alonso Briceño, Martin de Paz, Joan de la Torre."

[4] "Estos fueron los trece de la fama. Estos los que cercados de los mayores trabajos que pudo el Mundo ofrecer á hombres, y los que estando mas para esperar la muerte que las riquezas que se les prometian, todo lo pospusieron á la honra, y siguieron á su capitan y caudillo para egemplo de lealtad en lo futuro." Montesinos, Annales, MS., año 1527.

[5] Zarate, Conq. del Peru, lib. 1, cap. 2.—Montesinos, Annales, MS., año 1527.—Naharro, Relacion Sumaria, MS.—Herrera, Hist. General, dec. 3, lib. 10, cap. 3.

[6] This common sentiment is expressed with uncommon beauty by the fanciful Boiardo, where he represents Rinaldo as catching Fortune, under the guise of the fickle fairy Morgana, by the forelock. The Italian reader may not be displeased to refresh his memory with it.

"Chi cerca in questo mondo aver tesoro, O diletto, e piacere, honore, e stato, Ponga la mano a questa chioma d' oro, Ch' io porto in fronte, e lo farò beato; Ma quando ha in destro si fatto lavoro, Non prenda indugio, che 'l tempo passato Perduto è tutto, e non ritorna mai, Ed io mi volto, e lui lascio con guai." Orlando, Innamorato, lib. 2, canto 8.

[7] "Cada Mañana daban gracias á Dios: à las tardes decian la Salve, i otras Oraciones, por las Horas: sabian las Fiestas, i tenian cuenta con los Viernes, i Domingos." Herrera, Hist. General, dec. 3, lib. 10, cap. 3.

[8] "Al cabo de muchos Dias aguardando, estaban tan angustiados, que los salages, que se hacian bien dentro de la Mar, les parecia, que era el Navio." Herrera, Hist. General, dec. 3, lib. 10, cap. 4.

[9] "Estubieron con estos trabajos con igualdad de animo siete meses." Montesinos, Annales, MS., año 1527.

[10] Xerez, Conq. del Peru, ap. Barcia, tom. III. p. 182.—Montesinos, Annales, MS., año 1527.—Naharro, Relacion Sumaria, MS.—Herrera, Hist. General, dec. 3, lib. 10, cap. 4. —Pedro Pizarro, Descub. y Conq., MS.

[11] According to Garcilasso, two years elapsed between the departure from Gorgona and the arrival at Tumbez. (Com. Real., Parte 2, lib. 1, cap. 11.) Such gross defiance of chronology is rather uncommon even in the narratives of these transactions, where it is as difficult to fix a precise date, amidst the silence, rather than the contradictions, of contemporary statements, as if the events had happened before the deluge.

[12] The text abridges somewhat the discourse of the military polemic; which is reported at length by Herrera, Hist. General, dec. 3, lib. 10, cap. 4.—See also Montesinos, Annales, MS., año 1527—Conq. i Pob. del Piru, MS.—Naharro, Relacion Sumaria, MS.— Relacion del Primer. Descub., MS.

[13] "No se cansaban de mirarle, hacianle labar, para vèr si se le quitaba la Tinta negra, i èl lo hacia de buena gana, riendose, i mostrando sus Dientes blancos." Herrera, Hist. General, dec. 3, lib. 10, cap. 5.

[14] Ibid., ubi supra.

[15] "Cerca del solia estar una fortaleza muy fuerte y de linda obra, hecha por los Yngas reyes del Cuzco y señores de todo el Peru. . . . . . Ya esta el edificio desta fortaleza muy gastado y deshecho: mas no para que dexe de dar muestra de lo mucho que fue." Cieza de Leon, Cronica, cap. 4.

[16] Conq. i Pob. del Piru, MS.—Herrera, Hist. General, loc. cit.—Zarate, Conq. del Peru, lib. 1, cap. 2.

[17] It is moreover stated that the Indians, desirous to prove still further the superhuman nature of the Spanish cavalier, let loose on him a tiger—a jaguar probably—which was caged in the royal fortress. But Don Pedro was a good Catholic, and he gently laid the cross which he wore round his neck on the animal's back, who, instantly forgetting his ferocious nature, crouched at the cavalier's feet, and began to play round him in innocent gambols. The Indians, now more amazed than ever, nothing doubted of the sanctity of their guest, and bore him in triumph on their shoulders to the temple.—This credible anecdote is repeated, without the least qualification or distrust, by several contemporary writers. (See Naharro, Relacion Sumaria, MS.—Herrera, Hist. General, dec. 3, lib. 10, cap. 5.—Cieza de Leon, Cronica, cap. 54.—Garcilasso, Com. Real., Parte 2, lib. 1, cap. 12.) This last author may have had his version from Candia's own son, with whom he tells us he was brought up at school. It will no doubt find as easy admission with those of the present day, who conceive that the age of miracles has not yet past.

[18] "Que habia visto un jardin donde las yerbas eran de oro imitando en un todo á las naturales, arboles con frutas de lo mismo, y otras muchas cosas á este modo, con que aficionó grandemente á sus compañeros á esta conquista." Montesinos, Annales, año 1527.

[19] The worthy knight's account does not seem to have found favor with the old Conqueror, so often cited in these pages, who says, that, when they afterwards visited Tumbez, the Spaniards found Candia's relation a lie from beginning to end, except, indeed, in respect to the temple; though the veteran acknowledges that what was deficient in Tumbez was more than made up by the magnificence of other places in the empire not then visited.

"Lo cual fué mentira; porque despues que todos los Españoles entramos en ella, se vió por vista de ojos haber mentido en todo, salvo en lo del templo, que este era cosa de ver, aunque mucho mas de lo que aquel encareció, lo que faltó en esta ciudad, se halló despues en otras que muchas leguas mas adelante se descubrieron." Relacion del Primer. Descub., MS.

[20] Cieza de Leon, who crossed this part of the country in 1548, mentions the wanton manner in which the hand of the Conqueror had fallen on the Indian edifices, which lay in ruin, even at that early period. Cronica, cap. 67.

[21] "I si le recibiesen con amor, hiciese su Mrd. lo que mas conveniente le pareciese al efecto de su conquista: porque tenia entendido, que el haverlos traido Dios erá para que su santa fé se dilatase i aquellas almas se salvasen." Naharro, Relacion Sumaria, MS.

[22] "Que resplandecian como el Sol. Llamabanles hijos del Sol por esto." Montesinos, Annales, MS., año 1528.

[23] Pizarro wished the natives to understand, says Father Naharro, that their good alone, and not the love of gold, had led him to their distant land! "Sin haver querido recibir el oro, plata i perlas que les ofrecieron, á fin de que conociesen no era codicia, sino deseo de su bien el que les habia traido de tan lejas tierras á las suyas." Relacion Sumaria, MS.

[24] "Lo que mas me admiro, quando passe por este valle, fue ver la muchedumbre que tienen de sepolturas: y que por todas las sierras y secadales en los altos del valle: ay numero grande de apartados, hechos a su usaña, todo cubiertas de huessos de muertos. De manera que lo que ay en este valle mas que ver, es las sepolturas de los muertos, y los campos que labraron siendo vivos." Cieza de Leon, Cronica, cap. 70.

[25] Conq. i Pob. del Piru, MS. — Montesinos, Annales, MS., año 1528. — Naharro, Relacion Sumaria, MS. — Pedro Pizarro, Descub. y Conq., MS. — Herrera, Hist. General, dec. 4, lib. 2, cap. 6, 7. — Relacion del Primer. Descub., MS.

[26] "No entendia de despoblar su Governacion, para que se fuesen à poblar nuevas Tierras, muriendo en tal demanda mas Gente de la que havia muerto, cebando à los Hombres con la muestra de las Ovejas, Oro, i Plata, que havian traido." Herrera, Hist. General, dec. 4, lib. 3, cap. 1.

[27] "E por pura importunacion de Almagro cupole á Pizarro, porque siempre Almagro le tubo respeto, é deseó honrarle." Oviedo, Hist. de las Indias, MS, Parte 3, lib. 8, cap. 1.

[28] "Plegue à Dios, Hijos, que no os hurteis la bendicion el uno al otro, que yo todavia holgaria, que à lo menos fuerades entrambos." Herrera, Hist. General, dec. 4, lib. 3, cap. 1.

[29] "Juntaronle mil y quinientos pesos de oro, que dió de buena voluntad Dⁿ Fernando de Luque." Montesinos, Annales, MS., año 1528.

Of all the writers on ancient Peruvian history, no one has acquired so wide celebrity, or been so largely referred to by later compilers, as the Inca Garcilasso de la Vega. He was born at Cuzco, in 1540; and was a *mestizo*, that is, of mixed descent, his father being European, and his mother Indian. His father, Garcilasso de la Vega, was one of that illustrious family whose achievements, both in arms and letters, shed such lustre over the proudest period of the Castilian annals. He came to Peru, in the suite of Pedro de Alvarado, soon after the country had been gained by Pizarro. Garcilasso attached himself to the fortunes of this chief, and, after his death, to those of his brother Gonzalo, — remaining constant to the latter, through his rebellion, up to the hour of his rout at

Xaquixaguana, when Garcilasso took the same course with most of his faction, and passed over to the enemy. But this demonstration of loyalty, though it saved his life, was too late to redeem his credit with the victorious party; and the obloquy which he incurred by his share in the rebellion threw a cloud over his subsequent fortunes, and even over those of his son, as it appears, in after years.

The historian's mother was of the Peruvian blood royal. She was niece of Huayna Capac, and granddaughter of the renowned Tupac Inca Yupanqui. Garcilasso, while he betrays obvious satisfaction that the blood of the civilized European flows in his veins, shows himself not a little proud of his descent from the royal dynasty of Peru; and this he intimated by combining with his patronymic the distinguishing title of the Peruvian princes,—subscribing himself always Garcilasso Inca de la Vega.

His early years were passed in his native land, where he was reared in the Roman Catholic faith, and received the benefit of as good an education as could be obtained amidst the incessant din of arms and civil commotion. In 1560, when twenty years of age, he left America, and from that time took up his residence in Spain. Here he entered the military service, and held a captain's commission in the war against the Moriscos, and, afterwards, under Don John of Austria. Though he acquitted himself honorably in his adventurous career, he does not seem to have been satisfied with the manner in which his services were requited by the government. The old reproach of the father's disloyalty still clung to the son, and Garcilasso assures us that this circumstance defeated all his efforts to recover the large inheritance of landed property belonging to his mother, which had escheated to the Crown. "Such were the prejudices against me," says he, "that I could not urge my ancient claims or expectations; and I left the army so poor and so much in debt, that I did not care to show myself again at court; but was obliged to withdraw into an obscure solitude, where I lead a tranquil life for the brief space that remains to me, no longer deluded by the world or its vanities."

The scene of this obscure retreat was not, however, as the reader might imagine from this tone of philosophic resignation, in the depths of some rural wilderness, but in Cordova, once the gay capital of Moslem science, and still the busy haunt of men. Here our philosopher occupied himself with literary labors, the more sweet and soothing to his wounded spirit, that they tended to illustrate the faded glories of his native land, and exhibit them in their primitive splendor to the eyes of his adopted countrymen. "And I have no reason to regret," he says in his Preface to his account of Florida, "that Fortune has not smiled on me, since this circumstance has opened a literary career which, I trust, will secure to me a wider and more enduring fame than could flow from any worldly prosperity."

In 1609, he gave to the world the First Part of his great work, the *Commentarios Reales*, devoted to the history of the country under the Incas; and in 1616, a few months before his death, he finished the Second Part, embracing the story of the Conquest, which was published at Cordova the following year. The chronicler, who thus closed his labors with his life, died at the ripe old age of seventy-six. He left a considerable sum for the purchase of masses for his soul, showing that the complaints of his poverty are not to be taken literally. His remains were interred in the cathedral church of Cordova, in a chapel which bears the name of Garcilasso; and an inscription was placed on his monument, intimating the high respect in which the historian was held both for his moral worth and his literary attainments.

The First Part of the *Commentarios Reales* is occupied, as already noticed, with the ancient history of the country, presenting a complete picture of its civilization under the Incas, —far more complete than has been given by any other writer. Garcilasso's mother was but ten years old at the time of her cousin Atahuallpa's accession, or rather usurpation, as it is called by the party of Cuzco. She had the good fortune to escape the massacre which, according to the chronicler, befell most of her kindred, and with her brother continued to reside in their ancient capital after the Conquest. Their conversations naturally turned to the good old times of the Inca rule, which, colored by their fond regrets, may be presumed to have lost nothing as seen through the magnifying medium of the past. The young Garcilasso listened greedily to the stories which recounted the magnificence and prowess of his royal ancestors, and though he made no use of them at the time, they sunk deep into his memory, to be treasured up for a future occasion. When he prepared, after the lapse of many years, in his retirement at Cordova, to compose the history of his country, he wrote to his old companions and schoolfellows, of the Inca family, to obtain fuller information than he could get in Spain on various matters of historical interest. He had witnessed in his youth the ancient ceremonies and usages of his countrymen, understood the science of their quipus, and mastered many of their primitive traditions. With the assistance he now obtained from his Peruvian kindred, he acquired a familiarity with the history of the great Inca race, and of their national institutions, to an extent that no person could have possessed, unless educated in the midst of them, speaking the same language, and with the same Indian blood flowing in his veins. Garcilasso, in short, was the representative of the conquered race; and we might expect to find the lights and shadows of the picture disposed under his pencil, so as to produce an effect very different from that which they had hitherto exhibited under the hands of the Conquerors.

Such, to a certain extent, is the fact; and this circumstance affords a means of comparison which would alone render his works of great value in arriving at just historic conclusions. But Garcilasso wrote late in life, after the story had been often told by Castilian writers. He naturally deferred much to men, some of whom enjoyed high credit on the score both of their scholarship and their social position. His object, he professes, was not so much to add any thing new of his own, as to correct their errors and the misconceptions into which they had been brought by their ignorance of the Indian languages and the usages of his people. He does, in fact, however, go far beyond this; and the stores of information which he has collected have made his work a large repository, whence later laborers in the same field have drawn copious materials. He writes from the fulness of his heart, and illuminates every topic that he touches with a variety and richness of illustration, that leave little to be desired by the most importunate curiosity. The difference between reading his Commentaries and the accounts of European writers is the difference that exists between reading a work in the original and in a bald translation. Garcilasso's writings are an emanation from the Indian mind.

Yet his Commentaries are open to a grave objection, —and one naturally suggested by his position. Addressing himself to the cultivated European, he was most desirous to display the ancient glories of his people, and still more of the Inca race, in their most imposing form. This, doubtless, was the great spur to his literary labors, for which previous education, however good for the evil time on which he was cast, had far from qualified him. Garcilasso, therefore, wrote to effect a particular object. He stood forth as counsel for his unfortunate countrymen, pleading the cause of that degraded race before the tribunal of posterity. The exaggerated tone of panegyric consequent on this becomes apparent in every page of his work. He pictures forth a state of society, such as an Utopian philosopher would hardly venture to depict. His royal ancestors became the types of every imaginary excellence, and the golden age is revived for a nation, which, while the war of proselytism is raging on its borders, enjoys within all the blessings of tranquillity and peace. Even the material splendors of the monarchy, sufficiently great in this land of gold, become heightened, under the glowing imagination of the Inca chronicler, into the gorgeous illusions of a fairy tale.

Yet there is truth at the bottom of his wildest conceptions, and it would be unfair to the Indian historian to suppose that he did not himself believe most of the magic marvels which he describes. There is no credulity like that of a Christian convert,—one newly converted to the faith. From long dwelling in the darkness of paganism, his eyes, when first opened to the light of truth, have not acquired the power of discriminating the just proportions of objects, of distinguishing between the real and the imaginary. Garcilasso was not a convert, indeed, for he was bred from infancy in the Roman Catholic faith. But he was surrounded by converts and neophytes,—by those of his own blood, who, after practising all their lives the rites of paganism, were now first admitted into the Christian fold. He listened to the teachings of the missionary, learned from him to give implicit credit to the marvellous legends of the Saints, and the no less marvellous accounts of his own victories in his spiritual warfare for the propagation of the faith. Thus early accustomed to such large drafts on his credulity, his reason lost its heavenly power of distinguishing truth from error, and he became so familiar with the miraculous, that the miraculous was no longer a miracle.

Yet, while large deductions are to be made on this account from the chronicler's reports, there is always a germ of truth which it is not difficult to detect, and even to disengage from the fanciful covering which envelopes it; and after every allowance for the exaggerations of national vanity, we shall find an abundance of genuine information in respect to the antiquities of his country, for which we shall look in vain in any European writer.

Garcilasso's work is the reflection of the age in which he lived. It is addressed to the imagination, more than to sober reason. We are dazzled by the gorgeous spectacle it perpetually exhibits, and delighted by the variety of amusing details and animated gossip sprinkled over its pages. The story of the action is perpetually varied by discussions on topics illustrating its progress, so as to break up the monotony of the narrative, and afford an agreeable relief to the reader. This is true of the First Part of his great work. In the Second there was no longer room for such discussion. But he has supplied the place by garrulous reminiscences, personal anecdotes, incidental adventures, and a host of trivial details,—trivial in the eyes of the pedant,—which historians have been too willing to discard, as below the dignity of history. We have the actors in this great drama in their private dress, become acquainted with their personal habits, listen to their familiar sayings, and, in short, gather up those minutiæ which in the aggregate make up so much of life, and not less of character.

It is this confusion of the great and the little, thus artlessly blended together, that constitutes one of the charms of the old romantic chronicle,—not the less true that, in this respect, it approaches nearer to the usual tone of romance. It is in such writings that we may look to find the form and pressure of the age. The worm-eaten state-papers, official correspondence, public records, are all serviceable, indispensable, to history. They are the framework on which it is to repose; the skeleton of facts which gives it its strength and proportions. But they are as worthless as the dry bones of the skeleton, unless clothed with the beautiful form and garb of humanity, and instinct with the spirit of the age.—Our debt is large to the antiquarian, who with conscientious precision lays broad and deep the foundations of historic truth; and no less to the philosophic annalist who exhibits man in the dress of public life,—man in masquerade; but our gratitude must surely not be withheld from those, who, like Garcilasso de la Vega, and many a romancer of the Middle Ages, have held up the mirror—distorted though it may somewhat be—to the interior of life, reflecting every object, the great and the mean, the beautiful and the deformed, with their natural prominence and their vivacity of coloring, to the eye of the spectator. As a work of art, such a production may be thought to be below criticism. But, although it defy the rules of art in its composition, it does not necessarily violate the principles of taste; for it conforms in its spirit to the spirit of the age in which it was written. And the critic, who coldly condemns it on the severe principles of art, will find a charm in its very simplicity, that will make him recur again and again to its pages, while more correct and classical compositions are laid aside and forgotten.

I cannot dismiss this notice of Garcilasso, though already long protracted, without some allusion to the English translation of his Commentaries. It appeared in James the Second's reign, and is the work of Sir Paul Rycaut, Knight. It was printed at London, in 1688, in folio, with considerable pretension in its outward dress, well garnished with wood-cuts, and a frontispiece displaying the gaunt and rather sardonic features, not of the author, but his translator. The version keeps pace with the march of the original, corresponding precisely in books and chapters, and seldom, though sometimes, using the freedom, so common in these ancient versions, of abridgment and omission. Where it does depart from the original, it is rather from ignorance than intention. Indeed, as far as the plea of ignorance will avail him, the worthy knight may urge it stoutly in his defence. No one who reads the book will doubt his limited acquaintance with his own tongue, and no one who compares it with the original will deny his ignorance of the Castilian. It contains as many blunders as paragraphs, and most of them such as might shame a schoolboy. Yet such are the rude charms of the original, that this ruder version of it has found considerable favor with readers; and Sir Paul Rycaut's translation, old as it is, may still be met with in many a private, as well as public library.

BOOK III
CHAPTER I

[1] Pedro Pizarro, Descub. y Conq., MS.—Naharro, Relacion Sumaria, MS.—Conq. i Pob. del Piru, MS.

"Hablaba tan bien en la materia, que se llevó los aplausos y atencion en Toledo donde el Emperador estaba diole audiencia con mucho gusto, tratolo amoroso, y oyole tierno, especialmente cuando le hizo relacion de su consistencia y de los trece compañeros en la Isla en medio de tantos trabajos." Montesinos, Annales, MS., año 1528.

[2] This remarkable document, formerly in the archives of Simancas, and now transferred to the *Archivo General de las Indias* in Seville, was transcribed for the rich collection of the late Don Martin Fernandez de Navarrete, to whose kindness I am indebted for a copy of it.—It will be found printed entire, in the original, in *Appendix, No. 7*.

[3] "Al fin se capituló, que Francisco Piçarro negociase la Governacion para si: i para Diego de Almagro, el Adelantamiento: i para Hernando de Luque, el Obispado: i para Bartolomé

Ruiz, el Alguacilazgo Maior: i Mercedes para los que quedeban vivos, de los trece Compañeros, afirmando siempre Francisco Piçarro, que todo lo queria para ellos, i prometiendo, que negociaria lealmente, i sin ninguna cautela." Herrera, Hist. General, dec. 4, lib. 3, cap. 1.

[4] "Y don Francisco Piçarro pidio conforme á lo que llevava capitulado y hordenado con sus compañeros ya dicho, y en el consejo se le rrespondio que no avia lugar de dar governacion á dos compañeros, á caussa de que en santa marta se avia dado ansi á dos compañeros y el uno avia muerto al otro. . . . . . Pues pedido, como digo, muchas vezes por don Francisco Piçarro se les hiziese la merced á ambos compañeros, se le rrespondio la pidiesse parassi sino que se daria á otro, y visto que no avia lugar lo que pedia y queria pedio se le hiziese la merced á el, y ansi se le hizo." Descub. y Conq., MS.

[5] Xerez, Conq. del Peru, ap. Barcia, tom. III. p. 182.—Oviedo, Hist. de las Indias, MS., Parte 3, lib. 8, cap. 1.—Caro de Torres, Historia de las Ordenes Militares, (ed. Madrid, 1629,) p. 113.

[6] "Caroli Cæsaris auspicio, et labore, ingenio, ac impensa Ducis Piçarro inventa, et pacata." Herrera, Hist. General, dec. 4, lib. 6, cap. 5.

[7] "Trujo tres o cuatro hermanos suyos tan soberbios como pobres, é tan sin hacienda como deseosos de alcanzarla." Hist. de las Indias, MS., Parte 3, lib. 8, cap. 1.

[8] Oviedo's portrait of him is by no means flattering. He writes like one too familiar with the original. "É de todos ellos el Hernando Pizarro solo era legitimo, é mas legitimado en la soberbia, hombre de alta estatura é grueso, la lengua é labios gordos, é la punta de la nariz con sobrada carne é encendida, y este fue el desavenidor y estorbador del sosiego de todos y en especial de los dos viejos compañeros Francisco Pizarro é Diego de Almagro." Hist. de las Indias, MS., ubi supra.

[9] Pizarro y Orellana, Varones Ilustres, p. 143.

[10] Herrera, Hist. General, dec. 4, lib. 7, cap. 9.—Pedro Pizarro, Descub. y Conq., MS.

[11] Pedro Pizarro, Descub. y Conq., MS.—Naharro, Relacion Sumaria, MS.—Montesinos, Annales, MS., año 1529.—Relacion del Primer. Descub., MS.—Zarate, Conq. del Peru, lib. 1, cap. 3.—Oviedo, Hist. de las Indias, MS., Parte 3, lib. 8, cap. 1.

There seems to have been little good-will, at bottom, between any of the confederates; for Father Luque wrote to Oviedo that both of his partners had repaid his services with ingratitude.—"Padre Luque, compañero de estos Capitanes, con cuya hacienda hicieron ellos sus hechos, puesto que el uno é el otro se lo pagaron con ingratitud segun a mi me lo escribió el mismo electo de su mano." Ibid., loc. cit.

[12] The numerical estimates differ, as usual. I conform to the statement of Pizarro's secretary, Xerez, Conq. del Peru, ap. Barcia, tom., III. p. 182.

[13] "El qual haviendo hecho bendecir en la Iglesia mayor las banderas i estandarte real dia de San Juan Evangelista de dicho año de 1530, i que todos los soldados confesasen i comulgasen en el convento de Nuestra Señora de la Merced, dia de los Inocentes en la misa cantada que se celebró con toda solemnidad i sermon que predicó el P. Present[do] Fr. Juan de Vargas, uno de los 5 religiosos que en cumplimiento de la obediencia de sus prelados i orden del Emperador pasaban à la conquista." Naharro, Relacion Sumaria, MS.

[14] "Pues llegados á este pueblo de Coaque dieron de supito sin savello la gente del porque si estuvieran avisados. No se tomara la cantidad de oro y esmeraldas que en el se tomaron." Pedro Pizarre, Descub. y Conq., MS.

[15] Herrera, Hist. General, dec. 4, lib. 7, cap. 9.

[16] Relacion del Primer. Descub., MS.—Zarate, Conq. del Peru, lib. 1, cap. 4.

"Á lo que se ha entendido en las esmeraldas ovo gran hierro y torpedad en algunas Personas por no conoscellas. Aunque quieren decir que algunos que las conoscieron las guardaron. Pero ffinalmente muchos vbieron esmeraldas de mucho valor; vnos las provavan en yunques, dandolas con martillos, diziendo que si hera esmeralda no se quebraria; otros las despreciaban, diziendo que era vidrio." Pedro Pizarro, Descub. y Conq., MS.

[17] Pedro Pizarro, Descub. y Conq., MS.—Herrera, Hist. General, dec. 4, lib. 7, cap. 9.

[18] "Los Españoles las rrecoxeron y juntaron el oro y la plata, porque asi estava mandado y hordenado sopena de la vida el que otra cossa hiziese, porque todos lo avian de tract á monton para que de alli el governador lo rrepartiese, dando á cada uno confforme á su persona y meritos de servicios; y esta horden se guardo en toda esta tierra en la conquista della, y al que se le hallara oro ó plata escondido muriera por ello, y deste medio nadie oso escondello." Pedro Pizarro, Descub. y Conq., MS.

[19] The booty was great, indeed, if, as Pedro Pizarro, one of the Conquerors present, says, it amounted in value to 200,000 gold castellanos. "Aqui se hallo mucha chaquira de oro y de plata, muchas coronas hechas de oro á manera de imperiales, y otras muchas piezas en que se avaleo montar mas de dozientos mill castellanos." (Descub. y Conq., MS.) Naharro, Montesinos, and Herrera content themselves with stating that he sent back 20,000 castellanos in the vessels to Panamá.

[20] "Fueron a dar en vn pueblo que se dezia Coaque que fue nuestro Señor servido tapasen con el, porque con lo que en el se hallo se acredito la tierra y vino gente a ella." Pedro Pizarro, Descub. y Conq., MS.

[21] Naharro, Relacion Sumaria, MS.—Pedro Pizarro, Descub. y Conq., MS.—Montesinos, Annales, MS., año 1530.

[22] Garcilasso, Com. Real., Parte 2, lib. 1, cap. 15.

[23] "Aunque ellos no ninguno por aver venido, porque como avian dexado el paraiso de mahoma que hera Nicaragua y hallaron la isla alzada y falta de comidas y la mayor parte de la gente enfferma y no oro ni plata como atras avian hallado, algunos y todos se holgaran de volver de adonde avian venido." Pedro Pizarro, Descub. y Conq., MS.

[24] Xeres, Conq. del Peru, ap. Barcia, tom. III. p. 183.

[25] "Y el marques don Francisco Piçarro, por tenellos por amigos y estuviesen de paz quando alla passasen, les dio algunos principales los quales ellos matavan en presencia de los españoles, cortandoles las cavezas por el cogote." Pedro Pizarro, Descub. y Conq., MS.

[26] The city of San Miguel was so named by Pizarro to commemorate the event,—and the existence of such a city may be considered by some as establishing the truth of the miracle.—"En la batalla de Puná vieron muchos, ya de los Indios, ya de los nuestros, que habia en el aire otros dos campos, uno acaudillado por el Arcangel S^n Miguel con espada y rodela, y otro por Luzbel y sus secuaces; mas apenas cantaron los Castellanos la victoria huyeron los diablos, y formando un gran torvellino de viento se oyeron en el aire unas terribles voces que decian, Vencistenos! Miguel vencistenos! De aqui tornó D^n Francisco Pizarro tanta devocion al sto Arcangel, que prometió llamar la primera ciudad que fundase de su nombre; cumpliolo asi como veremos adelante." Montesinos, Annales, MS., año 1530.

[27] The transactions in Puná are given at more or less length by Naharro, Relacion Sumaria, MS.—Conq. i Pob. del Peru, MS.—Pedro Pizarro, Descub. y Conq., MS.—Montesinos, Annales, MS., ubi supra.—Relacion del Primer. Descub., MS.—Xerez, Conq. del Peru, ap. Barcia, tom. III. pp. 182, 183.

CHAPTER II

[1] Sarmiento, an honest authority, tells us he had this from some of the Inca lords who heard it. Relacion, MS., cap. 65.

[2] A minute relation of these supernatural occurrences is given by the Inca Garcillasso de la Vega, (Com. Real., Parte 1, lib. 9, cap. 14,) whose situation opened to him the very best sources of information, which is more than counterbalanced by the defects in his own character as an historian,—his childish credulity, and his desire to magnify and mystify every thing relating to his own order, and, indeed, his nation. His work is the source of most of the facts and the falsehoods—that have obtained circulation in respect to the ancient Peruvians. Unfortunately, at this distance of time, it is not always easy to distinguish the one from the other.

[3] *Huascar*, in the Quichua dialect, signifies "a cable." The reason of its being given to the heir apparent is remarkable. Huayna Capac celebrated the birth of the prince by a festival, in which he introduced a massive gold chain for the nobles to hold in their hands as they performed their national dances. The chain was seven hundred feet in length, and the links nearly as big round as a man's wrist! (See Zarate, Conq. del Peru, lib. 1, cap. 14.—Garcilasso, Com. Real., Parte 1, lib. 9, cap. 1.) The latter writer had the particulars, he tells us, from his old Inca uncle,—who seems to have dealt largely in the marvellous; not too largely for his audience, however, as the story has been greedily circulated by most of the Castilian writers, both of that and of the succeeding age.

[4] "Atabalipa era bien quisto de los Capitanes viejos de su Padre y de los Soldados, porque andubo en la guerra en su niñez y porque él en vida le mostró tanto amor que no le dejaba comer otra cosa que lo que él le daba de su plato." Sarmiento, Relacion, MS., cap. 66.

[5] Oviedo, Hist. de las Indias, MS., Parte 1, lib. 8, cap. 9.—Zarate, Conq. del Peru, lib. 1, cap. 12.—Sarmiento, Relacion, MS., cap. 65.—Xerez, Conq. del Peru, ap. Barcia, tom. III. p. 201.

[6] The precise date of this event, though so near the time of the Conquest, is matter of doubt. Balboa, a contemporary with the Conquerors, and who wrote at Quito, where the Inca died, fixes it at 1525. (Hist. du Perou, chap. 14.) Velasco, another inhabitant of the same place, after an investigation of the different accounts, comes to the like conclusion. (Hist. de Quito, tom. I. p. 232.) Dr. Robertson, after telling us that Huayna Capac died in 1529, speaks again of this event as having happened in 1527. (Conf. America, vol. III. pp. 25, 381.) Any one, who has been bewildered by the chronological snarl of the ancient chronicles, will not be surprised at meeting occasionally with such inconsistencies in a writer who is obliged to take them as his guides.

[7] One cannot doubt this monarch's popularity with the female part of his subjects, at least, if, as the historian of the Incas tells us, "he was never known to refuse a woman, of whatever ago or degree she might be, any favor that she asked of him"! Com. Real., Parte 1, lib. 8, cap. 7.

[8] Sarmiento, Relacion, MS., cap. 65.—Herrera, Hist. General, dec. 5, lib. 3, cap. 17.

[9] Garcilasso denies that any thing but insignificant skirmishes took place before the decisive action fought on the plains of Cuzco. But the Licentiate Sarmiento, who gathered his accounts of these events, as he tells us, from the actors in them, walked over the field of battle at Ambato, when the ground was still covered with the bones of the slain. "Yo hé pasado por este Pueblo y he visto el Lugar donde dicen que esta Batalla se dió y cierto segun hay la osamenta devieron aun de morir mas gente de la que cuentan." Relacion, MS., cap. 69.

[10] "Cuentan muchos Indios á quien yo lo oi, que por amansar su ira, mandaron á un escuadron grande de niños y á otto de hombres de toda edad, que saliesen hasta las ricas andas donde venia con gran pompa, llevando en las manos ramos verdes y ojas de palma, y que le pidiesen la gracia y amistad suya para el pueblo, sin mirar la injuria pasada, y que en tantos elamores se lo suplicaron, y con tanta humildad, que bastara quebrantar corazones de piedra; mas poca impresion hicieron en el cruel de Atabalipa, porque dicen que mandó á sus capitanes y gentes que matasen á todos aquellos que habian venido, lo cual fué hecho, no perdonando sino á algunos niños y á las mugeres sagradas del Templo." Sarmiento, Relacion, MS., cap. 70.

[11] Cieza de Leon, Cronica, cap. 77.—Oviedo, Hist. de las Indias, MS., Parte 3, lib. 8, cap. 9. —Xerez, Conq. del Peru, ap. Barcia, tom. III. p. 202.—Zarate, Conq. del Peru, lib. 1, cap. 12.—Sarmiento, Relacion, MS., cap. 70.—Pedro Pizarro, Descub. y Conq., MS.

[12] Garcilasso, Com. Real., Parte 1, lib. 9, cap. 35-39.

"A las Mugeres, Hermanas, Tias, Sobrinas, Primas Hermanas, y Madrastras de Atahuallpa, colgavan de los Arboles, y de muchas Horcas mui altas que hicieron: à unas colgaron de los cabellos, à otras por debajo de los braços, y à otras de otras maneras feas, que por la honestidad se callan: davanles sus hijuelos, que los tuviesen en braços, tenianlos hasta que se les caìan, y se aporreavan." (Ibid., cap. 37.) The variety of torture shows some invention in the writer, or, more probably, in the writer's uncle, the ancient Inca, the *raconteur* of these Bluebeard butcheries.

[13] "Las crueldades, que Atahuallpa en los de la Sangre Real hiço, diré de Relacion de mi Madre, y de un Hermano suio, que se llamó Don Fernando Huallpa Tupac Inca Yupanqui, que entonces eran Niños de menos de diez Años." Ibid., Parte 1, lib. 9, cap. 14.

[14] This appears from a petition for certain immunities, forwarded to Spain in 1603, and signed by five hundred and sixty-seven Indians of the royal Inca race. (Ibid., Parte 3, lib. 9, cap. 40.) Oviedo says that Huayna Capac left a hundred sons and daughters, and that *most of them were alive at the time of his writing.* "Tubo cien hijos y hijas, y la mayor parte de ellos son viros." Hist. de las Indias, MS., Parte 3, lib. 8, cap. 9.

[15] I have looked in vain for some confirmation of this story in Oviedo, Sarmiento, Xerez, Cieza de Leon, Zarate, Pedro Pizarro, Gomara,—all living at the time, and having access to the best sources of information; and all, it may be added, disposed to do stern justice to the evil qualities of the Indian monarch.

[16] No one of the apologists of Atahuallpa goes quite so far as Father Velasco, who, in the overflowings of his loyalty for a Quito monarch, regards his massacre of the Cañares as a very fair retribution for their offences. "Si les auteurs dont je viens de parler s'étaient trouvés dans les mêmes circonstances qu' Atahuallpa et avaient éprouvé autant d'offenses graves et de trahisons, je ne croirai jamais qu'ils eussent agi autrement"! Hist. de Quito, tom. I. p. 253.

[17] "Οὐ γάρ πω πάντεσσι θεοὶ φαίνονται ἐναργεῖς." v. 161.

CHAPTER III

[1] Xerez, Conq. del Peru, ap. Barcia, tom. III. p. 185.

"Aunque lo del templo del Sol en quien ellos adoran era cosa de ver, porque tenian grandes edificios, y todo el por de dentro y de fuera pintado de grandes pinturas y ricos matizes de colores, porque los hay en aquella tierra." Relacion del Primer. Descub., MS.

[2] For the account of the transactions in Tumbez, see Pedro Pizarro, Descub. y Conq., MS.— Oviedo, Hist. de las Indias, MS., Parte 3, lib. 8, cap. 1.—Relacion del Primer. Descub., MS.—Herrera, Hist. General, dec. 4, lib. 9, cap. 1, 2.—Xerez, Conq. del Peru, ap Barcia, tom. III. p. 185.

[3] "Mando el Gobernador por pregon é so graves penas que no le fuese hecha fuerza ni descortesia é que se les hiciese muy buen tratamiento por los Españoles é sus criados." Oviedo, Hist. de las Indias, MS., Parte 3, lib. 8, cap. 2.

[4] "E mandabales notificar ó dar á entender con las lenguas el requerimiento que su Magestad manda que se les haga á los Indios para traellos en conocimiento de nuestra Santa fé catolica, y requiriendoles con la paz, é que obedezcan á la Iglesia e Apostolica de Roma, é en lo temporal den la obediencia á su Magestad é á los Reyes sus succesores en los regnos de Castilla i de Leon; respondieron que asi lo querian é harian, guardarian é cumplirian enteramente; e el Gobernador los recibio por tales vasallos de sus Magestades por auto publico de notarios." Ibid., MS., ubi supra.

[5] Pedro Pizarro, Descub. y Conq., MS.—Conq. i Pob. del Peru, MS.—Cieza de Leon, Cronica, cap. 55.—Relacion del Primer. Descub., MS.

"Porque los Vecinos, sin aiuda i servicios de los Naturales no se podian sostener, ni poblarse el Pueblo. . . . . .A esta causa, con acuerdo de el Religioso, i de los Oficiales que los parecio convenir asi al servicio de Dios, i bien de los Naturales, el Gobernador depositò los Caciques, i Indios en los Vecinos de este Pueblo, porque los aiudasen a sostener, i los Christianos los doctrinasen en nuestra Santa Fé, conforme á los Mandamientos de su Magestad." Xerez, Conq. del Peru, ap. Barcia, tom. III. p. 187.

[6] "E sacado el quinto para su Magestad, lo restante que perteneció al Egercito de la Conquista, el Gobernador le tomó prestado de los compañeros para se lo pagar del primer oro que se obiese." Oviedo, Hist. de las Indias, MS., Parte 3, lib. 8, cap. 2.

[7] Xerez, Conq. del Peru, ap. Barcia, tom. III. p. 187.—Pedro Pizarro, Descub. y Conq., MS. —Oviedo, Hist. de las Indias, MS., Parte 3, lib. 8, cap. 10.

[8] Oviedo, Hist. de las Indias, MS., Parte 3, lib. 8, cap. 4.—Naharro, Relacion Sumaria, MS. —Conq. i Pob. del Piru, MS.—Relacion del Primer. Descub., MS.

[9] There is less discrepancy in the estimate of the Spanish force here than usual. The paucity of numbers gave less room for it. No account carries them as high as two hundred. I have adopted that of the Secretary Xerez, (Conq. del Peru, ap. Barcia, tom. III. p. 187,) who has been followed by Oviedo, (Hist. de las Indias, MS., Parte 3, lib. 1, cap. 3,) and by the judicious Herrera, Hist. General, dec. 5, lib. 1, cap. 2.

[10] "Que todos los que quiriesen bolverse á la ciudad de San Miguel y avecindarse alli demas de los vecinos que alli quedaban el los depositaria repartimientos de Indios con que se sortubiesen como lo habia hecho con los otros vecinos; é que con los Españoles quedasen, pocos ó muchos, iria á conquistar é pacificar la tierra en demanda y persecucion del camino que llevaba." Oviedo, Hist. de las Indias, MS., Parte 3, lib. 8, cap. 3.

[11] Ibid., MS., loc. cit.—Herrera, Hist. General, dec. 5, lib. 1, cap. 2.—Xerez, Conq. del Peru, ap. Barcia, tom. III. p. 187.

[12] Conq. i Pob. del Piru, MS.

[13] "Dos Fortaleças, à manera de Fuente, figuradas en Piedra, con que beba, i dos cargas de Patos sccos, desollados, para que hechos polvos, se sahume con ellos, porque asi se usa entre los Señores de su Tierra: i que le embiaba à decir, que èl tiene voluntad de ser su Amigo, i esperalle de Paz en Caxamalca." Xerez, Conq. del Peru, ap. Barcia, tom. III. p. 189.

[14] Pedro Pizarro, Descub. y Conq., MS.—Oviedo, Hist. de las Indias, MS., Parte 3, lib. 8, cap. 3.—Relacion del Primer. Descub., MS.—Xerez, Conq. del Peru, ap. Barcia, tom. III. p. 189.

Garcilasso de la Vega tells us that Atahuallpa's envoy addressed the Spanish commander in the most humble and deprecatory manner, as Son of the Sun and of the great God Viracocha. He adds, that he was loaded with a prodigious present of all kinds of game, living and dead, gold and silver vases, emeralds, turquoises, &c., &c., enough to furnish out the finest chapter of the Arabian Nights. (Com. Real., Parte 2, lib. 1, cap. 19.) It is extraordinary that none of the Conquerors, who had a quick eye for these dainties, should allude to them! One cannot but suspect that the "old uncle" was amusing himself at his young nephew's expense; and, as it has proved, at the expense of most of his readers, who receive the Inca's fairy tales as historic facts.

[15] "I mandò, que le diesen de comer à el, i à los que con èl venian, i todo lo que huviesen menester, i fuesen bien aposentados, como Embajadores de tan Gran Señor." Xerez, Conq. del Peru, ap. Barcia, tom. III. p. 189.

[16] "Los Indios de la tierra se entendian muy bien con los Españoles, porque aquellos mochachos Indios que en el descubrimiento de la tierra Pizarro truxo á España, entendian muy bien nuestra lengua, y los tenia alli, con los cuales se entendia muy bien con todos los naturales de la tierra." (Relacion del Primer. Descub., MS.) Yet it is a proof of the ludicrous blunders into which the Conquerors were perpetually falling, that Pizarro's secretary constantly confounds the Inca's name with that of his capital. Huayna Capac, he always styles "old Cuzco," and his son Huascar "young Cuzco."

[17] "A la entrada del Pueblo havia ciertos Indios ahorcados de los pies: i supo de este Principal, que Atabalipa los mandò matar, porque uno de ellos entrò en la Casa de las Mugeres à dormir con una: al qual, i à todos los Porteros que consintieron, ahorcò." Xerez, Conq. del Peru, ap. Barcia, tom. III. p. 188.

[18] "Van por este camino caños de agua de donde los caminantes beben, traidos de sus nacimientos de otras partes, y a cada jornada una Casa á manera de Venta donde se aposentan los que van é vienen." Oviedo, Hist. de las Indias, MS., Parte 3, lib. 8, cap. 3.

[19] "A la entrada de este Camino en el Pueblo de Cajas esta una casa al principio de una puente donde reside una guarda que recibe el Portazgo de todos los que van e vienen, é paganló en la misma cosa que llevan, y ninguno puede sacar carga del Pueblo sino la mete, y esta costumbre es alli antigua." Oviedo, Hist. de las Indias, MS., ubi supra.

[20] "Piezas de lana de la tierra, que era cosa mucho de ver segun su primer é gentileza, e no se sabian determinar si era seda ó lana segun su fineza con muchas labores i figuras de oro de martillo de tal manera asentado en la ropa que era cosa de marabillar." Oviedo, Hist. de las Indias, MS., Parte 3, lib. 8, cap. 4.

[21] Oviedo, Hist. de las Indias, MS., Parte 3, lib. 8, cap. 4.—Conq. i Pob. del Piru, MS.—Relacion del Primer. Descub., MS.—Xerez, Conq. del Peru, ap. Barcia, tom. III. p. 190.

[22] "Que todos se animasen y esforzasen á hacer como de ellos esperaba y como buenos españoles lo suelen hacer, é que no les pusiese temor la multitud que se decia que habia de gente ni el poco numero de los cristianos, que aunque menos fuesen é mayor el egercito contrario, la ayuda de Dios es mucho mayor, y en las mayores necesidades socorre y faborece a los suyos para desbaratar y abajar la soberbia de los infieles è traerlos en conocimiento de nuestra Sta fe catolica." Oviedo, Hist. de las Indias, MS., Parte 3, lib. 8, cap. 4.

[23] "Todos digeron que fuese por el Camino que quisiese i viese que mas convenia, que todos le seguirian con buena voluntad é obra al tiempo del efecto, y veria lo que cada uno de ellos haria en servicio de Dios é de su Magestad." Ibid., MS., loc. cit.

CHAPTER IV

[1] "Tan ancha la Cerca como qualquier Fortaleça de España, con sus Puertas: que si en esta Tierra oviese los Maestros, i Herramientas de España, no pudiera ser mejor labrada la Cerca." Xerez, Conq. del Peru, ap. Barcia, tom. III. p. 192.

[2] "Es tanto el frio que hace en esta Sierra, que como los Caballos venian hechos al calor, que en los Valles hacia, algunos de ellos se resfriaron." Ibid., p. 191.

[3] "É aposentaronse los Españoles en sus toldos ó pabellones de algodon de la tierra que llevaban, é haciendo fuegos para defenderse del mucho frio que en aquella Sierra hacen, porque sin ellos no se pudieron valer sin padecer mucho trabajo; y segun á los cristianos les pareció, y aun como era lo cierto, no podia haber mas frio en parte de España en invierno." Oviedo, Hist. de las Indias, MS., Parte 3, lib. 8, cap. 4.

[4] Xerez, Conq. del Peru, ap. Barcia, tom. III. p. 193.—Oviedo, Hist. de las Indias, MS., Parte 3, lib. 8, cap. 5.

[5] "Este Embajador traìa servicio de Señor, i cinco, ò seis Vasos de Oro fino, con que bebia, i con ellos daba à beber à los Españoles de la Chicha que traìa." Xerez, Conq. del Peru, ap. Barcia, tom. III. p. 193.—Oviedo, Hist. de las Indias, MS., ubi supra.

The latter author, in this part of his work, has done little more than make a transcript of that of Xerez. His indorsement of Pizarro's secretary, however, is of value, from the fact that, with less temptation to misstate or overstate, he enjoyed excellent opportunities for information.

[6] Xerez, Conq. del Peru, ap. Barcìa, tom. III. p. 194.—Oviedo, Hist. de las Indias, MS., ubi supra.

[7] Xerez, Conq. del Peru, ap. Barcia, tom. III. p. 195.

[8] "Y eran tantas las tiendas que parecian, que cierto nos puso harto espanto, porque no pensabamos que Indios pudiesen tener tan soberbia estancia, ni tantas tiendas, ni tan á punto, lo cual hasta alli en las Indias nunca se vió, que nos causó á todos los Españoles harta confusion y temor; aunque no convenia mostrarse, ni menos volver atras, porque si alguna flaqueza en nosotros sintieran, los mismos Indios que llevabamos nos mataran, y ansi con animoso semblante, despues de haber muy bien atalayado el pueblo y tiendas que he dicho, abajamos por el valle abajo, y entramos en el pueblo de Cajamalca." Relacion del Primer. Descub., MS.

[9] This was evidently the opinion of the old Conqueror, whose imperfect manuscript forms one of the best authorities for this portion of our narrative. "Teniendonos en muy poco, y no haciendo cuenta que 190 hombres le habian de ofender, dió lugar y consintió que pasasemos por aquel paso y por otros muchos tan malos como él, porque realmente, á lo que despues se supo y averiguó, su intencion era vernos y preguntarnos, de donde veniamos? y quien nos habia hechado alli? y que queriamos? Porque *era muy sabio y discreto, y aunque sin luz ni escriptura, amigo de saber y de sotil entendimiento;* y despues de holgadose con nosotros, tomarnos los caballos y las cosas que á el mas le aplacian, y sacrificar á los demas." Relacion del Primer. Descub., MS.

[10] According to Stevenson, this population, which is of a very mixed character, amounts, or did amount some thirty years ago, to about seven thousand. That sagacious traveller gives an animated description of the city, in which he resided some time, and which he seems to have regarded with peculiar predilection. Yet it does not hold probably the relative rank at the present day, that it did in that of the Incas. Residence in South America, vol. II. p. 131.

[11] Carta de Hern. Pizarro, ap. Oviedo, Hist. de las Indias, MS., Parte 3, lib. 8, cap. 15.—Xerez, Conq. del Peru, ap. Barcia, tom. III. p. 195.

[12] "Fuerças son, que entre Indios no se han visto tales." Xerez, Conq. del Peru, ap. Barcia, tom. III. p. 195.—Relacion del Primer. Descub., MS.

[13] "Desde à poco rato començo à llover, i caer graniço." (Xerez, Conq. del Peru, ap. Barcia, tom. III. p. 195.) Caxamalca, in the Indian tongue, signifies "place of frost"; for the temperature, though usually bland and genial, is sometimes affected by frosty winds from the east, very pernicious to vegetation. Stevenson, Residence in South America, vol. II. p. 129.

[14] Carta de Hern. Pizarro, MS.

The Letter of Hernando Pizarro, addressed to the Royal Audience of St. Domingo, gives a full account of the extraordinary events recorded in this and the ensuing chapter, in which that cavalier took a prominent part. Allowing for the partialities incident to a chief actor in the scenes he describes, no authority can rank higher. The indefatigable Oviedo, who resided in St. Domingo, saw its importance, and fortunately incorporated the document in his great work, Hist. de las Indias, MS., Parte 3, lib. 8, cap. 15.—The anonymous author of the Relacion del Primer. Descub., MS., was also detached on this service.

[15] Pedro Pizarro, Descub. y Conq., MS.—Carta de Hern. Pizarro, MS.

[16] Xerez, Conq. del Peru, ap. Barcia, tom. III. p. 202.

"Y al estanque venian dos caños de agua, uno caliente y otro frio, y alli se templava la una con la otra, para quando el Señor se queria bañar ó sus mugeres que otra persona no osava entrar en el so pena de la vida." Pedro Pizarro, Descub. y Conq., MS.

[17] Stevenson, Residence in South America, vol. II. p. 164.

[18] Xerez, Conq. del Peru, ap. Barcia, tom. III. p. 196.—Carta de Hern. Pizarro, MS.

The appearance of the Peruvian monarch is described in simple but animated style by the Conqueror so often quoted, one of the party. "Llegados al patio de la dicha casa que tenia delante della, vimos estar en medio de gran muchedumbre de Indios asentado aquel gran Señor Atabalica (de quien tanta noticia, y tantas cosas nos habian dicho) con una corona en la cabeza, y una borla que le salia della, y le cubria toda la frente, la cual era la insinia real, sentado en una sillecita muy baja del suelo, como los turcos y moros acostumbran sentarse, el cual estaba con tanta magestad y aparato cual nunca se ha visto jamas, porque estaba cercado de mas de seiscientos Señores de su tierra." Relacion del Primer. Descub., MS.

[19] "Las cuales por él oidas, con ser su inclinacion preguntarnos y saber de donde veniamos, y que queriamos, y ver nuestras personas y caballos, tubo tanta serenidad en el rostro, y tanta gravedad en su persona, que no quiso responder palabra á lo que se le decia, salvo que un Señor de aquellos que estaban par de el respondia: bien esta." Relacion del Primer. Descub., MS.

[20] "Visto por el dicho Hernando Pizarro que él no hablaba, y que aquella tercera persona respondia de suyo, tornó le á suplicar, que el hablase por su boca, y le respondiese lo que quisiese." Ibid., MS., ubi supra.

[21] "El cual á esto volvió la cabeza á mirarle sonriendose y le dijo: Decid á ese Capitan que os embia acá; que yo estoy en ayuno, y le acabo mañana por la mañana, que en bebiendo una vez, yo iré con algunos destos principales mios á verme con el, que en tanto él se aposente en esas casas que estan en la plaza que son comunes á todos, y que no entren en otra ninguna hasta que Yo vaya, que Yo mandaré lo que se ha de hacer." Ibid., MS., ubi supra.

In this singular interview I have followed the account of the cavalier who accompanied Hernando Pizarro, in preference to the latter, who represents himself as talking in a lordly key, that savours too much of the vaunt of the hidalgo.

[22] Pedro Pizarro, Descub. y Conq., MS.—Relacion del Primer. Descub., MS.

"I algunos Indios, con miedo, se desviaron de la Carrera, por lo qual Atabalipa los hiço luego matar." (Zarate, Conq. del Peru, lib. 2, cap. 4.)—Xerez states that Atahuallpa confessed this himself, in conversation with the Spaniards after he was taken prisoner.—Soto's charger might well have made the Indians start, if, as Balboa says, he took twenty feet at a leap, and this with a knight in armour on his back! Hist. du Perou, chap. 22.

[23] Relacion del Primer. Descub., MS.—Xerez, Conq. del Peru, ap. Barcia, tom. III. p. 196.

[24] "Hecho esto y visto y atalayado la grandeza del ejercito, y las tiendas que era bien de ver, nos bolvimos á donde el dicho capitan nos estabá esperando, harto espantados de lo que habiamos visto, habiendo y tomando entre nosotros muchos acuerdos y opiniones de lo que se debia hacer, estando todos con mucho temor por ser tan pocos, y estar tan metidos en la tierra donde no podiamos ser socorridos." (Relacion del Primer. Descub., MS.) Pedro Pizarro is honest enough to confirm this account of the consternation of the Spaniards. (Descub. y Conq., MS.) Fear was a strange sensation for the Castilian cavalier. But if he did not feel some touch of it on that occasion, he must have been akin to that doughty knight who, as Charles V. pronounced, "never could have snuffed a candle with his fingers."

[25] "Hecimos la guardia en la plaza, de donde se vian los fuegos del ejercito de los Indios, lo cual era cosa espantable, que como estaban en una ladera la mayor parte, y tan juntos unos de otros, no parecia sino un cielo muy estrellado." Relacion del Primer. Descub., MS.

[26] Xerez, Conq. del Peru, ap. Barcia, tom. III. p. 197.—Naharro, Relacion Sumaria, MS.

CHAPTER V

[1] Pedro Pizarro, Descub. y Conq., MS.—Relacion del Primer. Descub., MS.—Xerez, Conq. del Peru, ap. Barcia tom. III. p. 197.—Carta de Hern. Pizarro, MS.—Oviedo, Hist. de las Indias, MS., Parte 3, lib. 8, cap. 7.

² "Los Eclesiasticos i Religiosos se ocuparon toda aquella noche en oracion, pidiendo a Dios el mas conveniente suceso á su sagrado servicio, exaltacion de la fé é salvacion de tanto numero de almas, derramando muchas lagrimas i sangre en las disciplinas que tomaron. *Francisco Pizarro animó á los soldados con una mui cristiana platica que les hizo:* con que, i asegurarles los Eclesiasticos de parte de Dios i de su Madre Santisima la vitoria, amanecieron todos mui deseosos de dar la batalla, diciendo á voces, Exsurge Domine, et judica causam tuam." Naharro, Relacion Sumaria, MS.

³ "El governador respondió: Dì à tu Señor, que venga en hora buena como quisiere, que de la manera que viniere lo recebirè como Amigo, i Hermano." Xerez, Conq. del Peru, ap. Barcia, tom. III. p. 197.—Oviedo, Hist. de las Indias, MS., Parte 3, lib. 8, cap. 7.—Carta de Hern. Pizarro, MS.

⁴ "Hera tanta la pateneria que traian d'oro y plata que hera cossa estraña lo que Reluzia con el Sol." Pedro Pizarro, Descub. y Conq., MS.

⁵ To the eye of the old Conqueror so often quoted, the number of Peruvian warriors appeared not less than 50,000; "mas de cincuenta mil que tenia de guerra." (Relacion del Primer. Descub., MS.) To Pizarro's secretary, as they lay encamped along the hills, they seemed about 30,000. (Xerez, Conq. del Peru, ap. Barcia, tom. III. p. 196.) However gratifying to the imagination to repose on some precise number, it is very rare that one can do so with safety, in estimating the irregular and tumultuous levies of a barbarian host.

⁶ Pedro Pizarro says that an Indian spy reported to Atahuallpa, that the white men were all huddled together in the great halls on the square, in much consternation, *llenos de miedo*, which was not far from the truth, adds the cavalier. (Descub. y Conq., MS.)

⁷ Pedro Pizarro, Descub. y Conq., MS.

"Asentados sus toldos envió á decir al gobernador que ya era tarde, que él queria dormir allí, que por la mañana vernia: el gobernador le envió á decir que le rogaba que viniese luego, porque le esperaba á cenar, é que no habia de cenar, hasta que fuese." Carta de Hern. Pizarro, MS.

⁸ "Él queria vernir luego, é que venia sin armas. E luego Ataballiva se movió para venir, é dejó allí la gente con las armas, é llevò consigo hasta cinco ó seis mil indios sin armas, salvo que debajo de las camisetas traían unas porras pequeñas, é hondas, é bolsas con piedras." Carta de Hern. Pizarro, MS.

⁹ Xerez, Conq. del Peru, ap. Barcia, tom. III. p. 197.

¹⁰ Relacion del Primer. Descub., MS.

¹¹ "Blanca y colorada como las casas de un ajedrez." Ibid., MS.

¹² "Con martíllos en las manos de cobre y plata." Ibid., MS.

¹³ "El asiento que traia sobre las andas era un tablon de oro que pesó un quintal de oro segun dicen los historiadores 25,000 pesos ó ducados." Naharro, Relacion Sumaria, MS.

¹⁴ "Luego venia mucha Gente con Armaduras, Patenas, i Coronas de oro i Plata: entre estos venia Ataballiba, en una Litera, aforrada de Pluma de Papagaios, de muchas colores, guarnecida de chapas de Oro, i Plata." Xerez, Conq. del Peru, ap. Barcia, tom. III. p. 198.

¹⁵ Pedro Pizarro, Descub. y Conq., MS.

"Venia la persona de Atabalica, la cual traian ochenta Señores en hombros todos bestidos de una librea azul muy rica, y el bestido su persona muy ricamente con su corona en la cabeza, y al cuello un collar de emeraldas grandes." Relacion del Primer. Descub., MS.

[16] Montesinos says that Valverde read to the Inca the regular formula used by the Spaniards in their Conquests. (Annales, MS., año 1533.) But that address, though absurd enough, did not comprehend the whole range of theology ascribed to the chaplain on this occasion. Yet it is not impossible. But I have followed the report of Fray Naharro, who collected his information from the actors in the tragedy, and whose minuter statement is corroborated by the more general testimony of both the Pizarros and the secretary Xerez.

[17] "Por dezir Dios trino y uno, dixo Dios tres y uno son quatro, sumando los numeros por darse á entender." Com. Real., Parte 2, lib. 1, cap. 23.

[18] See *Appendix, No.* 8, where the reader will find extracts in the original from several contemporary MSS., relating to the capture of Atahuallpa.

[19] Some accounts describe him as taxing the Spaniards in much more unqualified terms. (See *Appendix, No.* 8.) But language is not likely to be accurately reported in such seasons of excitement. — According to some authorities, Atahuallpa let the volume drop by accident. (Montesinos, Annales, MS., año 1533. — Balboa, Hist. du Perou, chap. 22.) But the testimony, as far as we have it, of those present, concurs in representing it as stated in the text. And, if he spoke with the heat imputed to him, this act would only be in keeping.

[20] "Visto esto por el Frayle y lo poco que aprovechaban sus palabras, tomó su libro, y abajó su cabeza, y fuese para donde estaba el dicho Pizarro, casi corriendo, y dijole: No veis lo que pasa: para que estais en comedimientos y requerimientos con este perro lleno de soberbia que vienen los campos llenos de Indios? Salid á el, — que yo os absuelvo." (Relacion del Primer. Descub., MS.) The historian should be slow in ascribing conduct so diabolical to Father Valverde, without evidence. Two of the Conquerors present, Pedro Pizarro and Xerez, simply state that the monk reported to his commander the indignity offered to the sacred volume. But Hernando Pizarro and the author of the Relacion del Primer. Descub., both eyewitnesses, and Naharro, Zarate, Gomara, Balboa, Herrera, the Inca Titucussi Yupanqui, all of whom obtained their information from persons who were eyewitnesses, state the circumstance, with little variation, as in the text. Yet Oviedo indorses the account of Xerez, and Garcilasso de la Vega insists on Valverde's innocence of any attempt to rouse the passions of his comrades.

[21] Pedro Pizarro, Descub. y Conq., MS. — Xerez, Conq. del Peru, ap. Barcia, tom. III. p. 198. — Carta de Hern. Pizarro, MS. — Oviedo, Hist. de las Indias, MS., Parte 3, lib. 8, cap. 7. — Relacion del Primer. Descub., MS. — Zarate, Conq. del Peru, lib. 2, cap. 5. — Instruccion del Inga Titucussi Yupanqui, MS.

[22] The author of the Relacion del Primero Descubrimiento speaks of a few as having bows and arrows, and of others as armed with silver and copper mallets or maces, which may, however, have been more for ornament than for service in fight. — Pedro Pizarro and some later writers say that the Indians brought thongs with them to bind the captive white men. — Both Hernando Pizarro and the secretary Xerez agree that their only arms were secreted under their clothes; but as they do not pretend that these were used, and as it was announced by the Inca that he came without arms, the assertion may well be doubted, — or rather discredited. All authorities, without exception, agree that no attempt was made at resistance.

[23] "El marquez dio bozes diciendo. Nadie hiera al indio so pena de la vida." Pedro Pizarro, Descub. y Conq., MS.

[24] Whatever discrepancy exists among the Castilian accounts in other respects, *all* concur in this remarkable fact,—that no Spaniard, except their general, received a wound on that occasion. Pizarro saw in this a satisfactory argument for regarding the Spaniards, this day, as under the especial protection of Providence. See Xerez, Conq. del Peru, ap. Barcia, tom. III. p. 199.

[25] Miguel Estete, who long retained the silken diadem as a trophy of the exploit, according to Garcilasso de la Vega, (Com. Real., Parte 2, lib. 1, cap. 27,) an indifferent authority for any thing in this part of his history. This popular writer, whose work, from his superior knowledge of the institutions of the country, has obtained greater credit, even in what relates to the Conquest, than the reports of the Conquerors themselves, has indulged in the romantic vein to an unpardonable extent, in his account of the capture of Atahuallpa. According to him, the Peruvian monarch treated the invaders from the first with supreme deference, as descendants of Viracocha, predicted by his oracles as to come and rule over the land. But if this flattering homage had been paid by the Inca, it would never have escaped the notice of the Conquerors. Garcilasso had read the Commentaries of Cortés, as he somewhere tells us; and it is probable that that general's account, well founded, it appears, of a similar superstition among the Aztecs suggested to the historian the idea of a corresponding sentiment in the Peruvians, which, while it flattered the vanity of the Spaniards, in some degree vindicated his own countrymen from the charge of cowardice, incurred by their too ready submission; for, however they might be called on to resist men, it would have been madness to resist the decrees of Heaven. Yet Garcilasso's romantic version has something in it so pleasing to the imagination, that it has ever found favor with the majority of readers. The English student might have met with a sufficient corrective in the criticism of the sagacious and skeptical Robertson.

[26] Xerez, Conq. del Peru, ap. Barcia, tom. III. p. 199.

[27] "Los mataron á todos con los Cavallos con espadas con arcabuzes como quien mata ovejas —sin hacerles nadie resistencia que no se escaparon de mas de diez mil, doscientos." Instruc. del Inga Titucussi, MS.

This document, consisting of two hundred folio pages, is signed by a Peruvian Inca, grandson of the great Huayna Capac, and nephew, consequently, of Atahuallpa. It was written in 1570, and designed to set forth to his Majesty Philip II. the claims of Titucussi and the members of his family to the royal bounty. In the course of the Memorial, the writer takes occasion to recapitulate some of the principal events in the latter years of the empire; and though sufficiently prolix to tax even the patience of Philip II., it is of much value as an historical document, coming from one of the royal race of Peru.

[28] Montesinos, Annales, MS., año 1532.

According to Naharro, the Indians were less astounded by the wild uproar caused by the sudden assault of the Spaniards, though "this was such that it seemed as if the very heavens were falling," than by a terrible apparition which appeared in the air during the on-slaught. It consisted of a woman and a child, and, at their side, a horseman all clothed in white on a milk-white charger,—doubtless the valiant St. James,—who, with his sword glancing lightning, smote down the infidel host, and rendered them incapable of resistance. This miracle the good father reports on the testimony of three of his Order, who were present in the action, and who received it from numberless of the natives. Relacion Sumaria, MS.

[29] "Diciendo que era uso de Guerra vencer, i ser vencido." Herrera, Hist. General, dec. 5, lib. 2, cap. 12.

[30] "Haciendo admiracion de la traza que tenia hecha." Relacion del Primer. Descub., MS.

[31] "And in my opinion," adds the Conqueror who reports the speech, "he had good grounds for believing he could do this, since nothing but the miraculous interposition of Heaven could have saved us." Ibid., MS.

[32] Xerez, Conq. del Peru, ap. Barcia, tom. III. p. 203.

[33] "Nosotros vsamos de piedad con nuestros Enemigos vencidos, i no hacemos Guerra, sino à los que nos la hacen, i pudiendolos destruir, no lo hacemos, antes los perdonamos." Ibid., tom. III. p. 199.

[34] Ibid., ubi supra.—Pedro Pizarro, Descub. i Conq., MS.

[35] From this time, says Ondegardo, the Spaniards, who hitherto had been designated as the "men with beards," *barbudos,* were called by the natives, from their fair-complexioned deity, *Viracochas.* The people of Cuzco, who bore no goodwill to the captive Inca, "looked upon the strangers," says the author, "as sent by Viracocha himself." (Rel. Prim., MS.) It reminds us of a superstition, or rather an amiable fancy, among the ancient Greeks, that "the stranger came from Jupiter."

$$\text{"Πρὸς γὰρ Διός εἰσιν ἅπαντες Ξεῖνοί τε."} \quad ΟΔΥΣ. ξ, v. 57.$$

[36] "Algunos fueron de opinion, que matasen à todos los Hombres de Guerra, ò les cortasen las manos." Xerez, Hist. del Peru, ap. Barcia, tom. III. p. 200.

[37] "Cada Español de los que alli ivan tomaron para si mui gran cantidad tanto que como andava todo a rienda suelta havia Español que tenia docientas piezas de Indios i Indias de servicio." Conq. i Pob. del Piru, MS.

[38] "Se matan cada Dia, ciento i cinquenta." Xerez, Conq. del Peru, ap. Barcia, tom. III. p. 202.

[39] Cieza de Leon, Cronica, cap. 80.—Ondegardo, Rel. Seg., MS.

"Hasta que los destruian todos sin haver Español ni Justicia que lo defendiese ni amparase." Conq. i Pob. del Piru, MS.

[40] Xerez, Conq. del Peru, ap. Barcia, tom. III. p. 200.

There was enough, says the anonymous Conqueror, for several ship-loads. "Todas estas cosas de tiendas y ropas de lana y algodon eran en tan gran cantidad, que à mi parecer fueran menester muchos navios en que supieran." Relacion del Primer. Descub., MS.

[41] I have adopted the dimensions given by the secretary Xerez, (Conq. del Peru, ap. Barcia, tom. III. p. 202.) According to Hernando Pizarro, the apartment was nine feet high, but thirty-five feet long by seventeen or eighteen feet wide. (Carta, MS.) The most moderate estimate is large enough.

Stevenson says that they still show "a large room, part of the old palace, and now the residence of the Cacique Astopilca, where the ill-fated Inca was kept a prisoner"; and he adds that the line traced on the wall is still visible. (Residence in South America, vol. II. p. 163.) Peru abounds in remains as ancient as the Conquest; and it would not be surprising that the memory of a place so remarkable as this should be preserved,—though any thing but a memorial to be cherished by the Spaniards.

[42] The facts in the preceding paragraph are told with remarkable uniformity by the ancient chroniclers. (Conf. Pedro Pizarro, Descub. y Conq., MS.—Carta de Hern. Pizarro, MS.—Xerez, Conq. del Peru, ap. Barcia, ubi supra.—Naharro, Relacion Sumaria, MS.—Zarate,

Conq. del Peru, lib. 2, cap. 6.—Gomara, Hist. de las Ind., cap. 114.—Herrera, Hist. General, dec. 5, lib. 2, cap. 1.)

Both Naharro and Herrera state expressly that Pizarro promised the Inca his liberation on fulfilling the compact. This is not confirmed by the other chroniclers, who, however, do not intimate that the Spanish general declined the terms. And as Pizarro, by all accounts, encouraged his prisoner to perform his part of the contract, it must have been with the understanding implied, if not expressed, that he would abide by the other. It is most improbable that the Inca would have stripped himself of his treasures, if he had not so understood it.

[43] Relacion del Primer. Descub., MS.—Naharro, Relacion Sumaria, MS.—Zarate, Conq. del Peru, lib. 2, cap. 6.

[44] "I mas dijo Atabalipa, que estaba espantado de lo que el Governador le havia dicho: que bien conocia que aquel que hablaba en su Idolo, no es Dios verdadero, pues tan poco le aiudò." Xerez, Conq. del Peru, ap. Barcia, tom. III. p. 203.

[45] Both the place and the manner of Huascar's death are reported with much discrepancy by the historians. All agree in the one important fact, that he died a violent death at the instigation of his brother. Conf. Herrera, Hist. General, dec. 5, lib. 3, cap. 2.—Xerez, Conq. del Peru, ap. Barcia, tom. III. p. 204.—Pedro Pizarro, Descub. y Conq., MS.—Naharro, Relacion Sumaria, MS.—Zarate, Conq. del Peru, lib. 2, cap. 6.—Instruc. del Inga Titucussi, MS.

[46] Both Garcilasso de la Vega and Titucussi Yupanqui were descendants from Huayna Capac, of the pure Peruvian stock, the natural enemies, therefore, of their kinsman of Quito, whom they regarded as a usurper. Circumstances brought the Castilians into direct collision with Atahuallpa, and it was natural they should seek to darken his reputation by contrast with the fair character of his rival.

[47] "Sabido esto por el Gobernador, mostrò, que le pesaba mucho: i dijo que era mentira, que no le havian muerto, que lo trujesen luego vivo: i sino, que èl mandaria matar à Atabalipa." Xerez, Conq. del Peru, ap. Barcia, tom. III. p. 204.

CHAPTER VI

[1] Zarate, Conq. del Peru, lib. 2, cap. 6.—Naharro, Relacion Sumaria, MS.—Xerez, Conq. del Peru, ap. Barcia, tom. III. p. 204.

[2] Pedro Pizarro, Descub. y Conq., MS.—Xerez, Conq. del Peru, ap. Barcia, tom. III. pp. 203, 204.—Naharro, Relacion Sumaria, MS.

[3] "El demonio Pachacama alegre con este concierto, afirman que mostraua en sus respuestas gran contento: pues con lo vno y lo otro era el seruido, y quedauan las animas de los simples malauenturados presas en su poder." Cieza de Leon, Cronica, cap. 72.

[4] "El camino de las sierras es cosa de ver, porque en verdad en tierra tan fragosa en la cristiandad no se han visto tan hermosos caminos, toda la mayor parte de calzada." Carta, MS.

[5] "Todos los arroyos tienen puentes de piedra ó de madera: en un rio grande, que era muy caudaloso é muy grande, que pasamos dos veces, hallamos puentes de red, que es cosa maravillosa de ver; pasamos por ellas los caballos; tienen en cada pasaje dos puentes, la una por donde pasa la gente comun, la otra por donde pasa el señor de la tierra ó sus capitanes: esta tienen siempre cerrada é indios que la guardan; estos indios cobran portazgo de los que pasan." Carta de Hern. Pizarro, MS.—Also Relacion del Primer. Descub., MS.

[6] A comical blunder has been made by the printer, in M. Ternaux-Compans's excellent translation of Xerez, in the account of this expedition. "On trouve sur toute la route beaucoup de porcs, de lamas." (Relation de la Conquête du Pérou, p. 157.) The substitution of *porcs* for *parcs* might well lead the reader into the error of supposing that swine existed in Peru before the Conquest.

[7] Carta de Hern. Pizarro, MS.—Estete, ap. Barcia, tom. III. pp. 206, 207.—Relacion del Primer. Descub., MS.

Both the last-cited author and Miguel Estete, the royal *veedor* or inspector, accompanied Hernando Pizarro on this expedition, and, of course, were eyewitnesses, like himself, of what they relate. Estete's narrative is incorporated by the secretary Xerez in his own.

[8] "Esta puerta era muy tejida de diversas cosas de corales y turquesas y cristales y otras cosas." Relacion del Primer. Descub., MS.

[9] "Aquel era Pachacama, el cual les sanaba de sus enfermedades, y á lo que alli se entendió, el Demonio aparecia en aquella cueba á aquellos sacerdotes y hablaba con ellos, y estos entraban con las peticiones y ofrendas de los que venian en romeria, que es cierto que del todo el Señorio de Atabalica iban alli, como los Moros y Turcos van á la casa de Meca." Relacion del Primer. Descub., MS.—Also Estete, ap. Barcia, tom. III. p. 209.

[10] "É á falta de predicador les hice mi sermon, diciendo el engaño en que vivian." Carta de Hern. Pizarro, MS.

[11] Ibid., MS.—Relacion del Primer. Descub., MS.—Estete, ap. Barcia, tom. III. p. 209.

[12] "Y andando los tiẽpos el capitan Rodrigo Orgoñez, y Francisco de Godoy, y otros sacaron grã summa de oro y plata de los enterramientos. Y aun se presume y tiene por cierto, que ay mucho mas: pero como no se sabe donde esta enterrado, se pierde." Cieza de Leon, Cronica, cap. 72.

[13] "Hicieron hacer herrage de herraduras é clavos para sus Caballos de Plata, los cuales hicieron los cien Indios fundidores muy buenos é cuantos quisieron de ellos, con el cual herrage andubieron dos meses." (Oviedo, Hist. de las Indias, MS., Parte 3, lib. 8, cap. 16.) The author of the Relacion del Primero Descubrimiento, MS., says they shod the horses with silver and copper. And another of the Peruvian Conquerors assures us they used gold and silver. (Relatione d'un Capitano Spagnuolo, ap. Ramusio, Navigationi et Viaggi, Venetia, 1565, tom. III. fol. 376.) All agree in the silver.

[14] "Era mucha la Gente de aquel Pueblo, i de sus Comarcas, que al parecer de los Españoles, se juntaban cada Dia en la Plaça Principal cien mil Personas." Estete, ap. Barcia, tom. III. p. 230.

[15] Pedro Pizarro, Descub. y Conq., MS.

"The like of it," exclaims Estete, "was never before seen since the Indies were discovered." Ibid., p. 231.

[16] Pedro Pizarro, Descub. y Conq., MS.

[17] This account of the personal habits of Atahuallpa is taken from Pedro Pizarro, who saw him often in his confinement. As his curious narrative is little known, I have extracted the original in *Appendix, No.* 9.

[18] Rel. d'un Capitano Spagn., ap. Ramusio, tom. III. fol. 375.—Pedro Pizarro, Descub. y Conq., MS.—Herrera, Hist. General, dec. 5, lib. 2, cap. 12, 13.

[19] "I de las Chapas de oro, que esta Casa tenia, quitaron setecientas Planchas. . . . . à manera de Tablas de Caxas de à tres, i à quarto palmos de largo." Xerez, Conq. del Peru, ap. Barcia, tom. III. p. 232.

[20] Herrera, Hist. General, ubi supra.

[21] So says Pizarro's secretary. "I vinieron docientas cargas de Oro, i veinte i cinco de Plata." (Xerez, Conq. del Peru, ap. Barcia, ubi supra.) A load, he says, was brought by four Indians. "Cargas de Paligueres, que las traen quatro Indios." The meaning of *paligueres*—not a Spanish word—is doubtful. Ternaux-Compans supposes, ingeniously enough, that it may have something of the same meaning with *palanquin*, to which it bears some resemblance.

[22] Pedro Pizarro, Descub. y Conq., MS.—Xerez, Conq. del Peru, ap. Barcia, tom. III. pp. 204, 205.—Relacion Sumaria, MS.—Conq. i Pob. del piru, MS.—Relacion del Primer. Descub., MS.—Herrera, Hist. General, dec. 5, lib. 3, cap. 1.

[23] Rel. d'un Capitano Spagn., ap. Ramusio, tom. III. fol. 377.—Cieza de Leon, Cronica, cap. 65.

CHAPTER VII

[1] Relatione de Pedro Sancho, ap. Ramusio, Viaggi, tom. III. fol. 399.—Xerez, Conq. del Peru, ap. Barcia, tom. III. p. 233.—Zarate, Conq. del Peru, lib. 2, cap. 7.

Oviedo saw at St. Domingo the articles which Ferdinand Pizarro was bearing to Castile; and he expatiates on several beautifully wrought vases, richly chased, of very fine gold, and measuring twelve inches in height and thirty round. Hist. de las Indias, MS., Parte 3, lib. 8, cap. 16.

[2] Herrera, Hist. General, dec. 5, lib. 2, cap. 3.

[3] According to Oviedo it was agreed that Hernando should have a share, much larger than he was entitled to, of the Inca's ransom, in the hope that he would feel so rich as never to desire to return again to Peru. "Trabajaron de le embiar rico por quitarle de entre ellos, y porque yendo muy rico como fue no tubiese voluntad de tornar á aquellas partes." Hist. de las Indias, MS., Parte 3, lib. 8, cap. 16.

[4] Acta de Reparticion del Rescate de Atahuallpa, MS.—Xerez, Conq. del Peru, ap. Barcia, tom. III. p. 232.

In reducing the sums mentioned in this work, I have availed myself—as I before did, in the History of the Conquest of Mexico—of the labors of Señor Clemencin, formerly Secretary of the Royal Academy of History at Madrid. This eminent scholar, in the sixth volume of the Memoirs of the Academy, prepared wholly by himself, has introduced an elaborate essay on the value of the currency in the reign of Ferdinand and Isabella. Although this period—the close of the fifteenth century—was somewhat earlier than that of the Conquest of Peru, yet his calculations are sufficiently near the truth for our purpose, since the Spanish currency had not as yet been much affected by that disturbing cause,—the influx of the precious metals from the New World.

In inquiries into the currency of a remote age, we may consider, in the first place, the specific value of the coin,—that is, the value which it derives from the weight, purity, &c., of the metal, circumstances easily determined. In the second place, we may inquire into the commercial or comparative worth of the money,—that is, the value founded on a comparison of the difference between the amount of commodities which the same sum would purchase formerly, and at the present time. The last inquiry is attended with great embarrassment, from the difficulty of finding any one article which my be taken as the true standard of value. Wheat, from its general cultivation and use, has usually been selected by political economists as this standard; and Clemencin has adopted it in his calculations. Assuming wheat as the standard, he has endeavoured to ascertain the value of the principal coins in circulation, at the time of the "Catholic Kings." He makes no mention in his treatise of the *peso de oro,* by which denomination the sums in the early part of the sixteenth century were more frequently expressed than by any other. But he ascertains both the specific and the commercial value of the *castellano,* which several of the old writers, as Oviedo, Herrera, and Xerez, concur in stating as precisely equivalent to the *peso de oro.* From the results of his calculations, it appears that the specific value of the castellano, as stated by him in reals, is equal to *three dollars and seven cents of our own currency,* while the commercial value is nearly four times as great, or *eleven dollars sixty-seven cents, equal to two pounds twelve shillings and sixpence sterling.* By adopting *this as the approximate value of the peso de oro, in the early part of the sixteenth century,* the reader may easily compute for himself the value, at that period, of the sums mentioned in these pages; most of which are expressed in that denomination.

I have been the more particular in this statement, since, in my former work, I confined myself to the commercial value of the money, which, being much greater than the specific value, founded on the quality and weight of the metal, was thought by an ingenious correspondent to give the reader an exaggerated estimate of the sums mentioned in the history. But it seems to me that it is only this comparative or commercial value with which the reader has any concern; indicating what amount of commodities any given sum represents, that he may thus know the real worth of that sum;—thus adopting the principle, though conversely stated, of the old Hudibrastic maxim, —

"What is *worth* in any thing, But so much money as 't will bring?"

[5] "Segun Dios Nuestro Señor le diere á entender teniendo su conciencia y para lo mejor hazer pedia el ayuda de Dios Nuestro Señor, é imboco el auxilio divino." Acta de Reparticion del Rescate, MS.

[6] The particulars of the distribution are given in the *Acta de Reparticion del Rescate,* an instrument drawn up and signed by the royal notary. The document, which is therefore of unquestionable authority, is among the MSS. selected for me from the collection of Muñoz.

[7] "Se diese á la gente que vino con el Capitan Diego de Almagro para ayuda á pagar sus deudas y fletes y suplir algunas necesidades que traian veinte mil pesos." (Acta de Reparticion del Rescate, MS.) Herrera says that 100,000 *pesos* were paid to Almagro's men. (Hist. General, dec. 5, lib. 2, cap. 3.) But it is not so set down in the instrument.

[8] "En treinta personas que quedaron en la ciudad de san Miguel de Piura dolientes y otros que no vinieron ni se hallaron en la prision de Atagualpa y toma del oro porque algunos son pobres y otros tienen necesidad señalaba 15,000 p^s de oro para los repartir S. Señoria entre las dichas personas." Ibid., MS.

[9] Montesinos, Annales, MS., año 1533.

[10] The "Spanish Captain," several times cited, who tells us he was one of the men appointed to guard the treasure, does indeed complain that a large quantity of gold vases and other articles remained undivided, a palpable injustice, he thinks, to the honest Conquerors, who had earned all by their hardships. (Rel. d'un Capitano Spagn., ap. Ramusio, tom. III. fol. 378, 379.) The writer, throughout his Relation, shows a full measure of the coarse and covetous spirit which marked the adventurers of Peru.

[11] "Y esto tenia por justo, pues era provechoso." It is the sentiment imputed to Pizarro by Herrera, Hist. General, dec. 5, lib. 3, cap. 4.

[12] "I como no ahondaban los designios que tenia le replicaban; pero èl respondia, que iba mirando en ello." Herrera, Hist. General, dec. 5, lib. 3, cap. 4.

[13] "Fatta quella fusione, il Governatore fece vn atto innanzi al notaro nel quale liberaua il Cacique Atabalipa et l'absolueua della promessa et parola che haueua data a gli Spagnuoli che lo presero della casa d'oro c'haueua lor côcessa, il quale fece publicar publicamête a suon di trombe nella piazza di quella città di Caxamalca." (Pedro Sancho, Rel., ap. Ramusio, tom. III. fol. 399.) The authority is unimpeachable,—for any fact, at least, that makes against the Conquerors,—since the *Relatione* was by one of Pizarro's own secretaries, and was authorized under the hands of the general and his great officers.

[14] "De la Gente Natural de Quito vienen docientos mil Hombres de Guerra, i treinta mil Caribes, que comen Carne Humana." Xerez, Conq. del Peru, ap. Barcia, tom. III. p. 233. —See also Pedro Sancho, Rel., ap. Ramusio, ubi supra.

[15] "Pues estando asi atravesose un demonio de una lengua que se dezia ffelipillo uno de los muchachos que el marquez avia llevado á España que al presente hera lengua y andava enamorado de una muger de Atabalipa." Pedro Pizarro, Descub. y Conq., MS.

The amour and the malice of Felipillo, which, Quintana seems to think, rest chiefly on Garcilasso's authority, (see Españoles Célebres, tom. II. p. 210, nota,) are stated very explicitly by Zarate, Naharro, Gomara, Balboa, all contemporaneous, though not, like Pedro Pizarro, personally present in the army.

[16] "Diciendo que sentia mas aquel desacato, que su prision." Zarate, Conq. del Peru, lib. 2, cap. 7.

[17] Ibid., loc. cit.

[18] "È le habian tomado sus mugeres é repartidolas en su presencia é usaban de ellas de sus adulterios." Oviedo, Hist. de las Indias, MS., Parte 3, lib. 8, cap. 22.

[19] "Burlaste conmigo? siempre me hablas cosas de burlas? Què parte somos Yo, i toda mi Gente, para enojar à tan valientes Hombres como vosotros? No me digas esas burlas." Xerez, Conq. del Peru, ap. Barcia, tom. III. p. 234.

[20] "De que los Españoles que se las han oìdo, estan espantados de vèr en vn Hombre Barbaro tanta prudencia." Ibid., loc. cit.

[21] "Pues si Yo no lo quiero, ni las Aves bolaràn en mi Tierra." Zarate, Conq. del Peru, lib. 2, cap. 7.

[22] Pedro Pizarro, Descub. y Conq., MS.—Relacion del Primer. Descub., MS.—Ped. Sancho, Rel., ap. Ramusio, tom. III. fol. 400.

These cavaliers were all present in the camp.

[23] "Aunque contra voluntad del dicho Gobernador, que nunca estubo bien en ello." Relacion del Primer. Descub., MS.—So also Pedro Pizarro, Descub. y Conq., MS.—Ped. Sancho, Rel., ap. Ramusio, ubi supra.

[24] The specification of the charges against the Inca is given by Garcilasso de la Vega. (Com. Real., Parte 2, lib. 1, cap. 37.) One could have wished to find them specified by some of the actors in the tragedy. But Garcilasso had access to the best sources of information, and where there was no motive for falsehood, as in the present instance, his word may probably be taken.—The fact of a process being formally instituted against the Indian monarch is explicitly recognized by several contemporary writers, by Gomara, Oviedo, and Pedro

Sancho. Oviedo characterizes it as "a badly contrived and worse written document, devised by a factious and unprincipled priest, a clumsy notary without conscience, and others of the like stamp, who were all concerned in this villany." (Hist. de las Indias, MS., Parte 3, lib. 8, cap. 22.) Most authorities agree in the two principal charges,—the assassination of Huascar, and the conspiracy against the Spaniards.

[25] "Doppo l'essersi molto disputato, et ragionato del danno et vtile che saria potuto auuenire per il viuere o morire di Atabalipa, fu risoluto che si facesse giustitia di lui." (Ped. Sancho, Rel., ap. Ramusio, tom. III. fol. 400.) It is the language of a writer who may be taken as the mouthpiece of Pizarro himself. According to him, the conclave, which agitated this "question of expediency," consisted of the "officers of the Crown and those of the army, a certain doctor learned in the law, that chanced to be with them, and the reverend Father Vicente de Valverde."

[26] "Respondió, que firmaria, que era bastante, para que el Inga fuese condenado à muerte, porque aun en lo exterior quisieron justificar su intento." Herrera, Hist. General, dec. 5, lib. 3, cap. 4.

[27] Garcilasso has preserved the names of some of those who so courageously, though ineffectually, resisted the popular cry for the Inca's blood. (Com. Real., Parte 2, lib. 1, cap. 37.) They were doubtless correct in denying the right of such a tribunal to sit in judgment on an independent prince, like the Inca of Peru; but not so correct in supposing that their master, the Emperor, had a better right. Vattel (Book II. ch. 4.) especially animadverts on this pretended trial of Atahuallpa, as a manifest outrage on the law of nations.

[28] Pedro Pizarro, Descub. y Conq., MS.—Herrera, Hist. General, dec. 5, lib. 3, cap. 4.—Zarate, Conq. del Peru, lib. 2, cap. 7.

[29] "I myself," says Pedro Pizarro, "saw the general weep." "*Yo vide llorar* al marques de pesar por no podelle dar la vida porque cierto temio los requirimientos y el rriezgo que avia en la tierra si se soltava." Descub. y Conq., MS.

[30] Xerez, Conq. del Peru, ap. Barcia, tom. III. p. 234.—Pedro Pizarro, Descub. y Conq., MS.—Conq. i Pob. del Piru, MS.—Ped. Sancho, Rel., ap. Ramusio, tom. III. fol. 400.

The *garrote* is a mode of execution by means of a noose drawn round the criminal's neck, to the back part of which a stick is attached. By twisting this stick, the noose is tightened and suffocation is produced. This was the mode, probably, of Atahuallpa's execution. In Spain, instead of the cord, an iron collar is substituted, which, by means of a screw, is compressed round the throat of the sufferer.

[31] Velasco, Hist. de Quito, tom. I. p. 372.

[32] "Ma quando se lo vidde appressare per douer esser morto, disse che raccomandaua al Governatore i suoi piccioli figliuoli che volesse tenersegli appresso, & con queste vltime parole, & dicendo per l'anima sua li Spagnuoli che erano all' intorno il Credo, fu subito affogato." Ped. Sancho, Rel., ap. Ramusio, tom. III. fol. 399.

Xerez, Conq. del Peru, ap. Barcia, tom. III. p. 234.—Pedro Pizarro, Descub. y Conq., MS.—Naharro, Relacion Sumaria, MS.—Conq. i Pob. del Piru, MS.—Relacion del Primer. Descub., MS.—Zarate, Conq. del Peru, lib. 2, cap. 7.

The death of Atahuallpa has many points of resemblance with that of Caupolican, the great Araucanian chief, as described in the historical epic of Ercilla. Both embraced the religion of their conquerors at the stake, though Caupolican was so far less fortunate than the Peruvian monarch, that his conversion did not save him from the tortures of a most agonizing death. He was impaled and shot with arrows. The spirited verses reflect so faithfully the character of these early adventurers, in which the fanaticism of the Crusader was mingled with the cruelty of the conqueror, and they are so germane to the present subject, that I would willingly quote the passage were it not too long. See La Araucana, Parte 2, canto 24.

[33] "Thus he paid the penalty of his errors and cruelties," says Xerez, "for he was the greatest butcher, as all agree, that the world ever saw; making nothing of razing a whole town to the ground for the most trifling offence, and massacring a thousand persons for the fault of one!" (Conq. del Peru, ap. Barcia, tom. III. p. 234.) Xerez was the private secretary of Pizarro. Sancho, who, on the departure of Xerez for Spain, succeeded him in the same office, pays a more decent tribute to the memory of the Inca, who, he trusts, "is received into glory, since he died penitent for his sins, and in the true faith of a Christian." Ped. Sancho, Rel., ap. Ramusio, tom. III. fol. 399.

[34] "El hera muy regalado, y muy Señor," says Pedro Pizarro. (Descub. y Conq., MS.) "Mui dispuesto, sabio, animoso, franco," says Gomara. (Hist. de las Ind., cap. 118.)

[35] The secretary Sancho seems to think that the Peruvians must have regarded these funeral honors as an ample compensation to Atahuallpa for any wrongs he may have sustained, since they at once raised him to a level with the Spaniards! Ibid., loc. cit.

[36] Relacion del Primer. Descub., MS.

See *Appendix, No. 10*, where I have cited in the original several of the contemporary notices of Atahuallpa's execution, which being in manuscript are not very accessible, even to Spaniards.

[37] "Oi dicen los indios que está su sepulcro junto á una Cruz de Piedra Blanca que esta en el Cementerio del Convento de S^n Francisco." Montesinos, Annales, MS., año 1533.

[38] Oviedo, Hist. de las Indias, MS., Parte 3, lib. 8, cap. 22.

According to Stevenson, "In the chapel belonging to the common gaol, which was formerly part of the palace, the altar stands on the stone on which Atahuallpa was placed by the Spaniards and strangled, and under which he was buried." (Residence in South America, vol. II. p. 163.) Montesinos, who wrote more than a century after the Conquest, tells us that "spots of blood were still visible on a broad flagstone, in the prison of Caxamalca, on which Atahuallpa was *beheaded*." (Annales, MS., año 1533.) — Ignorance and credulity could scarcely go farther.

[39] "Hallaronle monstrando mucho sentimiento con un gran sombrero de fieltro puesto en la cabeza por luto é muy calado sobre los ojos." Oviedo, Hist. de las Indias, MS., Parte 3, lib. 8, cap. 22.

[40] Ibid., MS., ubi supra. — Pedro Pizarro, Descub. y Conq., MS. — See *Appendix, No. 10*.

[41] This remarkable account is given by Oviedo, not in the body of his narrative, but in one of those supplementary chapters, which he makes the vehicle of the most miscellaneous, yet oftentimes important gossip, respecting the great transactions of his history. As he knew familiarly the leaders in these transactions, the testimony which he collected, somewhat at random, is of high authority. The reader will find Oviedo's account of the Inca's death extracted, in the original, among the other notices of this catastrophe, in *Appendix, No. 10*.

[42] "Contra su voluntad sentencio á muerte á Atabalipa." (Pedro Pizarro, Descub. y Conq., MS.) "Contra voluntad del dicho Gobernador." (Relacion del Primer. Descub., MS.)

"Ancora che molto li dispiacesse di venir a questo atto." (Ped. Sancho, Rel., ap, Ramusio, tom. III. fol. 399.) Even Oviedo seems willing to admit it possible that Pizarro may have been somewhat deceived by others. "Que tambien se puede creer que era engañado." Hist. de las Indias, MS., Parte 3, lib. 8, cap. 22.

[43] The story is to be found in Garcilasso de la Vega, (Com. Real., Parte 2, cap. 38,) and in no other writer of the period, so far as I am aware.

[44] I have already noticed the lavish epithets heaped by Xerez on the Inca's cruelty. This account was printed in Spain, in 1534, the year after the execution. "The proud tyrant," says the other secretary, Sancho, "would have repaid the kindness and good treatment he had received from the governor and every one of us with the same coin with which he usually paid his own followers, without any fault on their part,—by putting them to death." (Ped. Sancho, Rel., ap. Ramusio, tom. III. fol. 399.) "He deserved to die," says the old Spanish Conqueror before quoted, "and all the country was rejoiced that he was put out of the way." Rel. d'un Capitano Spagn., ap. Ramusio, tom. III. fol. 377.

[45] "Las demostraciones que despues se vieron bien manifiestan lo mui injusta que fué,. . . . puesto que todos quantos entendieron en ella tuvieron despues mui desastradas muertes." (Naharro, Relacion Sumaria, MS.) Gomara uses nearly the same language. "No ai quo reprehender à los que le mataron, pues el tiempo, i sus pecados los castigaron despues; cà todos ellos acabaron mal." (Hist. de las Ind., cap. 118.) According to the former writer, Felipillo paid the forfeit of his crimes sometime afterwards,—being hanged by Almagro on the expedition to Chili,—when, as "*some say*, he confessed having perverted testimony given in favor of Atahuallpa's innocence, directly against that monarch." Oviedo, usually ready enough to excuse the excesses of his countrymen, is unqualified in his condemnation of this whole proceeding, (see *Appendix, No.* 10,) which, says another contemporary, "fills every one with pity who has a spark of humanity in his bosom." Conq. i Pob. del Piru, MS.

[46] The most eminent example of this is given by Quintana in his memoir of Pizarro, (Españoles Celebres, tom. II.,) throughout which the writer, rising above the mists of national prejudice, which too often blind the eyes of his countrymen, holds the scale of historic criticism with an impartial hand, and deals a full measure of reprobation to the actors in these dismal scenes.

CHAPTER VIII

[1] "Such was the awe in which the Inca was held," says Pizarro, "that it was only necessary for him to intimate his commands to that effect, and a Peruvian would at once jump down a precipice, hang himself, or put an end to his life in any way that was prescribed." Descub. y Conq., MS.

[2] Oviedo tells us, that the Inca's right name was *Atabaliva*, and that the Spaniards usually misspelt it, because they thought much more of getting treasure for themselves, than they did of the name of the person who owned it. (Hist. de las Indias, MS., Parte 3, lib. 8, cap. 16.) Nevertheless, I have preferred the authority of Garcilasso, who, a Peruvian himself, and a near kinsman of the Inca, must be supposed to have been well informed. His countrymen, he says, pretended that the cocks imported into Peru by the Spaniards, when they crowed, uttered the name of Atahuallpa; "and I and the other Indian boys," adds the historian, "when we were at school, used to mimic them." Com. Real., Parte 1, lib. 9, cap. 23.

[3] "That which the Inca gave the Spaniards, said some of the Indian nobles to Benalcazar, the conqueror of Quito, was but as a kernel of corn, compared with the heap before him." (Oviedo, Hist. de las Indias, MS., Parte 3, lib. 8, cap. 22.) See also Pedro Pizarro, Descub. y Conq., MS.—Relacion del Primer. Descub., MS.

[4] The "first conquerors," according to Garcilasso, were held in especial honor by those who came after them, though they were, on the whole, men of less consideration and fortune than the later adventurers. Com. Real., Parte 1, lib. 7, cap. 9.

[5] Pedro Pizarro, Descub. y Conq., MS.—Naharro, Relacion Sumaria, MS.—Ped. Sancho, Rel., ap. Ramusio, tom. III. fol. 400.

[6] "Va todo el camino de una traza y anchura hecho á mano." Relacion del Primer. Descub., MS.

[7] "En muchas partes viendo lo que está adelante, parece cosa impossible poderlo pasar." Ibid., MS.

[8] Ped. Sancho, Rel., ap. Ramusio, tom. III. fol. 404.

[9] Ibid., ubi supra.—Relacion del Primer. Descub., MS.

[10] "La notte dormirono tutti in quella campagna senza coperto alcuno, sopra la neue, ne pur hebber souuenimento di legne ne da mangiare." Ped. Sancho, Rel., ap. Ramusio, tom. III. fol. 401.

[11] Carta de la Justicia y Regimiento de la Ciudad de Xauja, MS.—Pedro Pizarro, Descub. y Conq., MS.—Conq. i Pob. del Piru, MS.—Herrera, Hist. General, dec. 5, lib. 4, cap. 10. —Relacion del Primer. Descub., MS.

[12] Ped. Sancho, Rel., ap. Ramusio, tom. III. fol. 405.

[13] Ibid., loc. cit.

[14] Pedro Pizarro, Descub. y Conq., MS.—Herrera, Hist. General, dec. 5, lib. 5, cap. 3.

[15] The account of De Soto's affair with the natives is given in more or less detail, by Ped. Sancho, Rel., ap. Ramusio, tom. III. fol. 405,—Conq. i Pob. del Piru, MS.,—Relacion del Primer. Descub., MS.,—Pedro Pizarro, Descub. y Conq., MS.,—parties all present in the army.

[16] Pedro Pizarro, Descub. y Conq., MS.—Ped. Sancho, Rel., ap. Ramusio, tom. III. fol. 406.

[17] Ibid., ubi supra.

[18] It seems, from the language of the letter addressed to the Emperor by the municipality of Xauxa, that the troops themselves were far from being convinced of Challcuchima's guilt. "Publico fue, aunque dello no ubo averiguacion in certenidad, que el capitan Chaliconiman le abia dado ierbas o a beber con que murio." Carta de la Just. y Reg. de Xauja, MS.

[19] According to Velasco, Toparca, whom, however, he calls by another name, tore off the diadem bestowed on him by Pizarro, with disdain, and died in a few weeks of chagrin. (Hist. de Quito, tom. I. p. 377.) This writer, a Jesuit of Quito, seems to feel himself bound to make out as good a case for Atahuallpa and his family, as if he had been expressly retained in their behalf. His vouchers—when he condescends to give any—too rarely bear him out in his statements to inspire us with much confidence in his correctness.

[20] "Auia en este valle muy sumptuosos aposentos y ricos adonde los señores del Cuzco salian a tomar sus plazeres y solazes." Cieza de Leon, Cronica, cap. 91.

[21] Ibid., ubi supra.

[22] Hist. General, dec. 5, lib. 6, cap. 3.

[23] Ped. Sancho, Rel., ap. Ramusio, tom. III. fol. 406.

[24] Ibid., loc. cit.

[25] Ibid., loc. cit.—Pedro Pizarro, Descub. y Conq., MS.

The MS. of the old Conqueror is so much damaged in this part of it, that much of his account is entirely effaced.

[26] Ped. Sancho, Rel., ap. Ramusio, tom. III. fol. 406.—Pedro Pizarro, Descub. y Conq., MS.

[27] "Y dos horas antes que el Sol se pusiese, llegaron á vista de la ciudad del Cuzco." Relacion del Primer. Descub., MS.

[28] The chronicles differ as to the precise date. There can be no better authorities than Pedro Sancho's narrative and the Letter of the Magistrates of Xauxa, which I have followed in the text.

[29] Ped. Sancho, Rel., ap. Ramusio, tom. III. fol. 407.—Garcilasso, Com. Real., Parte 1, lib. 7, cap. 10.—Relacion del Primer. Descub., MS.

[30] "Esta ciudad era muy grande i mui populosa de grandes edificios i comarcas, quando los Españoles entraron la primera vez en ella havia gran cantidad de gente, seria pueblo de mas de 40 mill. vecinos solamente lo que tomaba la ciudad, que arravalles i comarca en deredor del Cuzco á 10 ó 12 leguas creo yo que havia docientos mill. Indios porque esto era lo mas poblado de todos estos reinos." (Conq. i Pob. del Piru, MS.) The *vecino* or "householder" is computed, usually, as representing five individuals.—Yet Father Valverde, in a letter written a few years after this, speaks of the city as having only three or four thousand houses at the time of its occupation, and the suburbs as having nineteen or twenty thousand. (Carta al Emperador, MS., 20 de Marzo, 1539.) It is possible that he took into the account only the better kind of houses, not considering the mud huts, or rather hovels, which made so large a part of a Peruvian town, as deserving notice.

[31] "Heran tantos los atambores que de noche se oian por todas partes bailando y cantando y beviendo que toda la mayor parte de la noche se los pasava en esto cotidianamente." Pedro Pizarro, Descub. y Conq., MS.

[32] "La maggior parte di queste case sono di pietra, et l'altre háno la metà della facciata di pietra." Ped. Sancho, Rel., ap. Ramusio, tom. III. fol. 413.

[33] "Che sono le principali della città dipinte et lauorate, et di pietra: et la miglior d'esse è la casa di Guainacaba Cacique vecchio, et la perta d'esse è di marmo bianco et rosso, et d'altri colori." (Ibid., ubi supra.) The buildings were usually of freestone. There may have been porphyry from the neighbouring mountains mixed with this, which the Spaniards mistook for marble.

[34] "Todo labrado de piedra muy prima, que cierto toda la canteria desta cibdad hace gran ventaja á la de España, aunque carecen de teja que todas las casas sine es la fortaleza, que era hecha de azoteas son cubiertas de paja, aunque tan primamente puesta, que parece bien." Relacion del Primer. Descub., MS.

[35] Ped. Sancho, Rel., ap. Ramusio, tom. III., ubi supra.

A passage in the Letter of the Municipality of Xauxa is worth quoting, as confirming on the best authority some of the interesting particulars mentioned in the text. "Esta cibdad es la mejor e maior que en la tierra se ha visto, i aun en Yndias; e decimos a V. M. ques tan hermosa i de tan buenos edeficios que en España seria muy de ver; tiene las calles por mucho concierto en pedradas i por medio dellas un caño enlosado. la plaza es hecha en cuadra i empedrada de quijas pequeñas todas, todas las mas de las casas son de Señores Principales hechas de canteria. esta en una ladera de un zerro en el cual sobre el pueblo esta una fortaleza mui bien obrada de canteria, tan de ver que por Españoles que han andado Reinos estraños dicen no haver visto otro edeficio igual al della." Carta de la Just. y Reg. de Xauja, MS.

[36] "Un rio, el cual baja por medio de la cibdad y desde que nace, mas de veinte leguas por aquel valle abajo donde hay muchas poblaciones, va enlosado todo por el suelo, y las varrancas de una parte y de otra hechas de canteria labrada, cosa nunca vista, ni oida." Relacion del Primer. Descub., MS.

[37] The reader will find a few repetitions in this chapter of what I have already said, in the Introduction, of Cuzco under the Incas. But the facts here stated are for the most part drawn from other sources, and some repetition was unavoidable in order to give a distinct image of the capital.

[38] "Pues mando el marquez dar vn pregon que ningun español fuese á entrar en las casas de los naturales ó tomalles nada." Pedro Pizarro, Descub. y Conq., MS.

[39] Gomara, Hist. de las Ind., cap. 123.

[40] "Et fra l'altre cose singolari, era veder quattro castrati di fin oro molto grandi, et 10 ò 12 statue di dône, della grandezza delle dône di quel paese tutte d'oro fino, cosi belle et ben fatte come se fossero viue. . . . . . Queste furono date nel quinto che toccaua a S. M." (Ped. Sancho, Rel., ap. Ramusio, tom. III. fol. 409.) "Muchas estatuas y figuras de oro y plata enteras, hecha la forma toda de una muger, y del tamaño della, muy bien labradas." Relacion del Primer. Descub., MS.

[41] "Avia ansi mismo otras muchas plumas de diferentes colores para este efecto de hacer rropas que vestian los señores y señoras y no otro en los tiempos de sus fiestas; avia tambien mantas hechas de chaquira, de oro, y de plata, que heran vnas quentecitas muy delicadas, que parecia cosa de espanto ver su hechura." Pedro Pizarro, Descub. y Conq., MS.

[42] Ondegardo, Rel. Prim., MS.

[43] "Pues andando yo buscando mahiz ó otras cosas para comer, acaso entre en vn buhio donde halle estos tablones de plata que tengo dicho que heran hasta diez y de largo tenian veinte pies y de anchor de vno y de gordor de tres dedos, di noticia dello al marquez y el y todos los demas que con el estavan entraron á vello." Pedro Pizarro, Descub. y Conq., MS.

[44] Descub. y Conq., MS.

[45] Ped. Sancho, Rel., ap. Ramusio, tom. III. fol. 409.

[46] Garcilasso, Com. Real., Parte 1, lib. 3, cap. 20.

[47] Xerez, Conq. del Peru, ap. Barcia, tom. III. p. 233.

VOLUME II

BOOK III (CONTINUED)

CHAPTER IX

[1] Pedro Pizarro, Descub. y Conq., MS.—Ped. Sancho, Rel., ap. Ramusio, tom. III. fol. 407.

[2] Pedro Pizarro, Descub. y Conq., MS.

"Luego por la mañana iba al enterramiento donde estaban cada uno por orden embalsamados como es dicho, y asentados en sus sillas, y con mucha veneracion y respeto, todos por orden los sacaban de alli y los trahian á la ciudad, teniendo cada uno su litera, y hombres con su librea, que le trujesen, y ansi desta manera todo el servicio y aderezos como si estubiera vivo." Relacion del Primer. Descub., MS.

[3] Ped. Sancho, Rel., ap. Ramusio, tom. III. fol. 409.—Montesinos, Annales, MS., año 1534. —Actto de la fundacion del Cuzco, MS.

This instrument, which belongs to the collection of Muñoz, records not only the names of the magistrates, but of the *vecinos* who formed the first population of the *Christian* capital.

[4] Actto de la fundacion del Cuzco, MS.—Pedro Pizarro, Descub. y Conq., MS.—Garcilasso, Com. Real., Parte 1, lib. 7, cap. 9, et seq.

When a building was of immense size, as happened with some of the temples and palaces, it was assigned to two or even three of the Conquerors, who each took his share of it. Garcilasso, who describes the city as it was soon after the Conquest, commemorates with sufficient prolixity the names of the cavaliers among whom the buildings were distributed.

[5] Montesinos, Annales, año 1534.

[6] Garcilasso, Com. Real., Parte 1, lib. 3, cap. 20; lib. 6, cap. 21.—Naharro, Relacion Sumaria, MS.

[7] Ulloa, Voyage to S. America, book 7, ch. 12.

"The Indian nuns," says the author of the Relacion del Primer. Descub., "lived chastely and in a holy manner."—"Their chastity was all a feint," says Pedro Pizarro, "for they had constant amours with the attendants on the temple." (Descub. y Conq., MS.)—What is truth?—In statements so contradictory, we may accept the most favorable to the Peruvian. The prejudices of the Conquerors certainly did not lie on that side.

[8] Such, however, it is but fair to Valverde to state, is not the language applied to him by the rude soldiers of the Conquest. The municipality of Xauxa, in a communication to the Court, extol the Dominican as an exemplary and learned divine, who had afforded much serviceable consolation to his countrymen. "Es persona de mucho exemplo i Doctrina i con quien todos los Españoles an tenido mucho consuelo." (Carta de la Just. y Reg. de Xauxa, MS.) And yet this is not incompatible with a high degree of insensibility to the natural rights of the natives.

[9] Pedro Pizarro, Descub. y Conq., MS.—Naharro, Relacion Sumaria, MS.—Oviedo, Hist. de las Indias, MS., Parte 3, lib. 8, cap. 20.—Ped. Sancho, Rel., ap. Ramusio, tom. III. fol. 408.—Relacion del Primer. Descub., MS.

[10] The number is variously reported by historians. But from a legal investigation made in Guatemala, it appears that the whole force amounted to 500, of which 230 were cavalry. —Informacion echa en Santiago, Set. 15, 1536, MS.

[11] "It began to rain earthy partitles from the heavens," says Oviedo, "that blinded the men and horses, so that the trees and bushes were full of dirt." Hist. de las Indias, MS., Parte 3, lib. 8, cap. 20.

[12] Garcilasso says the shower of ashes came from the "volcano of Quito." (Com. Real., Parte 2, lib. 2, cap. 2.) Cieza de Leon only says from one of the volcanoes in that region. (Cronica, cap. 41.) Neither of them specify the name. Humboldt accepts the common opinion, that Cotopaxi was intended. Researches, I. 123.

[13] A popular tradition among the natives states, that a large fragment of porphyry near the base of the cone was thrown out in an eruption, which occurred at the moment of Atahuallpa's death.—But such tradition will hardly pass for history.

[14] A minute account of this formidable mountain is given by M. de Humboldt, (Researches, I. 118, et seq.,) and more circumstantially by Condamine. (Voyage à l'Equateur, pp. 48-56, 156-160.) The latter philosopher would have attempted to scale the almost perpendicular walls of the volcano, but no one was hardy enough to second him.

[15] By far the most spirited and thorough record of Alvarado's march is given by Herrera, who has borrowed the pen of Livy describing the Alpine march of Hannibal. (Hist. General, dec. 5, lib. 6, cap. 1, 2, 7, 8, 9.) See also Pedro Pizarro, Descub. y Conq., MS.,— Oviedo, Hist. de las Indias, MS., Parte 3, lib. 8, cap. 20,—and Carta de Pedro de Alvarado al Emperador, San Miguel, 15 de Enero, 1535, MS.

Alvarado, in the letter above cited, which is preserved in the Muñoz collection, explains to the Emperor the grounds of his expedition, with no little effrontery. In this document he touches very briefly on the march, being chiefly occupied by the negotiations with Almagro, and accompanying his remarks with many dark suggestions as to the policy pursued by the Conquerors.

[16] Pedro Pizarro, Descub. y Conq., MS.—Herrera, Hist. General, dec. 5, lib. 4, cap. 11, 18; lib. 6, cap. 5, 6.—Oviedo, Hist. de las Indias, MS., Parte 3, lib. 8, cap. 19.—Carta de Benalcazar, MS.

[17] Conq. i Pob. del Piru, MS.—Naharro, Relacion Sumaria, MS.—Pedro Pizarro, Descub. y Conq., MS.—Herrera, Hist. General, dec. 5, lib. 6, cap. 8-10.—Oviedo, Hist. de las Indias, MS., Parte 3. lib. 8, cap. 20.—Carta de Benalcazar, MS.

The amount of the *bonus* paid to Alvarado is stated very differently by writers. But both that cavalier and Almagro, in their letters to the Emperor, which have hitherto been unknown to historians, agree in the sum given in the text. Alvarado complains that he had no choice but to take it, although it was greatly to his own loss, and, by defeating his expedition, as he modestly intimates, to the loss of the Crown. (Carta de Alvarado al Emperador, MS.)—Almagro, however, states that the sum paid was three times as much as the armament was worth; "a sacrifice," he adds, "which he made to preserve peace, never dear at any price."—Strange sentiment for a Castilian conqueror! Carta de Diego de Almagro al Emperador, MS., Oct. 15, 1534.

[18] Carta de la Just. y Reg. de Xauja, MS.—Relacion del Primer. Descub., MS.—Herrera, Hist. General, dec. 5, lib. 6, cap. 16.—Montesinos, Annales, MS., año 1534.

At this place, the author of the *Relacion del Primer Descubrimiento del Perú*, the MS. so often quoted in these pages, abruptly terminates his labors. He is a writer of sense and observation; and, though he has his share of the national tendency to exaggerate and overcolor, he writes like one who means to be honest, and who has seen what he describes.

At Xauxa, also, the notary Pedro Sancho ends his *Relacion*, which embraces a much shorter period than the preceding narrative, but which is equally authentic. Coming from the secretary of Pizarro, and countersigned by that general himself, this Relation, indeed, may be regarded as of the very highest authority. And yet large deductions must obviously be made for the source whence it springs; for it may be taken as Pizarro's own account of his doings, some of which stood much in need of apology. It must be added, in justice both to the general and to his secretary, that the Relation does not differ substantially from other contemporary accounts, and that the attempt to varnish over the exceptionable passages in the conduct of the Conquerors is not obtrusive.

For the publication of this journal, we are indebted to Ramusio, whose enlightened labors have preserved to us more than one contemporary production of value, though in the form of translation.

[19] Naharro, Relacion Sumaria, MS.—Pedro Pizarro, Descub. y Conq., MS.—Carta de Francisco Pizarro al Señor de Molina, MS.

Alvarado died in 1541, of an injury received from a horse which rolled down on him as he was attempting to scale a precipitous hill in New Galicia. In the same year, by a singular coincidence, perished his beautiful wife, at her own residence in Guatemala, which was overwhelmed by a torrent from the adjacent mountains.

[20] So says Quintana, who follows in this what he pronounces a sure authority, Father Bernabe Cobo, in his book entitled *Fundacion de Lima*. Españoles Celebres, tom. II. p. 250, nota.

[21] The MSS. of the old Conquerors show how, from the very first, the name of Lima superseded the original Indian title. "Y el marquez se passo á Lima y fundo la ciudad de los rreyes que agora es." (Pedro Pizarro, Descub. y Conq., MS.) "Asimismo ordenaron que se pasasen el pueblo que tenian en Xauxa poblado á este Valle de Lima donde agora es esta ciudad de los i aqui se poblo." Conq. i Pob. del Piru, MS.

[22] Montesinos, Annales, MS., año 1535.—Conq. i Pob. del Piru, MS.

The remains of Pizarro's palace may still be discerned in the *Callejon de Petateros*, says Stevenson, who gives the best account of Lima to be found in any modern book of travels which I have consulted. Residence in South America, vol. II. chap. 8.

[23] Herrera, Hist. General, dec. 5, lib. 6, cap. 13.—Lista de todo lo que Hernando Pizarro trajo del Peru, ap. MSS. de Muñoz.

[24] The country to be occupied received the name of New Toledo, in the royal grant, as the conquests of Pizarro had been designated by that of New Castile. But the present attempt to change the Indian name was as ineffectual as the former, and the ancient title of Chili still designates that narrow strip of fruitful land between the Andes and the ocean, which stretches to the south of the great continent.

[25] Ibid., loc. cit.

[26] In point of discipline, they presented a remarkable contrast to the Conquerors of Peru, if we may take the word of Pedro Pizarro, who assures us that his comrades would not have plucked so much as an ear of corn without leave from their commander. "Que los que pasamos con el Marquez á la conquista no ovo hombre que osase tomar vna mazorca de mahiz sin licencia." Descub. y Conq., MS.

[27] "Se entraron de paz en la ciudad del Cuzco i los salieron todos los naturales á rescibir i les tomaron la Ciudad con todo quanto havia de dentro llenas las casas de mucha ropa i algunas oro i plata i otras muchas cosas, i las que no estaban bien llenas las enchian de lo que tomaban de las demas casas de la dicha ciudad, sin pensar que en ello hacian ofensa alguna Divina ni humana, i porquesta es una cosa larga i casi incomprehensible, la dexase al juicio de quien mas entiende aunque en el daño rescebido por parte de los naturales cerca deste articulo yo sé harto por mis pecados que no quisiera saber ni haver visto." Conq. i Pob. del Piru, MS.

[28] Pedro Pizarro, Descub. y Conq., MS.—Herrera, Hist. General, dec. 5, lib. 7, cap. 6.—Conq. i Pob. del Piru, MS.

[29] "E suplicamos á su infinita bondad que á qualquier de nos que fuere en contrario de lo asi convenido, con todo rigor de justicia permita la perdicion de su anima, fin y mal acavamiento de su vida, destruicion y perdimientos de su familia, honrras y hacienda." Capitulacion entre Pizarro y Almagro, 12 de Junio, 1535, MS.

[30] This remarkable document, the original of which is preserved in the archives of Simancas, may be found entire in the Castilian, in *Appendix, No. 11*.

[31] "El Adelantado Almagro despues que se vido en el Cuzco descarnado de su jente temio al Marquez no le prendiese por las alteraciones pasadas que havia tenido con sus hermanos como ya hemos dicho, i dicen que por ser avisado dello tomó la posta i se fue al pueblo de Paria donde estava su Capitan Saavedra." Conq. i Pob. del Piru, MS.

[32] Carta de F. Pizarro a Molina, MS.

[33] I have before me two copies of grants of *encomiendas* by Pizarro, the one dated at Xauxa, 1534, the other at Cuzco, 1539.—They emphatically enjoin on the colonist the religious instruction of the natives under his care, as well as kind and considerate usage. How ineffectual were the recommendations may be inferred from the lament of the anonymous contemporary often cited, that "from this time forth, the pest of personal servitude was established among the Indians, equally disastrous to body and soul of both the master and the slave." (Conq. i Pob. del Piru, MS.) This honest burst of indignation, not to have been expected in the rude Conqueror, came probably from an ecclesiastic.

[34] "El Marques hizo encomiendas en los Españoles, las quales fueron por noticias que ni el sabia lo que dava ni nadie lo que rescebia sino a tiento ya poco mas ó menos, y asi muchos que pensaron que se les dava pocos se hallaron con mucho y al contrario." Ondegardo, Rel. Prim., MS.

CHAPTER X

[1] So says the author of the *Conquista i Poblacion del Piru*, a contemporary writer, who describes what he saw himself as well as what he gathered from others. Several circumstances, especially the honest indignation he expresses at the excesses of the Conquerors, lead one to suppose he may have been an ecclesiastic, one of the good men who attended the cruel expedition on an errand of love and mercy. It is to be hoped that his credulity leads him to exaggerate the misdeeds of his countrymen.

According to him, there were full six thousand women of rank, living in the convents of Cuzco, served each by fifteen or twenty female attendants, most of whom, that did not perish in the war, suffered a more melancholy fate, as the victims of prostitution.—The passage is so remarkable, and the MS. so rare, that I will cite it in the original.

"De estas señoras del Cuzco es cierto de tener grande sentimiento el que tuviese alguna humanidad en el pecho, que en tiempo de la prosperidad del Cuzco quando los Españoles entraron en el havia grand cantidad de señoras que tenian sus casas i sus asientos mui quietas i sosegadas i vivian mui politicamente i como mui buenas mugeres, cada señora acompañada con quince o veinte mugeres que tenia de servicio en su casa bien traidas i aderezadas, i no salian menos desto i con grand onestidad i gravedad i atavio a su usanza, i es a la cantidad destas señoras principales creo yo que en el . . . . . que avia mas de seis mil sin las de servicio que creo yo que eran mas de veinte mil mugeres sin las de servicio i mamaconas que eran las que andavan como beatas i dende á dos años casi no se allava en el Cuzco i su tierra sino cada qual i qual porque muchas murieron en la guerra que huvo i las otras vinieron las mas á ser malas mugeres. Señor perdone a quien fue la causa desto i aquien no lo remedia pudiendo." Conq. i Pob. del Piru, MS.

[2] Ibid., ubi supra.

[3] Pedro Pizarro, Descub. y Conq., MS.—Herrera, Hist. General, dec. 5, lib. 8, cap. 1, 2.—Conq. i Pob. del Piru, MS.—Zarate, Conq. del Peru, lib. 2, cap. 3.

[4] "Es gente," says Oviedo, "muy belicosa é muy diestra; sus armas son picas, é ondas, porras é Alabardas de Plata é oro é cobre." (Hist. de las Indias, MS., Parte 3, lib. 8, cap. 17.) Xerez has made a good enumeration of the native Peruvian arms. (Conq. del Peru, ap. Barcia, tom. III. p. 200.) Father Velasco has added considerably to this catalogue. According to him they used copper swords, poniards, and other European weapons. (Hist. de Quito, tom. I. pp. 178-180.) He does not insist on their knowledge of fire-arms before the Conquest!

[5] "Pues junta toda la gente quel ynga avia embiado á juntar que á lo que se entendio y los indios dixeron fueron dozientos mil indios de guerra los que vinieron á poner este cerco." Pedro Pizarro, Descub. y Conq., MS.

[6] Pedro Pizarro, Descub. y Conq., MS.—Conq. i Pob. del Piru, MS.—Herrera, Hist. General, dec. 5, lib. 8, cap. 4.—Gomara, Hist. de las Ind., cap. 133.

[7] "Y los pocos Españoles que heramos aun no dozientos todos." Pedro Pizarro, Descub. y Conq., MS.

[8] "Pues de noche heran tantos los fuegos que no parecia sino vn cielo muy sereno lleno de estrellas." Pedro Pizarro, Descub. y Conq., MS.

[9] "Unas piedras rredondas y hechallas en el fuego y hazellas asqua embolvianlas en vnos algodones y poniendolas en hondas las tiravan a las cassas donde no alcanzavan á poner fuego con las manos, y ansi nos quemavan las cassas sin entendello. Otras veces con flechas encendidas tirandolas á las casas que como heran de paja luego se encendian." Ibid., MS.

[10] "I era tanto el humo que casi los oviera de aogar i pasaron grand travajo por esta causa i sino fuera porque de la una parte de la plaza no havia casas i estava desconorado no pudieran escapar porque si por todas partes les diera el humo i el calor siendo tan grande pasaron travajo, pero la divina providencia lo estorvó." Conq. i Pob. del Piru, MS.

[11] The temple was dedicated to Our Blessed Lady of the Assumption. The apparition of the Virgin was manifest not only to Christian but to Indian warriors, many of whom reported it to Garcilasso de la Vega, in whose hands the marvellous rarely loses any of its gloss. (Com. Real., Parte 2, lib. 2, cap. 25.) It is further attested by Father Acosta, who came into the country forty years after the event. (lib. 7, cap. 27.) Both writers testify to the seasonable aid rendered by St. James, who with his buckler, displaying the device of his Military Order, and armed with his flaming sword, rode his white charger into the thick of the enemy. The patron Saint of Spain might always be relied on when his presence was needed; *dignus vindice nodus.*

[12] Garcilasso, Com. Real., Parte 2, lib. 2, cap. 24.

Father Valverde, Bishop of Cuzco, who took so signal a part in the seizure of Atahuallpa, was absent from the country at this period, but returned the following year. In a letter to the emperor, he contrasts the flourishing condition of the capital when he left it, and that in which he now found it, despoiled, as well as its beautiful suburbs, of its ancient glories. "If I had not known the site of the city," he says, "I should not have recognized it as the same." The passage is too remarkable to be omitted. The original letter exists in the archives of Simancas.—"Certifico á V. M. que si no me acordara del sitio desta Ciudad yo no la conosciera, á lo menos por los edificios y Pueblos della; porque quando el Gobernador D. Franzisco Pizarro entró aqui y entré yo con él estava este valle tan hermoso en edificios y poblazion que en torno tenia que era cosa de admiracion vello, porque aunque la Ciudad en si no ternia mas de 3 o 4000 casas, ternia en torno quasi á vista 19 o 20,000; la fortaleza que estava sobre la Ciudad parescia desde á parte una mui gran fortaleza de las de España: agora la mayor parte de la Ciudad esta toda derivada y quemada; la fortaleza no tiene quasi nada enhiesso; todos los pueblos de alderredor no tienē sino las paredes que por maravilla ai casa cubierta! La cosa que mas contentamiento me dio en esta Ciudad fue la Iglesia, que para en Indias es harto buena cosa, aunque segun la riqueza a havido en esta tierra pudiera ser mas semejante al Templo de Salomon." Carta del Obispo F. Vicente de Valverde al Emperador, MS., 20 de Marzo, 1539.

[13] Pedro Pizarro, Descub. y Conq., MS.

"Los Indios ganaron el Cuzco casi todo desta manera que enganando la calle hivan haciendo una pared para que los cavallos ni los Españoles no los pudiesen romper." Conq. i Pob. del Piru, MS.

[14] Ibid., MS.—Herrera, Hist. General, dec. 5, lib. 8, cap. 4.

[15] Ibid., ubi supra.—Conq. i Pob. del Piru, MS.

[16] "Pues Hernando Piçarro nunca estuvo en ello y les respondia que todos aviamos de morir y no desamparar el cuzco. Juntavanse á estas consultas Hernando Piçarro y sus hermanos, Graviel de Rojas, Hernan Ponce de Leon, el Thesorero Riquelme." Pedro Pizarro, Descub. y Conq., MS.

[17] Herrera assures us, that the Peruvians even turned the fire-arms of their Conquerors against them, compelling their prisoners to put the muskets in order, and manufacture powder for them. Hist. General, dec. 5, lib. 8, cap. 5, 6.

[18] Pedro Pizarro, Descub. y Conq., MS.—Conq. i Pob. del Piru, MS.—Herrera, Hist. General, dec. 5, lib. 8, cap. 4, 5.

[19] Conq. i Pob. del Piru, MS.

[20] Pedro Pizarro, Descub. y Conq., MS.

[21] "Y estando batallando con ellos para echallos de alli Joan Piçarro se descuido descubrirse la cabeça con la adarga y con las muchas pedradas que tiravan le acertaron vna en la caveça que le quebraron los cascos y dende á quince dias murio desta herida y ansi herido estuvo forcejando con los yndios y españoles hasta que se gano este terrado y ganado le abaxaron al Cuzco." Pedro Pizarro, Descub. y Conq., MS.

[22] "Hera valiente," says Pedro Pizarro, "y muy animoso, gentil hombre, magnanimo y afable." (Descub. y Conq., MS.) Zarate dismisses him with this brief panegyric:—"Fue gran pèrdida en la Tierra, porque era Juan Piçarro mui valiente, i experimentado en las Guerras de los Indios, i bien quisto, i amado de todos." Conq. del Peru, lib. 3, cap. 3.

[23] "Y mando hernando piçarro á los Españoles que subian que no matasen á este yndio sino que se lo tomasen á vida, jurando de no matalle si lo avia bivo." Pedro Pizarro, Descub. y Conq., MS.

[24] "Visto este orejon que se lo avian ganado y le avian ganado y le avian tomado por dos ó tres partes el fuerte, arrojando las armas se tapo la caveça y el rrostro con la manta y se arrojo del cubo abajo mas de cien estados, y ansi se hizo pedazos. Á hernando Piçarro le peso mucho por no tomalle á vida." Ibid., MS.

[25] Garcilasso, Com. Real., Parte 2, lib. 2, cap. 24.

[26] Zarate, Conq. del Peru, lib. 4, cap. 5.—Herrera, Hist. General, dec. 5, lib. 8, cap 5.—Garcilasso, Com. Real., Parte 2, lib. 2, cap. 28.

According to the historian of the Incas, there fell in these expeditions four hundred and seventy Spaniards. Cieza de Leon computes the whole number of Christians who perished in this insurrection at seven hundred, many of them, he adds, under circumstances of great cruelty. (Cronica, cap. 82.) The estimate, considering the spread and spirit of the insurrection, does not seem extravagant.

[27] "É crea V. Sª sino somos socorridos se perderá el Cusco, ques la cosa mas señalada é de mas importancia que se puede descubrir, é luego nos perderémos todos; porque somos pocos é tenemos pocas armas, é los Indios estan atrevidos." Carta de Francisco Pizarro á D. Pedro de Alvarado, desde la Ciudad le los Reyes, 29 de julio, 1536, MS.

[28] Ondegardo, Rel. Prim. y Seg., MS.

[29] "Recoximos hasta dos mil cavezas de ganado." Pedro Pizarro, Descub. y Conq., MS.

[30] Pedro Pizarro recounts several of these deeds of arms, in some of which his own prowess is made quite apparent. One piece of cruelty recorded by him is little to the credit of his commander, Hernando Pizarro, who, he says, after a desperate rencontre, caused the right hands of his prisoners to be struck off, and sent them in this mutilated condition back to their countrymen! (Descub. y Conq., MS.) Such atrocities are not often noticed by the chroniclers; and we may hope they were exceptions to the general policy of the Conquerors in this invasion.

[31] "Tambo tan fortalescido que hera cosa de grima, porquel assiento donde Tambo esta es muy fuerte, de andenes muy altos y de muy gran canterias fortalescidos." Pedro Pizarro, Descub. y Conq., MS.

[32] "El rio de yucay ques grande por aquella parte va muy angosto y hondo." Ibid., MS.

[33] "Parecia el Inga à caballo entre su gente, con su lança en la mano." Herrera, Hist. General, dec. 5, lib. 8, cap. 7.

[34] "Pues hechos dos ó tres acometimientos á tomar este pueblo tantas vezes nos hizieron bolver dando de manos. Ansi estuvimos todo este dia hasta puesta de sol; los indios sin entendello nos hechavan el rrio en el llano donde estavamos, y aguardar mas perescieramos aqui todos." Pedro Pizarro, Descub. y Conq., MS.

[35] Ibid., MS.—Herrera, Hist. General, dec. 5, lib. 8, cap. 7.

Among the manuscripts for which I am indebted to the liberality of that illustrious Spanish scholar, the lamented Navarrete, the most remarkable, in connection with this history, is the work of Pedro Pizarro; *Relaciones del Descubrimiento y Conquista de los Reynos del Peru.* But a single copy of this important document appears to have been preserved, the existence of which was but little known till it came into the hands of Señor de Navarrete; though it did not escape the indefatigable researches of Herrera, as is evident from the mention of several incidents, some of them having personal relation to Pedro Pizarro himself, which the historian of the Indies could have derived through no other channel. The manuscript has lately been given to the public as part of the inestimable collection of historical documents now in process of publication at Madrid, under auspices which, we may trust, will insure its success. As the printed work did not reach me till my present labors were far advanced, I have preferred to rely on the manuscript copy for the brief remainder of my narrative, as I had been compelled to do for the previous portion of it.

Nothing, that I am aware of, is known respecting the author, but what is to be gleaned from incidental notices of himself in his own history. He was born at Toledo in Estremadura, the fruitful province of adventurers to the New World, whence the family of

Francis Pizarro, to which Pedro was allied, also emigrated. When that chief came over to undertake the conquest of Peru, after receiving his commission from the emperor in 1529, Pedro Pizarro, then only fifteen years of age, accompanied him in quality of page. For three years he remained attached to the household of his commander, and afterwards continued to follow his banner as a soldier of fortune. He was present at most of the memorable events of the Conquest, and seems to have possessed in a great degree the confidence of his leader, who employed him on some difficult missions, in which he displayed coolness and gallantry. It is true, we must take the author's own word for all this. But he tells his exploits with an air of honesty, and without any extraordinary effort to set them off in undue relief. He speaks of himself in the third person, and, as his manuscript was not intended solely for posterity, he would hardly have ventured on great misrepresentation, where fraud could so easily have been exposed.

After the Conquest, our author still remained attached to the fortunes of his commander, and stood by him through all the troubles which ensued; and on the assassination of that chief, he withdrew to Arequipa, to enjoy in quiet the *repartimiento* of lands and Indians, which had been bestowed on him as the recompense of his services. He was there on the breaking out of the great rebellion under Gonzalo Pizarro. But he was true to his allegiance, and chose rather, as he tells us, to be false to his name and his lineage than to his loyalty. Gonzalo, in retaliation, seized his estates, and would have proceeded to still further extremities against him, when Pedro Pizarro had fallen into his hands at Lima, but for the interposition of his lieutenant, the famous Francisco de Carbajal, to whom the chronicler had once the good fortune to render an important service. This, Carbajal requited by sparing his life on two occasions, — but on the second coolly remarked, "No man has a right to a brace of lives; and if you fall into my hands a third time, God only can grant you another." Happily, Pizarro did not find occasion to put this menace to the test. After the pacification of the country, he again retired to Arequipa; but, from the querulous tone of his remarks, it would seem he was not fully reinstated in the possessions he had sacrificed by his loyal devotion to government. The last we hear of him is in 1571, the date which he assigns as that of the completion of his history.

Pedro Pizarro's narrative covers the whole ground of the Conquest, from the date of the first expedition that sallied out from Panamá, to the troubles that ensued on the departure of President Gasca. The first part of the work was gathered from the testimony of others, and, of course, cannot claim the distinction of rising to the highest class of evidence. But all that follows the return of Francis Pizarro from Castile, all, in short, which constitutes the conquest of the country, may be said to be reported on his own observation, as an eyewitness and an actor. This gives to his narrative a value to which it could have no pretensions on the score of its literary execution. Pizarro was a soldier, with as little education, probably, as usually falls to those who have been trained from youth in this rough school, — the most unpropitious in the world to both mental and moral progress. He had the good sense, moreover, not to aspire to an excellence which he could not reach. There is no ambition of fine writing in his chronicle; there are none of those affectations of ornament which only make more glaring the beggarly condition of him who assumes them. His object was simply to tell the story of the Conquest, as he had seen it. He was to deal with facts, not with words, which he wisely left to those who came into the field after the laborers had quitted it, to garner up what they could at second hand.

Pizarro's situation may be thought to have necessarily exposed him to party influences, and thus given an undue bias to his narrative. It is not difficult, indeed, to determine under whose banner he had enlisted. He writes like a partisan, and yet like an honest one, who is no further warped from a correct judgment of passing affairs than must necessarily come from preconceived opinions. There is no management to work a conviction in his reader on this side or the other, still less any obvious perversion of fact. He evidently believes what he says, and this is the great point to be desired. We can make allowance for the natural influences of his position. Were he more impartial than this, the critic of the present day, by making allowance for a greater amount of prejudice and partiality, might only be led into error.

Pizarro is not only independent, but occasionally caustic in his condemnation of those under whom he acted. This is particularly the case where their measures bear too unfavorably on his own interests, or those of the army. As to the unfortunate natives, he no more regards their sufferings than the Jews of old did those of the Philistines, whom they considered as delivered up to their swords, and whose lands they regarded as their lawful heritage. There is no mercy shown by the hard Conqueror in his treatment of the infidel.

Pizarro was the representative of the age in which he lived. Yet it is too much to cast such obloquy on the age. He represented more truly the spirit of the fierce warriors who overturned the dynasty of the Incas. He was not merely a crusader, fighting to extend the empire of the Cross over the darkened heathen. Gold was his great object; the estimate by which he judged of the value of the Conquest; the recompense that he asked for a life of toil and danger. It was with these golden visions, far more than with visions of glory, above all, of celestial glory, that the Peruvian adventurer fed his gross and worldly imagination. Pizarro did not rise above his caste. Neither did he rise above it in a mental view, any more than in a moral. His history displays no great penetration, or vigor and comprehension of thought. It is the work of a soldier, telling simply his tale of blood. Its value is, that it is told by him who acted it. And this, to the modern compiler, renders it of higher worth than far abler productions at second hand. It is the rude ore, which, submitted to the regular process of purification and refinement, may receive the current stamp that fits it for general circulation.

Another authority, to whom I have occasionally referred, and whose writings still slumber in manuscript, is the Licentiate Fernando Montesinos. He is, in every respect, the opposite of the military chronicler who has just come under our notice. He flourished about a century after the Conquest. Of course, the value of his writings as an authority for historical facts must depend on his superior opportunities for consulting original documents. For this his advantages were great. He was twice sent in an official capacity to Peru, which required him to visit the different parts of the country. These two missions occupied fifteen years; so that, while his position gave him access to the colonial archives and literary repositories, he was enabled to verify his researches, to some extent, by actual observation of the country.

The result was his two historical works, *Memorias Antiguas Historiales del Peru,* and his *Annales,* sometimes cited in these pages. The former is taken up with the early history of the country,—very early, it must be admitted, since it goes back to the deluge. The first part of this treatise is chiefly occupied with an argument to show the identity of Peru with the golden Ophir of Solomon's time! This hypothesis, by no means original with the author, may give no unfair notion of the character of his mind. In the progress of his work he follows down the line of Inca princes, whose exploits, and names even, by no means coincide with Garcilasso's catalogue; a circumstance, however, far from establishing their inaccuracy.

But one will have little doubt of the writer's title to this reproach, that reads the absurd legends told in the grave tone of reliance by Montesinos, who shared largely in the credulity and the love of the marvellous which belong to an earlier and less enlightened age.

These same traits are visible in his Annals, which are devoted exclusively to the Conquest. Here, indeed, the author, after his cloudy flight, has descended on firm ground, where gross violations of truth, or, at least, of probability, are not to be expected. But any one who has occasion to compare his narrative with that of contemporary writers will find frequent cause to distrust it. Yet Montesinos has one merit. In his extensive researches, he became acquainted with original instruments, which he has occasionally transferred to his own pages, and which it would be now difficult to meet elsewhere.

His writings have been commended by some of his learned countrymen, as showing diligent research and information. My own experience would not assign them a high rank as historical vouchers. They seem to me entitled to little praise, either for the accuracy of their statements, or the sagacity of their reflections. The spirit of cold indifference which they manifest to the sufferings of the natives is an odious feature, for which there is less apology in a writer of the seventeenth century than in one of the primitive Conquerors, whose passions had been inflamed by long-protracted hostility. M. Ternaux-Compans has translated the *Memorias Antiguas* with his usual elegance and precision, for his collection of original documents relating to the New World. He speaks in the Preface of doing the same kind office to the *Annales*, at a future time. I am not aware that he has done this; and I cannot but think that the excellent translator may find a better subject for his labors in some of the rich collection of the Muñoz manuscripts in his possession.

BOOK IV
CHAPTER I

[1] Herrera, Hist. General, dec. 5, lib. 10, cap. 1-3.—Oviedo, Hist. de las Indias, MS., Parte 3, lib. 9, cap. 4.—Conq. i Pob. del Piru, MS.

[2] Conq. i Pob. del Piru, MS.

The writer must have made one on this expedition, as he speaks from personal observation. The poor natives had at least one friend in the Christian camp. "I si en el Real havia algun Español que era buen rancheador i cruel i matava muchos Indios tenianle por buen hombre i en grand reputacion i el que era inclinado á hacer bien i a hacer buenos tratamientos a los naturales i los favorecia no era tenido en tan buena estima, *he apuntado esto que vi con mis ojos i en que por mis pecados anduve* porque entiendan los que esto leyeren que de la manera que aqui digo i con mayores crueldades harto se hizo esta jornada i descubrimiento de Chile."

[3] "I para castigarlos por la muerte destos tres Españoles juntolos en un aposento donde estava aposentado i mandó cavalgar la jente de cavallo i la de apie que guardasen las puertas i todos estuviesen apercividos i los prendio i en conclusion hizo quemar mas de 30 señores vivos atados cada uno a su palo" (Conq. i Pob. del Piru, MS.) Oviedo, who always shows the hard feeling of the colonist, excuses this on the old plea of necessity,—*fue necesario este castigo,*—and adds, that after this a Spaniard might send a messenger from one end of the country to the other, without fear of injury. Hist. de las Indias, MS., Parte 3, lib. 9, cap. 4.

[4] It is the language of a Spaniard; "i como no le parecio bien la tierra por no ser quajada de oro." Conq. i Pob. del Piru, MS.

[5] According to Oviedo, a hundred and fifty leagues, and very near, as they told him, to the end of the world; *cerca del fin del mundo.* (Hist. de las Indias, MS., Parte 3, lib. 9, cap. 5.) One must not expect to meet with very accurate notions of geography in the rude soldiers of America.

[6] "Peleando en un tiempo con los Enemigos, con los Elementos, i con la Hambre." Herrera, Hist. General, dec. 5, lib. 10, cap. 2.

[7] Pedro Pizarro, Descub. y Conq., MS.—Conq. i Pob. del Piru, MS.—Oviedo, Hist. de las Indias, MS., Parte 3, lib. 9, cap. 6.

[8] Zarate, Conq. del Peru, lib. 3, cap. 4.—Conq. i Pob. del Piru, MS., Parte 3, lib. 8, cap. 21.

[9] "Contando diez i siete leguas i media per grado." Herrera, Hist. General, dec. 6, lib. 3, cap. 5.

[10] The government had endeavoured early to provide against any dispute in regard to the limits of the respective jurisdictions. The language of the original grants gave room to some misunderstanding; and, as early as 1536, Fray Jomás de Berlanga, Bishop of Tierra Firme, had been sent to Lima with full powers to determine the question of boundary, by fixing the latitude of the river of Santiago, and measuring two hundred and seventy leagues south on the meridian. But Pizarro, having engaged Almagro in his Chili expedition, did not care to revive the question, and the Bishop returned, *re infectâ,* to his diocese, with strong feelings of disgust towards the governor. Ibid., dec. 6, lib. 3, cap. 1.

[11] "All say," says Oviedo, in a letter to the emperor, "that Cuzco falls within the territory of Almagro." Oviedo was, probably, the best-informed man in the colonies. Yet this was an error. Carta desde Sto. Domingo, MS., 25 de Oct. 1539.

[12] According to Zarate, Almagro, on entering the capital, found no appearance of the designs imputed to Hernando, and exclaimed that "he had been deceived." (Conq. del Peru, lib. 3, cap. 4.) He was probably easy of faith in the matter.

[13] Carta de Espinall, Tesorero de N. Toledo, 15 de Junio, 1539.—Conq. i Pob. del Piru, MS.—Pedro Pizarro, Descub. y Conq., MS.—Oviedo, Hist. de las Indias, MS., Parte 3, lib. 8, cap. 21.

[14] So it would appear from the general testimony; yet Pedro Pizarro, one of the opposite faction, and among those imprisoned by Almagro, complains that that chief plundered them of their horses and other property. Descub. y Conq., MS.

[15] Pizarro's secretary Picado had an *encomienda* in that neighbourhood, and Alvarado, who was under personal obligations to him, remained there, it is said, at his instigation. (Herrera, Hist. General, dec. 5, lib. 8, cap. 7.) Alvarado was a good officer, and largely trusted, both before and after, by the Pizarros; and we may presume there was some explanation of his conduct, of which we are not possessed.

[16] "El muerto no mordia." Ibid., dec. 6, lib. 2, cap. 8.

[17] Carta de Francisco Pizarro al Obispo de Tierra Firme, MS., 28 de Agosto, 1539.—Pedro Pizarro, Descub. y Conq., MS.—Oviedo, Hist. de las Indias, MS., ubi supra.—Conq. i Pob. del Piru, MS.—Carta de Espinall, MS.

[18] "Fernando Cortès embiò con Rodrigo de Grijalva en vn proprio Navio suio, desde la Nueva España, muchas Armas, Tiros, Jaeces, Adereços, Vestidos de Seda, i vna Ropa de Martas." Gomara, Hist. de las Ind., cap. 136.

[19] Herrera, Hist. General, dec. 6, lib. 2, cap. 7.

[20] Carta de Pizarro al Obispo de Tierra Firme, MS.—Herrera, Hist. General, dec. 6, lib. 2, cap. 13.—Carta de Espinall, MS.

[21] He incurred some odium as presiding officer in the trial and condemnation of the unfortunate Vasco Nuñez de Balboa. But it must be allowed, that he made great efforts to resist the tyrannical proceedings of Pedrarias, and he earnestly recommended the prisoner to mercy. See Herrera, Hist. General, dec. 2, lib. 2, cap. 21, 22.

[22] Pedro Pizarro, Descub. y Conq., MS.—Conq. i Pob. del Piru, MS.

[23] Carta de Gutierrez al Emperador, MS., 10 de Feb. 1539.—Carta de Espinall, MS.—Oviedo, Hist. de las Ind., MS., ubi supra.—Herrera, Hist. General, dec. 6, lib. 2, cap. 8-14.—Pedro Pizarro, Descub. y Conq., MS.—Zarate, Conq. del Peru, lib. 3, cap. 8.—Naharro, Relacion Sumaria, MS.

[24] It was said that Gonzalo Pizarro lay in ambush with a strong force in the neighbourhood to intercept the marshal, and that the latter was warned of his danger by an honorable cavalier of the opposite party, who repeated a distich of an old ballad,

> "Tiempo es el Caballero
> Tiempo es de andar de aqui."

(Herrera, Hist. General, dec. 6, lib. 3, cap. 4.) Pedro Pizarro admits the truth of the design imputed to Gonzalo, which he was prevented from putting into execution by the commands of the governor, who, the chronicler, with edifying simplicity, or assurance, informs us, was a man that scrupulously kept his word. "Porque el marquez don Francisco Piçarro hera hombre que guardava mucho su palabra." Descub. y Conq., MS.

[25] Pedro Pizarro, Descub. y Conq., MS.—Carta de Espinall, MS.

[26] Espinall, Almagro's treasurer, denounces the friar "as proving himself a very devil" by this award. (Carta al Emperador, MS.) And Oviedo, a more dispassionate judge, quotes, without condemning, a cavalier who told the father, that "a sentence so unjust had not been pronounced since the time of Pontius Pilate"! Hist. de las Indias, MS., Parte 3, lib. 8, cap. 21.

[27] "I tomando la barba con la mano izquierda, con la derecha hiço señal de cortarse la cabeça, diciendo: Orgoñez, Orgoñez, por el amistad de Don Diego de Almagro te han de cortar esta." Herrera, Hist. General, dec, 6, lib. 3, cap, 9.

[28] Ibid., loc. cit.—Carta de Gutierrez, MS.—Pedro Pizarro, Descub. y Conq., MS.—Zarate, Conq. del Peru, lib. 3, cap. 9.

CHAPTER II

[1] Herrera, Hist. General, dec. 6, lib. 3, cap. 10.

[2] "Cayó enfermo i estuvo malo a punto de muerte de bubas i dolores." (Carta de Espinall, MS.) It was a hard penalty, occurring at this crisis, for the sins, perhaps, of earlier days; but

> "The gods are just, and of our pleasant vices
> Make instruments to scourge us."

[3] Carta de Gutierrez, MS.—Pedro Pizarro, Descub. y Conq., MS.—Herrera, Hist. General, dec. 6, lib. 4, cap. 1-5.—Carta de Espinall, MS.—Zarate, Conq. del Peru, lib. 3, cap. 10, 11.—Garcilasso, Com. Real., Parte 2, lib. 2, cap. 36, 37.

[4] Herrera, Hist. General, dec. 6, lib. 4, cap. 5, 6.

[5] Ibid., ubi supra.

[6] "I fue cosa de notar, que se estuvieron toda la Noche, sin que nadie de la vna i otra parte pensase en mover tratos de Paz: tanta era la ira i aborrecimiento de ambas partes." Ibid., cap. 6.

[7] A church dedicated to Saint Lazarus was afterwards erected on the battle-ground, and the bodies of those slain in the action were interred within its walls. This circumstance leads Garcilasso to suppose that the battle took place on Saturday, the sixth, — the day after the Feast of Saint Lazarus, — and not on the twenty-sixth of April, as commonly reported. Com. Real., Parte 2, lib. 2, cap. 38. See also Montesinos, (Annales, MS., año 1538,) — an indifferent authority for any thing.

[8] Zarate, Conq. del Peru, lib. 3, cap. 8. — Garcilasso, Com. Real., Parte 2, lib. 2, cap. 36.

[9] The Araucana of Ercilla may claim the merit, indeed, — if it be a merit, — of combining both romance and history in one. Surely never did the Muse venture on such a specification of details, not merely poetical, but political, geographical, and statistical, as in this celebrated Castilian epic. It is a military journal done into rhyme.

[10] Herrera, Hist. General, dec. 6, lib. 4, cap. 6. — Pedro Pizarro, Descub. y Conq., MS. — Carta de Espinall, MS. — Zarate, Conq. del Peru, lib. 3, cap. 11.

Every thing relating to this battle, — the disposition of the forces, the character of the ground, the mode of attack, are told as variously and confusedly, as if it had been a contest between two great armies, instead of a handful of men on either side. It would seem that truth is nowhere so difficult to come at, as on the battle-field.

[11] Pedro Pizarro, Descub. y Conq., MS. — Herrera, Hist. General, ubi supra. — Zarate, Conq. del Peru, ubi supra.

[12] Herrera, Hist. General, ubi supra. — Garcilasso, Com. Real., Parte 2, lib. 2, cap. 36.

Hernando Pizarro wore a surcoat of orange-colored velvet over his armour, according to Garcilasso, and before the battle sent notice of it to Orgoñez, that the latter might distinguish him in the *mêlée*. But a knight in Hernando's suite also wore the same colors, it appears, which led Orgoñez into error.

[13] "Murieron en esta Batalla de las Salinas casi dozientos hombres de vna parte y de otra." (Pedro Pizarro, Descub. y Conq., MS.) Most authorities rate the loss at less. The treasurer Espinall, a partisan of Almagro, says they massacred a hundred and fifty after the fight, in cold blood. "Siguieron el alcanze la mas cruelmente que en el mundo se ha visto, porque matavan a los hombres rendidos e desarmados, e por les quitar las armas los mataban si presto no se las quitaban, e trayendo á las ancas de un caballo a un Ruy Diaz viniendo rendido e desarmado le mataron, i desta manera mataron mas de ciento è cinquenta hombres." Carta, MS.

[14] Carta de Espinall, MS. — Garcilasso, Com. Real., Parte 2, lib. 2, cap. 38.

He was hanged for this very crime by the governor of Puerto Viejo, about five years after this time, having outraged the feelings of that officer and the community by the insolent and open manner in which he boasted of his atrocious exploit.

[15] "Los Indios viendo la Batalla fenescida, ellos tambien se dejaron de la suia, iendo los vnos i los otros à desnudar los Españoles muertos, i aun algunos vivos, que por sus heridas no se podian defender, porque como pasò el tropel de la Gente, siguiendo la Victoria, no huvo quien se lo impidiese; de manera que dexaron en cueros à todos los caìdos." Zarate, Conq. del Peru, lib. 3, cap. 11.

[16] "Respondia Hernando Pizarro, que no le haria Dios tan gran mal, que le dexase morir, sin que le huviese á las manos." Herrera, Hist. General, dec. 6, lib. 4, cap. 5.

[17] Ibid., dec. 6, lib. 4, cap. 9.

[18] "De tal manera que los Escrivanos no se davan manos, i ià tenian escritas mas de dos mil hojas." Ibid., dec. 6, lib. 4, cap. 7.

Naharro, Relacion Sumaria, MS.—Conq. i Pob. del Piru, MS.—Carta de Gutierrez, MS.—Pedro Pizarro, Descub. y Conq., MS.—Carta de Espinall, MS.

[19] "I que pues tuvo tanta gracia de Dios, que le hiço Christiano, ordenase su Alma, i temiese á Dios." Herrera, Hist. General, dec. 6, lib. 5, cap. 1.

[20] Ibid., ubi supra.

The marshal appealed from the sentence of his judges to the Crown, supplicating his conqueror, (says the treasurer Espinall, in his letter to the emperor,) in terms that would have touched the heart of an infidel. "De la qual el dicho Adelantado apelo para ante V. M. i le rogo que por amor de Dios hincado de rodillas le otorgase el apelacion, diciendole que mirase sus canas e vejez e quanto havia servido á V. M. i qᵉ el havia sido el primer escalon para que el i sus hermanos subiesen en el estado en que estavan, i diciendole otras muchas palabras de dolor e compasion que despues de muerto supe que dixo, que á qualquier hombre, aunque fuera infiel, moviera á piedad." Carta, MS.

[21] Carta de Espinall, MS.—Montesinos, Annales, MS., año 1538.

Bishop Valverde, as he assures the emperor, remonstrated with Francisco Pizarro in Lima, against allowing violence towards the marshal; urging it on him, as an imperative duty, to go himself at once to Cuzco, and set him at liberty. "It was too grave a matter," he rightly added, "to trust to a third party." (Carta al Emperador, MS.) The treasurer Espinall, then in Cuzco, made a similar ineffectual attempt to turn Hernando from his purpose.

[22] Carta de Espinall, MS.—Herrera, Hist. General, loc. cit.—Carta de Valverde al Emperador, MS.—Carta de Gutierrez, MS.—Pedro Pizarro, Descub. y Conq., MS.—Montesinos, Annales, MS., año 1538.

The date of Almagro's execution is not given; a strange omission; but of little moment, as that event must have followed soon on the condemnation.

[23] Ante, vol. I. p. 207.

[24] Montesinos, for want of a better pedigree, says,—"He was the son of his own great deeds, and such has been the parentage of many a famous hero!" (Annales, MS., año 1538.) It would go hard with a Castilian, if he could not make out something like a genealogy,—however shadowy.

[25] "Hera vn hombre muy profano, de muy mala lengua, que en enojandose tratava muy mal á todos los que con el andavan aunque fuesen cavalleros." (Descub. y Conq., MS.) It is the portrait drawn by an enemy.

[26] "Los Indios lloraban amargamente, diciendo, que de él nunca recibieron mal tratamiento." Herrera, Hist. General, dec. 6, lib. 5, cap. 1.

[27] If we may credit Herrera, he distributed a hundred and eighty loads of silver and twenty of gold among his followers! "Mandò sacar de su Posada mas de ciento i ochenta cargas de Plata i veinte de Oro, i las repartiò." (Dec. 5, lib. 7, cap. 9.) A load was what a man could easily carry. Such a statement taxes our credulity, but it is difficult to set the proper limits to one's credulity, in what relates to this land of gold.

CHAPTER III

[1] "I dixo, que no tuviese ninguna pena, porque no consentiria, que su Padre fuese muerto." Herrera, Hist. General, dec. 6, lib. 6, cap. 3.

[2] "Que lo haria asi como lo decia, i que su de seo no era otro, sino ver el Reino en paz; i que en lo que tocaba al Adelantado, perdiese cuidado, que bolveria à tener el antigua amistad con èl." Ibid., dec. 6, lib. 4, cap. 9.

[3] Pedro Pizarro, Descub. y Conq., MS.

He even shed many tears, *derramó muchas lagrimas*, according to Herrera, who evidently gives him small credit for them. Ibid., dec. 6, lib. 6, cap. 7.—Conf. lib. 5, cap. 1.

[4] "Respondiò, que hiciese de manera, que el Adelantado no los pusiese en mas alborotos." (Ibid., dec. 6, lib. 6, cap. 7.) "De todo esto," says Espinall, "fue sabidor el dicho Governador Pizarro á lo que mi juicio i el de otros que en ello quisieron mirar alcanzo." Carta de Espinall, MS.

[5] Ibid., dec. 6, lib. 5, cap. 1.

Herrera's testimony is little short of that of a contemporary, since it was derived, he tells us, from the correspondence of the Conquerors, and the accounts given him by their own sons. Lib. 6, cap. 7.

[6] Carta de Valverde al Emperador, MS.

[7] "En este medio tiempo vino á la dicha cibdad del Cuzco el Gobernador D. Fran^co Pizarro, el qual entro con tronpetas i chirimias vestido con ropa de martas que fue el luto con que entro." Carta de Espinall, MS.

[8] Carta de Espinall, MS.

"Mui asperamente le respondiò el Governador, diciendo, que su Governacion no tenia Termino, i que llegaba hasta Flandes." Herrera, Hist. General, dec. 6, lib. 6, cap. 7.

[9] "Avia querido hazer amigos de los principales de Chile, y ofrecidoles daria rrepartimientos y no lo avian aceptado ni querido." Pedro Pizarro, Descub. y Conq., MS.

[10] "Viendolas oy en dia, muertos de ambre, fechos pedazos e adeudados, andando por los montes desesperados por no parecer ante gentes, porque no tienen otra cosa que se vestir sino ropa de los Indios, ni dineros con que lo comprar." Carta de Espinall, MS.

[11] "Con la quietud," writes Hernando Pizarro to the emperor, "questa tierra agora tiene han descubierto i descubren cada dia los vecinos muchas minas ricas de oro i plata, de que los quintos i rentas reales de V. M. cada dia se le ofrecen i hacer casa á todo el Mundo." Carta al Emperador, MS., de Puerto Viejo, 6 de Julii, 1539.

[12] Carta de Carbajal al Emperador, MS., del Cuzco, 3 de Nov. 1539.—Pedro Pizarro, Descub. y Conq., MS.—Montesinos, Annales, MS., año 1539.

The story is well known of the manner in which the mines of Potosí were discovered by an Indian, who pulled a bush out of the ground to the fibres of which a quantity of silver globules was attached. The mine was not registered till 1545. The account is given by Acosta, lib. 4, cap. 6.

[13] Herrera, Hist. General, dec. 6, lib. 6, cap. 10.—Zarate, Conq. del Peru, lib. 3, cap. 12.— Gomara, Hist. de las Ind., cap. 142.

"No consienta vuestra señoria que se junten diez juntos en cinquenta leguas alrrededor de adonde vuestra señoria estuviere, porque si los dexa juntar le an de matar. Si á Vuestra Señoria matan, yo negociare mal y de vuestra señoria no quedara memoria. Estas palabras dixo Hernando Piçarro altas que todos le oymos. Y abraçando al marquez se partio y se fue." Pedro Pizarro, Descub. y Conq., MS.

[14] Carta de Hernando Pizarro al Emperador, MS.—Herrera, Hist. General, dec. 6, lib. 6, cap. 10.—Montesinos, Annales, MS., año 1539.

[15] Gomara, Hist. de las Ind., cap. 143.

[16] "Pero todo lo atajó la repentina muerte de Diego de Alvarado, que sucedió luego en cinco dias, no sin sospecha de veneno." Herrera, Hist. General, dec. 6, lib. 8, cap. 9.

[17] This date is established by Quintana, from a legal process instituted by Hernando's grandson, in vindication of the title of Marquess, in the year 1625.

[18] Naharro, Relacion Sumaria, MS.—Pizarro y Orellana, Varones Ilustres p 341.—Montesinos, Annales, M., año 1539.—Gomara, Hist. de las Ind., cap. 142.

[19] Caro de Torres gives a royal *cédula* in reference to the working of the silver mines of Porco, still owned by Hernando Pizarro, in 1555; and another document of nearly the same date, noticing his receipt of ten thousand ducats by the fleet from Peru. (Historia de las Ordenes Militares Madrid, 1629, p. 144.) Hernando's grandson was created by Philip IV. Marquess of the Conquest, *Marques de la Conquista*, with a liberal pension from government. Pizarro y Orellana, Varones Ilustres, p. 342, and Discurso, p. 72.

[20] "Multos da, Jupiter, annos"; the greatest boon, in Pizarro y Orellana's opinion, that Heaven can confer! "Diole Dios, por todo, el premio mayor desta vida, pues fue tan larga, que excedio de cien años." (Varones Ilustres, p. 342) According to the same somewhat partial authority, Hernando died, as he had lived, in the odor of sanctity! "Viviendo aprender a morir, y saber morir, quando llegò la muerte.

[21] Pedro Pizarro, Descub. y Conq., MS.—Gomara, Hist. de las Ind., cap. 146.—Herrera, Hist. General, dec. 6, lib. 8, cap. 9.—Montesinos, Annales, MS., año 1540.

This latter writer sees nothing short of a "divine mystery" in this forecast of government, so singularly sustained by events. "Prevencion del gran espiritu del Rey, no sin misterio." Ubi supra.

[22] Or, as the port should rather be called, *Mala Ventura*, as Pedro Pizarro punningly remarks. "Tuvo tan mal viaje en la mar que vbo de desembarcar en la Buena Ventura, aunque yo la llamo Mala." Descub. y Conq., MS.

[23] "Piensan que les mienten los que aca les dizen que ai un gran Señor en Castilla, viendo que aca pelean unos capitanes contra otros; y piensan que no ai otro Rei sino aquel que venze al otro, porque aca entrellos no se acostumbra que un capitan pelee contra otro, estando entrambos debaxo de un Señor." Carta de Valverde al Emperador, MS.

[24] Herrera, Hist. General, dec. 6, lib. 6, cap. 7.—Pedro Pizarro, Descub. y Conq., MS.—Carta de Espinall, MS.—Carta de Valverde al Emperador, MS.

[25] The Inca declined the interview with the bishop, on the ground that he had seen him pay obeisance by taking off his cap to Pizarro. It proved his inferiority to the latter, he said, and that he could never protect him against the governor. The passage in which it is related is curious. "Preguntando a indios del inca que anda alzado que si sabe el inca que yo soi venido á la tierra en nombre de S. M. para defendellos, dixo que mui bien lo sabia; y preguntado que porque no se benia á mi de paz, dixo el indio que dezia el inca que

porque yo quando vine hize la mocha al gobernador, que quiere dezir que le quité el Bonete; que no queria venir á mi de paz, que él que no havia de venir de paz sino á uno que viniese de castilla que no hiziese la mocha al gobernador, porque le paresze á él que este lo podrá defender por lo que ha hecho y no otro." Carta de Valverde al Emperador, MS.

[26] At least, we may presume they did so, since they openly condemn him in their accounts of the transaction. I quote Pedro Pizarro, not disposed to criticise the conduct of his general too severely. "Se tomo una muger de mango ynga que le queria mucho y se guardo, creyendo que por ella saldria de paz. Esta muger mando matar al marquez despues en Yncay, haziendola varear con varas y flechar con flechas por una burla que mango ynga le hizo que aqui contare, y entiendo yo que por esta crueldad y otra hermana del ynga que mando matar en Lima quando los yndios pusieron cerco sobrella que se llamava Açarpay. me paresce á mi que nuestro señor le castigo en el fin que tuvo." Descub. y Conq., MS.

[27] Cieza de Leon notices the uncommon beauty and solidity of the buildings at Guamanga. "La qual han edificado las mayores y mejores casas que ay en todo el Peru, todas de piedra, ladrillo, y teja, con grandes torres: de manera que no falta aposentos. La plaça esta llana y bien grande." Cronica, cap. 87.

[28] "I con que ià começaba á haver en aquellas Tierras cosecha de Trigo, Cevada, i otras muchas cosas de Castilla." Herrera, Hist. General, dec. 6, lib. 10, cap. 2.

[29] Carta de Carvajal al Emperador, MS.—Montesinos, Annales, MS., años 1539 et 1541.—Pedro Pizarro, Descub. y Conq., MS.—Herrera, Hist. General, dec. 6, lib. 7, cap. 1.—Cieza de Leon, Cronica, cap. 76 et alibi.

[30] The cavalier Pizarro y Orellana has given biographical notices of each of the brothers. It requires no witchcraft to detect that the blood of the Pizarros flowed in the veins of the writer to his fingers' ends. Yet his facts are less suspicious than his inferences.

CHAPTER IV

[1] Herrera, Hist. General, dec. 6, lib. 8, cap. 6, 7.—Garcilasso, Com. Real., Parte 2, lib. 3, cap. 2.—Zarate, Conq. del Peru, lib. 4, cap. 1, 2.—Gomara, Hist. de las Ind., cap. 143.—Montesinos, Annales, año 1539.

Historians differ as to the number of Gonzalo's forces,—of his men, his horses, and his hogs. The last, according to Herrera, amounted to no less than 5000; a goodly supply of bacon for so small a troop, since the Indians, doubtless, lived on parched corn, *coca*, which usually formed their only support on the longest journeys.

[2] Zarate states the number with precision at five hundred houses. "Sobrevino vn tan gran Terremoto, con temblor, i tempestad de Agua, i Relampagos, i Raios, i grandes Truenos, que abriendose la Tierra por muchas partes, se hundieron quinientas Casas." (Conq. del Peru, lib. 4, cap. 2.) There is nothing so satisfactory to the mind of the reader as precise numbers; and nothing so little deserving of his confidence.

[3] *Canela* is the Spanish for cinnamon.

[4] This, allowing six feet for the spread of a man's arms, would be about ninety-six feet in circumference, or thirty-two feet in diameter; larger, probably, than the largest tree known in Europe. Yet it falls short of that famous giant of the forests mentioned by M. de Humboldt as still flourishing in the intendancy of Oaxaca, which, by the exact measure-

ment of a traveller in 1839, was found to be a hundred and twelve feet in circumference at the height of four feet from the ground. This height may correspond with that of the measurement taken by the Spaniards. See a curious and learned article on Forest-trees in No. 124 of the North American Review.

[5] The dramatist Molina, in his play of "*Las Amazonas en las Indias,*" has devoted some dozen columns of *redondillas* to an account of the sufferings of his countrymen in the expedition to the Amazon. The poet reckoned confidently on the patience of his audience. The following verses describe the miserable condition to which the Spaniards were reduced by the incessant rains.

> "Sin que el Sol en este tiempo
> Su cara vèr nos permita,
> Ni las nubes taberneras
> Cessen de echarnos encima
> Dilubios inagotables,
> *Que hasta el alma nos bautizan.*
> Cayeron los mas enfermos,
> Porque las ropas podridas
> Con el eterno agua và,
> Nos dexò en las carnes vivas."

[6] Capitulacion con Orellana, MS.—Pedro Pizarro, Descub. y Conq., MS.—Gomara, Hist. de las Ind., cap. 143.—Zarate, Conq. del Peru, lib. 4, cap. 2.—Herrera, Hist. General, dec. 6, lib. 8, cap. 6, 7.—Garcilasso, Com. Real., Parte 2, lib. 3, cap. 2.

The last writer obtained his information, as he tells us, from several who were present in the expedition. The reader may be assured that it has lost nothing in coming through his hands.

[7] "Al cabo de este largo camino hallaron que el rio hazia vn salto de una peña de mas de dozientas braças de alto: que hazia tan gran ruydo, que lo oyeron mas de seys leguas antes que llegassen a el." (Garcilasso, Com. Real., Parte 2, lib. 3, cap. 3.) I find nothing to confirm or to confute the account of this stupendous cataract in later travellers, not very numerous in these wild regions. The alleged height of the falls, twice that of the great cataract of the Tequendama in the Bogotá, as measured by Humboldt, usually esteemed the highest in America, is not so great as that of some of the cascades thrown over the precipices in Switzerland. Yet the estimates of the Spaniards, who, in the gloomy state of their feelings, were doubtless keenly alive to impressions of the sublime and the terrible, cannot safely be relied on.

[8] "Yeruas y rayzes, y fruta siluestre, sapos, y culebras, y otras malas sauandijas, si las auia por aquellas montañas que todo les hazia buen estomago a los Españoles; que peor les yua con la falta de cosas tan viles." Garcilasso, Com. Real., Parte 2, lib. 3, cap. 4.—Capitulacion con Orellana, MS.—Herrera, Hist. General, dec. 6, lib. 8, cap. 7.—Zarate, Conq. del Peru, lib. 4, cap. 3, 4.—Gomara, Hist. de las Ind., cap. 143.

[9] This statement of De Vargas was confirmed by Orellana, as appears from the language of the royal grant made to that cavalier on his return to Castile. The document is preserved entire in the Muñoz collection of MSS.

"Haviendo vos ido con ciertos compañeros un rio abajo á buscar comida, con la corriente fuistes metidos por el dicho rio mas de 200 leguas donde no pudistes dar la buelta é por esta necesidad é por la mucha noticia que tuvistes de la grandeza é riqueza de la tierra, posponiendo vuestro peligro, sin interes ninguno por servir á S. M. os aventurastes á saber lo que havia en aquellas provincias, é ansi descubristes é hallastes grandes poblaciones." Capitulacion con Orellana, MS.

[10] Condamine, who, in 1743, went down the Amazon, has often occasion to notice the perils and perplexities in which he was involved in the navigation of this river, too difficult, as he says, to be undertaken without the guidance of a skilful pilot. See his Relation Abregée d'un Voyage fait dans l'Interieur de l'Amérique Méridionale. (Maestricht, 1778.)

[11] It has not been easy to discern the exact line in later times, with all the lights of modern discovery. Condamine, after a careful investigation, considers that there is good ground for believing in the existence of a community of armed women, once living somewhere in the neighbourhood of the Amazon, though they have now disappeared. It would be hard to disprove the fact, but still harder, considering the embarrassments in perpetuating such a community, to believe it. Voyage dans l'Amérique Méridionale, p. 99, et seq.

[12] "His crime is, in some measure, balanced by the glory of having ventured upon a navigation of near two thousand leagues, through unknown nations, in a vessel hastily constructed, with green timber, and by very unskilful hands, without provisions, without a compass, or a pilot." (Robertson, America, (ed. London, 1796,) vol. III. p. 84.) The historian of America does not hold the moral balance with as unerring a hand as usual, in his judgment of Orellana's splendid enterprise. No success, however splendid, in the language of one, not too severe a moralist,

"Can blazon evil deeds or consecrate a crime."

[13] An expedition more remarkable than that of Orellana was performed by a delicate female, Madame Godin, who, in 1769, attempted to descend the Amazon in an open boat to its mouth. She was attended by seven persons, two of them her brothers, and two her female domestics. The boat was wrecked, and Madame Godin, narrowly escaping with her life, endeavoured with her party to accomplish the remainder of her journey on foot. She saw them perish, one after another, of hunger and disease, till she was left alone in the howling wilderness. Still, like Milton's lady in Comus, she was permitted to come safely out of all these perils, and, after unparalleled sufferings, falling in with some friendly Indians, she was conducted by them to a French settlement. Though a young woman, it will not be surprising that the hardships and terrors she endured turned her hair perfectly white. The details of the extraordinary story are given in a letter to M. de la Condamine by her husband, who tells them in an earnest, unaffected way that engages our confidence. Voyage dans l'Amérique Méridionale, p. 329, et seq.

[14] Garcilasso, Com. Real., Parte 2, lib. 3, cap. 5.—Herrera, Hist. General, dec. 6, lib. 8, cap. 8.—Zarate, Conq. del Peru, lib. 4, cap. 5.—Gomara, Hist. de las Ind., cap. 143.

One must not expect from these wanderers in the wilderness any exact computation of time or distance, destitute, as they were, of the means of making a correct observation of either.

[15] Pedro Pizarro, Descub. y Conq., MS.—Zarate, Conq. del Peru, lib. 4, cap. 5.—Gomara, Hist. de las Ind., cap. 143.—Garcilasso, Com. Real., Parte 2, lib. 3, cap. 15.—Herrera, Hist. General, dec. 7, lib. 3, cap. 14.

The last historian, in dismissing his account of the expedition, passes a panegyric on the courage and constancy of his countrymen, which we must admit to be well deserved.

"Finalmente, Gonçalo Piçarro entró en el Quito, triunfando del valor, i sufrimiento, i de la constancia, recto, é immutable vigor del animo, pues Hombres Humanos no se hallan haver tanto sufrido, ni padecido tantas desventuras." Ibid., ubi supra.

[16] Zarate, Conq. del Peru, lib. 4, cap. 5.

CHAPTER V

[1] Carta de Almagro, MS.

[2] Herrera, Hist. General, dec. 6, lib. 8, cap. 6.

[3] Gomara, Hist. de las Ind., cap. 144.

[4] Garcilasso, Com. Real., Parte 2, lib. 3, cap. 6.

[5] "My sufferings," says Almagro, in his letter to the Royal Audience of Panamá, "were enough to unsettle my reason." See his Letter in the original, *Appendix, No.* 12.

[6] "Hizo Picado el secretario del Marquez mucho daño a muchos, porque el marquez don Francisco Piçarro como no savia ler ni escrivir fiavase del y no hacia mas de lo que el le aconsejava y ansi hizo este mucho mal en estos rreinos, porque el que no andava á su voluntad sirviendole aunque tuviese meritos le destruya y este Picado fue causa de que los de Chile tomasen mas odio al marquez por donde le mataron. Porque queria este que todos lo reverenciasen, y los de chile no hazian caso dél, y por esta causa los perseguia este mucho, y ansi vinieron á hazer lo que hizieron los de Chile." Pedro Pizarro, Descub. y Conq., MS.—Also Zarate, Conq. del Peru, lib. 4, cap. 6.

[7] Pedro Pizarro, Descub. y Conq., MS.—Garcilasso, Com. Real., Parte 2, lib. 3, cap. 6.— Herrera, Hist. General, dec. 6, lib. 10, cap. 2.

[8] Pedro Pizarro, Descub. y Conq., MS.—Montesinos, Annales, MS., año 1541.—Zarate, Conq. del Peru, lib. 4, cap. 6.

[9] Yet this would seem to be contradicted by Almagro's own letter to the audience of Panamá, in which he states, that, galled by intolerable injuries, he and his followers had resolved to take the remedy into their own hands, by entering the governor's house and seizing his person. (See the original in *Appendix, No.* 12.) It is certain, however, that in the full accounts we have of the affair by writers who had the best means of information, we do not find Almagro's name mentioned as one who took an active part in the tragic drama. His own letter merely expresses that it was his purpose to have taken part in it, with the further declaration, that it was simply to seize, not to slay, Pizarro;—a declaration that no one who reads the history of the transaction will be very ready to credit.

[10] "Mancebo virtuoso, i de grande Animo, i bien enseñado: i especialmente se havia exercitado mucho en cavalgar a Caballo, de ambas sillas, lo qual hacia con mucha gracia, i destreça, i tambien en escrevir, i leer, lo qual hacia mas liberalmente, i mejor de lo que requeria su Profesion. De este tenia cargo, como Aio, Juan de Herrada." Zarate, Conq. del Peru, lib. 4, cap. 6.

[11] "Pues un dia antes un sacerdote clerigo llamado Benao fue de noche y avisso a Picado el secretario y dixole mañana Domingo quando el marquez saliere á misa tienen concertado los de Chile de matar al marquez y á vos y á sus amigos. Esto me a dicho

vno en confision para que os venga á avisar. Pues savido esto Picado se fue luego y lo conto al marquez y el le rrespondio. Ese clerigo obispado quiere." Pedro Pizarro, Descub. y Conq., MS.

[12] "El Juan Velazquez le dixo. No tema vuestra señoria que mientras yo tuviere esta vara en la mano nadie se atrevera." Pedro Pizarro, Descub. y Conq., MS.

[13] Herrera, Hist. General, dec. 6, lib. 10, cap. 6.—Pedro Pizarro, Descub. y Conq., MS.— Zarate, Conq. del Peru, lib. 4, cap. 8.—Naharro, Rel. Sumaria, MS.—Carta del Maestro, Martin de Arauco, MS., 15 de Julio, 1541.

[14] "Gomez Perez por haver alli agua derramada de una acequia, rodeo algun tanto por no mojarse; reparó en ello Juan de Rada, y entrandose atrevido por el agua le dijo: ¿Bamos á bañarnos en sangre humana, y rehusais mojaros los pies en agua? Ea volveos. hizolo volver y no asistió al hecho." Montesinos, Annales, MS., año 1541.

[15] "En lo qual no paresce haver quebrantado su palabra, porque despues huiendo (como adelante se dirá) al tiempo, que quisieron matar al Marques, se hecho de vna Ventana abajo, à la Huerta, llevando la Vara en la boca." Zarate, Conq. del Peru, lib. 4, cap. 7.

Pedro Pizarro, Descub. y Conq., MS.—Naharro, Relacion Sumaria, MS.—Carta del Maestro, Martin de Arauco, MS.—Carta de Fray Vicente de Valverde a la Audiencia de Panamá, MS., desde Tumbez, 15 Nov. 1541.—Gomara, Hist. de las Ind., cap. 145.

[16] Zarate, Conq. del Peru, lib. 4, cap. 8.—Naharro, Relacion Sumaria, MS.—Pedro Pizarro, Descub. y Conq., MS.—Herrera, Hist. General, dec. 6, lib. 10, cap. 6.—Carta de la Justicia y Regimiento de la Ciudad de los Reyes, MS., 15 de Julio, 1541.—Carta del Maestro, Martin de Arauco, MS.—Carta de Fray Vicente Valverde, desde Tumbez, MS.— Gomara, Hist. de las Ind., ubi supra.—Montesinos, Annales, MS., año 1541.

Pizarro y Orellana seems to have no doubt that his slaughtered kinsman died in the odor of sanctity.—"Alli le acabaron los traidores enemigos, dandole cruelissimas heridas, con que acabó el Julio Cesar Español, estando tan en si que pidiendo confession con gran acto de contricion, haziendo la señal de la Cruz con su misma sangre, y besandola murió." Varones Ilustres, p. 186.

According to one authority, the mortal blow was given by a soldier named Borregan, who, when Pizarro was down, struck him on the back of the head with a water-jar, which he had snatched from the table. (Herrera, Hist. General, dec. 6, lib. 10, cap. 6.) Considering the hurry and confusion of the scene, the different narratives of the catastrophe, though necessarily differing in minute details, have a remarkable agreement with one another.

[17] "No se olvidaron de buscar à Antonio Picado, i iendo en casa del Tesorero Alonso Riquelme, èl mismo iba diciendo: No sè adonde està el Señor Picado, i con los ojos le mostraba, i le hallaron debaxo de la cama." Herrera, Hist. General, dec. 6, lib. 10, cap. 7.

We find Riquelme's name, soon after this, enrolled among the municipality of Lima, showing that he found it convenient to give in his temporary adhesion, at least, to Almagro. Carta de la Justicia y Regimiento de la Ciudad de los Reyes, MS.

[18] "Muriò pidiendo confesion, i haciendo la Cruz, sin que nadie dijese, Dios te perdone." Gomara, Hist. de las Ind., cap. 144.

MS. de Caravantes.—Zarate, Conq. del Peru, lib. 4, cap. 8.—Carta del Maestro, Martin de Arauco, MS.—Carta de Fray Vicente Valverde, desde Tumbez, MS.

[19] "Sus huesos ençerrados en una caxa guarnecida de terciopelo morado con passamanos de oro que yo he visto." MS. de Caravantes.

[20] Ante, Book 2, chap. 2, note 1.

[21] MS. de Caravantes.—Quintana, Españoles Celebres, tom. II., p. 417.

See also the *Discurso, Legal y Político*, annexed by Pizarro y Orellana to his bulky tome, in which that cavalier urges the claims of Pizarro. It is in the nature of a memorial to Philip IV. in behalf of Pizarro's descendants, in which the writer, after setting forth the manifold services of the Conqueror, shows how little his posterity had profited by the magnificent grants conferred on him by the Crown. The argument of the Royal Counsellor was not without its effect.

[22] Gomara, Hist. de las Ind., cap. 144.—Zarate, Conq. del Peru, lib. 4, cap. 9.

The portrait of Pizarro, in the viceregal palace at Lima, represents him in a citizen's dress, with a sable cloak,—the *capa y espada* of a Spanish gentleman. Each panel in the spacious *sala de los Vireyes* was reserved for the portrait of a viceroy. The long file is complete, from Pizarro to Pezuela; and it is a curious fact, noticed by Stevenson, that the last panel was exactly filled when the reign of the viceroys was abruptly terminated by the Revolution. (Residence in South America, vol. I. p. 228.) It is a singular coincidence that the same thing should have occurred at Venice, where, if my memory serves me, the last niche reserved for the effigies of its doges was just filled, when the ancient aristocracy was overturned.

[23] Garcilasso, Com. Real., Parte 2, lib. 3, cap. 9.

[24] "Halló, i tuvo mas Oro, i Plata, que otro ningun Español de quantos han pasado á Indias, ni que ninguno de quantos Capitanes han sido por el Mundo." Gomara, Hist. de las Ind., cap. 144.

[25] MS. de Caravantes.—Pizarro y Orellana, Discurso Leg. y Pol., ap. Varones Ilust. Gonzalo Pizarro, when taken prisoner by President Gasca, challenged him to point out any quarter of the country in which the royal grant had been carried into effect by a specific assignment of land to his brother. See Garcilasso, Com. Real., Parte 2, lib. 5, cap. 36.

[26] Even so experienced a person as Muñoz seems to have fallen into this error. On one of Pizarro's letters I find the following copy of an autograph memorandum by this eminent scholar:— *Carta de Francisco Pizarro, su letra i buena letra.*

[27] "En este viage trató Pizarro de aprender á leer; no le dió su viveza lugar á ello; contentose solo con saber firmar, de lo que se veia Almagro, y decia, que firmar sin saber leer era lo mismo que recibir herida, sin poder darla. En adelante firmó siempre Pizarro por si, y por Almagro su Secretario." Montesinos, Annales, MS., año 1525.

[28] "Porque el marquez don Francisco Piçarro como no savia ler ni escrivir." Pedro Pizarro, Descub. y Conq., MS.

[29] "Siendo personas," says the author, speaking both of Pizarro and Almagro, "no solamente, no leidas, pero que de todo punto no sabian leer, ni aun firmar, que en ellos fue cosa de gran defecto. . . . . . Fue el Marquès tan confiado de sus Criados, i Amigos, que todos los Despachos, que hacia, asi de Governacion, como de Repartimientos de Indios, libraba haciendo èl dos señales, en medio de las quales Antonio Picado, su Secretario, firmaba el nombre de Francisco Piçarro." Zarate, Conq. del Peru, lib. 4, cap. 9.

[30] This tardiness of resolve has even led Herrera to doubt his resolution altogether; a judgment certainly contradicted by the whole tenor of his history. "Porque aunque era astuto, i recatado, por la maior parte fue de animo suspenso, i no mui resoluto." Hist. General, dec. 5, lib. 7, cap. 13.

[31] "Tenia por costumbre de quando algo le pedian dezir siempre de no. esto dezia el que hazia por no faltar su palabra, y no obstante que dezia no, correspondia con hazer lo que le pedian no aviendo inconvenimente. . . . . . Don Diego de Almagro hera á la contra que á todos dezia si, y con pocos lo cumplia." Pedro Pizarro, Descub. y Conq., MS.

[32] See Conquest of Mexico, Book 4, chap 8.

[33] The following vigorous lines of Southey condense, in a small compass, the most remarkable traits of Pizarro. The poet's epitaph may certainly be acquitted of the imputation, generally well deserved, of flattery towards the subject of it.

"FOR A COLUMN AT TRUXILLO.

"Pizarro here was born; a greater name
The list of Glory boasts not. Toil and Pain,
Famine, and hostile Elements, and Hosts
Embattled, failed to check him in his course,
Not to be wearied, not to be deterred,
Not to be overcome. A mighty realm
He overran, and with relentless arm
Slew or enslaved its unoffending sons,
And wealth and power and fame were his rewards.
There is another world, beyond the grave,
According to their deeds where men are judged.
O Reader! if thy daily bread be earned
By daily labor,—yea, however low,
However wretched, be thy lot assigned,
Thank thou, with deepest gratitude, the God
Who made thee, that thou art not such as he."

CHAPTER VI

[1] Zarate, Conq. del Peru, lib. 4, cap. 13.—Herrera, Hist. General, dec. 6, lib. 10, cap. 7.—Declaracion de Uscategui, MS.—Carta del Maestro, Martin de Arauco, MS.—Carta de Fray Vicente Valverde, desde Tumbez, MS.

[2] Herrera, Hist. General, dec. 6, lib. 10, cap. 4.—Carta de Benalcazar al Emperador, desde Cali, MS., 20 Septiembre, 1542.

Benalcazar urged Vaca de Castro to assume only the title of Judge, and not that of Governor, which would conflict with the pretensions of Almagro to that part of the country known as New Toledo, and bequeathed to him by his father "Porque yo le avisé muchas veces no entrase en la tierra como Governador, sino como Juez de V. M. que venia á desagraviar á los agraviados, porque todos lo rescibirian de buena gana." Ubi supra.

[3] Pedro Pizarro, Descub. y Conq., MS.—Carta de Barrio Nuevo, MS.—Carta de Fray Vicente Valverde, desde Tumbez, MS.

[4] "Siendo informado que andavan ordenando la muerte á Antonio Picado secretario del Marques que tenian preso, fui á Don Diego é á su Capitan General Joan de Herrada é á todos sus capitanes, i les puse delante el servicio de Dios i de S. M. i que bastase en lo

fecho por respeto de Dios, humillandome á sus pies porque no lo matasen: i no bastó que luego dende á pocos dias lo sacaron á la plaza desta cibdad donde le cortaron la cabeza." Carta de Fray Vicente de Valverde, desde Tumbez, MS.

[5] "Quel Señor obispo Fray Vicente de Balverde como persona que jamas ha tenido fin ni zelo al servicio de Dios ni de S. M. ni menos en la conversion de los naturales en los poner é dotrinar en las cosas de nuestra santa fée catholica, ni menos en entender en la paz é sosiego destos reynos, sino á sus intereses propios dando mal ejemplo á todos." (Carta de Almagro á la Audiencia de Panamá, MS., 8 de Nov. 1541.) The writer, it must be remembered, was his personal enemy.

[6] Pedro Pizarro, Descub. y Conq., MS.—Zarate, Conq. del Peru, lib. 4, cap. 10-14.— Gomara, Hist. de las Ind., cap. 147.—Declaracion de Uscategui, MS.—Carta de Barrio Nuevo, MS.—Herrera, Hist. General, dec. 6, lib. 10, cap. 13; dec. 7, lib. 3, cap. 1, 5.

[7] "Hiço mas que su edad requeria, porque seria de edad de veinte i dos años." Zarate, Conq. del Peru, lib. 4, cap. 20.

[8] "Y demas de esto hiço armas para la Gente de su Real, que no las tenia, de pasta de Plata, i Cobre, mezclado, de que salen mui buenos Coseletes: haviendo corregido, demàs de esto, todas las armas de la Tierra; de manera, que el que menos Armas tenia entre su Gente, era Cota, i Coracinas, ò Coselete, i Celadas de la mesma Pasta, que los Indios hacen diestramente, por muestras de las de Milàn." Zarate, Conq. del Peru, lib. 4, cap. 14.

[9] "Hombres de armas con tan buenas celadas borgoñesas como se hacen en Milan." Carta de Ventura Beltran al Emperador, MS., desde Vilcas, 8 Octubre, 1542.

[10] "El artilleria hera suficiente para hazer bateria en el castillo de Burgos." Dicho del Capitan Francisco de Carvajal sobre la pregunta 38 de la informacion hecha en el Cuzco en 1543, á favor de Vaca de Castro, MS.

[11] Pedro Pizarro, Descub. y Conq., MS.—Declaracion de Uscategui, MS.—Garcilasso, Com. Real., Parte 2, lib. 2, cap. 13.—Carta del Cabildo de Arequipa al Emperador, San Joan de la Frontera, MS., 24 de Sep. 1542.—Herrera, Hist. General, dec. 7, lib. 3, cap. 1, 2.

[12] Declaracion de Uscategui, MS.—Pedro Pizarro, Descub. y Conq., MS.—Herrera, Hist. General, dec. 7, lib. 1, cap. 1.—Carta de Barrio Nuevo, MS.—Carta de Benalcazar al Emperador, MS.

[13] The Municipality of Arequipa, most of whose members were present in the army, stoutly urge their claims to a compensation for thus promptly leaving their estates, and taking up arms at the call of government. Without such reward, they say, their patriotic example will not often be followed. The document, which is important for its historical details, may be found in the Castilian, in *Appendix, No. 13.*

[14] Pedro Pizarro, Descub. y Conq., MS.—Zarate, Conq. del Peru, lib. 4, cap. 15.—Carta de Barrio Nuevo, MS.

Carbajal notices the politic manner in which his commander bribed recruits into his service,—paying them with promises and fair words when ready money failed him. "Dando á unos dineros, é á otros armas i caballos, i á otros palabras, i á otros promesas, i á otros graziosas respuestas de lo que con él negoziaban para tenerlos á todos muy contentos i presttos en el servicio de S. M. quando fuese menestter." Dicho del Capitan Francisco de Carvajal sobre la informacion hecha en el Cuzco en 1543, á favor de Vaca de Castro, MS.

[15] Zarate, Conq. del Peru, lib. 4, cap. 15.

[16] Cieza de Leon, Cronica, cap. 85.

[17] Dicho del Capitan Francisco de Carbajal sobre la informacion hecha en el Cuzco en 1543, á favor de Vaca de Castro, MS.—Zarate, Conq. del Peru, lib. 4, cap. 16.—Herrera, Hist. General, dec. 7, lib. 3, cap. 8.—Carta de Ventura Beltran, MS.—Gomara, Hist. de las Ind., cap. 149.

[18] "Tuvieron tan gran tempestad de agua, Truenos, i Nieve, que pensaron perecer; i amaneciendo con dia claro, i sereno." Herrera, Hist. General, dec. 7, lib. 3, cap. 8.

[19] "Y asi Vaca de Castro signió su parescer, temiendo toda via la falta del Dia, i dijo, que quisiera tener el poder de Josue, para detener el Sol." Zarate, Conq. del Peru, lib. 4, cap. 18.

[20] "I visto esto por el dicho señor Governador, mandó dar al arma á mui gran priesa, i mando á este testigo que sacase toda la gente al campo, i el se entró en su tienda á se armar, i dende á poco salió della encima de un cavallo morcillo rabicano armado en blanco i con una ropa de brocado encima de las armas con el abito de Santiago en los pechos." Dicho del Capitan Francisco de Carbajal sobre la informacion hecha en el Cuzco en 1543, á favor de Vaca de Castro, MS.

[21] The governor's words, says Carbajal, who witnessed their effect, stirred the heart of the troops, so that they went to the battle as to a ball. "En pocas palabras comprehendió tan grandes cosas que la gente de S. M. covró tan grande animo con ellas, que tan determinadamente se partieron de alli para ir á los enemigos como si fueran á fiestas donde estuvieran convidados." Dicho del Capitan Francisco de Carbajal, sobre la informacion hecha en el Cuzco en 1543, á favor de Vaca de Castro, MS.

[22] Pedro Pizarro, Descub. y Conq., MS.—Zarate, Conq. del Peru, lib. 4, cap. 17-19.—Naharro, Relacion Sumaria, MS.—Herrera, Hist. General, dec. 7, lib. 3, cap. 11.—Dicho del Capitan Francisco de Carbajal sobre la informacion hecha en el Cuzco en 1543, á favor de Vaca de Castro, MS.—Carta del Cabildo de Arequipa al Emperador, MS.—Carta de Ventura Beltran, MS.—Declaracion de Uscategui, MS.—Gomara, Hist. de las Ind., cap. 149.

According to Garcilasso, whose guns usually do more execution than those of any other authority, seventeen men were killed by this wonderful shot. See Com. Real., Parte 2, lib. 3, cap. 16.

[23] The officers drove the men, according to Zarate, at the point of their swords, to take the places of their fallen comrades. "Porque vn tiro llevo toda vna hilera, è hiço abrir el Escuadron, i los Capitanes pusieron gran diligencia en hacerlo cerrar, amenaçando de muerte à los Soldados, con las Espadas desenvainadas, i se cerrò." Conq. del Peru, lib. 4, cap. 1.

[24] "Se encontraron de suerte, que casi todas las lanças quebraron, quedando muchos muertos, i caidos de ambas partes." (Ibid., ubi supra.) Zarate writes on this occasion with the spirit and strength of Thucydides. He was not present, but came into the country the following year, when he gleaned the particulars of the battle from the best informed persons there, to whom his position gave him ready access.

[25] It is the language of the Conquerors themselves, who, in their letter to the Emperor, compare the action to the great battle of Ravenna. "Fue tan reñida i porfiada, que despues de la de Rebena, no se ha visto entre tan poca gente mas cruel batalla, donde hermanos á hermanos, ni deudos a deudos, ni amigos á amigos no se davan vida uno á otro." Carta del Cabildo de Arequipa al Emperador, MS.

[26] The battle was so equally contested, says Beltran, one of Vaca de Castro's captains, that it was long doubtful on which side victory was to incline. "I la batalla estuvo mui gran rato en peso sin conoscerse vitoria de la una parte á la otra." Carta de Ventura Beltran, MS.

[27] "Gritaba, Victoria; i decia, Prender i no matar." Herrera, Hist. General, dec. 7, lib. 3, cap. 11.

[28] The letter of the municipality of Arequipa gives the governor credit for deciding the fate of the day by this movement, and the writers express their "admiration of the gallantry and courage he displayed, so little to have been expected from his age and profession." See the original in *Appendix, No.* 13.

[29] "Se arrojaron en los Enemigos, como desesperados, hiriendo à todas partes, diciendo cada vno por su nombre: Yo soi Fulano, que matè al Marquès; i asi anduvieron hasta, que los hicieron pedaços." Zarate, Conq. del Peru, lib. 4, cap. 19.

[30] Zarate estimates the number at three hundred. Uscategui, who belonged to the Almagrian party, and Garcilasso, both rate it as high as five hundred.

[31] The particulars of the action are gathered from Pedro Pizarro, Descub. y Conq., MS.— Carta de Ventura Beltran, MS.—Zarate, Conq. del Peru, lib. 4, cap. 17-20.—Naharro, Relacion Sumaria, MS.—Dicho del Capitan Francisco de Carbajal sobre la informacion hecha en el Cuzco en 1543, á favor de Vaca de Castro, MS.—Carta del Cabildo de Arequipa al Emperador, MS.—Carta de Barrio Nuevo, MS.—Gomara, Hist. de las Ind., cap. 149.— Garcilasso, Com. Real., Parte 2, lib. 3, cap. 15-18.—Declaracion de Uscategui, MS.

Many of these authorities were personally present on the field; and it is rare that the details of a battle are drawn from more authentic testimony. The student of history will not be surprised that in these details there should be the greatest discrepancy.

[32] Declaracion de Uscategui, MS.—Carta de Ventura Beltran, MS.—Zarate, Conq. del Peru, lib. 4, cap. 21.

The loyal burghers of Arequipa seem to have been well contented with these executions. "If night had not overtaken us," they say, alluding to the action, in their letter to the emperor, "your Majesty would have had no reason to complain; but what was omitted then is made up now, since the governor goes on quartering every day some one or other of the traitors who escaped from the field." See the original in *Appendix, No.* 13.

[33] Herrera, Hist. General, dec. 7, lib. 4, cap. 1.

[34] Pedro Pizarro, Descub. y Conq., MS.—Zarate, Conq. del Peru, lib. 4, cap. 21.—Naharro, Relacion Sumaria, MS.—Herrera, Hist. General, dec. 7, lib. 6, cap. 1.

[35] Pedro Pizarro, Descub. y Conq., MS.—Herrera, Hist. General, dec. 7, lib. 4, cap. 1; lib. 6, cap. 3.—Zarate, Conq. del Peru, lib. 4, cap. 22.

[36] Ibid., ubi supra.—Herrera, Hist. General, dec. 7, lib. 6, cap. 2.

[37] "I asi lo escrivieron al Rei la Ciudad del Cuzco, la Villa de la Plata, i otras Comunidades, suplicandole, que los dexase por Governador à Vaca de Castro, como Persona, que procedia con rectitud, i que ià entendia el Govierno de aquellos Reinos." Herrera, Ibid., loc. cit.

CHAPTER VII

[1] "Españoles hai que crian perros carniceros i los avezan á matar Indios, lo qual procuran á las veces por pasatiempo, i ver si lo hacen bien los perros." Relacion que dió el Provisor Morales sobre las cosas que convenian provarse en el Peru, MS.

[2] "Que los Justicias dan cedulas de Anaconas que por otros terminos los hacen esclavos é vivir contra su voluntad, diciendo: Por la presente damos licencia á vos Fulano, para que os podais servir de tal Indio ó de tal India é lo podais tomar é sacar donde quiera que lo hallaredes." Rel. del Provisor Morales, MS.

[3] "Es general el vicio del amancebamiento con Indias, i algunos tienen cantidad dellas como en serrallo." Ibid., MS.

[4] "Muchos Españoles han muerto i matan increible cantidad de ovejas por comer solo los sesos, hacer pasteles del tuetano i candelas de la grasa. De ai hambre general." Ibid., MS.

[5] "Se puede afirmar que hicieron mas daño los Españoles en solos quatro años que el Inga en quatrocientos." Ondegardo, Rel. Seg., MS.

[6] "Ahora no tienen que comer ni donde sembrar, i asi van á hurtallo como solian, delito por que han aorcado á muchos." Rel. del Provisor Morales, MS.

This, and some of the preceding citations, as the reader will see, have been taken from the MS. of the Bachelor Luis de Morales, who lived eighteen or twenty years in Cuzco; and, in 1541, about the time of Vaca de Castro's coming to Peru, prepared a Memorial for the government, embracing a hundred and nine chapters. It treats of the condition of the country, and the remedies which suggested themselves to the benevolent mind of its author. The emperor's notes on the margin show that it received attention at court. There is no reason, as far as I am aware, to distrust the testimony of the writer, and Muñoz has made some sensible extracts from it for his inestimable collection.

[7] Father Naharro notices twelve missionaries, some of his own order, whose zealous labors and miracles for the conversion of the Indians he deems worthy of comparison with those of the twelve Apostles of Christianity. It is a pity that history, while it has commemorated the names of so many persecutors of the poor heathen, should have omitted those of their benefactors.

"Tomó su divina Magestad por instrumento 12 solos religiosos pobres, descalzos i desconocidos, 5 del orden de la Merced, 4 de Predicadores, i 3 de San Francisco, obraron lo mismo que los 12 apostolos en la conversion de todo el universo mundo." Naharro, Relacion Sumaria, MS.

[8] "Todos los conventos de Dominicos i Mercenarios tienen repartimientos. Ninguno dellos ha dotrinado ni convertido un Indio. Procuran sacar dellos quanto pueden, trabajarles en grangerias; con esto i con otras limosnas enriquecen. Mal egemplo. Ademas convendrá no pasen frailes sino precediendo diligente examen de vida i dotrina." (Relacion de las cosas que S. M. deve proveer para los reynos del Peru, embiada desde los Reyes á la Corte por el Licenciado Martel Santoyo, de quien va firmáda en principios de 1542, MS.)

This statement of the licentiate shows a different side of the picture from that above quoted from Father Naharro. Yet they are not irreconcilable. Human nature has both its lights and its shadows.

[9] I have several of these Memorials or *Relaciones,* as they are called, in my possession, drawn up by residents in answer to queries propounded by government. These queries, while their great object is to ascertain the nature of existing abuses, and to invite the suggestion of remedies, are often directed to the laws and usages of the ancient Incas. The responses, therefore, are of great value to the historical inquirer. The most important of these documents in my possession is that by Ondegardo, governor of Cuzco, covering near four hundred folio pages, once forming part of Lord Kingsborough's

valuable colection. It is impossible to peruse these elaborate and conscientious reports without a deep conviction of the pains taken by the Crown to ascertain the nature of the abuses in the domestic government of the colonies, and their honest purpose to amend them. Unfortunately, in this laudable purpose they were not often seconded by the colonists themselves.

[10] The perpetual emancipation of the Indians is urged in the most emphatic manner by another bishop, also a Dominican, but bearing certainly very little resemblance to Las Casas. Fray Valverde makes this one of the prominent topics in a communication, already cited, to the government, the general scope of which must be admitted to do more credit to his humanity than some of the passages recorded of him in history.—"A V. M. representarán alla los conquistadores muchos servicios, dandolos por causa para que los dexen servir de los indios como de esclavos: V. M. se los tiene mui bien pagados en los provechos que han avido desta tierra, y no los ha de pagar con hazer á sus vasallos esclavos." Carta de Valverde al Emperador, MS.

[11] "La loi de Dieu défend de faire le mal pour qu'il en résulte du bien." Œuvres de Las Casas, évêque de Chiapa, trad. par Llorente, (Paris, 1822,) tom. I. p. 251.

[12] It is a curious coincidence, that this argument of Las Casas should have been first published—in a translated form, indeed—by a secretary of the Inquisition, Llorente. The original still remains in MS. It is singular that these volumes, containing the views of this great philanthropist on topics of such interest to humanity, should not have been more freely consulted, or at least cited, by those who have since trod in his footsteps. They are an arsenal from which many a serviceable weapon for the good cause might be borrowed.

[13] The provisions of this celebrated code are to be found, with more or less—generally less —accuracy, in the various contemporary writers. Herrera gives them *in extenso*. Hist. General, dec. 7, lib. 6, cap. 5.

[14] Las Casas pressed the matter home on the royal conscience, by representing that the Papal See conceded the right of conquest to the Spanish sovereigns on the exclusive condition of converting the heathen, and that the Almighty would hold him accountable for the execution of this trust. Œuvres de Las Casas, ubi supra.

[15] Carta de Gonzalo Pizarro a Pedro de Valdivia, MS., desde Los Reyes, 31 de Oct., 1538.— Zarate, Conq. del Peru, lib. 5, cap. 1.—Herrera, Hist. General, dec. 7, lib. 6, cap. 10, 11.

Benalcazar, in a letter to Charles the Fifth, indulges in a strain of invective against the ordinances, which, by stripping the planters of their Indian slaves, must inevitably reduce the country to beggary. Benalcazar was a conqueror, and one of the most respectable of his caste. His argument is a good specimen of the reasoning of his party on this subject, and presents a decided counterblast to that of Las Casas. Carta de Benalcazar al Emperador, MS., desde Cali, 20 de Diciembre, 1544.

[16] Ibid., ubi supra.—Zarate, Conq. del Peru, ubi supra.—Pedro Pizarro, Descub. y Conq., MS.—Carta de Gonzalo Pizarro a Valdivia, MS.—Montesinos, Annales, MS., año 1543.

[17] Carta de Gonzalo Pizarro a Valdivia, MS.—Herrera, Hist. General, dec. 7, lib. 6, cap. 9.— Fernandez, Hist. del Peru, Parte 1, lib. 1, cap. 6.—Zarate, MS.

[18] "Estas y otras cosas le dixo el Licenciado Çarate: que no fueron al gusto del Virey: antes se enojò mucho por ello, y respondio con alguna aspereza: jurando, que auia de executar las ordenanças como en ellas se contenia: sin esperar para ello terminos algunos, ni dilaciones." Fernandez, Hist. del Peru, Parte 1, lib. 1, cap. 6.

[19] Zarate, Conq. del Peru, lib. 5, cap. 2.—Fernandez, Hist. del Peru, ubi supra.—Carta de Gonzalo Pizarro a Valdivia, MS.—Montesinos, Annales, MS., año 1544.

[20] "It was not fair," the viceroy said, "that the country should remain longer in the hands of muleteers and swineherds, (alluding to the origin of the Pizarros,) and he would take measures to restore it to the Crown."

"Que asi me la havia de cortar á mi i á todos los que havian seido notablemente, como el decia, culpados en la batalla de las Salinas i en las diferencias de Almagro, i que una tierra como esta no era justo que estuviese en poder de gente tan vaxa que llamava el á los desta tierra porqueros i arrieros, sino que estuviese toda en la Corona real." Carta de Gonzalo Pizarro a Valdivia, MS.

[21] "Diciendo que no queria nada para si, sino para el beneficio universal, i que por todos havia de poner todas sus fuerças." Herrera, Hist. General, dec. 7, lib. 7, cap. 20.

[22] "Acepté lo por ver que en ello hacia servicio á Dios i á S. M. i gran bien á esta tierra i generalmente á todas las Indias." Carta de Gonzalo Pizarro a Valdivia, MS.

Herrera, Hist. General, dec. 7, lib. 7, cap. 19, 20.—Zarate, Conq. del Peru, lib. 5, cap. 4, 8.—Fernandez, Hist. del Peru, Parte 1, lib. 1, cap. 8.—Carta do Gonzalo Pizarro a Valdivia, MS.—Montesinos, Annales, MS., año 1544.

CHAPTER VIII

[1] "A quien me viniere á quitar mi hacienda, quitarle he la vida." Herrera, Hist. General, dec. 7, lib. 7, cap. 18.

[2] "Entró en la cibdad de Lima á 17 de Mayo de 1544: saliole á recibir todo el pueblo á pie y á caballo dos tiros de ballesta del pueblo, y á la entrada de la cibdad estaba un arco triunfal de verde con las Armas de España, y las de la misma cibdad; estaban le esperando el Regimiento y Justicia, y oficiales del Rey con ropas largas, hasta en pies de carmesi, y un palio del mesmo carmesi aforrado en lo mesmo, con ocho baras guarnecidas de plata y tomaronle debajo todos á pie, cada Regidor y justicia con una bara del palio, y el Virrey en su caballo con las mazas delante tomaronle juramento en un libro misal, y juró de las guardar y cumplir todas sus libertades y provisiones de S. M.; y luego fueron desta manera hasta la iglesia, salieron los clerigos con la cruz á la puerta y le metieron dentro cantando *Te deum laudamus,* y despues que obo dicho su oracion, fué con el cabildo y toda la ciudad á su palacio donde fué recebido y hizo un parlamento breve en que contentó á toda la gente." Relacion de los sucesos del Peru desde que entró el virrey Blasco Nuñez acaecidos en mar y tierra, MS.

[3] "Porque llanamente el confesaba, que asi para su Magestad, como para aquellos Reinos, eran perjudiciales." Zarate, Conq. del Peru, lib. 5, cap. 5.

[4] Fernandez, Hist. del Peru, Parte 1, lib. 1, cap. 2-5.

[5] Zarate, Conq. del Peru, lib. 5, cap. 8.

[6] Herrera, Hist. General, dec. 7, lib. 7, cap. 22.

[7] Pedro Pizarro, Descub. y Conq., MS.—Garcilasso, Com. Real., Parte 2, lib. 4, cap. 7.

[8] Fernandez, Hist. del Peru, Parte 1, lib. 1, cap. 14, 16.—Zarate, Conq. del Peru, lib. 5, cap. 9, 10.—Herrera, Hist. General, dec. 7, lib. 8, cap. 5-9.—Carta de Gonzalo Pizarro a Valdivia, MS.—Relacion de los Sucesos del Peru, MS.

[9] Zarate, Conq. del Peru, lib. 5, cap. 3.—Pedro Pizarro, Descub. y Conq., MS.—Fernandez, Hist. del Peru, Parte 1, lib. 1, cap. 10.

[10] Loaysa, the bishop, was robbed of his despatches, and not even allowed to enter the camp, lest his presence should shake the constancy of the soldiers. (See Relacion de los Sucesos del Peru, MS.) The account occupies more space than it deserves in most of the authorities.

[11] "Hiço hacer gran Copia de Arcabuces, asi de Hierro, como de Fundicion, de ciertas Campanas de la Iglesia Maior, que para ello quitó." Zarate, Conq. del Peru, lib. 5, cap. 6.

[12] Blasco Nuñez paid, according to Zarate, who had the means of knowing, twelve thousand ducats for thirty-five mules.—"El Visorrei les mandó comprar, de la Hacienda Real, treinta i cinco Machos, en que hiciesen la Jornada, que costaron mas de doce mil ducados." (Zarate, Conq. del Peru, lib. 5, cap. 10.) The South-American of our day might well be surprised at such prices for animals since so abundant in his country.

[13] Fernandez, Hist. del Peru, Parte 1, lib. 1, cap. 10.—Herrera, Hist. General, dec. 7, lib. 8, cap. 2, 10.—Carta de Gonzalo Pizarro a Valdivia, MS.

[14] "He struck him in the bosom with his dagger, as some say, but the viceroy denies it."—So says Zarate, in the *printed* copy of his history. (Lib. 5, cap. 11.) In the original manuscript of this work, still extant at Simancas, he states the fact without any qualification at all. "Luego el dicho Virrei echó mano á una daga, i arremetió con él, i le dió una puñalada, i á grandes voces mandó que le matasen." (Zarate, MS.) This was doubtless his honest conviction, when on the spot soon after the event occurred. The politic historian thought it prudent to qualify his remark before publication.—"They say," says another contemporary, familiar with these events and friendly to the viceroy, "that he gave him several wounds with his dagger." And he makes no attempt to refute the charge. (Relacion de los Sucesos del Peru, MS.) Indeed, this version of the story seems to have been generally received at the time by those who had the best means of knowing the truth.

[15] Zarate, Conq. del Peru, ubi supra.

[16] Ibid., lib. 5, cap. 12.—Fernandez, Parte 1, lib. 1, cap. 18.

[17] Relacion de los Sucesos del Peru, MS.—Relacion Anonima, MS.—Pedro Pizarro, Descub. y Conq., MS.—Fernandez, Hist. del Peru, Parte 1, lib. 1, cap. 19.—Zarate, Conq. del Peru, lib. 5, cap. 11.—Carta de Gonzalo Pizarro a Valdivia, MS.

Gonzalo Pizarro devoutly draws a conclusion from this, that the revolution was clearly brought about by the hand of God for the good of the land. "E hizóse sin que muriese un hombre, ni fuese herido, como obra que Dios la guiava para el bien desta tierra." Carta, MS., ubi supra.

[18] Carta de Gonzalo Pizarro a Valdivia, MS.—Relacion de los Sucesos del Peru, MS.

The story of the seizure of the viceroy is well told by the writer of the last MS., who seems here, at least, not unduly biased in favor of Blasco Nuñez, though a partisan.

[19] Zarate, Conq. del Peru, lib. 5, cap. 13.

It required some courage to carry the message of the Audience to Gonzalo and his desperate followers. The historian Zarate, the royal comptroller, was the envoy; not much, as it appears, to his own satisfaction. He escaped, however, unharmed, and has made a full report of the affair in his chronicle.

[20] "Le queria dar su muerte con una preëminencia señalada, que escogiese en qual de las Ramas de aquel Arbol queria que le colgasen." Zarate, Conq. del Peru, lib. 5, cap. 13.— See also Relacion Anonima, MS.—Fernandez, Parte 1, lib. 1, cap. 25.

[21] According to Gonzalo Pizarro, the Audience gave this invitation in obedience to the demands of the representatives of the cities. — "Y á esta sazon llegué yo á Lima, i todos los procuradores de las cibdades destos reynos suplicaron al Audiencia me hiciesen Governador para resistir los robos é fuerzas que Blasco Nuñez andava faciendo, i para tener la tierra en justicia hasta que S. M. proveyese lo que mas á su real servicio convenia. Los Oydores visto que asi convenia al servicio de Dios i al de S. M. i al bien destos reynos," &c. (Carta de Gonzalo Pizarro a Valdivia, MS.) But Gonzalo's account of himself must be received with more than the usual grain of allowance. His letter, which is addressed to Valdivia, the celebrated conqueror of Chili, contains a full account of the rise and progress of his rebellion. It is the best vindication, therefore, to be found of himself, and, as a counterpoise to the narratives of his enemies, is of inestimable value to the historian.

[22] He employed twelve thousand Indians on this service, says the writer of the *Relacion Anónima, MS.* But this author, although living in the colonies at the time, talks too much at random to gain our implicit confidence.

[23] "Y el armado y con una capa de grana cubierta con muchas guarniciones de oro é con sayo de brocado sobre las armas." Relacion de los Sucesos del Peru, MS. — Also Zarate, Conq. del Peru, lib. 5, cap. 13.

[24] For the preceding pages relating to Gonzalo Pizarro, see Relacion Anonima, MS. — Fernandez, Hist. del Peru, Parte 1, lib. 1, cap. 25. — Pedro Pizarro, Descub. y Conq., MS. — Carta de Gonzalo Pizarro a Valdivia, MS. — Zarate, loc. cit. — Herrera, Hist. General, dec. 7, lib. 8, cap. 16-19. — Relacion de los Sucesos del Peru, MS. — Montesinos, Annales, MS., año 1544.

CHAPTER IX

[1] Pedro Pizarro, Descub. y Conq., MS.

The honest soldier, who tells us this, was more true to his king than to his kindred. At least, he did not attach himself to Gonzalo's party, and was among those who barely escaped hanging on this occasion. He seems to have had little respect for his namesake.

[2] Zarate, the judge, must not be confounded with Zarate, the historian, who went out to Peru with the Court of Audience, as *contador real,* royal comptroller, — having before filled the office of secretary of the royal council in Spain.

[3] Gomara, Hist. de las Ind., cap. 172. — Garcilasso, Com. Real., Parte 2, lib. 4, cap. 21.

[4] Zarate, Conq. del Peru, lib. 5, cap. 15. — Relacion Anonima, MS. — Relacion de los Sucesos del Peru, MS. — Montesinos, Annales, MS., año 1545. — Fernandez, Hist. del Peru, Parte 1, lib. 1, cap. 28.

[5] Carta de Gonzalo Pizarro a Valdivia, MS. — Zarate, Conq. del Peru, lib. 5, cap. 14, 15. — Herrera, Hist. General, dec. 7, lib. 8, cap. 19, 20. — Relacion Anonima, MS. — Fernandez, Hist. del Peru, Parte 1, lib. 1, cap. 23. — Relacion de los Sucesos del Peru, MS.

The author of the document last cited notices the strong feeling for the Crown existing in several of the cities; and mentions also the rumor of a meditated assault on Cuzco by the Indians. — The writer belonged to the discomfited party of Blasco Nuñez; and the facility with which exiles credit reports in their own favor is proverbial.

[6] "Mas Francisco Caruajal q̃ los yua siguiendo, llegó quatro horas de la noche á dõde estauan: y con vna Trompeta que lleuaua les tocó arma: y sentido por el Virey se leuantó luego el primero." Fernandez, Hist. del Peru, Parte 1, lib. 1, cap. 40.

[7] Ibid., ubi supra.—Herrera, Hist. General, dec. 7, lib. 9, cap. 22.—Garcilasso, Com. Real., lib. 4, cap. 26.

[8] "Caminando, pues, comiendo algunas Jervas, que cocian en las Celadas, quando paraban à dar aliento a los Caballos." Herrera, Hist. General, dec. 7, lib. 9, cap. 24.

[9] "I sin que en todo el camino los vnos, ni los otros, quitasen las Sillas à los Caballos, aunque en este caso estaba mas alerta la Gente del Visorei, porque si algun pequeño rato de la Noche reposaban, era vestidos, i teniendo siempre los Caballos del Cabestro, sin esperar à poner Toldos, ni à adereçar las otras formas, que se suelen tener para atar los Caballos de Noche." Zarate, Conq. del Peru, lib. 5, cap. 29.

[10] "I en cansandose el Caballo, le desjarretaba, i le dexaba, porque sus contrarios no se aprovechasen de él." Ibid., loc. cit.

[11] "Had it not been for Gonzalo Pizarro's interference," says Fernandez, "many more would have been hung up by his lieutenant, who *pleasantly* quoted the old Spanish proverb,— 'The fewer of our enemies the better.'" *De los enemigos, los menos.* Hist. del Peru, Parte 1, lib. 1, cap. 40.

[12] "Los afligidos Soldados, que por el cansancio de los Caballos iban à pie con terrible angustia, por la persecution de los Enemigos, que iban cerca, i por la fatiga de la hambre, quando vieron los Cuerpos de los dos Capitanes muertos en aquel camino quedaron atonitos." Herrera, Hist. General, dec. 7, lib. 9, cap. 25.

[13] Fernandez, who held a loyal pen, and one sufficiently friendly to the viceroy, after stating that the officers, whom the latter put to death, had served him to that time with their lives and fortunes, dismisses the affair with the temperate reflection, that men formed different judgments on it. "Sobre estas muertes uuo en el Perù varios y contrarios juyzios y opiniones, de culpa y de su descargo." (Hist. del Peru, Parte 1, lib. 1, cap. 41.) Gomara says, more unequivocally, "All condemned it." (Hist. de las Ind., cap. 167.) The weight of opinion seems to have been against the viceroy.

[14] Some of these omens recorded by the historian—as the howling of dogs—were certainly no miracles. "En esta lamentable, i angustiosa partida, muchos afirmaron, haver visto por el Aire muchos Cometas, i que quadrillas de Perros andaban por las Calles, dando grandes i temerosos ahullidos, i los Hombres andaban asombrados, i fuera de si." Herrera, Hist. General, dec. 7, lib. 10, cap. 4.

[15] Ibid., ubi supra.

[16] This retreat of Blasco Nuñez may undoubtedly compare, if not in duration, at least in sharpness of suffering, with any expedition in the New World,—save, indeed, that of Gonzalo Pizarro himself to the Amazon. The particulars of it may be found, with more or less amplification, in Zarate, Conq. del Peru, lib. 5, cap. 19, 29.—Carta de Gonzalo Pizarro a Valdivia, MS.—Herrera, Hist. General, dec. 7, lib. 9, cap. 20-26.—Fernandez, Hist. del Peru, Parte 1, lib. 1, cap. 40, et seq.—Relacion de los Sucesos del Peru, MS.— Relacion Anonima, MS.—Montesinos, Annales, MS. año 1545.

[17] "Proveiò, que se tragese alli todo el hierro que se pudo haver en la Provincia, i buscò Maestros, i hiço adereçar Fraguas, i en breve tiempo se forjaron en ellas docientos Arcabuces, con todos sus aparejos." Zarate, Conq. del Peru, lib. 5, cap. 34.

[18] "Que se llegaron à hablar los Corredores de ambas partes, llamandose Traidores los vnos à los otros, fundando, que cada vno sustentaba la voz del Rei, i asi estuvieron toda aquella noche aguardando." Ibid., ubi supra.

[19] For the preceding pages, see Zarate, Conq. del Peru, lib. 5, cap. 34, 35.—Gomara, Hist. de las Ind., cap. 167.—Carta de Gonzalo Pizarro a Valdivia, MS.—Montesinos, Annales, MS., año 1546.—Fernandez, Hist. del Peru, Parte 1, lib. 1, cap. 50-52.

Herrera, in his account of these transactions, has fallen into a strange confusion of dates, fixing the time of the viceroy's entry into Quito on the 10th of January, and that of his battle with Pizarro nine days later. (Hist. General, dec. 8, lib. 1, cap. 1.) This last event, which, by the testimony of Fernandez, was on the eighteenth of the month, was, by the agreement of such contemporary authorities as I have consulted,—as stated in the text,—on the evening of the same day in which the viceroy entered Quito. Herrera, though his work is arranged on the chronological system of annals, is by no means immaculate as to his dates. Quintana has exposed several glaring anachronisms of the historian in the earlier period of the Peruvian conquest. See his Españoles Celebres, tom. II. Appendix, *No.* 7.

[20] "Yo os prometo, que la primera lâça que se rompa en los enemigos, sea la mia (y assi lo cumplio)." Fernandez, Hist. del Peru, Parte 1, lib. 1, cap. 53.

[21] "Que de Dios es la causa, de Dios es la causa, de Dios es la causa." Zarate, Conq. del Peru, lib. 5, cap. 35.

[22] "Un quarto de legua de la ciudad." Carta de Gonzalo Pizarro a Valdivia, MS.

[23] The amount of the numbers on both sides is variously given, as usual, making, however, more than the usual difference in the relative proportions, since the sum total is so small. I have conformed to the statements of the best-instructed writers. Pizarro estimates his adversary's force at four hundred and fifty men, and his own at only six hundred; an estimate, it may be remarked, that does not make that given in the text any less credible.

[24] Zarate, Conq. del Peru, lib. 5, cap. 35.

[25] He wore this dress, says Garcilasso de la Vega, that he might fare no better than a common soldier, but take his chance with the rest. (Com. Real., Parte 2, lib. 4, cap. 34.) Pizarro gives him credit for no such magnanimous intent. According to him, the viceroy assumed this disguise, that, his rank being unknown, he might have the better chance for escape.—It must be confessed that this is the general motive for a disguise. "I Blasco Nuñez puso mucha diligencia por poder huirse si pudiera, porque venia vestido con una camiseta de Yndios por no ser conocido, i no quiso Dios porque pagase quantos males por su causa se havian hecho." Carta de Gonzalo Pizarro a Valdivia, MS.

[26] Fernandez, Hist. del Peru, Parte 1, lib. 1, cap. 54.—Zarate, Conq. del Peru, lib. 5, cap. 35.

"Mandò à un Negro que traìa, que le cortase la Cabeça, i en todo esto no se conoció flaqueça en el Visorrei, ni hablò palabra, ni hiço mas movimiento, que alçar los ojos al Cielo, dando muestras de mucha Christiandad, i constancia." Herrera, Hist. General, dec. 8, lib. 1, cap. 3.

[27] "Aviendo algunos capitanes y personas arrancado y pelado algunas de sus blancas y leales baruas, para traer por empresa, y Juã de la Torre las traxo despues publicamente en la gorra por la ciudad de los Reyes." Fernandez, Hist. del Peru, Parte 1, lib. 1, cap. 54.

[28] The estimates of killed and wounded in this action are as discordant as usual. Some carry the viceroy's loss to two hundred, while Gonzalo Pizarro rates his own at only seven killed and but a few wounded. But how rarely is it that a faithful bulletin is issued by the parties engaged in the action!

[29] For the accounts of the battle of Añaquito, rather summarily despatched by most writers, see Carta de Gonzalo Pizarro a Valdivia, MS.—Gomara, Hist. de las Ind., cap. 170.—Herrera, Hist. General, dec. 8, lib. 1, cap. 1-3.—Pedro Pizarro, Descub. y Conq., MS.—Zarate, Conq. del Peru, lib. 5, cap. 35.—Montesinos, Annales, MS., año 1546.—Garcilasso, Com. Real., Parte 2, lib. 4, cap. 33-35.—Fernandez, Hist. del Peru, Parte 1, lib. 1, cap. 53, 54.

Gonzalo Pizarro seems to regard the battle as a sort of judicial trial by combat, in which Heaven, by the result, plainly indicated the right. His remarks are edifying. "Por donde parecerá claramente que Nuestro Señor fuè servido este se viniese á meter en las manos para quitarnos de tantos cuidados, i que pagase quantos males havia fecho en la tierra, la qual quedó tan asosegada i tan en paz i servicio de S. M. como lo estuvo en tiempo del Marques mi hermano." Carta de Gonzalo Pizarro a Valdivia, MS.

[30] Garcilasso's reflections on this point are commendably tolerant. "Assi acabò este buen cauallero, por querer porfiar tanto en la execucion de lo que ni a su Rey ni a aquel Reyno conuenia: donde se causaron tantas muertes y daños de Españoles, y de Yndios: aunque no tuuo tanta culpa como se le atribuye, porque lleuó preciso mandato de lo que hizó." Com. Real., Parte 2, lib. 4, cap. 34.

[31] Blasco Nuñez characterized the four judges of the Audience in a manner more concise than complimentary,—a boy, a madman, a booby, and a dunce! "Decia muchas veces Blasco Nuñez, que le havian dado el Emperador, i su Consejo de Indias vn Moço, un Loco, un Necio, vn Tonto por Oìdores, que asi lo havian hecho como ellos eran. Moço era Cepeda, i llamaba Loco a Juan Alvarez, i Necio à Tejada, que no sabia Latin." Gomara, Hist. de las Ind., cap. 171.

[32] The account of Blasco Nuñez Vela rests chiefly on the authority of loyal writers, some of whom wrote after their return to Castile. They would, therefore, more naturally lean to the side of the true representative of the Crown, than to that of the rebel. Indeed, the only voice raised decidedly in favor of Pizarro is his own,—a very suspicious authority. Yet, with all the *prestiges* in his favor, the administration of Blasco Nuñez, from universal testimony, was a total failure. And there is little to interest us in the story of the man, except his unparalleled misfortunes, and the firmness with which he bore them.

[33] "Nunca Piçarro, en ausencia de Francisco de Carvajal, su Maestre de Campo, matò, ni consintió matar Español, sin que todos, los mas de su Consejo, lo aprobasen: i entonces con Proceso en forma de Derecho, i confesados primero." Gomara, Hist. de las Ind., cap. 172.

[34] Ibid., ubi supra.—Fernandez gives a less favorable picture of Gonzalo's administration. (Hist. del Peru, Parte 1, lib. 1, cap. 54; lib. 2, cap. 13.) Fernandez wrote at the instance of the Court; Gomara, though present at court, wrote to please himself. The praise of Gomara is less suspicious than the censure of Fernandez.

[35] "Victorioso Principe, hagate Dios dichoso, i bienaventurado, èl te mantenga, i te conserve." Herrera, Hist. General, dec. 8, lib. 2, cap. 9.

[36] For an account of this pageant, see Pedro Pizarro, Descub. y Conq., MS.—Herrera, Hist. General, dec. 8, lib. 2, cap. 9.—Zarate, Conq. del Peru, lib. 6, cap. 5.—Carta de Gonzalo Pizarro a Valdivia, MS.

[37] *Poblando los arboles con sus cuerpos,* "peopling the trees with their bodies," says Fernandez, strongly; alluding to the manner in which the ferocious officer hung up his captives on the branches.

[38] For the expedition of Carbajal, see Herrera, Hist. General, dec. 8, lib. 1, cap. 9, et seq.—Zarate, Conq. del Peru, lib. 6, cap. 1.—Garcilasso, Com. Real., Parte 2, lib. 4, cap. 28, 29, 36, 39.—Fernandez, Hist. del Peru, Parte 1, lib. 2, cap. 1, et seq.—Carta de Gonzalo Pizarro a Valdivia, MS.

It is impossible to give, in a page or two, any adequate idea of the hairbreadth escapes and perilous risks of Carbajal, not only from the enemy, but from his own men, whose strength he overtasked in the chase. They rival those of the renowned Scanderbeg, or our own Kentucky hero, Colonel Boone. They were, indeed, far more wonderful than theirs, since the Spanish captain had reached an age when the failing energies usually crave repose. But the veteran's body seems to have been as insensible as his soul.

[39] The vein now discovered at Potosí was so rich, that the other mines were comparatively deserted in order to work this. (Zarate, Conq. del Peru, lib. 6, cap. 4.) The effect of the sudden influx of wealth was such, according to Garcilasso, that in ten years from this period an iron horseshoe, in that quarter, came to be worth nearly its weight in silver. Com. Real., Parte 1, lib. 8, cap. 24.

[40] "Traia Guarda de ochenta Alabarderos, i otros muchos de Caballo, que le acompañaban, i ià en su presencia ninguno se sentaba, i à mui pocos quitaba la Gorra." Zarate, Conq. del Peru, lib. 6, cap. 5.

[41] Garcilasso, Com. Real., Parte 2, lib. 4, cap. 42.

Garcilssso had opportunities of personal acquaintance with Gonzalo's manner of living; for, when a boy, he was sometimes admitted, as he tells us, to a place at his table. This courtesy, so rare from the Conquerors to any of the Indian race, was not lost on the historian of the Incas, who has depicted Gonzalo Pizarro in more favorable colors than most of his own countrymen.

[42] Ibid., Parte 2, lib. 4, cap. 40.—Gomara, Hist. de las Ind., cap. 172.—Fernandez, Hist. del Peru, Parte 1, lib. 2, cap. 13.

The poet Molina has worked up this scene between Carbajal and his commander with good effect, in his *Amazonas en las Indias,* where he uses something of a poet's license in the homage he pays to the modest merits of Gonzalo. Julius Cæsar himself was not more magnanimous.

> "Sepa mi Rey, sepa España,
> Que muero por no ofendería,
> Tan facil de conservarla,
> Que pierdo por no agraviarla,
> Quanto infame en poseerla,
> Una Corona ofrecida."

Among the biographical notices of the writers on Spanish colonial affairs, the name of Herrera, who has done more for this vast subject than any other author, should certainly not be omitted. His account of Peru takes its proper place in his great work, the *Historia General de las Indias,* according to the chronological plan on which that history is arranged. But as it suggests reflections not different in character from those suggested by other portions of the work, I shall take the liberty to refer the reader to the Postscript to Book Third of the *Conquest of Mexico,* for a full account of these volumes and their learned author.

Another chronicler, to whom I have been frequently indebted in the progress of the narrative, is Francisco Lopez de Gomara. The reader will also find a notice of this author in the *Conquest of Mexico,* Vol. III. Book 5, Postscript. But as the remarks on his writings are there confined to his *Crónica de Nueva España,* it may be well to add here some reflections on his greater work, *Historia de las Indias,* in which the Peruvian story bears a conspicuous part.

The "History of the Indies" is intended to give a brief view of the whole range of Spanish conquest in the islands and on the American continent, as far as had been achieved by the middle of the sixteenth century. For this account, Gomara, though it does not appear that he ever visited the New World, was in a situation that opened to him the best means of information. He was well acquainted with the principal men of the time, and gathered the details of their history from their own lips; while, from his residence at court, he was in possession of the state of opinion there, and of the impression made by passing events on those most competent to judge of them. He was thus enabled to introduce into his work many interesting particulars, not to be found in other records of the period. His range of inquiry extended beyond the mere doings of the Conquerors, and led him to a survey of the general resources of the countries he describes, and especially of their physical aspect and productions. The conduct of his work, no less than its diction, shows the cultivated scholar, practised in the art of composition. Instead of the *naïveté,* engaging, but childlike, of the old military chroniclers, Gomara handles his various topics with the shrewd and piquant criticism of a man of the world; while his descriptions are managed with a comprehensive brevity that forms the opposite to the long-winded and rambling paragraphs of the monkish annalist. These literary merits, combined with the knowledge of the writer's opportunities for information, secured his productions from the oblivion which too often awaits the unpublished manuscript; and he had the satisfaction to see them pass into more than one edition in his own day. Yet they do not bear the highest stamp of authenticity. The author too readily admits accounts into his pages which are not supported by contemporary testimony. This he does, not from credulity, for his mind rather leans in an opposite direction, but from a want, apparently, of the true spirit of historic conscientiousness. The imputation of carelessness in his statements—to use a temperate phrase—was brought against Gomara in his own day; and Garcilasso tells us, that, when called to account by some of the Peruvian cavaliers for misstatements which bore hard on themselves, the historian made but an awkward explanation. This is a great blemish on his productions, and renders them of far less value to the modern compiler, who seeks for the well of truth undefiled, than many an humbler but less unscrupulous chronicle.

There is still another authority used in this work, Gonzalo Fernandez de Oviedo, of whom I have given an account elsewhere; and the reader curious in the matter will permit me to refer him for a critical notice of his life and writings to the *Conquest of Mexico,* Book 4, Postscript.—His account of Peru is incorporated into his great work, *Natural é General Historia de las Indias, MS.,* where it forms the forty-sixth and forty-seventh books. It extends from Pizarro's landing at Tumbez to Almagro's return from Chili, and thus covers the entire portion of what may be called the conquest of the country. The style of its execution, corresponding with that of the residue of the work to which it belongs, affords no ground for criticism different from that already passed on the general character of Oviedo's writings.

545

This eminent person was at once a scholar and a man of the world. Living much at court, and familiar with persons of the highest distinction in Castile, he yet passed much of his time in the colonies, and thus added the fruits of personal experience to what he had gained from the reports of others. His curiosity was indefatigable, extending to every department of natural science, as well as to the civil and personal history of the colonists. He was, at once, their Pliny and their Tacitus. His works abound in portraitures of character, sketched with freedom and animation. His reflections are piquant, and often rise to a philosophic tone, which discards the usual trammels of the age; and the progress of the story is varied by a multiplicity of personal anecdotes, that give a rapid insight into the characters of the parties.

With his eminent qualifications, and with a social position that commanded respect, it is strange that so much of his writings—the whole of his great *Historia de las Indias,* and his curious *Quincuagenas*—should be so long suffered to remain in manuscript. This is partly chargeable to the caprice of fortune; for the History was more than once on the eve of publication, and is even now understood to be prepared for the press. Yet it has serious defects, which may have contributed to keep it in its present form. In its desultory and episodical style of composition, it resembles rather notes for a great history, than history itself. It may be regarded in the light of commentaries, or as illustrations of the times. In that view his pages are of high worth, and have been frequently resorted to by writers who have not too scrupulously appropriated the statements of the old chronicler, with slight acknowledgments to their author.

It is a pity that Oviedo should have shown more solicitude to tell what was new, than to ascertain how much of it was strictly true. Among his merits will scarcely be found that of historical accuracy. And yet we may find an apology for this, to some extent, in the fact, that his writings, as already intimated, are not so much in the nature of finished compositions, as of loose memoranda, where every thing, rumor as well as fact,—even the most contradictory rumors,—are all set down at random, forming a miscellaneous heap of materials, of which the discreet historian may avail himself to rear a symmetrical fabric on foundations of greater strength and solidity.

Another author worthy of particular note is Pedro Cieza de Leon. His *Crónica del Peru* should more properly be styled an Itinerary, or rather Geography, of Peru. It gives a minute topographical view of the country at the time of the Conquest; of its provinces and towns, both Indian and Spanish; its flourishing sea-coast; its forests, valleys, and interminable ranges of mountains in the interior; with many interesting particulars of the existing population,—their dress, manners, architectural remains, and public works, while, scattered here and there, may be found notices of their early history and social polity. It is, in short, a lively picture of the country in its physical and moral relations, as it met the eye at the time of the Conquest, and in that transition period when it was first subjected to European influences. The conception of a work, at so early a period, on this philosophical plan, reminding us of that of Malte-Brun in our own time,—*parva componere magnis,*—was, of itself, indicative of great comprehensiveness of mind in its author. It was a task of no little difficulty, where there was yet no pathway opened by the labors of the antiquarian; no hints from the sketchbook of the traveller, or the measurements of the scientific explorer. Yet the distances from place to place are all carefully jotted down by the industrious compiler, and the bearings of the different places and their peculiar features are exhibited with sufficient precision, considering the nature of the obstacles he had to encounter. The literary execution of the work, moreover, is highly respectable, sometimes even rich and picturesque; and the author describes the grand and beautiful scenery of the Cordilleras with a sensibility to its charms, not often found in the tasteless topographer, still less often in the rude Conqueror.

Cieza de Leon came to the New World, as he informs us, at the early age of thirteen. But it is not till Gasca's time that we find his name enrolled among the actors in the busy scenes of civil strife, when he accompanied the president in his campaign against Gonzalo Pizarro. His Chronicle, or, at least, the notes for it, was compiled in such leisure as he could snatch from his more stirring avocations; and after ten years from the time he undertook it, the First Part—all we have—was completed in 1550, when the author had reached only the age of thirty-two. It appeared at Seville in 1553, and the following year at Antwerp; while an Italian translation, printed at Rome, in 1555, attested the rapid celebrity of the work. The edition of Antwerp—the one used by me in this compilation—is in the duodecimo form, exceedingly well printed, and garnished with wood-cuts, in which Satan,—for the author had a full measure of the ancient credulity,—with his usual bugbear accompaniments, frequently appears in bodily presence. In the Preface, Cieza announces his purpose to continue the work in three other parts, illustrating respectively the ancient history of the country under the Incas, its conquest by the Spaniards, and the civil wars which ensued. He even gives, with curious minuteness, the contents of the several books of the projected history. But the First Part, as already noticed, was alone completed; and the author, having returned to Spain, died there in 1560, at the premature age of forty-two, without having covered any portion of the magnificent ground-plan which he had thus confidently laid out. The deficiency is much to be regretted, considering the talent of the writer, and his opportunities for personal observation. But he has done enough to render us grateful for his labors. By the vivid delineation of scenes and scenery, as they were presented fresh to his own eyes, he has furnished us with a background to the historic picture,—the landscape, as it were, in which the personages of the time might be more fitly portrayed. It would have been impossible to exhibit the ancient topography of the land so faithfully at a subsequent period, when old things had passed away, and the Conqueror, breaking down the landmarks of ancient civilization, had effaced many of the features even of the physical aspect of the country, as it existed under the elaborate culture of the Incas.

BOOK V

CHAPTER I

[1] "Que aquello era contra una cédula que tenian del Emperador que les daba el repartimiento de los indios de su vida, y del hijo mayor, y no teniendo hijos á sus mugeres, con mandarles espresamente que se casasen como lo habian ya hecho los mas de ellos; y que tambien era contra otra cédula real que ninguno podia ser despojado de sus indios sin ser primero oido á justicia y condenado." Historia de Don Pedro Gasca, Obispo de Siguenza, MS.

[2] MS. de Caravantes.—Hist. de Don Pedro Gasca, MS.

One of this council was the great Duke of Alva, of such gloomy celebrity afterwards in the Netherlands. We may well believe his voice was for coercion.

[3] "Ventilose la forma del remedio de tan grave caso en que huvo dos opiniones; la una de imbiar un gran soldado con fuerza de gente á la demostracion de este castigo; la otra que se llevase el negocio por prudentes y suaves medios, por la imposibilidad y falto de dinero para llevar gente, cavallos, armas, municiones y vastimentos, y para sustentarlos en tierra firme y pasarlos al Pirú." MS. de Caravantes.

[4] "Pasando á España vinieron á tierra de Avila y quedó del nombre dellos el lugar y familia de Gasca; madandose por la afinidad de la pronunciacion, que hay entre las dos letras consonantes *c. y. g.* el nombre de Casca en Gasca." Hist. de Don Pedro Gasca, MS.

Similarity of name is a peg quite strong enough to hang a pedigree upon in Castile.

[5] This account of the early history of Gasca I have derived chiefly from a manuscript biographical notice written in 1465, during the prelate's life. The name of the author, who speaks apparently from personal knowledge, is not given; but it seems to be the work of a scholar, and is written with a certain pretension to elegance. The original MS. forms part of the valuable collection of Don Pascual de Gayangos of Madrid. It is of much value for the light it throws on the early career of Gasca, which has been passed over in profound silence by Castilian historians. It is to be regretted that the author did not continue his labors beyond the period when the subject of them received his appointment to the Peruvian mission.

[6] "Era tanta la opinion que en Valencia tenian de la integridad y prudencia de Gasca, que en las Cortes de Monzon los Estados de aquel Reyno le pidieron por Visitador contra la costumbre y fuero de aquel Reyno, que no puede serlo sino fuere natural de la Corona de Araugon, y consintiendo que aquel fuero se derogase el Emperador lo concedió á instancia y peticion dellos." Hist. de Don Pedro Gasca, MS.

[7] "Que parece cierto," says his enthusiastic biographer, "que por disposicion Divina vino á hallarse Gasca entónces en la Ciudad de Valencia, para remedio de aquel Reyno y Islas de Mallorca y Menorca é Iviza, segun la órden, prevencion y diligencia que en la defensa contra las armadas del Turco y Francia tuvo, y las provisiones que para ello hizo." Hist. de Don Pedro Gasca, MS.

[8] "Finding a lion would not answer, they sent a lamb," says Gomara; — "Finalmente, quiso embiar una Oveja, pues un Leon no aprovecho; y asi escogiò al Licenciado Pedro Gasca." Hist. de las Ind., cap. 174.

[9] Gasca made what the author calls *una breve y copyosa relacion* of the proceedings to the emperor in Valencia; and the monarch was so intent on the inquiry, that he devoted the whole afternoon to it, notwithstanding his son Philip was waiting for him to attend a *fiesta!* irrefragable proof, as the writer conceives, of his zeal for the faith.—"Queriendo entender muy de raizo todo lo que pasaba, como Principe tan zeloso que era de las cosas de la religion." Hist. de Don Pedro Gasca, MS.

[10] These instructions, the patriarchal tone of which is highly creditable to the government, are given *in extenso* in the MS. of Caravantes, and in no other work which I have consulted.

[11] "De suerte que juzgassen que la mas fuerça que lleuaua, era su abito de clerigo y breuiario." Fernandez, Hist. del Peru, Parte 1, lib. 2, cap. 16.

[12] MS. de Caravantes.—Hist. de Don Pedro Gasca, MS.—Fernandez, Hist. del Peru, Parte 1, lib. 2, cap. 16, 17.

Though not for himself, Gasca did solicit one favor of the emperor,—the appointment of his brother, an eminent jurist, to a vacant place on the bench of one of the Castilian tribunals.

[13] Zarate, Conq. del Peru, lib. 6, cap. 6.—Herrera, Hist. General, dec. 8, lib. 1, cap. 6.—
MS. de Caravantes.—Fernandez, Hist. del Peru, Parte 1, lib. 2, cap. 17, 18.—Gomara,
Hist. de las Ind., cap. 174.—Hist. de Don Pedro Gasca, MS.

[14] "Especialmente, si alla muriesse ó le matassen: que entôces de nada le podria ser buena,
sino para partir desta vida, con mas congoxa y pena de la poca cuenta que daua de la
prouision que auia aceptado." Fernandez, Hist. de Peru, Parte 1, lib. 2, cap. 18.

[15] From this cavalier descended the noble house of the counts of Villamor in Spain.
MS. de Caravantes.

[16] Fernandez, Hist. del Peru, Parte 1, lib. 2, cap. 21.

[17] "Especialmente muchos de los soldados, que estauan desacatados, y decian palabras feas,
y desuergõçadas. A lo qual el Presidente (viendo que era necessario) hazia las orejas sor-
das." Ibid., Parte 1, lib. 2, cap. 23.

[18] Ibid., ubi supra.—Carta de Gonzalo Pizarro a Valdivia, MS.—Montesinos, Annales,
MS., año 1546.—Zarate, Conq. del Peru, lib. 6, cap. 6.—Herrera, Hist. General, dec.
8, lib. 2, cap. 5.

[19] Fernandez, Hist. del Peru, Parte 1, lib. 2, cap. 25.—Zarate, Conq. del Peru, lib. 6, cap. 7.
—MS. de Caravantes.

[20] "El Licenciado Cepeda que tengo yo agora por teniente, de quien yo hago mucho caso i
le quiero mucho." Carta de Gonzalo Pizarro a Valdivia, MS.

[21] The letters noticed in the text may be found in Zarate, Conq. del Peru, lib. 6, cap. 7, and
Fernandez, Hist. del Peru, Parte 1, lib. 2, cap. 29, 30. The president's letter covers several
pages. Much of it is taken up with historic precedents and illustrations, to show the folly,
as well as wickedness, of a collision with the imperial authority. The benignant tone of
this homily may be inferred from its concluding sentence; "Nuestro señor por su infinita
bõdad alumbre a vuestra merced, y a todos los demas para que acierten a hazer en este
negocio lo que cõuiene a sus almas, honras, vidas y haziendas: y guarde en su sancto servicio la Illustre persona de vuestra merced."

[22] Fernandez, Hist. del Peru, Parte 1, lib. 2, cap. 27.—Herrera, Hist. General, dec. 8, lib. 2,
cap. 7.—MS. de Caravantes.

[23] "Y con esto, estaua siempre en fiestas y recozijo, holgandose mucho que le diessen musi-
cas, cantando romances, y coplas, de todo lo que auia hecho: encaresciendo sus hazañas,
y victorias. En lo qual mucho se deleytaua como hombre de gruesso entẽdimiento."
Fernandez, Hist. del Peru, Parte 1, lib. 2, cap. 32.

[24] Gonzalo, in his letter to Valdivia, speaks of Gasca as a clergyman of a godly reputation,
who, without recompense, in the true spirit of a missionary, had come over to settle the
affairs of the country. "Dicen ques mui buen christiano i hombre de buena vida i clerigo,
i dicen que viene a estas partes con buena intencion i no quiso salario ninguno del Rey
sino venir para poner paz en estos reynos con sus cristiandades." Carta de Gonzalo
Pizarro a Valdivia, MS.

[25] "Porque perdõ ninguno de nosotros le pide, porque no entendemos que emos errado,
sino seruido à su Magestad: conseruãdo nuestro derecho; que por sus leyes Reales à sus
vasallos es permitido." Fernandez, Hist. del Peru, Parte 1, lib. 2, cap. 33.

[26] "Porque el por sus virtudes es muy amado de todos: y tenido por padre del Perú"
Ibid., ubi supra.

[27] Ibid., loc. cit.—Herrera, Hist. General, dec. 8, lib. 2, cap. 10.—Zarate, Conq. del Peru, lib. 6, cap. 8.—Gomara, Hist. de las Ind., cap. 177.—Montesinos, Annales, MS., año 1546.

Pizarro, in his letter to Valdivia, notices this remonstrance to Gasca, who, with all his *reputation as a saint, was as deep as any man in Spain,* and had now come to send him home, as a reward, no doubt, of his faithful services. "But I and the rest of the cavaliers," he concludes, "have warned him not to set foot here." "Y agora que yo tenia puesta esta tierra en sosiego embiava su parte al de la Gasca, que aunque arriba digo que dicen ques un santo, es un hombre mas mañoso que havia en toda España é mas sabio; é asi venia por presidente é Governador, é todo quanto el quiera; é para poderme embiar á mi á España, i á cabo de dos años que andavamos fuera de nuestras casas queria el Rey darme este pago, mas yo con todos los cavalleros deste Reyno le embiavamos á decir que se vaya, sino que harémos con él como con Blasco Nuñez." Carte de Gonzalo Pizarro a Valdivia, MS.

[28] With Aldana's mission to Castile Gonzalo Pizarro closes the important letter, so often cited in these pages, and which may be supposed to furnish the best arguments for his own conduct. It is a curious fact, that Valdivia, the conqueror of Chili, to whom the epistle is addressed, soon after this openly espoused the cause of Gasca, and his troops formed part of the forces who contended with Pizarro, not long afterwards, at Huarina. Such was the friend on whom Gonzalo relied!

[29] Pedro Pizarro, Descub. y Conq., MS.—Zarate, Conq. del Peru, lib. 6, cap. 9.—Fernandez, Hist. del Peru, Parte 1, lib. 2, cap. 38, 42.—Gomara, Hist. de las Indias, cap. 178.—MS. de Caravantes.

Garcilasso de la Vega,—whose partiality for Gonzalo Pizarro forms a wholesome counterpoise to the unfavorable views taken of his conduct by most other writers,—in his notice of this transaction, seems disposed to allow little credit to that loyalty which is shown by the sacrifice of a benefactor. Com. Real., Parte 2, lib. 5, cap. 4.

CHAPTER II

[1] "Y ponia sus fuerças con tanta llaneza y obediencia, que los Obispos y clerigos y los capitanes y mas principales personas eran los que primero echauan mano, y tirauan de las gumenas y cables de los nauios, para los sacar à la costa." Fernandez, Hist. del Peru, Parte 1, lib. 2, cap. 70.

[2] Ibid., ubi supra.—Montesinos, Annales, MS., año 1546.—Gomara, Hist. de las Ind., cap. 178.—Zarate, Conq. del Peru, lib. 6, cap. 9.—Herrera, Hist. General, dec. 8, lib. 3, cap. 3.

[3] "Que eran mas de temer aquellas cartas que a las lâças del Rey de Castilla." Fernandez, Hist. del Peru Parte 1, lib. 2, cap. 45.

[4] "Y le enladrillen los caminos por do viniere con barras de plata, y tejos de Oro." Garcilasso, Com. Real., Parte 2, lib. 5, cap. 5.

[5] "Que no lo embiauan por hombre sencillo y llano, sino de grandes cautelas, astucias, falsedades y engaños." Ibid., loc. cit.

[6] "Por lo demas, quãdo acaezca otra cosa, ya yo he viuido muchos años, y tengo tan buẽ palmo de pescueço para la soga, como cada uno de vuesas mercedes." Ibid., loc. cit.

[7] "Loca y luciferina soberuia," as Fernandez characterizes the aspiring temper of Gonzalo. Hist. del Peru, Parte 1, lib. 2, cap. 15.

[8] MS. de Caravantes.

According to Garcilasso, Paniagua was furnished with secret instructions by the president, empowering him, in case he judged it necessary to the preservation of the royal authority, to confirm Pizarro in the government, "it being little matter if the Devil ruled there, provided the country remained to the Crown!" The fact was so reported by Paniagua, who continued in Peru after these events. (Com. Real., Parte 2, lib. 5, cap. 5.) This is possible. But it is more probable that a credulous gossip, like Garcilasso, should be in error, than that Charles the Fifth should have been prepared to make such an acknowledgment of his imbecility, or that the man selected for Gasca's confidence should have so indiscreetly betrayed his trust.

[9] Pedro Pizarro, Descub. y Conq., MS.—Zarate, Conq. del Peru, lib. 6, cap. 11, 13.—Fernandez, Hist. del Peru, Parte 1, lib. 2, cap. 45, 59.—Montesinos, Annales, MS., año 1547.

[10] "Mil Hombres tan bien armados i adereçados, como se han visto en Italia, en la maior prosperidad, porque ninguno havia, demas de las Armas, que no llevase Calças, i Jubon de Seda, i muchos de Tela de Oro, i de Brocado, i otros bordados, i recamados de Oro, i Plata, con mucha Chaperia de Oro por los Sombreros, i especialmente por Frascos, i Caxas de Arcubuces." Zarate, Conq. del Peru, lib. 6, cap. 11.

[11] Ibid., ubi supra.

Some writers even assert that Pizarro was preparing for his coronation at this time, and that he had actually despatched his summons to the different towns to send their deputies to assist at it. "Queria apresurar su coronacion, y para ello despachó cartas á todas las ciudades del Perú." (Montesinos, Annales, MS., año 1547.) But it is hardly probable he could have placed so blind a confidence in the colonists at this crisis, as to have meditated so rash a step. The loyal Castilian historians are not slow to receive reports to the discredit of the *rebel*.

[12] "El qual en este tiempo, oluidado de lo que conuenia a sus letras, y profession, y officio de Oydor; salio en calças jubon, y cuera, de muchos recamados: y gorra con plumas." Fernandez, Hist. del Peru, Parte 1, lib. 2, cap. 62.

[13] Ibid., ubi supra.—Zarate, Conq. del Peru, lib. 6, cap. 11.—Herrera, Hist. General, dec. 8, lib. 3, cap. 5.—Montesinos, Annales, año 1547.

[14] Fernandez, Parte 1, lib. 2, cap. 62.—Montesinos, Annales, MS., año 1547.

[15] Gomara, Hist. de las Ind., cap. 172.

[16] "Andaba la Gente tan asombrada con el temor de la muerte, que no se podian entender, ni terian animo para huir, i algunos, que hallaron mejor aparejo, se escondieron por los Cañaverales, i Cuevas, enterrando sus Haciendas." Zarate, Conq. del Peru, lib. 6, cap. 15.

[17] Rel. Anonima, MS.—Montesinos, Annales, MS., año 1547. "Assi mismo echó Gōzalo Piçarro a toda la plata que gastaua y destribuya su marca, que era una G. rebuelta en una P. y pregonò que so pena de muerte, todos recibiessen por plata fina la que tuuiesse aquella marca: sin ensayo, ni otra diligencia alguna. Y desta suerte hizo passar mucha plata de ley baja por fina." Fernandez, Hist. del Peru, Parte 1, lib. 2, cap. 62.

[18] "Riose mucho entonces Caruajal y dixo; que segū auia hecho la instancia, que auia entendido, que la justicia como rayo, auia de yr luego a justiciarlos. Y dezia que si el los tuuiesse presos, no se le daria vn clauo por su sentēcia, ni firmas." (Ibid., Parte 1, lib. 2, cap. 55.) Among the jurists in Lima who thus independently resisted Cepeda's requisition to sign the paper was the Licentiate Polo Ondegardo, a man of much discretion, and one of the best authorities for the ancient institutions of the Incas.

[19] Pedro Pizarro, Descub. y Conq., MS.—Fernandez, Hist. del Peru, Parte 1, lib. 2, cap. 61.
—Montesinos, Annales, MS., año 1547.—Zarate, Conq. del Peru, lib. 6, cap. 11, 14.

[20] "Entre otras cosas dixo a Gonçalo Pizarro vuesa Señoria mandò quemar cinco angeles que tenia en su puerto para guarda y defensa de la costa del Peru." Garcilasso, Parte 2, lib. 5, cap. 6.

[21] Pedro Pizarro, Descub. y Conq., MS.—Gomara, Hist. de las Ind., cap. 180.—Fernandez, Hist. del Peru, Parte 1, lib. 2, cap. 63, 65.—Zarate, Conq. del Peru, lib. 6, cap. 15, 16.

[22] "Estos mis Cabellicos, Madre,

Dos a dos me los lleva el Aire."

Gomara, Hist. de las Ind., cap. 180.

[23] "Aunque siempre dijo: que con diez Amigos que le quedasen, havia de conservarse, i conquistar de nuevo el Perù: tanta era su saña, ò su sobervia." Ibid., loc. cit.

[24] "Y los truenos y relãpagos eran tantos y tales; que siempre parecia que estauan en llamas, y que sobre ellos venian Rayos (que en todas aquellas partes caen muchos)." (Fernandez, Hist. del Peru, Parte 1, lib. 2, cap. 71.) The vivid coloring of the old chronicler shows that he had himself been familiar with these tropical tempests on the Pacific.

[25] "Y con lo poco que en aquella sazon, el Presidente estimaua la vida si no auia de hazer la jornada: y el gran desseo que tenia de hazerla se puso cõtra ellos diziendo, que qual quiera que le tocasse en abaxar vela, le costaria la vida." Fernandez, Parte 1, lib. 2, cap. 71.

[26] The phosphoric lights, sometimes seen in a storm at sea, were observed to hover round the masts and rigging of the president's vessel; and he amused the seamen, according to Fernandez, by explaining the phenomenon, and telling the fables to which they had given rise in ancient mythology.—This little anecdote affords a key to Gasca's popularity with even the humblest classes.

[27] For the preceding pages, see Pedro Pizarro, Descub. y Conq., MS.—Zarate, Conq. del Peru, lib. 7, cap. 1.—Herrera, Hist. General, dec. 8, lib. 3, cap. 14, et seq.—Fernandez, Hist. del Peru, Parte 1, lib. 2, cap. 71-77.—MS. de Caravantes.

This last writer, who held an important post in the department of colonial finance, had opportunities of information which have enabled him to furnish several particulars not to be met with elsewhere, respecting the principal actors in these turbulent times. His work, still in manuscript, which formerly existed in the archives of the University of Salamanca, has been transferred to the King's library at Madrid.

[28] Pedro Pizarro, Descub. y Conq., MS.—Garcilasso, Com. Real., Parte 2, lib. 5, cap. 16.—Zarate, Conq. del Peru, lib. 7.

[29] In the estimate of Centeno's forces,—which ranges, in the different accounts, from seven hundred to twelve hundred,—I have taken the intermediate number of a thousand adopted by Zarate, as, on the whole, more probable than either extreme.

[30] *Flor de la milicia del Peru,* says Garcilasso de la Vega, who compares Carbajal to an expert chess-player, disposing his pieces in such a manner as must infallibly secure him the victory. Com. Real., Parte 2, lib. 5, cap. 18.

[31] Garcilasso, Com. Real., ubi supra.

The historian's father—of the same name with himself—was one of the few noble cavaliers who remained faithful to Gonzalo Pizarro, in the wane of his fortunes. He was present at the battle of Huarina; and the particulars which he gave his son enabled the latter to supply many deficiencies in the reports of historians.

[32] "A las manos, á las manos: á ellos, á ellos." Fernandez, Hist. del Peru, Parte 1, lib. 2, cap. 79.

[33] Garcilasso, Com. Real., ubi supra.

[34] "Los de Diego Centeno, como yuan con la pujança de vna carrera larga, lleuaron a los de Gonçalo Piçarro de encuentro, y los tropellaron como si fueran ouejas, y cayeron cauallos y caualleros." Ibid., Parte 2, lib. 5, cap. 19.

[35] Cepeda's wound laid open his nose, leaving so hideous a scar that he was obliged afterwards to cover it with a patch, as Garcilasso tells us, who frequently saw him in Cuzco.

[36] According to most authorities, Pizarro's horse was not only wounded but slain in the fight, and the loss was supplied by his friend Garcilasso de la Vega, who mounted him on his own. This timely aid to the rebel did no service to the generous cavalier in after times, but was urged against him by his enemies as a crime. The fact is stoutly denied by his son, the historian, who seems anxious to relieve his father from this honorable imputation, which threw a cloud over both their fortunes. Ibid., Parte 2, lib. 5, cap. 23.

[37] The booty amounted to no less than one million four hundred thousand *pesos*, according to Fernandez. "El saco que vuo fue grande: que se dixo ser de mas de vn millon y quatrociētos mil pesos." (Hist. del Peru, Parte 1, lib. 2, cap. 79.) The amount is, doubtless, grossly exaggerated. But we get to be so familiar with the golden wonders of Peru, that, like the reader of the "Arabian Nights," we become of too easy faith to resort to the vulgar standard of probability.

[38] "La mas sangrienta batalla que vuo en el Perù." Ibid., loc. cit.

In the accounts of this battle there are discrepancies, as usual, which the historian must reconcile as he can. But on the whole, there is a general conformity in the outline and in the prominent points. All concur in representing it as the bloodiest fight that had yet occurred between the Spaniards in Peru, and all assign to Carbajal the credit of the victory.—For authorities, besides Garcilasso and Fernandez, repeatedly quoted, see Pedro Pizarro, Descub. y Conq., MS. (He was present in the action.)—Zarate, Conq. del Peru, lib. 7, cap. 3.—Herrera, Hist. General, dec. 8, lib. 4, cap. 2.—Gomara, Hist. de las Indias, cap. 181.—Montesinos, Annales, MS., año 1547.

[39] Pedro Pizarro, Descub. y Conq., MS.—Fernandez, Hist. del Peru, ubi supra.—Zarate, lib. 7, cap. 3.—Garcilasso, Com. Real., Parte 2, lib. 5, cap. 21, 22.

[40] Ibid., Parte 2, lib. 5, cap. 27.—Pedro Pizarro, Descub. y Conq., MS.—Zarate, Conq. del Peru, lib. 7, cap. 3.

Garcilasso de la Vega, who was a boy at the time, witnessed Pizarro's entry into Cuzco. He writes, therefore, from memory; though after an interval of many years. In consequence of his father's rank, he had easy access to the palace of Pizarro; and this portion of his narrative may claim the consideration due not merely to a contemporary, but to an eyewitness.

CHAPTER III

[1] "Y salio a la Ciudad de los Reyes, sin que Carbajal, ni alguno de los suyos supiesse por donde fue, sino que parecio encantamiento." Garcilasso, Com. Real., Parte 2, lib. 5, cap. 22.

[2] Gasca, according to Ondegardo, supported his army, during his stay at Xauxa, from the Peruvian granaries in the valley, as he found a quantity of maize still remaining in them sufficient for several years' consumption. It is passing strange that these depositaries

should have been so long respected by the hungry Conquerors. — "Cuando el Señor Presidente Gasca passó con la gente de castigo de Gonzalo Pizarro por el Valle de Jauja, estuvo alli siete semanas á lo que me acuerdo, se hallaron en deposito maiz de cuatro y de tres y de dos años mas de 15,000 hanegas junto al camino, é alli comió la gente." Ondegardo, Rel. Seg., MS.

[3] Zarate, Conq. del Peru, lib. 7, cap. 4.—Fernandez, Hist. del Peru, Parte 1, lib. 2, cap. 82-85.—Pedro Pizarro, Descub. y Conq., MS.—Cieza do Leon, cap. 90.

[4] At least, so says Valdivia in his letter to the emperor. "I dixo publico que estimara mas mi persona que á los mejores ochocientos hombres de guerra que le pudieran venir aquella hora." Carta de Valdivia, MS.

[5] Zarate, MS.

[6] Cieza de Leon, Cronica, cap. 90.

The old chronicler, or rather geographer, Cieza de Leon, was present in the campaign, he tells us; so that his testimony, always good, becomes for the remaining events of more than usual value.

[7] Valdivia, indeed, claims to have had the whole command intrusted to him by Gasca. "Luego me dio el autoridad toda que traia de parte de V. M. para en los casos tocantes à la guerra, i me encargó todo el exercito, i le puso baxo de mi mano rogando i pidiendo por merced de su parte á todos aquellos caballeros capitanes e gente de guerra, i de la de V. M. mandandoles me obedesciesen en todo lo que les mandase acerca de la guerra, i cumpliesen mis mandamientos como los suyos." (Carta de Valdivia, MS.) But other authorities state it, with more probability, as given in the text. Valdivia, it must be confessed, loses nothing from modesty. The whole of his letter to the emperor is written in a strain of self-glorification, rarely matched even by a Castilian hidalgo.

[8] Cieza de Leon, Cronica, cap. 91.

[9] MS. de Caravantes.

[10] Fernandez, Hist. del Peru, Parte 1, lib. 2, cap. 86, 87.—Zarate, Conq. del Peru, lib. 7, cap. 5.—Pedro Pizarro, Descub. y Conq., MS.—MS. de Caravantes.—Carta de Valdivia, MS.—Relacion del Lic. Gasca, MS.

[11] "La gente quo estaua, de la vna parte y de la otra, todos tirauan y trabajauan al poner, y apretar de las Criznejas: sin que el Presidente ni Obispos, ni otra persona quisiesse tener preuilegio para dexar de trabajar." Fernandez, Hist. del Peru, Parte 1, lib. 2, cap. 87.

[12] "Aquel dia pasaron mas de quatrocientos Hombres, llevando los Caballos à nado, encima de ellos atadas sus armas, i arcabuces, caso que se perdieron mas de sesenta Caballos, que con la corriente grande se desataron, i luego daban en vnas peñas, donde se hacian pedaços, sin darles lugar el impetu del rio, à que pudiesen nadar." Zarate, Conq. del Peru, lib. 7, cap. 5.—Gomara, Hist. de las Indias, cap. 184.

[13] Ibid., ubi supra.—Fernandez, Hist. del Peru, Parte 1, lib. 2, cap. 87.—Zarate, Conq. del Peru, lib. 7, cap. 5.—Pedro Pizarro, Descub. y Conq., MS.—MS. de Caravantes.—Carta de Valdivia, MS.—Cieza de Leon, Cronica, cap. 91.—Relation del Lic. Gasca, MS.

[14] "Andaua siempre en vna mula crescida de color entre pardo y bermejo, yo no le vi en otra caualgadura en todo el tiempo que estuuo en el Cozco antes de la batalla de Sacsahuana. Era tan contino y diligēte on solicitar lo que a su exercito conuenia, que a todas horas del dia y de la noche le topauan sus soldados haziendo su oficio, y los agenos." Garcilasso, Com. Real., Parte 1, lib. 5, cap. 27.

[15] Garcilasso, Com. Real., Parte 2, lib. 5, cap. 27.—Gomara, Hist. de las Indias, cap. 182.—Fernandez, Hist. del Peru, Parte 1, lib. 2, cap. 88.

"Finalmente, Gonçalo Pizarro dixo que queria prouar su ventura: pues siempre auia sido vencedor, y jamas vencido." Ibid.,.ubi supra.

[16] "Paresceme vuestra Señoria se vaya á la vuelta del Collao y me deje cien hombres, los que yo escojiere, que yo me iré á vista deste capellan, que ansi llamaba él al presidente." Pedro Pizarro, Descub. y Conq., MS.

[17] Garcilasso, Com. Real., Parte 2, lib. 5, cap. 31.

[18] Pedro Pizarro, Descub. y Conq., MS.—Fernandez, Hist del Peru, Parte 1, lib. 2, cap. 88.—Zarate, Conq. del Peru, lib. 7, cap. 5.—Carta de Valdivia, MS.

Valdivia's letter to the emperor, dated at Concepcion, was written about two years after the events above recorded. It is chiefly taken up with his Chilian conquests, to which his campaign under Gasca, on his visit to Peru, forms a kind of brilliant episode. This letter, the original of which is preserved in Simancas, covers about seventy folio pages in the copy belonging to me. It is one of that class of historical documents, consisting of the despatches and correspondence of the colonial governors, which, from the minuteness of the details and the means of information possessed by the writers, are of the highest worth. The despatches addressed to the Court, particularly, may compare with the celebrated *Relazioni* made by the Venetian ambassadors to their republic, and now happily in the course of publication, at Florence, under the editorial auspices of the learned Albèri.

[19] Carta de Valdivia, MS.—Garcilasso, Com. Real., Parte 2, lib. 5, cap. 33, 34.—Pedro Pizarro, Descub. y Conq., MS.—Gomara, Hist. de las Indias, cap. 185.—Fernandez, Hist. del Peru, Parte 1, lib. 2, cap. 88.

[20] The fact is not mentioned by any of the parties present at these transactions. It is to be found, with some little discrepancy of circumstances, in Gomara (Hist. de las Indias, cap. 185) and Zarate (Conq. del Peru, lib. 7, cap. 6); and their positive testimony may be thought by most readers to outweigh the negative afforded by the silence of other contemporaries.

[21] "Salió á Xaquixaguana con toda su gente y allí nos aguardó en un llano junto á un cerro alto por donde bajábamos; y cierto nuestro Señor le cegó el entendimiento, porque si nos aguardaran al pie de la bajada, hicieran mucho daño á nosotros. Restiráronse á un llano junto á una ciénaga, creyendo que nuestro campo allí les acometiera y con la ventaja que nos tenian del puesto nos vencieran." Pedro Pizarro, Descub. y Conq., MS.—Carta de Valdivia, MS.—Relacion del Lic. Gasca, MS.

[22] "Porq. muchas pelotas dieron en medio de la gente, y una dellas matò jũto à Gonçalo Pizarro vn criado suyo que se estaua armando: y matò otro hombre y vn cauallo: que puso grande alteracion en el campo, y abatieron todas las tiẽdas y toldos." Fernandez, Hist. del Peru, Parte 1, lib. 2, cap. 89.—Carta de Valdivia, MS.—Relacion del Lic. Gasca, MS.

[23] "I asi estuvo el Campo toda la Noche en Arma, desarmadas las Tiendas, padesciendo mui gran frio que no podian tener las Lanças en las manos." Zarate, Conq. del Peru, lib. 7, cap. 6.

[24] "Y assi quando vio Francisco de Caruajal el campo Real; pareciendole que los esquadrones venian biẽ ordenados dixo, Valdiuia està en la tierra, y rige el campo, ò el diablo." Fernandez, Hist. del Peru, Parte 1, lib. 2, cap. 89.—Relacion del Lic. Gasca, MS.—Carta de Valdivia, MS.—Gomara, Hist. de las Indias, cap. 185.—Zarate, Conq. del Peru, lib. 7, cap. 6.—Garcilasso, Com. Real., Parte 2, lib. 5, cap. 34.—Pedro Pizarro, Descub. y Conq., MS.

[25] "Iba mui galàn, i gentil hombre sobre vn poderoso caballo castaño, armado de Cota, i Coracinas ricas, con vna sobre ropa de Raso bien golpeada, i vn Capacete de Oro en la cabeça, con su barbote de lo mismo." Gomara, Hist. de las Indias, cap. 185.

[26] "Porque el Maesse de campo Francisco de Caruajal, como hombre desdeñado de que Gonçalo Piçarro no huuiesse querido seguir su parecer y consejo (dandose ya por vencido), no quiso hazer oficio de Maesse de campo, como solia, y assi fue a ponerse en el esquadron con su compañia, como vno de los capitanes de ynfanteria." Garcilasso, Com. Real., Parte 2, lib. 5, cap. 35.

[27] Ibid., ubi supra.

[28] "Gasca abraçò, i besò en el carrillo à Cepeda, aunque lo llevaba encenagado, teniendo por vencido à Piçarro, con su falta." Gomara, Hist. de las Indias, cap. 185.

[29] "Ça, segun pareciò, Cepeda le huvo avisado con Fr. Antonio de Castro, Prior de Santo Domingo en Arequipa, que si Piçarro no quisiesse concierto ninguno, èl se pasaria al servicio del Emperador à tiempo qus lo deshiciese." Ibid., ubi supra.

[30] "Visto por Gonzalo Pizarro i Caravajal su Maestre de Campo que se les iva gente procuraron de caminar en su orden hacia el campo de S. M. i que viendo esto los lados i sobre salientes del exercito real se empezaron á llegar á ellos i á disparar en ellos i que lo mesmo hizo la artilleria, i todo el campo con paso bien concertado i entera determinacion se llegó á ellos. Relacion del Lic. Gasca, MS.

[31] "Los Indios qua tenian los enemigos que diz que eran mucha cantidad huyeron mui á furia." (Relacion del Lic. Gasca, MS.) For the particulars of the battle, more or less minute, see Carta de Valdivia, MS.—Garcilasso, Com. Real., Parte 2, lib. 5, cap. 35.— Pedro Pizarro, Descub. y Conq., MS.—Gomara, Hist. de las Indias, cap. 185.— Fernandez, Hist. del Peru, Parte 1, lib. 2, cap. 90.—Zarate, Conq. del Peru, lib. 7, cap. 7. —Herrera, Hist. General, dec. 8, lib. 4, cap. 16.

[32] "Gonçalo Piçarro boluiendo el rostro, a Juan de Acosta, que estaua cerca del, le dixo, que haremos hermano Juan? Acosta presumiendo mas de valiente que de discreto respondiò, Señor arremetamos, y muramos como los antiguos Romanos. Gonçalo Piçarro dixo mejor es morir como Cristianos." Garcilasso, Com. Real., Parte 2, lib. 5, cap. 36.—Zarate, Conq. del Peru, lib. 7, cap. 7.

[33] Garcilasso, Com. Real., ubi supra.

[34] Fernandez, Hist. del Peru, Parte 1, lib. 2, cap. 90.

Historians, of course, report the dialogue between Gasca and his prisoner with some variety. See Gomara, Hist. de las Indias, cap. 185.—Garcilasso, Com. Real., Parte 2, lib. 5, cap. 36.—Relacion del Lic. Gasca, MS.

[35] "Luego llevaron antel dicho Licenciado Caravajal Maestre de campo del dicho Pizarro i tan cercado de gentes que del havian sido ofendidas que le querian matar, el qual diz que mostrava que olgara que le matáran alli." Relacion del Lic. Gasca, MS.

[36] "Diego Centeno reprehendia mucho à los que le offendian. Por lo qual Caruajal le mirò, y le dixo, Señor quien es vuestra merced que tanta merced me haze? à lo qual Centeno respondio, Que no conoce vuestra merced a Diego Centeno? Dixo entonces Caruajal, Por Dios señor que como siempre vi à vuestra merced de espaldas, que agora teniendo le de cara, no le conocia." Fernandez, Hist. del Peru, Parte 1, lib. 2, cap. 90.

[37] Ibid., ubi supra.

It is but fair to state that Garcilasso, who was personally acquainted with the bishop of Cuzco, doubts the fact of the indecorous conduct imputed to him by Fernandez, as inconsistent with the prelate's character. Com. Real., Parte 2, lib. 5, cap. 39.

[38] Zarate, Conq., del Peru, lib. 7, cap. 8.

[39] "Temióse que en esta batalla muriria mucha gente de ambas partes por haver en ellas mill i quatrocientos arcabuceros i seiscientos de caballo i mucho numero de piqueros i diez i ocho piezas de artilleria, pero plugo á Dios que solo murió un hombre del campo de S. M. i quince de los contrarios como está dicho." Relacion del Lic. Gasca, MS.

The MS. above referred to is supposed by Muñoz to have been written by Gasca, or rather dictated by him to his secretary. The original is preserved at Simancas, without date, and in the character of the sixteenth century. It is principally taken up with the battle, and the events immediately connected with it; and although very brief, every sentence is of value as coming from so high a source. Alcedo, in his *Biblioteca Americana, MS.*, gives the title of a work from Gasca's pen, which would seem to be an account of his own administration, *Historia del Peru, y de su Pacificacion,* 1576, fol.—I have never met with the work, or with any other allusion to it.

CHAPTER IV

[1] The sentence passed upon Pizarro is given at length in the *manuscript* copy of Zarate's History, to which I have had occasion more than once to refer. The historian omitted it in his printed work; but the curious reader may find it entire, cited in the original, in *Appendix, No.* 14.

[2] "Basta matar." Fernandez, Hist. del Peru, Parte 1, lib. 2, cap. 91.

[3] "En esso no tengo que confessar: porque juro à tal, que no tengo otro cargo, si no medio real que deuo en Seuilla à vna bodegonera de la puerta del Arenal, del tiempo que passè a Indias." Ibid., ubi supra.

[4] "Niño en cuna, y viejo en cuna." Ibid., loc. cit.

[5] "Murió como gentil, porque dicen, que yo no le quise ver, que ansí le dí la palabra de no velle; mas á la postrer vez que me habló llevandole á matar le decia el sacerdote que con él iba, que se encomendase á Dios y dijese el Pater Noster y el Ave María, y dicen que dijo Pater Noster, Ave María, y que no dijo otra palabra." Pedro Pizarro, Descub. y Conq., MS.

[6] I quote from memory, but believe the reflection may be found in that admirable digest of worldly wisdom, The Characters of La Bruyère.

[7] Pedro Pizarro bears testimony to Carbajal's endeavours to leave the country, in which he was aided, though ineffectually, by the chronicler, who was, at that time, in the most friendly relations with him. Civil war parted these ancient comrades; but Carbajal did not forget his obligations to Pedro Pizarro, which he afterwards repaid by exempting him on two different occasions from the general doom of the prisoners who fell into his hands.

[8] Out of three hundred and forty executions, according to Fernandez, three hundred were by Carbajal. (Hist. del Peru, Parte 1, lib. 2, cap. 91.) Zarate swells the number of these executions to five hundred. (Conq. del Peru, lib. 7, cap. 1.) The discrepancy shows how little we can confide in the accuracy of such estimates.

[9] Fidelity, indeed, is but one of many virtues claimed for Carbajal by Garcilasso, who considers most of the tales of cruelty and avarice circulated of the veteran, as well as the hardened levity imputed to him in his latter moments, as inventions of his enemies. The Inca chronicler was a boy when Gonzalo and his chivalry occupied Cuzco; and the kind treatment he experienced from them, owing, doubtless, to his father's position in the rebel army, he has well repaid by depicting their portraits in the favorable colors in which they appeared to his young imagination. But the garrulous old man has recorded several individual instances of atrocity in the career of Carbajal, which form but an indifferent commentary on the correctness of his general assertions in respect to his character.

[10] "Fue maior sufridor de trabajos, que requeria su edad, porque à maravilla se quitaba las Armas de Dia, ni de Noche, i quando era necesario, tampoco se acostaba, ni dormia mas de quanto recostado en vna Silla, se le cansaba la mano en que arrimaba la Cabeça." Zarate, Conq. del Peru, lib. 5, cap. 14.

[11] Pedro Pizarro, who seems to have entertained feelings not unfriendly to Carbajal, thus sums up his character in a few words. "Era mui lenguaz: hablaba muy discreptamente y á gusto de los que le oian: era hombre sagaz, cruel, bien entendido en la guerra. . . . . . Este Carbajal era tan sabio que decian tenia familiar." Des cub. y Conq., MS.

[12] "Al tiempo que lo mataron, diò al Verdugo toda la Ropa, que traìa que era mui rica, i de mucho valor, porque tenia vna Ropa de Armas de Terciopelo amarillo, casi toda cubierta de Chaperia de Oro, i vn Chapeo de la misma forma." Zarate, Conq. del Peru, lib. 7, cap. 8.

[13] "The executioner," says Garcilasso, with a simile more expressive than elegant, "did his work as cleanly as if he had been slicing off a head of lettuce!" "De vn reues le cortò la cabeça con tanta facilidad, como si fuera vna hoja de lechuga, y se quedò con ella en la mano, y tardò el cuerpo algun espacio en caer en el suelo." Garcilasso, Com. Real., Parte 2, lib. 5, cap. 43.

[14] "Esta es la cabeza del traidor de Gonzalo Pizarro que se hizo justicia del en el valle de Aquixaguana, donde dió la batalla campal contra el estandarte real queriendo defender su traicion e tirania: ninguno sea osado de la quitar de aqui so pena de muerte natural." Zarate, MS.

[15] "Y las sepulturas vna sola auiendo de ser tres: que aun la tierra parece que les faltò para auer los de cubrir." Garcilasso, Com. Real., Parte 2, lib. 5, cap. 43.

For the tragic particulars of the preceding pages, see Ibid., cap. 39-43.—Relacion del Lic. Gasca, MS.—Carta de Valdivia, MS. —
MS. de Caravantes.—Pedro Pizarro, Descub. y Conq., MS.—Gomara, Hist. de las Indias, cap. 186.—Fernandez, Hist. del Peru, Parte 1, lib. 2, cap. 91.—Zarate, Conq. del Peru, lib. 7, cap. 8.—Herrera, Hist. General, dec. 8, lib. 4, cap. 16.

[16] "Quando Gonçalo Pizarro, que aya gloria, se veya en su zaynillo, no hazia mas caso de esquadrones de Yndios, que si fueran de moscas." Garcilasso, Parte 2, lib. 5, cap. 43.

[17] "Dezian que no era falta de entendimiento, pues lo tenia bastante, sino que deuia de ser sobra de influencia de signos y planetas, que le cegauan y forçauan a que pusiesse la garganta al cuchillo." Garcilasso, Com. Real., Parte 2, lib. 5, cap. 33.

[18] "Ὅταν δὲ Δαίμων ἀνδρὶ πορσύνῃ κακὰ,

Τὸν νοῦν ἔβλαψε πρῶτον."

Eurip. Fragmenta.

[19] The cunning lawyer prepared so plausible an argument in his own justification, that Yllescas, the celebrated historian of the Popes, declares that no one who read the paper attentively, but must rise from the perusal of it with an entire conviction of the writer's innocence, and of his unshaken loyalty to the Crown. See the passage quoted by Garcilasso, Com. Real., Parte 2, lib. 6, cap. 10.

[20] Pedro Pizarro, Descub. y Conq., MS.—Fernandez, Hist. del Peru, Parte 1, lib. 2, cap. 91.—Carta de Valdivia, MS.—Zarate, Conq. del Peru, lib. 7, cap. 8.—Relacion del Lic. Gasca, MS.

[21] MS. de Caravantes.—Pedro Pizarro, Descub. y Conq., MS.—Zarate, Conq. del Peru, lib. 7, cap. 9.—Fernandez, Hist. del Peru, Parte 1, lib. 2, cap. 92.

[22] The *peso ensayado,* according to Garcilasso, was one fifth more in value than the Castilian ducat. Com. Real., Parte 2, lib. 6, cap. 3.

[23] "Entre los caballeros capitanes y soldados que le ayudaron en esta ocasion repartió el Presidente Pedro de la Gasca 135,000 pesos ensayados de renta que estaban vacos, y no un millon y tantos mil pesos, como dize Diego Fernandez, que escrivió en Palencia estas alteraciones, y de quien lo tomó Antonio de Herrera: y porque esta ocasion fué la segunda en que los benemeritos del Pirú fundan con razon los servicios de sus pasados, porque mediante esta batalla aseguro la corona de Castilia las provincias mas ricas que tiene en America, pondré sus nombres para que se conserbe con certeza su memoria como pareze en el auto original que proveyó en el asiento de Guainarima cerca de la ciudad del Cuzco en diez y siete de Agosto de 1548, que está en los archivos del govierno." MS. de Caravantes.

The sum mentioned in the text, as thus divided among the army, falls very far short of the amount stated by Garcilasso, Fernandez, Zarate, and, indeed, every other writer on the subject, none of whom estimate it at less than a million of *pesos.* But Caravantes, from whom I have taken it, copies the original act of partition preserved in the royal archives. Yet Garcilasso de la Vega ought to have been well informed of the value of these estates, which, according to him, far exceeded the estimate given in the schedule. Thus, for instance, Hinojosa, he says, obtained from the share of lands and rich mines assigned to him from the property of Gonzalo Pizarro no less than 200,000 *pesos* annually, while Aldana, the Licentiate Carbajal, and others, had estates which yielded them from 10,000 to 50,000 *pesos.* (Ibid., ubi supra.) It is impossible to reconcile these monstrous discrepancies. No sum seems to have been too large for the credulity of the ancient chronicler; and the imagination of the reader is so completely bewildered by the actual riches of this El Dorado, that it is difficult to adjust his faith by any standard of probability.

[24] Caravantes has transcribed from the original act a full catalogue of the pensioners, with the amount of the sums set against each of their names.

[25] The president found an ingenious way of remunerating several of his followers, by bestowing on them the hands of the rich widows of the cavaliers who had perished in the war. The inclinations of the ladies do not seem to have been always consulted in this politic arrangement. See Garcilasso, Com. Real., Parte 2, lib. 6, cap. 3.

[26] Fernandez has collected these flowers of colonial poesy, which prove that the old Conquerors were much more expert with the sword than with the pen. Hist. del Peru, Parte 1, lib. 2, cap. 93.

[27] "Fue recibimiento mui solemne, con universal alegria del Pueblo, por verse libre de Tiranos; i toda la Gente, à voces, bendecia al Presidente, i le llamaban: Padre, Restaurador, i Pacificador, dando gracias à Dios, por haver vengado las injurias hechas à su Divina Magestad." Herrera, Hist. General, dec. 8, lib. 4, cap. 17.

[28] "El Presidente Gasca mando visitar todas las provincias y repartimientos deste reyno, nombrando para ello personas de autoridad y de quien se tenia entendido que tenian conoscimento de la tierra que se les encargavan, que ha de ser la principal calidad, que se ha buscar en la persona, a quien se comete semejante negocio despues que sea Cristiana: lo segundo se les dio instruccion de lo que hauian de averiguar, que fueron muchas cosas: el numero, las haciendas, los tratos y grangerias, la calidad de la gente y de sus tierras y comarca, y lo que davan de tributo." Ondegardo, Rel. Prim, MS.

[29] "El Presidente, i el Audiencia dieron tales ordenes, qua este negocio se asentò, de manera, que para adelante no se platicò mas este nombre de Esclavos, sino que la libertad fue general por todo el Reino." Herrera, Hist. Gen., dec. 8, lib. 5, cap. 7.

[30] MS. de Caravantes.—Gomara, Hist. de las Indias, cap. 187.—Fernandez, Hist. del Peru, Parte 1, lib. 2, cap. 93-95.—Zarate, Conq. del Peru, lib. 7, cap. 10.

[31] "Recogiò tanta suma de dinero, que pagò novecientos mil pesos de Oro, que se hallò haver gastado, desde el Dia que entrò en Panamá, hasta que se acabò la Guerra, los quales tomò prestados." Herrera, Hist. General, dec. 8, lib. 5, cap. 7.—Zarate, Conq. del Peru, lib. 7, cap. 10.

[32] "Aviendo pagado el Presidente las costas de la guerra que fueron muchas, remitió á S. M. y lo llevó consigo 264,422 marcos de plata, que á seis ducados valieron 1 millon 588, 332 ducados." MS. de Caravantes.

[33] "No tubo ni quiso salario el Presidente Gasca sino cedula para que á un mayordomo suyo diosen los Oficiales reales lo necesario de la real Hacienda, que como pareze de los quadernos de su gasto fué muy moderado." (MS. de Caravantes.) Gasca, it appears, was most exact in keeping the accounts of his disbursements for the expenses of himself and household, from the time he embarked for the colonies.

[34] "En lo qual hizo mas que en vencer y ganar todo aquel Ympe rio: porque fue vencerse assi pro prio." Garcilasso, Com. Real., Parte 2, lib. 6, cap. 7.

[35] Fernandez, Hist. del Peru, Parte 1, lib. 2, cap. 95.

[36] MS. de Caravantes.—Gomara, Hist. de las Indias, cap. 183.—Fernandez, Hist. del Peru, Parte 2, lib. 1, cap. 10.—Zarate, Conq. del Peru, lib. 7, cap. 13.—Herrera, Hist. General, dec. 8, lib. 6, cap. 17.

[37] Ibid., ubi supra.—MS. de Caravantes.—Gomara, Hist. de las Indias, cap. 182.—Fernandez, Hist. del Peru, Parte 2, lib. 1, cap. 10.—Zarate, Conq. del Peru, lib. 7, cap. 13.

[38] I have met with no account of the year in which Gasca was born; but an inscription on his portrait in the sacristy of St. Mary Magdalene at Valladolid, from which the engraving prefixed to this volume is taken, states that he died in 1567, at the age of seventy-one. This is perfectly consistent with the time of life at which he had probably arrived when we find him a collegiate at Salamanca, in the year 1522.

[39] "Murió en Valladolid, donde mandó enterrar su cuerpo en la Iglesia de la advocacion de la Magdalena, que hizo edificar en aquella ciudad, donde se pusieron las vanderas que ganó á Gonzalo Pizarro." MS. de Caravantes.

[40] The memory of his achievements has not been left entirely to the care of the historian. It is but a few years since the character and administration of Gasca formed the subject of an elaborate panegyric from one of the most distinguished statesmen in the British parliament. (See Lord Brougham's speech on the maltreatment of the North American colonies, February, 1838.) The enlightened Spaniard of our day, who contemplates with sorrow the excesses committed by his countrymen of the sixteenth century in the New World, may feel an honest pride, that in this company of dark spirits should be found one to whom the present generation may turn as to the brightest model of integrity and wisdom.

[41] "Era muy pequeño de cuerpo con estraña hechura, que de la cintura abaxo tenia tanto cuerpo, como qualquiera hombre alto, y de la cintura al hombro no tenia vna tercia. Andando a cauallo parescia a vn mas pequeño de lo que era, porque todo era piernas: de rostro era muy feo: pero lo que la naturaleza le nego de las dotes del cuerpo, se los dobló en los del animo." Garcilasso, Com. Real. Parte 2, lib. 5, cap. 2.

[42] "Fue tan recatado y estremado en esta virtud, que puesto que de muchos quedó mal quisto, quando del Perù se partio para España, por el repartimiento que hizo: con todo esso, jamas nadie dixo del, ni sospechò; que en esto, ni otra cosa, se vuiesse mouido por codicia." Fernandez, Hist. del Peru, Parte 1, lib. 2, cap. 95.

Augustin de Zarate—a highly respectable authority, frequently cited in the later portion of this work—was *Contador de Mercedes*, Comptroller of Accounts, for Castile. This office he filled for fifteen years; after which he was sent by the government to Peru to examine into the state of the colonial finances, which had been greatly deranged by the recent troubles, and to bring them, if possible, into order.

Zarate went out accordingly in the train of the viceroy Blasco Nuñez, and found himself, through the passions of his imprudent leader, entangled, soon after his arrival, in the inextricable meshes of civil discord. In the struggle which ensued, he remained with the Royal Audience; and we find him in Lima, on the approach of Gonzalo Pizarro to that capital, when Zarate was deputed by the judges to wait on the insurgent chief, and require him to disband his troops and withdraw to his own estates. The historian executed the mission, for which he seems to have had little relish, and which certainly was not without danger. From this period, we rarely hear of him in the troubled scenes that ensued. He probably took no further part in affairs than was absolutely forced on him by circumstances; but the unfavorable bearing of his remarks on Gonzalo Pizarro intimates, that, however he may have been discontented with the conduct of the viceroy, he did not countenance, for a moment, the criminal ambition of his rival. The times were certainly unpropitious to the execution of the financial reforms for which Zarate had come to Peru. But he showed so much real devotion to the interests of the Crown, that the emperor, on his return, signified his satisfaction by making him Superintendent of the Finances in Flanders.

Soon after his arrival in Peru, he seems to have conceived the idea of making his countrymen at home acquainted with the stirring events passing in the colony, which, moreover, afforded some striking passages for the study of the historian. Although he collected notes and diaries, as he tells us, for this purpose, he did not dare to avail himself of them till his return to Castile. "For to have begun the history in Peru," he says, "would have alone been enough to put my life in jeopardy; since a certain commander, named Francisco de Carbajal, threatened to take vengeance on any one who should be so rash as to attempt the relation of his exploits,—far less deserving, as they were, to be placed on record, than to be consigned to eternal oblivion." In this same commander, the reader will readily recognize the veteran lieutenant of Gonzalo Pizarro.

On his return home, Zarate set about the compilation of his work. His first purpose was to confine it to the events that followed the arrival of Blasco Nuñez; but he soon found, that, to make these intelligible, he must trace the stream of history higher up towards its sources. He accordingly enlarged his plan, and, beginning with the discovery of Peru, gave an entire view of the conquest and subsequent occupation of the country, bringing the narrative down to the close of Gasca's mission. For the earlier portion of the story, he relied on the accounts of persons who took a leading part in the events. He disposes more summarily of this portion than of that in which he himself was both a spectator and an actor; where his testimony, considering the advantages his position gave him for information, is of the highest value.

Alcedo in his *Biblioteca Americana, MS.*, speaks of Zarate's work as "containing much that is good, but as not entitled to the praise of exactness." He wrote under the influence of party heat, which necessarily operates to warp the fairest mind somewhat from its natural bent. For this we must make allowance, in perusing accounts of conflicting parties. But there is no intention, apparently, to turn the truth aside in support of his own cause; and his access to the best sources of knowledge often supplies us with particulars not within the reach of other chroniclers. His narrative is seasoned, moreover, with sensible reflections and passing comments, that open gleams of light into the dark passages of that eventful period. Yet the style of the author can make but moderate pretensions to the praise of elegance or exactness; while the sentences run into that tedious, interminable length which belongs to the garrulous compositions of the regular thoroughbred chronicler of the olden time.

The personalities, necessarily incident, more or less, to such a work, led its author to shrink from publication, at least during his life. By the jealous spirit of the Castilian cavalier, "censure," he says, "however light, is regarded with indignation, and even praise is rarely dealt out in a measure satisfactory to the subject of it." And he expresses his conviction that those do wisely, who allow their accounts of their own times to repose in the quiet security of manuscript, till the generation that is to be affected by them has passed away. His own manuscript, however, was submitted to the emperor; and it received such commendation from this royal authority, that Zarate, plucking up a more courageous spirit, consented to give it to the press. It accordingly appeared at Antwerp, in 1555, in octavo; and a second edition was printed, in folio, at Seville, in 1577. It has since been incorporated in Barcia's valuable collection; and, whatever indignation or displeasure it may have excited among contemporaries, who smarted under the author's censure, or felt themselves defrauded of their legitimate guerdon, Zarate's work has taken a permanent rank among the most respectable authorities for a history of the time.

The name of Zarate naturally suggests that of Fernandez, for both were laborers in the same field of history. Diego Fernandez de Palencia, or *Palentino,* as he is usually called, from the place of his birth, came over to Peru, and served as a private in the royal army raised to quell the insurrections that broke out after Gasca's return to Castile. Amidst his military occupations, he found leisure to collect materials for a history of the period, to which he was further urged by the viceroy, Mendoza, Marques de Cañete, who bestowed on him, as he tells us, the post of Chronicler of Peru. This mark of confidence in his literary capacity intimates higher attainments in Fernandez than might be inferred from the humble station that he occupied. With the fruits of his researches the soldier-chronicler returned to Spain, and, after a time, completed his narrative of the insurrection of Giron.

The manuscript was seen by the President of the Council of the Indies, and he was so much pleased with its execution, that he urged the author to write the account, in like manner, of Gonzalo Pizarro's rebellion, and of the administration of Gasca. The historian was further stimulated, as he mentions in his dedication to Philip the Second, by the promise of a guerdon from that monarch, on the completion of his labors; a very proper, as well as politic, promise, but which inevitably suggests the idea of an influence not altogether favorable to severe historic impartiality. Nor will such an inference be found altogether at variance with truth; for while the narrative of Fernandez studiously exhibits the royal cause in the most favorable aspect to the reader, it does scanty justice to the claims of the opposite party. It would not be meet, indeed, that an apology for rebellion should be found in the pages of a royal pensioner; but there are always mitigating circumstances, which, however we may condemn the guilt, may serve to lessen our indignation towards the guilty. These circumstances are not to be found in the pages of Fernandez. It is unfortunate for the historian of such events, that it is so difficult to find one disposed to do even justice to the claims of the unsuccessful rebel. Yet the Inca Garcilasso has not shrunk from this, in the case of Gonzalo Pizarro; and even Gomara, though living under the shadow, or rather in the sunshine, of the Court, has occasionally ventured a generous protest in his behalf.

The countenance thus afforded to Fernandez from the highest quarter opened to him the best fountains of intelligence, — at least, on the government side of the quarrel. Besides personal communication with the royalist leaders, he had access to their correspondence, diaries, and official documents. He industriously profited by his opportunities; and his narrative, taking up the story of the rebellion from its birth, continues it to its final extinction, and the end of Gasca's administration. Thus the First Part of his work, as it was now called, was brought down to the commencement of the Second, and the whole presented a complete picture of the distractions of the nation, till a new order of things was introduced, and tranquillity was permanently established throughout the country.

The diction is sufficiently plain, not aspiring to rhetorical beauties beyond the reach of its author, and out of keeping with the simple character of a chronicle. The sentences are arranged with more art than in most of the unwieldy compositions of the time; and, while there is no attempt at erudition or philosophic speculation, the current of events flows on in an orderly manner, tolerably prolix, it is true, but leaving a clear and intelligible impression on the mind of the reader. No history of that period compares with it in the copiousness of its details; and it has accordingly been resorted to by later compilers, as an inexhaustible reservoir for the supply of their own pages; a circumstance that may be thought of itself to bear no slight testimony to the general fidelity, as well as fulness, of the narrative. — The Chronicle of Fernandez, thus arranged in two parts, under the general title of *Historia del Peru*, was given to the world in the author's lifetime, at Seville, in 1571, in one volume, folio, being the edition used in the preparation of this work.

INDEX

Felipillo, Pizarro's interpreter, I. 116. His hostility to Atahuallpa, 172, 193. Intrigue of, 503, *note*. Perverts the testimony of witnesses against the Inca, 195. Hanged by Almagro, 506, *note*.

Fernandez, loyalty of, II. 539, *note*. Remarks upon, 549, *note*. Critical notice of, 560.

Festivals, religious, I. 39.

Feast of Raymi, 39-41.

Fish brought from the Pacific to Cuzco by runners, I. 454, *note*.

Forests, Spaniards entangled in, I. 84, 85, 99.

Fornication, punishment of, in Peru, I. 450, *note*.

Fortresses, massive work of, at Cuzco, I. 7, 210. A part of the Peruvian military policy, 8.

For the accommodation of the Inca's armies, 25, 445, *note*, 184. Seen by the Spaniards, 155, 159.

Future life, Peruvian ideas respecting, I. 35. Intended only for the higher classes, 456, *note*.

G.

Gallo, Isle of, Ruiz anchors at, I. 97. Pizarro lands at, 100. Spaniards left on, 102. Tafur arrives at, 105.

Garcilasso de la Vega, not trustworthy in his geography, I. 443, *note*. Fulness of, 450, *note*. Authority of, contradicted, 457, *note*, 459, *note*. Critical notice of, 118. Defects of, as an historian, 488. *note*. Probably imposed upon, 491, *note*. Fond of romancing, 497, *note*. A Peruvian by birth, 506, *note*. Is partial to Gonzalo Pizarro, II. 346, *note*, 550, *note*, 554, *note*. The father of, 552, *note*, 552, *note*, 387. An eyewitness of Gonzalo's proceedings in Lima, 553, *note*, 551, *note*.

Gardens of Yucay, I. 12.

Garrote, I. 504, *note*. Atahuallpa dies by the, 196.

Gasca, Pedro de la, II. 350. Birth and early life of, 450, *note*. His able conduct at Valencia, 351. Appointed to the Peruvian mission, 352. Demands unlimited powers, 352. Writes to the emperor, 353. His request granted, 353. Refuses a mitre, 354. Arrives at Santa Martha, 354. Crosses to Nombre de Dios, 355. Politic conduct of, 355, 356. Gains over Mexia, 356. Sends manifestoes through the land, 356. Sends to Gonzalo Pizarro, 357. Writes to him and Cepeda, 358, 359, *note*. Refuses to seize Hinojosa, 358. Gains over Aldana, 360. Receives the fleet from Hinojosa, 360. Raises levies, 362. Condemned by Cepeda, 366. Sails from Panamá, 381. Quiets the apprehensions of the seamen, 369. Fixes his head-quarters at Xauxa, 370. His vigorous proceedings, 377. Marches to Andaguaylas, 378. Compliments Valdivia, 378. His army, 379. Crosses the Abancay and Apurimac, 379, 380, 381. Offers terms to Pizarro, 384. Arrives at Xaquixaguana, 385. His reception of Cepeda, 387; of Gonzalo Pizarro, 388; of Carbajal, 389. *Relacion* of, 553, *note*. Enters Cuzco, 397. His difficulties in making repartimientos, 397. Enters Lima, 399. His care of the natives, 399. His wise reforms, 400. His wisdom and economy, 401. Refuses presents, 401. Leaves Peru, 402. Arrives in Spain, 403. Visits the emperor, and appointed bishop of Siguenza, 403. Dies, 403. His character, 404-405.

Geography, knowledge of, by the Peruvians, I. 48. Causes of the slow advance in, 72. Of ancient nations, 72. Of Middle Ages, 73.

Gnomon, used for determining the equinoxes, I. 48. In Florence, 462, *note*.

God, elevated conceptions of, on the American continent, I. 34. See *Religion*.

Mendoza, releases Hernando Pizarro, II.
270. Prudent conduct of, in respect to
ordinances, 325.

Mexia, Hernan, governor of Nombre de
Dios, II. 355. His interview with Gasca,
355. Gives his allegiance to him, 356.
Sent by Gasca to Hinojosa, 356.

Mexicans, established currency among, I.
60.

Middle Ages, geographical science in, I. 73.

Military weapons and tactics of Peruvians, I.
28. Expeditions, 29.

Milk, use of, not known on the American
continent, I. 465, *note*.

Mines, working of, I. 12, 21, 452, *note*, 21,
note. Exclusive property of the Incas,
21. Of Potosi, II. 270, 524, *note*, 320,
345.

Minstrelsy, Peruvian national, I. 20, 47.

Missionaries, II. 217, 317. Twelve, commemorated by Naharro, 536 *note*.

Mitimaes, I. 31, 456, *note*.

Molina, Alonso de, visits Tumbez, I. 111. Is
left there by Pizarro, 116.

Money, use of, unknown to Peruvians, I. 60.

Montenegro sent for aid to Panamá, I. 85.
Returns to Pizarro, 87. Rescues him
from Indians, 89.

Montesinos, critical notice of, II. 516, *note*.
A poor authority, 522, *note*.

Monuments of the dead, I. 35. Treasure
concealed in, 456, *note*, 211.

Moon, temple to, I. 37.

Morales, Luis de, memorial of, II. 536, *note*.

Morasses crossed by the Spaniards, I. 84,
85, 99.

Morton, work of, on skulls, I. 449, *note*.

Motupe, Pizarro halts at, I. 151.

Mummies of Peruvian princes, I. 448, *note*,
211. Brought out at the coronation of
Manco, II. 216.

Muskets manufactured from the church-
bells of Lima, II. 328.

Muyscas, astronomy of, I. 48. Piedrahita's
account, of, 462, *note*.

N.

Naharro, I. 496, *note*.

Napo, river of, discovered by Gonzalo
Pizarro, II. 278. His difficult passage of,
279.

Nasca, II. 259.

Navigation, improvements in the art of, I.
73. Of the first discoverers, 87.

New World, emigration to, I. 473, *note*, II.
225. Romantic adventure in, I. 74.

Nombre de Dios, Pizarro sails from, I. 121.
Returns to, 127. Sufferings of
Hernando Pizarro's followers at, II.
226. Blasco Nuñez lands at, 321.
Secured for Gonzalo Pizarro, 345.
Given up to Gasca, 356.

Nuñez Vela, Blasco, appointed viceroy of
Peru, II. 321. Arrives at Nombre de
Dios, 321. His high-handed measures,
321. Goes to Tumbez, 322. At Lima,
324. Determines to enforce the ordinances, 325. Confines Vaca de Castro,
328. Prepares for war with Gonzalo
Pizarro, 328. Assassinates Carbajal,
329. His unpopularity, 329. Made prisoner by the Royal Audience, 330. Sent
to Panamá, 331. Escapes to Tumbez,
335. Musters an army, 335. Pursued by
Gonzalo, 336, 337. Driven to Popayan,
338. Moves south, 339. Gives battle to
Pizarro, 340. Defeated and killed, 341,
342. His character, 343. See *Gonzalo
Pizarro* and *Carbajal*.

O.

Ojeda, Alonso de, I. 81.

Olmedo, Father, II. 299.

Omens, at Feast of Raymi, I. 41. Seen in
Peru on the arrival of the white men,
135. At Quito, II. 121.

Ondegardo, ingenious views of, respecting
the property laws of Peru, I. 453, *note*.
Conscientiousness of, 454, *note*. Critical
notice of, 549. Notice of, II. 470, *note*.

SUGGESTED READING

ANDRIEN, KENNETH J. *Andean Worlds: Indigenous History, Culture and Consciousness.* Albuquerque, NM: University of New Mexico Press, 2001.

BAUER, BRIAN S. *The Development of the Inca State.* Austin, TX: University of Texas Press, 1992.

BINGHAM, HIRAM. *Lost City of the Incas.* London: Phoenix Press, 2003.

BLANCHARD, PETER, ED. *Markham in Peru: The Travels of Clements R. Markham, 1852-1853.* Austin, TX: University of Texas Press, 1991.

BURKHOLDER, MARK A., LYMAN L. JOHNSON. *Colonial Latin America.* New York: Oxford University Press, 2003.

CARR, RAYMOND, ED. *Spain: A History.* New York: Oxford University Press, 2000.

CIEZA LEON, PEDRO DE. *The Discovery and Conquest of Peru.* Trans. Alexandra Parma Cook and Noble David Coiok. Durham, NC: Duke University Press, 1999.

CONRAD, GEOFFREY W. *Arthur Demarest. Religion and Empire: The Dynamics of Aztec and Inca Expansion.* New York: Cambridge University Press, 1990.

DAVIES, NIGEL. *Ancient Kingdoms of Peru.* New York: Penguin, 1997.

GARDINER, C. HARVEY. *William Hickling Prescott: A Biography.* Austin, TX: University of Texas Press, 1969.

HEMMING, JOHN. *The Conquest of the Incas.* New York: Harcourt Brace, 1970.

HYMANS, EDWARD, AND GEORGE ORDISH. *The Last of the Incas: The Rise and Fall of an American Empire.* New York: Dorset Press, 1983.

MARTIN, LUIS. *Kingdom of the Sun.* New York: Scribner, 1974.

MOSELEY, MICHAEL. *The Incas and Their Ancestors.* New York: Thames and Hudson, 2001.

PAYNE, STANLEY G. *History of Spain and Portugal.* Madison, WI: University of Wisconsin Press, 1973.

SARMIENTO DE GAMBOA, PEDRO. *History of the Incas.* New York: Dover, 1998.

SILVERBLATT, IRENE MARSHA. *Moon, Sun and Witches: Gender Ideologies and Class and Colonial Peru.* Princeton, NJ: Princeton University Press, 1990.

STARN, ORIN, ED. *The Peru Reader: History, Culture, Politics.* Durham, NC: Duke University Press, 1995.

TICKNOR, GEORGE. *Life of William Hickling Prescott.* Boston: Ticknor & Fields, 1864.

VEGA, GARCILASO DE LA. *The Royal Commentaries of the Inca.* Trans. Harold Livermore. Austin, TX: University of Texas Press, 1987.

Look for the following titles, available now from
The Barnes & Noble Library of Essential Reading.

Visit your Barnes & Noble bookstore,
or shop online at www.bn.com/loer

FICTION AND LITERATURE

Abbott, Edwin A.	Flatland	0-7607-5587-6	$5.95
Apuleius	Golden Ass	0-7607-5598-1	$7.95
Austen, Jane	Love and Freindship and Other Early Works	0-7607-6856-0	$6.95
Braddon, Mary Elizabeth	Lady Audley's Secret	0-7607-6304-6	$7.95
Burroughs, Edgar Rice	Land That Time Forgot	0-7607-6886-2	$7.95
Burroughs, Edgar Rice	Martian Tales Trilogy	0-7607-5585-X	$9.95
Butler, Samuel	Way of All Flesh	0-7607-6585-5	$9.95
Cather, Willa	Alexander's Bridge	0-7607-6887-0	$6.95
Chesterton, G. K.	Man Who Was Thursday	0-7607-6310-0	$5.95
Childers, Erskine	Riddle of the Sands	0-7607-6523-5	$6.95
Cleland, John	Fanny Hill	0-7607-6591-X	$6.95
Conan Doyle, Sir Arthur	Lost World	0-7607-5583-3	$5.95
Defoe, Daniel	Journal of the Plague Year	0-7607-5237-0	$5.95
Dos Passos, John	Three Soldiers	0-7607-5754-2	$7.95
Franklin, Benjamin	Poor Richard's Almanack	0-7607-6201-5	$6.95
Goethe	Sorrows of Young Werther	0-7607-6833-1	$5.95
Grey, Zane	Riders of the Purple Sage	0-7607-5755-0	$6.95
Haggard, H. Rider	She	0-7607-5240-0	$7.95
Hudson, W. H.	Green Mansions	0-7607-5595-7	$7.95
Huxley, Aldous	Crome Yellow	0-7607-6050-0	$5.95
Jerome, Jerome K.	Three Men in a Boat	0-7607-5759-3	$7.95
Lardner, Ring W.	You Know Me Al	0-7607-5833-6	$7.95
Lawrence, D. H.	Sea and Sardinia	0-7607-6583-9	$7.95
Mansfield, Katherine	Garden Party and Other Stories	0-7607-6579-0	$7.95

Maugham, W. Somerset	Three Early Novels	0-7607-6862-5	$9.95
Rabelais, François	Gargantua and Pantagruel	0-7607-6314-3	$14.95
Radcliffe, Ann	Mysteries of Udolpho	0-7607-6315-1	$12.95
Radcliffe, Ann	Romance of the Forest	0-7607-5753-4	$7.95
Sabatini, Rafael	Captain Blood	0-7607-5596-5	$7.95
Sienkiewicz, Henryk	Quo Vadis	0-7607-6309-7	$12.95
Somerville, Edith, and Martin Ross	Some Experiences of an Irish R. M.	0-7607-6580-4	$6.95
Sterne, Laurence	Life and Opinions of Tristram Shandy, Gentleman	0-7607-6305-4	$9.95
Swift, Jonathan	Modest Proposal and Other Prose	0-7607-6051-9	$7.95
Tolstoy, Leo	Gospels in Brief	0-7607-5762-3	$7.95
Tolstoy, Leo	What Is Art?	0-7607-6581-2	$6.95
Verne, Jules	From the Earth to the Moon	0-7607-6522-7	$6.95
Von, Leopold Sacher-Masoch	Venus in Furs	0-7607-6308-9	$6.95
Wallace, Lew	Ben-Hur	0-7607-6306-2	$9.95
Walpole, Horace	Castle of Otranto	0-7607-6307-0	$5.95
Wells, H. G.	Island of Dr. Moreau	0-7607-5584-1	$4.95
Zitkala-Ša	American Indian Stories	0-7607-6550-2	$5.95

NONFICTION

Age of Revolution	Winston Churchill	0-7607-6859-5	$9.95
American Democrat	James Fenimore Cooper	0-7607-6198-1	$6.95
Autobiography of Benjamin Franklin	Benjamin Franklin	0-7607-6199-X	$6.95
Babylonian Life and History	E. A. Wallis Budge	0-7607-6549-9	$7.95
Birth of Britain	Winston Churchill	0-7607-6857-9	$9.95
Book of the Courtier	Baldesar Castiglione	0-7607-6832-3	$7.95
Chemical History of a Candle	Michael Faraday	0-7607-6522-7	$6.95
Common Law	Oliver Wendell Holmes, Jr.	0-7607-5498-5	$9.95
Creative Evolution	Henri Bergson	0-7607-6548-0	$7.95
Critique of Judgment	Immanuel Kant	0-7607-6202-3	$7.95
Critique of Practical Reason	Immanuel Kant	0-7607-6094-2	$7.95
Critique of Pure Reason	Immanuel Kant	0-7607-5594-9	$12.95
Dark Night of the Soul	St. John of the Cross	0-7607-6587-1	$5.95
Democracy and Education	John Dewey	0-7607-6586-3	$9.95
Democracy in America	Alexis de Tocqueville	0-7607-5230-3	$14.95
Discourse on Method	Rene Descartes	0-7607-5602-3	$4.95
Edison: His Life and Inventions	Frank Lewis Dyer and Thomas C. Martin	0-7607-6582-0	$14.95

Egyptian Book of the Dead	E. A. Wallis Budge	0-7607-6838-2	$9.95
Eminent Victorians	Lytton Strachey	0-7607-4993-0	$7.95
Enquiry concerning Human Understanding	David Hume	0-7607-5592-2	$7.95
Essay Concerning Human Understanding	John Locke	0-7607-6049-7	$9.95
Essence of Christianity	Ludwig Feuerbach	0-7607-5764-X	$7.95
Ethics and On the Improvement of the Understanding	Benedict de Spinoza	0-7607-6837-4	$8.95
Extraordinary Popular Delusions and the Madness of Crowds	Charles Mackay	0-7607-5582-5	$9.95
Fall of Troy	Quintus of Smyrna	0-7607-6836-6	$6.95
Fifteen Decisive Battles of the Western World	Edward Shepherd Creasy	0-7607-5495-0	$12.95
Florentine History	Niccolò Machiavelli	0-7607-5601-5	$9.95
From Manassas to Appomattox	James Longstreet	0-7607-5920-0	$14.95
Great Democracies	Winston Churchill	0-7607-6860-9	$9.95
Guide for the Perplexed	Moses Maimonides	0-7607-5757-7	$12.95
Happy Hunting-Grounds	Kermit Roosevelt	0-7607-5581-7	$5.95
History of the Conquest of Mexico	William H. Prescott	0-7607-5922-7	$17.95
History of the Conquest of Peru	William H. Prescott	0-7607-6137-X	$14.95
History of the Donner Party	Charles F. McGlashan	0-7607-5242-7	$6.95
History of the English Church and People	Bede	0-7607-6551-0	$9.95
History of Wales	J. E. Lloyd	0-7607-5241-9	$19.95
How the Other Half Lives	Jacob A. Riis	0-7607-5589-2	$9.95
How to Sing	Lilli Lehmann	0-7607-5231-1	$5.95
Hunting the Grisly and Other Sketches	Theodore Roosevelt	0-7607-5233-8	$5.95
Imitation of Christ	Thomas à Kempis	0-7607-5591-4	$7.95
Influence of Sea Power upon History, 1660–1783	Alfred Thayer Mahan	0-7607-5499-3	$14.95
In His Steps	Charles M. Sheldon	0-7607-5577-9	$5.95
Interior Castle	St. Teresa of Avila	0-7607-7024-7	$9.95
Introduction to Mathematics	Alfred North Whitehead	0-7607-6588-X	$7.95
Investigation of the Laws of Thought	George Boole	0-7607-6584-7	$9.95
Kingdom of God Is Within You	Leo Tolstoy	0-7607-6552-9	$9.95
Lady's Life in the Rocky Mountains	Isabella Bird	0-7607-6313-5	$6.95

Leonardo da Vinci and a Memory of His Childhood	Sigmund Freud	0-7607-4992-2	$6.95
Letters and Sayings of Epicurus	Epicurus	0-7607-6328-3	$5.95
Leviathan	Thomas Hobbes	0-7607-5593-0	$9.95
Lives of the Caesars	Suetonius	0-7607-5758-5	$9.95
Manners, Customs, and History of the Highlanders of Scotland	Sir Walter Scott	0-7607-5869-7	$7.95
Meditations	Marcus Aurelius	0-7607-5229-X	$5.95
Montcalm and Wolfe	Francis Parkman	0-7607-6835-8	$12.95
Montessori Method	Maria Montessori	0-7607-4995-7	$7.95
New World	Winston Churchill	0-7607-6858-7	$9.95
Nicomachean Ethics	Aristotle	0-7607-5236-2	$7.95
Notes on Nursing	Florence Nightingale	0-7607-4994-9	$4.95
On Education	Immanuel Kant	0-7607-5588-4	$6.95
On Liberty	John Stuart Mill	0-7607-5500-0	$4.95
On the Nature of Things	Lucretius	0-7607-6834-X	$8.95
On War	Carl von Clausewitz	0-7607-5597-3	$14.95
Oregon Trail	Francis Parkman	0-7607-5232-X	$7.95
Outline of History: Volume 1	H. G. Wells	0-7607-5866-2	$12.95
Outline of History: Volume 2	H. G. Wells	0-7607-5867-0	$12.95
Passing of the Armies	Joshua Lawrence Chamberlain	0-7607-6052-7	$7.95
Personal Memoirs	Ulysses S. Grant	0-7607-4990-6	$14.95
Philosophy of History	G. W. F. Hegel	0-7607-5763-1	$9.95
Political Economy for Beginners	Millicent Garrett Fawcett	0-7607-5497-7	$6.95
Pragmatism	William James	0-7607-4996-5	$5.95
Praise of Folly	Desiderius Erasmus	0-7607-5760-7	$6.95
Principia Ethica	G. E. Moore	0-7607-6546-4	$5.95
Principles of Political Economy and Taxation	David Ricardo	0-7607-6536-7	$7.95
Principle of Relativity	Alfred North Whitehead	0-7607-6521-9	$7.95
Problems of Philosophy	Bertrand Russell	0-7607-5604-X	$5.95
Recollections and Letters	Robert E. Lee	0-7607-5919-7	$9.95
Relativity	Albert Einstein	0-7607-5921-9	$6.95
Rights of Man	Thomas Paine	0-7607-5501-9	$5.95
Rough Riders	Theodore Roosevelt	0-7607-5576-0	$7.95
Russia and Its Crisis	Paul Miliukov	0-7607-6863-3	$12.95
Second Treatise of Government	John Locke	0-7607-6095-0	$5.95
Theory of Moral Sentiments	Adam Smith	0-7607-5868-9	$12.95
Totem and Taboo	Sigmund Freud	0-7607-6520-0	$7.95

Tractatus Logico-Philosophicus	Ludwig Wittgenstein	0-7607-5235-4	$5.95
Trial and Death of Socrates	Plato	0-7607-6200-7	$4.95
Up From Slavery	Booker T. Washington	0-7607-5234-6	$6.95
Violin Playing As I Teach It	Leopold Auer	0-7607-4991-4	$5.95
Vindication of the Rights of Woman	Mary Wollstonecraft	0-7607-5494-2	$6.95
Voyage of the Beagle	Charles Darwin	0-7607-5496-9	$9.95
Wealth of Nations	Adam Smith	0-7607-5761-5	$9.95
Wilderness Hunter	Theodore Roosevelt	0-7607-5603-1	$7.95
Worst Journey in the World	Apsley Cherry-Garrard	0-7607-5759-3	$14.95

THE BARNES & NOBLE
LIBRARY OF ESSENTIAL READING

This newly developed series has been established to provide affordable access to books of literary, academic, and historic value—works of both well-known writers and those who deserve to be rediscovered. Selected and introduced by scholars and specialists with an intimate knowledge of the works, these volumes present complete, original texts in a modern, readable typeface— welcoming a new generation of readers to influential and important books of the past. With more than 100 titles already in print and more than 100 forthcoming, the *Library of Essential Reading* offers an unrivaled variety of thought, scholarship, and entertainment. Best of all, these handsome and durable paperbacks are priced to be exceptionally affordable. For a full list of titles, visit www.bn.com/loer.